WOMAN of VISION

Ellen White

WOMAN of VISION

ARTHUR L. WHITE

REVIEW AND HERALD® PUBLISHING ASSOCIATION
HAGERSTOWN, MD 21740

This book was
Edited by Kenneth H. Wood
Copyedited by Jocelyn Fay, Delma Miller, James Cavil
Designed by Trent Truman
Desktop technician by Shirley M. Bolivar
Typeset: Goudy 11/13

PRINTED IN U.S.A.

04 03 02 01 00   5 4 3 2 1

R&H Cataloging Service
White, Arthur L., 1907-1991
    Ellen White: woman of vision.

    1. White, Ellen Gould Harmon, 1827-1915.   2. Seventh-day Adventists—
United States—Biography.

286.7'3 [B]

ISBN 0-8280-1412-4

ELLEN G. WHITE AND HER WRITINGS

Who was Ellen G. White, and why do millions consider her writings of special value and significance?

In brief, she was a woman of remarkable spiritual gifts who lived most of her life during the nineteenth century (1827-1915), yet through her writings and public ministry has made a revolutionary impact on millions of people around the world.

During her lifetime she wrote more than 5,000 periodical articles and 26 books; but today, including compilations from her 55,000 pages of manuscript, more than 126 titles are available in English. She may well be the most translated woman writer in the entire history of literature, and the most translated American author of either gender. Her writings cover a broad range of subjects, including education, health, prophecy, nutrition, and cultural and ethnic-linguistic issues, creationism, and the origin of life. Her life-changing masterpiece on successful Christian living, *Steps to Christ*, has been published in more than 144 languages.

Seventh-day Adventists believe that Mrs. White was more than a gifted writer; they believe she was appointed by God as a special messenger to draw the world's attention to the Holy Scriptures and help prepare people for Christ's second advent. From the time she was 17 years old until she died 70 years later, God gave her approximately 2,000 visions and dreams. The visions varied in length from less than a minute to nearly four hours. The knowledge and counsel received through these revelations she wrote out to be shared with others. Thus her special writings are accepted by Seventh-day Adventists as inspired, and their exceptional quality is recognized even by casual readers.

As stated in *Seventh-day Adventists Believe*, "the writings of Ellen White are not a substitute for Scripture. They cannot be placed on the same level. The Holy Scriptures stand alone, the unique standard by which her and all other writings must be judged and to which they must be subject" (*Seventh-day Adventists Believe* [Washington, D.C.: Ministerial Association, General

Conference of Seventh-day Adventists, 1988], p. 227).

Yet as Ellen White herself noted, "the fact that God has revealed His will to men through His Word has not rendered needless the continued presence and guiding of the Holy Spirit. On the contrary, the Spirit was promised by our Saviour, to open the Word to His servants, to illuminate and apply its teachings" (GC, p. vii).

This book tells the story of this remarkable woman who, meeting all the tests of a true prophet as set forth in the Holy Scriptures, helped found the Seventh-day Adventist Church.

FOREWORD

In 1913 F. M. Wilcox, editor of the *Review and Herald*, wrote of Ellen G. White: "The story of her life is the story of this movement. The two are identified in experience" (RH, Feb. 27, 1913). Being a seasoned evangelist, a church executive, and then editor of the general church paper, Elder Wilcox was in a unique position to make such an appraisal.

It was a busy and fruitful life that Ellen White lived from 1827 to 1915. It produced a story not fully told until the six-volume biography of Ellen White, written by Arthur L. White, appeared. True biographical sketches and several books had been published down through the years. These began with the seven pages devoted to her experience printed in July 1851 in her first book, a diminutive volume of 64 pages. They have included the 480-page *Life Sketches*, hurried into the field on her death in 1915. It had to be limited in detail.

In writing the six-volume biography, Elder Arthur White had before him 11 aims and objectives:

1. To write for the average reader, but in such detail and with such documentation as would meet the expectations of the scholar.

2. To leave the reader with the feeling that he or she had become acquainted with Ellen White as a very human person.

3. To portray accurately her life and work as the Lord's messenger in the Seventh-day Adventist Church, not by a slavish chronicle of each day of her active ministry, but by a selection from her experience of events and happenings that illustrate her lifework and make a contribution to the cause.

4. As far as possible, to keep these events in a year-by-year development, picturing her home life, her travels, her weaknesses and strengths, her burden of heart, and her earnest devotional life.

5. To select and present in detail significant events, two or three in a given year, that best illustrate her prophetic mission, depicting the interplay between the prophet and church leaders, institutions, and individuals, and recounting the sending of testimonies and the response to these messages.

6. To provide a knowledge of the principal points of the history of the

church in a unique way as it was seen especially through the eyes of, or in relation to, the messenger of the Lord.

7. Not only to make the work an interesting narrative but to provide a selection of illustrative experiences with which readers might at times vicariously associate themselves.

8. To keep constantly before readers the major role the visions played in almost every phase of the experiences comprising the narrative.

9. Where convenient to the purposes of the manuscript, to let Ellen White speak in her own words, rather than providing a paraphrase. This would ensure an accurate conveyance of the unique and fine points of the messages in the very expressions of the prophetic messenger herself. Thus, many important statements are provided in a form that will be of value to all readers.

10. To provide a documented running account of the literary work done by Ellen White and her literary assistants in the production of her articles and books.

11. And in all of this, to present in the narrative, in a natural way, confidence-confirming features.

Mention should be made here of Ellen White's conversation with the angel in connection with the commission that she should present to others what had been opened up to her. Having observed the experience of some especially favored by God, she feared she might become exalted, but the angel of the Lord responded: "If this evil that you dread threatens you, the hand of God will be stretched out to save you; by affliction He will draw you to Himself and preserve your humility" (1LS, p. 196).

The sources from which the author worked were voluminous. They included the Ellen G. White diaries, the tens of thousands of pages of her letters and manuscripts, her many articles as they have appeared in the *Review and Herald* and *Signs of the Times* and other journals, her books and pamphlets, the correspondence she and her office received through the years, and letters and historical articles in the White Estate Document File. Also, for general historical backgrounds, the *Review and Herald* in its entirety.

Arthur White's six-volume biography of his grandmother was given wide circulation throughout the world and was so well received that almost immediately requests began coming in to the White Estate for a single-volume abridged edition. Adventist publishers and church leaders throughout the world felt that a work of this kind would meet a real need. Thus, in retirement Elder White asked Mrs. Margaret Rossiter Thiele to reduce the six volumes to one. Her work was submitted to the White Estate, where it was edited by Kenneth H. Wood. If through this volume Ellen White becomes better known as an individual—a wife and mother, a neighbor and friend, as well as the messenger of the Lord, laboring tirelessly in the pulpit and on the public platform in declaring God's messages and in counseling often and writing incessantly, with influence felt the world around—the objectives of the author and of the White Estate will have been met.

—THE TRUSTEES OF THE ELLEN G. WHITE ESTATE

ABBREVIATIONS

AGD	Arthur G. Daniells
AR	*Advent Review*
AUCR	Australasian *Union Conference Record*
AY	*An Appeal to the Youth*
BE	*Bible Echo*
CCC	Clarence C. Crisler
CM	*Colporteur Ministry*
CW	*Counsels to Writers and Editors*
DF	Ellen G. White Document File
EGW	Ellen G. White
Ev	*Evangelism*
EW	*Early Writings*
FE	*Fundamentals of Christian Education*
GC	*The Great Controversy*
GCB	*General Conference Bulletin*
GSAM	*The Great Second Advent Movement*
HTL	*Health, or How to Live*
HR	*Health Reformer*
HS	*Historical Sketches of Foreign Missions*
JNL	John N. Loughborough
JW	James White
Letter	Ellen G. White letter
1LS	*Life Sketches*, 1880 ed. (2LS, 1888 ed.; 3LS, 1915 ed.)
MKW	Mary K. White
MM	*Medical Ministry*
MR	*Ellen G. White, Messenger to the Remnant*
MS	Ellen G. White manuscript
MYP	*Messages to Young People*
PT	*Present Truth*
PUR	*Pacific Union Recorder*
RH	*Review and Herald*
1SG	*Spiritual Gifts*, Vol. I (2SG, etc., for Vols. II-IV)
SHM	*The Story of Our Health Message*
1SM	*Selected Messages*, book 1 (2SM, etc., for books 2, 3)
1SP	*The Spirit of Prophecy*, vol. 1 (2SP, etc., for vols. 2-4)
Sp. T	*Special Testimonies*
ST	*Signs of the Times*
1T	*Testimonies*, vol. 1 (2T, etc., for vols. 2-9)
TM	*Testimonies to Ministers*
WCW	William C. White
1 WCW	William C. White letter file, volume 1 (2 WCW for volume 2, etc.)
WLF	*Word to the "Little Flock"*
YI	*Youth's Instructor*

Contents

About the Author

Arthur Lacey White, one of seven grandchildren of James and Ellen White, was born to William C. (Willie) and Ethel May White on October 7, 1907. He grew up in picturesque Pratt Valley, just below the St. Helena Sanitarium in northern California. This small valley cradled the W. C. White home; Elmshaven, the home of Ellen White; and several others. Arthur attended the nearby 10-grade church school and then continued his education at Pacific Union College. He received a certificate in business administration in 1928 and that same year was united in marriage with a classmate, Frieda Belle Swingle. The newlyweds moved to Madison College in Tennessee, he to serve as assistant accountant and she as secretary to college and hospital personnel.

The following year Arthur was called to the office of the Ellen G. White Estate at Elmshaven to serve as accountant and general assistant to his 74-year-old father. The latter, one of five church leaders appointed by Ellen White in her will to administer her estate, was secretary of the board of trustees when Arthur joined him in 1929. During the next nine years Arthur was given increasing responsibilities, and in 1933 he was appointed assistant secretary of the board. Shortly after the death of W. C. White at the age of 83, in late 1937, Arthur was elected as a life member of the board and secretary of the estate, a position he held for 41 years.

On the death of his father, in harmony with plans of long standing, Arthur supervised the transfer of the office and E. G. White files to the world headquarters of the Seventh-day Adventist Church in Washington, D.C. Principal tasks included working with the world field in the development of the available Spirit of Prophecy literature and assembling E. G. White materials for publication, in compilations such as *Evangelism*, *The Adventist Home*, and *Selected Messages*, climaxed by the three-volume *Comprehensive Index to the Writings of Ellen G. White*.

With the development of the Seventh-day Adventist Theological Seminary, Arthur White was drawn into a teaching program in Washington, Berrien Springs, and overseas. He taught in 13 overseas Seminary Extension Schools. As secretary of the White Estate he also wrote many periodical articles and produced substantial monographs dealing with various matters relating to Ellen White and her teachings. In 1973 Andrews University conferred on him the honorary degree of Doctor of Divinity.

In 1966 the White Estate board of trustees, in counsel with the General Conference officers, asked Elder White to author a definitive biography of Ellen White. Hesitant because of his personal relationship to the subject of the biography, but conditioned by his stance taken early in his ministry that he would relate to Ellen White as would any other loyal Seventh-day Adventist, viewing her as "Sister White" and not as "my grandmother," he accepted the assignment. In 1978 he resigned as secretary of the Ellen G. White Estate to devote his energies almost exclusively to the biography project. Adhering to a careful schedule, he produced one volume each year—six in all—doing his work largely in his study at home, where he could give undivided attention to research and writing while at the same time maintaining easy access to the rich sources in the White Estate vault.

With this monumental task completed, Arthur and Frieda White moved to their retirement home at Deer Park, California, with its garden, orchard, and workshop situated on the crest of the hill above the St. Helena Health Center and the Pratt Valley, where Arthur was born. Six years later, on January 12, 1991, he died at the age of 83.

—THE PUBLISHERS

THE TIME WAS RIGHT

In 1837 a traumatic event occurred in the life of a small girl in Portland, Maine. This event eventually would have far-reaching consequences in all parts of the world.

In 1837 the groundswell of expectation that Christ would come in 1844 was moving toward a crisis.

In 1837 appointments for lectures in Vermont alone filled many pages in William Miller's memorandum book.

In 1837 the United States was struck by a depression. Robert Harmon, a hatmaker and father of eight, the youngest being his 9-year-old twins, Ellen and Elizabeth, had moved his family from the rural farm in Gorham, Maine, to the city of Portland, where he thought to find a better market for hats. But even the hat business had been affected. So one day in the winter of 1837-1838 he decided to take his supply of hats to Georgia in hope of a more ready sale. Doubtless there was an air of excitement in the family the night before he was to leave, as they helped wrap the hats and place them in a large leather bag.

In imagination we can see the whole family following the father to the stage depot early the next morning. Together they walked the dirt paths near their home, and then on the wooden sidewalks down to the old "Elm House" to catch the western stage for Boston and points south.

As Robert Harmon placed his hat box on top of the stage, he climbed in and turned to wave goodbye. Lovingly he looked at the cheerful, well-formed features of Ellen's face. The next time he was to see his precious daughter she would be much changed.

It was midafternoon. Ellen and Elizabeth, with a classmate, were crossing a park when they noticed that an older girl who also attended Portland's Brackett Street School was following them. Carrying a stone, she shouted some angry words. The Harmon children had been taught never to retaliate, so they ran toward home.

As they ran, Ellen turned to see how far behind them the girl was. When she turned, the stone hit her directly in the face. She fell to the ground unconscious, blood streaming from her nose and staining her clothes. Someone gave her first aid in a nearby store. Then a customer, a total stranger, offered to take

Ellen home in his carriage. But Ellen, fearing that she might soil his carriage with blood, refused. However, as she made the attempt by foot, she soon became faint and collapsed to the ground. Elizabeth and the classmate managed to carry her home, a block or two away.

Anxious days followed. Ellen lay in a coma for three weeks. When consciousness returned, she remembered nothing of the experience. All she knew was that she was lying on her cot in great weakness. Then one day she heard a visitor say, "What a pity! I should not know her."

"Let me see," Ellen said.

They handed her a mirror. The shock was almost more than she could bear.

> Every feature of my face seemed changed. . . . The bone of my nose proved to be broken. The idea of carrying my misfortune through life was insupportable. I could see no pleasure in my life. I did not wish to live, and I dared not die, for I was not prepared (2SG, p. 9).

Ellen soon learned the tremendous difference one's personal appearance makes in the way one is treated. Though she slowly regained her strength for play, her young friends spurned her.

Another consequence of her accident was that she found it impossible to study. She could not retain what she learned, and her hand was too unsteady to write. Her teacher advised her to drop out of school until her health improved. She recalled:

> It was the hardest struggle of my young life to yield to my feebleness and decide that I must leave my studies and give up the hope of gaining an education (1T, p. 13).

Ellen often felt unreconciled to being a near-invalid. She also felt a deep sense of sin and guilt. At times, almost overwhelmed with distress, she turned to Jesus for comfort, and received from Him consolation.

"I believed that Jesus did love even me," she said (2SG, p. 11).

Later on Ellen realized that the cruel blow that made her life miserable proved to be a blessing in disguise. "I might never have known Jesus, had not the sorrow that clouded my early years led me to seek comfort in Him" (RH, Nov. 25, 1884).

In March 1840 William Miller conducted a series of revival meetings in Portland, Maine. In the series he lectured on the second coming of Christ and other Bible prophecies. Earnestly he preached that the end of the world was near. With her family and friends Ellen attended the meetings. Miller's powerful and solemn sermons brought "terrible conviction" to the entire city, and comfort and hope to 12-year-old Ellen (1LS, p. 137).

ELLEN'S DEVELOPING CHRISTIAN EXPERIENCE

In the summer of 1842 Ellen and her parents attended the Methodist camp meeting at Buxton, Maine. One sermon in particular led her to an understanding of justification by faith. Later she wrote:

> In his remarks the speaker referred to those who were wavering between hope and fear, longing to be saved from their sins and receive the pardoning love of Christ, yet held in doubt and bondage by timidity and fear of failure. He counseled such ones to surrender themselves to God and venture upon His mercy without delay (*ibid.*, p. 140).

Soon after her return to Portland from the camp meeting Ellen was taken into the Methodist Church on probation, with baptism to follow. In those days baptism as a means of acceptance into the Methodist Church was administered either by sprinkling or immersion. Ellen chose immersion. On Sunday afternoon, June 26, 1842, she and 11 others were baptized in the rather rough waters of Portland's Casco Bay.

About this time—in 1842—William Miller was back in Portland for another series of meetings on the Second Advent. Ellen attended faithfully and observed closely his demeanor and manner of preaching. Convinced that the doctrine he preached was the truth, she fully accepted his message, as did her older brother, Robert. Both decided it was their duty and privilege to prepare for the Saviour's coming.

In spite of her faith, Ellen's joy and confidence often were shadowed by periods of perplexity and deep concern. When she confided her anxieties to her mother, she was advised to ask counsel from Levi F. Stockman, who was then preaching the Advent doctrine in Portland.

Ellen told Elder Stockman about a dream she had had in which she was taken up some steps to see Jesus. Jesus received her with a smile and said, "Fear not."

Elder Stockman placed his hand on her head and said, with tears in his eyes, "Ellen, you are only a child. Yours is a most singular experience for one of your tender age. Jesus must be preparing you for some special work" (*ibid.*, p. 158).

This was the turning point in Ellen's experience. That evening she attended a prayer meeting and offered her first prayer in public.

"I praised God from the depths of my heart," she said. "Everything seemed shut out from me but Jesus and His glory, and I lost consciousness of what was passing around me" (*ibid.*, p. 159).

From this time forward Ellen's whole purpose in life was to do the will of God and keep Jesus continually in mind. She shared this newfound joy with her young friends, arranging meetings with them and telling them in a simple way the story of her experience.

BEARING PUBLIC WITNESS

Ellen's father and mother, Robert and Eunice Harmon, had been faithful members of the Chestnut Street Methodist Church for several years. They also were earnest believers in the soon coming of Christ. Young Robert and Ellen often attended class meetings in private homes. At one such meeting Ellen told in a simple way of her recent experience and the blessings she enjoyed as her life had been brought into full conformity to the will of God and confidence in Jesus' soon coming. She expected that her friends would understand and rejoice with her, but she was disappointed.

The class leader questioned her and suggested it would be better to look forward to the temporal millennium when the earth would be filled with the knowledge of God.

On another occasion, when it came time for her to testify, Ellen's heart was so full that she again spoke of looking forward in glad expectation to soon meeting her Redeemer. She said that this hope stirred her to seek sanctification of the Spirit of God.

"You received sanctification through Methodism," interjected the class leader. "Through *Methodism*, sister, not through an erroneous theory."

Ellen felt compelled to confess the truth. It was not through Methodism that she had received the new blessing, but by the stirring truths related to the soon coming of Jesus. This was the last testimony Ellen was to bear to this Methodist class.

Her brother, Robert, followed with a clear and impressive talk. Although some were much moved, others coughed with dissent and seemed quite uneasy. After leaving the classroom, Robert and Ellen again talked over their faith and marveled that their Christian brothers and sisters could not endure having their Saviour's coming discussed. They decided that they should no longer attend the Methodist class meeting.

CAST OUT FROM THE METHODIST CHURCH

Not long after this, the officers of the Chestnut Street Methodist Church took steps to separate the Harmon family from its membership. The minister made them a special visit. He did not inquire as to the reasons for their beliefs, but stated that they had adopted a new and strange belief that the Methodist Church could not accept.

"This is a very old doctrine," said Mr. Harmon, "and bears no taint of heresy." Mr. Harmon was prepared to quote Scripture in defense of his faith, including the promise of Jesus Himself that He would come again. But the minister was not willing to enter into any discussion. He advised the family to withdraw quietly from the church and avoid the publicity of a trial. But this proposition Robert

Harmon refused to accept. Soon the family was notified to be present at a meeting to be held in the church vestry. Of this meeting Ellen reported:

> There were but few present. The influence of my father and my family was such that our opposers had no desire to present our cases before a larger number of the congregation. The single charge preferred was that we had walked contrary to their rules (*ibid.*, p. 174).

Thus, on a Sunday in September 1843, the presiding elder read off the seven names of the Harmon family as discontinued from the church. He stated that they were not expelled on account of any wrong or immoral conduct, but because they were guilty of walking contrary to the rules of the Methodist Church. He also declared that all who were guilty of a similar breach of the rules would be dealt with in like manner.

1844—AND FOLLOWING

During the last few weeks leading up to April 21, 1844—the time first thought to be the end of the 2300-day prophecy—preparations for the glorious advent of Christ intensified. The rich and the poor, the high and the low, ministers and laymen, crowded into Portland's Beethoven Hall to hear the final exhortations to repent. Ellen White recalled the unity and peace among those of the sincere believers in her circle of friends and family:

> How carefully and tremblingly did we approach the time of expectation. We sought, as a people, with solemn earnestness to purify our lives that we might be ready to meet the Saviour at His coming. . . .
>
> Worldly business was for the most part laid aside for a few weeks. We carefully scrutinized every thought and emotion of our hearts as if upon our deathbeds. . . . There was no making "ascension robes" for the great event; we felt the need of internal evidence that we were prepared to meet Christ. . . .
>
> But the time of expectation passed. . . . The disappointment of God's waiting people was great (*ibid.*, pp. 180-184).

Although perplexed and disappointed, they did not renounce their faith. Ellen said:

> We fully believed that God, in His wisdom, designed that His people should meet with a disappointment, which was well calculated to reveal hearts and develop the true characters of those who had professed to look for and rejoice in the coming of the Lord (*ibid.*, p. 186).

Their confidence seemed well founded, for even scholars who had no conviction about the near advent of Christ saw no flaw in the reckoning of the prophecy. Ardently the believers had proclaimed what they understood to be the message of the first angel of Revelation, "The hour of his judgment is come" (Rev. 14:7). The Bible contained numerous prophecies concerning the second advent of Christ, foremost of which was given by Jesus Himself: "I go to prepare a place for you. And if I go and prepare a place for you, I will come again, and receive you unto myself; that where I am, there ye may be also" (John 14:2, 3).

Some of these promises seemed linked with the judgment. Basic was the prophecy of Daniel 8:14: "Unto two thousand three hundred days; then shall the sanctuary be cleansed." They thought this earth to be the sanctuary; it would be cleansed by fire at the second advent of Christ.

When April 21, 1844, passed and Jesus did not come, the believers checked and rechecked the basis of their reckoning.

> Calculation of the time was so simple and plain that even the children could understand it. From the date of the decree of the king of Persia, found in Ezra 7, which was given in 457 before Christ, the 2300 years of Daniel 8:14 must terminate with 1843. Accordingly we looked to the end of this year for the coming of the Lord. We were sadly disappointed when the year entirely passed away and the Saviour had not come.
>
> It was not at first perceived that if the decree did not go forth at the beginning of the year 457 B.C., the 2300 years would not be completed at the close of 1843. But it was ascertained that the decree was given near the close of the year 457 B.C. . . . Therefore the vision of time did not tarry, though it had seemed to do so (*ibid.*, pp. 185, 186).

A careful study of types and antitypes led to the observation that the crucifixion of Christ took place on the very day in the yearly round of ceremonies given to Israel when the Passover lamb was slain. Would not the cleansing of the sanctuary typified in the Day of Atonement—falling on the tenth day of the seventh month—likewise take place on the very day in the year celebrated in the type? This, according to the true Mosaic reckoning of time, would be October 22.

Early in August 1844, at a camp meeting at Exeter, New Hampshire, this view was presented and accepted as the date for the fulfillment of the prophecy of the 2300 days. The parable of the 10 virgins in Matthew 25:1-13 took on particular significance—the tarrying of the bridegroom, the waiting and slumbering of those who awaited the marriage, the cry at midnight, the shutting of the door, etc. The message that Christ was coming on October 22 came to be known as the "midnight cry." "The 'midnight cry,'" wrote Ellen White, "was heralded by thousands of believers" (GC 400).

Their hopes now centered in the coming of the Lord on October 22, 1844.

> This was also the time for the message of the second angel, who, flying through the midst of heaven, cried, "Babylon is fallen, is fallen, that great city." Many left the churches in obedience to the message of the second angel. Near its close the Midnight Cry was given: "Behold, the bridegroom cometh; go ye out to meet Him"! (1LS, p. 187).

This was "the happiest year of my life," recalled Ellen. "My heart was full of glad expectation; but I felt great pity and anxiety for those who were in discouragement and had no hope in Jesus."

> Light was being given concerning this message in every part of the land, and the cry aroused thousands. It went from city to city, from village to village, and into the remote country regions. It reached the learned and talented, as well as the obscure and humble (ibid).

In spite of the evidences of a work sweeping across the land and drawing thousands into the fellowship of the Second Advent, and some 200 ministers from various churches united in spreading the message,* the Protestant churches as a whole spurned it and used every means at their command to prevent the belief in Christ's soon coming from spreading. No one dared to mention in a church service the hope of the soon coming of Jesus, but to those awaiting the event it was quite different. Ellen White described what it was like:

> Every moment seemed precious and of the utmost importance to me. I felt that we were doing work for eternity, and that the careless and uninterested were in the greatest peril. My faith was unclouded, and I appropriated the precious promises of Jesus to myself. . . .
>
> With diligent searching of hearts and humble confession we came prayerfully up to the time of expectation. Every morning we felt that it was our first business to secure the evidence that our lives were right before God. We realized that if we were not advancing in holiness we were sure to retrograde. Our interest for each other increased; we prayed much with and for one another.
>
> We assembled in the orchards and groves to commune with God and to offer up our petitions to Him, feeling more clearly His presence when surrounded by His natural works. The joys of salvation were more necessary to us than our food and drink. If clouds obscured our minds we dared not rest or sleep till they were swept away by the consciousness of our acceptance with the Lord (ibid., pp. 188, 189).

THE GREAT DISAPPOINTMENT OF OCTOBER 22, 1844

With bated breath the Adventists, no fewer than 50,000 and probably nearer 100,000 scattered largely across the northeastern portion of North America, arose to greet the eventful day, Tuesday, October 22, 1844.

Some sought vantage points where they could peer into the clear heavens, hoping to catch a first glimpse of the coming of their returning Lord. When would Jesus come? The morning hours passed slowly. Noon came, then midafternoon. Finally darkness settled upon the earth. But it was still October 22, and it would be till midnight. At last that hour came, but Jesus did not come.

Their disappointment was almost beyond description. In later years some wrote of the experience. Hiram Edson gave a vivid account of how they looked for the coming of the Lord "until the clock tolled twelve at midnight. Then our disappointment became a certainty."

> Our fondest hopes and expectations were blasted, and such a spirit of weeping came over us as I never experienced before. It seemed that the loss of all earthly friends could have been no comparison. We wept and wept, till the day dawn.
>
> I mused in my own heart, saying, "My advent experience has been the richest and brightest of all my Christian experience. If this has proved a failure, what was the rest of my Christian experience worth? Has the Bible proved a failure? Is there no God, no heaven, no golden home city, no Paradise? Is all this but a cunningly devised fable? Is there no reality to our fondest hopes and expectation of these things?" And thus we had something to grieve and weep over, if all our fondest hopes were lost. And as I said, we wept, till the day dawn (DF 588, Hiram Edson manuscript [see also RH, June 23, 1921]).

Ellen White gave this eyewitness account:

> We were disappointed but not disheartened. We resolved to submit patiently to the process of purifying that God deemed needful for us; to refrain from murmuring at the trying ordeal by which the Lord was purging us from the dross and refining us like gold in the furnace. We resolved to wait with patient hope for the Saviour to redeem His tried and faithful ones.
>
> We were firm in the belief that the preaching of definite time was of God. It was this that led men to search the Bible diligently, discovering truths they had not before perceived. . . .
>
> Our disappointment was not so great as that of the disciples. When the Son of man rode triumphantly into Jerusalem they expected Him to

be crowned king. . . . Yet in a few days these very disciples saw their beloved Master, whom they believed would reign on David's throne, stretched upon the cruel cross above the mocking, taunting Pharisees. Their high hopes were drowned in bitter disappointment, and the darkness of death closed about them. Yet Christ was true to His promises (1LS, pp. 190-192).

ELLEN HARMON RECEIVES HER FIRST VISION

During this period of uncertainty and bitter disappointment Ellen's health, already impaired, worsened rapidly. Tuberculosis, it seemed, would take her life. She could speak only in a whisper or broken voice. Her heart was seriously affected. She found it difficult to breathe lying down, and at night was often bolstered to almost a sitting position. She was frequently awakened from sleep by coughing and bleeding in her lungs.

While in this condition Ellen responded to an invitation from a close friend, Mrs. Elizabeth Haines, just a little older than she, to visit her in her home across the causeway in south Portland. It was December, and cold, but even so Ellen went to spend a few days with her. Mrs. Haines was perplexed because of the seeming failure of the fulfillment of prophecy in October. Ellen, too, no longer had confidence in the validity of the October date. For her and her fellow believers, October 22 seemed to have no real significance. They now considered as yet in the future the events they had expected to take place on October 22 (letter 3, 1847; WLF, p. 22).

At morning family worship three other young women joined Mrs. Haines and Ellen. The commonly held belief is that this worship experience occurred in a second-floor room of the house at the corner of Ocean and C streets. The exact date is not known, but in 1847 Ellen White placed it in December 1844. She later recalled:

> While I was praying at the family altar, the Holy Ghost fell upon me, and I seemed to be rising higher and higher, far above the dark world. I turned to look for the Advent people in the world, but could not find them, when a voice said to me, "Look again, and look a little higher."
>
> At this I raised my eyes, and saw a straight and narrow path, cast up high above the world. On this path the Advent people were traveling to the city, which was at the farther end of the path. They had a bright light set up behind them at the beginning of the path, which an angel told me was the Midnight Cry. This light shone all along the path and gave light for their feet so that they might not stumble. If they kept

their eyes fixed on Jesus, who was just before them, leading them to the city, they were safe.

But soon some grew weary, and said the city was a great way off, and they expected to have entered it before. Then Jesus would encourage them by raising His glorious right arm, and from His arm came a light which waved over the Advent band, and they shouted, "Alleluia!"

Others rashly denied the light behind them and said that it was not God that had led them out so far. The light behind them went out, leaving their feet in perfect darkness, and they stumbled and lost sight of the mark and of Jesus, and fell off the path down into the dark and wicked world below. Soon we heard the voice of God like many waters, which gave us the day and hour of Jesus' coming. The living saints, 144,000 in number, knew and understood the voice, while the wicked thought it was thunder and an earthquake. When God spoke the time, He poured upon us the Holy Ghost, and our faces began to light up and shine with the glory of God, as Moses' did when he came down from Mount Sinai.

The 144,000 were all sealed and perfectly united. On their foreheads was written, God, New Jerusalem, and a glorious star containing Jesus' new name.

At our happy, holy state the wicked were enraged, and would rush violently up to lay hands on us to thrust us into prison, when we would stretch forth the hand in the name of the Lord, and they would fall helpless to the ground. Then it was that the synagogue of Satan knew that God had loved us who could wash one another's feet and salute the brethren with a holy kiss, and they worshiped at our feet.

Soon our eyes were drawn to the east, for a small black cloud[†] had appeared, about half as large as a man's hand, which we all knew was the sign of the Son of man. We all in solemn silence gazed on the cloud as it drew nearer and became lighter, glorious, and still more glorious, till it was a great white cloud. The bottom appeared like fire; a rainbow was over the cloud, while around it were ten thousand angels, singing a most lovely song; and upon it sat the Son of man. His hair was white and curly and lay on His shoulders; and upon His head were many crowns. His feet had the appearance of fire; in His right hand was a sharp sickle; in His left, a silver trumpet. His eyes were as a flame of fire, which searched His children through and through.

Then all faces gathered paleness, and those that God had rejected gathered blackness. Then we all cried out, "Who shall be able to stand? Is my robe spotless?" Then the angels ceased to sing, and there was some time of awful silence, when Jesus spoke: "Those who have clean hands and pure hearts shall be able to stand; My grace is sufficient for you." At this our faces lighted up, and joy filled every heart. And the angels struck a note higher and sang again, while the cloud drew still nearer the earth.

Then Jesus' silver trumpet sounded, as He descended on the cloud, wrapped in flames of fire. He gazed on the graves of the sleeping saints, then raised His eyes and hands to heaven, and cried, "Awake! awake! awake! ye that sleep in the dust, and arise." Then there was a mighty earthquake. The graves opened, and the dead came up clothed with immortality. The 144,000 shouted, "Alleluia!" as they recognized their friends who had been torn from them by death, and in the same moment we were changed and caught up together with them to meet the Lord in the air.

We all entered the cloud together, and were seven days ascending to the sea of glass (EW, pp. 14-16 [see also *The Day-Star*, Jan. 24, 1846]).

---

*See C. M. Maxwell, *Tell It to the World*, pp. 19, 20.
† See the expanded account in GC, pp. 640-642.

CALLED TO BE A MESSENGER

Difficult days challenged the Advent believers in Portland, Maine, following the great disappointment of October 22, 1844. Some clung to the hope that the mistake involved a miscalculation of only a few days, and lived in constant expectancy. They believed that Jesus would come at almost any moment and that probation was closed. But as the days stretched into weeks and Jesus did not come, their faith began to waver.

"Why, oh, why were we disappointed?" their hearts cried out. They had been confident that God had been leading them as they studied, worked, and prayed. How could they be mistaken in the integrity of the 1844 date?

By December most of the believers in the Portland area had abandoned their confidence in Miller's interpretation. Every passing day drove home the conviction that nothing of prophetic significance had taken place on October 22.

Nothing could have been more timely and calculated to cheer the spirits of the dedicated believers than the vision given to Ellen Harmon in December in the Haines home. This presented an entirely different picture. *God had led His people.* The light behind them that shone all along the path was the Midnight Cry. The vision revealed that they were at the beginning of the path rather than at the end. If they trusted the light and kept their eyes fixed on Jesus, they would safely enter into their reward.

About one week later Ellen was given a second vision. The vision troubled her much, for in it she was commissioned to go out among the people and present the truths that God had revealed to her. Her health was poor; she was in constant bodily suffering; tuberculosis ravaged her lungs; and in every way she appeared "marked for the grave." Her family was without money; it was midwinter in Maine; she was timid, and entertained serious misgivings about traveling and coming before the people with the claim to have had visions.

For several days and far into the night Ellen prayed that God would remove the burden from her and place it on someone more capable of bearing it. But constantly the words of the angel sounded in her ears: "Make known to others what I have revealed to you" (1LS, p. 194).

The first telling of the vision in her parents' home in Portland apparently took place within a few days of the vision itself, which she later pinpointed as having occurred in December 1844. What a relief this brought to the

Adventists in Portland! They knew her family. They had heard that a vision had been given to her, and when they heard it from her own lips they accepted what she told them as a message from God. It met a need in their experience. According to James White, about 60 belonging to the Advent band in Portland accepted the vision and through it regained their confidence in the fulfillment of prophecy concerning October 22, 1844 (WLF, p. 22).

But the task of traveling and sharing the vision seemed to her impossible to accomplish and doomed to failure. Oh, how welcome death would have been, for it would have released her from the responsibilities that were crowding in upon her. She talked with her father of her perplexities. He repeatedly assured her that if God had called her to a public ministry, He would not fail her. But to Ellen it seemed impossible to submit to the commission.

Soon the peace of God that she had enjoyed left her. She even refused to attend the meetings held in her home. But one evening she was persuaded to be present. At this meeting John Pearson encouraged her to surrender her will to the will of God. In her distress she could not muster courage to bring her own will into play. But now her heart united with the petitions of her friends. She later recounted:

> While prayer was offered for me, that the Lord would give me strength and courage to bear the message, the thick darkness that had encompassed me rolled back, and a sudden light came upon me. Something that seemed to me like a ball of fire struck me right over the heart. My strength was taken away, and I fell to the floor. I seemed to be in the presence of the angels. One of these holy beings again repeated the words, "Make known to others what I have revealed to you" (3LS, p. 71).

When Ellen regained consciousness, Elder Pearson, who because of rheumatism could not kneel, stood and declared:

> "I have seen a sight such as I never expected to see. A ball of fire came down from heaven, and struck Sister Ellen Harmon right on the heart. *I saw it! I saw it!* I can never forget it. It has changed my whole being. Sister Ellen, have courage in the Lord. After this night I will never doubt again" *(ibid.)*.

FEAR OF EXALTATION

One reason Ellen shrank from the trying ordeal was that she recalled the experience of some who had become proud after being entrusted by God with large responsibilities. In vision she discussed this with the angel. "If I must go and relate what thou hast shown me," she pleaded, "preserve me from undue exaltation." Replied the angel:

"Your prayers are heard and shall be answered. If this evil that you dread threatens you, the hand of God will be stretched out to save you; by affliction He will draw you to Himself and preserve your humility.

"Deliver the message faithfully. Endure unto the end and you shall eat the fruit of the tree of life and drink of the water of life" (1LS, p. 196).

With this assurance Ellen committed herself to the Lord, ready to do His bidding, whatever that might be or whatever the cost.

Providence quickly opened the way for Ellen to enter upon her work. One day in late January 1845 her brother-in-law, Samuel Foss, from Poland, Maine, stopped in at the house and told her that Mary was eager for her to come and visit her.

"I thought this was an opening from the Lord," Ellen wrote later (letter 37, 1890). She decided to go with him. In the bitter cold and in spite of feeble health, she made the 30-mile (50-kilometer) journey with her brother-in-law—crouched on the bottom of the sleigh with a buffalo robe over her head. When she reached Poland she learned that there would soon be a meeting of the Adventists at the little chapel on McGuire's Hill. Mary invited Ellen to attend. She consented, and at the meeting stood to relate what God had shown her in vision. For five minutes she spoke in only a whisper, then her voice broke clear and she addressed the audience for nearly two hours. This was the first time that she related her vision outside of Portland. She reported, "In this meeting the power of the Lord came upon me and on the people" *(ibid.)*.

Before continuing with our story, we should review a bit of history. During the months that led up to October 22, 1844, the believers were absolutely united in their confidence that Jesus would come on the appointed day. But as the weeks stretched into months a wedge began to separate the Adventists. Fanatical teachings and actions on the part of some divided the little group who clung to their confidence that prophecy had been fulfilled on October 22. A few, following what they interpreted to be the biddings of God's Word, but lacking balance and a true understanding of what it means to follow Christ, became involved in strange and sometimes wild fanaticism.

A small group, however, having cut loose from church creeds and church discipline, maintained their purpose to find their guidance in God's Word alone. They patiently awaited the dawning of light, that they might gain a true understanding of their position and work. These became the spiritual forebears of the Seventh-day Adventist Church.

Into this scene the 17-year-old Ellen Harmon was cast. She began her work by encouraging the believers and countering fanaticism, a work that was to continue through the next year or two.

After a few days in Poland at her sister's home, Ellen was back again in Portland, convinced that she must follow the intimations of God's will. She had promised to go if the Lord opened the way, and now she was invited by William Jordan and his sister, Sarah, to journey with them to eastern Maine. "I was urged to go with them," she wrote, "and relate my visions" (2SG, p. 38). The Jordans were driving by sleigh the 100 miles (160 kilometers) to Orrington, on the Penobscot River.

Mr. Jordan had a horse that belonged to a young Adventist minister, James White. As he had business that would take him to certain parts of eastern Maine, he decided to return the horse and invited Miss Harmon to accompany them so that she might bear her witness in a wider circle. Little did Ellen realize what was before her. She had now assumed a confident trust in God. Financial resources for her journey did not concern her. Just where her itinerary might take her she did not know. As to the message she might bear, she would depend wholly upon God.

At Orrington Jordan delivered the horse to James White. Here Ellen met the youthful but earnest Adventist minister, firm in his confidence in the fulfillment of prophecy.

James had become aware of Ellen on an earlier trip to Portland, and was glad that she had come and he would have a chance to hear her relate her visions. As she stood up to speak, James took in every detail of her face and dress and manner. She seemed so young, so shy, so humble that he was surprised she would have the courage to speak to this gathering. He knew well the nature of some of the people in the audience. As she began to speak, her voice was low—hardly above a whisper. She faltered a little, and it appeared that she might not go on. But after a few minutes her voice became clear and strong. She seemed perfectly at ease, and all hesitation and embarrassment were gone. Her message was one of simple faith and encouragement.

Following this visit in Orrington, Ellen gave her witness in eastern Maine for several months, traveling day and night and speaking almost every day until she had visited most of the Advent bands in Maine and in the eastern part of New Hampshire. James White accompanied her and a woman traveling companion.

Her message was always attended with the Holy Ghost, and, wherever it was received as from the Lord, it melted hearts, strengthened the weak, and encouraged the believers to hold on to the faith.

VISION OF MINISTRY IN THE HEAVENLY SANCTUARY

Ellen had been in eastern Maine only a short time when, at Exeter, she was given the significant vision she described in two early letters. One, dated February 15, 1846, was to Enoch Jacobs; the other, dated July 13, 1847, was to Joseph Bates. Of this vision she wrote:

It was then I had a view of Jesus rising from His mediatorial throne and going to the Holiest as Bridegroom to receive His kingdom (letter 3, 1847).

I saw the Father rise from the throne and in a flaming chariot go into the Holy of Holies within the veil, and did sit. . . . I saw a cloudy chariot with wheels like flaming fire. Angels were all about the chariot as it came where Jesus was; He stepped into it and was borne to the Holiest, where the Father sat. Then I beheld Jesus as He was before the Father, a great high priest (letter 1, 1846 [see also *The Day-Star*, Mar. 14, 1846]).

In her ministry she mentioned this vision from time to time, for it confirmed the results of Bible study—of which she knew nothing at the time—in western New York State by Hiram Edson and O.R.L. Crosier. In a letter to J. N. Loughborough, written August 24, 1874, she recounted:

It was on my first journey east to relate my visions that the precious light in regard to the heavenly sanctuary was opened before me and I was shown the open and shut door. We believed that the Lord was soon to come in the clouds of heaven. I was shown that there was a great work to be done in the world for those who had not the light. . . . Some accused me of saying my Lord delayeth His coming, especially the fanatical ones. I saw that in 1844 God had opened a door and no man could shut it, and shut a door and no man could open it (letter 2, 1874).

In eastern Maine Ellen was traveling and working in the atmosphere of the spiritualizers who had allegorized away heaven, God, Jesus, and the Advent hope. In the vision at Exeter in mid-February she seemed to be in the presence of Jesus, and she was eager to obtain answers to some vital questions.

I asked Jesus if His Father had a form like Himself. He said He had, but I could not behold it, for said He, "If you should once behold the glory of His person, you would cease to exist" (EW, p. 54).

The spiritualization of heaven, God, Christ, and the coming of Christ lay at the foundation of much of the fanatical teachings that 17-year-old Ellen Harmon was called by God to meet in those formative days. The visions firmly established the personality of God and Christ, the reality of heaven, the reward of the faithful, and the resurrection. This sound guidance saved the emerging church.

A large number of people at this time were bitter and disappointed when the period passed without bringing the event that was expected. For these Ellen was given a message of good cheer and encouragement. She called their attention to the fact that God had granted the world more time to prepare for His coming; that the warning of the judgment could be heard more widely; and that the people could be tested with greater light. Although the expected event did not occur (as in the case of Jonah), the message was nonetheless of God and accomplished the purpose He designed it should.

Subsequent light upon the prophecies revealed the event that did take place—the entering of the High Priest into the Most Holy Place of the sanctuary in heaven to finish the atonement for the sins of humanity.

IT WAS NOT EASY

It was not easy to be a messenger of the Lord. Particularly at the beginning of Ellen Harmon's ministry it was important that the gift of prophecy promised to the remnant church be established with unusual phenomena.

Through false representations some of the believers were led to believe that the visions were of the devil, that James White mesmerized her, and that she could not have a vision if he was not present. Some attributed her visions to magnetism (hypnotism) or mesmerism.

At times because of all the suggestions and accusations that were made, she was led to question her own experience. She wrote:

> All these things weighed heavily upon my spirits, and in the confusion I was sometimes tempted to doubt my own experience. While at family prayers one morning, the power of God began to rest upon me, and the thought rushed into my mind that it was mesmerism, and I resisted it. Immediately I was struck dumb and for a few moments was lost to everything around me. I then saw my sin in doubting the power of God, and that for so doing I was struck dumb, and that my tongue would be loosed in less than twenty-four hours.
>
> A card was held up before me, on which were written in letters of gold the chapter and verse of fifty texts of Scripture. [Texts are given in *Early Writings*, pp. 24-31.] After I came out of vision, I beckoned for the slate, and wrote upon it that I was dumb, also what I had seen, and that I wished the large Bible.
>
> I took the Bible and readily turned to all the texts that I had seen upon the card. I was unable to speak all day. Early the next morning my soul was filled with joy, and my tongue was loosed to shout the high praises of God. After that I dared not doubt or for a moment resist the power of God, however others might think of me (EW, pp. 22, 23).

The Bible Ellen called for after this experience in her home in Portland was, presumably, the "big Bible" now in the White Estate vault with the names of Robert and Eunice Harmon stamped in gold on the spine. This Bible is 18 inches (46 centimeters) long, 11 inches (28 centimeters) wide, four inches (10 centimeters) thick, and weighs 18½ pounds (seven kilograms). On one occasion, during family prayers in 1845, Ellen stepped over to a bureau upon which this large volume rested and picked it up. Placing it on her left hand, she easily held it with her arm extended for an estimated half hour. During the vision she referred, in short exclamations, to the value of the Word of God. Although in frail health she was in no way fatigued by the experience.

On another occasion Ellen encountered a group of obstinate opposers. By invitation of Brother and Sister Otis Nichols, Ellen and her sister Sarah were in Massachusetts making their home with the Nichols family. There was in Boston and vicinity a company of fanatical persons who held that it was a sin to work. Two of their leaders were named Sargent and Robbins. Their principal message was "Sell that ye have, and give alms." They had denounced Ellen's visions as being of the devil because she had been shown their errors.

One day when Sargent and Robbins were visiting at the Nichols home they agreed to Nichols' proposal that they hear Ellen's testimony at their meeting in Boston the next Sunday. But that evening Ellen was shown their hypocrisy and that they were not having a meeting in Boston; it would be in Randolph. So the next morning, instead of driving north into Boston, they drove 13 miles (22 kilometers) south to Randolph, arriving rather late in the morning. They found Sargent and Robbins and a roomful of people meeting in the Thayer home. Wrote Ellen,

> As we entered, Robbins and Sargent looked at each other in surprise and began to groan. They had promised to meet me in Boston, but thought they would disappoint us by going to Randolph, and while we were in Boston, warn the brethren against us" (1LS, p. 232).

Closing the morning services rather early, Sargent announced that they would have a short intermission. Ellen Harmon learned during the intermission that one of the critics remarked that "good matter would be brought out in the afternoon." Robbins told Sarah Harmon that Ellen could not have a vision where he was.

Assembling again about 1:00 in the afternoon, several engaged in prayer, including Ellen Harmon.

OTIS NICHOLS' EYEWITNESS ACCOUNT

Writing in 1859 or 1860, Otis Nichols gave this account of the meeting:

> About one o'clock p.m. the meeting was opened by singing and praying by Sargent, Robbins, and French; then one of us prayed for the Lord

to lead this meeting. Then Sister White commenced praying and was soon afterwards taken off in vision with extraordinary manifestations and continued talking in vision with a shrill voice which could be distinctly understood by all present, until about sundown.

Sargent, Robbins, and French were much exasperated as well as excited to hear Sister White talk in vision, which they declared was of the devil. They exhausted all their influence and bodily strength to destroy the effect of the vision. They would unite in singing very loud, and then alternately would talk and read from the Bible in a loud voice in order that Ellen might not be heard, until their strength was exhausted and their hands would shake, so they could not read from the Bible.

But amidst all this confusion and noise, Ellen's clear and shrill voice as she talked in vision was distinctly heard by all present. The opposition of these men continued as long as they could talk and sing, notwithstanding some of their own friends rebuked them and requested them to stop.

"But," said Robbins, "you are bowed to an idol. You are worshiping a golden calf."

Mr. Thayer, the owner of the house, was not fully satisfied that her vision was of the devil, as Robbins declared it to be. He wanted it tested in some way. He had heard that visions of satanic power were arrested by opening the Bible and laying it on the person in vision, and asked Sargent if he would test it in this way, which he declined to do.

Then Thayer took a heavy, large quarto family Bible which was lying on the table and seldom used, opened it, and laid it open upon the breast of Ellen while in vision, as she was then inclined backward against the wall in one corner of the room. Immediately after the Bible was laid upon her, she arose upon her feet and walked into the middle of the room, with the Bible open in one hand and lifted up as high as she could reach, and with her eyes steadily looking upward, declared in a solemn manner, "The inspired testimony of God," or words of the same import, and then she continued for a long time, while the Bible was extended in one hand and her eyes [were] looking upward and not on the Bible, to turn over the leaves with the other hand and place her finger upon certain passages and correctly utter their words with a solemn voice.

Many present looked at the passages where her finger was pointed to see if she spoke them correctly, for her eyes at the same time were looking upward. Some of the passages referred to were judgments against the wicked and blasphemous; and others were admonitions and instructions relative to our present condition.

In this state she continued all the afternoon until nearly sundown when she came out of vision.

When Ellen arose in vision upon her feet with the heavy open Bible upon her hand, and walked the room uttering the passages of Scripture, Sargent, Robbins, and French were silent. For the remainder of the time they were troubled, with many others, but they shut their eyes and braved it out without making any acknowledgment of their feelings (DF 105, "Statement by Otis Nichols" [see also 1LS, pp. 232-234; 2SG, pp. 77-79]).

Not long after this these men confessed publicly to some of the most shameful acts of their lives. This had the effect of breaking up the meetings at Randolph and separating the honest believers from their unholy influence. Within a short time the "No-work Party" of fanatics gave up their faith in the Bible and scattered as Ellen had predicted.

Some stalwart souls who later became pillars in the church were initially hesitant about accepting the visions of Ellen Harmon. Outstanding among these was Joseph Bates.

Joseph Bates had been an earnest worker in the Advent awakening of 1840-1844. A sea-captain-turned-minister, he invested his property and his strength in heralding the soon coming of Christ. As Ellen and her sister were in New Bedford, Massachusetts, they became acquainted with him and his family. He, of course, learned of the visions given to Ellen, and this troubled him. He wrote of his experience two years later:

Although I could see nothing in them that militated against the Word, yet I felt alarmed and tried exceedingly, and for a long time unwilling to believe that it was anything more than what was produced by a protracted debilitated state of her body.

I therefore sought opportunities in the presence of others, when her mind seemed freed from excitement (out of meeting), to question and cross-question her, and her friends which accompanied her, especially her elder sister [Sarah], to get if possible at the truth (3LS, pp. 97, 98).

Bates had been troubled with serious doubts as to the visions, but the evidence in the experience at Topsham, Maine, at the home of Eli Curtis in November 1846, was such that he accepted them wholeheartedly from that time forth. Bates told the story to his friend J. N. Loughborough, who recorded it in his book *The Great Second Advent Movement*.

Mrs. White, while in vision, began to talk about the stars, giving a glowing description of rosy-tinted belts which she saw across the surface of some planet, and added, "I see four moons."

"Oh," said Elder Bates, "she is viewing Jupiter!"

Then having made motions as though traveling through space, she began giving a description of belts and rings in their ever-varying beauty, and said, "I see seven moons."

Elder Bates exclaimed, "She is describing Saturn."

Next she said, "I see six moons," and at once began a description of Uranus, with its six moons; then a wonderful description of the "opening heavens," with its glory, calling it an opening into a region more enlightened. Elder Bates said that her description far surpassed any account of the opening heavens he had ever read from any author.

While she was talking and still in vision, he arose to his feet, and exclaimed, "Oh, how I wish Lord John Rosse was here tonight!" Elder White inquired, "Who is Lord John Rosse?"

"Oh," said Elder Bates, "he is the great English astronomer. I wish he was here to hear that woman talk astronomy, and to hear that description of the 'opening heavens.' It is ahead of anything I ever read on the subject" (GSAM, p. 258).

Ellen White reported of this experience that took place in the Eli Curtis home:

After I came out of vision I related what I had seen. Elder Bates then asked if I had studied astronomy. I told him I had no recollection of ever looking into an astronomy.

Said he, "This is of the Lord."

I never saw him as free and happy before. His countenance shone with the light of heaven, and he exhorted the church with power (1LS, p. 239).

Another pioneer of the Advent movement who had witnessed the early manifestation of the gift of the Spirit through Ellen Harmon was John N. Loughborough, who first saw her in vision in 1852 and later in life declared that he had seen her in vision 50 times. He wrote:

In passing into vision she gives three enrapturing shouts of "Glory!" which echo and re-echo, the second, and especially the third, fainter, but more thrilling than the first, the voice resembling that of one quite a distance from you, and just going out of hearing.

For about four or five seconds she seems to drop down like a person in a swoon, or one having lost his strength; she then seems to be instantly filled with superhuman strength, sometimes rising at once to her feet and walking about the room. There are frequent movements of the hands and arms, pointing to the right or left as her head turns. All these movements are made in a most graceful manner. In whatever position the hand or arm may be placed, it is impossible for anyone to move it.

Her eyes are always open, but she does not wink; her head is raised, and she is looking upward, not with a vacant stare, but with a pleasant expression, only differing from the normal in that she appears to be looking intently at some distant object.

She does not breathe, yet her pulse beats regularly. Her countenance is pleasant, and the color of her face as florid as in her natural state (GSAM, pp. 204, 205).

Individual visions were marked by various characteristics, but James White pointed out four:

1. She is utterly unconscious of everything transpiring around her, as has been proved by the most rigid tests, but views herself as removed from this world, and in the presence of heavenly beings.

2. She does not breathe. During the entire period of her continuance in vision, which has at different times ranged from fifteen minutes to three hours, there is no breath, as has been repeatedly proved by pressing upon the chest, and by closing the mouth and nostrils.

3. Immediately on entering vision, her muscles become rigid, and joints fixed, so far as any external force can influence them. At the same time her movements and gestures, which are frequent, are free and graceful, and cannot be hindered nor controlled by the strongest person.

4. On coming out of vision, whether in the daytime or a well-lighted room at night, all is total darkness. Her power to distinguish even the most brilliant objects, held within a few inches of the eyes, returns but gradually. . . .

She has probably had, during the past twenty-three years, between one and two hundred visions. These have been given under almost every variety of circumstance, yet maintaining a wonderful similarity (*Life Incidents*, p. 272).

While Ellen had no part in the divine procedure that selected her as the one to whom the gift of prophecy would be given for the remnant church, the responsibility of delivering special light, truth, and counsel troubled her very much. She often prayed that God would remove the burden from her and place it upon someone more capable of bearing it. Many times she felt that death would have been welcome to relieve her of the responsibilities.

"Deliver the message faithfully," the angel had said. "Endure unto the end, and you shall eat of the fruit of the tree of life and drink of the water of life" (3LS, p. 72). With this assurance Ellen committed herself to the Lord, ready to do His bidding whatever the cost.

Jesus did not tell His disciples that their work would be easy. When Ellen accepted the call to be God's special messenger, she was not told that it would be easy. Finding acceptance for the role to which she was committed was not easy.

But one of the most difficult problems that confronted her and her family at the beginning of her ministry was the matter of transportation. How could an 18-year-old girl, frail and in poor health, get around and visit the scattered believers in Maine, Massachusetts, New Hampshire, and other places? Frequently on the steamboats or on the train she would faint and remain breathless for minutes.

James White explained:

> It was necessary that she should have one or more attendants. Either her sister Sarah or Sister Foss traveled with her. And as neither her aged father nor feeble brother were suitable persons to travel with one so feeble, and introduce her and her mission to the people, the writer, fully believing that her wonderful experience and work was of God, became satisfied that it was his duty to accompany them.

> And as our thus traveling subjected us to the reproaches of the enemies of the Lord and His truth, duty seemed very clear that the one who had so important a message to the world should have a legal protector, and that we should unite our labors (1LS, p. 238).

James and Ellen had been closely associated in travel and labor through much of 1845, but apparently neither had given thought to marriage. Of their situation James White later wrote that they both shared the view that the coming of Christ was "near, even at the doors. . . . Most of our brethren who believed with us that the Second Advent movement was the work of God were opposed to marriage in the sense that as time was very short it was a denial of faith, as such a union contemplated long years of married life" (*ibid.*, p. 126).

Now as her work would spread out into a larger field, they took the matter to the Lord and were convinced that God had a great work for both of them, and that they could greatly assist each other in that work.

THE WEDDING

On Sunday, August 30, 1846, James Springer White and Ellen Gould Harmon stood before Charles Harding, justice of the peace, in Portland, Maine, and were married. The marriage certificate, preserved through the years, is just a small slip of paper carrying a brief form and the signature of the one who officiated. Of their experience James White later wrote:

> We were married August 30, 1846, and from that hour to the present

she has been my crown of rejoicing. . . . It has been in the good providence of God that both of us had enjoyed a deep experience in the Advent movement. . . . This experience was now needed as we should join our forces and, united, labor extensively from the Atlantic Ocean to the Pacific. . . .

We entered upon this work penniless, with few friends, and broken in health. Mrs. White has suffered ill health from a child, . . . and although I had inherited a powerful constitution, imprudence in study at school, and in lecturing . . . had made me a dyspeptic.

In this condition, without means, with very few who sympathized with us in our views, without a paper, and without books, we entered upon our work. We had no houses of worship at that time, and the idea of using a tent had not then occurred to us. Most of our meetings were held in private houses. Our congregations were small. It was seldom that any came into our meetings, excepting Adventists, unless they were attracted by curiosity to hear a woman speak (*ibid.*, pp. 126, 127).

The Harmon home in Gorham became the first place of residence for the newlyweds.

STEP BY STEP

The first seed that was to grow into the worldwide Seventh-day Adventist publishing work was planted in January 1846. It came about in rather an unpremeditated manner.

Soon after her eighteenth birthday Ellen had learned that Enoch Jacobs, of Cincinnati, Ohio, one of the believers who had been disappointed in 1844, had been wavering in his confidence in the fulfillment of prophecy. She wrote to him from Portland on December 20, 1845, recounting the highlights of her first vision. Although she stated that the letter was not written for publication, Jacobs printed it in the *Day-Star* issue of January 24, 1846.

Through the next few years it was republished in various forms until it was carried into her first little book, *Christian Experience and Views*, published in 1851, and from there into *Early Writings*.

Sometime later when Ellen was visiting in the home of Otis Nichols in Dorchester, near Boston, she discovered that the editor of *The Day-Star* had published her letter, including her statement that it was not written for publication. Seeing this, on February 15, 1846, she wrote a second letter to Jacobs stating that had she known he was going to publish her first letter she would have written more fully of what God had revealed to her. "As the readers of *The Day-Star* have seen a part of what God has revealed to me, . . . I humbly request you to publish this also in your paper" (*The Day-Star*, Mar. 14, 1846). She presented the vision given to her at Exeter, Maine, "one year ago this month." This was the vision in which she was shown the heavenly sanctuary and the transfer of the ministry of Christ from the holy place to the "Holy of Holies."

THE PLACE OF THE VISION IN CONFIRMING THE SANCTUARY TRUTH

Significantly, *The Day-Star Extra* dated February 7, 1846, had been devoted to the Bible study of Hiram Edson and O.R.L. Crosier in which they set forth from the Scriptures the evidence for the understanding that the two phases of ministry in the earthly sanctuary service were a type of Christ's ministry in the heavenly sanctuary. Consequently, according to Edson and Crosier, events that were to come to pass, beginning on October 22, 1844, were events taking place in heaven.

The investigation supporting these conclusions had taken place at the

Hiram Edson home in western New York State over a period of a number of months. The existence of this Bible study was unknown to Ellen Harmon when she was given the vision in Exeter in mid-February 1845, nor had there been time for the February 7, 1846, issue of *The Day-Star* to reach her before she wrote of the vision for the readers of that journal. The vision, as published on March 14, gave unique confirmation to the conclusions of the Edson and Crosier Bible study. A year later, April 21, 1847, Ellen White wrote in a letter to Eli Curtis:

> The Lord showed me in vision, more than one year ago, that Brother Crosier had the true light on the cleansing of the sanctuary, et cetera, and that it was His will that Brother C. should write out the view which he gave us in *The Day-Star Extra*, February 7, 1846. I feel fully authorized by the Lord to recommend that *Extra* to every saint (WLF, p. 12).

Step by step God was leading His children. The great Second Advent Awakening, so powerful, so free from extremes and fanaticism, was to the sincere believers the work of God. The disappointment of October 22 was a bitter experience, but they were confident that God had led them and would continue to lead those who kept their eyes on Jesus. Earnest, prayerful Bible study pointed the way to an understanding of the ministry of Jesus in the heavenly sanctuary. In vision Ellen Harmon witnessed Christ entering the Most Holy Place in the heavenly sanctuary to begin another phase of ministry, closing one door and opening another, thus confirming the integrity of their 1844 experience. It also confirmed the conclusions reached through earnest Bible study. It would take time to grasp fully the various aspects of unfolding truth.

THE SEVENTH-DAY SABBATH

Soon after their marriage Ellen and James began keeping the seventh-day Sabbath. Scriptural evidence for this had first been given to them by Joseph Bates, a retired sea captain living in Fairhaven, near New Bedford, the Massachusetts whaling seaport center. Bates had taken his stand in 1845, having had his attention called to it through an article in *The Hope of Israel*, written by T. M. Preble. A man of conviction and action, Bates in turn prepared a 48-page pamphlet, which he published in August 1846 under the title *The Seventh-day Sabbath a Perpetual Sign From the Beginning to the Entering Into the Gates of the Holy City According to the Commandment*. James White took a copy home with him after a funeral service he conducted at Falmouth. As he and Ellen studied the biblical evidences for the sacredness of the seventh day, they took their stand and began to teach it as they met with their fellow Adventists. At this time there were about 50 Sabbathkeepers in New England and New York State (1T, p. 77).

James and Ellen White had accepted the Sabbath solely on the evidence of Scripture called to their attention by the Joseph Bates tract. On Sabbath, April 3, 1847, while visiting with the Howlands in their well-constructed home in Topsham, Maine, Ellen was given a significant vision confirming the Sabbath. She wrote of it in a letter to Joseph Bates:

> In the city I saw a temple, which I entered. I passed through a door before I came to the first veil. This veil was raised, and I passed into the holy place. I saw the altar of incense, the candlestick with seven lamps, and the table on which was the shewbread, et cetera. After viewing the glory of the holy, Jesus raised the second veil, and I passed into the Holy of Holies.
>
> In the Holiest I saw an ark; on the top and sides of it was purest gold. On each end of the ark was a lovely cherub, with their wings spread over it. Their faces were turned towards each other, and they looked downwards. Between the angels was a golden censer. Above the ark, where the angels stood, was an exceeding bright glory, that appeared like a throne where God dwelt. Jesus stood by the ark (WLF, p. 18 [see also EW, pp. 32-35]).

In the vision Ellen saw Jesus ministering in the Most Holy Place in behalf of the saints, and then the ark was opened to enable her to see its contents. She describes what she saw:

> In the ark was the golden pot of manna, Aaron's rod that budded, and the tables of stone which folded together like a book. Jesus opened them, and I saw the Ten Commandments written on them with the finger of God. On one table was four, and on the other six. The four on the first table shone brighter than the other six. But the fourth, the Sabbath commandment, shone above them all; for the Sabbath was set apart to be kept in honor of God's holy name. The holy Sabbath looked glorious—a halo of glory was all around it (*ibid.*).

In successive scenes she was carried through a review of the factors that give validity to the Sabbath and its observance. She was shown that the Sabbath is the point at which all humanity must make a decision to serve God or an apostate power. The vision was climaxed with a view of the second coming of Christ and the ascension of the redeemed to the Holy City, where Jesus opens the gates to welcome those who have "kept *the 'commandments of God,'*" and have a "'right to the tree of life'" (*ibid.*, p. 20).

A letter containing this message was sent to Joseph Bates. James White suggested to Bates that he have 1,000 copies printed on a broadside and send him the bill. This Bates did. When James received the bill of $7.50 he borrowed the money to pay it. Writing to Elvira Hastings, of New Ipswich, New Hampshire, he stated that he would "trust in the Lord for the money to be sent in" (JW to Elvira Hastings, May 21, 1847).

The intense urgency that had motivated both Ellen and James to spread the news of Christ's second coming before the disappointment in 1844 now was intensified by the impact of the visions and the assurance that came with the revelation of God's gentle guiding of His faithful believers. But how could they get this wonderful news across to the widely separated, somewhat bewildered people? Without funds, backing from any source, or experience, James White plunged ahead.

April 1847 marked James White's first major publishing accomplishment—the issuance of a 24-page pamphlet that he titled A Word to the "Little Flock." The type was small and the margins narrow, yielding a page with twice the normal content of a book page of today.

Just a year earlier, on April 6, 1846, he had arranged for the broadside publication of Ellen's first vision—a single large sheet printed on one side only. Two hundred fifty copies were struck off in Portland, Maine. H. S. Gurney, blacksmith of Fairhaven, Massachusetts, shared the printing costs. It carried the significant title "To the Little Remnant Scattered Abroad." A little more than two of the three columns were given to Ellen's first vision. Half of the third column was devoted to the vision of mid-February 1845 concerning the heavenly sanctuary and the events at the end of the 2300 days (EW, pp. 54-56).

Very clearly A Word to the "Little Flock" represented the joint ministry of both James and Ellen White. James had written several articles for publication in Crosier's short-lived Day-Dawn, but by the time they were ready, that paper had ceased publication. So after talking with the Howlands and some others, he decided to present the materials in pamphlet form. In his opening paragraph he explained: "I wish to call the attention of the 'little flock' to those things which will very soon take place on this earth" (WLF, p. 1).

The pamphlet was Bible-based with copious Scripture references and quotations. It seems clear that the visions given to Ellen helped James sort things out and clarify the order of events. It will be remembered that in 1845 a move toward time setting had been averted when Ellen was shown that before Christ would come, "the saints must pass through the 'time of Jacob's trouble,' which was future" (ibid., p. 22).

The Whites were in Topsham through much of April and May while James was getting his pamphlet published in nearby Brunswick. They then returned to Gorham, where, through the summer, awaiting the birth of their first child. James engaged in such labor as he could find, determined not to be dependent on others for their livelihood.

In August 1847 their first son, Henry Nichols, was born.

NEW RESPONSIBILITIES

From this point on, James and Ellen White had to take into account the fact that they were a family. The Howlands soon invited the couple to set up housekeeping in the upstairs rooms of their home in Topsham. Of this Ellen White wrote:

> In October, Brother and Sister Howland kindly offered us a part of their dwelling, which we gladly accepted, and commenced housekeeping with borrowed furniture. We were poor and saw close times (1LS, pp. 241, 242).

Many incidents might be cited illustrating their poverty. The young people were determined to be independent financially, so James engaged in daily labor. He secured work hauling stone as a railroad cut was thrust through close to Brunswick. He wore the skin on his hands to the bleeding point in many places, and then had difficulty in collecting his wages. Freely the Howlands divided what they had with the young couple in the economically depressed times. James then cut cordwood in a nearby forest, working from early till late, to earn 50 cents a day. Severe pain in his side made for sleepless nights. But the young couple resolved to live within their means—and to suffer want rather than to run into debt. On their very limited budget Ellen could afford only one pint of milk a day for her child and herself. Then came a day when she had to cut out the nine-cent allowance for the milk supply for three days to have enough money to buy some cloth for a simple garment for the baby. "I gave up the milk," she wrote, "and purchased the cloth for an apron to cover the bare arms of my child" (*ibid.*, p. 243). She wrote of their experience:

> We endeavored to keep up good courage and trust in the Lord. I did not murmur. . . . One day when our provisions were gone, husband went to his employer to get money or provisions. It was a stormy day, and he walked three miles and back in the rain, passing through the village of Brunswick, where he had often lectured, carrying a bag of provisions on his back, tied in different apartments.
>
> As he entered the house very weary my heart sank within me. My first feelings were that God had forsaken us. I said to my husband, "Have we come to this? Has the Lord left us?" I could not restrain my tears, and wept aloud for hours until I fainted (*ibid.*, p. 242).

The young mother had reached an all-time low. Why, oh, why were their lives so hard when they had been dedicated to the cause of God? Regaining consciousness, she felt the cheering influence of the Spirit of God.

For six months they maintained their home in the Howland residence, but it was indeed a trying time. According to James, he suffered more in mind and body than he could show with pen and paper (JW to Leonard and Elvira Hastings, Apr. 27, 1848).

Then James and Ellen discovered a true understanding of what their difficult time was all about. She had thought that now that they had a child it would be impossible for her to travel and a change must come about in their program. A vision from God revealed the purpose of the trials they were facing:

> I was shown that the Lord had been trying us for our good, and to prepare us to labor for others; that He had been stirring up our nest, lest we should settle down in ease, and that our work was to labor for souls; that if we had been prospered, home would be so pleasant that we would be unwilling to leave it to travel, and that we had been suffering trial to prepare us for still greater conflicts that we would suffer in our travels (1LS, p. 243).

A heart-rending experience enforced the message of the vision. Henry was taken very ill and soon lapsed into unconsciousness. Nothing they or their friends could do brought relief. Recognizing that they had made their little Henry "an excuse for not traveling and laboring for the good of others," they feared that God was about to remove the basis for their excuses. Agonizing in prayer, they pledged God that if the child's life were spared they would go forth trusting in Him wherever He might send them. By faith they claimed the promises of God. From the hour of this resolution and consecration the fever turned, and Henry began to recover. Wrote Ellen White: "Light from heaven was breaking through the clouds, and shining upon us again. Hope revived. Our prayers were graciously answered" (ibid., p. 244).

CAREERS CHANGED

James and Ellen White could now see that regardless of home comforts, pleasures, and responsibilities, their life was to be a life of dedicated service involving travel, suffering, and earnest labor for others.

ESTABLISHING THE PILLARS OF FAITH

After the disappointment of 1844 little companies of believers throughout New England met together from time to time to study the prophecies and compare views. As news of the visions and the significance of the Sabbath truth, being publicized and promoted by Joseph Bates, became more widely known, the need to draw together accelerated.

In April 1848 Ellen and James White received an invitation to attend a conference of Sabbathkeeping Adventists in Connecticut. They went, taking their 7-month-old Henry with them in their arms. James had received $10 for his work cutting wood. They used half of the money in preparation for the trip, and kept the other half for transportation. With all their earthly possessions only partially filling a trunk, they went to Boston, where they stayed with the Nichols family. They did not make known their penniless plight to the family, but, as they left, Mrs. Nichols handed James $5. With all but 50 cents of this they purchased tickets to Middletown, Connecticut, the closest rail point to Rocky Hill and the Albert Belden home, where the conference was to begin on Thursday night, April 20. When the meeting opened, 15 people had come together. Ellen White described what took place as the conference got under way:

> Friday morning the brethren came in until we numbered about fifty. These were not all fully in the truth. Our meeting that day was very interesting. Brother Bates presented the commandments in a clear light, and their importance was urged home by powerful testimonies. The word had effect to establish those already in the truth and to awaken those who were not fully decided (1LS, p. 245).

It was this meeting in the unfinished chamber of Albert Belden's home at Rocky Hill that Ellen White later referred to as "the first conference that was ever held among Seventh-day Adventists" (MS 76, 1886). James White spoke of it as "the first under the message" (RH, Sept. 29, 1863).

Soon after this the Whites were invited to attend a conference at Volney, New York, in August 1848. They had no money for travel, so James was glad to find an opportunity to earn means by cutting hay on nearby farms. To his friend Stockbridge Howland at Topsham he wrote on July 2:

> I mow five days for unbelievers and Sunday for believers and rest on the seventh day, therefore I have but very little time to write. My health is good, God gives me strength to labor hard all day. I have mowed eight days right off and felt hardly a pain. Brother Holt, Brother John Belden, and I have taken 100 acres [41 hectares] of grass to mow at 87½ cents per acre [.41 hectare] and board ourselves. Praise the Lord. I hope to get a few dollars here to use in the cause of God (JW to S. Howland, July 2, 1848).

That summer James White earned $40 in the hayfield. He used part of the money for needed clothing for the family and part for travel to western New York State. Reluctantly James and Ellen left Baby Henry in Middletown in the care of Clarissa Bonfoey. With E.L.H. Chamberlain accompanying them, they took the steamboat for New York City en route to Volney, where the conference was to be held in David Arnold's barn.

THE VOLNEY CONFERENCE

On Friday, August 18, about 35 people gathered in the Arnold barn to hear the leading workers, including Joseph Bates, Chamberlain, and James and Ellen White. Hardly two agreed on doctrines. Each was strenuous for his or her views, declaring that they were according to the Bible.

Some of these points of view were in conflict with what had been shown to Ellen White in vision. She wrote of her reactions and of subsequent happenings:

> These strange differences of opinion rolled a heavy weight upon me, especially as Brother A. spoke of the thousand years being in the past. I knew that he was in error, and great grief pressed my spirits, for it seemed to me that God was dishonored. I fainted under the burden. Brethren Bates, Chamberlain, Gurney, Edson, and my husband prayed for me. . . . The light of Heaven rested upon me. I was soon lost to earthly things.

> My accompanying angel presented before me some of the errors of those present, and also the truth in contrast with their errors. That these discordant views, which they claimed to be according to the Bible, were only according to their opinion of the Bible, and that their errors must be yielded, and they unite upon the third angel's message (2SG, pp. 98, 99).

Ellen White summed up the outcome in two sentences: "Our meeting ended victoriously. Truth gained the victory" (*ibid.*, p. 99).

But there was more to it than that. To these people with divergent views—people who had not seen Ellen White before—the Lord gave very convincing evidences beyond the fact that she was shown by the angel "the truth in contrast with their errors." Just a few years later J. N. Loughborough visited with David Arnold and some others who were present at the conference in 1848, and some interesting sidelights emerged. Loughborough wrote:

> As the circumstance was related to me, Sister White, while in vision, arose to her feet and took the family Bible upon her left arm, the book being an ordinary-sized one. While holding it thus, her eyes looking upward and in an opposite direction from the Bible, with her right hand she would turn from text to text, placing her finger on the text, and would repeat the same.

> Brother Ross looked at many of the texts to see if she was repeating the one to which she pointed. He or some of the company looked at them all. In every case she not only repeated the texts to which she pointed, but she did so while her eyes were fastened upward and in an opposite direction from the Bible. It was these scriptures quoted in this wonderful manner which overthrew the false theories of the

Sabbathkeepers assembled at Volney, in August, 1848, and caused them to unite upon the truth (JNL, in RH, Mar. 3, 1885).

More conferences followed in this year of development, clarifying and binding together the basic doctrines held by Seventh-day Adventists. The early records speak of meetings at Rocky Hill; Topsham, Maine; and Dorchester, Massachusetts, in November. The basic team of workers from conference to conference was much the same: James and Ellen White, Joseph Bates, H. S. Gurney. At times, Hiram Edson, E.L.H. Chamberlain, and Otis Nichols joined forces with the basic group.

BIBLE STUDY AIDED BY SPECIAL REVELATION

How were these conferences conducted and what was accomplished? Looking back at them in later years, Ellen White described their activities:

> We would come together burdened in soul, praying that we might be one in faith and doctrine; for we knew that Christ is not divided. One point at a time was made the subject of investigation. The Scriptures were opened with a sense of awe. Often we fasted, that we might be better fitted to understand the truth. After earnest prayer, if any point was not understood it was discussed, and each one expressed his opinion freely; then we would again bow in prayer, and earnest supplications went up to heaven that God would help us to see eye to eye, that we might be one as Christ and the Father are one. Many tears were shed.

> We spent many hours in this way. Sometimes the entire night was spent in solemn investigation of the Scriptures, that we might understand the truth for our time. On some occasions the Spirit of God would come upon me, and difficult portions were made clear through God's appointed way, and then there was perfect harmony. We were all of one mind and one spirit.

> We sought most earnestly that the Scriptures should not be wrested to suit any man's opinions. We tried to make our differences as slight as possible by not dwelling on points that were of minor importance, upon which there were varying opinions. But the burden of every soul was to bring about a condition among the brethren which would answer the prayer of Christ that His disciples might be one as He and the Father are one (TM, pp. 24, 25).

The Lord manifested Himself in a manner that made it forever clear that what took place was beyond human manipulation. Ellen White explained:

> During this whole time I could not understand the reasoning of the

brethren. My mind was locked, as it were, and I could not comprehend the meaning of the scriptures we were studying. This was one of the greatest sorrows of my life. I was in this condition of mind until all the principal points of our faith were made clear to our minds, in harmony with the Word of God. The brethren knew that when not in vision, I could not understand these matters, and they accepted as light direct from heaven the revelations given (MS 46, 1904 [see also 1SM, p. 207]).

For two or three years my mind continued to be locked to the Scriptures. . . . It was some time after my second son was born [July 1849] that we were in great perplexity regarding certain points of doctrine. I was asking the Lord to unlock my mind, that I might understand His Word. Suddenly I seemed to be enshrouded in clear, beautiful light, and ever since, the Scriptures have been an open book to me (MS 135, 1903).

She explained, "Many theories were advanced, bearing a semblance of truth, but so mingled with misinterpreted and misapplied scriptures, that they led to dangerous errors. Very well do we know how every point of truth was established" (MS 31, 1896 [see also 2SM, pp. 103, 104]).

In the experience of Seventh-day Adventists the visions were not given to take the place of Bible study. They were, however, a definite aid in Bible study, correcting erroneous interpretations and pointing to what was truth. "He [God] wants us to go to the Bible," she wrote in 1888, "and get the Scripture evidence" (MS 9, 1888). In 1903 she wrote:

The leading points of our faith as we hold them today were firmly established. Point after point was clearly defined, and all the brethren came into harmony. The whole company of believers were united in the truth. There were those who came in with strange doctrines, but we were never afraid to meet them. Our experience was wonderfully established by the revelation of the Holy Spirit (MS 135, 1903).

STREAMS OF LIGHT
(STORY OF THE PUBLISHING WORK: PRESENT TRUTH AND THE REVIEW AND HERALD)

THE EIGHT-PAGE PRESENT TRUTH

Joseph Bates was among the small company gathered for a conference in the home of Otis Nichols in Dorchester, Massachusetts, November 18, 1848. Here Ellen White was given a vision in which God made it clear that the time had come to publish. Coming out of the vision, she turned to her husband and said:

> I have a message for you. You must begin to print a little paper and send it out to the people. Let it be small at first; but as the people read, they will send you means with which to print, and it will be a success from the first. From this small beginning it was shown to me to be like streams of light that went clear round the world (3LS, p. 125).

But how could he? Where would he get financial and moral support? Nonetheless, James White pondered the words spoken in the commission. He was in great doubt and perplexity. He was penniless. He had no steady income. According to him, "there were those who had means, but they chose to keep it" (1LS, p. 259).

Not long after this, when the Whites were in a quandary to know how to plan for their summer work, and Ellen was within two months of giving birth to their second child, they received a generous invitation from friends. Albert Belden in Rocky Hill, Connecticut, urged them to come and live with his family.

"We will consider it a privilege to administer to all your wants," he said. Enclosed with the letter was money to buy tickets. Accepting this as the leading of God, James and Ellen left little Henry with the Howlands at Topsham, and were soon on their way to Connecticut. Rocky Hill was not far from Middletown, where little Henry had spent some time with Clarissa Bonfoey. Of God's providence Ellen White wrote:

> Sister Clarissa M. Bonfoey proposed to live with us. Her parents had recently died, and a division of furniture at the homestead had given her everything necessary for a small family to commence housekeeping. She cheerfully gave us the use of these things, and did our work. We occupied a part of Brother Belden's house at Rocky Hill. Sister Bonfoey was a precious child of God. She possessed a cheerful and happy disposition, never gloomy, yet not light and trifling (ibid., p. 258).

While comfortably established with the Beldens, James again felt the burden to publish. The need to get the message to the people pressed upon him. He was still penniless, but he recalled the words of the promise "As the people read, they will send you means to print."

The year before, he had gone into the field to mow hay to earn money on which to live and to travel to the Sabbath and Sanctuary conferences. Perhaps, he thought, now he should again go into the field to earn money with which to print. He started out in search of work. But God had other plans. Ellen White wrote:

> As he left the house, a burden was rolled upon me, and I fainted. Prayer

was offered for me, and I was blessed, and taken off in vision. I saw that the Lord had blessed and strengthened my husband to labor in the field one year before; that he had made a right disposition of the means he there earned; and that he would have a hundredfold in this life, and, if faithful, a rich reward in the kingdom of God; but that the Lord would not now give him strength to labor in the field, for He had another work for him; that if he ventured into the field he would be cut down by sickness; but that he must write, write, write, and walk out by faith (*ibid.*, pp. 259, 260).

WRITING FOR THE PRESS

In harmony with the vision, James White took up his pen. It required faith, as he later recalled:

> We sat down to prepare the matter for that little sheet, and wrote every word of it, our entire library comprising a three-shilling pocket Bible, *Cruden's Condensed Concordance*, and Walker's old dictionary, minus one of its covers. [We were] destitute of means; our hope of success was in God (RH, June 17, 1880).

Ellen was close by his side. She recalled: "When he came to some difficult passage we would call upon the Lord to give us the true meaning of His word" (1LS, p. 260). While preparing copy for the new publication, James White sought out a printer in Middletown, one who would print an eight-page paper for a total stranger and wait for his pay until the prospective readers would send the editor donations to cover printing costs. On the third floor of a brick building in the heart of Middletown, James found the man—Charles Pelton—and walked back to Rocky Hill to finish preparing copy. Its subject matter would be the Sabbath truth. He decided to name the paper *The Present Truth*, and introduced his first-page editorial with words quoted from 2 Peter 1:12: "Wherefore I will not be negligent to put you always in remembrance of these things, though ye know them, and be established in the PRESENT TRUTH."

It was the Sabbath truth that burned in James White's heart, and his writing related to various aspects of the integrity and importance of the seventh-day Sabbath. He had in mind quite a wide spectrum of articles that would be printed at first in eight-page sheets sent out semimonthly. Then he would bind them in pamphlets (PT, July 1849). The readers would be Adventists—those who had been through the first and second angels' messages—and it would carry to them the Sabbath truth of the third angel's message.

Back and forth between Rocky Hill and Middletown, James White trudged the eight miles (13 kilometers), limping at each step (from an earlier foot injury), first with copy and then with proofs. When the sheets were finally printed, he borrowed Albert Belden's buggy to transport the 1,000 copies of the precious document to the Belden home.

Ellen White described the scene:

> When he brought the first number from the printing office, we all bowed around it, asking the Lord, with humble hearts and many tears, to let His blessing rest upon the feeble effort of His servant (1LS, p. 260).

Together they folded the papers and prepared them for mailing. James "directed the paper to all he thought would read it," then carried the copies in a carpetbag to the post office.

The visions had given assurance that God's blessing would attend James White as he wrote; that money would come in as the papers were sent out and read. It would be a success from the first; but the most staggering prediction was that from this small beginning, it would be like "streams of light that went clear round the world."

The articles that followed James White's opening editorial explanation carried such titles as "The Weekly Sabbath Instituted at Creation, and Not at Sinai"; "The Sabbath a Perpetual Weekly Memorial"; "The Law of God, or the Ten Commandments"; "Scriptures Usually Quoted to Prove the Abolition of the Sabbath Examined." He declared that the little sheet was free to all, then added, "Those who are interested in *Present Truth*, and esteem it a privilege, are invited to help pay the expense." To swell the mailing list, he asked:

> Will some brother or sister in each place where this sheet is received send me in plain writing the names and post office address of all who are seeking present truth. Write soon. My post office address is Middletown, Connecticut (PT, July 1849).

The precise date when the *Present Truth* was brought home, prayed over, folded, addressed, and mailed is not recorded, but it was late July 1849. Almost simultaneously there was an important event in the White family, and that does carry a date. Ellen White wrote: "July 28, 1849, my second child, James Edson White, was born" (1LS, p. 260).

BEGINNING THE *REVIEW AND HERALD*

Present Truth, in 10 issues published over a period of 11 months, heralded the third angel's message, with the Sabbath truth as the focal point. But the eye of the Lord saw a need extending beyond this. Far beyond. *Present Truth* was the forerunner of the paper that would be known by a number of names until the present day: *Advent Review, Advent Review and Sabbath Herald, Review and Herald,* and *Adventist Review.*

God had shown Ellen White in vision the need for those now studying the prophecies to understand that the work done by the leaders in the Advent movement of 1844 was the work of God.

James said, "Now this is my first work. I expect to get out a journal called the *Advent Review,* sixteen pages, the size of the *Present Truth.*" He declared his intention to republish the writings of the leaders of the Advent cause and to "show that they once boldly advocated, and published to the world, the same position . . . that we now occupy."

In August 1850 the Whites moved from the Belden home in Connecticut to the Harris home at Port Byron, New York. There James began his new journal, and had it printed in nearby Auburn. He explained the object of the paper in an opening editorial statement:

> Our design in this review is to cheer and refresh the true believer, by showing the fulfillment of prophecy in the past wonderful work of God, in calling out, and separating from the world and the nominal church, a people who are looking for the second advent of the dear Saviour (AR, August 1850).

As James began to publish, Ellen was given advance warning that although Satan would try to hinder, they must continue, and struggle for the victory. What took place in rather quick succession came as no surprise but showed that the great adversary would do all in his power to block the spread of truth:

1. One-year-old Edson was afflicted to the point of death.

2. Ellen was tempted to think that God had left her or the child would have been healed when they first asked God to heal him.

3. Clarissa Bonfoey was overcome by depression.

4. James was prostrated by cholera, and lay helpless on his sickbed until they sought God with special anointing.

5. James and Ellen were thrown out of a wagon in which they were traveling, but were saved from injury by angels of God.

The Whites believed that these attempts to destroy them showed how important was their work in publishing the *Advent Review.* Ellen was shown that "it was as necessary for the paper to be published as for messengers to go," and "that the paper would go where messengers could not go" (letter 28, 1850).

It was soon apparent that the *Advent Review* was doing an effective work and fulfilling its God-appointed mission.

Significant changes could be noted:

1. Greater contributions from the followers

2. New names in correspondence
3. Larger numbers attending the conferences
4. Preaching forces materially increased
5. A "brighter turn" in reporting the conferences
6. An increased spirit of unity among the brethren

Four issues of the *Advent Review* were published at Oswego during August and September. The type was saved, and a 48-page combined number was issued as a "Special" almost immediately. During the next few years it was given a wide distribution.

In late October 1850 the Whites took up residence in Paris, Maine, for the purpose of publishing the three angels' messages. James had suspended the publication of *Present Truth* while they made an itinerary to Vermont, Canada, and Maine from mid-May to mid-July, and while he was publishing the first four numbers of the *Advent Review* at Auburn, New York. In early November at Paris he picked up the *Present Truth* again and put out number 11. In this he stated, "The brethren may now expect to receive a few numbers," and he called for those who could do so to write for the paper. He also brought out number 5 of the *Advent Review*, the final issue. It was devoted entirely to a reprint of portions of Joseph Bates's *Second Advent Way Marks and High Heaps*, a significant pamphlet reviewing the 1844 experience.

Within a few days publishing plans changed. At the conference in Paris on Sabbath and Sunday, November 16 and 17, it was decided to combine *Present Truth* and the *Advent Review*. The new periodical would be called *The Second Advent Review and Sabbath Herald*.

The page size was 9½" x 13" (24 centimeters x 33 centimeters), as compared to the 7¾" x 10" (20 centimeters x 25 centimeters) for *Present Truth* and the *Advent Review*. The masthead carried four names as the Publishing Committee (Joseph Bates, S. W. Rhodes, J. N. Andrews, and James White), and the subscription terms were "gratis, except the reader desires to aid in its publication."

> If any are not able to send means, we beseech them not to let this stop them from writing. We greatly desire to hear from such and will cheerfully pay the postage on their letters (RH, November 1850).

Very early in his many years of publishing James White demonstrated a selfless generosity and commitment that was not always realistic.

DIFFICULT DAYS IN PARIS

James and Ellen White faced difficult times in Paris. She wrote of it:

> We suffered many privations. . . . We were willing to live cheaply

that the paper might be sustained. My husband was a dyspeptic. We could not eat meat or butter, and were obliged to abstain from all greasy food. Take these from a poor farmer's table and it leaves a very spare diet. Our labors were so great that we needed nourishing food.

We had much care, and often sat up as late as midnight, and sometimes until two or three in the morning, to read proof-sheets. We could have better borne these extra exertions could we have had the sympathy of our brethren in Paris, and had they appreciated our labors and the efforts we were making to advance the cause of truth. Mental labor and privation reduced the strength of my husband very fast (1LS, p. 278).

They did have with them in Paris their horse, Charlie, and the carriage. They had a very special affection for Charlie because he had come to them in a time of great distress. About a year previous when Ellen White had suffered a painful 40-mile (64-kilometer) stagecoach trip to Sutton, Vermont, the believers in Sutton realized the difficulties that attended the Whites in their journeys, and united in making up a purse of $175 with which to provide a horse and carriage. James and Ellen were given the choice of several horses brought for their inspection. The process of selecting one did not take long, for in vision the night before Ellen seemed to be at the crossroads appointed, and as horses were led before them the angel had given counsel.

The first was a high-spirited, light reddish-brown, rather nervous animal, and the angel said, "No." "Not that one" was the verdict on the second, a large gray horse. Then, as a beautiful dapple chestnut, somewhat swaybacked, horse was led before them, the angel said, "That is the one for you." His name was Charlie, and he lightened their journey to Canada and through a period of many years (WCW, "Sketches and Memories of James and Ellen G. White," RH, Apr. 25, 1935).

At the Waterbury conference they ran into distressing criticism. A whispering campaign had been started against James White in which many joined, even the venerable Joseph Bates. It was based on the opinion that the Whites had too good a horse, and as James had been very liberal in contributing to the conference, he must be making money. Wrote Ellen White:

This was the reward he received. We were forced to wade through a tide of oppression. It seemed that the deep waters would overflow us, and that we should sink (1LS, p. 280).

One discouraging episode followed another. Severe colds that took hold of him on the journey to and from Waterbury settled in James's lungs. Ellen White reported the result:

He sank beneath his trials. He was so weak he could not get to the printing office without staggering. Our faith was tried to the uttermost. We had willingly endured privation, toil, and suffering, yet but few seemed to appreciate our efforts, when it was even for their good we had suffered. We were too much troubled to sleep or rest (*ibid.*, pp. 280, 281).

The situation finally came to the point where James declared, "Wife, it is no use to try to struggle on any longer. These things are crushing me, and will soon carry me to the grave. I cannot go any farther. I have written a note for the paper stating that I shall publish no more" (*ibid.*). As he stepped out of the door to take the note to the printing office, Ellen fainted. He returned, and she rallied in response to earnest prayer. The next morning at family worship she was taken off in vision. She wrote of what she was shown:

I saw that my husband must not give up the paper, for such a step was just what Satan was trying to drive him to take, and he was working through agents to do this. I was shown that he must continue to publish, and that the Lord would sustain him (*ibid.*, p. 281).

So the *Second Advent Review and Sabbath Herald* continued to come from the press one or two issues a month until number 13 was put out on June 9, 1851. This closed the first volume, and the Whites terminated their stay in Paris.

With the end of volume 1, James thought it would be well to find a more central place from which to send out the paper and other printed materials. They began looking for a place near Saratoga Springs where they would be only a few miles from the printing office. Within a few days the Whites found a house, borrowed furniture from fellow believers, and set up housekeeping. The first number of volume 2 came from the press on August 5, 1851. Ellen's sister Sarah and Stephen Belden (Sarah's husband) arrived soon to help with publishing. And Clarissa Bonfoey came, bringing 2-year-old Edson, who had been in her care. Soon 23-year-old Annie Smith, the very talented sister of Uriah Smith, joined the publishing family. She gave much-needed help in issuing the *Advent Review and Sabbath Herald*, the newly shortened name of the paper. Writing to the Howlands on November 12, Ellen White stated:

Annie Smith is with us. She is just the help we need; she takes right hold with James and helps him much. We can leave her now to get off the papers and can go out more among the flock (letter 8, 1851).

So through the fall and winter of 1851-1852 the Whites divided their time between publishing and field work.

EXPANDING BY PUBLISHING

In December 1851 James and Ellen White left Saratoga Springs for a midwinter tour, visiting scattered groups of believers and churches in northern and western New York. James's report in the *Review* at the end of the seven-week tour was optimistic:

> We reached home the thirteenth, and found our friends in good health and spirits. Sister [Annie] Smith, who has had the care of the paper in our absence, seems happy with her charge. Our health is improved by traveling. We are all very happy to see the cause of truth rapidly advancing (RH, Feb. 17, 1852).

On the back page of the same issue he made an interesting proposition regarding the work of publishing the message:

> We think the time has come when a press should be owned by Sabbathkeepers. Now our work is being done on the Sabbath, which is very unpleasant and inconvenient. It also costs much more than it would if we had an office of our own. Will the committee take this matter in hand? (*ibid.*).

James called a conference to meet on Friday, March 12, 1852, in the home of Jesse Thompson, nine miles (15 kilometers) from Saratoga Springs where the 14 numbers of volume 2 of the *Review and Herald* had been published. Among those attending that conference were Joseph Bates, Hiram Edson, S. W. Rhodes, and James and Ellen White. They were joined by the *Review* staff and nearby believers. The report of the work done that Friday was faith challenging.

> The subject of publishing the paper was introduced. Several brethren spoke of the disadvantages of having it published as it has been, and of the propriety of having an office at the control of Sabbathkeepers. And after investigating the matter it was decided by a unanimous vote (1) that a press, type, et cetera, should be purchased immediately, (2) that the paper should be published at Rochester, New York, (3) that Brethren E. A. Pool, Lebbeus Drew, and Hiram Edson compose a committee to receive donations from the friends of the cause to purchase the press, type,

et cetera, and to conduct the financial concerns of the paper, (4) that the brethren abroad be requested through the next number of the *Review and Herald* to choose agents in their churches to receive donations for the purpose of establishing the press, and carrying forward the publishing of the paper, and (5) that those donations that are immediately sent in should be sent to Hiram Edson, Port Byron, New York.

It was thought that $600 would be sufficient to establish the press at Rochester (RH, Mar. 23, 1852).

ESTABLISHING A PUBLISHING OFFICE IN ROCHESTER, NEW YORK

Steps were taken immediately to carry out the actions of the conference held on March 12. A printing press was purchased in New York City, and the stocks of papers and pamphlets, along with the Whites' meager household equipment and personal belongings, were packed and shipped from Saratoga Springs. As money was scarce, they had to borrow to pay the freight westward across the state.

In Rochester they found, at 124 Mount Hope Avenue, a home thought sufficiently large to accommodate the publishing house family and the printing equipment. The rent of $14.50 a month seemed to be within their ability to pay. As the house stood on about an acre of land, there was space for a garden. Ellen White described their circumstances in a letter written to the Howland family on April 16.

> We are just getting settled here in Rochester. We have rented an old house for $175 a year. We have the press in the house. Were it not for this, we should have to pay $50 a year for office room.
>
> You would smile could you look in upon us and see our furniture. We have bought two old bedsteads for 25 cents each. My husband brought me home six old chairs, no two of them alike, for which he paid $1, and soon he presented me with four more old chairs without any seating, for which he paid 62 cents for the lot. The frames were strong, and I have been seating them with drilling.
>
> Butter is so high we do not purchase it, neither can we afford potatoes. Our first meals were taken on a fireboard placed upon two empty flour barrels. We are willing to endure privations if the work of God can be advanced. We believe the Lord's hand was in our coming to this place (1LS, p. 287).

THE PUBLISHING HOUSE FAMILY

At first there were James and Ellen White; little Edson, and his nurse Clarissa Bonfoey; Stephen and Sarah Belden; and Annie Smith. Soon Jennie Fraser was employed as cook. For a short time Thomas and Mary Mead were members of the family and office force. Then came Oswald Stowell, who acted as pressman.

In the autumn, Warren Bacheller, a boy of 13, joined the force and served as roller boy while learning typesetting. In the spring of 1853, Uriah Smith joined the family, and in the autumn, George Amadon, a young man of 17, also became a member of the little company. These three were to grow gray in the service of the *Review and Herald*. Later on they were joined by Fletcher Byington, a son of John Byington, of northern New York. . . .

It was necessary to employ a skilled printer to superintend the work and teach the beginners. For this position a very competent man was found in Lumen V. Masten, with whom Elder White had become acquainted in Saratoga Springs (WCW, "Sketches and Memories," RH, June 13, 1935).

The Washington hand press, other needed equipment, and the type purchased in New York cost more than $600. Hiram Edson advanced the money on a short-term loan; James White called for donations with which to pay this debt, if possible by mid-June, and work began. The first issue of volume 3 of the *Review*, bearing the publication date of May 6, was ready in type before the press arrived, so was "struck off" on another press in the town. The masthead lists as a publishing committee Joseph Bates, J. N. Andrews, and Joseph Baker; James White was named editor. The paper would appear semimonthly. The "terms" were stated: "Gratis. It is expected that all the friends of the cause will aid in its publication, as the Lord has prospered them" (*ibid.*, May 6, 1852). A poem from the pen of Annie Smith titled "The Blessed Hope" filled column one and half of column two of the first page. The articles related to the third angel's message, and Elder White's editorial reviewed the past and dealt with present work.

THE TOUR EAST

Soon after the Whites had settled in Rochester, a letter from Ellen's mother informed them that her brother Robert was dying of tuberculosis at the family home in Gorham, Maine. James had trained the staff quite well while at Saratoga Springs, and Lumen Masten was on hand to manage the office. So with their faithful horse Charlie to convey them by carriage, he and Ellen planned a trip east that would take two months. The *Review* of June 24 set his plans before the companies of believers:

We now design making a tour east, and spending several weeks, holding conferences where they are most needed (*ibid.*, June 24, 1852).

In mid-June, while visiting a nearby company of believers over the weekend, they were pleasantly surprised. James White wrote about this:

> Brother Drew being informed of our intended eastern tour, and seeing that our carriage was about falling to pieces, purchased and gave us a suitable carriage for which he paid $85. For this we thank God, also our brother, His steward (*ibid.*, July 8, 1852).

The couple planned to take 3-year-old Edson with them. As the summer wore on, cholera struck Rochester with heavy mortality. Just as they were to start on their carriage tour east, little Edson was stricken. Their first resort, of course, was to pray for his healing. "I took him in my arms," wrote Ellen White, "and in the name of Jesus rebuked the disease." He felt relief at once. As a sister commenced praying for the Lord to heal him, Edson looked up and said, "They need not pray any more, for the Lord has healed me" (3LS, p. 144). But James did not dare start on their journey until Edson had improved sufficiently to call for food. He did that afternoon, Wednesday, July 21, and they started, for they had nearly 100 miles (160 kilometers) to cover in the next two days to fill their first appointment at Oswego.

James had charted the itinerary, allowing time to drive from one appointment to the next and giving word in advance through the *Review*. The journey by carriage rested both James and Ellen White.

Charlie was very fond of apples. As they drove where apple orchards lined the roads and big red apples lay in the path of the travelers, James would loosen the checkrein. Charlie would gently slow down from a seven-mile (11-kilometer) pace, select a good apple within easy reach, pick it up, and then throw his head high and dash on at full speed, chewing the apple as he journeyed (WCW, "Sketches and Memories," RH, Apr. 25, 1935).

Ellen White described their travel experience:

> The Lord greatly blessed us on our journey to Vermont. My husband had much care and labor. At the different conferences he did most of the preaching, sold books, and took pay for the papers. And when one conference was over, we would hasten to the next.
>
> At noon we would feed the horse by the roadside and eat our lunch. Then my husband, with paper and pencil upon the cover of our dinner box, or the top of his hat, would write articles for the *Review* and *Instructor* (1LS, p. 292).

The *Youth's Instructor* was a monthly journal James White had started recently to reach the youth of the emerging church. Each copy contained Sabbath school lessons, the first prepared for children and young people. James later recalled that he thought out the lessons while the "carriage was in motion"; then, while the horse was eating, he wrote them out.

With faithful Charlie pulling their carriage, James and Ellen White drove into their yard in Rochester on the afternoon of Wednesday, October 6, returning from their 1852 trip east.

The *Review* office staff had not missed an issue in the 11 weeks the editor was absent. This proved to James White that others could carry many of the routine tasks to which he had given attention in the previous three years. Every other Thursday 2,000 copies were "struck off" on the hand press and mailed to 1,600 homes (WCW, "Sketches and Memories," RH, June 27, 1935). The *Youth's Instructor*, started in August, was mailed to nearly 1,000 homes. Now there was need for more space in which to work. The first important action after getting back was to rent office space in downtown Rochester on South Saint Paul Street, on the third floor of an office building, and move the printing work to this new location.

PUBLISHING THE VISIONS

In 1849 when James White began to publish *Present Truth*, the reading audience was limited to those who had been in the first and second angels' messages. It was this same group he addressed in 1850 in the five numbers of the *Advent Review*. To a large degree it was this same group that he hoped to reach through the *Second Advent Review and Sabbath Herald*.

The marked change now appearing in the attitudes of the general public presented a challenge in setting forth truths that would win, and not be cut off through prejudice. James White cautiously refrained from publishing the visions in the 13 issues of volume 1 of the combined journal issued at Paris, Maine. Nor did he make direct reference to the special experience of Ellen White. In the issue of April 21, 1851, he did introduce an article he titled "The Gifts of the Gospel Church."

He defended the proposition of the gift of prophecy in the church, but he did not mention Ellen White. By mid-June 1851 the growing number of church members were calling for the visions in published form. This led him to plan for the issuance of *Extras* of the *Review* just for the believers. He explained this in the first, *and* only, issue of an *Extra*. It carried the date of July 21, 1851, and was published between volume 1 of the *Review*, which closed with the June 9 issue, and volume 2, which opened August 5.

It took longer to get out the *Extra* than was first expected. The printing was done at Saratoga Springs. On July 21, the date carried by the yet-unprinted *Extra*, Ellen White mentioned the pamphlet in a letter to friends in Michigan:

> The visions trouble many. They [know] not what to make of them. ... If you desire it, I can write it off for you. As it was coming out so soon in the pamphlet, I thought that you would not wish me to write them all off for you. We now think that you can have the book in about four weeks (letter 4, 1851).

Elder White promised that it would contain 64 pages (four printing forms), and that 2,000 copies would be printed, at a cost of $5 per 100.

As they were publishing the *Extra* they decided to turn to a pamphlet or book as a means of making the visions available in permanent form. To begin with, they could use the same type already set for the *Extra*, and a little book would be more serviceable than the periodical.

ELLEN WHITE'S FIRST BOOK

Even though the pamphlet contained only 64 pages, *A Sketch of the Christian Experience and Views of Ellen G. White*, with more than 20 chapters, is considered the first Ellen G. White book. Most of the chapters were made up of her messages to the church, first published in broadsides or articles. The entire work was republished in 1882 and is the first section of *Early Writings*.

During its first five years the *Review and Herald* had not included even one vision given by God to Ellen White, and very little had been said about God's communicating through the visions to encourage, guard, and counsel His people.

True, in 1851 Ellen White's first little 64-page book, which presented many of the visions of the previous seven years, had been published and circulated. But with the intent of not offending the general public, the *Review* was silent on the visions, and its editor had done no more than maintain that visions in the last days are scriptural. Now, with the confessions of neglect and the determination to place the gift in its proper place in the church, the whole atmosphere changed. The minutes of the conference and the conference address were published December 4, 1855, in the first issue of the *Review* printed in Battle Creek. This issue carried Uriah Smith's name on the masthead as resident editor, and James White as one of the corresponding editors.

Immediately a change in policy became evident. In the issue of December 18, in a two-page editorial titled "The Testimony of Jesus," James White defended the appearance of the Spirit of prophecy in the remnant church. Beginning with Revelation 12:17, he carried through the scriptural support for the continuing ministry of the gift of prophecy till earth's last days, and closed with the biblical tests of the true prophet.

The events and experiences at the conference of November 1855 may well be considered as marking a turning point in Seventh-day Adventist history. With the church accepting the responsibility for its publishing work, and the Spirit of Prophecy now given its rightful place, added blessing attended the labors of the ministers, the publishing enterprise prospered, and the work moved forward.

EXPANDING BY TENT EVANGELISM

As the third angel's message accelerated, new talent joined the ranks of evangelists—men like 23-year-old J. N. Loughborough, M. E. Cornell, and J. N. Andrews, who were pioneering the message in Ohio, Wisconsin, and Michigan.

Sometimes overflow audiences created problems. Meetings had often been held in homes or schoolhouses or small meetinghouses. On one such occasion the attendance at Locke, Michigan, over the weekend of May 19 to 21, 1854, was so large that only half the audience could get into the schoolhouse secured for the occasion. The speakers stood near an open window where the larger, outside, portion of the audience could see and hear as they sat in their carriages and on the grass (JNL, in RH, Jan. 27, 1885). While they were driving the next day to Sylvan, they discussed the experience at Locke. James White suggested that by another year they might try using a tent to proclaim the message.

Cornell asked, "Why not have a tent at once?" As they discussed it they decided to propose it at coming conferences at Sylvan and Jackson. The response was enthusiastic, and money was raised and pledged. On Tuesday, Cornell hurried off to Rochester to buy a 60-foot (18-meter) round meeting tent (ibid.).

Quite naturally James and Ellen White had a special interest in the tent that he and Loughborough pitched in Battle Creek. Meetings were advertised for Friday, June 2, to Sunday, June 4. Thinking the meetings might run longer, the Whites hoped to get to Battle Creek in time to see the tent and preach in it. James wrote:

> We had a great desire to be at the Battle Creek meeting, and to speak to the people in the tent at least once before our return home. And when we arrived in Battle Creek we were happy to learn that the brethren had a cheering meeting, and the tent was on its way to Grand Rapids to our last appointment (RH, July 4, 1854).

Loughborough described this first attempt at tent meetings. The tent was located, he reported, on "Van Buren Street, just above the railroad, near the planing mill." He and Cornell worked together in this new, promising evangelistic thrust. Loughborough later reported:

Here, June 10 (Sabbath), the writer opened the tent meetings with a discourse on Daniel 2. This meeting continued only two days, and then we took our tent to Grand Rapids (*ibid.*, Feb. 24, 1885).

The *Review and Herald* of July 4, 1854, announced that 1,000 people attended the Sunday evening meeting, and a good interest was awakened.

Of the meeting in the tent at Grand Rapids, a week later, James White wrote:

On Sixth-day the brethren pitched it on a vacant lot in the city. We were much pleased with its appearance from without, and when we entered it to engage in the solemn worship of God, we felt that the Lord was indeed with us. We are perfectly satisfied that the brethren have moved none too fast in obtaining the tent for this season. On First-day probably about five hundred came out to hear, and if the brethren could have remained another week, the congregation doubtless would have increased to thousands. The people listened with great interest, and when publications were offered, crowded forward to obtain them. The way seems to be fully open to spread the truth (*ibid.*, July 4, 1854).

After the meetings at Grand Rapids were over, Ellen White was given a vision at the house of Brother Fitch. Loughborough described it as being "full of instruction, reproof, and counsel, for the church present, and also encouragement of success to the tent enterprise." He added:

The use of tents for meetings was a new business to us, and we had some things to learn by experience that may look a little strange to those now engaged in tent labor.

First, we did not then so fully realize that when an interest was first awakened in a place it was best to follow up that interest with a thorough effort, or with a full series of discourses, bringing as many as possible of the interested ones to a decision.

Secondly, we did not suppose people would be interested to come out evenings through the week, and so the most of our meetings were held only over Sabbath and first day of each week.

Thirdly, we looked upon tent meetings as a means for the general arousing of the public mind; and, with this idea, we tried to visit as many different places as possible in one season (*ibid.*, Feb. 24, 1885).

The use of a tent was a new approach in evangelism for Sabbathkeepers. Different plans were followed in the 14 tent meetings held in Michigan in the summer of 1854. The majority were two-day meetings in which Loughborough and Cornell gave a "condensed view of the prophecies, sanctuary, messages, and

Sabbath, earnestly urging the people to obey." This moved some to act.

Several meetings were held a little longer than two or three days, and one meeting was held over three consecutive weekends. Wrote Loughborough:

> It was not, however, until the Lord gave us instruction through the Spirit of Prophecy that we fully understood the best mode of prosecuting "the work of the ministry" in connection with tent labor (ibid.).

He was pleased to report that "in almost every place where our tent was erected there were some to obey the truth, but we saw the best results where we tarried the longest."

A most promising line of evangelism was now opening up. Before the summer ended, the *Review* was carrying reports of a second 60-foot (18-meter) tent in New England, and the enlargement of the Michigan tent to 90 feet (27 meters). The *Review* pages were also carrying appointments for meetings in the two evangelistic tents and thrilling reports of the success of these meetings.

At the close of the season James White summed up the success of what had been an experiment. He explained:

> Much can be done with tents, and but little can be accomplished in the summer season in any other way. For example: One year since at our conference in Springfield, Massachusetts, a good hall was obtained, and the people were notified by handbills, and through the daily paper, yet on First-day but few were present excepting believers. But on the sixth inst. 1,200 persons were assembled to hear the Word at the tent meeting held in that city (ibid., Oct. 24, 1854).

The big tent challenged the curiosity of the people and brought out the crowds.

THE MOVE TO BATTLE CREEK

At age 34 James White was putting all his life, health, and strength into the publishing of the *Review*. By early February 1855 he found himself in a desperate situation in regard to the *Review* office. Not only was he the proprietor, financial agent, and editor, he also was burdened with financial troubles. He was working 14 to 18 hours a day. He and Ellen needed to be free of the care of a large publishing house family who had been working for little more than their room and board in the White home.

He realized the need for a change. "Without capital, and without health," he said, "we cannot much longer bear the burden" (RH, Feb. 20, 1855).

Opportunity came in May for a hastily planned trip to Michigan where the brethren in Battle Creek were generally awake to the needs of the cause and eager to establish the *Review* office in that place.

The "conference" met in a private house, for as yet the Sabbathkeeping Adventists had no house of worship in Battle Creek. Here he had opportunity to discuss the future of the *Review* and the *Review* office.

A TRANSITION EVIDENCING THE MATURITY OF THE CHURCH
There were a number of men of good judgment in both Vermont and Michigan capable of assuming most of the responsibilities of which James White felt he must divest himself.

At this time Ellen was "shown" that "no longer should those connected with the office bear burdens they have borne. . . . They must be free in mind, and then their health will improve" (MS 3, 1855).

They spent most of May in Michigan attending and assisting in the tent meetings. Returning home, James reported: "My health gradually improves, and my spirit is getting perfectly free while freed from the cares of the office" (RH, May 29, 1855).

In mid-June they took off by carriage on an 11-week trip through New England. As James interviewed leading workers in Vermont he found them eager to move the *Review* office to Vermont and have the responsibility and burden of conducting it, unless the friends of the cause in some more central position would assume this responsibility.

THE *REVIEW* OFFICE TO GO TO BATTLE CREEK, MICHIGAN
Having consulted with the brethren in Michigan and Vermont, the two states from which there had been the strongest moral and financial support, on his return to Rochester on August 30, 1855, James White was prepared to make the announcement of what seemed to be the consensus of opinion. He did so in early September under the title of "The Office":

> We are happy to say that the brethren in Michigan cheerfully take upon themselves the responsibilities of the *Review* office. They will probably move it to that state this fall. Brethren in Vermont are willing and ready to do the same, but regard Michigan to be more the center of the future field of labor, and are willing that the press should be established in that state.
>
> The *Review* will probably be issued weekly after the press shall be established at Battle Creek, Michigan. It will be our duty and privilege to be freed from the office at present, at least. God has raised up others who are better able to conduct the *Review*, and bear these burdens, than we are (*ibid.*, Sept. 4, 1855).

The decision having been made that the press would go to Battle Creek, the men there went into action. The *Review* of October 2 placed before the church the plans and decisions the Michigan brethren were making:

1. The *Advent Review* office would remain the property of the church.
2. It would be moved to Battle Creek, Michigan.
3. A financial committee of three would be chosen, whose duty it was to move the office, and publish the *Advent Review*.
4. The church-at-large would be called upon to send their freewill offerings to defray the expenses of moving.
5. There was a call for a plan on which the editorial department of the *Advent Review* would be conducted (*ibid.*, Oct. 2, 1855).

The response from the field was uniform and favorable. The month of November was given over to erecting the little publishing house on the southeast corner of Washington and Main streets in the western edge of Battle Creek, and to moving both the press and the families connected with the *Advent Review* office. The White family moved into a little cottage that they rented for $1.50 a week. The general conference, which had been called for Friday, November 16, met in the newly constructed house of worship, a building 18' x 24' (six meters x seven meters), provided for the Battle Creek congregation of 24 (*ibid.*, Aug. 22, 1935). It was one of three church buildings erected in 1855.

Actions of the conference included the appointment of Henry Lyon, David Hewitt, and William M. Smith, all of Battle Creek, to be a committee to investigate the financial condition of the *Review* office, and the appointment of Uriah Smith as the resident (or managing) editor, and five corresponding editors. These were J. N. Andrews, of Iowa; James White and J. H. Waggoner, of Michigan; R. F. Cottrell, of New York; and Stephen Pierce, of Vermont. The minutes also recorded:

8. That a vote of thanks be tendered to Brother White for his valuable services as an editor, in spreading the light of present truth (*ibid.*, Dec. 5, 1855).

A POWER PRESS FOR THE *REVIEW* OFFICE

For five years the *Review and Herald* had been printed on a press owned and operated by Sabbathkeeping Adventists. The printing of each sheet was virtually a "custom job"—the type was inked, a sheet of paper laid on it, and the lever pulled, making the impression. The same was true of all other publications put out between 1852 and 1857. Wrote James White:

With our hand press, it takes three days of each week to print the

Review and Herald. Should the circulation of the *Review and Herald* be doubled (which we may hope it soon will be), there would be no room for the *Instructor*; and a large amount of work . . . would be shut out (*ibid.*, Mar. 19, 1857).

A special conference to consider this urgent need was called for Friday, April 10, 1857, in Battle Creek. Joseph Bates was chosen to preside. First attention was given to the matter of a power press.

Two resolutions were passed: (1) "That such a press be obtained for the *Review* office," and (2) "That all business pertaining to the purchasing [of] the press, et cetera, be confided to the hands of the publishing committee" (*ibid.*, Apr. 16, 1857).

It was thought that such a press could be secured for less than $2,500. James White made the purchase in Boston on their next trip to the East.

FINANCIAL SUPPORT
FOR THE CAUSE OF GOD

The movement was growing. As it spread to the West, families of means accepted the message. For some it was difficult to grasp their responsibility to give financial support to the cause they loved. During the years 1857 and 1858 the situation became desperate. There was no church organization; there was no church treasury. Those who felt called to enter the ministry faced great sacrifices, for they were dependent upon gifts placed in their hands as they moved from place to place. Dedication and sacrifice were called for.

John Loughborough reported concerning financial support for four months of service while holding tent meetings in Illinois, that he had received his board, lodging, and traveling expenses and about $15 in money. This did not leave him much to take home to his wife, Mary.

"For the whole winter of 1857-1858," he said, "I received three ten-pound [4-kilogram] cakes of maple sugar, ten bushels [40 pecks] of wheat, five bushels [20 pecks] of apples, five bushels [20 pecks] of potatoes, one ham, one half of a small hog, one peck [nine liters] of beans, and four dollars in cash. This with the small profit from our boarders brought me through the winter in better condition than other of our ministers" (PUR, Oct. 6, 1910).

James and Ellen White, too, were struggling. While some of the ministers had to drop out from time to time and work with their hands to support their families, James White found as he traveled among the believers that there were those in need of Bibles and other books. He bought supplies and carried some with him, or sent them from Battle Creek. These he sold at a profit.

Things had reached a state where a permanent plan had to be found to provide financial resources for the growing church. In these circumstances Ellen White said to her husband, "The Lord has shown me that if you will call the ministers together, and have J. N. Andrews come down from Waukon, and hold a Bible class, you will find that in the Scriptures there is a complete plan to sustaining . . . the work of the ministry" (*ibid.*).

James White did call for Andrews to come to Battle Creek for such a study, which was reported by J. N. Loughborough. Several workers, including J. N. Andrews, met for two days in Battle Creek to study a Bible-based system of finance for the emerging church. The plan that was developed was presented to the Battle Creek church in a business meeting the following Sunday night, January 16, 1859 . The aim was to induce all to sustain the cause of present truth and at the same time relieve some who had given beyond their real ability.

"Brethren Andrews, Frisbie, and White were chosen to prepare an address on Systematic Benevolence, founded on the declarations of Scripture (RH, Feb. 3, 1859). Two weeks later, January 29, after the hours of the Sabbath were passed, the church came together to hear the reading of the address. The report was adopted by a unanimous vote.

This plan, developed by leading men in the church, became known from the outset as "Systematic Benevolence." Almost from the first the close relation of Systematic Benevolence to the tithe was observed. In early 1861 James White, in a little-known and short-lived printed sheet, referred to the Systematic Benevolence as the tithe.

> We propose that the friends give a tithe, or a tenth of their income, estimating their income at 10 percent of what they possess (*Good Samaritan*, January 1861).

> Next come the personal donations. Let the young men who have no taxable property come up nobly here, also the young women (RH, Apr. 9, 1861).

Systematic Benevolence was early endorsed by Ellen White, and she linked it with the tithe. At the outset there was no separation of tithes and offerings. The demand for funds was mainly for the support of the ministers and the evangelistic outreach.

As the work of the church broadened, developments called for a separation of funds into two groups, "tithes" and "offerings." Also, the precise use of the tithe, sacred to the support of the ministry of the church, was repeatedly brought to the attention of the leaders and members.

THE BATTLE CREEK CONFERENCE

Because James White was eager to have the largest possible representation present for the consideration of plans for the financial support of the growing church, he placed several notices in the *Review* to believers "east, west, north, and south" to attend a conference at Battle Creek, Friday, June 3, to Monday, June 6, 1859. He was especially eager for a good attendance, for it was his plan to promote Systematic Benevolence.

The people were told to make provision for their own entertainment. "It will be impossible," he wrote, "to supply all with beds, or all their horses with stable room. Our sleeping rooms will be given up to females to be made as comfortable as possible, in camp meeting style. The brethren will have the next-best chance in our barns, in the tent, or on unoccupied floors in our houses. Blankets and buffalo robes will be in good demand" (*ibid.*, Apr. 21, 1859).

James White called for a business session to convene immediately after the Sabbath. Joseph Bates chaired the meeting. The address from the Battle Creek church, prepared in January setting forth the broad plans for Systematic Benevolence, was read and freely discussed. Waggoner declared he had seen the plan in operation, and "it worked well." Andrews said he heartily approved the plan. Steward compared it to taxes that people pay, even when they are increased. Cornell declared that "nothing could be brought against the position taken." Byington remarked that God is a God of order, and he thought it was a good plan. Rhodes had only one objection: "The . . . amount called for by the system was too small."

The record of the meeting stated: "Moved by Brother Loughborough that the address be adopted by the conference. Unanimously carried" (*ibid.*, June 9, 1859). This marked another step toward organization by the emerging church.

Ellen White was ill and discouraged and too feeble to attend this meeting. She did go to the tent meeting the following Sunday, but was too miserable to enjoy it. She soon wrote of the experience in introducing the pamphlet *Testimony* No. 5. Here she mentioned that her disease of the heart had a tendency "to depress" her spirits and "destroy" her "faith and courage." Often as she retired at night she felt that her life might be cut short at any moment. She reported that it was at this point that she fainted at midnight on this occasion, presumably Sunday, June 4.

Brethren Andrews and Loughborough were sent for, and offered earnest petitions to God in her behalf. She was taken off in vision. The heavy weight and depression were lifted from her heart and she was shown a number of things to present to the church (1T, p. 185).

First, she was instructed in regard to her personal experience. She saw "that Satan had tried to drive me into discouragement and despair, and to make me desire death rather than life" (*ibid.*).

She also saw that the Laodicean message applied at the present time, and "the message would not accomplish its work in a few short months. It is designed to arouse the people of God, to . . . be fitted for the loud cry of the third angel" (*ibid.*, p. 186).

Then the vision turned to the topic the conference had been considering that very evening. Of this she wrote:

> The plan of systematic benevolence is pleasing to God. I was pointed

back to the days of the apostles, and saw that God laid the plan by the descent of His Holy Spirit, and that by the gift of prophecy He counseled His people in regard to a system of benevolence. All were to share in this work (*ibid.*, p. 190).

The records indicate that this vision marked a turning of the tide in Ellen White's health.

THE AUTUMN TRIP EAST

On Wednesday, August 17, 1859, the Whites left by train for a three-month tour through the Eastern states. Her diary carries day-by-day accounts of conferences and meetings held, of old friends met, of comforting the bereaved, of preaching to large audiences, and, where presented, of the adoption of Systematic Benevolence. They were back home Monday, November 21.

James White summarized the trip east this way:

> The first ten weeks of our journey, till Brother Loughborough joined us, we traveled two thousand miles (3,200 kilometers), preached fifty times, and transacted business, from the sale of a penny tract up to a much larger sum, to the amount of $1,000. We returned with better health and courage to labor in the cause of truth than we had had for the past ten years (RH, Dec. 6, 1859).

GUIDING TOWARD ORGANIZATION
THE VITAL NEED FOR CHURCH ORGANIZATION

As the number of believers increased, it became clear that there was a pressing need for some guidance and controls. Except for the messages that came from God through the visions given to Ellen White, there was no authoritative voice, no voice of an organization, to endorse doctrinal holdings or to certify to the integrity and the qualifications of those who chose to represent themselves as ministers to the Sabbathkeeping remnant. Some who felt called gave no real evidence of such a call. Some organization was needed.

One matter that required agreement was the time to begin the Sabbath. Joseph Bates was considered the father of the Sabbath truth. As captain of his own vessels, he had sailed far and wide and was acquainted with the matter of time-keeping in various parts of the world. It was his conclusion that time as kept at the equator, with sunset uniformly at 6:00 p.m., was the proper guide to Sabbathkeeping, regardless of season of the year or location. The Scriptures called for evening to mark the beginning of the new day, and the words "from even unto even, shall ye celebrate your Sabbath" (Lev. 23:32) were cited in support of this view. The April 21, 1851, issue of the *Review* carried a three-column article by Joseph Bates in support of the 6:00 time.

In the state of Maine in 1847-1848 some took the position that the Sabbath commenced at sunrise, quoting as support, Matthew 28:1: "In the end of the sabbath, as it began to dawn toward the first day of the week" (see RH, Feb. 25, 1868). A vision given to Ellen White checked this error in principle, for the angel repeated the words of the scripture "From even unto even, shall ye celebrate your Sabbath."

There were a few who observed the Sabbath from sundown to sundown (JW to "My Dear Brother," July 2, 1848; see also RH, Feb. 25, 1868), but the majority stood with Bates, as did James and Ellen White. In June 1854 James White requested D. P. Hall in Wisconsin to study the matter and come up with an answer (RH, Dec. 4, 1855).

When this request failed to yield fruit, he asked John Andrews to take his Bible and bring evidence to settle the question. Andrews prepared a paper on the matter. As he passed through Battle Creek with his parents in November on his way to Iowa, he left this in the hands of James White. The reading of this paper became the Sabbath morning Bible study at the conference in Battle Creek. From nine texts in the Old Testament and two from the New, Andrews demonstrated that "even" and "evening" of the Sabbath were identical with sunset *(ibid.)*.

As the paper was read that Sabbath morning, it could be seen that while the 6:00 time advocated by Bates was in principle not incorrect—for it called for beginning the Sabbath in the evening—in detail there was an error. Now with the position of sunset time so amply supported by Scripture evidence, all the congregations, which included the church's leaders, readily accepted the light and were prepared to shift their practice. All, that is, but two—Joseph Bates and Ellen White.

Bates's position had been generally accepted and defended. He was the venerable apostle of the Sabbath truth. He was unready to accept what had been presented by the youthful John Andrews, and he would stand in defense of his position. The vision given to Ellen White in 1848, correcting the sunrise time and confirming "evening time," had nothing to say about the 6:00 time being in error.

Ellen White reasoned that the 6:00 time had been a matter of practice for nearly a decade. The Sabbath so kept had been a great blessing to her, and the angel had said nothing about its being in error. Must a change be made now? Thus matters stood through the rest of the Sabbath and through Sunday as the members met in conference, but this was a rather touchy point of division that was bound to widen as time went on. Then the God of heaven stepped in.

Of what took place Ellen White wrote:

November 20, 1855, while in prayer, the Spirit of the Lord came suddenly and powerfully upon me, and I was taken off in vision (1T, p. 113).

Her attention was called to many points, among them the time to commence the Sabbath. She discussed the matter with the angel. This conversation was very enlightening:

> I saw that it is even so: "From even unto even, shall ye celebrate your sabbath." Said the angel: "Take the Word of God, read it, understand, and ye cannot err. Read carefully, and ye shall find *what* even is and *when* it is."
>
> I asked the angel if the frown of God had been upon His people for commencing the Sabbath as they had. I was directed back to the first rise of the Sabbath, and followed the people of God up to this time, but did not see that the Lord was displeased, or frowned upon them.
>
> I inquired why it had been thus, that at this late day we must change the time of commencing the Sabbath. Said the angel: "Ye shall understand, but not yet, not yet." Said the angel: "If light come, and that light is set aside or rejected, then comes condemnation and the frown of God; but before the light comes, there is no sin, for there is no light for them to reject."
>
> I saw that it was in the minds of some that the Lord had shown that the Sabbath commenced at six o'clock, when I had only seen that it commenced at "even," and it was inferred that even was at six.
>
> I saw that the servants of God must draw together, press together (*ibid.*, p. 116).

And they did. The vision set Ellen White and Joseph Bates straight, and they accepted the vision wholeheartedly. The matter of the time to begin the Sabbath was settled—settled on the basis of Bible study, confirmed by vision.

INITIAL STEPS TOWARD CHURCH ORGANIZATION

Late in 1853 Ellen White prepared a comprehensive article on organization based largely on a vision given in September 1852. In it she pointed out:

> The Lord has shown me that gospel order has been too much neglected and feared. That formality should be shunned; but in so doing, order should not be neglected. There is order in heaven. There was order in the church when Christ was upon the earth; and after His departure, order was strictly observed among His apostles. And now in these last days, while God is bringing His children into the unity of faith, there is more real need of order than ever before (*Supplement to Christian Experience and Views*, p. 15 [see also EW, p. 97]).

In view of the great importance of this testimony in relation to the emerging church, let us consider some of the high points:

1. Men are hurried into the field who lack wisdom and judgment (EW, p. 97).

2. Men whose lives are not holy and who are unqualified to teach the present truth enter the field without being acknowledged by the church or the brethren generally, and confusion and disunion are the result (*ibid.*).

3. Some have a theory of the truth, and can present the argument, but lack spirituality, judgment, and experience; they fail in many things which it is very necessary for them to understand before they can teach the truth (*ibid.*, p. 98).

4. Others have not the argument, but . . . are pressed into the field to engage in a work for which God has not qualified them (*ibid.*).

5. The church should feel their responsibility and should look carefully and attentively at the lives, qualifications, and general course of those who profess to be teachers (*ibid.*, p. 100).

6. It is the duty of the church to act and let it be known that these persons [those who are not called of God, but profess to be teachers] are not acknowledged as teachers by the church (*ibid.*).

7. I saw that this door at which the enemy comes in to perplex and trouble the flock can be shut. I inquired of the angel how it could be closed. He said, "The church must flee to God's Word and become established upon gospel order, which has been overlooked and neglected" (*ibid.*).

JAMES WHITE JOINS IN CALLING FOR GOSPEL ORDER

Through December James White joined Ellen White's voice through four *Review* editorials. Under the same title, "Gospel Order," he came to grips with the matter in a practical way. In the first editorial he pointed out the confusion that exists when gospel order is overlooked. The result is "perfect Babylon." Was having a creed the answer? "What is the real condition of the churches with all their creeds to aid them?"

He then presented his basic position:

We go for order and strict discipline in the church of Christ. And while we reject all human creeds, or platforms, which have failed to effect the order set forth in the gospel, we take the Bible, the perfect rule of faith and practice, given by inspiration of God. This shall be our platform on which to stand, our creed and discipline (RH, Dec. 13, 1853).

In the second editorial James White made it clear that he saw a large task ahead in arriving at and preserving "gospel order in the church," but he declared that it "must be and will be accomplished."

In the third editorial he dealt with the "calling, qualifications, and the duties of a gospel minister." He asserted that "the united action of the church relative to those who take the watchcare of the flock would have a powerful influence to unite the church in love" (*ibid.*, Dec. 20, 1853).

The fourth editorial brought out the responsibilities of the individual church members in giving support in both prayers and finances.

The series closed with the words of the apostle Paul in Romans 12:1-18, setting forth God's ideal for His people. Ellen and James White had sown the seed—it would take time to mature. What was written tended to restrain a tendency to disunion in the ranks of the believers. Another factor, something not enjoyed by the other churches, was the guiding and restraining influence of the visions, which the believers accepted as having authority. The interplay of Bible instruction and the Spirit of Prophecy messages come into full view as church organization was consummated a few years later.

While Ellen White had written and published at some length on the need of order in managing the work of the church (see EW, pp. 97-104), and while James White had kept his need before the believers in addresses and *Review* articles, the church was slow to move. What had been presented in general terms was well received, but when it came to translating this into something constructive there was resistance and opposition. James White's brief articles in February aroused not a few from complacency, and now a great deal was being said.

J. N. Loughborough, working with White in Michigan, was the first to respond. His words were in the affirmative, but on the defensive:

> Says one, if you organize so as to hold property by law, you will be a part of Babylon. No; I understand there is quite a difference between our being in a position that we can protect our property by law and using the law to protect and enforce our religious views. If it is wrong to protect *church* property, why is it not wrong for individuals to hold any property legally? (RH, Mar. 8, 1860).

NEED FOR ORGANIZATION FOR PUBLISHING INTERESTS

James White had closed his statement in the *Review*, laying before the church the matter of the need for organization of the publishing interests with the words "If any object to our suggestions, will they please write out a plan on which we as a people can act?" (*ibid.*, Feb. 23, 1860). The first minister in the field to respond was R. F. Cottrell, a stalwart corresponding editor of the *Review*. His immediate reaction was decidedly negative:

Brother White has asked the brethren to speak in relation to his proposition to secure the property of the church. I do not know precisely what measure he intends in this suggestion, but understand it is to get incorporated as a religious body according to law. For myself, I think it would be wrong to "make us a name," since that lies at the foundation of Babylon. I do not think God would approve of it (*ibid.*, Mar. 22, 1860).

Cottrell was experienced and influential; his message, published in James White's absence, set the pace for a long-drawn-out battle. The matter seesawed back and forth through the next six months, with some reference to it in most issues of the *Review*. Then came the call for a general conference at Battle Creek opening Friday, September 28, to consider safeguarding the work through some type of organization. Because of the importance of the conference, its business proceedings were reported in great detail in the issues of the *Review and Herald* for October 9, 16, and 23. The business meetings began September 29 immediately after the Sabbath, with Joseph Bates serving as chairman. Having in mind the debate that had been running in the *Review*, those attending the conference moved immediately into a lengthy discussion. It was clear that most looked negatively on any steps toward organization. Meetings continued through the evening after the Sabbath and Sunday morning and afternoon, ending finally with the adoption of the following:

We recommend to the conference the organization of a publishing association that may legally hold the Review office (*ibid.*, Oct. 16, 1860).

With relief James White stood and said, "This is just what I have been pleading for, for the last six months" (*ibid.*, Oct. 23, 1860). On Monday at sunrise the conference met to adopt a constitution built upon this action. First, White made some remarks, "expressing his gratitude for the candor and good feeling and unity and regard for the principles of right, manifested by those present" (*ibid.*). The first of the 10 articles adopted that Monday morning read:

This Association shall be denominated *The Advent Review Publishing Association*, the object of which shall be the publication of periodicals, books, and tracts, calculated to convey instruction on Bible truth, especially the fulfillment of prophecy, the commandments of God, and the faith of Jesus (*ibid.*).

ADOPTING A DENOMINATIONAL NAME

The conference, having reached a consensus on the need for organizing the publishing association, now faced a further step. In order to own property legally a name needed to be chosen for the groups of Sabbathkeeping Adventists scattered widely in New England and the Midwest.

Cautiously the conference moved into this highly sensitive area. Brother Poole feared that to adopt a general name would hurt them as a people. J. B. Frisbie was opposed to a sectarian name but saw the need for some uniformity of the terms by which the body of Sabbathkeepers would be known. Moses Hull thought that the churches in various places might be known as "the church worshiping on the seventh day in such and such places." James White stated that he did not see how they could get along without some name, and they could not hold property without a name. The law was specific on that point. He could not see that this would be going into Babylon. M. E. Cornell was articulate in expressing his feelings:

> The commandments of God and the faith of Jesus is a distinguishing feature between us and the other denominations. . . . There is confusion in the names already chosen; and if something is not done here, churches will go on choosing different names still. A general name will bring us into unity and not confusion (*ibid.*).

The discussion continued in earnest terms through the morning hours till 11:00, when a recess seemed in order. The minutes of the discussions after lunch read:

> The question again [was] brought before the meeting, "Shall we adopt some name?" Some who had previously been averse to such a step here signified their change of opinion, and their readiness to cooperate with their brethren in this course (*ibid.*).

Brother Sperry was willing to lay his prejudice on the altar, believing that God would give wisdom. Stephen Belden, employed in the *Review* office, expressed his feeling that going without a name would be like publishing books without titles, or sending out a paper without a heading.

James White then took the floor and apologized for some of the brethren who seemed to be afraid of a name. The *Review* reported:

> He [James] had been in the same position once. In times past when we were comparatively few, he did not see the necessity of any such steps. But now large bodies of intelligent brethren are being raised up, and without some regulation of this kind will be thrown into confusion.
>
> He then gave a review of the past, mentioning the opposition which had been manifested by some all the way along, first against publishing a paper, then against issuing pamphlets, then against having an office,

then against the sale of publications, then against church order, then against having a power press. It had been hard to bring the minds of some of the brethren to the necessity of these things; but they had all been essential to the prosperity of the cause (ibid.).

The motion to adopt a name was finally put before the delegates, and it carried. The record states, "None dissented, though a few declined to vote." Turning again to the minutes of this 1860 conference, we find the story of the outcome, which gave birth to the name by which the Sabbathkeeping Adventists would be known.

SEVENTH-DAY ADVENTISTS THE NAME CHOSEN

Having voted to adopt a name, the discussion now turned on what that name should be. The name Church of God, was proposed and zealously advocated by some. It was objected that the name was already in use by some denominations, and on this account, was indefinite, besides having to the world an appearance of presumption. Brother White remarked that the name taken should be one which would be the least objectionable to the world at large.

The name Seventh-day Adventists was proposed as a simple name and one expressive of our faith and position. After some further remarks, Brother Hewitt offered the following resolution:

Resolved, That we take the name of Seventh-day Adventists (ibid.).

This resolution was discussed freely, and the wording was adjusted to "That we call ourselves Seventh-day Adventists." It was finally acted upon (ibid.).

Even so, T. J. Butler, of Ohio, dissented, and Elders Lawrence, Sperry, Andrews, and Ingraham refrained from voting. Now the Sabbathkeeping Adventists had a name, a name that Ellen White was shown carried Heaven's approval. It had been a momentous conference, clearly influenced by the Spirit of God.

The next step to be taken was the organization of the publishing work. On May 3, 1861, the Seventh-day Adventist Publishing Association was incorporated in harmony with laws newly formulated by the Michigan legislature, and on May 23, in Battle Creek, bylaws governing the operation of the corporation was adopted. Officers for the association were chosen as follows:

President, James White
Vice President, G. W. Amadon
Secretary, E. S. Walker
Treasurer, Uriah Smith

Auditor, J. N. Loughborough

James White was elected editor of the *Review and Herald*, and G. W. Amadon, editor of the *Youth's Instructor* (ibid., May 28, 1861).

WINNING THE STRUGGLE FOR CHURCH ORGANIZATION

With others sharing the responsibilities of the publishing work in Battle Creek, James and Ellen were more free to travel into the field and visit the churches.

But while there was unanimity at the conference in Battle Creek, this was not true in the field generally.

With repairs being made on their home, with the laying of plans for the new publishing house, with planning for a trip east to secure moral support for organization and for funds badly needed by the publishing association, James White, as reported by Ellen to Mary Loughborough, was "too busy to know whether he is sick or well" (letter 6, 1861). He was yet to discover the extent of the negative feelings in the field, particularly in New York State and Ohio.

MEETING OPPOSITION

James and Ellen White started on their eastern tour Tuesday, July 23, 1861. They spent Tuesday night with friends in Jackson, Michigan, and the next morning were on their way to Eagle Harbor, New York, where Moses Hull was leading out in tent meetings. A phrase in Hull's report of the meetings gives a hint of the erosion, in certain areas, of confidence in church leaders. He wrote: "Sister White's testimonies were very pointed, and seemed to remove prejudice which existed against her and her visions" (RH, Sept. 3, 1861). As resistance to organization deepened, and criticism of James White for his attempts to lead the church into organization proliferated, Ellen White and the visions came under attack, first covertly and then openly. Church order and spiritual gifts were closely linked together, as was seen as the eastern tour progressed.

VISION AT ROOSEVELT, NEW YORK

From Eagle Harbor the Whites made their way to Rochester and then to Roosevelt, New York. A conference was to be held in the house of worship there over the weekend of August 3 and 4. This was a difficult meeting. White reported that on Sabbath afternoon light began to break through, especially in a season of special prayer "for the afflicted and desponding among us, and for the return of the Holy Spirit to us as a people." He reported:

We had been assembled seven hours without taking food, and the interest of the occasion was such that no one appeared to be faint or weary.

God heard the united prayers of His afflicted people, and His Spirit came down upon them. Mrs. White shared largely in this blessed refreshing, and was soon in vision, in which she had messages of comfort for the desponding and afflicted, and of correction for the wayward and erring (*ibid.*, Aug. 20, 1861).

In the vision she was shown, among other things, "in regard to church order, and the struggle of our nation, and its effect upon the cause" (*ibid.*, Aug. 27, 1861). As they moved through the state and saw what was happening, James White was "stung with the thought that the balance of influence is either against, or silent upon, the subject of organization" (*ibid.*, Sept. 3, 1861). He wrote:

We seem to be wading through the influence of a stupid uncertainty upon the subject of organization. This is as might be expected from the circumstances connected with the introduction of the subject among us. Soon after we merely hinted at it about eighteen months since, an article appeared in the *Review* from one of the corresponding editors well calculated to arouse the fears of many that Brother White was in favor of something dreadful. . . .

The brethren in Pennsylvania voted down organization, and the cause in Ohio has been dreadfully shaken. It has suffered everywhere. If such ministers of experience as Brethren Ingraham, Andrews, and Wheeler could have spoken on the subject decidedly and in season, much might have been saved that has probably gone to ruin. There is everywhere someone to hold back. They have no valid reasons for so doing; still they hold back (*ibid.*, Aug. 27, 1861).

White then referred to the conference in Roosevelt. After a two-hour discussion on organization at which objections were removed, he called for a standing vote favoring organization. Pioneer worker Frederick Wheeler kept his seat. James White was devastated. He wrote, "A dreadful feeling of discouragement came over us that we have not been able to shake off," and he asked, "What can we expect of the people when the ministers stand thus?"

As James White bemoaned the situation, he observed that "instead of our being a united people, growing stronger, we are in many places but little better than broken fragments, still scattering and growing weaker" (*ibid.*).

This situation had been most obvious to James and Ellen and other leaders as they traveled widely and visited individual churches. They saw how important it was for individual churches to agree on such matters as qualifications of leaders, accepting new members, and teaching the beliefs.

Since the first steps had been taken in Battle Creek, in providing for the publishing work and having decided on a name, the members in Battle Creek were first to take the next step.

THE BATTLE CREEK CHURCH SETS THE PACE IN ORGANIZING

Though in August and September several companies of believers entered into some form of organization, it was left to the Battle Creek church to lead out again in well-defined steps in this direction. The annual meeting of the Seventh-day Adventist Publishing Association was called for Friday, October 4. This would bring together quite a group of Michigan ministers and laymen. J. N. Loughborough, E. S. Walker, and George Amadon saw this as an opportunity to further the interests of church order, carrying it to a third step, the organizing of local churches. In connection with the constituency meeting, they suggested meetings over the weekend at which attention could be given to "a more perfect organization of the church" (*ibid.*, Sept. 24, 1861).

So after the Sabbath, October 5, a meeting was held, with Joseph Bates serving as chairman and Uriah Smith as secretary.

The first business presented was the organization of churches.

Loughborough moved "that we consider the proper manner of organizing churches."

James White seconded it, and it was carried.

White then presented the following resolution:

> *Resolved,* That this conference recommend the following church covenant: We, the undersigned, hereby associate ourselves together as a church, taking the name Seventh-day Adventists, covenanting to keep the commandments of God, and the faith of Jesus Christ (*ibid.*, Oct. 8, 1861).

It was seconded by Moses Hull, and adopted. But the vote was not full, and White stated that he hoped that a matter of such importance would not be passed without some discussion. On this suggestion, Loughborough, by a motion, opened the way for a reconsideration of the matter. This led to the question whether White's proposal was not a creed—and a creed they would not tolerate. Hull felt that it was not a creed or articles of faith, but merely a pledge to do one thing: "Keep the commandments of God and the faith of Jesus." James White then led into a discussion of the involvements in the light of the fears sustained by some.

James said, in part: "I would like to hear remarks on this point. It will certainly be doing like those around us; and certain individuals will say that we are following Babylon; and this may be an objection in their minds" (*ibid.*).

Loughborough suggested that if this were true, they would be patterning after the other churches by building meetinghouses. "We call the churches

Babylon not because they covenant together to obey God," but for other reasons.

Cornell could not see that adopting such a covenant was "patterning after the churches."

Then James made a comprehensive and significant statement on the matter.

> I wish to say a word now in favor of the resolution. I prefer that the brethren should be uniform in this thing. This would tend to unity in the church. Let us set a right example here and let it go out from this meeting. . . . In Ephesians 4:11-13, we read, "And He gave some, apostles; and some, prophets," et cetera. Here we have the gifts of the church presented. Now I take the ground that creeds stand in a direct opposition to the gifts. Let us suppose a case: We get up a creed, stating just what we shall believe on this point and the other, and just what we shall do in reference to this thing and that, and say that we will believe the gifts, too.
>
> But suppose the Lord, through the gifts, should give us some new light that did not harmonize with our creed; then, if we remain true to the gifts, it knocks our creed all over at once. Making a creed is setting the stakes, and barring up the way to all future advancement. God put the gifts into the church for a good and great object; but men who have got up their churches have shut up the way or have marked out a course for the Almighty. They say virtually that the Lord must not do anything further than what has been marked out in the creed.
>
> A creed and the gifts thus stand in direct opposition to each other. Now what is our position as a people? The Bible is our creed. We reject everything in the form of a human creed. *We take the Bible and the gifts of the Spirit; embracing the faith that thus the Lord will teach us from time to time.* And in this we take a position against the formation of a creed. We are not taking one step, in what we are doing, toward becoming Babylon (*ibid.*; italics supplied).

Some discussion followed about statements in writing and covenants. Then the far-reaching action was taken—that of adopting the wording proposed. Before the meeting ended they adopted unanimously the covenant by which members would join the church:

> We, the undersigned, hereby associate ourselves together as a church, taking the name Seventh-day Adventists, covenanting to keep the commandments of God, and the faith of Jesus Christ (*ibid.*).

Another important step in church organization had been taken.

The matter of procedure in organizing churches was referred to the ministers present who were charged with holding a "Bible class" on the subject and were to write an address to the brethren, to be published in the *Review*.

THE FORMATION OF THE MICHIGAN CONFERENCE

James White then suggested another proposition:

> *Resolved*, That we recommend to the churches in the State of Michigan to unite in one conference with the name of the Michigan Conference of Seventh-day Adventists.

The resolution was quickly adopted. Then the ministers and delegates from the churches were declared members of the Michigan Conference. Appropriate officers and a conference committee were elected. The chairman, Joseph Bates, and the clerk, Uriah Smith, were voted in as the officers for the current year, and the time for the first session was set for October 5 to 8, 1862. There was one more important question, and that was "ministers' papers." Here is the action:

> *Resolved*, That our ministers' papers consist of a certificate of ordination, also credentials to be signed by the chairman and clerk of the conference, which credentials shall be renewed annually *(ibid.)*.

A significant milestone in the organization of the Seventh-day Adventist Church had now been put in place. The foundations were laid with Michigan as an example of what might be accomplished. The responsibility for the organization of local churches and state conferences now passed to the believers in other states.

The conference over, James White reported through the *Review and Herald*:

> A calm, sweet, melting spirit pervaded this meeting, making it the best of the kind we ever witnessed. We heard many brethren remark in regard to the conference that it was the best ever held at Battle Creek. . . .
>
> The unity existing among the brethren at this conference, the eagerness to take a decided position upon organization, and the general readiness to sustain the publishing association have greatly encouraged us. . . . We certainly made rapid progress during the three days of our conference *(ibid.)*.

OTHER STATES ORGANIZE

When the *Review* that reported the meeting of the Michigan Conference came to the hands of J. N. Andrews, who was working in Minnesota, he took the matter of organization to a conference held there. Believers and workers adopted a resolution patterned after the example of Michigan.

Soon Ohio followed, through the efforts of M. E. Cornell, who had gone there to meet appointments for James and Ellen White, who were exhausted.

The stage had been set, and now the believers in most states moved rather promptly into full organization.

The October 29 *Review and Herald* expressed James White's concern over the peril of inexperienced persons attempting to lead out in organizing local churches. He closed his editorial with these words:

> The question has been Shall we organize? That question being answered in the affirmative, the question now is How shall we organize? Beware, brethren, of moving hastily in this matter. By hard tugging, our experienced ministers may be induced to take hold of this work, and not leave it for novices in the faith to make still greater confusion by meddling with the organization of churches (*ibid.*, Oct. 29, 1861).

This was followed by an in-depth article from Loughborough titled "Church Discipline." He wrote at length of the relation of members to church officers, of the problems of dealing with those who had never been under discipline, of some who were inclined to rebel against the Spirit of Prophecy counsels, and of receiving and propagating rumors and accusations.

CONFESSIONS OF NEGATIVE ATTITUDES

Through all of this the *Review* carried statements from lay members and ministers confessing their wrong attitudes about both organization and the Spirit of Prophecy. Frederick Wheeler's "Confession," published in the *Review* of December 3, was typical. It was heartfelt and extended, and said in part:

> I have been slow . . . to engage in the work of organization. I regret this, and intend for the future to be more diligent, believing it will accomplish a work in bringing the church on higher and holier ground.
>
> I humbly ask forgiveness of God and all my brethren, and ask an interest in their prayers (*ibid.*, Dec. 3, 1861).

A confession was also made by J. N. Andrews, who, writing from Waukon, Iowa, on November 28, 1861, confessed his negative attitude and influence concerning "the testimony of the Spirit of God, given through vision to Sister White." He referred to his turning around, stating that "the present work of organization meets my hearty approval" (*ibid.*, Dec. 17, 1861).

There was one more step to be taken in church organization, and that was the binding of the state conferences together in the General Conference of Seventh-day Adventists.

84

THE CALL FOR A GENERAL CONFERENCE

The April 7, 1863, issue of the *Review* carried the call for a meeting of the General Conference, at which it was hoped that the state conferences could be bound together in a unified organization across the land. The delegates were called to meet on Wednesday, May 20. The notice stated:

> The several conference committees in the different states are requested to send delegates, or letters at their discretion. The brethren in those localities where there is no state conference can also be represented in the conference by delegates or letters (*ibid.*, Apr. 7, 1863).

On Wednesday afternoon, May 20, twenty ministers and laymen assembled in Battle Creek to present their credentials. The conference moved into its work in organizing the General Conference of Seventh-day Adventists.

The conference elected John Byington as president; Uriah Smith, secretary; and E. S. Walker, treasurer. James White was first unanimously elected to the presidency, but he thought it best to let another carry that responsibility. Byington would be joined by J. N. Andrews and G. W. Amadon, making an executive committee of three. The main thrust of the conference related to organization in both the state conferences and the General Conference.

This step in organization brought the church into a unified denominational structure in time to meet the emergencies of the military draft, and prepared to make advance steps as the health message came, through vision, two weeks after the session.

SEVENTH-DAY ADVENTISTS IN TIME OF WAR

As the year 1861 dawned, the United States was in somewhat of a turmoil. The recent presidential election had polarized the Northern states and the Southern states, where slaves were held. Before Lincoln's inauguration as president, South Carolina passed an ordinance seceding from the United States.

Sabbathkeeping Adventists had no sympathy with slavery and were aware, of course, of the tensions and excitement, but had kept aloof of matters relating to the political situation. Just at this time light concerning what was ahead was given to Ellen White in vision:

> I was shown that many do not realize the extent of the evil which has come upon us. They have flattered themselves that the national difficulties would soon be settled and confusion and war end, but all will be convinced that there is more reality in the matter than was anticipated. . . .
>
> The North and South were presented before me. The North have been deceived in regard to the South. They are better prepared for war than has been represented. Most of their men are well skilled in the use of arms, some of them from experience in battle, others from habitual sporting. They have the advantage of the North in this respect, but have not, as a general thing, the valor and the power of endurance that Northern men have (1T, pp. 264-266).

Seventh-day Adventists, just moving into church organization, were, as the War Between the States opened, forced to find their way in a very difficult and sensitive area. They had no guidelines to follow. While the Ten Commandments prohibited the taking of life and the desecration of the seventh-day Sabbath, the history of God's people of old under the theocracy was not a paradigm. But God did not leave His remnant people to flounder. They prayed and studied, and when God gave counsel through His messenger, Ellen White, they listened.

Even before the first shots of the Civil War were fired, Ellen had been given a view of the coming conflict and its ferocity. The visions given at Parkville, Michigan; Roosevelt, New York; and Battle Creek, Michigan, put Adventists in the unique position of knowing, first, of the coming war and its long duration, and then, its philosophy, with the assurance that God had a controlling hand in the affairs of the nation.

Ellen said, "I saw that both the South and the North were being punished."

> God is punishing the North, that they have so long suffered the accursed sin of slavery to exist; for in the sight of heaven it is a sin of the darkest dye. God is not with the South, and He will punish them dreadfully in the end (*ibid.*, p. 359).

She contrasted the guidance God would give with that of the great adversary, Satan himself:

> The great leading rebel general, Satan, is acquainted with the transactions of this war, and he directs his angels to assume the form of dead generals, to imitate their manners, and exhibit their peculiar traits of character. The leaders in the army really believe that the spirits of their friends, and of dead warriors, the fathers of the Revolutionary War, are guiding them (*ibid.*, p. 364).

THE BATTLE OF MANASSAS

In vision Ellen White was taken to the scene of the Battle of Manassas; she was shown God's hand in what took place there:

> I had a view of the disastrous battle at Manassas, Virginia. It was a most exciting, distressing scene. The Southern army had everything in their favor and were prepared for a dreadful contest. The Northern army was moving on with triumph, not doubting but that they would be victorious. Many were reckless and marched forward boastingly, as though victory were already theirs.
>
> As they neared the battlefield, many were almost fainting through weariness and want of refreshment. They did not expect so fierce an encounter. They rushed into battle and fought bravely, desperately. The dead and dying were on every side. Both the North and the South suffered severely. The Southern men felt the battle, and in a little while would have been driven back still further. The Northern men were rushing on, although their destruction was very great.
>
> Just then an angel descended and waved his hand backward. Instantly there was confusion in the ranks. It appeared to the Northern men that their troops were retreating, when it was not so in reality, and a precipitate retreat commenced. This seemed wonderful to me.
>
> Then it was explained that God had this nation in His own hand,

and would not suffer victories to be gained faster than He ordained, and would permit no more losses to the Northern men than in His wisdom He saw fit, to punish them for their sins. And had the Northern army at this time pushed the battle still further in their fainting, exhausted condition, the far greater struggle and destruction which awaited them would have caused great triumph in the South.

God would not permit this, and sent an angel to interfere. The sudden falling back of the Northern troops is a mystery to all. They know not that God's hand was in the matter (*ibid.*, pp. 266, 267).

Thus was revealed God's guiding hand in the affairs of the war.

EYEWITNESS ACCOUNT

W. W. Blackford, a lieutenant colonel in the Southern army, in his book *War Years With Jeb Stuart* gave a stirring account of what happened at Manassas in the battle of July 21, 1861:

It was now about four o'clock and the battle raged with unabated fury. The lines of blue were unbroken and their fire vigorous as ever while they surged against the solid walls of gray, standing immovable in their front. It was on that ridge earlier in the day that Jackson won the name of Stonewall.

But now the most extraordinary spectacle I have ever witnessed took place. I had been gazing at the numerous well-formed lines as they moved forward to the attack, some fifteen or twenty thousand strong in full view, and for some reason had turned my head in another direction for a moment, when someone exclaimed, pointing to the battlefield, "Look! Look!"

I looked, and what a change had taken place in an instant. Where those well-dressed, well-defined lines, with clear spaces between, had been steadily pressing forward, the whole field was a confused swarm of men, like bees, running away as fast as their legs could carry them, with all order and organization abandoned. In a moment more the whole valley was filled with them as far as the eye could reach.

They plunged through Bull Run wherever they came to it, regardless of fords or bridges, and there many were drowned. Muskets, cartridge boxes, belts, knapsacks, haversacks, and blankets were thrown away in their mad race, that nothing might impede their flight. In the reckless haste, the artillery drove over everyone who did not get out of their way. Ambulance and wagon drivers cut the traces and dashed off on the mules. In [their] crossing Cub Run, a shell exploded in a team and blocked the way and twenty-eight pieces of artillery fell into our hands (pp. 34, 35 [see also DF 956]).

THE WAR AND THE WORK OF THE CHURCH

For a time to those in Battle Creek, the war seemed far away. Little was happening on the battlefields, and James and Ellen White were involved in the various church interests.

But as the war progressed, the president issued calls for more soldiers. Each state was required to furnish a certain quota of men for each call, and this in turn was apportioned to each county, city, and ward. If the number of those who freely volunteered failed to reach the required quota, it would become necessary to institute a draft. To avoid this, ways had to be found to encourage the enlistment of men to make up the required number. To promote enlistment, citizens' committees were formed in many municipalities; they arranged to offer bounties to be paid to recruits. Beginning at $25, they were soon raised to as high as $100 as more and more men were called to the front.

Because Seventh-day Adventists were particularly anxious to avoid the threatened draft, which would involve Sabbathkeepers, James White heartily participated in the matter of raising funds to pay attractive bonuses to volunteers. Seventh-day Adventists as a rule were conscientiously opposed to the bearing of arms, yet they felt it to be their duty to raise money for the payment of the bonuses offered to volunteers who had no religious scruples against bearing arms.

James White, J. P. Kellogg, and other leading Adventists attended and took part in a number of mass meetings of Battle Creek citizens. In these meetings there was free discussion of the activities of the war, but particularly the problem of furnishing the quota of men, if possible, without the necessity of the draft. White made it clear that Sabbathkeeping young men had not refrained from volunteering because they were cowards or ease-loving. Though they were generally poor, they would willingly contribute as freely as the well-to-do.

The perplexities incident to the war increased as the rate of the bounty was raised, necessitating still heavier calls for means from Seventh-day Adventists. Workers in the field reported difficulties in connection with attempts in evangelism. William Ingraham reported that the Illinois tent was laid up because it was useless to pitch the tent in new fields during the war excitement (RH, Aug. 19, 1862). In Iowa J. H. Waggoner and B. F. Snook were arrested under martial law and detained till they secured a certificate from the county judge "setting forth their place of residence, their present occupation and calling." The judge advised them to repair immediately to their homes, as they would be daily more and more liable to troubles and difficulties (*ibid.*, Aug. 26, 1862).

From Rochester, New York, M. E. Cornell reported:

> The war excitement was so great we had to adjourn for two nights. Our tent was used for the war meetings. I never saw such an excitement as there is here in Rochester. The streets are blocked up with the tents of recruiting officers. The stores are all closed up 3:00 to 6:00 p.m., and all are trying to induce men to enlist. War meetings every night (*ibid.*).

THE TIDE BEGINS TO TURN

With President Lincoln's Emancipation Proclamation, effective January 1, 1863, the tide in the war began to turn. When a national fast was appointed for April 30, 1863, Seventh-day Adventists felt they could join in its observance, for the government was lining up more in harmony with the testimony of Isaiah 58. In early July a decisive battle was fought at Gettysburg, Pennsylvania, with the Union forces gaining the victory.

There were still many difficult days ahead, but the provision that by paying $300 a drafted Seventh-day Adventist could gain freedom from military service brought relief till well into 1864. The newly organized church had a breathing spell. Yet such a payment was equivalent to somewhat more than the wages for a year of employment, and James White saw the provision, as beneficial as it was, a threat to denominational income. He warned:

> Should our brethren be drafted, they should if necessary mortgage their property to raise the $300, rather than to accept means that should go into the Lord's treasury. We would say this even of our ministers. The draft will probably come closer and closer (*ibid.*, Nov. 24, 1863).

On March 3, 1863, the Congress of the United States passed a law calling for the enrollment of all men between the ages of 20 and 45; this would form the basis of a national draft. It now looked as if one man in three would be called to military service. Certain provisions of this act brought a sigh of relief to Seventh-day Adventists:

> That members of religious denominations, who shall by oath or affirmation declare that they are conscientiously opposed to the bearing of arms, and who are prohibited from doing so by the rules and articles of faith and practice of such religious denomination, shall, when drafted into the military service, be considered noncombatants, and shall be assigned by the Secretary of War to duty in the hospitals, or to the care of freedmen, or shall pay the sum of $300, to such person as the Secretary of War shall designate

to receive it, to be applied to the benefit of the sick and wounded soldiers.

Provided, That no person shall be entitled to the benefit of the provisions of this section, unless his declaration of conscientious scruples against bearing arms shall be supported by satisfactory evidence that his deportment has been uniformly consistent with such declaration ("The Views of Seventh-day Adventists Relative to Bearing Arms," pp. 3, 4).

Under these liberal provisions, Seventh-day Adventist generally, if drafted, paid $300 and were excused from serving. In the light of the counsel given by God through Ellen White, it seemed consistent to take this course and thus escape the many problems of military service. But the law was amended on July 4, 1864; the $300 commutation provision was revoked, but with Quakers seemingly in mind, the amendment declared:

"Nothing contained in this Act is to be construed to alter, or in any way affect the law relative to those conscientiously opposed to bearing arms" (*ibid.,* p. 4).

This meant that the $300 commutation provision now applied only to those officially recognized as noncombatants. Up to this point Seventh-day Adventists, although firmly of that persuasion, had not publicly declared this fact, nor was their position officially recognized. The church had to act quickly to obtain official noncombatant status. Church leaders, working through proper channels, took immediate steps to achieve this. The first step was to gain the endorsement of the governor of Michigan, Austin Blair. Hence, on August 3, 1864, a communication was taken to him by three men of the General Conference Committee:

We the undersigned, Executive Committee of the General Conference of Seventh-day Adventists, respectfully beg leave to present for your consideration the following statements:

The denomination of Christians calling themselves Seventh-day Adventists, taking the Bible as their rule of faith and practice, are unanimous in their views that its teachings are contrary to the spirit and practice of war; hence, they have ever been conscientiously opposed to bearing arms. . . . We would further represent that Seventh-day Adventists are rigidly anti-slavery, loyal to the government, and in sympathy with it against the rebellion.

But not having had a long existence as a distinct people, and our organization having but recently been perfected, our sentiments are not yet extensively known. The change in the law renders it necessary that we take a more public stand in the matter. For this reason we now lay before

Your Excellency the sentiments of Seventh-day Adventists, as a body, relative to bearing arms, trusting that you will feel no hesitation in endorsing our claim that, as a people, we come under the intent of the late action of Congress concerning those who are conscientiously opposed to bearing arms, and are entitled to the benefits of said laws.

> John Byington   General Conference
> J. N. Loughborough   Executive Committee
> George W. Amadon   of Seventh-day Adventists
> Battle Creek, August 2, 1864.

This communication addressed to the governor was accompanied by letters of introduction and a commendation from the mayor and the leading citizens of Battle Creek.

GOVERNOR BLAIR'S REPLY

The delegation carried back with them the governor's reply, brief and to the point, but adequate:

> I am satisfied that the foregoing statement of principles and practices of the Seventh-day Adventists is correct, and that they are entitled to all the immunities secured by law to those who are conscientiously opposed to bearing arms, or engaging in war.
>
> Austin Blair
> Governor of Michigan
> Dated, August 3, 1864.

The next step had to be taken in Washington. For this important mission, J. N. Andrews, armed with appropriate documents, was sent as the church's emissary. Reported James White in the *Review* of September 6, 1864.

> Brother J. N. Andrews left for Washington, Monday [August 29], well endorsed from the highest military authority in this city. He will report through the *Review* as soon as possible. May it be favorable for those who have enlisted to serve under the Prince of Peace.

Two weeks later the *Review* carried Andrews' Washington, D.C., report. He had successfully followed through, and now Adventists would be fully recognized as noncombatants. They would be assigned to duty in hospitals, or to the care of freedmen, or would be exempt on the payment of $300.

However, on the local level recognition of the claims of Adventist men was difficult to secure.

During this time the intensity of the war had been such that the General

Conference Committee made an appeal for Sabbath, August 27, to be m day of fasting and prayer.

Three points of concern were named in a brief article in the *Review*:

> 1. The existing war, which threatens to very much retard the progress of the third angel's message.
> 2. The condition of American slaves.
> 3. That God will direct His people to act wisely and humbly in reference to the draft, and overrule impending events to their good and His glory (RH, Aug. 9, 1864).

On October 20 the president of the United States, Abraham Lincoln, proclaimed "the last Thursday in November next, as a day . . . of thanksgiving and prayer to Almighty God, the beneficent Creator and Ruler of the universe." It was a day for humility and pleading with God for "peace, union, and harmony throughout the land" (*ibid.*, Nov. 8, 1864).

In January 1865 the president issued another call for 300,000 volunteers to fill up the ranks in the armies. It was expected that most of this need would be supplied by a draft, and this would take a number of Adventists. James White wearily commented in the *Review*:

> If this war continues, God only knows what it will do for even non-combatants. Unless Heaven interposes, they may not always be treated with that respect and mercy which they now receive (*ibid.*, Jan. 24, 1865).

A CALL TO IMPORTUNE GOD TO STOP THE WAR

The next week James White addressed the readers of the *Review*. After expressing gratitude for "the provision made by the government for the exemption of noncombatants from bearing carnal weapons," he proposed to fellow Adventists:

> Prayer and giving of thanks for those in authority constitute a proper portion of their Sabbath and other seasons of public worship, and also of family and private devotions. And besides this, we recommend that the second Sabbath in each month be especially set apart to fasting and prayer in view of the present terrible war (*ibid.*, Jan. 31, 1865).

By mid-February 1865 it was clear to the committee that if the war did not come to an early close, and if there was to be a call for more men every five or six months, "we must inevitably lose means, or lose our own numbers, and lose those who would embrace the truth, and lose the attention of the people" (*ibid.*, Feb. 21, 1865).

We are thus brought, as it plainly appears to us, to a place where if the war continues, we must stop. We repeat it, the war must stop, or our work in spreading the truth must stop. Which shall it be? (*ibid.*).

Then came a most unusual appeal:

We would recommend, nay more, earnestly request, all our churches and scattered brethren to set apart four days commencing Wednesday, March 1, and continuing till the close of the following Sabbath, as days of earnest and importunate prayer over this subject. Let business be suspended, and the churches meet at one o'clock on the afternoon of each of the weekdays, and twice on the Sabbath, to pour out their supplications before God. . . . During these days of prayer we recommend on the part of all a very abstemious and simple diet. . . . Labor will be suspended at the *Review* office (*ibid.*).

Seventh-day Adventists responded most heartily.

President Lincoln, in his second inaugural address, given on March 4, 1865, acknowledged the scourge of the war as a result of the crime of slavery. Here are his words:

Fondly do we hope, fervently do we pray, that this mighty scourge of war may speedily pass away. Yet, if God wills that it continue until all the wealth piled by the bondman's 250 years of unrequited toil shall be sunk, and until every drop of blood drawn with the lash shall be paid by another drawn with the sword, as was said three thousand years ago, so, still it must be said, that the judgments of the Lord are true and righteous altogether (*ibid.*, Mar. 21, 1865).

By this time the *Review and Herald* carried in almost every issue information concerning the draft situation and advice to draftees.

THE DEVASTATING WAR SUDDENLY ENDS

But suddenly a change came. On April 9 General Robert E. Lee surrendered at the Appomattox Courthouse in Virginia. The war was virtually over. Some activities remained to be quelled farther south and to the west, but on April 11, two days after Lee's surrender, Editor Smith of the *Review and Herald,* recognizing the visible answer to prayer, wrote:

They see in the prospect not only the immediate effects that others see, the cessation of slaughter and bloodshed, . . . but they see in it a fulfillment of prophecy, an answer to prayer, a bright token that the great Shepherd of Israel is going before His flock. We therefore thank God for the visible manifestation of His hand in our national affairs (*ibid.*, Apr. 11, 1865.).

A week later Smith referred to the wide acclaim of God's providential hand in the affairs of the nation:

> It is right and appropriate that God should be recognized in the national gratitude; for He it is who has given the victory. But to see so general an acknowledgment from the official under his seal of authority, to the humblest citizen, is more than could have been expected (*ibid.*, Apr. 18, 1865).

The recognition of God's providence in the speedy closing of the war was quite generally accepted. The readers of the *Review* were treated to a significant item in the *American Missionary* for April, calling attention to

> the strong *religious* element in the rejoicing over our victories. The ascription of our great successes to God was all but universal. In the high places of the land and on the busiest marts of trade, as well as in churches and around the domestic altars of Christian families, the same pious recognition was manifest. The brilliant transparency on the Capitol at Washington, "It is the Lord's doing and it is marvelous in our eyes," and the uncovered multitude in Wall Street joining reverently in prayer and singing the *Christian* Doxology were rare but representative facts (*ibid.*, June 6, 1865).

The Civil War came to a close too soon to test well the provisions made by the government to bring relief to drafted Seventh-day Adventists. But in World War I and subsequent military situations, the steps taken in 1864 and 1865 paved the way for relief of Seventh-day Adventists in the armed services.

And what was the significance of an act of Congress that directed that all new dies made at the United States Mint were to bear the motto "In God We Trust"?

The favorable trend led James White to appeal to the church:

> The holding of the winds, in the suppression of the rebellion, outstripping even our faith in the suddenness of its execution, is opening a wide door before us. Let the thousands of Sabbathkeepers whose prayer ascended two months since for the speedy accomplishment of this work, now so signally answered, again ascend that the great Captain of the Lord's host will meet with His people (*ibid.*, May 9, 1865).

And at the annual meeting of the General Conference in May a resolution was passed and recorded:

Resolved, That we acknowledge, with devout gratitude, the hand of God in this event, as a direct answer to prayer, and that in view of the increased responsibilities laid upon us in again opening the way for the progress of the message, we solemnly consecrate ourselves anew to this great work to which God has called us (*ibid.,* May 23, 1865).

THE CLOUDS OF WAR AND THE WHITE FAMILY

When the White family settled in the little cottage on Wood Street in Battle Creek in 1857, there was forest to the north and pastureland to the west. This gave promise of a quiet retreat and a wholesome atmosphere for rearing the family. Soon, however, the Michigan Fair Association secured considerable acreage almost adjoining the White property, and built a racetrack for trotting horses. As the war came on, this proved to be an excellent training ground for recruits in the Union Army. The activities on the fairgrounds came to be of special interest to the teenage boys. W. C. White later recalled:

The nearest neighbors to the south were the Jonah Lewis family, devout Adventists. While the White and Lewis families were noncombatants, the children took a lively interest in the war. The two younger Lewis boys, 16 and 18 years of age, and the two older White boys, 12 and 14, got hold of wartime songs and many a sunny afternoon sat on the fence and practiced "Tramp, Tramp, Tramp, the Boys Are Marching" and "We Are Coming, Father Abraham." They all had good voices, and I, about 7, was an admiring audience, and sat on the grass to listen.

My brothers went as far as they could in supplying themselves with warlike instruments. They built good bows and arrows with which they shot troublesome birds. They were good whistlers, but wanted a drum, so they bought two cheese boxes, knocking out the heads, putting the rims together, paper inside and out. They secured a sheepskin, took the wool off, and made rawhide heads (DF 780a, "Pioneer Days Are Recalled," Battle Creek *Enquirer,* Oct. 30, 1932).

The drum was quite successful and could be heard all over the neighborhood. In his account Willie included developments over a period of time:

When soldiers were in training on the old fairground, . . . Henry went to watch them and, boylike, was marching along with them, whistling in harmony with the fife. The captain gave the signal to the fifers to be silent, and the company of soldiers made their one-mile march keeping step to music of the drum and Henry's whistle.

He wanted to enter the war as a drummer, but love for his mother and respect for her wishes led him to give up the cherished thought of being in the Army (ibid.).

James and Ellen were distressed as they watched Henry and Edson in 1862 and early 1863 becoming more and more fascinated with the war activities, and at the same time losing the consecration they had enjoyed at the time of their baptism at the turn of the year. It seemed to them that they must get the children clear away from Battle Creek. James was now free from administrative responsibilities.

At the General Conference session in May 1863 actions had been taken calling for the production of a new prophetic chart and a chart of the Ten Commandments. The development and production of the charts called for him to spend two or three months in the vicinity of Boston, Massachusetts. And since his position as president of the SDA Publishing Association would not hold him continuously in Battle Creek, why not take the family and stay, say, a year in the East, possibly living at the Howland home in Topsham, Maine, just a few hours by train from Boston?

Learning that they would be welcome in the commodious and comfortable Howland home, James and Ellen White decided that the whole family would go east. They would take with them Adelia Patten, the young woman who lived with them and cared for the children when the parents were traveling. She also was beginning to give some assistance in copying the testimonies and other writings.

In addition to working on the charts, James White was eager to join Loughborough and Hull in evangelism in the Eastern cities. Ellen White wanted to put some time into writing Spiritual Gifts, Volume III, dealing with Old Testament history. Adelia would look after the children while the parents pursued their religious mission.

THE EXTENDED EASTERN TOUR
IN THE SUMMER AND AUTUMN OF 1863

James was now 42, and Ellen, 35. Henry was almost 16, Edson, 14, and Willie, nearly 9. Adelia Patten was 24. They all took the train at Battle Creek on Wednesday, August 19, bound for Boston, with two stopovers in New York State. In Boston, while James White was starting work on the charts, Henry Nichols and Ransom Lockwood took the three boys in hand and gave them a tour of the city. Adelia Patten mentions in her report that they visited places such as the public gardens, glassworks, Bunker Hill Monument, Prospect Hill, and the State House.

At Topsham, where the family would make their headquarters, they were joyfully welcomed by the Howlands. Henry was especially glad to see the Howlands, for he had spent some five years as an infant with them. Noting

Henry's interest in and love for music, Stockbridge Howland purchased a brand-new organ. The "old mansion in which a dozen years before was heard the innocent, merry laugh of the beautiful, prattling little Henry now resounded with the music of the instrument from his skillful touch, mingled with his own sweet voice." So wrote Adelia Patten, who accompanied the family and reported the journey.

She was one who fitted well into the family, leading James and Ellen White, who had no daughter, to accept and treat her as one. She was one of the first to be drawn into service as a literary assistant to Ellen White.

While in the home there in Topsham, where he and Ellen had first set up housekeeping when Henry was a newborn babe, James recalled those experiences of 16 years before:

> Here we had our first impressions of duty to preach and publish the message. In this place we chopped cordwood sixteen years since, to support our family, and get means to attend a conference in Connecticut, the first under the message. With this family we have ever found true friends and a hospitable home (RH, Sept. 29, 1863).

DIVERSIFIED ACTIVITIES IN NEW ENGLAND

But James and Ellen White felt they must press on, so after a few days of relaxation in the comfortable Howland home, they left for Massachusetts. Adelia described their departure:

> The children accompanied their parents to the depot, and before the family parted, Henry, Edson, and Willie, by request, sang "The Evergreen Shore," much to the gratification of the crowd waiting for another train. The whistle was heard, the "good-by" and "farewell" were said, and away sped the train, bearing the parents on their mission of love, and leaving the children again without their watchcare (AY, pp. 22, 23).

For the next three months Adelia and the children were at the Howland home. Although James and Ellen White considered this their headquarters while in the East, their time was divided, Ellen with her writing and James working on the charts, with weekends at the churches.

Ellen was endeavoring to complete the third volume of *Spiritual Gifts*, which was dealing with Old Testament history. So dedicated was she to this goal that James recounted this story about her:

> At Adams Center she wrote early and late, and between meetings. And First-day afternoon she wrote six pages of testimony while Brother

Andrews was preaching, which she afterwards read with other matter before the State conference. She sat within four feet [1 meter] of the pulpit and used her Bible for a writing desk. When asked what she thought of Brother Andrews as a speaker, she replied that she could not say, as it had been so long since she had heard him. When the sermon was finished she arose and addressed the congregation twenty minutes (RH, Dec. 8, 1863).

James was eager to introduce the new charts into the field. In the *Review* of October 6 he reported:

> The charts are both in the hands of the artist, and the work on them is progressing as fast as possible. We shall probably have some of them ready by the middle of October.
>
> The prophetic chart will be much improved in arrangement from the one in use. The sanctuary and angels will be larger and bolder, so that all the figures upon the chart can be seen equally plain. From what we have already seen of the work, we judge that it will be a beautifully executed thing (*ibid.*, Oct. 6, 1863).

He projected a price of $2 for the prophetic chart and $1.50 for the one of the law. He commented that if the chart had been done two years earlier the cost of production would have been less than half: the cotton cloth, "the principal item of expense, that could have been bought two years since for 10 cents, is now 30" (*ibid.*).

On October 21, "having obtained a large trunk full of finished charts," the Whites left Maine for the Newport, New Hampshire, meeting by way of Boston. Their itinerary took them by train, stages, and private conveyance to meet various appointments.

They were both in good health and good spirits. The Civil War had changed the economy considerably. The same issue of the *Review* that carried James White's report on the charts presented the financial statement of the Seventh-day Adventist Publishing Association rendered at its third annual meeting, October 2, 1863. It showed receipts for operations to be $20,104.84 as against expense of $18,956.36. Association assets of $19,649.41 were offset by liabilities of only $4,377.53, leaving a net worth of $15,271.88. How different from a few years before!

There were also noticeable changes in attitudes since they had been in Adams Center two years before when nearly all the brethren had been opposed to organization. "Thank God for what He has done for the cause and for us," observed James.

Interesting things had been happening at Adams Center. As White reported: "Here nearly a whole Seventh Day Baptist church, meetinghouse and all, has been converted to the Seventh-day Adventists" (*ibid.*, Nov. 24, 1863).

J. M. Aldrich, the conference secretary, reported of the conference: "The attendance was large, there being a good representation of brethren from all parts of the state" (*ibid.*, Dec. 1, 1863). Both James and Ellen spoke a number of times to very appreciative audiences.

Considering so many encouraging factors, the Whites offered to extend their work in the East for six months, one year, or longer, saying that to do so would be a considerable sacrifice, but that they were prepared to make such a sacrifice so that the work might advance.

LEARNING A NEW LIFESTYLE

Many factors common to New Englanders in the mid-nineteenth century determined their lifestyle:

1. Eating habits. There was very little store-bought food except meat, potatoes, salt, and sugar. Winters were long and cold. The people made up for the lack of fresh fruits and vegetables with rich breads and pastries. Cakes, pies, and doughnuts were common as breakfast foods. There were no vegetable oils or shortenings. Meat was expensive, and pork the most available.

2. Clothing. There was very little store-bought clothing. Cold winters necessitated heavy clothing and bedding.

3. No indoor plumbing. No electricity. No washing machines.

4. Heat. Homes were heated by wood-burning stoves and fireplaces. Windows were tightly closed at night. Night air was considered injurious.

5. Use of tea, coffee, alcohol, tobacco, and cider. These were just as habit-forming then as now. In lives with little recreation or change, they offered a solace of sorts!

6. Life expectancy. In 1900 in the United States the average was 47.3 years.

7. Proneness to disease. Caused by appalling ignorance of hygiene, sanitation, and the cause of sickness.

The relation of diet and the care of the body to health and the causes of disease was not realized.

Quite early in the years following the Disappointment, as the believers met together there was recognition of the evils of liquor and tobacco. In 1851 one man wrote to Ellen White asking if she had seen in vision that it was wrong to use tobacco. She replied on December 14:

> I have seen in vision that tobacco was a filthy weed, and that it must be laid aside or given up. Said my accompanying angel, "If it is an *idol*, it is high time it was given up, and unless it is given up, the frown of God will be upon the one that uses it. . . .
>
> I saw that Christ will have a church without *spot* or *wrinkle* or *any such thing* to present to His Father, . . . as He leads us through the pearly gates of the New Jerusalem. . . . After Jesus has done so much for us, will anyone be undecided whether to deny himself of the filthy *weed* for His sake?

> We must be perfect Christians, deny ourselves all the way along, tread the narrow, thorny pathway that our Jesus trod, and then if we are final overcomers, heaven, sweet heaven will be cheap enough (letter 5, 1851).

Ellen White wrote understandingly of the struggle some will have to leave off the use of tobacco, and suggested that they do as S. W. Rhodes did when he was battling to break away from its use. "He called for the brethren to pray for him, and we did. He was cured and has desired none since."

In 1856 there were a number of Sabbathkeeping Adventists still plagued with the use of tobacco in one form or another.

On February 7 the *Review* carried an article that included a compilation of statements by physicians on the use of tobacco. One in April written by J. N. Andrews, entitled "The Use of Tobacco a Sin Against God," drove the matter home. In a short editorial, James White, in an indirect way, indicted a good many of his fellow church members. He inquired of those who claimed to be too poor to pay for the church paper, "Do you use tea, coffee, and tobacco?"

Then in 1861 when the matter of church organization began to crystallize, the question came up:

> How do you manage in forming a church about taking in members who use tea, coffee, tobacco, and wear hoops, and some who do not believe in Sister White's visions? (RH, Nov. 5, 1861).

Loughborough worked very closely with James and Ellen White, and White was editor of the *Review*, where the answers would be published. So we may be certain there was some counseling together on these points—what appeared in print represented the mind of the three.

The reply was that no one, not even those who had been united in worshiping on Sabbath with a company of believers, should be taken into the church as a member unless he or she was in full harmony with the beliefs of the church.

It took time to lead people to recognize the importance of following sound health principles.

THE OTSEGO VISION

Of the visions given to Ellen White, one of those most remembered was that of June 6, 1863,* at Otsego, Michigan—the health reform vision. Otsego is about 30 (50 kilometers) miles northeast of Battle Creek. To give support to R. J. Lawrence and M. E. Cornell in their evangelistic meetings, James and Ellen White started for the place by carriage on Friday morning, June 5, along with Mr. and Mrs. George Amadon and several other families.

The Whites were entertained at the Aaron Hilliard home a few miles west of town. The Amadons and others came in for worship as the Sabbath was beginning.

Ellen White was asked to lead in prayer. She did so, pleading fervently with God. As she prayed for James, who was close by, she moved to his side, laid her hand on his shoulder, and poured out her heart. Then her voice changed, and she was heard to exclaim, "Glory to God!" Martha Amadon, daughter of John Byington, the newly elected president of the General Conference, commented:

> Many who have witnessed these things have often wished a description could be given of the servant of God when thus under the influence of the Holy Spirit—the illumination of the countenance, the graceful gestures of the hands, the dignity attending every movement, the musical intonations of the voice sounding as from a distance, and many, many other things which give an eyewitness confidence in their heavenly origin. . . . She was in vision about forty-five minutes (DF 105, "The Otsego Vision of 1863").

Many matters were opened to her in this vision, but the vision is noted particularly for what was shown to her in regard to health—the responsibility of all to live in harmony with principles that would prevent sickness and yield good health.

> I saw that now we should take special care of the health God has given us, for our work was not yet done. Our testimony must yet be borne and would have influence. I saw that I had spent too much time and strength in sewing and waiting upon and entertaining company. I saw that home cares should be thrown off. The preparing of garments is a snare; others can do that. God had not given me strength for such labor. . . .
>
> I saw that we should encourage a cheerful, hopeful, peaceful frame of mind, for our health depends upon our doing this. . . .
>
> I saw that when we tax our strength, overlabor and weary ourselves much, then we take colds and at such times are in danger of disease taking a dangerous form. We must not leave the care of ourselves for God to see to and to take care of that which He has left for us to watch and care for. It is not safe nor pleasing to God to violate the laws of health and then ask Him to take care of our health and keep us from disease when we are living directly contrary to our prayers.
>
> I saw that it was a sacred duty to attend to our health, and arouse others to their duty, and yet not take the burden of their cases upon us. Yet we have a duty to speak, to come out against intemperance of every kind— intemperance in working, in eating, in drinking, and in drugging—and

then point them to God's great medicine, water, pure soft water, for diseases, for health, for cleanliness, and for a luxury (MS 1, 1863).

Then there was a call for an active ministry on the part of James and Ellen White along health lines. What Ellen White had been shown in the vision at the Hilliard home was so different from concepts commonly held at the time that it was with hesitancy she faced the bidding in the vision to take the lead in guiding Seventh-day Adventists and others to a way of life in harmony with nature's laws. When she was in the home of Dr. H. S. Lay, he pressed her to tell him what she had been shown. She explained that much of what was presented to her was so different from the ordinarily accepted views that she feared she could not relate it so that it could be understood. She protested that she was not familiar with medical language and hardly knew how to present it. In the conversation that followed, she set forth in simple language what she later reduced to writing in the extended chapter entitled "Health," now found in *Spiritual Gifts*, Volume IV.

GENERAL COUNSELS ON HEALTH

She began with eating habits. These included the use of meat—she referred to the risks incurred of contracting disease thereby, because of the increasing prevalence of disease among animals. She also detailed the harmful effects of overeating and of eating too frequently.

She mentioned the use of stimulants and narcotics, speaking particularly of alcohol, tobacco, tea, and coffee. She emphasized the importance of cleanliness of person and of the home and its premises; the importance of physical exercise and of the proper exercise of the will. She told of what she was shown concerning the value of water and of pure air and sunshine. She spoke of how those who looked only to God to keep them from sickness, without doing what was in their power to maintain good health, would be disappointed, for God intended they should do their part.

For the medical world, and for almost everyone, these were days of great ignorance in health lines. Bacteria and viruses were unknown. When disease struck, the symptoms were treated with poisonous drugs, such as strychnine, mercury, and calomel; also alcohol, blisters, and bleeding.

In the vision of June 6, 1863, not only was there opened to Ellen White the basic principles of healthful living, but a solemn commission was given to her that would have a bearing on her work and that of her husband for many years to come. She and James were to be teachers of health reform. But before they could teach they must know what to teach. Though they were adults, parents, and alert, their knowledge in health lines was but little different from the average—and these were days of general ignorance.

The *Review and Herald*, edited by James White and Uriah Smith, occasionally carried items such as rest, fresh air, and exercise, selected from other journals or from the writings of a Dr. Dio Lewis. Quite often articles and admonition discouraging the use of tobacco, tea, and coffee were included. But in connection with the scourge of diphtheria in the winter of 1862 and 1863, although the obituary notices kept before its readers the death of many children, up to February 1863, the *Review* had little to offer terrified parents but the application of a poultice of "Spanish flies and turpentine."

Then there came to the attention of James and Ellen White Dr. James C. Jackson's method of treatment of diphtheria, embodying simple, rational methods in the proper use of water, fresh air, and rest. Earnestly employed, these remedies saved two of the White boys when stricken, and also Moses Hull's boy; but upon the recovery of the children the experience was soon forgotten. Then in the vision of June 6, 1863, among a number of situations and matters opened up to Ellen White, health was an important one. Many of its features were to her so revolutionary that she was for a time bewildered.

When James and Ellen were in Boston, some three months later, James saw some books on health advertised in a periodical called the *Voice of the Prophets*, published by Elder J. V. Himes. He ordered the works and received them at Topsham, Maine. But he was too busy to read them, and they remained in their wrappers for some time.

Ellen had been working under heavy pressure to complete writing out the vision before she and her husband would visit the "Home on the Hillside" of Dr. Jackson in Dansville, New York. But she was determined that before leaving she would cover in that book the main points that had been shown to her in the health reform vision. She did not want it to be said that what she presented as shown to her in vision could have been influenced by Dr. Jackson or anyone else.

She made an interesting statement of what she did *not* read before first writing out what the Lord had revealed to her:

> That which I have written in regard to health was not taken from books or papers. . . . My view was clear, and I did not want to read anything until I had fully completed my books. My views were written independent of books or of the opinions of others (MS 7, 1867).

She had talked freely with Dr. Lay and many others upon the things shown her in vision in reference to health, but she had not read a paper dealing with health.

FIRST VISIT TO DANSVILLE

Having completed the work on "Laws of Health," which was to be a part of

Volume IV of *Spiritual Gifts*, Ellen and James were now ready to make the trip to Dansville to spend a few weeks in learning all they could about health reform and new methods in the care of the sick. For weeks they had looked forward to visiting Dr. Jackson's "Our Home on the Hillside" at Dansville, New York. James White wrote regarding this health institution:

> In the month of September, 1864, Mrs. White and self spent three weeks at the health institution at Dansville, Livingston County, New York, called "Our Home." Our object in this visit was not to take treatment, as we were enjoying better health than usual, but to see what we could see and hear what we could hear, so as to be able to give to many inquiring friends a somewhat definite report (HL, No. 1, p. 12).

The institution was well located, and the guest list ran about 300. The physicians on the staff were listed as James C. Jackson, M.D., physician-in-chief; F. Wilson Hurd, M.D.; Miss Harriet N. Austin, M.D.; Mrs. Mary H. York, M.D.; and Horatio S. Lay, M.D.

Dr. Lay was the Seventh-day Adventist physician of 17 years' experience at Allegan, Michigan, with whom Ellen White had talked soon after the health reform vision. This visit had encouraged him to take his ill wife to the institution and to learn what he could of the so-called rational methods. At Dansville he was soon taken onto the staff, which gave him an excellent opportunity to study the practices and procedures employed there.

Accompanying James and Ellen White to Dansville were Edson and Willie, and also Adelia Patten. They were given routine physical examinations by Dr. Jackson. As to James and Ellen's health report, no data is available. But they conversed freely with the doctor and listened to his lectures, took treatments, observed the attire of the women there, and dined at the institution's tables. Both gave good reports on the general atmosphere, the dietary program, and the courses of treatments.

They observed the various forms of water therapy, as the half-bath, the "plunge," the cold sheet pack, the compresses, and fomentations. Ellen White said:

> I do think we should have an institution in Michigan to which our Sabbathkeeping invalids can resort (letter 6, 1864).

James White found the food program equally appealing and wrote of it in some detail:

> The tables are spread with an abundance of plain and nourishing food, which becomes a daily luxury to the patients, as the natural and healthful condition of the taste is restored. The glutton, who gratifies his

depraved appetite with swine's flesh, grease, gravies, spices, et cetera, et cetera, on looking over Dr. Hurd's tract on cookery, may in his ignorance regard this style of living as a system of starvation.

But a few weeks' experience at "Our Home" would correct his appetite, so that he would eat plain, simple, and nutritious food with a far better relish than he now does that which is unnatural and hurtful. We never saw men and women gather around tables more cheerfully, and eat more heartily, than the patients at Dansville. The uniformity and sharpness of appetite was wonderful for a crowd of patients. It was the general leanness and lankness of these persons alone that could give the idea that they were sick.

Besides the usual rounds of excellently cooked wheat-meal mushes, wheat-meal biscuits, cakes, and pies, and occasionally other varieties, we found the tables bountifully loaded with the fruits of the season, such as apples, peaches, and grapes. No one need fear of starving at "Our Home." There is greater danger of eating too much.

The appetite of the feeble patient, who has been pining with loss of appetite over fashionable food, becomes natural and sharp, so that simple food is eaten with all that keen relish with which healthy country schoolchildren devour plain food. The food being nutritious, and the appetite keen, the danger of that class of patients who have become feeble by self-indulgence is decidedly in the direction of eating too much (HL, No. 1, pp. 14, 15).

James recognized that changing from the common meat-eating diet to one that was plain and healthful could, with some, call for time to accomplish. He warned against sudden, sweeping changes. Dr. Jackson made a deep impression upon him as a physician who was a "master of his business," a "clear and impressive speaker," and "decidedly thorough" in whatever he undertook. James closed his report on a positive note, recommending the institution to those suffering critically. As to others he had this to say:

To those who are active yet suffering from failing health, we urgently recommend health publications, a good assortment of which we design to keep on hand. Friends, read up in time to successfully change your habits, and live in harmony with the laws of life.

And to those who call themselves well, we would say, As you value the blessings of health, and would honor the Author of your being, learn to live in obedience to those laws established in your being by High Heaven. A few dollars' worth of books that will teach you how to live may save you heavy doctor bills, save you months of pain upon a sickbed, save you suffering and feebleness from the use of drugs, and perhaps from a premature grave (*ibid.*, p. 18).

ACTIVE TEACHERS OF HEALTH REFORM

In the three weeks they spent at Dansville, James and Ellen White found what they were needing and seeking—a practical application of the principles of healthful living that would fit them for the position they were called to fill as teachers of health. There was still much to learn, but with open minds they continued their search for what would be a help to them and to the believers generally. Together they visited churches and met with the general public. When the Whites met seasoned believers, they dealt with the subject of disease and its causes, and reforms in habits of life. Their messages were well received.

THE *HEALTH REFORMER*

At the General Conference session in mid-May 1866, a resolution called for Dr. H. L. Lay to furnish a series of articles through the *Review* on the subject of health reform. In the days following the conference, plans were quickly laid and implemented to publish a monthly health journal, which Dr. Lay would edit. The *Review* of June 5, 1866, carried this notice:

> *Prospectus of the Health Reformer:* The first number of a monthly periodical, with the above title, sixteen pages, magazine form, with cover, will be issued at the Western Health Reform Institute, Battle Creek, Michigan, August 1, 1866. . . .
>
> It will advocate the cure of diseases by use of nature's own remedies, air, light, heat, exercise, food, sleep, recreation, et cetera. . . . Price $1.00 per volume of twelve numbers (RH, June 5, 1866).

In his editorial in the first number, published in August, Dr. Lay restated the aims and objects of the *Health Reformer*. He added that "its contributors will be persons of experience and of high mental and moral attainments. Its selections will be of the choicest kind."

Shortly after the launching of the journal, Ellen White wrote:

> The *Health Reformer* is the medium through which rays of light are to shine upon the people. It should be the very best health journal in our country. It must be adapted to the wants of the common people, ready to answer all proper questions and fully explain the first principles of the laws of life and how to obey them and preserve health (1T, pp. 552, 553).

EXTREMES TAUGHT IN THE *HEALTH REFORMER* BRING CRISIS

The publishing of extreme views in the *Health Reformer* in the summer of 1870 brought on a crisis, and at the camp meeting in Pleasanton, Kansas, in October the situation was more than ever clearly seen. In his report of that meeting, James White wrote of the unfortunate results of Ellen White's virtual silence on the subject of health because of his prolonged illness. The believers in the Midwest, having read the extreme positions being advocated in the *Reformer*, which would ban the use of milk, sugar, and salt, were asking:

> How do the friends of health reform live at Battle Creek? Do they dispense with salt entirely? If so, we cannot at present adopt the health reform. We can get but little fruit, and we have left off the use of meat, tea, coffee; and tobacco, but we must have something to sustain life (3T, p. 20).

Both James and Ellen White made it clear they could not stand by the extreme positions taken in the *Health Reformer*, especially by the non-Adventist contributing editor, Dr. R. T. Trall, and the editor, William C. Gage, a layman who did not in his own home carry out what he advocated in the journal. Explaining why Ellen White spoke often on health reform, her husband wrote:

> Since we have become active again, Mrs. White oftener feels called upon to speak upon the subject of health reform because of existing extremes of health reformers than from any other reason. The fact that all, or nearly all, of the existing extremes upon health reform among our people are supposed to receive her unqualified sanction is the reason why she feels called upon to speak her real sentiments (RH, Nov. 8, 1870).

ELLEN WHITE'S MODERATE POSITIONS

James White explained the moderate positions they held. He embodied this in his report from the Kansas camp meeting:

> In reference to the use of tobacco, tea, coffee, flesh meats, also of dress, there is general agreement. But at present she is not prepared to take the extreme position relative to salt, sugar, and milk. If there were no other reasons for moving carefully in reference to these things of so common and abundant use, there is a sufficient one in the fact that the minds of many are not prepared even to receive the facts relative to these things. . . .
>
> It may be well here to state, however, that while she does not regard milk, taken in large quantities as customarily eaten with bread, the best article of food, *her mind, as yet, has only been called* to the importance of the best and most healthy condition possible of the cow . . . whose milk

is used as an article of food. She cannot unite in circulating publications broadcast which take an extreme position on the important question of milk, with *her present light upon the subject* (*ibid.*; italics supplied).

Turning particularly to sugar and salt, he set forth her middle-of-the-road stance:

Mrs. White thinks that a change from the simplest kinds of flesh meats to an abundant use of sugar is going from "bad to worse." She would recommend a very sparing use of both sugar and salt. The appetite can, and should, be brought to a very moderate use of both (*ibid.*).

Then he sounded warnings in another line, that of making abrupt changes:

While tobacco, tea, and coffee may be left at once (one at a time, however, by those who are so unfortunate as to be slaves to all), changes in diet should be made carefully, one at a time. And while she would say this to those who are in danger of making changes too rapidly, she would also say to the tardy, Be sure and not forget to change (*ibid.*).

James and Ellen had spent most of the summer and fall of 1870 attending camp meetings. They had observed that the cause of health reform had been more or less left to flounder as those who had led out in teaching it looked on helplessly.

LIFESAVING THERAPY FOR THE *HEALTH REFORMER*

Going to the *Review* office, after a long absence from Battle Creek, James White found unoccupied both the *Review* editor's room and that of the editor of the *Health Reformer*. The latter was ill at home. "Our hands are full of business that has been waiting our return," James wrote, "and editing our periodicals" (*ibid.*, Nov. 15, 1870). Warren Bacheller, connected with the *Review* office since he was a teenager, was, with some assistance from traveling James White, keeping the *Review* going, but as for the *Health Reformer*, it stood not only waiting, but seemingly dying. James White, never reticent to get involved in time of special need, took the paper under his wing. He saw that if it was to survive, changes must be made quickly. Without formal authorization he took over, pulling things together for the already-late November issue. He furnished an editorial for this and succeeding issues, and Ellen White helped meet the emergency by furnishing an article for each of four monthly issues. These articles followed his editorials.

James had three objectives in view for the magazine: "First, to raise the interest of the journal; second, to increase its circulation; third, to establish a strict pay-in-advance system" (HR, April 1871).

In White's editorials he reviewed the rise and progress of health reform among Seventh-day Adventists. He made it plain that the journal was nonsectarian, but that it had its roots in the experience and convictions of Seventh-day Adventists. Ellen White's articles, keyed to experiences and observations in traveling, developed certain lines of practical counsel under such titles as "Creatures of Circumstance" in the November 1870 issue, followed in succeeding issues by "Convenient Food," "Willpower," and "Mothers and Their Daughters." The journal was enlarged from 20 pages to 32.

At the General Conference session held in February 1871, James White was elected editor of the *Health Reformer*. In his reorganization of the journal he continued Dr. Trall's Special Department and introduced a new one, Mrs. White's Department. Having observed the efficacy of his wife's work with the general public at camp meetings, he persuaded her to take hold with him in attempts to save the paper.

The changes James White instituted in behalf of the *Reformer* soon began to bear fruit. His editorials and articles added interest. He was able to persuade Dr. R. T. Trall to modify his stances, which were tending to extremes. Mrs. White's Department was well received. He solicited articles from Adventist ministers who had adopted the health reform program, and by May he had 12.

But the best barometer was in the increased circulation—300 new subscriptions were received in 25 days. By December the subscription list had almost doubled, at 5,000. The *Reformer* was generally conceded to be the best health journal in America (RH, Dec. 12, 1871).

PRACTICING NEW LIGHT

The year previous to the Whites' first visit to Dansville had been full of anxious days in which they had learned firsthand of the value of the light they were receiving on the care of their bodies and the treatment of the sick. First, in the winter of 1863, was a battle with the dreaded diphtheria. Helplessly physicians and parents reached out for means of combating the disease. The *Review* of January 13, 1863, reprinted an item, taken from an Illinois paper, under the title "The Diphtheria Scourge in Western Illinois." A portion read:

> The diphtheria has been raging throughout the country to an alarming extent, and seems, to a great extent, to baffle the skill of physicians. It is confined almost exclusively to children, and when once under headway, death is almost certain to be the result. It will pass through whole towns, missing scarcely a family, and in some instances whole families of children have been swept away by it.

TWO OF THE THREE WHITE CHILDREN STRICKEN

There was anxiety in every home in Battle Creek. Would the dread disease strike and lay low some of the precious children?

Then it happened! In the first week of February two of James and Ellen White's three boys complained of severe sore throats and high fever; they could hardly utter a word—undeniable, frightening symptoms. They had diphtheria.

Fortunately—in the providence of God, no doubt—there had come into their hands, probably through an "exchange" of papers at the *Review* office, either the *Yates County Chronicle*, of Penn Yan, New York, or some journal quoting from it, an extended article entitled "Diphtheria, Its Causes, Treatment and Cure." It was written by Dr. James Jackson, of Dansville, New York. Eagerly James and Ellen White read it. It made sense, and they immediately followed its treatment in every detail. The treatment outlined was simple—it required only a washtub, towels, sheets, and blankets—but demanded diligent attention and earnest labor. In great detail Dr. Jackson pointed out the procedures that would bring relief and finally a cure. These were attained by the simple means we today call hydrotherapy—with proper baths, packs, rest, fresh air, and, above all, absence of anxiety.

Jackson reported that over a period of years, while employing these means in hundreds of cases involving young and old, not one patient had died. The methods he set forth were those that he, a physician with a good understanding of physiology, had reasoned out and put together. He stated:

> Our success has been so great, while as yet our plan of treatment has been so simple, as really to introduce a decided change in the medical practice in the particular disease, in this locality. I do not know of a physician of any school in this town who has not practically abandoned the administration of cathartics in cases of diphtheria, and . . . adopted, in fact, our method (RH, Feb. 17, 1863).

To James and Ellen White, who already highly valued "air, water, and light" as "God's great remedies" (*ibid.*, Feb. 10, 1863), what Dr. Jackson wrote made more sense than either drugs or a poultice of Spanish flies compounded with turpentine. The symptoms had overtaken their children very rapidly, and the Whites lost little time in carrying out—scrupulously—the directions of Dr. Jackson. They had appointments to speak in Convis, Michigan, on Sabbath and Sunday, February 7 and 8. By following Jackson's method of treating diphtheria, which involved the better part of Friday night, on Sabbath morning they saw that they could safely leave the sick children in the hands of those who helped in the home. They drove the 15 miles (24 kilometers) to Convis Sabbath morning and took services both morning and afternoon, meeting with new converts to the Adventist message.

Sabbath evening they returned to Battle Creek for another night of broken sleep as they treated and watched over the children. Sunday morning they were off again to Convis for morning and afternoon meetings, as promised (*ibid.*).

While the White children were making a speedy recovery, Ellen White was called one evening to the home of Moses Hull and his wife. Their oldest child, 6 years old, had been suddenly and severely stricken. The parents were in Monterey, holding evangelistic meetings. As reported by James White in the *Review*, "Mrs. White pursued the same course of treatment as with our own children, and the child appeared well the next morning" (*ibid.*, Feb. 17, 1863).

HENRY: DEATH FROM PNEUMONIA

Six months after the health reform vision in Otsego, Henry, 16, their oldest son, took sick with pneumonia. James and Ellen were in Brookfield, New York, visiting the Abbeys. They were in good spirits planning to spend two or three more months in Maine, where Ellen would have opportunity to complete the third volume of *Spiritual Gifts*.

> While in Brookfield, New York, Elder White received impressions from a dream, which led him to feel that all was not well with the children, and that they must return to Maine without delay. Each day they anxiously waited for the arrival of the mail, but news from Topsham reported "all well." This did not satisfy their minds, and in accordance with their convictions of duty, when they had filled their appointments, they immediately returned to their children (AY, p. 23).

When on Friday, November 27, the parents reached Topsham, they found their three sons and Adelia waiting for them at the depot. Apparently all were in good health, except for Henry, who had a cold. But by the next Tuesday, December 1, Henry was very ill with pneumonia. Years later Willie, his youngest brother, reconstructed the story:

> During the absence of their parents Henry and Edson, under the supervision of Brother Howland, were busily engaged in mounting the charts on cloth, ready for sale. They worked in a rented store building about a block from the Howland home. At length they had a respite for a few days while they were waiting for charts to be sent from Boston. . . . Returning from a long tramp by the river, he [Henry] thoughtlessly lay down and slept on a few damp cloths used in backing the paper charts. A chilly wind was blowing in from an open window. This indiscretion resulted in a severe cold (WCW, "Sketches and Memories of James and Ellen G. White," RH, Dec. 10, 1936).

As the cold turned to pneumonia, a kindly, experienced physician was summoned, and Henry was treated in the conventional manner, which called for the employment of poisonous drugs. The attending physician was ignorant of hydrotherapy, which was just then being pioneered by a few practitioners. Although earlier in the year, following Dr. James Jackson's guidance, two of the boys had been nursed back to health from diphtheria by an appropriate use of water, fresh air, and rest, Ellen and James were not yet prepared to use hydrotherapy as a means of treating other illnesses, and the disease now confronting them was pneumonia.

Henry failed rapidly. Though the Whites and Howlands prayed earnestly for his healing, he grew worse. His parents did not hesitate to talk with him about death, and even to prepare for it. Henry's faith in Jesus remained firm. He had an opportunity to meditate on his life, and he deeply regretted that in Battle Creek he had set an example short of what it should have been. This he confessed to God, his parents, and brothers. As he confessed his waywardness and sins, he was drawn nearer and nearer to God and enjoyed peace of mind and the blessing of the Lord. His faith grew ever more firm.

One morning while his mother was attending him he said:

> "Promise me, Mother, that if I die I may be taken to Battle Creek, and laid by the side of my little brother, John Herbert, that we may come up together in the morning of the resurrection" (AY, p. 26).

He was given the assurance that this would be. From day to day he grew weaker. Medical science had little to offer in treating pneumonia, and it now seemed certain there would be no recovery. The record is:

> On the fifth [day], burdened with grief, his father retired to a place of prayer, and after returned to the sickroom, feeling the assurance that God would do all things well, and thus expressed himself to his suffering son. At this his countenance seemed to light up with a heavenly smile, and he nodded his assent and whispered, "Yes, He will" (ibid., p. 27).

In one conversation he said:

> "Father, you are losing your son. You will miss me, but don't mourn. It is better for me. I shall escape being drafted, and shall not witness the seven last plagues. To die so happy is a privilege" (ibid., p. 29).

On several occasions Henry dictated short messages of admonition and assurance to young friends in Battle Creek. The deathbed scene was recorded by Adelia Patten:

He said to his mother, "Mother, I shall meet you in heaven in the morning of the resurrection, for I know you will be there." He then beckoned to his brothers, parents, and friends, and gave them all a parting kiss, after which he pointed upward and whispered, "Heaven is sweet." These were his last words (*ibid.*, p. 31).

FUNERAL SERVICES IN TOPSHAM AND BATTLE CREEK

During the three months Henry and his brothers had been in Topsham he had made a number of acquaintances. At their request a funeral service was held in the Baptist church just across the street from the Howland home. M. E. Cornell, at that time working in Maine, was asked to officiate. Then the family took Henry's body, in a "metallic burial casket," back to Battle Creek. There Uriah Smith presided at the funeral, which was attended by many friends of the family. Henry's former schoolmates were there; in the closing exercises they sang a hymn and then accompanied the family and friends to Oak Hill Cemetery. Looking back at the experience, Ellen White wrote:

When our noble Henry died, at the age of 16—when our sweet singer was borne to the grave, and we no more heard his early song—ours was a lonely home. Both parents and the two remaining sons felt the blow most keenly. But God comforted us in our bereavements, and with faith and courage we pressed forward in the work He had given us, in bright hope of meeting our children who had been torn from us by death, in that world where sickness and death will never come (3LS, pp. 165, 166).

WILLIE'S BOUT WITH PNEUMONIA

Ellen and James had learned something of the value of water in the treatment of disease in their encounter with diphtheria when the plague struck Edson and Willie; they also had learned the futility of drug medication when they lost Henry to pneumonia. Then, two months later, during the second week of February 1864, when Willie was stricken with pneumonia, they were confronted with a dilemma that could mean life or death to one of their two remaining children. Ellen White reported their daring decision:

We decided that we would not send for a physician, but do the best we could with him ourselves by the use of water, and entreat the Lord in behalf of the child. We called in a few who had faith to unite their prayers with ours. We had a sweet assurance of God's presence and blessing (4aSG, p. 151).

Nor was there any delay in making a beginning:

> The next day Willie was very sick. He was wandering. He did not seem to see or hear me when I spoke to him. His heart had no regular beat, but was in a constant agitated flutter. We continued to look to God in his behalf, and to use water freely upon his head, and a compress constantly upon his lungs, and soon he seemed rational as ever. He suffered severe pain in his right side, and could not lie upon it for a moment. This pain we subdued with cold water compresses, varying the temperature of the water according to the degree of the fever. We were very careful to keep his hands and feet warm (*ibid.*, pp. 151, 152).

The anxious parents watched over him day and night until they were both nearly worn out. It was very clear that the application of hydrotherapy in such a case called for tireless effort. But it produced good results. Ellen White wrote later:

> We expected the crisis would come the seventh day. We had but little rest during his sickness, and were obliged to give him up into others' care the fourth and fifth nights. My husband and myself the fifth day felt very anxious. The child raised fresh blood, and coughed considerably. My husband spent much time in prayer.
>
> We left our child in careful hands that night. Before retiring, my husband prayed long and earnestly. Suddenly his burden of prayer left him, and it seemed as though a voice spoke to him and said, "Go lie down; I will take care of the child."
>
> I had retired sick, and could not sleep for anxiety for several hours. I felt pressed for breath. Although sleeping in a large chamber, I arose and opened the door into a large hall, and was at once relieved, and soon slept.
>
> I dreamed that an experienced physician was standing by my child, watching every breath, with one hand over his heart, and with the other feeling his pulse. He turned to us and said, "The crisis has passed. He has seen his worst night. He will now come up speedily, for he has not the injurious influence of drugs to recover from. Nature has nobly done her work to rid the system of impurities."
>
> I related to him my worn-out condition, my pressure for breath, and the relief obtained by opening the door. Said he, "That which gave you relief will also relieve your child. He needs air. You have kept him too warm. The heated air coming from a stove is injurious, and were it not for the air coming in at the crevices of the windows, would be poisonous, and destroy life. Stove heat destroys the vitality of the air, and weakens the lungs. The child's lungs have been weakened by the room being kept too warm. Sick

persons are debilitated by disease and need all the invigorating air that they can bear to strengthen the vital organs to resist disease. And yet in most cases air and light are excluded from the sickroom at the very time when most needed, as though dangerous enemies" (*ibid.*, pp. 152, 153).

What consolation this dream, and the assurance that came to her husband a few hours before, brought to them! She reported:

> We found in the morning that our boy had passed a restless night. He seemed to be in a high fever until noon. Then the fever left him, and he appeared quite well, except weak.
> He had eaten but one small cracker through his five days' sickness. He came up rapidly, and has had better health than he has had for several years before (*ibid.*, p. 153).

She added the significant words "This experience is valuable to us." What contrasting, thought-provoking object lessons James and Ellen White had experienced in just 11 weeks! Now, more than ever, they knew that they must dig deep, learn how to combat disease, and discover sound dietetic principles. In this experience they had learned the importance of clean, fresh air in the treatment of sickness.

To learn ways to prevent disease was just as important in the care of the body as treatment during illness.

ELLEN WHITE TRIES THE MEATLESS DIET

In the vision at Otsego, Michigan, light was given to Ellen White on major changes that would improve their health. She was shown the contrast between the human race today and Adam and Eve in Eden. Our first parents were noble in stature, perfect in symmetry and beauty, sinless, and in perfect health. "I inquired," she stated, "the cause of this wonderful degeneracy, and was pointed back to Eden" (*ibid.*, p. 120). It was the disobedience of our first parents, leading to intemperate desires and violation of the laws of health, that had led to degeneracy and disease. She called for reform in eating habits; these included eliminating meat from the diet. She referred to the risks of contracting disease because of the increased prevalence of disease among animals.

> I have thought for years that I was dependent upon a meat diet for strength. I have eaten three meals a day until within a few months. It has been very difficult for me to go from one meal to another without suffering from faintness at the stomach, and dizziness of the head. . . . Eating meat removed for the time these faint feelings. I therefore decided that meat was indispensable in my case.

But since the Lord presented before me, in June, 1863, the subject of meat eating in relation to health, I have left the use of meat. For a while it was rather difficult to bring my appetite to bread, for which, formerly, I have had but little relish. But by persevering, I have been able to do this. I have lived for nearly one year without meat. For about six months most of the bread upon our table has been unleavened cakes [gems], made of unbolted wheat meal and water, and a very little salt. We use fruits and vegetables liberally. I have lived for eight months upon two meals a day. I have applied myself to writing the most of the time for above a year. For eight months have been confined closely to writing. My brain has been constantly taxed, and I have had but little exercise. Yet my health has never been better than for the past six months (*ibid.*, pp. 153, 154).

In an address given in Battle Creek on March 6, 1869, Ellen White further described her experiences as a health reformer:

I suffered keen hunger. I was a great meat eater. But when faint, I placed my arms across my stomach and said: "I will not taste a morsel. I will eat simple food, or I will not eat at all." Bread was distasteful to me. I could seldom eat a piece as large as a dollar. Some things in the reform I could get along with very well, but when I came to the bread I was especially set against it.

When I made these changes, I had a special battle to fight. The first two or three meals, I could not eat. I said to my stomach: "You may wait until you can eat bread." In a little while I could eat bread, and graham bread, too. This I could not eat before; but now it tastes good, and I have had no loss of appetite (2T, pp. 371, 372).

She continued:

I left off these things [meat, butter, and three meals] from principle. I took my stand on health reform from principle. And since that time, brethren, you have not heard me advance an extreme view of health reform that I have had to take back. . . .

I do not regard it a great privation to discontinue the use of those things which leave a bad smell on the breath and a bad taste in the mouth.

Is it self-denial to leave these things and get into a condition where everything is as sweet as honey; where no bad taste is left in the mouth and no feeling of goneness in the stomach? These I used to have much of the time. I have fainted away with my child in my arms again and again.

I have none of this now, and shall I call this a privation when I can stand before you as I do this day? There is not one woman in a hundred that could endure the amount of labor that I do. I moved out from principle, not from impulse. I moved because I believed Heaven would approve of the course I was taking to bring myself into the very best condition of health, that I might glorify God in my body and spirit, which are His (*ibid.*, p. 372).

---

* The vision was on Friday night, June 5, but inasmuch as the sun had gone down, the pioneers gave it the June 6 date.

JAMES:
LEARNING THE HARD WAY

When James married Ellen at age 25 he possessed unusual physical strength and ability. He had grown strong and tall working on his father's farm. During the years immediately following the Disappointment his zeal for the cause propelled him along a course that made increasing demands on his time and strength.

By 1865 he was president of the General Conference; head of the General Conference Committee; president of the SDA Publishing Association; active in writing, publishing, traveling, and filling appointments. In addition he had been intimately involved in publishing the first of a series of Ellen's pamphlets, *Health; or How to Live.*

On Friday, August 18, at age 44, he suffered a stroke of paralysis. Here is what led up to this:

After the General Conference in May, James and Ellen were traveling with Elder Loughborough, visiting various churches, when they received word of a critical situation centering in Marion, Iowa. Convinced that this called for their counsel, they made a change in their travel plans and went together to Pilot Grove for a hastily called conference. As a result of most earnest labor the trouble was seemingly resolved, and the visiting workers were again on their way.

But it took a heavy toll on James. James and Ellen had looked forward to a little period of rest on returning from Iowa but were denied this, as they were called upon to contend with criticism and falsehoods. Then they faced an appointment with the church in Memphis, Michigan, across the state, just north of Detroit. A debt hung over the meetinghouse, and the members were discouraged. James White's presence was urged. Ellen White described the journey:

> When the time came to attend our appointment in Memphis, we needed rest of body and mind. A constant strain had been upon us for months. . . . Yet we urged up our exhausted energies, arose at midnight, walked about a mile to the depot, and stepped on board the train which was to take us to Detroit. . . . The meetings in Memphis were those of labor. My husband here performed the amount of labor which was sufficient for two

men who possessed a good degree of strength. His vital energies were exceedingly depressed, yet his zeal in the cause of God urged him on presumptuously to exhaust, by overlabor, the little strength that remained.

Our meetings closed on Sunday evening after eleven o'clock. We retired after midnight, and arose at daybreak to take the stage for the cars [train]. The cars missed connection, and we did not arrive at our home till past midnight.

My husband slept but little, and would not be prevailed upon to rest the next day. He thought his business required his presence at the office. Night found him exhausted. His sleep was broken and unrefreshing, yet we rose in the morning at five o'clock to take our usual walk before breakfast (RH, Feb. 20, 1866).

As they walked that early-morning hour, on Wednesday, August 16, they stopped for milk at Brother Lunt's home, and then stepped into the corn patch. Admiring the full ears, James plucked one and started to pull back the husk. Ellen, by his side, heard a strange noise. Looking up, she saw the face of her husband flushed, and then she saw his right arm drop to his side, helpless. He attempted to raise his arm but could not. He staggered, but did not fall. He was unable to speak. Ellen helped him into the Lunt home. Indistinctly James uttered the word "Pray," and repeated it. Ellen reported later:

> We dropped to our knees and cried to God, who had ever been to us a present help in time of trouble. He soon uttered words of praise and gratitude to God, that he could use his arm. His hand was partially restored, but not fully (ibid.).

Physicians were called, but they had little to offer, either as to what might be done for him or encouragement that he would survive.

Two days later, Friday, August 18, James White was carried on a couch to his own home. The next Tuesday, as the *Review and Herald* came from the press, it carried a notice that Elder White had been stricken by "a partial shock of paralysis."

SEEKING HELP AT DANSVILLE

For five weeks James was tenderly cared for by Ellen, joined by the Uriah Smiths, the George Amadons, and the M. J. Cornells (ibid., Nov. 7, 1865). Having spent a few weeks at "Our Home" in Dansville, New York, during the past year, Ellen White was convinced of the value of water as one of God's approved remedies, and having no confidence in the use of poisonous drugs, she turned to hydrotherapy. But this, in her worn-out condition, seemed more than she could undertake. There were none in Battle Creek who would dare to venture treating James with the little-known hydropathic remedies. This led her to consider taking him to Dansville. Dr. H. S. Lay, now in Battle Creek, was sent for and helped them decide that James should go back with him to "Our Home on the Hillside." And as will be seen from the notice placed in the *Review* by the acting editor, James White was not the only one who traveled with the doctor to Dansville:

> Journeyed, from this city, Thursday, the fourteenth inst., in quest of rest and health, a Seventh-day Adventist invalid party consisting of the following named persons: Elder James White and wife, Elder J. N. Loughborough, Sr., M. F. Maxson, and the editor of the *Adventist Review* [Uriah Smith].
>
> They were accompanied by Dr. H. S. Lay, recently by request from Dansville, New York, to which place they now direct their course. . . . We hope also these overworked and overburdened servants of the Lord will share largely in the prayers of the faithful, while they are obeying that very important, but much-neglected, command of Christ, to "rest a while" [Mark 6:31] (*ibid.*, Sept. 19, 1865).

The Whites were cordially welcomed by Dr. Jackson, and the next day all in the party were given physical examinations. A cottage close to the institution was found where the Whites had upstairs rooms. Treatments were begun, and each day they walked in the open air. Smith and Loughborough remained for rest and treatment.

Dr. Jackson's judgment in regard to James was that "it was very fortunate for him that he was arrested in his course of toil and labor when he was; for if nature had held up even but a short time longer under the same pressure, it would have eventually given way, and in such a manner as to produce a complete wreck, for which there would have been no remedy. As it is, under proper hygienic influences, he will fully recover, regaining more than his former health and strength; *but the causes which have led to this attack must for all time be avoided,* and to the work of recovery, quite a length of time, perhaps six or eight months, must be devoted" (*ibid.*, Oct. 3, 1865; italics supplied).

James and Ellen remained at Dansville for about three months. Here they had opportunity to observe methods of treatment and the wholesome diet.

In time the Whites were able to secure a ground-floor apartment. There were good days for James, and there were bad days. When disturbed with the extreme nervousness that accompanied his illness, he seemed to lose courage. But the good days outnumbered the bad. On October 23 Dr. Lay sent to the *Review* a report of the progress he was making:

> Though he has made marked progress toward recovery since coming

to this place, yet he is far from being well; and in order for him to fully recover, it seems indispensably necessary that he should devote at least several months to that special object; and in order to do this successfully, he needs rest, simple diet, judicious bathing, a certain amount of exercise in the open air, with the most pleasant social surroundings; consequently his family should be here with him. He should also have a team at his command, that he may ride every day when the weather will permit (*ibid.*, Oct. 31, 1865).

He wrote of the arduous labors of Ellen White in caring for her husband, and felt she should have some help and several months' treatment. He called for Adelia Patten, now Mrs. Van Horn, who had filled an extremely important place in the White family, to be sent to Dansville.

Dr. Lay's suggestions were taken seriously, for everyone was ready to do whatever was thought best to hasten James's recovery. On November 7 Adelia Van Horn and the children, Edson and Willie, left Battle Creek, and the next day there was a united White family at Dansville. Arrangements were also made for the use of a carriage and a team of horses that would augment James's physical activities.

The total expense for the White family was now running at $40 per week, and that of Loughborough about $20. The denomination had no plan for aiding workers who were ill, so fellow Adventists sent generous gifts to Battle Creek to help carry the burden. In six weeks' time Smith and Loughborough were fully recovered, but Loughborough stayed on to be a help to the Whites.

Morning, noon, and night those of like faith met to pray for James White, but he made very slow progress. In explanation Ellen White wrote:

> My husband could obtain but little rest or sleep nights. He suffered with the most extreme nervousness. I could not sew or knit in his room, or converse but very little, as he was easily agitated, and his brain confused almost beyond endurance. He required almost constant care, and the Lord gave me strength according to my need. . . .
>
> Many nights when my husband was suffering with pain, unable to rest or sleep, have I left my bed at midnight and bowed before God and earnestly prayed for Him to grant us this token of His love and care—that my husband might realize the soothing influence of His Holy Spirit, and find rest in sleep. . . . We had the evidence that God heard us pray, and my husband would drop into a quiet sleep (*ibid.*, Feb. 27, 1866).

> We did not doubt that God could work a miracle, and in a moment restore to health and vigor. But should He do this, would we not be in danger of again transgressing—abusing our strength by prolonged,

intemperate labor, and bringing upon ourselves even a worse condition of things? (*ibid.*, Feb. 20, 1866).

The fact that his illness was the result of overwork, together with the instructions of the Dansville physicians concerning the importance of entire rest, led him, in his feeble state, to shrink from all exertion. Here was one of the most serious obstacles to his recovery (2LS, pp. 353, 354).

With the coming of December, the family knew they would have to endure a winter in somewhat cramped quarters, and with the very slow recovery of James, there were days when he was so discouraged he thought he might not live. Ellen worked devotedly and untiringly in the care of her husband until she herself was in danger of a breakdown. She knew she could not keep up the program as it was at Dansville through the whole winter. Her thoughts turned to Battle Creek:

> I thought of our large and convenient house at Battle Creek, with its high and airy rooms, and asked myself the question Would we not make more rapid progress toward health were we at our own home? I thought of the large reservoir of hot water upon our stove—ready for use at any time—and our immense cistern of soft water, and our filter in the cellar, our various bathing pans, and bathroom fitted up with a stove.
>
> But all these convenient things had but little weight in my mind compared with my anxiety to get my husband, while I could, among his tried brethren who knew him, and who had been benefited by his labors (RH, Feb. 27, 1866).

Ellen White was convinced that they should return to Battle Creek. But she would not trust her judgment alone. She prayed that God would guide her and not allow her to take one wrong step. As she prayed, the conviction grew that she must take James where he could be among his brethren. She talked with Dr. Lay. He told her that she could not take him home, for he could not endure the journey. Then she talked with Dr. Jackson. He thought it would be well to try it, taking the journey in easy stages. She sought the counsel of Loughborough, who was surprised at first at such a sudden move, but saw light in it. James, overhearing her conversations, was soon enthusiastic to go. They packed that evening, finishing before 9:00.

On December 6 they took the train to Rochester. James had proposed that they call some of their trusted friends in that vicinity to come to Rochester to engage in seasons of prayer—J. N. Andrews, who lived in Rochester but was laboring in Maine; the Lindsays from Olcott; and friends in Roosevelt "who had faith in God, and felt it their duty." "These friends," wrote Ellen White, "came in answer to his call. For ten days we had special and earnest seasons of prayer. All who engaged in these seasons of prayer were greatly blessed" *(ibid.)*.

THE IMPORTANT VISION OF DECEMBER 25

Each morning the group met in the Andrews home in Rochester; in the afternoons they went to the Lamson home, where they could be with James as they prayed. This routine continued till December 25. Ellen White described what then took place:

> Christmas evening as we were humbling ourselves before God, and earnestly pleading for deliverance, the light of heaven seemed to shine upon us, and I was wrapped in a vision of God's glory. It seemed that I was borne quickly from earth to heaven, where all was health, beauty, and glory. Strains of music fell upon my ear, melodious, perfect, and enchanting. I was permitted to enjoy this scene awhile before my attention was called to this dark world *(ibid.)*.

Recounting the experience many years later, Loughborough declared:

> As she related the vision to us, she said: "Satan's purpose was to destroy my husband, and bring him down to the grave. Through these earnest prayers, his power has been broken" (PUR, Nov. 21, 1912).

Ellen had been caring for James for more than four months, but neither she nor the others had witnessed the progress for which they had hoped and prayed. Why? And what did the future hold? The answers came in the vision: "I had an encouraging view of the case of my husband, the particulars of which will be presented hereafter" (RH, Feb. 27, 1866).

> I was shown that God had suffered this affliction to come upon us to teach us much that we could not otherwise have learned in so short a time. It was His will that we should go to Dansville, for our experience could not have been thorough without it (1T, pp. 614, 615).

> I have been shown that Satan is angry with this company who have continued for three weeks praying earnestly in behalf of this servant of God, and he is now determined to make a powerful attack upon them. I was told to say to you, "Live very near to God that you may be prepared for what comes upon you" (PUR, Nov. 21, 1912).

Ellen White reported that shortly after the vision, with its encouragement to James, "my husband then proposed our returning to Battle Creek the next week on Monday [Jan. 1, 1866], New Year's evening. . . . I felt the evidence that the Lord would go with us on our journey, and bring us safely to our home again" (RH, Feb. 27, 1866).

New Year's day was set for the trip. Andrews proposed that he accompany them to Battle Creek, but Ellen replied that she wished them to go by themselves, trusting alone in God to sustain them. A number of their friends accompanied them to the railway station to see them off.

At Battle Creek later in the day they were met by friends and escorted to their home, which had been comfortably prepared for them. At 5:00 they sat down at their dining table, bountifully spread with good food that the women of the church had prepared. James rested well through the night and on the weekend participated in the services at the church. Wrote Ellen:

> I saw that God was fitting up my husband to engage in the solemn, sacred work of reform which He designs shall progress among His people. It is important that instructions should be given by ministers in regard to living temperately. They should show the relation which eating, working, resting, and dressing sustain to health. All who believe the truth for these last days have something to do in this matter (1T, p. 618).

ELLEN SHOCKS BATTLE CREEK (WITH UNCONVENTIONAL THERAPY)

The year following the Whites' return from Dansville was a "year of captivity." Ellen's attention was given almost wholly to James's care. Although there had been temporary gains, James had remained an invalid in spite of her efforts. But remembering the assurance given her in the vision at Rochester, Ellen White could not dismiss the picture in her mind of her and her husband working together to build up the cause. She feared, however, that James had been too much impressed with the counsel of the physicians at Dansville, who urged entire rest, both of body and mind, for those who had been prostrated by overwork.

Having become fully satisfied that James would not recover from his protracted sickness while remaining inactive, Ellen decided to "venture a tour in northern Michigan" with James "in his extremely feeble condition, in the severest cold of winter" (1T, p. 570).

She added,

> It required no small degree of moral courage and faith in God to bring my mind to the decision to risk so much, especially as I stood alone. . . . But I knew I had a work to do, and it seemed to me that Satan was determined to keep me from it. I had waited long for our captivity to

be turned and feared that precious souls would be lost if I remained longer from the work. To remain longer from the field seemed to me worse than death, and should we move out we could but perish *(ibid.)*.

In recounting the experience several years later, Ellen stated:

> We had the assurance that God could raise him up, and we believed he would yet be able to work in the cause of God. I thought my husband should have some change, and we took our team, faithful Jack and Jim, and ventured a journey to Wright, Michigan.
>
> In this matter I was obliged to move contrary to the judgment of my brethren and sisters in Battle Creek. They all felt that I was sacrificing my life in shouldering this burden; that for the sake of my children, for the cause of God, I should do all in my power to preserve my life (MS 1, 1867).

So, in a snowstorm, on December 19, 1866, they left Battle Creek with the team and Brother Rogers for northern Michigan, planning to make Wright, Ottawa County, their first stop. The weather was stormy, yet they drove 46 miles [74 kilometers] that day, and were obliged to put up at a noisy rum tavern.

The next morning they arose at 5:00 and before breakfast drove 15 miles [24 kilometers] against a keen north wind to Brother Hardy's. Here they thanked God for the hospitality and the simple, wholesome food. Driving another 23 miles [37 kilometers] brought them to Wright. Ellen reported:

> My husband stood the long and severe journey of ninety miles [144 kilometers] much better than I feared, and seemed quite as well when we reached our old home at Brother Root's as when we left Battle Creek (1T, p. 570).
>
> Here commenced our first effective labors since the sickness of my husband. Here he commenced to labor as in former years, though in much weakness *(ibid., p. 571)*.

At long last they were turning a corner, with the promise of better days ahead. But the battle was not fully won. It took some persuasion on her part to get James to prepare reports for the *Review*. But this was a significant step in his recovery.

Wright was off the beaten path; ministers seldom visited the church. Ellen wrote:

> We found this church in a very low condition. With a large portion of its members the seeds of disunion and dissatisfaction with one another were taking deep root, and a worldly spirit was taking possession

of them. And notwithstanding their low state they had enjoyed the labors of our preachers so seldom that they were hungry for spiritual food (*ibid.*, pp. 570, 571).

The situation was just the challenge James White needed to draw him into active spiritual labor. They conducted a series of meetings, lasting several weeks. Visions were given to Ellen presenting lines of instruction, counsel, and reproof for a number of the members of that church.

It was a critical time for a number in the church. They hardly knew how to relate to personal testimonies. It is not easy to receive and accept reproof. In the service Sabbath morning, January 12, James White saw an opportunity to help the church in a special way. He spoke on the testimony to the Laodiceans, drawing parallels and giving counsel. He pointed to the Saviour standing at the door, knocking, waiting, entreating. He reminded the audience:

> It is those He loves that He rebukes and chastens, whether by the cutting testimony of the Word of God or by a corresponding testimony, pointing out their errors and spiritual blindness. Let those, then, thus re-proved, rejoice, instead of being discouraged. It is the best of evidence that their salvation is possible (RH, Jan. 29, 1867).

This was a landmark experience in the history of the Wright church, bringing strength and stability. It also was a milestone in James White's finding his way back to active service. Ellen White was jubilant. During the six weeks that they were at Wright, she spoke 25 times, and James 12. Since James was recovering from a long illness, she carried the heavy part of the burden, but she was careful to see that her husband led out.

Ultimately nine baptisms resulted from this evangelistic thrust, and the church was spiritually revived. The Roots, who so graciously took the Whites into their home, cared for them as tenderly "as Christian parents can care for invalid children" (1T, p. 570). As a result, the Roots were blessed with health and temporal prosperity. Root reported that his wheat fields had produced 27 bushels [108 pecks] to the acre [.41 hectare] and some 40 [160 pecks], while the average yield of his neighbors' fields had been only seven bushels [28 pecks] to the acre [.41 hectare] (*ibid.*, pp. 574, 575).

Ellen insisted on keeping up James's exercise program. They took a long walk twice a day. Then came a snowstorm that left a heavy blanket on the ground, bringing a minor crisis. She later told of it:

> I went to Brother Root and said, "Brother Root, have you a spare pair of boots?"
>
> "Yes," he answered.

"I should be glad to borrow them this morning," I said. Putting on the boots and starting out, I tracked a quarter of a mile [.41 kilometer] in the deep snow. On my return, I asked my husband to take a walk.

He said he could not go out in such weather.

"Oh, yes, you can," I replied. "Surely you can step in my tracks."

He was a man who had great respect for women; and when he saw my tracks, he thought that if a woman could walk in that snow, he could. That morning he took his usual walk (MS 50, 1902 [see also 2SM, p. 307]).

On January 29, 1867, the Whites left Wright and rode to Greenville, Montcalm County, a distance of 40 miles [64 kilometers]. Ellen described the trip:

It was the most severely cold day of the winter, and we were glad to find a shelter from the cold and storm at Brother Maynard's. This dear family welcomed us to their hearts and to their home. We remained in this vicinity six weeks, laboring with the churches at Greenville and Orleans, and making Brother Maynard's hospitable home our headquarters (1T, p. 575).

The activities in the Greenville area were much the same as those at Wright. Meetings were frequent, and both James and Ellen participated. She noted the improvement in her husband's health:

His labors were received by the people, and he was a great help to me in the work. . . . The Lord sustained him in every effort which he put forth. As he ventured, trusting in God, regardless of his feebleness, he gained strength and improved with every effort (ibid.).

With the prospect improving that the two would work together again, Ellen's feeling of "gratitude was unbounded." Subjects dealt with in depth were primarily Systematic Benevolence and health reform in its broad aspects. They found the Word more readily received there than at Wright, prejudice breaking away as plain truth was spoken (RH, Feb. 19, 1867).

They were delighted with Greenville's surroundings. Of this James wrote:

One might suppose that Montcalm County was a very new, log-house country, it being seventy-five miles [120 kilometers] north of Calhoun County [and Battle Creek]. But this is the most beautiful portion of the State. The farmers are generally independent, many of them rich, with large, splendid houses, large, fertile farms, and beautiful orchards.

One traveling through this country passes a variety of scenery peculiar to Michigan, namely, rolling, oak openings, and plains covered with heavy maple and beech, and lofty pines. Then before he is aware of it, he comes upon a fine farm with buildings equal in size and style to the dwellings in our small cities (*ibid.*).

"The sleighing has been excellent for the last two months," he reported, "and the weather, generally, comparatively mild and fine" (*ibid.*). With their team of horses, which were a great blessing, they drove from five to 40 miles [eight to 64 kilometers] nearly every day. In his report written March 3, James informed the readers of the *Review*:

> Since we left home [Battle Creek on December 19], . . . we have ridden, with our team, one thousand miles [1,600 kilometers], and have walked some each day, in all amounting to one hundred miles [160 kilometers]. This, with our preaching, writing, baths, and rest hours, has filled up our time (*ibid.*, Mar. 12, 1867).

Other reports put his health at about one-half recovered. He was still frail, but determined to move on by faith, looking forward to full restoration. He closed his report of their work in the vicinity of Greenville:

> We have taken our leave of this people for the present, who express a desire that we should settle among them. And we feel the strongest desire, if the Lord will, to settle with this dear people where our testimony, as is most natural, is prized more than in those places where they are blessed with much ministerial labor, and the labors also of efficient local elders and experienced brethren.
>
> When men come from ten to fifteen miles [16-24 kilometers] on foot, and aged and feeble come from three to twelve miles [five-19 kilometers] on foot, at this season of the year, depend upon it, they come to hear (*ibid.*).

DISAPPOINTING RECEPTION IN BATTLE CREEK

With the spring thaws, the roads were getting bad, making weekly visits to the churches difficult. James was eager to see the church members in Battle Creek and to "rejoice with them in the work which God was doing for him" (1T, p. 577), so they planned the trip south in such a way that they could spend a few days visiting believers en route. One night Ellen White was given a disquieting dream. It warned of a cold reception in Battle Creek (*ibid.*, p. 578). They had reason to expect that after an absence of three months, during which James White had definitely improved in health, they would be heartily welcomed.

But no. False reports and criticism had done their work. Although James took services Sabbath morning and afternoon, March 16, speaking with clearness, and again Sunday morning, and Ellen White bore her testimony with freedom, they seemed to be held at a distance.

Ellen was crushed. James too was terribly disappointed at the cold reception. Little by little they discovered the reason. Part of the problem rested in Ellen White's refusal to take the counsel of friends and church leaders in Battle Creek that would have dissuaded her from taking her husband to Wright in December. Also, evil reports had been bandied about for some time to the effect that James White had a craze for money and that the Battle Creek church had not the slightest confidence in the testimonies of Sister White.

While painful, such reports were no great surprise to Ellen, for this had been revealed to her in a dream.

THE MOVE TO GREENVILLE

Under these circumstances James and Ellen White packed some of their goods and on Thursday, April 25, left by wagon for Greenville. They arrived at the Maynard home Tuesday afternoon, April 30. "Home again," they sighed. From the Maynard yard they could see the framework of their new home, rising half a mile away on farm acreage they had purchased before the trip to Battle Creek. "Before getting out of the carriage," wrote James White, they drove over to it "and viewed the premises." He added, "Today, May 2, we start the plow for garden. We hope, with the blessing of God, to prosper in our new home" (RH, May 14, 1867).

But they had hardly moved in when they returned to Battle Creek to attend the May 14 General Conference of 1867. Although weary from traveling and the move to Greenville, they spoke on "both Sabbath and First-day upon the coming of the Lord, and felt much as we used to feel on such occasions" (*ibid.*, May 28, 1867).

The Battle Creek church had not yet fully disabused themselves of their indifferent attitudes toward the Whites, but there was an exchange of formal statements published in the *Review*: the Battle Creek church expressed sympathy, and James and Ellen White expressed love and confidence in the church at Battle Creek. They requested the prayers of the church and all who had faith (*ibid.*). By the end of May they were back in Greenville.

FARMING IN GREENVILLE

It was a happy day for the Whites—James White, and Willie, now 12— when on Thursday, May 2, 1867, they could see the plow turn the rich soil on their little Greenville farm (*ibid.*, May 14, 1867), to be followed quickly by the setting out of grapes, blackberries, raspberries, and strawberries, and incidentally watch the construction of their new home. At some point about this time Ellen devised a plan to encourage James to engage in physical activity. He had been warned by the physicians at Dansville that physical activity could lead to another stroke. Ellen had been shown that without mental and physical activity he could not hope to recover fully. Here is her account:

> In the spring there were fruit trees to be set out and a garden to be made. "Willie," I said, "please buy three hoes and three rakes. Be sure to buy three of each." When he brought them to me, I told him to take one of the hoes, and Father another. Father objected, but took one. Taking one myself, we began to work; and although I blistered my hands, I led them in the hoeing. Father could not do much, but he went through the motions. It was by such methods as these that I tried to cooperate with God in restoring my husband to health (MS 50, 1902 [see also 2SM, p. 307]).

Rather triumphantly James White reported on Tuesday, June 18, that he harnessed his horses and went to town on business and brought home materials for the builders (RH, June 25, 1867). Sabbath, June 29, he and Ellen met with the church in Fairplains. He spoke in the morning for an hour and a half on baptism, and in the afternoon for an hour on Galatians 6:6, 7, on reaping what one sows. Ellen followed, speaking for an hour. The next morning he led four candidates into the nearby lake and baptized them. Willie was one of the four. James took Brother King into the water with him in case he needed assistance, but he needed none.

GETTING IN THE HAY

The work of recovery continued at a steady but slow pace. Thursday and Friday, July 18 and 19, were busy days for James White, for it was time to get in the hay. He arranged with the neighbors to cut the hay, and expected to invite them to help him get it in. But Ellen saw a good opportunity to draw her husband into further activity. While the hay was drying she slipped away and visited the neighbors. Through inquiry she learned that they were pressed with their own work, but were planning to help James get his hay in. To each she said, "When he sends for you, tell him what you have just told me, that you are pressed with your own work and it is not convenient to leave your own work, as you will suffer loss if you do" (see 2LS, p. 357). The neighbors were reluctant to do this, but when she explained her plan to encourage James in activity, they agreed to cooperate. The story is told in several places, but here is the account as related in *Life Sketches* of James and Ellen White, published in 1888:

> When the call was made for help, all the neighbors declared themselves too busy to respond. It was necessary that the hay be secured at

once, and Elder White was sorely disappointed. But Mrs. White was not at all despondent; she resolutely said: "Let us show the neighbors that we can attend to the work ourselves. Willie and I will rake the hay and pitch it on the wagon, if you will load it and drive the team." To this he consented; but how could they make the stack?

The farm was new, and they had no barn. Mrs. White volunteered to build the stack, if her husband would pitch up the hay, while Willie should be raking for another load (ibid.).

Some of the neighbors, as they passed by, were surprised to see Ellen White, the woman who spoke each week to a houseful of people, treading down the hay and building the stack. Reporting his activities for this week, James wrote: "I have worked from six to twelve hours each day, and have enjoyed blessed sleep from six to nine hours each night. . . . My work has been haying, plowing, grading about the house, hoeing, and putting down carpets" (RH, July 30, 1867).

The days in their new roomy home in Greenville marked the gradual recovery of James from the point of such weakness that he could carry neither purse nor watch, to an active, aggressive ministry. Years later Ellen commented:

After his recovery, my husband lived for a number of years, during which time he did the best work of his life. Did not those added years of usefulness repay me manyfold for the eighteen months of painstaking care? (MS 50, 1902 [see also 2SM, p. 308]).

RUGGED PIONEERS

In fact, they were so pleased with James's improvement that by the end of October 1867 they jubilantly set off for a three-month tour of the Eastern states, visiting the members in New England.

Wednesday, October 23, James and Ellen White, accompanied by D. T. Bourdeau, left for appointments with the churches in the East. Sabbath and Sunday they were at Roosevelt, New York, where J. N. Andrews joined them. It was soon seen at Roosevelt that much would be called for to get the work in full order.

Their next appointments were in Maine. The first was for Norridgewock, some 75 miles (120 kilometers) north of Portland. There delegates were being called together to organize the Maine Conference. J. N. Andrews, president of the General Conference, was with them. D. M. Canright had been doing good work there and at the time seemed to be the most prominent minister in that area. He reported the accomplishments of the meeting held from Friday through Sunday and emphasized the special value of the help given by both James and Ellen White.

Never before did I so fully realize the great importance of the gifts in the church, and never did I have so strong faith in them as now. Many, nay, nearly all, felt the same. *Thank God for the testimonies* (RH, Nov. 12, 1867).

On Friday, November 1, the delegates set about to organize the Maine Conference. Through November and till mid-December James and Ellen White were in Maine, visiting the churches and, when possible, relatives and friends of former days.

J. N. Andrews, who had done considerable work in Maine, described the experience of those who had not been acquainted with Ellen White and her special gift. He stated that "even those who have felt the greatest opposition to the reproofs they received have, with scarcely an exception, on calm and serious reflection, acknowledged that they were justly reproved," and accepted her messages to them. Andrews observed thoughtfully:

> I have had great opportunity to judge of the truthfulness of these testimonies by witnessing their faithful and exact delineations of character in a very large number of cases, presenting very widely dissimilar features. I have every reason to know that these things were almost entirely unknown to Sister White, and in some cases absolutely unknown, only as given her by the Spirit of God. Yet a most perfect and exact representation of the faults, as well as the virtues, of many persons has thus been given, so that even those who know them best have said they could not so well have described them (*ibid.*, Dec. 24, 1867).

It was this type of evidence that convinced many of the integrity of the visions given to Ellen White.

The Whites and Andrews filled appointments in Topsham, Maine; in Washington, New Hampshire; and in Vermont. Many places could be reached only by sleigh or carriage.

Monday, December 23, the meeting was held during the daylight hours in the William Farnsworth home. Farnsworth was the man who in 1844 had risen to his feet in the Washington, New Hampshire, church and declared that he was going to keep God's Sabbath. Others followed him in his decision.

Sitting in the group was 19-year-old Eugene Farnsworth, one of William's 22 children. As he heard Ellen White addressing one and then another with messages indicating that she had insights others did not have, an idea came to him. He said in his heart, I wish she would tackle my dad. He knew what most others did not know—that his father had slipped back to the use of tobacco. Their farm was quite isolated, and William did his chewing of tobacco on the sly, but Eugene had seen him spit tobacco juice into the snow and quickly scuff it out of sight with his boot. As these thoughts were forming in Eugene's head Ellen White turned and addressed William:

"I saw that this brother is a slave to tobacco. But the worst of the matter is that he is acting the part of a hypocrite, trying to deceive his brethren into thinking that he has discarded it, as he promised to do when he united with the church" (WCW, in RH, Feb. 11, 1937).

As Eugene saw these covered sins dealt with faithfully by Ellen White, he knew he was witnessing a manifestation of the prophetic gift. When she had finished with her messages to different ones in the room and there was an opportunity for a response, one after another stood and acknowledged the truthfulness of her message, and with repentance and confession yielded themselves anew to God. Then the parents made confession to their children. This touched the hearts of the young people who had been watching and listening, and whose hearts were being moved by the messages and invitations not only of Ellen but of James White and Andrews.

On Wednesday morning, Christmas Day, a meeting was held and 13 children and young people expressed their determination to be Christians.

Five young people were not present Christmas morning, but in response to the appeals of their young friends they too gave their hearts to the Lord, making 18 whose lives were changed during the five eventful days at Washington. Some of them wanted to be baptized without delay, so a hole was sawed in the ice on nearby Millan Pond, and with joy they went forward with this rite. Others waited till spring and warmer weather. Nine of the 18 became church workers in the cause of God, some filling prominent positions. Among them were Eugene, Elmer, and Orville Farnsworth, and their sister Loretta. The latter married A. T. Robinson and led out in developing the Bible instructor ministry. The two Mead children made their contributions, Rose in city mission work and Fred as a literature evangelist leader, and missionary to Africa.

Thursday morning, December 26, James and Ellen White and John Andrews hastened on to northern Vermont, where a conference was to begin in West Enosburg Friday evening in the church close to the A. C. and D. T. Bourdeau homes. A. C. Bourdeau reported in the *Review* that in the evening, after the Sabbath, 150 participated in the "ordinances of the Lord's house."

> Monday morning the meeting commenced with a good interest. The good work progressed till two o'clock p.m., when by request of Brother White, six long seats near the pulpit were vacated and then filled with those who during these meetings had decided to make a new start for the kingdom. . . .

> These were examined one by one and received into the church by

vote as candidates for baptism; and just before the setting of the sun, when the thermometer stood at 20 degrees below zero [–29° C], we went down to the branch nearly one mile [two kilometers] from the meeting-house, where I stepped down from the ice into a clear stream of water and baptized eleven, among whom were my aged and respected father and mother (RH, Jan. 21, 1868).

BACK IN BATTLE CREEK

Back in Battle Creek on Sabbath, January 11, James White took the morning service and preached on the parable of the lost sheep. In the afternoon Andrews and Ellen White spoke. Sunday morning Ellen had the meeting. She gave "an account of absorbing interest of what she had seen relative to the view given to Moses of the land of Canaan, typical and antitypical" (ibid., Jan. 14, 1868). James White reported concerning their Eastern tour:

We have, in this time [nearly three months], traveled by railroad 3,200 miles [5,120 kilometers], and by private conveyance 600 [960 kilometers]. Have held 140 meetings and preached 60 times, and have spoken more or less in nearly all these meetings. Mrs. White has spoken from half an hour to two hours in more than 100 of these meetings. We have assisted in the ordination of four ministers, and the dedication of one house of worship. Have presided in the examination of 150 candidates for baptism, and have baptized 18. . . .

We leave for our good home in Greenville the fifteenth, where we hope to hear from friends (ibid.).

No question, James and Ellen White were back in the harness again.

THE NEW HEALTH INSTITUTE
FORERUNNER OF THE BATTLE CREEK SANITARIUM

A DESPERATE NEED

As early as the Whites' first visit to Dansville, Ellen had been impressed with the desirability of a health institution for Sabbathkeeping Adventists. Instead of the rapid advance of the message expected at this time, the work was crippled by the illness of many of the leading workers.

James White was incapacitated by illness. But he was not the only one. Because of their poor health, Elders J. N. Loughborough, D. T. Bourdeau, A. S. Hutchins, J. B. Frisbie, and John Byington had been doing little or no field work during the year. All three children of Elder O. C. Taylor had been taken by death, and also one each in the families of Elders R. J. Lawrence and J. N. Andrews.

In the April 17, 1866, issue of the *Review*, Uriah Smith described the sad situation:

> Instead of an increase of laborers, many of the more efficient ones then in the field have been either entirely prostrated or afflicted in some way calculated to dishearten or cripple them. And as in times of prosperity it is proper to enumerate our blessings, so now in this time of adversity and humiliation let us enumerate our calamities.

Smith listed 13 cases of illness, death, and other misfortune. He declared:

> All this has intervened since our last conference, and what is the meaning of it all? If God is by these things designing to teach us an important lesson, we should not be slow to learn it (*ibid.*).

Not only was there a need for a health institution but a need for a change in the health habits of the believers.

For a year the church had had before it an outline of the basic health principles, in the six *How to Live* pamphlets.

When the General Conference session of 1866 met in Battle Creek in May, the matter of health reform was uppermost in the minds of the leaders. James White was not able to attend on account of illness. John Byington was asked to preside.

Sensing the need for immediate help from God, the General Conference

Committee appointed a four-day season of fasting and prayer, beginning Wednesday, May 9, and continuing to the close of the following Sabbath. Meetings were to be free from discussions, and characterized by humiliation, fasting, and prayer on the part of the church. Business was to be suspended; the members of each church would meet at 1:00 on weekdays, and both morning and afternoon on Sabbath. The following counsel was given concerning the fast:

> During these days of prayer we recommend on the part of all a very abstemious and simple diet, Daniel 10:3, while some may more or less abstain from food as their health may permit, or their feelings prompt (*ibid.*).

The churches responded well. J. N. Loughborough reported:

> The praying seasons for the reviving of God's people, and the restoration of His servants, were especially refreshing, so much so that it seemed evident to all that the Lord by giving us freely of His Spirit said to us, "Yes, I accept you, and will work for you" (*ibid.*, May 15, 1866).

On the last Sabbath Ellen White spoke twice in the Michigan tent, which was pitched on the west side of North Washington Street, about half a block from the publishing house.

Referring to the vision given her on December 25, 1865, at Rochester, she said:

> I was shown that the work of health reform has scarcely been entered upon yet. While some feel deeply and act out their faith in the work, others remain indifferent and have scarcely taken the first step in reform. . . .
>
> The health reform, I was shown, is a part of the third angel's message and is just as closely connected with it as are the arm and hand with the human body (1T, pp. 485, 486).

CHURCH CHALLENGED TO BUILD A HEALTH INSTITUTION

Ellen White was shown that:

> Our Sabbathkeeping people have been negligent in acting upon the light which God has given in regard to the health reform, that there is yet a great work before us, and that as a people we have been too backward to follow in God's opening providence as He has chosen to lead us (*ibid.*, p. 485).

> Our people should have an institution of their own, under their own control, for the benefit of the diseased and suffering among us who wish to have health and strength that they may glorify God in their bodies

and spirits, which are His. Such an institution, rightly conducted, would be the means of bringing our views before many whom it would be impossible for us to reach by the common course of advocating the truth (*ibid.*, pp. 492, 493).

Doubtless, some in the audience questioned how this small people with limited resources could ever start a medical institution. The audience, including J. N. Loughborough, was startled.

Since James was at that time in a critical condition of health and could not undertake such an enterprise, the matter seemed to fall upon the Michigan Conference, of which Loughborough was president.

Loughborough drew up a subscription paper, and went first to J. P. Kellogg, one of the most prosperous businessmen among the Adventists in Battle Creek, and father of J. H. and W. K. Kellogg. Loughborough said to him:

> Brother Kellogg, you heard the testimony that Sister White read to us in the tent. A few of us have decided to make an investment for the purpose presented to us in that testimony, "sink or swim." We thought we would like to have your name at the head of the list, as you have more money than any of us (PUR, Jan. 2, 1913).

Kellogg replied, "Let me take that paper." In a bold hand he wrote, "J. P. Kellogg, $500." "There it is," he said, "'sink or swim.'" Others were quick to follow with pledges: Ellen G. White, $500; J. M. Aldrich, $250; James White, $100; J. N. Loughborough, $50; et cetera. The committee followed the counsel of competent lawyers, and the emerging institution developed as a business enterprise on a dividend-paying share basis. Each share sold for $25, with the promise of returns to the investor from the earnings. Before long, however, on Ellen White's counsel, this was turned around. While the capital was built up on the basis of the purchase of shares, which provided voting rights, profits from the investment were plowed back into the enterprise.

HEALTH INSTITUTION OPENED

Within days after the call for such an institution, the residence of Judge Graves was purchased. This comprised nine acres [three hectares] of land, three short blocks north of the publishing house. A two-story structure for treatment rooms was added. Tanks were installed on the roof of the treatment rooms to hold water pumped by windmill from a nearby well. Loughborough reported:

> On the fifth of September, 1866, the institution was formally opened for patients and boarders, having Drs. Lay and Byington as physicians, two helpers, and one patient. . . . We had room for twelve patients. Ere

a month passed, the rooms were filled with patients, and we had to increase our help, and provide more room *(ibid.)*.

Denominational leaders were venturing into a new field that offered unique opportunities but was fraught with many perils. Ellen White shortly placed before them this caution:

> The health reform is a branch of the special work of God for the benefit of His people. I saw that in an institution established among us the greatest danger would be of its managers' departing from the spirit of present truth and from that simplicity which should ever characterize the disciples of Christ (1T, p. 560).

It would have been well if the health of James White had been such that he could have used his cautious managerial experience, and Ellen could have been in a position to give closer attention to the project. In the absence of this, men in all sincerity but with limited experience moved ahead, sometimes inadvisably.

The enthusiastic response from the general public led to premature plans for the rapid enlargement of the institution to accommodate all who applied for admission as patients.

James and Ellen White, in northern Michigan, watched the rapid developments with growing concern. It was clear to them that plans for expansion of the health institute were premature, and the way in which materials from Ellen White's pen were being used brought particular distress, for the testimonies written to bring the institution into being were now being used to support the plans for immediate enlargement.

Plans were drawn, an excavation was made, a stone foundation was laid, and materials were purchased for proceeding with the proposed enlargement. James and Ellen White watched at long range through the letters, the *Review*, and reports that reached them, and were greatly distressed. They were convinced that the denomination lacked much of what would be needed in skill, experience, and finance.

Then, by vision, God gave direction. Of this Ellen White wrote later:

> I was shown a large building going up on the site on which the Battle Creek Sanitarium was afterward erected. The brethren were in great perplexity as to who should take charge of the work. I wept sorely. One of authority stood up among us, and said, "Not yet. You are not ready to invest means in that building, or to plan for its future management." At this time the foundation of the Sanitarium had been laid. But we needed to learn the lesson of waiting (letter 135, 1903).

Ellen White knew she faced a difficult situation with those who were proceeding so enthusiastically in enlarging the health institute. The Whites knew they were already under considerable criticism, although they did not know just why.

THE CRUCIAL WEEKEND AT BATTLE CREEK

They met with the Battle Creek church on Sabbath, September 14, 1867, and entered upon the work they dreaded, establishing restraints on the premature enlargement of the health institute. They had come to Battle Creek "with trembling" to bear their testimony, and this they did. Ellen White reviewed some of the high points in the call for, and the rapid development of, the institute.

She pointed out that physicians might fail, through sickness or death or by some other cause; money might not come in as needed to put up the larger buildings; and there might be an insufficient number of patients, resulting in a lack of means to carry on. She had confidence that with proper efforts put forth in a "judicious manner, and with the blessing of God, the institution will prove a glorious success" (1T, p. 559).

In the evening after the Sabbath James White came forward and gave his counsel as a careful church administrator. This was the first meeting he had attended in 20 months. He spoke again Sunday morning at a well-attended meeting in the church.

A WHOLESOME RESPONSE

The days spent in Battle Creek were difficult, crucial, but successful. However, the large building was given up for the present. Hammers, saws, and trowels were laid aside, and church leaders were determined to follow the counsel given.

James was put on the board of directors, which helped to establish confidence. To hold things on an even keel, he told of plans that would make it possible for the institute to continue its activities within its resources. He assured everyone that the business was sound and urged them to manifest a gracious attitude toward those responsible for the current problems.

Four years later he was happy to report that:

> We have worked in accordance with our faith, and with the blessing of God, and the cooperation of faithful friends at the institute, and also abroad, it has been gradually rising, and is now enjoying a full tide of prosperity (RH, Sept. 12, 1871).

It was finally on a sound financial basis, under good management, and with four physicians on the staff. Enlargement of the main building was about finished, and the cottages had been refurbished; it seemed that there should be a rededication of the facilities. This would offer an opportunity to acquaint the city and surrounding community with the institution. A committee was formed to foster such a program, and the back page of the July 18 *Review* carried an announcement of a health convention to be held Thursday, July 27, with plans for a banquet. James White, as chairman of the committee on arrangements, signed the notice.

A GALA FESTIVAL

The committee chosen to foster the event, chaired by James White, sent out printed invitations to the principal families in the city and community to participate in a "hygienic festival" on the grounds of the institution. The response was excellent, and the dinner was an outstanding success. One of the guests, the Honorable George Willard, editor of the Battle Creek *Journal*, made the following statement:

> On Thursday, July 27, on the spacious and beautiful grounds of the Health Institute in this city, there was held a Health Reform Convention or Hygienic Festival, which was attended by about eight hundred persons, chiefly assembled from Battle Creek and the towns in the vicinity. The day was one of the finest of the season, and as the people began arriving about eleven o'clock in the forenoon, they found the amplest preparations made for their reception.
>
> On the south side of the grounds were five tables—each 128 feet [39 meters] in length, the total length being 640 feet [195 meters]—all set in the neatest style and appropriately decorated with vases of flowers, while on the north side a large platform had been fitted up for a speaker's stand, with seats arranged in front of it for accommodation of the guests during the speaking (HR, August 1871; quoted in RH, Aug. 22, 1871).

Before the guests sat down at the tables, there were some speeches from both James and Ellen White. They were listened to with close attention as they presented with force and clearness the new principles of hygiene.

After the invocation of the divine blessing and dinner was announced, the crowd surged toward the five tables. Six hundred seventy-five persons were served with a tempting meal. There were vegetables, of course, tastily prepared:

> New ripe potatoes, green beans, green corn, beets, squash, green peas, baked beans (*ibid.*).

There were breads and cakes:

> Gems, raised bread, hard biscuit, buns, fruit cake (graham), sponge

cake (graham), apple pie (graham), oatmeal pudding, manioca pudding with fruit, rice pudding with fruit (*ibid.*).

As to fruit there were peaches, dried prunes, figs, dates, apples, whortleberries (huckleberries), and blackberries. The editor stated:

> It is to be noticed that butter, grease of all kinds, tea, coffee, spice, pepper, ginger, and nutmeg were wholly discarded in the cookery and were not in use on the tables. Salt was provided for those who desired it (*ibid.*).

Going considerably into detail, the editor stated:

> The dinner was served in a most capital manner, and was relished and universally commended by the vast company of guests, most of whom for the first time sat at a public dinner got up on the hygienic plan (*ibid.*).

Then there was a visit to the facilities of the institute, and the crowd gathered again to listen further to James and Ellen White. Willard concluded his report: "The institute, it is needless to add, has gained greatly by this convention, in having its aims and objects, as well as its actual condition and prospects, brought more fully before the public at large" (*ibid.*).

This is precisely what the directors of the institute and the Adventist community had hoped for, and was a prelude to a long and interesting future that really put the name of Battle Creek on the map.

THE TENTH ANNUAL SESSION OF THE GENERAL CONFERENCE

The tenth annual session of the General Conference opened in Battle Creek, Friday morning, December 29, 1871. It was a meeting that to a degree would see the fruition of James White's determination to strengthen the base of the work to ensure its future and give him needed relief. It was a meeting of encouraging reports and the laying of long-range plans. The Publishing Association was prospering, having increased its assets by nearly $11,000 during the previous 10 months and erected a new building that was to be dedicated in a few days. The health institute was doing well; it was managed by Ira Abbey, the first of the "picked men" to join the business forces in Battle Creek. But James and Ellen White were spent; it was clear that they must get away from the burdens that inevitably rolled upon them when they were in Battle Creek.

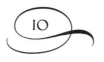

FIRST ANNUAL
CAMP MEETINGS

At the General Conference session of May 1868 some promising ventures were launched. One was the annual Adventist camp meeting. Convocations whereby believers, leaving their farms and occupations, could come together to worship for a few days living in tents had been a success off and on in various states for some years. Now, as it was discussed at the General Conference session, a resolution calling for "a general camp meeting annually" was passed, and the General Conference Committee was authorized to execute the plan (RH, May 26, 1868). Such meetings would give impetus to the messages and help solidify the work.

THE CAMP MEETING AT WRIGHT, MICHIGAN

When plans for an annual camp meeting were considered seriously in mid-July, the first thought was that there was not enough time to arrange for such a meeting that year. But then the leaders felt it could be done if they worked quickly. On the back page of the August 11 *Review*, under the heading "General Camp Meeting," readers were informed:

> It is now decided to hold a general camp meeting in the town of Wright, Ottawa County, Michigan, August 26-31.

Other notices and instructions followed quickly. Because of the closeness of time, the meeting was deferred a week, to open Tuesday, September 1, and run to Monday, September 7. On the editorial page in the *Review* of August 18, the General Conference Committee informed prospective attendees:

> This meeting has not been appointed for the purpose of spending a few days in recreation and vanity. Nor has it been appointed as a novelty, for the purpose of calling out the idle and the curious who might not otherwise be reached. Nor do we by this means merely seek to gather a large concourse of people that we may thereby make a display of our strength. We have a very different object in view.
> We desire to call out as many of our brethren, both preachers and

people, as we can, and also as many of our unconverted fellowmen as we may be able to interest in this meeting, that we may do them good.

We want all who shall come to this meeting to come for the purpose of seeking God. We want our brethren to come for the purpose of seeking a new conversion. We want our preachers to set them in this an example worthy of imitation.

We desire also to see many of our fellowmen who have no interest in Christ, or at least no knowledge of the present truth, converted to the Lord, and rejoicing in the light of His truth (*ibid.*, Aug. 18, 1868).

Directions were given on how to reach the campground, on the farm of E. H. Root, with the promise that "a beautiful grove will be prepared with seats for three thousand persons." Two 60-foot (18-meter) round tents would be pitched on the grounds, one of them new, and the hope was expressed that there would be many small, family tents. James and Ellen White would have theirs, and the *Review* of August 18 carried instruction on how to make simple tents at home, to serve families and churches.

THE CAMP LAYOUT

After about a week in Battle Creek the Whites returned to Greenville to get ready for the camp meeting at Wright (RH, Aug. 25, 1868). As the people began to assemble for the meeting on Tuesday, September 1, they found the site to be in a beautiful grove on the Root farm. Meetings were to be held in a natural amphitheater, the ground gently sloping to the speaker's stand. Two 60-foot (18-meter) tents had been erected, one well supplied with good clean straw with which to fill their bed ticks, and in which some of the men could sleep. Water came from a spring on the nearby crest of the incline, which furnished water for the livestock on the Root farm.

As the wagons drove up, family and church tents were unloaded and pitched in a circle around the speaker's stand—22 in all. Many of these were quite large—sleeping quarters were divided off by blankets or quilts, providing shelter for several families. Nineteen tents were from Michigan, one from New York State, and two from Wisconsin (*ibid.*, Sept. 15, 1868). There would have been more had there been more time between the announcement and the opening of the meeting.

The first brief meeting was held Tuesday morning at 11:00, but it was limited to a season of prayer. The rest of the day was given to pitching tents and getting settled. Cooking was done on small open fires. The meeting area in front of the stand was seated with planks on logs. Close by was a bookstand well supplied with the products of the SDA Publishing House: *Spiritual Gifts,*

Volumes I-IV; *Testimony* pamphlets; *Life Incidents; How to Live; Thoughts on Revelation*; and the newly issued Uriah Smith book—*The Visions of Mrs. E. G. White*, et cetera. There also were many, many pamphlets. The youthful John Corliss tended the bookstand, with 14-year-old Willie White assisting.

ACTIVITIES AND SPEAKERS

The camp meeting had its real beginning when at 5:00 in the afternoon those on the grounds assembled under the sugar maple trees facing the speaker's stand. Ellen White gave what might be called the keynote address.

Through the week of meetings, 16 discourses were given—six by James White, five by Ellen White, four by Andrews, and one by Nathan Fuller. Uriah Smith reported:

> We doubt if a series of more stirring, earnest, vehement, and pointed discourses were ever consecutively given. They were all aglow with the fire of present truth. The Spirit of the Lord is evidently calling the minds of His servants to the special duties and dangers of the church at the present time (*ibid.*, Sept. 15, 1868).

The weather was good. Meetings were held under the trees through Sabbath. Three hundred people tented on the grounds. It was estimated that 1,000 Sabbathkeepers attended most of the time, many staying in the homes of church members in the Wright area. Some thought that on Sunday as many as 3,000 were on the grounds as people from the surrounding country came in. But Sunday morning a hard rain fell, and attendance dropped to about 2,000. Meetings were held simultaneously in the two big tents.

Sunday afternoon, as the sky was clearing, Ellen White spoke. Tracts were distributed freely to the crowd. Then in the evening James White spoke from the stand on the law and the gospel. Meetings continued through Monday, the evening meeting bringing the camp meeting to a close. Smith reported of the weeklong convocation that "best of order reigned throughout, and no disturbance was experienced from any quarter" (*ibid.*). Joseph Clarke, a layman, declared in his report:

> The order and regularity observed at this meeting was unusual for a meeting of this kind. If all camp meetings could be conducted as this was, we should hear of glorious results (*ibid.*, Sept. 22, 1868).

TWO MORE CAMP MEETINGS PLANNED FOR 1868

So successful was the Wright camp meeting that before it closed, plans were laid for two more—at Clyde, Illinois, September 23 to 30, for the Wisconsin

Conference; and at Pilot Grove, Iowa, October 2 to 7, for Iowa. The Whites and Andrews were at both. Attendance was rather limited.

At these meetings James White and his brethren worked in close common interest, and mutual confidence was restored. The Battle Creek brethren urged the Whites to return and settle in the city, that the work of the cause might be carried on more efficiently and that they might have the pleasure of closer association. This was tempting, and as they journeyed from Wright to the camp meeting in Clyde, Illinois, they stopped in Battle Creek, selected a building lot, and got plans under way for putting up a house. Also they announced through a note on the back page of the *Review*, signed by both James and Ellen White, that after the two camp meetings they would attend the annual conferences in Ohio and New York. En route to these meetings they stopped again in Battle Creek. It is clear from the following report in the *Review* that James White was quickly becoming much involved with Battle Creek interests.

> Returning from the West, we reached Battle Creek October 13, and spent one week with Brother Andrews in matters of importance relative to the Health Institute, the Publishing Association, the Battle Creek School, religious meetings, besides our own personal interests in book matters, house building, and fitting up winter clothing. It was a busy week.
>
> The Health Institute is prospering. God's blessing is there. The church is still settling into the work. And the prospect is very encouraging for the establishment of a good school at Battle Creek, where not only the sciences may be taught, but the principles and spirit of the religion of Jesus may be impressed upon the children and youth who may attend it. . . . We left Battle Creek in company with Brother Andrews, the twenty-first, for the New York State Conference (*ibid.*, Nov. 17, 1868).

CAMP MEETING AGAIN

In the year 1870 four camp meetings were scheduled in the West in early summer, and 10 in the Eastern states in the late summer and fall. The first would be at Marion, Iowa, opening June 9. James and Ellen White had, at the turn of the year, purchased a modest home in Washington, Iowa, as a hideout where they could get away to relax and pursue their writing. They would spend a week there on their way to the Iowa camp meeting.

They spent eight weeks attending six Eastern camp meetings but then decided that this was too heavy a program. From this time on they would be in great demand to attend and speak at camp meetings. Their presence was a great attraction at these meetings, but as the years went by so much of their time and thought had to be given to solving personal problems and counseling that they had little time for rest.

CAMP MEETING TRAVEL VIGNETTES

Much of the program in attending camp meetings one after another, although strenuous, became somewhat routine, but in the 1870 season there were a few happenings of special interest.

The Carriage Journey to Marion, Iowa

We were awake at four. We were . . . on our journey at five o'clock. We halted for breakfast, five double wagons well loaded, at seven. Out on the open prairie James and self walked about one mile and half [2.4 kilometers]. We were willing to ride when the wagons came up. At noon we halted in a beautiful grove. We then overtook the teams from Pilot Grove. There were then thirteen wagons well filled with men and women and children. There were about one hundred in all.

At night we tarried in a grove. Tents were pitched and we then held a meeting in the large [family] tent. The neighbors flocked in. My husband spoke and I followed him. We had an interesting meeting, singing, talking, and praying. We retired to rest, but I was too weary to sleep, until about midnight.

We arose at half past three and were on our way at four. We found all had the tents down and packed. Ours was soon ready and again our caravan started. Order was observed by all. At half past six, we halted on the prairie and built a large fire, and all came together for a season of prayer. We then ate our humble fare and were soon on our way again.

At one o'clock we were on the campground and were faint and weary. We felt refreshed by eating a warm dinner. Our tent was pitched in the afternoon and we made our beds. Had a good straw bed to lie on and we slept sweetly (letter 9, 1870).

The next vignette comes from a James White report of traveling on a riverboat up the Mississippi.

Riverboat Activities

We have, on our upward trip, met many, and very large, rafts of lumber drifting down the river. On them are erected board shanties in which the men cook and sleep. We observed, as we passed a large raft, in which there were probably forty men, one man swimming toward the steamer, while others were swinging their hats and crying, "Papers!" These were immediately thrown overboard and gathered up by the swimmer and taken to the raft. In a few moments these could be dried, ready to be read.

This gave Willie a new idea. He immediately went to my traveling bag for present truth books and cord, and to the fireman for stone coal. Between two pamphlets he would tie a piece of coal, and as we passed within throwing distance we would land the books quite on the rafts. They were eagerly seized by the sturdy lumbermen. God bless the truth thus distributed (RH, July 5, 1870).

The White family were not the only Seventh-day Adventists on the river going to camp meeting. This gave an opportunity for an unwitting outreach in song, reported by James White:

A Shipboard Song Service

As the sun sank behind the bluffs on the Iowa side, the air grew cooler, and the evening was delightful. Our company was seated together in front of the clerk's office, on the bow of the boat, when we struck up the good tune and hymn "Resting By and By." This we did for our own diversion and devotion, not expecting to attract attention. But as soon as we had finished two verses and paused, hands were clapped and feet were tapped all around us, and as we looked around, our fellow passengers were all gathered forward standing just over our shoulders calling out, "Give us some more!" "Try that again!"

We made an apology for disturbing them with our poor singing. . . . But as they continued to call for more, we gave them two verses of the "Celestial Army," and begged to be excused (ibid.).

James wrote that somewhat fewer than 100 passengers were on the riverboat. One young man approached him, addressed him as Elder White, and told him that he had heard him preach at Johnstown, Wisconsin, in the fall of 1868. He must have mentioned this to other passengers, among them a man from Ohio, who was on his way to Minnesota to improve his health.

An Impromptu Evening Shipboard Meeting

The feeble gentleman from Ohio . . . said to us, "It is rumored about this boat, Mr. White, that your wife is a public speaker, and every passenger will unite in a request for her to speak in the ladies' cabin, if she will consent."

After a moment's consultation as to the propriety of the thing, and the right subject, we returned an affirmative answer. Soon the seats were arranged, a short prayer offered, and Mrs. White seized upon the great idea that God—His wisdom, love, and even His love of the beautiful— could be seen through the beauties of nature. The subject was made more interesting by references to the grand and beautiful scenery of the day's trip up the old Mississippi.

A more attentive audience we never saw. Nine in the evening came, and a dozen black-faced fellows were standing ready to prepare extra beds in the very room we were using as a chapel, so we closed and sought rest for the night (*ibid.*).

At times when James and Ellen White had planned some trip in their ministry, illness on her part seemed to make it entirely out of the question, but taking God's providence into account in their plans, they would start out by faith, and God sustained them. On the day they were to attend one camp meeting, Ellen was very ill. She had been in bed for two days, but she thought she must at least attempt to go. She wrote of it to Willie:

"Make Way for a Sick Woman"
I was not dressed Wednesday and but a short time Thursday in the morning, until I dressed to start on the cars. . . . When we arrived at Jackson it was state fair, and such a crowd I never saw before. They were determined to crowd upon the platform.

Your father rushed out with me on his arm. He put his shoulder against men and women, crying out, "Make way for a sick woman. Clear the track for a sick woman." He rushed through the crowd, took me to one side, and found me a seat. Adelia Van Horn was by my side. He went for Brother Palmer's team (letter 13, 1870).

Their travels took them into newly settled country where the roads were sometimes very difficult to negotiate. On one occasion in Missouri this left them in a distressing but somewhat comical situation, described in a letter to Edson and Willie:

Stranded in a Sea of Mud
I spoke five times in Hamilton. We started to visit an afflicted family who had lost a child 14 years old. Father preached the funeral sermon in the Methodist meetinghouse. We were provided a double wagon and horses by Brother McCollester.

We rode finely for two miles [three kilometers] when we tried to cross a mud slough. When in the center of rods of mud, the horses were stuck (stalled is the Western phrase). The mud was up to the horses' bellies. They could go no farther. They were struggling until they lay flat in the mud.

We were puzzled to know what to do. Father walked out on the pole [tongue] of the wagon and separated them from each other [and the wagon] and then used the whip and they, after making a terrible effort, struggled to terra firma, leaving us in the wagon in a sea of mud.

Father decided to venture out on the pole and ran lightly over the stiffest part of the mud. The stiff mud bore him up. He tried to get a board for me to walk on over the mud. I had no rubbers. The board refused to come off the oak posts.

I decided to follow your father's example. I ran out on the pole and his hand met mine and I got safe on terra firma. We left the wagon [in the mud] and horses [tied to the fence] and walked back to Hamilton, two miles [three kilometers] (letter 11, 1870).

We told the donor of the team where his horses were, and with strong ropes he has gone to see if he can get them home (letter 17, 1870).

James and Ellen White spent eight weeks attending six Eastern camp meetings, first at Oneida, New York; followed by South Lancaster, Massachusetts; Bordeauville, Vermont; Skowhegan, Maine; Clyde, Ohio; and one close at hand in Charlotte, Michigan. Wearily James took his pen and wrote:

Our labors have been too great for us; and we decide that we should not hold more than two camp meetings a month, especially if we are to commence in May and continue into October (RH, Oct. 4, 1870).

ON TO THE KANSAS CAMP MEETING

These were brave words of good intentions, but they were soon forgotten. After the Whites had caught their breath at the Ohio meeting, they were ready to go on. Wrote James:

On the Ohio campground the burden rolled upon us, and we have decided to hold camp meetings in Indiana and Kansas in the month of October. . . .

We make the sacrifice in our much worn condition to hold these meetings for the good of perishing souls. Who wish to share with us? Such are invited to assist with their prayers and their means (ibid., Sept. 27, 1870).

With renewed spirits they journeyed to Indiana and then Kansas, and entered wholeheartedly into the meetings. Near the close of the Kansas meeting, held near Fort Scott, 75 miles (120 kilometers) south of Kansas City, James White, on Sunday, October 16, described the circumstances:

Here are ten family tents, several covered wagons in which families live, a provision stand, and the Iowa large tent, of inestimable value to us during the heavy storm. A coal stove has been set up in the big tent, which has added much to our comfort during the storm. In fact, nearly all the tents are furnished with stoves. As far as we can learn, our people have been quite comfortable, even in the midst of the storm. All are cheerful, and enjoy the meeting very much (*ibid.,* Nov. 8, 1870).

He added, "Mrs. White has spoken on the health question in a manner to give entire satisfaction."

Instead of returning home to Battle Creek promptly, as they first planned, they felt sufficiently rejuvenated to hold a few meetings in Missouri. This swing to the south and west added five weeks to their 1870 camp meeting work. They reached home Monday, November 7 (*ibid.,* Nov. 15, 1870).

FIRST DENOMINATIONAL SCHOOL

No one was more aware of the need for qualified men in the ministry of the denomination than James White. He recognized that the important work of the third angel's message required a special type of education. As the work expanded, the need for training schools became urgent.

Because of his zeal and foresight, Elder White was always taking on more responsibilities than he had strength to bear. At the General Conference of 1869 he had agreed to serve as:

President of the General Conference
President of the SDA Publishing Association
Director of the Health Institute

But now he was beginning to promote the idea of a denominational school. In January he had proposed through the *Review* that a school be started in Battle Creek, and he called for pledges for such an enterprise. But the idea did not catch fire.

Then in 1870 he proposed that a series of lectures be presented after the General Conference session. The following year he made a similar proposal, but without significant response. Finally, in early April 1872 James and Ellen White called the Battle Creek church together to give serious study to establishing a school there. Among the questions asked were:

Shall we take hold, as a people, of the subject of education, and form an Educational Society?

Shall we have a denominational school . . . to qualify young men and women to act some part, more or less public, in the cause of God?

Shall there be some place provided where our young people can go to learn such branches of the sciences as they can put into immediate and practical use, and at the same time be instructed on the great themes of prophetic and other Bible truth? (RH, Apr. 16, 1872).

It was proposed that with shares costing $10 each, the church form a society "to raise funds for the purpose of renting, purchasing, or erecting school buildings, and procuring school apparatus." Steps were taken to determine what the interest was and what support could be expected. A standing committee consisting of Uriah Smith and E. W. Whitney was formed to foster the interest. With James White joining this committee, the following definite and significant steps were taken:

> "*Resolved*, That we invite the General Conference Committee to employ suitable teachers for the contemplated school, to take such steps as they may deem proper to raise the necessary means for the support till it becomes self-sustaining, and to take the general oversight of this enterprise."

> This being a movement in behalf of the cause at large, the General Conference Committee are the proper persons to act in the premises. In accordance with the foregoing resolution, its management will hereafter be in their hands.

> It is now decided to commence the school on Monday, the third of June next. A place is provided, and teacher engaged. The first term will continue twelve weeks, to August 26. Tuition from $3 to $6, according to studies taken.

> The chief object has been stated to aid those who contemplate becoming public laborers in the cause of truth. Of course, those who have no such object in view, but who wish merely to acquire an education under the advantages and in the society here offered, are at perfect liberty to attend. Let all come who can, in season to be here at the commencement, and others as soon thereafter as possible (*ibid.*, May 14, 1872).

George Butler, the new president of the General Conference, quickly joined in support of the school idea. On May 22 he wrote:

> We want a school to be controlled by our people where influences of a moral character may be thrown around the pupils which will tend to preserve them from those influences which are so common and injurious in the majority of the schools of the present day; and in this school we want a department in which those who would labor in the ministry, or in other public positions of usefulness, may receive the instruction which will qualify them for the duties of those positions (*ibid.*, June 4, 1872).

Announcement that the school had opened was made the next week in the

June 11 issue of the *Review* under the heading "The S. D. A. School." The announcement opened with the words:

> This school commenced in Battle Creek at the time appointed, June 3, with twelve scholars, Brother G. H. Bell, teacher. Two have since joined. This is a better beginning than we had ventured to anticipate, in view of the brief time taken to commence the enterprise, and the short notice that was necessarily given (*ibid.*, June 11, 1872).

George I. Butler came in quickly with a second article, titled "Mental Culture and the Pulpit." In it he emphasized the importance of a proper education for those who engage in the highest and noblest work God has committed to human beings.

At midterm there were 25 regular students, but between 40 and 50 attended the grammar class, which was held in the evenings for the convenience of *Review* employees. The school was well on its way (*ibid.*, July 16, 1872).

Those who might feel that this was a small beginning were reminded of the parable of the mustard seed.

This mustard seed grew into the Seventh-day Adventist education system, which includes Andrews University, Loma Linda University, various colleges in North America, universities and colleges in countries outside North America, academies, and elementary schools.

The "school" met temporarily in rooms in the newly constructed *Review and Herald* third building.

The Whites were not present for the opening of the school, as they were planning their first trip to California about this time. But they eagerly waited to hear news of its progress and plan for choosing a location and building.

About a year later, having spent a number of months promoting the work of evangelism and attending camp meetings in California, the Whites returned to Battle Creek to attend the eleventh annual meeting of the General Conference. In his opening address James emphasized the needs of the school:

> Probably there is no branch of this work that suffers so much at the present time as the proper education of men and women to proclaim the third angel's message. . . . Now, I say, we want a school. We want a denominational school, if you please. . . .
>
> We want a school in which the languages, especially the spoken and written languages of the present day, can be taught, and learned by young men and women to prepare them to become printers, editors, and teachers; and if we can do no more, where our young men that are about entering the ministry, and women, too, who are to be laborers in this

great work, can be instructed thoroughly in the common branches, where their minds can be disciplined to study, where, if it is not for more than three months, our young men may have the best instruction, and may, during that time, at least, learn how to study (*ibid.*, May 20, 1873).

He had no misgivings about the ability of Seventh-day Adventists to provide the money for a school enterprise, noting the liberality shown in erecting the second *Review and Herald* building.

James's vision reached far beyond the immediate need of the school in Battle Creek. He launched into a presentation of the church's position in fulfilling prophecy, and then the responsibilities that devolve on the church in advocating a message far beyond the limitations of the English language. This called for publishing in other languages, and also for a school in which, among other things, ministers could be trained to work in the languages of Europe.

Little wonder that when the conference got down to business one of the first actions read:

> *Resolved*, That we regard it as the imperative duty of S. D. Adventists to take immediate steps for the formation of an educational society, and the establishment of a denominational school (*ibid.*, Mar. 18, 1873).

One deep concern shared by James and Ellen White was for a well-qualified ministry. A large part of the working forces in the field were self-trained, strongly dedicated men who, having reached a good degree of proficiency through diligent study and the blessing of God, had been pressed into public ministry. Stephen N. Haskell and Dudley M. Canright were typical examples. Canright, the oldest son in a southern Michigan farm family, had listened favorably to the preaching of the third angel's message at a tent meeting. He secured and devoured Adventist books, studied his Bible day and night, and soon longed to convert others to his newfound faith. His first convert was his own mother.

At about the age of 21, Canright felt the call to the ministry. He went to Battle Creek, sought out James White, and spent an hour with him. White related the incident:

> I said to him, "Do not content yourself with being a small preacher, but be somebody, or die trying. Do not go out to be a pet, but go out into the field, with the weight of the work upon you, with steady principles, and stand your ground."
>
> The last thing I did was to present him with one of our English Bibles, and a pair of charts, saying as I did so, "Here, Dudley, take these, and go out and try it. When you become satisfied that you have made a mistake, bring them back."

The next May, at the conference, I met him and asked him, "What about those charts and the Bible?"

He replied, "Brother White, you have lost them."

Thank God! I would like to lose more in the same way. We raised means to purchase a library for Brother Canright and Brother Van Horn. And said I to them, "When you study, study with all your might, and when you visit, visit with all your might, and exercise briskly. Whatever you do, do it with all your might" (*ibid.*, May 20, 1873 [see also Carrie Johnson, *I Was Canright's Secretary*, pp. 12-14]).

With James White's dividing his time between the interests of the Publishing Association and the initial steps in getting a denominational school going, he was held close to Battle Creek. The brethren had sought to press him into the presidency of the General Conference, as well as of the Publishing Association, but he had refused, and Ellen sustained him in this. She knew he must have rest or he would sink under the pressure.

She was right, for on Tuesday, April 22, he had his third stroke of paralysis. The stroke was not as crippling as the first one, in August 1865. It was, however, the most severe. Ellen reported what happened:

I had taken about half my dinner when a messenger came with the word my husband had another shock of paralysis. I hastened to the house and found my husband's right arm partially paralyzed. We anointed with oil and then engaged in prayer for his recovery. The Lord came near by His Holy Spirit. My husband was greatly blessed. His arm was strengthened. We felt assured that by the blessing of the Lord he would recover. We moved to the institute. My husband feels cheerful and happy. He now is settled in regard to his duty to drop everything like burdens at Battle Creek and spend the summer in the Colorado mountains (MS 6, 1873).

The next day, although it was chilly, they rode out, and there was evidence that James was exercising his mind. He was soon able to engage in various activities, but with impaired strength, and at times with considerable suffering. It was clear now to everyone that he was working on too narrow a margin to remain in Battle Creek. James and Ellen fixed their eyes on Colorado, but it was too early in the year to go to the mountains, and there were matters in Battle Creek that they needed to care for. So they stayed on. Ellen continued with her writing, and James spent some time at the office and in committees. Both of them spoke occasionally in the church.

While waiting in Battle Creek for James to recoup his strength, they had a short visit from G. I. Butler, president of the General Conference. Elder Butler lived in Mount Pleasant, Iowa, and visited Battle Creek only occasionally. They were glad to counsel with him about a number of important matters. They had found "a most desirable place" for the school and on May 6, 1873, they discussed the location for the buildings.

DEDICATION OF BATTLE CREEK COLLEGE

James and Ellen White watched with interest as the walls for a denominational college building rose to a height of three stories in the summer and fall of 1874. Dedication was to be Monday, January 4, 1875.

Between the closing of classes for the fall term and the dedication of the new buildings, there would be a three-week period. This would provide a unique opportunity for the ministers of the denomination to gather for a training period, reasoned James White. As early as September 29, 1874, he made the proposal through the pages of the *Review*. He headed it "Biblical Institute." The response was enthusiastic. The biblical institute opened on Tuesday evening, December 15, according to plan, with about 150 in attendance and the promise of "abundant success."

James and Ellen White had delayed their return to California for the winter months until after the biblical institute and the dedication of Battle Creek College. The institute would close on Sunday night, January 3, the night before the college dedication. But as they approached the time a cloud hung over their cherished plans. Ellen White was very ill with influenza. W. C. White tells the story:

> After three or four days of the usual run of the disease, we expected her to recover, but she did not improve. Rather she grew worse, and the sanitarium physicians feared that she was in danger of pneumonia. They urged that she be brought without delay to the sanitarium for treatment. . . . Father was distressed at the thought of her not being able to bear her testimony before the members of the Bible institute, the Battle Creek church, and the many visiting brethren who had gathered to witness the dedication of the college. . . .
>
> I shall never forget the solemnity of the occasion. Mother had been brought down from her sickroom into the parlor. She was seated in a large armchair, warmly wrapped in blankets. Uriah Smith and J. H. Waggoner had come up from the *Review* office with Father, to unite with him in prayer, and four members of our family were also permitted to be present.
>
> Elder Waggoner prayed. Elder Smith followed in prayer, and then Father prayed. It seemed that heaven was very near to us. Then Mother

undertook to pray, and in a hoarse, labored voice, she uttered two or three sentences of petition.

Suddenly her voice broke clear and musical, and we heard the ringing shout, "Glory to God!" We all looked up, and saw that she was in vision. Her hands were folded across her breast. Her eyes were directed intently upward, and her lips were closed. There was no breathing, although the heart continued its action.

As she looked intently upward, an expression of anxiety came into her face. She threw aside her blankets, and, stepping forward, walked back and forth in the room. Wringing her hands, she moaned, "Dark! Dark! All dark! So dark!" Then after a few moments' silence she exclaimed with emphasis, and a brightening of her countenance, "A light! A little light! More light! Much light!" (RH, Feb. 10, 1938).

In his narration W. C. White explained concerning this exclamation:

This we understood afterward, when she told us that the world was presented to her as enshrouded in the mists and fog of error, of superstition, of false tradition, and of worldliness. Then as she looked intently and with distress upon this scene, she saw little lights glimmering through the darkness. These lights increased in power. They burned brighter, and they were lifted higher and higher. Each one lighted other lights, which also burned brightly, until the whole world was lighted.

Following her exclamatory remarks regarding the lights, she sat down in her chair. After a few minutes, she drew three long, deep breaths, and then resumed her natural breathing. Her eyes rested upon the company that had been assembled for prayer. Father, knowing that after a vision everything looked strange to her, knelt by her side, and spoke in her ear, saying, "Ellen, you have been in vision."

"Yes," she said, her voice sounding far away, as though she were speaking to someone in another room.

"Were you shown many things?" Father asked.

"Yes," she replied.

"Would you like to tell us about them now?" he asked.

"Not now," was her response. So the company was dismissed, and she went back to her room (*ibid.*).

W. C. White continued his account of the vision:

Father then hastened down to the *Review* office to meet the brethren who were coming in from the East and the West to attend the dedication. About sundown he came up from the office, walking through the snow, for it had been snowing quite heavily during the afternoon. Entering the house, he threw off his overcoat in the kitchen, and hastened up to Mother's room. There, after a few words of inquiry about the experience of the afternoon, he said, "Ellen, there is to be an important meeting in the church this evening. Do you wish to attend?"

"Certainly," she answered. So she dressed for the meeting, and with Father, walked down through the snow to the church (ibid.).

In the next few evenings she rehearsed the many subjects revealed to her in the vision. She made an appeal to her hearers to take a broader view of the work. She said:

> The time was not far distant when we should send ministers to many foreign lands, that God would bless their labors, and that there would be in many places a work of publishing the present truth.
>
> She said that in the vision she had seen printing presses running in many foreign lands, printing periodicals, tracts, and books containing truths regarding the sacredness of the Sabbath and the soon coming of Jesus.
>
> At this point Father interrupted and said, "Ellen, can you tell us the names of those countries?" She hesitated a moment and then said, "No, I do not know the names. The picture of the places and of the printing presses is very clear, and if I should ever see them, I would recognize them. But I did not hear the names of the places. Oh, yes, I remember one; the angel said, 'Australia'" (ibid., Feb. 17, 1938 [see also GCB 1909, pp. 92, 93]).

A decade later, while visiting Europe, she recognized the presses in the publishing house in Switzerland as shown to her in this 1875 vision; the same can be said of the presses she saw in Australia still later.

This was the last vision given to Ellen White accompanied by physical phenomena concerning which we have detailed information and published reports attesting to it.

It is significant that this vision, with its far-reaching view of the worldwide work of the Advent movement, was given in connection with the dedication of Battle Creek College on Monday, January 4, 1875. Battle Creek College was to be different from the secular colleges. Its purpose was to train workers to preach the gospel and the soon coming of Christ. Instruction was to be Christ-centered. The teachers were to be dedicated men and women. It was intended to be a model on which the whole system of Adventist education was to be patterned.

CALIFORNIA—HERE WE COME

"Anyone for California?" asked James White.

At the close of the General Conference session held in mid-May 1868, the ministers in attendance were given an opportunity to express their preferences as to the fields in which they would work during the coming year. California was as yet an unentered field as far as any denominational workers were concerned.

But eight years previously Merritt G. Kellogg had trekked with his family by ox team to California and worked in San Francisco as a carpenter. Then, as health reform was being promoted among Seventh-day Adventists, he returned to the East to take a medical course. He enrolled at Dr. Trall's Medical College, Florence Heights, New Jersey, where a few months later he was granted a diploma as a qualified physician and surgeon. He lingered in Michigan following his graduation, and at the General Conference session in mid-May made an earnest appeal for the General Conference to send a missionary to California to help him in his work in raising up a company of believers in San Francisco. The brethren agreed that in time such might be done.

But James was not ready to let it drop there. "Has no one had any impressions of duty with reference to the California field?" Up to this time J. N. Loughborough had remained silent; now he stood and spoke of his impressions and offered his services for work in the West.

Loughborough had come to the conference with the deep impression that he should go to California, but he had revealed this to no one. In no fewer than 20 dreams he seemed to be working there!

Loughborough reported on what followed:

> Brother White then remarked, "When the Lord sent forth His servants, He sent them two and two, and it seems as though two ministers should go to that distant field." . . . Then Elder [D. T.] Bourdeau arose and stated how his mind had been exercised, and that he had come to the meetings with his companion and all his earthly substance ready to go where the conference might say (PUR, July 3, 1913).

White counseled, "Will Brethren Bourdeau and Loughborough pray over this together and separately until the day the *Review* goes to press, that they may be sure of the mind of the Lord in the matter?" (*ibid.*).

At the appropriate time, when White called for their word, the two brethren replied, "California, or nothing." White then called for $1,000 to buy a tent and start the mission. At this time the rails extended only to the Rocky Mountains; the journey had to be made by ship to the Isthmus of Panama and then by another ship to San Francisco. For the next year and beyond, readers of the *Review* were thrilled by reports from the missionaries, first on the trip itself, and then on the tent meetings and the organization of churches in the valleys north of San Francisco.

They began their work in Petaluma, and from there worked northward. Soon they had established churches in Santa Rosa, Healdsburg, Bloomfield, and other places.

Loughborough reported:

> Shortly after our arrival in California we received a letter from Mrs. White, in which she related a vision given her in Battle Creek on Friday evening of June 12—a day that we had spent in Lancaster, New York, before starting for California. She had never been in California, and had no personal knowledge of the habits of the people. In fact, at that time she had never been west of the Missouri River. Any knowledge she possessed concerning things there was derived from what the Lord was pleased to reveal to her.
>
> In the instruction in her letter, she delineated the liberal ways of the people of California, and what would be the effect of labor among them on a close, "pennywise" plan. In preaching to the people in California, they must be approached in something of the liberal spirit in which they work, and yet not in a spendthrift manner (GSAM, p. 385).

Looking back years later, Loughborough testified:

> As I witness the results of following the instruction given, I can say that our cause advanced more in three months than it would have done in one year had we not been helped "in the work of the ministry" by the instruction received through the gift of prophecy. Up to the spring of 1871, as the result of the efforts in Sonoma County, five churches of Sabbathkeepers had been raised up (*ibid.*, p. 386).

James and Ellen eagerly looked forward to the time when they would be able to visit the brethren there and see for themselves how the work was progressing. In fact, a year later James was already talking about attending a camp meeting in California. But their trip was delayed a number of times. In the summer of 1872 they had planned to attend most of the Western camp meetings

(Iowa, Illinois, Wisconsin, and Minnesota), and then join J. N. Loughborough in California for a camp meeting to be held in late September. But when the Iowa meeting closed, they saw that in their state of health the strain would be greater than they could bear. After a few days' rest they decided to go at once, thinking to arrive in California in late June. They had to have some rest.

A SURPRISE VACATION IN THE ROCKY MOUNTAINS

It had been 25 years since Ellen had been with her older sister, Caroline Clough, who lived in Ottawa, Kansas. "Why not stop and make a brief visit on our way to California?" This they did. The reunion was a very happy one. In a letter to Edson, Ellen described her sister, 15 years her senior:

> She is an understanding, intelligent woman, living, I think, up to the best light she has had. She is a powerful singer. This is as much her talent as speaking is mine. I think I never heard a voice that would thrill the soul like hers (letter 10, 1872).

They had thought to remain for only two days, but Caroline had many ideas for their pleasure and for speaking, and insisted that they extend their visit.

> Brother and Sister Clough informed us that they had four children in Colorado Territory, and expressed a strong desire that we should visit them. We decided to stop at Denver and spend a day or two with their daughter, Mrs. Walling (ibid.).

When the party arrived in Denver, a city of 12,000 (WCW, in YI, December 1872), Willie was sent out to find the Walling home. He soon returned to the station in a carriage with Mr. Walling. At the Walling home the White party met two of Ellen's nieces, Mrs. Walling and Miss Mary L. Clough. She described Mr. Walling as "very free and kind," and engaged in a large, profitable lumber business. Being quite well-to-do (letter 25, 1872), he spared no expense to please and entertain them. His lumber mills were some 40 miles west (64 kilometers), at the edge of the Rocky Mountains, but he had his home in Denver so that the children might have the benefit of a school. Instead of staying a couple days, the Whites accepted an invitation to remain for a while.

It was Mr. Walling's business to furnish lumber for the houses, and timbers for the mines in this region. Walling's Mills, near Black Hawk, was not in a steep ravine but in an expansive area above. Here was a cottage that he made available to the White party, and here they lived, read, wrote, and took their walks.

Through the entire month of August the Whites vacationed. They hiked; picked raspberries as they ripened; visited interesting places, such as the stamping mills in which the ore was broken up and then processed; gathered samples of minerals for an exhibit they proposed to set up; and, of course, wrote.

"Mr. Walling is very earnest that we should go with him across the Snowy Mountain Range to what is called the Park, on the other side of the Snowy Range" (letter 12, 1872). She saw in the proposed trip over the Snowy Range the needed incentive and opportunity for James to "be at liberty to enjoy the scenery, get tired, camp and rest, and become hardened for California" (letter 13a, 1872).

In a letter to Edson and Emma, Ellen wrote on August 22:

> Last night Father and I rode six miles [nine kilometers] on the Indian ponies, that we might get accustomed to riding. We have decided it would be better for Father to go up the mountains over the Snowy Range and be benefited with the exercise he would obtain in so doing than to go to California just now. . . . We feel much encouraged in regard to Father, but we dare not yet go to California (ibid.).

CARAVAN TO HOT SULPHUR SPRINGS

James White describes the start of the Snowy Range trip:

> It was on Monday, 11:00 a.m., September 2, 1872, when we mounted our horses and ponies for the trip over the Snowy Range into Middle Park. . . . Our course lay along through Rollinsville, Boulder Park, up the mountains through Boulder Pass (HR, January 1873).

By midafternoon a heavy storm came up, and the travelers took refuge in an empty log shanty, where they built a fire in a big stone fireplace. By the time the storm was over, night had almost fallen. As they had brought all their gear in with them, they decided to spend the night there.

> The four ladies were on ponies. Mr. Walling had the principal part of the baggage in a wagon drawn by two powerful horses, while Willie and his father were each on a good horse, ready to help in packing baggage up the sharpest ascents, or to assist the ladies in the most dangerous places (ibid.).

Soon after starting the ascent again, Ellen White was involved in a bad accident. She had her pony well under control when the strap holding her bedding roll gave way. In a letter to Edson and Emma she described what followed:

> As I was in the best of spirits, enjoying the scenery very much, my pack behind me became unloosened and dangled against the horse's heels. Your father had tarried behind to arrange his pack more securely.

I was between two companies—three of our company ahead and five behind me. I saw the situation of things, slipped my feet from the stirrup, and was just ready to slip from the saddle to the ground and in one moment should have been safe. But the pony was frightened and threw me over his back. I struck my back and my head. I knew I was badly hurt, but felt assured no bones were broken. I could scarcely breathe or talk for some time, but finally improved a little. I was in great pain through my head, neck, shoulders, and back, and bowels (letter 14, 1872).

James White picks up the story: "We soon became satisfied that bones were not broken. Neither could we discover external injuries of any kind; but as breathing and speaking were so very difficult, we feared internal injuries." With towels that Mrs. Hall brought, and water, hydrotherapy was applied. James reported:

Patient improved, and was soon able to take the writer's arm, and walk a few rods from the company, where we asked the following questions: 1. Shall we pitch our tents here, and go into camp, let Mr. Walling return to his business, and we remain till we see how your case shall turn? 2. Or shall we apply to the Great Physician, and, by faith in the efficacy of prayer, move on our journey?

Mrs. White decided, as she frequently has done under circumstances alike trying, to go forward. As we bowed in prayer, evidences of Divine Presence caused us to weep for joy. And in a few moments we were in our saddles, moving joyfully, and yet solemnly, along, resolving that we would not leave camp another morning without first thanking God for mercies past, and imploring His care and protection for time to come (HR, January 1873).

Ellen's injuries were more extensive than at first fully sensed, and she suffered for many years. In 1907 she made reference to her left leg, which had troubled her long after the accident: "The ligaments were torn from the ankle." When she sought medical help, some time after the accident, the word was "You will never be able to use your foot, for it has been so long without close investigation that nothing can relieve the difficulty and unite the ligaments torn from the ankle bone" (MS 156, 1907).

With the decision to continue the trip, the party was soon faced with a very steep climb, the steepest of the journey. The wagon was lightened of its supplies and equipment, and with difficulty the horses pulled it up the ascent, leaving tents, equipment, and supplies to be taken up piecemeal by James and Willie with their horses. At noontime they stopped by an old log shanty in a forest of pines. Here Ellen White took a warm bath and seemed to be improving. Just before reaching the timberline, they found a good camping spot for the night.

CROSSING THE CONTINENTAL DIVIDE

Pressing on early the next morning, they found it a steady climb to the 11,000-foot mark. "Here," wrote James White, "the air was so light that the climbing horses breathed and panted as though they would lose their breath; and their riders were frequently disposed to take a long breath, which did not seem to hit the spot, nor satisfy the usual demands of the breathing apparatus. This gave an excellent opportunity to expand the lungs and chest. . . .

"We hastened on, and up the sharp ascent, to the summit of the range, which we reached at 11:00 a.m. . . . From this grand range, the backbone of the continent, waters rise from springs, within a gunshot of each other, which flow, one to the Atlantic, and the other to the Pacific. We had now reached an altitude too cold for trees of any kind to exist" (HR, March 1873).

At the top of the range the terrain was rather level but rough and "untrodden, rocky, mountain way." Then they must descend. Ellen White elected to ride in the wagon with Mr. Walling, but soon she found the jerking wagon seat so uncomfortable she chose to ride with the baggage, sprawled over and clinging to the big bundle of tents. Willie described the descent:

> As we descend, the cold winds and snowbanks are left behind, but the roads are fearful. They go down so steep you are in danger of slipping over your horse's head, then through little marshes which are numerous near the top of the range, and where you must work sharp to keep your horse above ground, and the rest of the way over loose rocks and boulders, through creeks and over logs, up and down, but mostly down till we reach the park [Middle Park].
>
> Lame and weary, we were glad to stop and camp in the edge of a thick forest surrounding a little meadow through which wound a crooked mountain brook, clear and cold, and full of speckled trout. As usual, we tied the horses where there was good grass, pitched the tents, cut spruce boughs for our beds, and then, building a big fire in front of the tents, retired to rest, and slept well till sunrise (YI, January 1873).

A WEEK AT HOT SULPHUR SPRINGS

Now it was an easy trip across the valley to Hot Sulphur Springs, their destination. They picked wild strawberries as they traveled, adding to their dinner rations. An old hunter, Mr. Byers, known as "Buckskin," had leased the hot springs. He helped the newcomers find a good camping place, lent them a sheet-iron cookstove, and left them much to themselves. But not his Newfoundland dog, who soon challenged Lion, Mr. Walling's Newfoundland. Lion won the contest and was put in charge of guarding camp for the week they were there. They found 20 or 30 people camped near the hot springs, and people coming and going. In addition to the sulphur springs, people were attracted by the beautiful scenery and fishing and/or hunting possibilities.

CALLS FROM CALIFORNIA CUT SHORT THE VACATION

The Whites hoped they might remain at Hot Sulphur Springs for three or four weeks, but on Thursday afternoon, September 12, after they had been there just a week, Mr. Walling came, bringing mail and the word that the California camp meeting, which had been postponed so the Whites might be present, would open on Thursday, October 3. They must be there. Friday morning they broke camp and started back to Black Hawk. Hardened to fatigue by camp life, they were able to make the return trip, which had taken four days in coming, in two traveling days. They spent the Sabbath en route, resting.

On Friday, September 20, they journeyed the 110 miles (176 kilometers) from Denver to Cheyenne, where they caught the Union and Central Pacific train bound for San Francisco. They were amazed at the railroad trestles spanning rivers and gorges, and the tunnels and snowsheds as they crossed the Sierras, then on to the broad Sacramento Valley. At last they had reached California.

THE WHITES DISCOVER CALIFORNIA

James and Ellen White received a most hearty reception when they arrived in California on Wednesday evening, September 25, 1872. At the end of the rail line in Oakland they were met by brothers Conkrite and Stockton, who ushered them to the San Francisco Ferry and on to the Rowland home. Mrs. Rowland was a well-to-do Scottish woman on the verge of taking her stand for the Adventist message. It was midnight when they reached this home. Ellen White wrote, "We met and were introduced to twenty brethren and sisters who greeted us as cordially as we were ever greeted in our lives. These friends had waited at the house of Sister Rowland until twelve o'clock at night to receive us. We did not get to rest until a still later hour" (letter 16, 1872).

This was the beginning of the Whites' lifelong love affair with California. Such was their enthusiasm about the flowers, the scenery, the weather, the people, that they admitted privately:

James: "Nothing but stern duty will ever call us from this country."

Ellen: "We shall not neglect the work of God to view the work of nature."

James and Ellen White had their eyes on Santa Rosa and looked forward to meeting Elder and Mrs. J. N. Loughborough, who resided there, and to attend the camp meeting. They made the 37-mile (59-kilometer) ferry trip across the bay and up the Petaluma River to the city of Petaluma, then a 15-mile (24-kilometer) train trip to Santa Rosa. This was a route they would often travel as they moved about in northern California. They were cordially received at the Loughborough home in Santa Rosa, and attended the Sabbath morning service in the house of worship. James spoke on the reasons of Adventist faith, and Ellen followed for another 15 minutes. Then nearly all the congregation crowded onto the platform to shake hands with them (letter 17, 1872).

The camp meeting was to be held in a grove at Windsor, a town 10 miles (16 kilometers) south, situated between Santa Rosa and Petaluma. James and Ellen White, together with Lucinda Hall and Willie, were on the grounds for the opening meetings, Thursday, October 3. James wrote:

> We are now writing in a tent upon the California campground, near Windsor, Sonoma County, fifth-day, October 3, at the close of the afternoon service. The location is good and the weather is fine. It is as warm as August in Michigan, very much warmer than at any point since we crossed the plains the first of July.
>
> Notwithstanding the brief notice of this meeting, there are, at the early stage of the meeting, thirty-three tents upon the ground, besides the large congregation tent and the provision stand.
>
> Three tents are marked San Francisco; two, Green Valley; one, Sebastopol; four, Bloomfield; one, Mendocino County; three, Windsor; six, Healdsburg; nine, Santa Rosa; two, Petaluma; two, Woodland. . . . We spoke in the morning upon the subject of the waiting, watching time, in answer to the question, Where are we? . . . Mrs. White spoke in the afternoon, and Elder Cornell spoke in the evening (RH, Oct. 15, 1872).

After the camp meeting James and Ellen were eager to spend some time in San Francisco, having merely passed through the city. So, with Loughborough and Cornell, they went to San Francisco by train and by ferry on Thursday morning, October 10. On Friday Loughborough and Cornell took the tent by train to Woodland.

IN SAN FRANCISCO

The Whites were again cordially received in the home of Mrs. Rowland. Spending the afternoon there, Ellen had an opportunity to write a report to Edson and Emma of her impressions of the camp meeting and of California:

> Our camp meeting was a success. We have not a doubt but that the Lord has directed our course to this coast, and we believe the cause of God will be advanced by our labors, which seem to be very necessary. Your father labored very hard during the meeting. He seemed to be full

of matter and he could not restrain his labors. The people hung upon his words with intense interest.

I think I never saw a company together all so intelligent, so sincere, so exceptional in every way, as the company we met upon the camp-ground. Twenty homes have been offered us already and such urgent, hearty invitations that we desire to gratify them all (letter 18, 1872).

She wrote of a committee of five who had waited upon them at the camp meeting, urging them to make their headquarters in San Francisco; they also offered to hire a five-room house, furnish it, and turn it over to them for their home. Further, they would furnish all they needed to live on, and even provide domestic help.

Ellen reported: "We declined. We should not be prescribed in our liberty at all. We should go among the brethren just when we choose and stay one, two, or three weeks."

Making their home with Mrs. Rowland, they shopped some, did some writing, and from day to day visited the believers in the city. They had a glimpse into the situation of the Sabbathkeepers in San Francisco.

TENT EFFORT IN SAN FRANCISCO

Friday evening, November 8, James White opened the tent meetings in San Francisco. A good crowd attended. In early winter the weather in that area is usually pleasantly warm. On November 17 they had to raise the tent wall to be comfortable. After 18 meetings Loughborough reported of the interest:

Brother White has preached six times, Sister White seven times, and I have spoken five times. Our congregations have been both large and deeply attentive. The preaching has been about an even mixture of close, searching, practical discourses, alternated with the theory of the truth, presented in a clear, concise, solemn, and pointed manner, spiced with exhortation, and close appeals to the consciences (RH, Dec. 3, 1872).

During the winter months of December, January, and February the Whites moved about among the six California churches—San Francisco, Santa Rosa, Healdsburg, Petaluma, Woodland, and Bloomfield.

ORGANIZATION OF THE CALIFORNIA CONFERENCE

The California state meeting was held February 14-18, in Bloomfield, and of course the Whites were there. In his report for the *Review*, Loughborough stated:

Everything moved off with perfect harmony and good feeling, and it was the source of deepest gratitude to us all that we were favored in our deliberations and meetings with the presence of Brother and Sister White (*ibid.*, Mar. 4, 1873).

During this formal meeting, with delegates present from the six churches in California, the California Conference of Seventh-day Adventists was formed, with a membership of 238. J. N. Loughborough was elected president; S. B. Bresee, also of Santa Rosa, secretary; and T. M. Chapman, of Petaluma, treasurer (*ibid.*, Mar. 11, 1873).

Word had just been received that the General Conference session would be held in Battle Creek, opening on March 11. James, of course, would attend, but Ellen wanted to get on with her writing. She was working on the book *The Spirit of Prophecy*, volume 2, on the life of Christ.[1]

But when the next issue of the *Review* came it carried this note:

> *A Special Request:* We deem it of the utmost importance that Brother and Sister White attend this meeting; and we therefore invite and urge, in the strongest terms, their attendance at this session of the General Conference, if their health will permit them to do so (*ibid.*, Feb. 11, 1873).

Ellen White would go East with her husband. It would be a full 21 months before the Whites would be able to return to California.

INTERLUDE

During this period James and Ellen attended two General Conference sessions and enjoyed another vacation in the Colorado mountains.

Soon after their arrival in Battle Creek they were deluged with callers and fellow workers who came in for consultations and appointments for speaking. This was "par for the course," and became somewhat tiring as the years passed by.

At the eleventh annual meeting of the General Conference (1873) James was unanimously elected president of the SDA Publishing Association. At first he declined to serve, but finally gave in to pressure and agreed.

His great interest at this time was to get the denominational school going, so he divided his time between the interests of the publishing association and the school.[2] He also was one of the directors of the health institute.

Ellen, as usual, was deeply involved in writing testimonies, and when she could get at it, the life of Christ for *Spirit of Prophecy*, volume 2. They also were involved in selling their house and finding a place to work.

All this culminated in James having his fourth stroke of paralysis. He was anointed with oil, and prayer was offered for his recovery. "We felt assured," Ellen reported, "that by the blessing of the Lord he would recover. We moved to the institute. My husband feels cheerful and happy. He now is settled in regard to his duty to drop everything like burdens at Battle Creek and spend the summer in the Colorado mountains" (MS 6, 1873).

They had not intended to remain long in Battle Creek. In fact, Ellen concluded that "every hour that they remained in Battle Creek was a positive danger to his life."

BACK TO COLORADO

It was 7:30 Wednesday evening, June 25, 1873, when James and Ellen White, Willie, and Lucinda Hall reached Denver. They were cordially received at the Walling home. Thursday and Friday they made preparation for the summer in the Rocky Mountains. To ensure comfortable beds, they arranged to have two hair mattresses made, and bought pillows. Mr. Walling came from the mountains Sabbath afternoon and found the visiting party in the city park enjoying the Sabbath rest. After the Sabbath they started out for Golden City, in the mountains (MS 8, 1873). Late Sunday afternoon they were at Walling's Mills and getting settled in the cottage that was to be their home for the summer.

Following much the same program and enjoying the same activities as they had on their previous sojourn here, including a camping trip, James regained his strength. The several months spent in Colorado had given him an opportunity to stand back and survey the cause as a whole. As he did so he wrote several articles for the *Review* proposing daring and broad steps for advance.

He had escaped the constant day-to-day pressures of Battle Creek, but his own ambition to see the work of God advance filled his mind with pressures and ideas for broadening the work. In a series of articles for the *Review*, he proposed the following:

A branch office for publishing on the Pacific Coast

A health institute on the Pacific Coast

He called for the responsible men in Battle Creek to move ahead quickly with the development of the school there and for enlarging the health institute to accommodate 300 guests. He pointed out that there was a need for two new power presses in the *Review* office and more capital with which to operate. Then he made a bold proposal:

> The General Conference should expend, before the close of 1874, the sum of $20,000 in the preparation, translation, and publication of works in the German, French, Danish, and Swedish languages. And the General Conference must extend its missions to Europe, to the Pacific, and, in fact, in all directions, as far as the calls can be supplied (*An Earnest Appeal*, p. 29).

Rested and strengthened after their four months in Colorado, the Whites looked forward happily to continuing their journey to California. There were several days of anguish trying to decide whether to attend the session or go directly to California, taking Lucinda Hall and the two Walling children with them. They decided for California.

This decision having been made, that evening, Thursday, November 6, they took the train in Denver for Cheyenne, Wyoming, presumably to catch the train the next day for San Francisco. But that night, feeling impressed that they should follow another course, James went to the front of the coach to meditate and pray. Of the experience he wrote:

> We felt a power turning our mind around, against our determined purpose, toward the General Conference to be holden in a few days in Battle Creek.
>
> In our mind we debated the probabilities of another shock of paralysis which would doubtless prove fatal, and decided that we would not count our life too dear to risk all in doing the will of God. And with this consecration, we became very happy before our train reached Cheyenne.
>
> It was then midnight, and after a few hours' sleep at the depot hotel, we laid the matter before Mrs. White, who for the first time seemed willing to risk another journey to the scene of our toils, trials, sicknesses, and sufferings. And in a few hours we were repacked, Sister Hall on her way to San Francisco to make ready for us at Santa Rosa in about ten days, as we supposed, and we ticketed and checked for Chicago. At Battle Creek we were greeted heartily, not only by our denominational friends, but by businessmen and leading citizens (RH, Dec. 30, 1873).

When the twelfth annual session of the General Conference opened on Friday morning, November 14, at 9:00, James and Ellen White were there. They stayed throughout, not continuing their journey to California until December 18.

AT HOME IN SANTA ROSA

James and Ellen arrived in San Francisco on Sunday evening, December 28. They were met the next day by J. N. Loughborough, president of the California Conference, now living in Woodland. He accompanied them to Santa Rosa, where Lucinda Hall had set up housekeeping for them in a commodious rented home.

Loughborough had called the officers of the California Conference to meet here for a two-day council. Isaac and Adelia Van Horn had traveled west with the Whites, and they joined the worker group meeting in Santa Rosa. Everyone rejoiced in the reports of the victories won in Battle Creek. James's bold proposals envisioned during the Colorado interlude would bring forth fruit.

He wrote to the *Review*, "There is good evidence that the Guiding Hand turned our course at Cheyenne, from the most desirable route to San Francisco, to the General Conference at Battle Creek" (*ibid.*).

The whole experience brought great relief and freedom to James.

During the Whites' previous stay in California—the six months when they had made the Rowland home their headquarters—they enjoyed being guests and visitors. But when they arrived in Santa Rosa in December 1873 they settled down as residents.

Ellen reported in a letter to her children: "We have plenty of house room and all the furniture we need. We are comfortably situated" (letter 8, 1874).

Their home seemed to be a center of attraction to many visitors and a place where the state conferences were held. On one occasion she reported, "We had thirty for dinner, lodged eighteen and fed them straight through. The meeting passed off very pleasantly" (letter 10, 1874).

But as the winter rains dragged on, they were hindered from riding out and visiting as they wished. But they kept busy. Loughborough reported:

> We esteem it a great privilege to have in our midst Brother and Sister White, who during the rainy season are vigorously prosecuting their writings, and are even now giving us good counsel and aid in the work here; and when spring opens, and they have the opportunity of speaking to our people in different places, as the providence of God may indicate, they are prepared to greatly help our people (*ibid.*, Feb. 24, 1874).

They followed with great interest the work that Cornell and Canright were doing. These brethren studied plans for an evangelistic thrust with the California tent, being inclined to work the smaller towns.

Years ago, before Ellen had come to California, she had been impressed that methods of evangelism in California should be different from those in the East. She had written Elder Loughborough that the people in California must be approached in the liberal spirit in which they work.

On the night of April 1 a dream was given to Ellen White. She wrote:

> I dreamed that several of the brethren in California were in council, considering the best plan for labor during the coming season. Some thought it wise to shun the large cities, and work in smaller places. My husband was earnestly urging that broader plans be laid, and more extended efforts be made, which would better compare with the character of our message.
>
> Then a young man whom I had frequently seen in my dreams came

into the council. He listened with interest to the words that were spoken, and then, speaking with deliberation and authoritative confidence, said:

"The cities and villages constitute a part of the Lord's vineyard. They must hear the messages of warning. . . . You are entertaining too limited ideas of the work for this time" (3LS, pp. 208, 209).

At the quarterly meeting that began in Bloomfield on April 24, Ellen urged the workers "not to pitch their tents in the smallest places." Writing to Edson and Emma about the meeting, she said, "We wished to know whether they would hug the shore or launch into the deep and let down their nets for a draught of fish in the deep waters. . . . San Francisco and Oakland, Santa Clara, San Jose (which is pronounced Sanas A) are large, influential cities. . . . We have a great and important work before us" (letter 23, 1874).

> The ideas of our brethren have been too narrow and the work too limited. We told them if they were not calculating to do more the present tent season than heretofore, we wished to return east and attend the camp meetings. They should not pitch their tents in the smallest places, but imitate the example of Christ. He placed Himself in the great thoroughfares of travel where people were going to and from all nations of the world, and here in a most impressive manner did He give His lessons upon important truth (*ibid.*).

Ellen White had called for something to be done "now." Her appeal set the workers on fire for God. A few days later James and Ellen were on their way to Oakland, prepared to set up headquarters there. Thursday the tent was up in the heart of the city, and that night Cornell preached on spiritualism. There was a keen interest in the subject because of spirit manifestations in the city. James White had rented the "Fountain Farm" four miles (six kilometers) from the city, and Ellen White and two young men were giving the eight-room house (letter 19h, 1874) a thorough cleaning. Friday afternoon, May 1, they moved in. Lucinda Hall and the Walling children were with them (letter 19f, 1874).

A few days later Ellen White, in a letter to Willie, described their rented residence:

> We are now getting settled in our new home four miles [six kilometers] from the city. It is rural here. There was once a very good "water cure" upon this place. The large three-story house is standing desolate, shattered and dilapidated. We live in a neat square house a few rods from this building. We have not got settled as yet, but we shall soon. This is a very pleasant place to live. There are trees and flowers; no fruit, but our neighbors have fruit in abundance, so we can purchase of them (letter 26, 1874).

THE FIRST ISSUE OF THE *SIGNS OF THE TIMES*

James White had a double interest in moving to Oakland in late April. The idea of a weekly paper published on the Pacific Coast had been conceived by James White while he was in the Rocky Mountains in the summer of 1873. He had made the proposal in an article in the *Review*, and at the General Conference session in November. Now in Oakland, in connection with the evangelistic meetings, he moved ahead in starting the journal. He did so on his own responsibility, not waiting for formal committee authorization or promise of sound financial support. He worked through May in getting the first copy of *Signs of the Times* edited, set in type, and printed. It appeared on June 4, 1874.

The paper was to be evangelistic in nature but also a means of communication among Seventh-day Adventists in the West. Now that the journal was under way, there were questions as to how it would be managed and supported. And James White envisioned something additional. If the project was to succeed, and if the church in the West was to have inexpensive literature for its use, it must have a publishing house at its command.

But how could James gain both the moral and financial support of the constituency east of the Plains? He felt he could not go east and leave the newly started journal unattended. The Whites agonized in prayer over this matter.

> While [we were] bowed before God in prayer in an upper chamber, the blessing of the Lord came upon us in such a manner that duty was made plain. It was as if an audible voice said, "Go [east] to the churches and solicit money from those whom I have made stewards of means" (MS 62, 1895).

James and Ellen had rarely been separated. Here was a crisis indeed! But now they were convinced it was the will of God for Ellen to travel east, seeking support. James wept aloud and said, "Ellen, you must go. I dare not withstand the Lord. You must go. But what shall I do without you?" (*ibid.*).

Preparations for the trip across the continent were hasty and brief:

> All that there was cooked were a few gems. I put these in a paper box, the horses were harnessed, and I was on my way for the cars. My husband said, "If I had not given my consent, I would now say it is inconsistent. I cannot have you go. I cannot be left with these terrible responsibilities" (*ibid.*).

Starting on such short notice, Ellen could not secure a berth in the sleeping car, so she had to make the trip in the chair car. This made it necessary for her to change trains both in the day and in the night. The handling of the baggage, checking it here and there, was a new experience for her.

> I had never traveled alone, but I took this long journey of eight days alone, and attended the camp meetings in the States alone until Willie White met me at Wisconsin and accompanied me.
>
> On that journey I set forth our situation, and money was raised at every meeting. I told them that California would return their loan sometime in the future, for I had been shown that prosperity would attend the work done there, that there were many souls that would be added to the church, and we should see the salvation of God (ibid.).

From one camp meeting to another Ellen White went, telling her story and appealing for support for the struggling but promising work in California. Those attending the camp meetings were overjoyed when she arrived on the grounds, and, of course, she was pressed in for full service in the speaking schedules. She thrived on it.

THE SEPARATION ENDED

The Michigan camp meeting, during which the General Conference session would be held, would open on Thursday, August 6, and the word was that James White would arrive a little after midnight on Tuesday, the fourth. Although usually retiring early, Ellen stayed up to greet him. She busied herself in writing to Edson and Emma, whom James had called to Oakland to help with the new paper. While she was writing, her eyes grew heavy and she dozed off. On hearing a familiar voice, she awakened with a start to greet her beloved husband, James. Likely he had walked the few blocks from the station to their home.

How she rejoiced that at long last they could be together again and unite their lives and their labor.

Evidently James's health had improved during his months alone in California. Throughout the 11 days of meetings he preached six times and spoke with "great power and clearness." Uriah Smith reported.

> Never, we believe, did he make better points, or present the great truths of this message with more clearness and force. The involuntary response of many hearts was Thank God for the freedom He gives His servant, and the physical strength that is granted for the ardent labors into which his truth-inspired soul is constantly leading him (RH, Aug. 18, 1874).

Of course, James White brought an encouraging report of the work on the Pacific Coast. He told of his commencing to publish *Signs of the Times*, and of his vision for a publishing house to be established soon in the West. It was his hope to return shortly with the full endorsement of the General Conference and the promise of support for what was being done there.

Among other actions taken at this General Conference was one that supported the tract enterprise and that called for drawing its interests together into a general organization to be known as the General Conference Tract and Missionary Society of Seventh-day Adventists. An action of renewed consecration also was taken, and one relating to the thrust that would shortly be made in missionary endeavor in sending J. N. Andrews to Europe as soon as practicable.

Other actions taken brought an unexpected and complete change in the life of both James and Ellen White. When the nominating committee brought in its report, James's name headed the list, calling for him to be president of the General Conference.

By what reasoning could he accept this great responsibility? He had recently refused responsibilities because of his poor health. In the *Review* that carried the report of the General Conference, he presented his reactions to the sudden changes and challenges that this action would bring to them.

1. He recognized the marked indication of providence. "We now resign all to the will of God and the choice of His dear people" (*ibid.*, Aug. 25, 1874).

2. Within the past year, in the providence of God, his health had improved greatly in body and mind. He had gained 25 pounds (nine kilograms). This, he said, was because of "the practice of continued cheerfulness and courage in God, and by ignoring Satan's dark schemes to discourage and dishearten me."

3. Then, turning more particularly to the interests in California with which he had been so closely linked, he explained:

> The General Conference has approved of what steps we have taken in establishing the press upon the Pacific, and take the responsibilities as well as the liabilities off our hands. They send Elder Butler to the California camp meeting to counsel with that conference as to the proper steps to be taken to advance the cause on the Pacific. . . . We shall ever cherish the tenderest regard for our dear people on the Pacific Coast. . . . But for the present we must heed the calls of those who have greater claims upon us (*ibid.*).

4. The greater responsibilities: Now, with others to share James's special interest in the California work—the *Signs of the Times*, a publishing house in the West, and evangelism—James would turn his attention to the needs of the church as a whole:

> the development of the denominational school
> the Health Institute
> the need of workers in new fields at home and overseas
> the organization of the General Conference Tract and Missionary Society

the publication of literature in other languages
continuing the preparation and publishing of Ellen's writings

Accepting this challenge of leadership meant drastic changes in their own plans and lifestyle. Battle Creek would now be their base of operations. But with his usual zeal James made no delay in shaping up his plans and adapting his schedules.

JAMES WHITE AGAIN IN THE SADDLE

The Whites postponed their return to California, and moved immediately. The outgoing General Conference treasurer, to whom they had rented their home in Battle Creek, vacated it, and they moved in. But they were somewhat uncertain concerning the immediate future. Ellen White felt very comfortable living in Battle Creek, but their hearts were in California.

The Eastern camp meetings were scheduled to open in Vermont on August 20, and run till September 28 in Indiana. It had been James White's hope, and that of the believers in the several states, that both he and his wife could attend. But the duties in Battle Creek were too pressing; therefore Ellen White, accompanied by Lucinda Hall, started out with the second eastern meeting at South Lancaster. There would be many times when they felt the necessity of going their separate ways and working alone.

A few weeks after attending the dedication of the school in Battle Creek on January 4, 1875, they left for California to assist in forming a publishing association and locating and putting up a publishing house.

> We were very happy to find in Oakland and San Francisco two active and well-united churches of about seventy-five members each. In our younger days Mrs. White always attended the same service with us, at which we would take turns in speaking; but the situation of things in the two cities seemed to demand that we should divide our efforts, so that we have generally occupied both stands, alternating, when not laboring in other churches.

> We have both labored at Petaluma, Napa, and Santa Clara, and Mrs. White, with our son, W. C. White, has spent one week with the church at Woodland. . . .

> Besides speaking, we have had the general care of the *Signs* office, and have written considerable for our papers. Add to this the labors of the principal duties which called us to this coast last winter (*ibid.*, Apr. 29, 1875).

BACK IN THE EAST FOR CAMP MEETINGS

After three months in California James and Ellen returned to the East.

Soon after arriving in Battle Creek to attend camp meetings, James White declared his general plan for working:

> We hope to be able to attend all the camp meetings the coming season with Mrs. White. We shall come to our brethren, not to do the work, but to help them do it in the name and strength of the Lord. We have neither strength nor disposition to labor as we have done. It is important to be in season. We have many suggestions to make, and we think it important at this early date to call the attention of the preachers of the several conferences to the fact that if duty calls them from important labor to the camp meeting, it calls them to labor at these meetings and not depend on those from abroad to do all the work (*ibid.*, Apr. 8, 1875).

The Whites did not spare themselves, but put in an active season attending camp meetings in Illinois, Iowa, Wisconsin, Minnesota, Vermont, Maine, and New York. Their participation was heavy. Often the burden of preaching was borne largely by James, Ellen, and Uriah Smith.

"To say that we are weary only faintly expresses our physical condition," remarked James on one occasion. "But we are not weary of the work," he added, "and we are filled with hope, courage, and faith" (*ibid.*, Sept. 23, 1875).

THE FOURTEENTH SESSION OF THE GENERAL CONFERENCE

As the delegates met together on August 10, 1875, they were cheered by the presence of James White back in the chair after an absence of several sessions.

The business was quite routine, but handled with dispatch. In his *Review and Herald* report of the General Conference session and the Michigan camp meeting, Uriah Smith stated:

> A greater amount of business was transacted during the seven days of this meeting than during the fourteen days of the meeting of 1874; and yet there was a fair proportion of time to devote to religious services, which were not without their interest and good results.
>
> The happy disposal of so much business was due to the energy and tact of Brother White, who took hold to lift in every direction, and whose executive ability, when his way is clear from any serious hindrances and drawbacks, is equal to the occasion (*ibid.*, Aug. 26, 1875).

Some far-reaching resolutions were passed. There were resolutions recognizing the school and its contributions; on health reform, recognizing the benefits of following its principles and calling for greater energy in the promulgation of its truths; and on the work on the Pacific Coast, urging strong support in the development of the Pacific SDA Publishing Association.

An action was taken calling for marked advance in Europe and in other parts of the world:

> *Resolved*, That we recommend the Executive Committee to take immediate steps to establish a printing office in Europe, to issue periodicals and publications in the French and German languages, and also to enter the openings presenting themselves in Great Britain, France, Germany, Holland, Italy, Hungary, Africa, and Australia (*ibid.*).

Naturally, James and Ellen White were eager to get back to their new home in Oakland and to the publishing house now in operation, stocked with the machinery and supplies purchased by James White in New York City and sent by train to Oakland. Before leaving for California, however, they attended camp meetings in Vermont, Maine, and New York.

After an absence of five months they reached Oakland on the evening of September 24 and spent the night at their own home on Eleventh Street. The carpenters had begun construction of this house when they had left in April. The next thing that attracted their attention was the office building on the same block, commenced some weeks after they had left, and brought nearly to completion about a month previously.

In an article published in both the *Signs of the Times* and the *Review and Herald*, titled "How We Found Things," James gave a glowing report:

> The appearance of this building from the outside is fine. The arrangement inside from the basement to the attic is admirable. The room in the basement is valuable. The several rooms of the two stories of the building are next to perfection in arrangement and conveniences. And there are four valuable finished rooms in the attic. In the rear of the main building and separated from it the distance of eleven feet is the brick engine house.
>
> And all will cost less than first calculated, and are much better than first expected, owing principally to the ability and faithfulness of Brother O. B. Jones, who took successful charge of our three printing houses and our college building at Battle Creek, Michigan (ST, Oct. 7, 1875).
>
> We found the Cottrell and Babcock, first-class, four-roller, air-spring, drum-cylinder printing press, and the Universal job press in the new building in complete running order, driven by the New York safety engine from Babcock and Wilcox. Only six weeks before these were doing good printing on the Pacific Coast they were lying at the freight warehouse across the continent in New York City waiting for shipment (*ibid.*).

He reported that friends of the cause in California were meeting their pledges, and it was his hope that by New Year's enough would have come in to pay for both the office building and the building site. He added:

> Our eastern brethren have come nobly up to the work of raising means to furnish the Oakland office with presses, engine, types, binders' machinery, et cetera. We have already two presses, engine, paper cutter and book trimmer, standing press, and types and material sufficient to print the *Signs*. These are all paid for at a cost, including transportation and setting up, of $6,500, and there are eastern funds on hand to purchase more material, and more pledged by our liberal eastern people to make the *Signs* office a complete book and job printing office where as good work may be done as anywhere on the continent *(ibid.)*.

LOOKING AHEAD

As James White looked ahead, it was with courage. His heart was in the publishing of the *Signs of the Times*. Addressing the readers of the journal, he declared:

> With the new year the *Signs* starts in to make its weekly visits to its patrons, and to all who may become such during the year. Its prospects of success are cheering. . . .
>
> We commence the series of articles setting forth the reasons of our faith and hope in this number, with the article on another page upon the millennium. These articles will continue in proper order quite through the year. Sketches of the life of Mrs. White will also continue, and will be very important to those who should know the facts of her remarkable experience.
>
> And we shall very soon commence a series of articles under the caption "The Matter Reversed, or Christ in the Old Testament and the Sabbath in the New." We design to thoroughly ventilate the question *(ibid.,* Jan. 6, 1876).

As White was editor of both the *Signs of the Times* and the *Review and Herald,* both journals had been replete with his editorials and articles through 1875. Ellen had made large contributions also: 14 major articles in the *Review* and 29 in the *Signs*. Both James and Ellen were enjoying good health and seemed to be at the apex of vigor and vitality. The new year held great promise.

---

[1] The four-volume Spirit of Prophecy Series was published between 1870 and 1884. In approximately 1,700 pages it expanded on the great controversy theme, which had been covered sketchily in *Spiritual Gifts,* Volumes I to IV. Later the theme was expanded in the 3,700-plus pages of the five-volume Conflict of the Ages Series.

[2] See chapter 21.

Encouraging Prospects

The clouds and cold drizzle that dampened the Bay cities of northern California on New Year's Day 1876 in no way typified the spirits of James and Ellen White, who were residing in Oakland. It was the Sabbath and a special day, a day for the edification and building up of the church, a day set apart by the General Conference Committee to be spent in prayer, fasting, and humiliation before God.

The prospects were encouraging. The *Signs of the Times* was to be published every week instead of every other week. This called for bold plans to fill its eight almost-newspaper-size pages every seven days. In his editorial column in the January 6 issue James White promised, "Our friends may depend upon the *Signs* weekly."

A well-established publishing house functioned near midcontinent in Battle Creek, Michigan.

A medical institution in Battle Creek, Michigan, which would in a few months have its tenth birthday, was now getting supplied with professional personnel.

Across the street from it was Battle Creek College, a year old and enjoying good patronage.

The outreach action of the 1874 General Conference session had been implemented, and J. N. Andrews was now pioneering the work of the church in Europe, pleading for someone to help him.

The Seventh-day Adventist Church had grown to a membership of just a little more than 10,000.

MINISTRY IN THE BAY AREA

In January, February, and March James and Ellen White ministered to the churches in the Bay area—Oakland, with 80 members, and San Francisco, with somewhat fewer.

The San Francisco church had moved ahead in building a house of worship on Laguna Street. O. B. Jones, the very capable builder whom James White had brought from Battle Creek to erect a building for the Pacific Press, was asked to construct the San Francisco house of worship. J. N. Loughborough, president of the California Conference, wrote in describing the progress in San Francisco:

This church one year since regarded it almost an impossibility to build a house of worship; but the house is now erected, and the basement rented for a sufficient sum to meet all the interest on the money it was necessary to hire to complete the house (ST, Jan. 6, 1876).

Though the Whites were fond of California, they did not intend that Oakland should be their permanent residence, for they must keep close to Battle Creek and the church's many interests there. Wrote James White:

There our first college, our Health Institute, and our main printing house are located. There is a church of more than two hundred members who regard us as their pastor, though we are from them six months at a time, and are with them only a few Sabbaths in a year. We can never have as much interest at any other point as at Battle Creek (*ibid.*, Nov. 11, 1875).

James White had in mind to return to the East soon. Important developments at headquarters summoned him as president of the General Conference to be present. An extra session of the General Conference had been appointed to convene March 31. Discussions would include the fact that the board of directors of the health reform institute in Battle Creek had decided to put up a large main building and had invited James White and O. B. Jones to direct the carrying out of these plans; the advancing cause in Europe required an office of publication; and plans needed to be laid for the camp meeting season.

James White was soon on his way. J. H. Waggoner, working on the Pacific Coast, announced:

Brother James White, president of the General Conference, left Oakland yesterday morning, the twenty-second, for Battle Creek, Michigan, to attend this conference. We are happy to say that Brother White left California in good health and with good courage. He has labored very hard here for nearly six months past under circumstances which might have discouraged one of less faith and less consecration to the cause of truth. The work of the publishing house has prospered wonderfully under his careful management (*ibid.*, Mar. 23, 1876).

When James White left for Battle Creek, Ellen remained in their Oakland home. With the help of Mary Clough, she was looking forward to making great strides in writing on the life of Christ.

Probably Ellen White never had such an opportunity to write as she did in April and May of 1876. She had good literary help in her niece Mary Clough, and the two worked together comfortably. The interests of the cause in the East that had called for James White to go to Battle Creek held him there. Although

Ellen missed James, home life became simple, and she did very little public work. She determined to make the most of this opportunity.

CAMP MEETING VERSUS WRITING AND PUBLISHING

Ever since the beginning of the annual camp meetings (see chapter 20) it was generally recognized by the leaders in the church, and by James and Ellen in particular, that there was a direct relationship between the growth of the church and the presence of James and Ellen White at these gatherings.

Two compelling personalities; two soul-stirring speakers; two staunch pillars of faith. Undoubtedly disappointment was great if either of them failed to attend. But year after year the strain was greater and the demands on their time and energy more exhausting.

To complicate the problem, each of them had personal goals they were committed to achieving. Since James had assumed the responsibilities of being president of the General Conference and also carried many other positions of leadership, to continue their usual rigorous program of attending camp meetings brought up questions of priorities. And Ellen was at this time earnestly engaged in finishing the writing of the book that would become *The Spirit of Prophecy*, volume 2, on the life of Christ, later to be incorporated into *The Desire of Ages*.

To James she wrote:

> The precious subjects open to my mind well. I trust in God and He helps me to write. I am some twenty-four pages ahead of Mary [Clough]. She does well with my copy. It will take a clear sense of duty to call me from this work to camp meetings. I mean to finish my writings on one book at any rate, before I go anywhere. I see no light in my attending camp meetings. You and I decided this before you left. . . .
>
> I have no will of mine own; I want to do God's will. At present His will is to tarry in California and make the most of my time in writing. I shall be doing more for the cause in this than in going across the plains to attend camp meetings (letter 4, 1876).

She shunned all outside responsibilities. She told James in a letter:

> I want time to have my mind calm and composed. I want to have time to meditate and pray while engaged in this work. I do not want to be wearied myself or be closely connected with our people who will divert my mind. This is a great work, and I feel like crying to God every day for His Spirit to help me to do this work all right. . . . I must do this work to the acceptance of God (letter 59, 1876).

However, when the time came for the first camp meeting of the season to open in Kansas on May 25 Ellen and Mary Clough were on the train bound for the East. Whatever work was yet to be done on the life of Christ would have to be done as they traveled. James White triumphantly placed a last-page note in the *Review* of May 25:

> We have received a telegram from Mrs. White stating that her niece, Miss M. L. Clough, and herself would meet us at the Kansas camp meeting the twenty-sixth. We shall probably go the rounds of the camp meetings for 1876, and retire from the northern climate in October, either to the South or to California.

James White was overjoyed to receive Ellen's telegram that she, with Mary Clough, would meet him at the Melvern, Kansas, camp meeting. He hastened off 20 postcards to as many points in Kansas, giving the welcome word. He had summoned J. H. Waggoner to come from California to assist him, for he felt the need of help through the camp meeting season. This he now canceled, for Ellen would be taking many of the meetings.

He assured Willie and Mary, in Oakland, that he would be on the grounds with ample preparations made, and he was, but Ellen White's train was delayed; instead of arriving on Friday, she was driven onto the grounds early Sabbath morning. She was weary after six days of travel, including a 20-mile (32-kilometer) trip by farm wagon over bad roads, a journey broken by a stop for the night at the home of a friend.

"Weary, of course," reported James White, "short of sleep, and trembling with nervous headache, she takes the speaker's stand at half past ten and is wonderfully sustained in her effort" (ST, June 8, 1876). She spoke that evening also to a congregation increasing in numbers.

At the special session of the General Conference that had been held in late March, James White had participated in laying plans that called for one meeting to follow another, week by week, usually with a parting meeting Tuesday morning. The first meeting was now in the past, but there were 13 more to attend: Missouri, Iowa, two in Wisconsin, Minnesota, Ohio, Vermont, Massachusetts, Maine, New York, Indiana, Michigan (including the General Conference session), and Illinois.

On one occasion Ellen, writing from the campground to Willie and Mary, said, "Children, I believe it was my duty to attend this meeting. I am coming out all right as far as health is concerned if I rest and do not labor too hard" (letter 30, 1876).

Another time she reported that James was so "fearfully worn" that she took the principal burden through the meeting (letter 34, 1876).

At the close of the sixth meeting in July they had a breathing spell until the series in the East would begin on August 10.

She reported in a letter:

> I have kept on the strain so long I am now finding my level and I am not very intelligent. We cannot, Father, Mary, or myself, do anything now. We are debilitated and run down like an old clock (letter 33, 1876).

After getting some rest, Ellen White picked up her work of writing on the life of Christ. It was a rugged season.

CAMP MEETINGS AGAIN

The program for the camp meetings in the East was much the same as the six already finished. The reports gave little glimpses of joyous and sometimes awkward situations, and, of course, of triumph as God blessed in the work. The late-summer meetings opened at Norwalk, Ohio. James White's older brother John, a Baptist minister, resided in Ohio, and they managed to get in a little visit en route.

> On Sunday the morning was cold and rainy, but before noon the clouds had dispersed, and fair weather smiled upon the encampment. In the afternoon, by actual count, 551 teams came through the gate of the campground, averaging four persons to each team. These, with the Sabbathkeepers upon the ground, made a congregation of 2,500 to whom Brother White spoke with great liberty on the reasons of our faith and hope (RH, Aug. 1, 1876).

Ellen White gave one evening discourse, but she was confined much of the time to their tent, and for two days to her bed. "Your father and mother are worked down," she wrote to Willie.

> We work hard. Your father does the work of three men at all these meetings. I never saw a man work so energetically, so constantly, as your father. God does give him more than mortal energy. If there is any place that is hard, your father takes it. We pray God that we may have strength to do the work necessary to be done in these special occasions (letter 39, 1876).

THE GROVELAND CAMP MEETING

For attendance, the camp meeting held at Groveland, Massachusetts, reached an all-time high. It opened Thursday, August 24, and ran for five days. The grounds, near Haverhill, some 30 miles (50 kilometers) north of Boston, were easily reached by train and river excursion boats from both Boston and Haverhill. There were 55 tents, including the three pavilions—45, 55, and 65 feet (14, 17, and 20 meters) in diameter—pitched in the beautiful grove. The weather was so fine the meetings were held under the trees, and the three large tents were used for sleeping quarters. The women occupied one, and men the other two. Five hundred camped on the grounds. The "auditorium" swept up in a natural amphitheater from the speakers' stand, the well-cleared grove affording delightful shade.

River steamers ran twice a day from Haverhill, four miles (seven kilometers) away, and every hour on Sunday. Eighteen trains ran each day, all stopping at the campground. The Sabbath meetings were well attended, but Sunday brought its surprises. Mary Clough reported:

> Sunday was a lively day on the campground. Special trains were run from the cities of Lawrence, Newburyport, Haverhill, et cetera, and at 9:00 a.m. the auditorium was filled with intelligent people to whom Elder White preached about one hour.
>
> Still the people poured in from the towns about, and the trains came loaded with their living freight. After an intermission of thirty minutes, Mrs. White ascended the platform, amid the profound stillness of that vast multitude, and addressed the people on the subject of Christian temperance. Her original and comprehensive manner of handling this subject elicited the highest commendation of all that heard.
>
> The morning trains were crowded, but the noon trains flooded the grove, and the two-thirty train from Lawrence brought fifteen cars literally packed with people, the platform and steps were full also, and the conductor was obliged to take the roof in order to signal the engineer. He reported that it would have taken twenty-five cars to bring all the people who were waiting at the depot to take passage for the campground (ST, Sept. 14, 1876).

Of the experience Ellen White wrote:

> What a scene is before me! It is estimated that twenty thousand people are assembled in this grove. The third train, of fifteen cars, has just arrived. Every seat was filled and every foot of standing room, also the platform and the steps. A sea of human heads is already before me, and still the cars are to come. This is to me the most solemn sight I ever beheld. Hundreds in carriages are driving away because they cannot get within sound of the speaker's voice (ibid.).

All standing room throughout the entire enclosure was taken, and some, like Zacchaeus, climbed trees to get sight of the speaker. The vast throng gave good attention. Ellen White, speaking slowly with a low, well-supported voice, made them hear.

When the camp meetings were over and the Whites and Mary Clough returned to Battle Creek on Wednesday, October 4, they were utterly worn and exhausted. They had succeeded, but for it they paid a price—the price human beings pay for overwork, a price paid gladly to see the cause of God prosper.

Elder Uriah Smith made this evaluation of the presence of the Whites at these camp meetings:

> Here [Sparta, Wisconsin], as in Iowa, the presence of Brother and Sister White constituted, in a large measure, the life of the meeting, their counsel and labors giving tone to the exercises and progress of the work. Sister White, especially, was at times called out in powerful appeals, and most forcible descriptions of scenes in the life of Christ from which lessons can be drawn applicable to everyday Christian experience. These were of absorbing interest to all the congregation.
>
> These servants of the church, though now of so long and large experience, and notwithstanding all their wearing labors, are still growing in mental and spiritual strength (RH, June 29, 1876).

PIONEERING IN TEXAS

One action taken at the 1878 General Conference session was a recommendation that a camp meeting be held in Texas during the autumn, when James and Ellen White could attend (RH, Oct. 24, 1878).

Tuesday afternoon, November 5, the Whites, with S. N. Haskell and Emma White, were off by train across the "Indian Territory" (Oklahoma), bound for Dallas, Texas.

AT THE MCDEARMON HOME

Of their arrival in Texas, James White reported to the readers of the *Review*:

> Wednesday [Nov. 6] we reached Dallas, dusty and weary, but glad that our journey of about one thousand miles [1600 kilometers) from Battle Creek, Michigan, to Dallas, Texas, was at an end. We tarried the night at the home of Brother Cole and family, and Thursday came to the good and comfortable home of Brother McDearmon [at Grand Prairie, west of Dallas]. Here our daughter [in-law] met her parents, brother, and sister, who have all been brought near the door of death by the fever which has prevailed in this state during the past season. Our coming was timely. They have a large house and warm hearts, but as they move about they look more like walking corpses than living men and women (*ibid.*, Nov. 21, 1878).

White declared that it would "take two of them to make a shadow." The Whites found the McDearmons destitute and ill. "We tried to help them," wrote Ellen White.

> I gave Sister McDearmon $40 from my own purse to use for the necessities of life. Father bought bags of flour, a barrel of apples, nuts, sugar, et cetera. He bought one cotton mattress and one husk [mattress] overlaid with cotton. It is seldom I have seen such destitution. I have bought several things for their comfort. Father left McDearmon his fur coat to use, for his blood is so low he cannot bear the least chilliness of the air. We have done what we could for them (letter 54, 1878).

THE PLANO CAMP MEETING

After spending a week at the McDearmon home, James and Ellen White went on north some 20 miles (32 kilometers) to Plano. The camp meeting had opened there, three miles (five kilometers) from the village, on Tuesday, November 12. About 200 believers came in for a very successful camp meeting. From Peoria, about 100 miles (160 kilometers) away, nine families came by private conveyance (MS 3, 1878).

Ellen White pictured the accommodations awaiting her and her party:

> We found a tent prepared for us with board floor, and carpeted, provided with bedsteads, tables, chairs, and stove. Nothing was wanting to make us comfortable. Our friends who had recently embraced the truth at Plano had anticipated our wants and liberally supplied them in the furnishing of our tent (ibid.).

As to the meetings, James White wrote:

> Twenty-four discourses were preached during the camp meeting. Elder Haskell was on the ground two days in advance and gave eleven discourses. Mrs. White and the writer gave six discourses each, and Elder Kilgore, one. In consequence of the distance, the rains, and deep mud, the outside attendance was small. Sunday afternoon Mrs. White gave a discourse on Christian temperance before a large congregation (RH, Dec. 5, 1878).

During the camp meeting 13 people were baptized, the Texas Conference was formed, and aggressive plans were laid for tent evangelism. It was decided to purchase two evangelistic tents, one 60 feet (18 meters) in diameter, the other 50 feet (15 meters).

The Whites elected to settle for the winter in Denison, some 60 miles

(100 kilometers) north of Dallas and not far from the Red River, which forms the boundary for the northeast part of the state. Denison was somewhat of a railroad center, situated on sandy land. Roads were fairly good and the surroundings pleasant.

In Denison the Whites were to occupy a home being built by the Bahlers. Just as soon as the plaster was dry they settled down for the winter. They had to secure furniture and furnishings, and assemble materials for their writing. It seems that Ellen White left Battle Creek in such haste that she did not have time or strength to assemble either adequate clothing for the winter or the writing materials and reference works she would need.

The requests she addressed to Willie and Mary included bedding, materials for sewing—patterns for dresses for herself and pants for James—and some food items for the table. But of top priority were materials needed for her writing.

On November 22 she stated, "We intend to commence writing at once and to make the most of our time" (letter 56, 1878).

MARIAN DAVIS JOINS THE WHITE FORCES

On New Year's Day Miss Marian Davis, who was with the *Youth's Instructor* staff in Battle Creek, joined the Whites in Texas to assist them in literary work. At the time she was not well, but she had some of the skills they badly needed. "Marian . . . is splendid help" (letter 4, 1879), Ellen White wrote Willie and Mary a few days later. Thus began a close personal and working relationship between the two women that was to continue through the next 25 years, until Marian's death in 1904. Now Ellen White was able to forge ahead with the preparation of personal testimonies.

THE HOME SITUATION

On January 6 Ellen White wrote to Edson of the home situation:

> Father is well, cheerful, and happy. Very kind and tender of me and my comfort. He is very active (letter 3a, 1879).

A week later she exclaimed, "I do not know as we ever enjoyed the society of each other as we do now" (letter 5a, 1879). Near the close of winter, she wrote feelingly to William and Mary:

> [Father] is in a good state of mind, willing to be counseled and advised. He is not so determined and set to carry out his ideas. We have had as pleasant and harmonious a winter as we have ever enjoyed in our lives (letter 18, 1879).

OUTREACH IN MISSIONARY ENDEAVOR

As the weather mellowed, and it did quickly, James and Ellen White were eager to engage in local evangelistic ministry. On weekends they held meetings in nearby communities. On Thursday, February 13, they were off for Dallas, 75 miles (120 kilometers) by carriage. Writing of this to Willie, James described one missionary facet of the trip:

> Brother [Arthur] Daniells takes my carriage with trunk, and [he plans] to sell and canvass in cities and villages by the way. He will take a fine pair of mules for which I paid $180. . . . We shall be gone about a week (JW to WCW, Feb. 12, 1879).

The 21-year-old Arthur G. Daniells was in Texas at his own expense, assisting R. M. Kilgore in tent evangelism. He had been lent to James White to assist him as a secretary. Daniells' wife, Mary, was brought into the White home in Denison as cook. Thus began a long personal and professional relationship between the president of the General Conference, the messenger of the Lord, and a young man who in time would himself serve as leader of the church for 21 years.

When James and Ellen White went to Texas, their general long-range plans were to remain there for the winter, then in early May travel to Colorado, where they might spend a few weeks (RH, Nov. 21, 1878). But their plans fluctuated. Ever in search of a place where he could lay off the stress of leadership and write without interruptions, and where there could be an improvement of health, James White turned first in one direction and then in another. Forgetful of good resolutions to temper his schedule, he would get caught up in the stimulus of the work of the church, which he had nurtured since its inception. He had a clear long-range vision, shared by only a few, of the great days the church was entering upon, and had a natural urge to stand in the lead.

He was the president of the General Conference and was one of those who served on the General Conference Committee. He also was president of several auxiliary organizations—publishing, medical, and educational—and was chief editor of both the *Review and Herald* and the *Signs of the Times*. While such responsibility was exhilarating, it also was enervating. Repeatedly he saw that in the interests of his own survival he must withdraw from the forefront of the battle.

TEXAS, A NEEDY FIELD OF LABOR

In writing of their mid-February visit to Dallas, Ellen White disclosed their hopes and plans:

> Yesterday we bore pointed testimony to the church in Dallas upon

the subject of health reform. My husband spoke from the text "Preach the Word." The Spirit of the Lord was in our midst, softening hearts and breaking up the fallow ground. Many testimonies were borne, and the church encouraged.

We now expect to commence labor here with a tent in about two weeks. We shall also hold meetings in Denison and vicinity. Angels of God are at work impressing souls everywhere, and we want to be at work doing all we can for the Master (ST, Mar. 6, 1879).

One thing that was clear to the Whites was that some Adventist families in the Dallas area, especially the McDearmons, should, for the sake of their very survival, move to a more healthful climate. To James White Colorado seemed to be just the place.

As plans were discussed, the interested families increased in number until between 20 and 30 church members were ready to join a minor exodus from northern Texas. James White would lead this expedition. The early-March trip from Dallas to Denison was a sort of trial run. Ellen White described the two-day trip:

We left Dallas last Wednesday morning [March 19] with two heavy wagons, loaded, two two-seated wagons called "hacks," and our phaeton, Brother McDearmon and family and goods. We were moving to Denison. We had our large family tent and pitched it and for two nights occupied it. Fifteen composed our caravan: Elder Kilgore and his brother Scott; Brother and Sister McDearmon—their two children, Hattie and Joseph—their niece Nettie Cole, and grandson Homer Salisbury, Brother Moore and his son Willie, Brother and Sister Daniells, Sister [Marian] Davis, Brother and Sister White.

We found that Brother and Sister McDearmon and family endured the journey much better than they feared. They will go through with the company to Colorado. I believe that they will enjoy good health there. We arrived at home in Denison before the Sabbath and were well arranged before sundown (letter 45, 1879).

To provide transportation for some of the families that had been reduced to poverty, James White bought or traded teams of horses and mules, upgrading them step by step. He figured these could be used to travel to Colorado, and then when the caravan reached Walling's Mills, near Boulder, could be sold at a profit.

TRIP BY CARAVAN

"We have started on our journey to Colorado." From their camp James White wrote to children William and Mary; they were midway between

Denison and the Red River, which separated Texas from the Indian Territory (Oklahoma). It was Sabbath, April 26, and the campers had been reading the *Review, Good Health,* and the *Youth's Instructor.*

Rains had delayed their getting off, and now the river was so high they would have to wait for the ferry.

Concerning the same camp Ellen White wrote in her diary:

> We remained until [Wednesday] April 30 in a waiting position, for the sick to be able to travel [W. H. Moore, from food poisoning, having eaten some partly decomposed bear meat, and James Cornell; Moore was desperately ill, and even when he was well enough to travel at all, did so for many days on a mattress in one of the covered wagons] and the ferry so that we could cross. We then started on our way with eight covered wagons and one covered spring wagon with two seats. Thirty composed our party. About noon we crossed the ferry with special instruction to drive quickly as soon as off the boat because of danger through quicksands (MS 4, 1879).
>
> We were having our first experience of overland journeying in transporting our sick and those too poor to pay car [railway] expenses, but the Lord cared for us *(ibid.)*.

The caravan pushed north into Indian Territory for five miles (eight kilometers). As night came on they made camp in the open prairie. Besides the covered wagons, their equipment included three tents, two cookstoves, and a sheet-iron camp stove.

The precautions they took were in line with those generally followed in like circumstances. The wagons were placed in a circle surrounding the horses and mules. Two men carrying guns stood guard in two-hour shifts.

Tents were pitched, but before they were fully prepared a severe storm struck. Ellen White described the experience in a letter to the children in Battle Creek:

> Before the tent was trenched, the beds were made on the ground and on the bedstead. When the storm struck us we were found unprepared and in ten minutes there were several inches of water in the tent. We got the two girls up and placed the bed and bedding on our own bedstead, and such a mess as we were in.
>
> After a time we decided, all four of us—Marian [Davis], Adelia Cole, Etta Bears, and myself—to sleep crossways on the bed and [that] Father [would] lodge with the doctor in the wagon, Corliss in our carriage. Thus we returned to rest. . . . The next night we lodged the same way (letter 20a, 1879).

Sunday morning they were on their way again. As they camped for the night at a place referred to as Stone Wall, she reported to the children at Battle Creek:

> We have reached thus far on our journey to Colorado. We have traveled four days. Rested yesterday. Spoke under our tent to our party of thirty-one. Was very free in speaking. Today we picked nearly a quart of strawberries. I have just gathered a large bundle of greens to cook for our breakfast. While Father is buying water buckets and cornmeal, I am writing.
>
> Father rides horseback a considerable part of the time. He is enjoying the journey much. . . .We are in sight of a meetinghouse. We are now being urged to speak in the Indian Territory. We shall ride out, camp, and then return to meet with the people. We will thus work our way along, preaching as we go. I will finish this tomorrow morning. . . . Last night I spoke to one hundred people assembled in a respectable meetinghouse. We find here an excellent class of people. . . .
>
> I had great freedom in presenting before them the love of God evidenced to man in the gift of His Son. All listened with the deepest interest. The Baptist minister arose and said we had heard the gospel that night and he hoped all would heed the words spoken (letter 36, 1879).

James White also spoke a short time, and the Whites were urged to remain and hold more meetings, but this could not be, for they needed to press on. It was a mile and a half (two and a half kilometers) back to the camp, but the success of the meeting warmed their hearts.

THE CARAVAN DIVIDES

At some point as they journeyed north, the Whites, accompanied by eight or 10 of the group, broke away from the caravan to hasten on to the camp meeting they had promised to attend in Emporia, Kansas; the rest turned west en route to Boulder.

While James White reveled in the venture, Ellen did not. She and Marian carried the burden of housekeeping and of providing the meals for their part of the traveling group. Marian often worked late in the night with inconvenient camping equipment. There was another point that perplexed Ellen White—was all this necessary and in the line of duty? She wrote to the children in Battle Creek, no doubt with some hyperbole:

> I had rather attend twenty camp meetings with all their wear, knowing I was doing good to souls, than to be here traveling through the country. The scenery is beautiful, the changes and variety enjoyable; but I have so many fears that I am not in the line of my duty. Oh, when will

this fearful perplexity end? . . . God hangs a mist over my eyes (letter 20a, 1879).

STILL ON THE CARAVAN TRAIL

The group heading for the camp meeting at Emporia, Kansas, reached Okmulgee, Indian Territory, on Friday, May 9. They had logged 160 miles (256 kilometers) since leaving Denison, and were 200 miles (320 kilometers) from Emporia. That evening James White was invited to speak in the Indian council house; Ellen White addressed the people the following evening (JW to WCW, May 10, 1879).

James White outlined his plans:

Here we shall take in some supplies. We shall not go to Coffeyville [Kansas], but keep up to Newton with the teams, then Elder Corliss, mother, and I will take the cars east to Emporia. Then at the close of the meetings we will take the cars west to meet the train [caravan bound for Colorado] (*ibid.*, May 11, 1879).

ON TO EMPORIA

By the third Sabbath on their trek the Whites had reached southeastern Kansas, and Ellen White spoke Sabbath afternoon and evening in a schoolhouse close to where they camped. The meetings were well attended, and she pressed home the subject of temperance and the necessity of self-denial and self-sacrifice in order to preserve physical, mental, and moral health. "I had special freedom in speaking to the people," she noted in her diary. "The Lord indeed gave me His Spirit and power in speaking the truth, and all seemed interested" (MS 4, 1879).

Sunday night there was a downpour, but since their tent was "staked and thoroughly ditched," they kept dry. The next morning the women in the party washed their clothes in the trenches about the tents. In her diary, Ellen wrote:

It is a beautiful morning. The sun is shining and all in camp are astir for breakfast, while some are packing the wagons for another move.

We are on the way again, slowly making our way over the broad prairies of Kansas. At nine o'clock we turned out to let the horses feed on grass. At noon we all drew up upon the broad prairie to take our dinner. . . . Teams are now being prepared for another move, while Marian and I, Adelia and Etta, are gathering up, washing the dishes, and putting the food in baskets. The order comes, "Move on." In one hour and a half we shall be at Brother Glover's (*ibid*).

James White had called for the Kansas camp meeting to be postponed for a week beyond the time first announced in the *Review*, but the Glovers had not received the word, hence had already left for Emporia. This led to a rapid change in plans. With less than an hour's time, the Whites took their two trunks and without changing from their camping attire, caught the train for Emporia, leaving the rest of the party to continue the journey with the wagons. Ellen White recorded in her diary the story of arriving in Emporia and driving onto the campground Tuesday morning "in style" (letter 20, 1879):

> We arrived at Emporia about seven o'clock [in the morning]. We engaged an omnibus to take us to the campground, about two miles (three kilometers). Four powerful horses were put before the bus and we were carried speedily to camp. All seemed glad to meet us. We pitched our tent and one and another brought us a piece of bedding, so we had a passable comfortable bed (MS 4, 1879).

At the end of the caravan experience Ellen reported to their children:

> I have just read your letters and cried like a child. . . . I suppose I was babyish, but I have been sick the entire journey. Lost twelve pounds (six kilograms). No rest, not a bit of it, for poor Marian and me. We have worked like slaves. We cooked repeatedly half the night. Marian, the entire night. . . .
>
> I have spoken every Sabbath to our camp because no one else seemed to feel the burden, and every Sabbath evening or Sunday in towns and villages. I am worn and feel as though I was about 100 years old. . . . My ambition is gone; my strength is gone, but this will not last. . . .
>
> I hope that by the cheering light of the countenance of my Saviour, I shall have the springback power. . . . I have not had even time to keep a diary or write a letter. Unpack and pack, hurry, cook, set table, has been the order of the day. . . . Marian astonishes us all. She is really forgetting herself and is efficient help. What I could have done unless she had taken the burden is more than I can tell (letter 20, 1879).

Writing to the children on the same day, James White reported that his health was the best it had been in four years (JW to WCW, May 20, 1879).

THE KANSAS CAMP MEETING

The camp meeting opened on Thursday, May 22, and was attended by about 300 believers (MS 5, 1879), some 30 of whom drove 200 miles (320 kilometers) in their wagons to attend. That day the wagons in the White caravan also drove onto the grounds. The weather was good, and there was a reasonably good attendance of the citizens of Emporia. Ellen White began her ministry the first day, joining her husband and J. O. Corliss. At the request of the General Conference, G. I. Butler was there, and on Friday reinforcements were present from Battle Creek. W. C. White was there in the interests of the Sabbath school work being developed in the state conferences, and Dr. J. H. Kellogg came, representing the health and temperance work and to assist in organizing a Health and Temperance Society in Kansas.

THE HEALTH AND TEMPERANCE SOCIETY

The American Health and Temperance Association had been formed in Battle Creek in January, with the intention of drawing Seventh-day Adventists together in an effective organization promoting both health and temperance. The Kansas camp meeting offered the first opportunity to launch the program in the field.

James and Ellen White had vowed to avoid camp meetings, but having attended two, they now had the camp meeting fever in their systems. They postponed their trip to Colorado and left to others the business of disposing of the teams of horses, mules, and ponies in Colorado. To James White it was an easy and quick switch, and to Ellen White the end of a perplexing experience.

Wednesday afternoon, June 4, 1879, James and Ellen White lighted from the train in Battle Creek, having made the trip overnight from Missouri. The note in the *Review* announcing their arrival remarked on the good degree of health and strength James White evidenced. He spoke in the tabernacle at the commencement of the Sabbath, June 6, and again Sabbath morning and afternoon.

Sunday evening both James and Ellen White spoke to a large congregation at a temperance rally in the tabernacle, and the "teetotal pledge" was circulated and signed. On Wednesday evening they held another temperance meeting. The next morning they were off for camp meetings in the West (RH, June 19, 1879). These included meetings in Wisconsin, Minnesota, Iowa, and Dakota. The latter, their sixth camp meeting of the season, was followed with the long-looked-forward-to break, a quick visit to the nearby mountains of Colorado. This gave opportunity for nearly four weeks' change.

HOME AGAIN IN BATTLE CREEK

James White had decided that he and his wife would attend but one camp meeting in 1879, for he expected that they would devote their time to writing while staying in their little cabin on "Whites' Ranch" in the mountains of Colorado. As it turned out, they attended more than 10 such gatherings. The adjusted summer program allowed them but a few days in their newly acquired Colorado home. Now back in Battle Creek at the close of the camp meeting season, James White in early October reviewed the situation and reported: "In many respects Mrs. White's general health is in advance of what it was a year ago, and the writer is able to report better health than for several years. God is good" (*ibid.*, Oct. 9, 1879).

TIME OF MELLOWING

As the work proliferated, Ellen and James faced the problem of where they should most profitably devote their time and add their presence. They could not be in Battle Creek and California at the same time. They could not be in New England and pioneer the work in Texas and Kansas. No wonder Ellen on their caravan trip questioned, "Was all this necessary and in the line of duty?" And no wonder James inquired again and again, "Where are the men to do the work?"

They had not been in the West since 1878. Now reports were coming from California that since Loughborough had been assigned to the newly opened work in England proper provision had not been made for the growing work in the West. Help was needed. It was thought advisable to send S. N. Haskell and W. C. White to spend a few months in California.

Two weeks later these men, accompanied by Ellen White, were on their way to California.

James remained in the East to care for the many administrative duties he had willingly accepted at the General Conference session, to pastor the church and to push ahead with such publishing interests as the issuance of *Life Sketches of James and Ellen White.*

After her arrival in Oakland, Ellen threw herself into the program of strengthening the church. She spoke that first Sabbath in the Oakland church, and the San Francisco members were invited to attend.

Two camp meetings were planned for late spring in the North Pacific Conference, which comprised the state of Oregon and the Washington Territory. The first was to be east of the Cascade Mountains at Milton, May 20 to 31; the second, west of the mountains, June 9 to 15, in the vicinity of Salem. "Mrs. E. G. White will be present at both our camp meetings," read the notice in the April 22 issue of the *Signs of the Times.* "It will be a most favorable opportunity for all our brethren and sisters to become acquainted with her, and receive the valuable instruction she is able to give." After wrestling with the matter of the proposed trip for some days, she wrote to James:

> If the Lord places the burden on me, I must go however unpleasant
> I may regard the matter. I do not want to move one step farther than the

Lord shall direct by His Holy Spirit. I fear sometimes it is a cowardly dread of the water that makes me not decide at once to go to Oregon. But I mean not to study my will but the will of God. . . . Oh, I tremble for myself, lest after I have preached to others, "I myself should be a castaway" (letter 22, 1880).

The Lord did place the burden on her. Three days later she wrote: "I shall go to Oregon the sixth of May—shall remain two months unless I see more clear light" (letter 24, 1880). She made the trip, accompanied by Mary White and S. N. Haskell. They sailed from San Francisco on the steamer *California*, Thursday, May 6, arriving at Portland Sunday morning, May 9 (ST, May 13, 1880). Then they hastened on up the Columbia River to eastern Oregon and Walla Walla. For a few days she and Haskell held meetings there, speaking Sabbath and Sunday, May 15 and 16. She also spoke in Walla Walla on three nights. Other meetings followed—one at Milton, Oregon, and another at Salem. Haskell then returned to California. Ellen and Mary left a few days later. Between meetings she was busy writing.

RETURN TO BATTLE CREEK (1880)

For several weeks Ellen White ministered in northern California, speaking several times in the tent in Chico. In her mind she debated as to whether she should remain in California or return East to attend the later camp meetings. Then she received a letter from James, written July 21:

> My dear wife, the enclosed is a sample of the appeals that are coming to me for you to attend our camp meeting. Such appeals are coming to me from Maine to Dakota, and from Michigan to Kentucky. I have nothing to say, only that it seems to me that our testimony was never needed so much in the wide field as at the present time.

From Oakland she responded by telegram that she expected to be in Battle Creek August 4. That would be on a Wednesday (RH, July 29, 1880).

With Lucinda Hall she took the train for the trip east on Monday, July 26. Traveling by "slow train"—it cost less—they were nine days on the way, arriving Wednesday noon (ST, Aug. 26, 1880). Then at 8:00 she, with her husband, caught the train for a two-hour trip to Jackson. They spent the night at the Palmer home and the next morning were on the train for Alma in central Michigan, arriving just before dark. Both immediately entered into the usual arduous camp meeting labor, Ellen speaking the night they arrived.

THE EASTERN CAMP MEETINGS

The next trip took them to the province of Quebec, Canada, where at

Magog a camp meeting opened on Thursday, August 12. They did not arrive till Friday evening. James reported the grounds good, the weather fine, and non-Adventist attendance large and orderly (*ibid.*, Sept. 2, 1880). About 2,000 heard Ellen's address on temperance Sunday afternoon. On Tuesday, the last day of the meeting, with 100 believers present, Elder White led out in organizing "The Seventh-day Adventist Conference of the Province of Quebec."

JAMES'S LAST YEAR

On August 15, 1880, while at the Magog camp meeting in Quebec, James wrote an item for the *Review*:

> The past fifteen years of our life have been marked with labor, care, and periods of illness and despondency. But God has been gracious. When we have fallen under affliction, His hand has lifted us up. When we have erred in our efforts to advance the cause of truth, the Lord has corrected in love and has reached down His arm to point the way and to sustain. God is good. Christ is worthy of all praise. We are unworthy of the care, love, and mercy of the Lord during the past fifteen years, which enables us to say, to the praise of God, August 15, 1880, we are free from pain and feebleness, and have been able to do as much work during the last as at any year of our life.

James did not know it, but he was entering the last year of his life. He was almost 59; Ellen was 52.

It was a time of mellowing for James, but not always at an even pace. He sensed that he must lay off the burdens of leadership. His sometimes erratic movements and statements, and the light given to Ellen in vision, as well as her own judgment, indicated clearly that the time had come. And he really tried.

Through the rest of August and September James and Ellen went from camp meeting to camp meeting, spending three to five days at each, but always including Sabbath and Sunday: Waterville, Maine; West Boylston, Massachusetts; Morrisville, Vermont; Hornellsville, New York; Clyde, Ohio; Rochester, Indiana (attended by E. G. White only); and the national camp meeting at Battle Creek, Michigan, October 2 and 9.

Although James was theoretically in agreement with the idea that he should step aside and let others carry the burden of leadership in the church, it was not easy for him to stand back and have no say in what should be done and how. He was distressed when he saw moves made in administrative lines that he felt could result in failure or would injure the cause.

As the time neared for the General Conference session with its election of officers and committees, the White household experienced some tense moments. James was trying to divest himself of responsibilities. Before the session opened, Ellen reported to the children in California, "Father has already sent in his resignation of every office except in connection with the publishing work. I think there will be no disagreeable issue" (letter 42, 1880).

The national camp meeting opened on September 28. The first meeting of the General Conference session was held on Wednesday afternoon, October 6.

As president of the General Conference, James White was in the chair. Twenty delegates were present, and by vote of the conference their number was increased to 38 by drawing in from those present several from conferences who had limited delegations. The appropriate committees were appointed.

Monday morning, October 11, the nominating committee reported with the following recommendations:

> For president, George I. Butler
> For secretary, Uriah Smith
> For treasurer, Mrs. M. J. Chapman
> For Conference Committee,
>   G. I. Butler, S. N. Haskell, and H. W. Kellogg

James White, serving as chairman of the meeting, called for the vote. "The nominees were . . . unanimously elected" (RH, Oct. 14, 1880).

Now James and Ellen turned their thoughts to the future. On Wednesday, October 14, she wrote:

> We are now deciding to spend this winter and next summer in preparing books. First I get articles prepared for *Signs*. 2. I get out articles for private testimony, health institutions. 3. Get out Testimony No. 30. 4. Letters to her children by a mother. 5. [*Spirit of Prophecy*] Volume 4. 6. Life of Christ, both books, the most sharp and interesting matter in one large book for canvassers to use for public sale (letter 43, 1880).

They instituted an immediate search for a place to make their home for the year before them. A three-acre (one-hectare) property in Grand Ledge was available but it did not suit. The house was run down. They finally settled on a three-story well-built brick home on a 30-acre (12-hectare) tract of land between the city of Battle Creek and Goguac Lake, a mile (two kilometers) from the city. It stood on a prominence overlooking Battle Creek, and on it was a young orchard of 225 trees—apples, pears, peaches, and cherries (JW to WCW, Nov. 3, 1880)—and an attractive 10-acre (four-hectare) oak grove. The 10-year-old house, explained Ellen, had "all the advantages of a country residence," and it could be secured for $6,000.

They moved in on Sunday, December 19. Observing that it would soon be

Christmas, Ellen noted in a letter to a friend: "My Christmas will be spent in seeking Jesus to be a welcome guest in my heart. His presence will drive all the shadows away" (letter 51, 1880).

James buried himself in writing and in doing chores on the little farm and about the new home. He was still editor of the *Review and Herald,* and this kept the way open for him to speak to the church each week in reports and editorials. But why, he pondered and fretted, didn't the members of the General Conference consult with him, and why didn't Willie, in Oakland?

Moving more in a pastoral role, James White frequently spoke in the tabernacle. Occasionally he baptized new converts and performed marriages. Among the latter was the marriage of the man to become widely known for his cornflakes, W. K. Kellogg, marrying Ella Davis. She was a sister to Marian, who assisted Ellen White in her literary work.

But plans for the winter's work were rudely broken on New Year's Day. Going by sleigh to a vesper meeting in the tabernacle, Ellen fell, tearing loose the ligaments in one ankle.

For more than four months she was on crutches and was quite miserable, her pen largely laid aside. She did fill a speaking appointment at the tabernacle on Sabbath morning, January 15. Two months later she resumed her public ministry, with services in the tabernacle and outlying churches (RH, Jan. 18, Apr. 5, Apr. 12, 1881).

James found satisfaction in visiting and mingling with the members. These loved and respected him, and were less concerned about his sometimes erratic movements than were the leaders in Battle Creek. With the aid of her nieces, Addie and May Walling, Ellen kept house in the big brick home and did a little writing. On a few occasions, as her ankle recovered from the accident, she accompanied her husband on his visits to nearby churches and to one or two weekend tent meetings (RH, June 7, 1881).

When the camp meeting season opened, James gave out word through the *Review* (May 24, 1881) that "Mrs. White is not in a condition of health to go the rounds of camp meetings as in years past."

But in spite of her physical weakness and injured ankle she attempted to attend the Michigan camp meeting, which began June 1 at Spring Arbor. Arriving on the grounds she felt pressed for breath and too ill to go on, so stopped with an Adventist family near the campgound. Early Sabbath morning James went to the grounds alone. Of her experience that day she wrote Willie and Mary in Oakland:

> I knelt with Brother Weed's family and felt that God indited prayer. I
> importuned the Lord for help, for light, for strength to bear my testimony

to the people of God. Light came. I went upon the ground and spoke to a large congregation with great power and clearness. I endured the effort. Sunday I spoke in the afternoon upon temperance and was so much encouraged that I left appointment for evening and spoke in the evening (letter 5a, 1881).

James reported that at that evening meeting his wife addressed the people, "with clearness, point, and power, probably equal to any effort of her life" (RH, June 7, 1881). Tuesday morning the deep impression came to her distinctly, "Go to Iowa; I have work for you to do." The Iowa camp meeting would open on Thursday. "I should as soon have thought of going to Europe," she commented, "but I told your father my convictions, that I should go with him or alone. He seemed surprised and said, 'We will go'" (letter 5a, 1881).

The camp meeting was to be held at Des Moines, opening Thursday, June 9. James and Ellen arrived about noon on Friday. A heavy rainstorm came up, calling for extra effort on her part to make the people hear. Following the meeting she went to her tent and retired early for the night. But "in one hour, a message came for me to repair to the tent and speak to some points introduced in their business meetings, upon the right of voting in favor of prohibition. I dressed and spoke to them about twenty minutes, and then returned to the tent" (letter 5a, 1881).

GUIDANCE REGARDING VOTING

She related a dream in which she seemed to be in a large gathering where the temperance movement was being discussed. A fine-looking man with pen in hand was circulating a temperance pledge, but no one would sign. As the visitor was leaving, he turned and said:

> God designs to help the people in a great movement on this subject. He also designed that you, as a people, should be the head and not the tail in the movement; but now the position you have taken will place you at the tail (in DF 274, "The Des Moines, Iowa, Temperance Experience").

When Ellen was asked, "Should we vote on prohibition?" she answered, "Yes, to a man, everywhere, and perhaps I shall shock some of you if I say, 'If necessary, vote on the Sabbath day for prohibition if you cannot at any other time'" (ibid.).

From Iowa James and Ellen White went to the Wisconsin camp meeting. It was their plan to attend the Minnesota meeting also, but division of feelings between Butler and Haskell on the one hand and James White on the other led the Whites to withdraw and hasten back from Wisconsin to Battle Creek. It had been Ellen's hope that as she and James attended these camp meetings there could be a reconciliation.

There was another matter that also gave her deep concern. The two leading men in the General Conference were doing little to exert a right influence on the sanitarium, which she mentioned as being "managed by one man's mind and one man's judgment" and that man veering from the "light God has given" (letter 8, 1881). Taking the several situations into account, she wrote Butler and Haskell expressing her distress and concern:

> I had a dream. I saw Dr. Kellogg in close conversation with men and with ministers. He adroitly would make statements born of suspicion and imagination to draw them out, and then would gain expression from them, while I saw him clap his hands over something very eagerly. I felt a pang of anguish at heart as I saw this going on.
>
> I saw in my dream yourself [probably Haskell] and Elder Butler in conversation with him. You made statements to him which he seemed to grasp with avidity, and close his hand over something in it. I then saw him go to his room, and there upon the floor was a pile of stones systematically laid up, stone upon stone. He placed the additional stones on the pile and counted them up. Every stone had a name—some report gathered up—and every stone was numbered.
>
> The young man who often instructs me came and looked upon the pile of stones with grief and indignation, and inquired what he had and what he purposed to do with them. The doctor looked up with a sharp, gratified laugh. "These are the mistakes of Elder White. I am going to stone him with them, stone him to death."
>
> The young man said, "You are bringing back the stoning system, are you? You are worse than the ancient Pharisees. Who gave you this work to do? The Lord raised you up, the Lord entrusted you with a special work. The Lord has sustained you in a most remarkable manner, but it was not for you to degrade your powers for this kind of work. Satan is an accuser of the brethren."
>
> I thought the doctor seemed very defiant and determined. Said he, "Elder White is trying to tear us to pieces. He is working against us, and to save our reputation and life we must work against him. I shall use every stone to the last pebble here upon this floor to kill him. This is only self-defense, a disagreeable necessity."
>
> And then said the young man solemnly, "What have you gained? Have you in the act righted your wrongs? Have you opened your heart to Jesus Christ, and does He sit there enthroned? Who occupies the citadel

of the soul under this administration of the stoning system?" . . .

I then saw my husband engaged in a similar work, gathering stones, making a pile and ready to begin the stoning system. Similar words were repeated to him with additional injunctions, and I awoke (MS 2, 1880).

Through late June and into July, James and Ellen continued their ministry in Battle Creek—James through his editorials and back-page notes in the *Review*, Ellen with her writing; the two united in efforts in the Battle Creek Tabernacle church. Often they repaired to the grove near their home for seasons of prayer. One particular occasion Ellen especially remembered:

> While walking to the usual place for prayer, he [James] stopped abruptly; his face was very pale, and he said, "A deep solemnity is upon my spirit. I am not discouraged, but I feel that some change is about to take place in affairs that concern myself and you. What if you should not live? Oh, this cannot be! God has a work for you to do. . . . It continues so long that I feel much anxiety as to the result. I feel a sense of danger, and with it comes an unutterable longing for the special blessing of God, an assurance that all my sins are washed away by the blood of Christ.

Both James and Ellen had an overwhelming burden for the Battle Creek church.

Continuing, with tears in his eyes, James expressed his anxiety for the institutions in Battle Creek. He said:

> My life has been given to the upbuilding of these institutions. It seems like death to leave them. They are as my children, and I cannot separate my interest from them. These institutions are the Lord's instrumentalities to do a specific work. Satan seeks to hinder and defeat every means by which the Lord is working for the salvation of men. If the great adversary can mold these institutions according to the world's standard, his object is gained. It is my greatest anxiety to have the right men in the right place. If those who stand in responsible positions are weak in moral power, and vacillating in principle, inclined to lead toward the world, there are enough who will be led. Evil influences must not prevail. I would rather die than live to see these institutions mismanaged, or turned aside from the purpose for which they were brought into existence (*In Memoriam*, p. 45).

Uriah Smith, resident editor of the *Review and Herald* and James's closest associate in the work of the church, had labored at his side for nearly three decades. Smith was well aware of the bruising conflicts; indeed, they had been out in the open for a year or two. He viewed the situation in the light of White's total dedication to the cause of God. Understandingly he declared:

> Some have thought that he was deficient in social qualities, and sometimes rigid, harsh, and unjust, even toward his best friends. But these feelings, we are persuaded, come from a failure to comprehend one of the strongest traits in his character, which was his preeminent love for the cause in which he was engaged. To that he subordinated all else; for that he was willing to renounce home and friends.
>
> No man would have been more glad than he to enjoy continuously the pleasures of domestic and social life, and the intercourse of friends, had he not thought that integrity to the cause called him to take a different course (*ibid.*, pp. 34, 35).

THE CARRIAGE TRIP TO CHARLOTTE

An invitation to spend the weekend at Charlotte, 30 miles (50 kilometers) northeast of Battle Creek, had come to the Whites. A. O. Burrill was holding evangelistic tent meetings there. James was glad that he had given word that he and his wife would drive over, for it would provide her the change and rest she needed. The weekend activities were like a camp meeting. James spoke three times and Ellen four. Many from the community attended the meetings. There was none of the strain of the preceding week in Battle Creek, and Ellen claimed she gained some rest (RH, July 26, 1881; letter 8a, 1881). Not long after this carriage trip she recalled their conversation as they drove through the countryside:

> My husband seemed cheerful, yet a feeling of solemnity rested upon him. He repeatedly praised the Lord for mercies and blessings received, and freely expressed his own feelings concerning the past and the future: ... "The future seems cloudy and uncertain, but the Lord would not have us distressed over these things. When trouble comes, He will give us grace to endure it. What the Lord has been to us, and what He has done for us, should make us so grateful that we would never murmur or complain" (MS 6, 1881).

Returning to their comfortable Battle Creek home on Wednesday, July 27, they picked up their tasks there. One of the first things Ellen did was to write to the children in California of the experience of the past two weeks and of the meeting she and James had with Dr. Kellogg. "I have been alarmed at the state of things," she wrote, but was glad to add:

> I think Father views matter in a different light. In some things I

think he is striving hard for the Spirit of God. He seems more humble, more guarded in words and actions. He has a hard battle before him. I shall help him all I can. . . .

As the new week dawned they were looking forward to more labor in the field. The *Review* of August 2 carried the following back-page note signed by both James and Ellen:

The Eastern Camp Meetings: We have been urged to attend the camp meetings to be holden at Magog, P. Q. [Province of Quebec], Morrisville, Vermont, and Waterville, Maine. We shall attend these meetings, and others, as the providence of God opens the way for us, and we have health and strength to labor.

But James and Ellen were not at these meetings. Instead, the next issue of the *Review* carried the notice of James White's death.

THE TIRED WARRIOR AT REST

On Sabbath morning, July 30, 1881, three days after the carriage trip to Charlotte, James and Ellen walked to the grove where they often prayed together. James prayed most fervently three times. He seemed to be reluctant to cease pleading with God for special guidance and blessing.

Then they went to the tabernacle, and James opened the service with singing and prayer. This would be the last time he would stand beside Ellen in the pulpit. Later Ellen recounted:

Monday he had a severe chill. Tuesday he did not rally as expected, but we thought the disease an attack of fever and ague [malaria], and supposed that it would soon yield to treatment (MS 6, 1881).

About 4:00 p.m. a message was sent to Dr. J. H. Kellogg requesting him to call on James at his home. The doctor went over immediately and found him suffering with a high fever, his pulse being 112 and his temperature 103¼° F (40° C). The doctor learned that about 10:00 a.m. of the same day James had suffered with a very severe congestive chill. At this time his head was greatly congested, and he complained of severe pain in the spine, extending into the lower limbs. He seemed to be greatly prostrated and was very restless.

Tuesday night Ellen also was attacked with chills and was very sick, being unable to sit up.

On Wednesday when Dr. Kellogg came over he proposed that they both be removed to the sanitarium where they could be given better treatment. A mattress was placed in a hack, James and Ellen were laid side by side (for the last time), and thus they were taken to the sanitarium.

Treatment to relieve James's fever and pain was immediately ordered, and administered by a bath attendant from the sanitarium. After a short time copious perspiration appeared, and he was greatly relieved.

Ellen recounted their experience:

> On Friday my symptoms were more favorable. The doctor then informed me that my husband was inclined to sleep, and that danger was apprehended. I was immediately taken to his room, and as soon as I looked upon his countenance I knew that he was dying.
>
> I tried to arouse him. He understood all that was said to him, and responded to all questions that could be answered by Yes or No, but seemed unable to say more.
>
> When I told him I thought he was dying, he manifested no surprise. I asked if Jesus was precious to him. He said, "Yes, oh, yes."
>
> "Have you no desire to live?" I inquired. He answered, "No."
>
> We then knelt by his bedside, and I prayed for my husband in that solemn hour. A peaceful expression rested upon his countenance. I said to him, "Jesus loves you. The everlasting arms are beneath you." He responded, "Yes, yes."
>
> I wished to be certain that he recognized us, and I asked him to tell who we were. He said, "You are Ellen. You"—looking at our eldest son—"are Edson. I know you all."
>
> Brother Smith and other brethren then prayed around his bedside, and retired to spend much of the night in prayer. My husband said he felt no pain; but he was evidently failing fast. Dr. Kellogg and his helpers did all that was in their power to hold him back from death. He slowly revived, but continued very weak. I remained with him through the night.
>
> The next morning he took some nourishment, and seemed slightly to revive. About noon he had a chill, which left him unconscious, and he quietly breathed his life away, without a struggle or a groan. I was mercifully spared the anguish of seeing my husband in agony battling with death. The scene was as pleasant as it was possible for a deathbed to be (MS 6, 1881 [see also *In Memoriam*, pp. 52-54]).

Plans for the funeral called for some delay, for W. C. White and his wife, Mary, were across the continent, almost a week's travel time away. James's brother John, for many years a presiding elder of the Methodist Conference in Ohio, was close, but might need a little time to arrange to come. Another brother, Samuel, a Baptist minister in Massachusetts, was summoned, but was too feeble to come. A sister, Mary Chase, lived with the Whites in Battle Creek.

The funeral was set for Sabbath afternoon, just a week after James's death. Through the week Ellen White's health and strength dipped to an all-time low.

JAMES WHITE'S FUNERAL

On Sabbath afternoon, August 13, some 2,500 Seventh-day Adventists and Battle Creek townspeople assembled in the tabernacle for the funeral of James White. Even though very ill, Ellen attended. She recounted:

> We then went in hacks to the Tabernacle, and I was carried in a chair while the mourners followed. I was laid upon the sofa prepared with pillows. I was carefully watched by the doctor (letter 9, 1881).

In his funeral address Uriah Smith eulogized the deceased and spoke of his activities in connection with the origin and rise of the Seventh-day Adventist Church:

> Before us, shrouded for the tomb, lies the man with whom it had its very beginning. Taking hold of this work while as yet it had neither form nor substance, under the leadings of what he regarded as the clearest indications of Divine Providence, he bore it in his arms heroically forward, making ways where none appeared, removing obstacles calculated to arrest its progress, defending it from enemies without and within, devising means for the development of strength, until it has reached its present growth, and stands today in its highest attainment of vitality.
>
> With every advance movement, with every new enterprise connected with this work, with all its outreachings to occupy new territory, and with the employment of new agencies to accomplish desired ends, his name has been connected, and his efforts have been inseparably interwoven (*In Memoriam*, p. 23).

Smith enumerated in some detail, giving illustrations, predominating traits, and characteristics of the man with whom he had worked intimately for so many years:

> We first notice that in times of confusion and excitement he was always calm and cool. . . .
> Secondly, he was a man never given to fanaticism. . . .
> Thirdly, he was endued with remarkable acuteness of perception to determine the most judicious moves to be made. . . .
> Fourthly, he was a man who would never yield to discouragement. The word "fail" was not in his vocabulary. . . .

Fifthly, he was a man who would look forward to the future wants of his work, and make provision for them. He foresaw that certain elements of stability must be wrought into the work, which could be secured only through organization. . . .

Sixthly, he was a man of strong personal friendships, and of a remarkably generous nature. To have a regard for the interest of others, and to see that their circumstances were rendered as favorable as possible, was a part of his nature (*ibid.*, pp. 29-33).

REMARKS BY ELLEN G. WHITE

As Smith concluded his remarks, Ellen quite unexpectedly arose from her couch to speak to the large audience. She later described the experience:

After Elder Smith had given the funeral discourse I did so long to say something to let all know that the Christian's hope was mine and sustained me in that hour of bereavement, but I feared I could not stand upon my feet. I finally determined to make the trial, and the Lord sustained me. The doctor stood ready to catch me, he said, if I fell. . . . Brother John and Willie and Edson were also watching to aid me, but I went through with what I had to say with clearness (letter 9, 1881).

"As I arose," she declared later, "strength was given me, and I spoke about ten minutes, exalting the mercy and love of God in the presence of that crowded assembly" (1S, p. 252). Her remarks were stenographically reported. Standing and steadying herself with a hand on the casket, she spoke in a clear voice:

I want to say a few words to those present on this occasion. My dear Saviour has been my strength and support in this time of need. When taken from my sickbed to be with my husband in his dying moments, at first the suddenness of the stroke seemed too heavy to bear, and I cried to God to spare him to me—not to take him away, and leave me to labor alone. . . .

At times I felt that I could not have my husband die. But these words seemed to be impressed on my mind: "Be still, and know that I am God." . . . I keenly feel my loss, but I dare not give myself up to useless grief. This would not bring back my husband. And I am not so selfish as to wish, if I could, bring him from his peaceful slumber to engage again in the battles of life. Like a tired warrior, he has lain down to sleep (*In Memoriam*, pp. 40-55).

Ninety-five carriages joined in the funeral procession to Oak Hill Cemetery; in addition, nearly 100 people went on foot. James White was laid to rest in the family plot where his two sons and his father and mother, John and Elizabeth White, were buried.

After the funeral Ellen was taken back to the sanitarium for the night. On Sunday she was taken on a bed out to their home, where she was joined by the members of the family who had attended the funeral. James's brother John was delighted with the place, but as for Ellen, she declared:

> The light of my home had gone and henceforth I should love it for his sake who thought so much of it. It just met his taste. . . . But how can I ever regard it as I could if he had lived? (letter 9, 1881).

THE PUBLIC PRESS

James White was known quite well across the land, not only as one of the founders of the Seventh-day Adventist Church—a church that had grown to 17,000 in his lifetime—but also as an astute businessman managing large publishing interests and closely connected with the educational and medical interests in Battle Creek. He was highly esteemed by the Honorable George Willard, one-time congressman from the state of Michigan and publisher of the Battle Creek *Daily Journal*. In his editorial on page one of the August 8 issue, Willard eulogized:

> He was a man of the patriarchal pattern, and his character was cast in the heroic mold. If the logical clearness to formulate a creed; if the power to infect others with one's own zeal, and impress them with one's own convictions; if the executive ability to establish a sect and to give it form and stability; if the genius to shape and direct the destiny of great communities, be a mark of true greatness, Elder White is certainly entitled to the appellation, for he possessed not one of these qualities only, but all of them in a marked degree.
>
> The essential feature of his life's work was constructive. He had the rare power of social organization and laid the foundation and marked the design for the erection of a social and religious structure for others to develop and further complete. . . . As with all founders of communities, his life is not a broken shaft, but an enduring column, whereon others are to build.

The public press across the land also gave him favorable notice.

ELLEN COPES WITH GRIEF

The next Monday, August 22, with her two daughters-in-law, Emma and Mary, Ellen left for Colorado, where she expected to spend a few weeks in retirement and rest and rejuvenation.

Several days were spent in Boulder, where lived the McDearmons, Emma's parents. Ellen spent most of one day writing out the circumstances connected with her husband's death (MS 6, 1881) for use in the *In Memoriam* pamphlet being prepared at Battle Creek. In this statement she dwelt quite fully upon their experience during the two weeks previous to his death, especially their praying seasons and conversation that showed that James had some foreboding of a change and that he was prepared. Ellen closed her statement with words of appreciation to friends in Battle Creek and those who assisted her:

> Especially would I acknowledge with gratitude Dr. Kellogg's skillful care as a physician, as well as his kindness and sympathy as a brother and friend, in my sickness and bereavement.

Then with Mary she was off to "Whites' Ranch" and the little cottage they owned on a few acres in the mountains near Rollinsville, Colorado.

ALONE IN THE MOUNTAINS

Although her health was improving and she was sleeping quite well, Ellen was not yet able to apply herself to writing. As she looked from the cottage to the pine-covered hills close by, she was reminded of the many happy times she and James had enjoyed there. But this time he was not there to share her thoughts and feelings.

Willie had remained in Battle Creek to work with Edson in taking care of the financial affairs relating to James White's estate. To him she wrote on September 12:

> I miss Father more and more. Especially do I feel his loss while here in the mountains. I find it a very different thing being in the mountains with my husband and in the mountains without him. I am fully of the opinion that my life was so entwined or interwoven with my husband's that it is about impossible for me to be of any great account without him (letter 17, 1881).

For her, Colorado with its beautiful mountains had lost its lure. She did some sewing to while away the time, but not much writing. Butler was urging her to attend the General Conference session being planned for November or December. The California camp meeting would be held a little before that, and she was debating in her mind whether to return for the winter to their comfortable home in Battle Creek or to go to California and occupy their Oakland home. As to the General Conference session, she told Mary that she "must have further light before consenting to go in her present state of health" (MKW to WCW, Sept. 14, 1881). She finally decided in favor of California, for she felt it would not be prudent to return to the East with the burdens she would have to face there.

With the California camp meeting to be held in Sacramento in the offing, she, with her helpers, left Boulder for Oakland on October 2. Physically she was steadily gaining ground, and when the camp meeting opened on Thursday evening, October 13, at East Park Grove, she was there. In light of her severe illness, it was thought that she would not be able to speak much, but she spoke almost every afternoon.

J. H. Waggoner reported that her address Sabbath afternoon, October 15, "was equal to the best effort we ever knew her to put forth" (ST, Oct. 27, 1881). Waggoner added, "Besides this, her counsel was of great value throughout the meeting."

Perhaps the most important business item introduced at the meeting was to take steps "to establish a school by Seventh-day Adventists in California." A committee was appointed to carry this intention into effect as soon as possible; also to examine and report in regard to a permanent location. A school board was elected, with W. C. White as chairman. In addition to J. H. Waggoner, editor of the *Signs*, five prominent businessmen and farmers served on the board.

ELLEN STILL HOLDING THE REINS

Through the remaining months of 1881 and into the early part of 1882 Ellen White, residing first in Oakland and then in Healdsburg, spent much of her time visiting the churches. At first she went to those nearby, in Oakland and San Francisco. Then she added Petaluma, Healdsburg, St. Helena, Napa, Williams, Arbuckle, and Santa Rosa. She was not ready to apply herself to a heavy program of writing. On occasion she was invited to speak in other than Seventh-day Adventist churches. Then, using the subject matter of her addresses here and there, she prepared a series of weekly articles for the *Signs* that ran under the general heading "Among the Churches." Much of the travel was by carriage, Ellen doing the driving. One report concerning the 35 mile (56-kilometer) trip from Healdsburg to St. Helena is highly descriptive:

> Brother and Sister Harmon [in whose comfortable home she had spent a few days] thought it unsafe for Sister Rogers and myself to make the journey alone at this season of the year. Hence they accompanied us, their team leading the way, while ours followed. When we left Healdsburg, the fog was so dense that we could see but a short distance before us, but in a few hours the mists dispersed, and we enjoyed beautiful sunshine.
>
> The road through Knight's Canyon, always perilous to the inexperienced traveler, is often impassable in the rainy season. We were very thankful for a pilot in this part of our journey. I dared not look either to

the right or left to view the scenery, but, holding the lines firmly, and guiding my horse in the narrow passage, I followed our leader. Carelessness here would have been fatal. Had our horse turned out of the right path, we should have plunged down a steep precipice, into the ravine below.

As we rode along in almost breathless silence, I could but think how forcibly this dangerous ride illustrates the Christian's experience. We are making life's journey amid the perils of the last days. We need to watch carefully every step, and to be sure that we are following our great Leader (*ibid.*, Jan. 26, 1882).

HEALDSBURG COLLEGE OPENS
AND
BATTLE CREEK COLLEGE CLOSES

Soon after returning to Oakland, Ellen attended the camp meeting held at Sacramento where the delegates took action to establish an educational institution at Healdsburg, less than 100 miles (160 kilometers) north of the Bay cities of San Francisco and Oakland.

A school committee of seven was appointed four days later. W. C. White, as chairman, was authorized, among other responsibilities, to "select a building at some eligible point in the State [in northern California]." Less than a month later a well-built school building was found at Healdsburg. It had cost $10,000 but could be secured, with furniture, for $3,750.

Just at this point W. C. White had to leave for Battle Creek and the General Conference session. But he was back in time to attend a meeting of the school board in Healdsburg January 28 and 29, 1882. Five of the seven members, W. C. White, John Morrison, J. H. Waggoner, T. M. Chapman, and William Saunders, were present. Ellen was invited to meet with them. The minutes record:

> At the first meeting, Mrs. E. G. White made appropriate remarks upon what should be the aims and ends of a denominational school, such as is purposed to be established in this State by Seventh-day Adventists, the gist of which was that "the fear of the Lord is the beginning of wisdom," and that it was necessary to have a school of our own in order to take the children away from the evil influences found in nearly all the common schools and colleges of the day (ST, Feb. 16, 1882).

To attain some of the objectives set forth by Ellen White called for some departures from the program at the Battle Creek school: (1) There must be regular classes in Bible study, not just chapel lectures; (2) there must be a school home, or dormitory; (3) there must be a program that would provide physical activity with study—in other words, an industrial program. These were basic in the planning for Healdsburg Academy. It would take time to implement some of the elements, particularly the providing of a school home.

Some of the problems that the college at Battle Creek was having should be avoided:

    a. The college did not have dormitories.

    b. Students boarded with families in the community or on their own.

    c. This exacerbated problems of discipline. Hosts naturally were inclined to sympathize with and accredit the reports of the students.

    d. Disagreements among the faculty, board, and community were common regarding the school policies and goals.

Appropriate actions were taken toward an early opening of the school. Professor Sidney Brownsberger, now recovered from illness, was invited to take charge, and his wife was asked to become one of the teachers. Without delay earnest Adventist families started moving to Healdsburg to take advantage of the academy. It was announced to open Tuesday, April 11 (ST, Apr. 6, 1882). That first day 26 students were on hand to register—more than had been expected (ibid., Apr. 20, 1882). The whole school enterprise was carried forward on a wave of enthusiasm and goodwill among its constituents and also the community of Healdsburg.

On Monday, April 24, the annual meeting of the Pacific SDA Publishing Association was held in Oakland, bringing together a good representation from the churches. Time was found at that meeting to discuss the school project. At 2:30 in the afternoon, less than two weeks after the opening of the school, a large group assembled in the Oakland church to hear reports and review plans for the new enterprise. Professor Brownsberger reported on the phenomenal progress being made.

The first 20-week term closed in mid-June with an enrollment of 38 (ibid., July 13, 1882). By this time an Adventist woman of some means had made a gift of $5,000, and work could begin on the school home, or "boardinghouse," as it was known. In the basement would be the kitchen, laundry, and bakery; on the first floor, classrooms and a working parlor. The second story would accommodate the young women, and the third would be a dormitory for the young men (ibid., July 20 and Oct. 26, 1882).

ELLEN WHITE FINDS A HOME BASE

After traveling out from Oakland to visit among the churches in northern California through the early winter months, Ellen decided that she would make Healdsburg her California headquarters. She and James had built a home on a little farm on West Dry Creek Road, about three miles (five kilometers) from the village, and she still owned it. On February 7, 1882, she wrote to Willie, who was managing the Pacific Press in Oakland, "Now I am decided to go to my Healdsburg place."

On Thursday, February 23, her personal belongings and some furniture arrived from Oakland and were moved into the little home on the farm.

She drew in her family of literary and home helpers, hoping soon to settle down to a serious program of writing. But this she found hard to do. She took pleasure in scouting around the country, buying grain and hay, chickens, a cow with its calf, and horses for transportation and to work the place. Here she spent four months happily working in her garden and building up her health. She wrote in a letter to her children:

> My health is good. I have some trouble in sleeping all I want to. I exercise considerably, picking up wood, and if it were not for weak ankles, would exercise more. I put rubber bandages on my ankles and this helps them. I feel then I can walk anywhere (letter 4, 1882).

In a letter written April 16, in which she mentioned some of the afflictions of those about her, she said, "I find, after all, your mother can endure about as much as the younger people" (letter 9, 1882). Up to this point she had to force herself to spend time writing.

But as the home on West Dry Creek Road was several miles from the town of Healdsburg, and she wanted to be closer to the college, early in August she bought a two-story house on Powell Street, which bordered the town. It stood on a two-and-a-half-acre (one-hectare) tract of good land with an orchard of fruit trees of choice varieties. As the college's "boardinghouse" was still under construction, her house was at once fitted up to board the carpenters. She canned a heavy yield of plums and peaches for the college and the health retreat at St. Helena. W. C. White reported that "Mother engaged in this work with great interest, saying, in answer to our cautions, that it was a rest to her weary brain" (RH, Sept. 26, 1882). When she was on the West Coast, this was her home until she went to Australia in 1891.

A MIRACULOUS HEALING

In late August, while in Oakland, Ellen suffered a severe chill followed by fever. This serious illness lasted several weeks. As she began to recover, she was taken to the health retreat at St. Helena. But she did not improve. As the time for the California camp meeting to be held at Healdsburg drew near, she pleaded to be taken back to her Healdsburg home. She hoped to be strong enough to bear her testimony at the camp meeting and to work for the support of the new school. Resting on a mattress in the back of a carriage driven by her son Willie, and accompanied by Jenny Ings, she started out on the trip to Healdsburg.

The day grew very warm. As W. C. White later recounted the experience to members of his family, he told how his mother, in time, failed to answer his questions. At once he knew she had lapsed into unconsciousness. He urged the horses on, hoping to reach Healdsburg with his mother still alive. In her own home she rallied a bit. It was her hope and the hope of her family that in the environment of the camp meeting she might experience a renewal of life and strength. Camp meeting opened in early October in a grove about a half mile (one kilometer) from her home. Although very feeble and hardly able to leave her bed, she gave instruction at noon on the first Sabbath:

> Prepare me a place in the large tent where I can hear the speaker. Possibly the sound of the speaker's voice will prove a blessing to me. I am hoping for something to bring new life (3LS, p. 262).

A sofa was arranged for her on the broad speaker's stand, and she was carried into the big tent and placed upon it. Those close by observed not only her weakness but also the deathly paleness of her face. Recalling the experience some years later, Ellen said that not only was the large tent full, but "it seemed as if nearly all Healdsburg was present" (letter 82, 1906).

J. H. Waggoner, editor of the *Signs of the Times*, spoke that Sabbath afternoon "on the rise and early work of the message, and its progress and present state" (ST, Oct. 26, 1882). When Waggoner had finished his address, Ellen turned to Willie and Mrs. Ings, who were at her side, and said, "Will you help me up, and assist me to stand on my feet while I say a few words?" They aided her to the desk. "For five minutes I stood there," she later recalled, "trying to speak, and thinking that it was the last speech I should ever make—my farewell message." With both hands she steadied herself at the pulpit.

> All at once I felt a power come upon me, like a shock of electricity. It passed through my body and up to my head. The people said that they plainly saw the blood mounting to my lips, my ears, my cheeks, my forehead (letter 82, 1906).

Every eye in the audience seemed fixed on her. Mr. Montrose, a businessman from the town, stood to his feet and exclaimed, "We are seeing a miracle performed before our eyes; Mrs. White is healed!" (WCW account). Her voice strengthened, her sentences came clear and full, and she bore a testimony such as the audience had never before heard. Waggoner filled out the story in his report in the *Signs*:

> Her voice and appearance changed, and she spoke for some time with clearness and energy. She then invited those who wished to make a start

in the service of God, and those who were far backslidden, to come forward, and a goodly number answered to the call (ST, Oct. 26, 1882).

Uriah Smith, who was present, in his report in the *Review and Herald* published October 31 mentioned that after the miraculous healing "she was able to attend meetings . . . as usual, and spoke six times with her ordinary strength of voice and clearness of thought." Referring to the experience, Ellen said, "It was as if one had been raised from the dead. . . . This sight the people in Healdsburg were to have as a witness for the truth" (letter 82, 1906).

This event, which seemed to be a turning point in her physical condition, opened the way for a strong ministry. In reporting her two-month illness, she remarked that she had expected it would gradually pass. Instead, she was healed instantaneously.

She was glad to be in the large group that during the camp meeting went to see the new college. First was the visit to the new building—the boardinghouse under construction—and then the school building. A brief dedication service was held in the "audience room," which could not contain all the visitors. After Waggoner offered the dedicatory prayer, Ellen called for singing a verse of "Hold the Fort." The whole congregation sang heartily.

THE CRISIS AT BATTLE CREEK

Four months after the school at Healdsburg had opened, the college at Battle Creek closed. During the summer of 1882, while Ellen was immersed in writing and publication problems at Healdsburg, she was not unaware of the situation in Battle Creek.

As early as December of the previous year she had presented this warning before conference delegates and leading workers in the *Review and Herald* office, sanitarium, and college:

> There is danger that our college will be turned away from its original design. God's purpose has been made known, that our people should have an opportunity to study the sciences and at the same time to learn the requirements of His word. . . . But for one or two years past there has been an effort to mold our school after other colleges. . . .
>
> I was shown that it is Satan's purpose to prevent the attainment of the very object for which the college was established. Hindered by his devices, its managers reason after the manner of the world and copy its plans and imitate its customs. But in thus doing, they will not meet the mind of the Spirit of God (5T, pp. 21-23).

A change of administration because of the illness of the president, Sidney

Brownsberger, had brought in a gradual change in policies. G. I. Butler reported in the *Review*:

> The board of directors whom the stockholders placed in control found themselves powerless to hold in check these influences. . . . A majority of the faculty, sustained by a large portion of the church, threatened to resign in a body if certain measures taken by the board were not retracted. Mass meetings of the students were held to sustain their favorites in the faculty. . . . The board virtually had nothing to do with the management of the college for months during the past year. . . .
>
> The tide ran so high that those teachers who had done most in founding the college lost their influence, and were looked upon with dislike. Their lot was made very hard, and stories were circulated against some of them which were calculated to ruin their reputation as Christians, and even as moral men, and these have been circulated through the land (RH, Sept. 12, 1882).

Faced with these conditions and unable to see the possibility of operating "such a school as the Lord had shown we ought to have," "the board finally [during the summer recess] decided to close the college" with no definite plan to reopen *(ibid.)*. It was a sad day.

Particularly painful to Ellen was the stance taken by the *Review* editor, Uriah Smith, in connection with the deteriorating Battle Creek College situation. Since the spring of 1853 when Smith had joined the office force in Rochester, New York, he had been a pillar of strength in the development and growth of the church. Now when the Spirit of Prophecy was being challenged, his support was especially needed.

Smith's children, who were attending the school, sided with the liberal element. His own sympathies tended in the same direction. During this period an occasional interchange of letters took place between him and Ellen. In her testimonies relating to Battle Creek, the church, and the college, she had probed the matter and given counsel based on her insights into the conflict and the attitude of various individuals. One key to the problem came to light later by way of Smith's letter to her written August 10, 1882. He explained his hesitancy to accept her counsel regarding some of these matters by saying: "I had always supposed that a testimony was based on a vision, and I did not understand that you had any vision since the recent trouble in the college commenced." Based on this philosophy, Smith attributed reproof and counsel that she wrote concerning school matters to reports she had received or to her own opinions.

Ellen's great concern as she learned of the trend at the college is revealed in this portion of a letter she sent to the church in Battle Creek:

Dear Brethren and Sisters in Battle Creek:

When I went to Colorado, I was so burdened for you, that, in my weakness, I wrote [in September 1881] many pages to be read at your camp meeting. Weak and trembling, I arose at three o'clock in the morning, to write to you. God was speaking through clay. But the document was entirely forgotten; the camp meeting passed, and it was not read until the General Conference. You might say that it was only a letter. Yes, it was a letter, but prompted by the Spirit of God, to bring before your minds things that had been shown me. . . .

While visiting Healdsburg last winter, I was much in prayer and burdened with anxiety and grief. But the Lord swept back the darkness at one time while I was in prayer, and a great light filled the room. An angel of God was by my side, and I seemed to be in Battle Creek. I was in your councils; I heard words uttered, I saw and heard things that, if God willed, I wish could be forever blotted from my memory. My soul was so wounded, I knew not what to do or what to say. Some things I cannot mention. I was bidden to let no one know in regard to this, for much was yet to be developed.

I was told to gather up the light that had been given me, and let its rays shine forth to God's people. I have been doing this in articles in the papers (*Testimony for the Battle Creek Church*, p. 49).

During the year that followed the closing of the college the work of Ellen G. White was carefully scrutinized and consideration was given to inspiration-revelation as it related to her experience and writings. Much was published by dissidents to destroy confidence in the Testimonies. Then a trio of dissidents united in the production of an "Extra" of the *Sabbath Advocate*, in which were presented a number of criticisms of Ellen White. At first the criticism was ignored. Then its wide distribution, especially among Adventists, gave rise to questions demanding answers. The first answer came from the pen of Wolcott Littlejohn in the *Review* in May 1883.

THE BEGINNING OF A TURNAROUND IN BATTLE CREEK

To aid in the crisis situation at Battle Creek, Littlejohn had been asked in January to take charge of "District No. 3." The Battle Creek church, with its 497 members (RH, Apr. 17, 1883), comprised the largest part of the district.

With a strong base of support in the majority of the church officers and members, Littlejohn began to get positive materials into the *Review*. The issue of May 8 carried the first of a series of three rather scholarly articles on "Seventh-day Adventists and the Testimony of Jesus Christ."

Ellen was aware, of course, of the warfare against her work and was particularly alert to the deplorable conditions existing in the Battle Creek church. Of these she wrote:

> Many are in reality fighting his [Satan's] battles while they profess to serve under the banner of Christ. These traitors in the camp may not be suspected, but they are doing their work to create unbelief, discord, and strife. Such are the most dangerous of foes. While they insinuate themselves into our favor and gain our confidence and sympathy, they are busy suggesting doubts and creating suspicion. They work in the same manner as did Satan in heaven when he deceived the angels by his artful representations (*ibid.*, Aug. 28, 1883).

As summer came and her book work was going well, she fixed her eyes on the dates for the Eastern camp meetings to start August 22 at Worcester, Massachusetts. Finally her communication to the president of the General Conference led him to feel he could count on her help. He notified the readers of the August 7 *Review and Herald* that "Sister E. G. White may be able to attend [the New England meeting], if her health is sufficient to endure the long journey from California."

With Sara McEnterfer as a traveling companion, Ellen White left California by train for Battle Creek. Arriving Friday, August 17, she went to the home of Edson and Emma for the night and then to the sanitarium. Almost immediately she was involved in meetings.

She did not sleep well Friday night, but on Sabbath morning she spoke in the tabernacle.

Sunday was a full day. In the morning she spoke to the workers in the Review and Herald office. In the afternoon at 4:00 she spoke to a crowd of about 400 in the public square. Her subject was temperance.

On Sunday evening she spoke to the patients at the sanitarium.

On Monday evening, August 20, she spoke to the employees of the Review and Herald.

Uriah Smith, whose attitude toward her had been noticeably cool, had planned to attend the camp meetings in New England, but at the last minute he felt he must remain in Battle Creek and attend to some important writing.

Now, having sounded an earnest but kind warning that she hoped would help to stabilize those who might have been wavering, she pressed on to Massachusetts.

Though meeting a busy schedule of camp meetings in Massachusetts, Vermont, Maine, New York, Nebraska, Michigan, and Indiana, Ellen followed with interest what was happening in Battle Creek.

BATTLE CREEK COLLEGE REOPENS

With a more accurate comprehension of the whole situation on the part of the Battle Creek church, and upon its members making a thorough confession and a pledge of loyalty to the Spirit of Prophecy and to church leadership, the board of trustees of Battle Creek College looked forward to the reopening of the college. Butler, chairman of the board as well as president of the General Conference, presented an extended statement on the situation in the *Review* of July 31, 1883, under the title "Our College at Battle Creek." The statement said, in part:

> Let us consider some of the questions involved in the reopening of the college. It has remained closed for one year. Why? Because as conducted for some time previous to its closing it did not answer the purpose for which it was established. And further, because the state of feeling existing in the community surrounding it was such that those to whom its management was entrusted felt that there was no reasonable hope that a better state of things could then be obtained. . . .
>
> A very different spirit is manifest in the church at Battle Creek the present year from that which was seen last year. . . .
>
> Yet there are great difficulties to be met if we have such a school as will meet the mind of the Spirit of God. It will require men of sound judgment, deep piety, and those whose whole hearts are enlisted in the work of God, to mold and manage it, if it ever fully succeeds. . . .
>
> To bring about the true spirit in our college will require a great effort. To secure proper officers and teachers who will exert the right influences, and bring into the school the Spirit of Christ, and lead the minds of the pupils to the truth, is a difficult problem, and one which the board of trustees is now trying to solve. We hope for such success as will enable us soon to announce the time when our college will open.

It was recognized that the main purpose of the college was to train ministers, missionaries, colporteurs, Bible "readers" (instructors), and teachers for auxiliary schools. A new day had dawned for Battle Creek College.

The *Review and Herald* of August 14, 1883, carried the announcement that Battle Creek College would open Wednesday, September 5, for the coming college year.

Eighty students were present for the opening. W. H. Littlejohn, who had shown his loyalty to the church and to the Spirit of Prophecy counsels, had been chosen president. He served for two years.

Especially gratifying and heartening to Ellen White was the turnaround of Uriah Smith. Using his editorial report on the Michigan camp meeting to herald to the church the marked change that had come in his personal relationship to the Spirit of Prophecy, Smith stated:

> The presence of Brethren Haskell and W. C. White from the Pacific Coast added to the interest of the meeting. . . . The benefit of the labors and attendance of Sister White at this meeting cannot be overestimated. Her exhortations moved the people to seek the Lord with earnestness and contrition of heart, as could have been done by no others. . . .
>
> Sister White has a work to do, and is trying faithfully to perform it, which no others can do. It is one which has a most intimate connection with the prosperity of the cause. For this she is especially qualified by the gift she has in exercise of "visions and revelations of the Lord." Through this she is able to perceive more vividly the dangers and duties pertaining to these closing moments of time, and thus more understandingly instruct and warn the little flock; and he who would try to destroy confidence in her work, or weaken her hands, is taking a course hostile to the best interests of this cause. . . .
>
> From the very beginning, now nearly forty years ago, the manifestation of the Spirit of Prophecy in the visions of Sister White has been connected with this work, and interwoven with every step of its progress. To suppose that during the brief time remaining it is to be separated from it would be to look for a singular providence indeed. A change in this respect is now no more possible than it is desirable.
>
> Rather than stop now to question the wisdom of God's providence, in the constitution or history of this work, and spend time and strength in efforts to introduce fundamental changes, we think all would do better to accept it as a whole, give their attention to a careful examination of their own hearts in view of the soon-coming judgment, and be willing to receive instruction from whatever source, and by whatever means the Lord may see fit to send it (*ibid.*, Oct. 9, 1883).

Ellen White Ventures Abroad

An invitation for Ellen White to visit Europe had come from the members of the Central European Mission. Thus the General Conference of 1884 voted:

> *Resolved*, That we extend to Sister White a hearty and urgent invitation to visit the different fields in Europe as soon as practicable.

At first Mrs. White was overwhelmed with the idea of traveling to Europe. She was in her late 50s and considered herself old. Following the strenuous activities connected with the Battle Creek crisis and then at the numerous camp meetings in the East, she found herself depleted in strength and aware that she must take steps to recoup her physical forces.

OH, TO KNOW WHAT TO DO!

Ellen did not relish traveling to Europe, especially in time to attend the missionary council in September 1885. "To travel across the continent in the heat of summer and in my condition of health," she wrote, "seemed almost presumptuous" (RH, Sept. 15, 1885). She wished for positive guidance to know what course to follow.

> As the appointed time for starting drew near, my faith was severely tested. I so much desired someone of experience upon whom I could rely for counsel and encouragement. My courage was gone, and I longed for human help, one who had a firm hold from above, and whose faith would stimulate mine (*ibid.*).

As the time for the final decision was at hand, W. C. White slipped away from Oakland for a few days at Healdsburg. He spoke courage to his mother. He pointed her to the past, when, under the most forbidding circumstances, she had moved out by faith according to the best light she had, and the Lord strengthened and supported her. Of the experience she reported:

> I did so, and decided to act in the judgment of the General Conference, and start on the journey, trusting in God. My trunk was

packed, and I returned with him to Oakland. Here I was invited to speak to the church Sabbath afternoon. I hesitated; but these words came to me with power, "My grace is sufficient for you" (ibid.).

Writing of the experience in her diary, she said, "I was no longer uncertain. I would venture to go with the party across the plains" (MS 16a, 1885). There were 12 who left Oakland for the East on Monday, July 13. Among them were her son, Willie; his wife, Mary, and their daughter, Ella; also, Miss Sara McEnterfer, whom Ellen chose to go with her as a traveling companion not only across the country but also to Europe.

This was her twenty-fifth trip to or from the West Coast. The party made brief stops at Battle Creek and South Lancaster. On Friday, after writing for a few hours, at 10:00 in the morning she left for Boston, where she and those traveling with her were to embark for Southampton, England. As the S.S. Cephalonia was to leave Sabbath afternoon, the party went aboard Friday afternoon so as to be settled before the Sabbath. She noted that "we accomplished this nearly." Her stateroom was large enough for the company to gather for Friday evening worship. She reported, "All take part. The Lord seems very near, and I feel peaceful and restful" (ibid.).

The voyage across the Atlantic took more than a week. Most of it was pleasant, but one storm was encountered, followed by foggy weather. Ellen White was able to do quite a bit of writing—articles and letters, with the help of Mary and Sara McEnterfer. She noted: "We used the calligraph [typewriter] with good effect" (ibid.).

TWO WEEKS IN ENGLAND

At Liverpool they were met by George Drew, who accompanied them to Grimsby, the city in which the mission headquarters was located. Thursday they went to the beach, but, finding it cold and windy, Mrs. White was glad to get back to their living quarters.

She spent two weeks in England, the first Sabbath at Grimsby. Of this day's activities she reported:

> Sabbath afternoon, when the little company of Sabbathkeepers assembled for worship, the room was full, and some were seated in the hall. I have ever felt great solemnity in addressing large audiences, and have tried to place myself wholly under the guidance of the Saviour. But I felt even more solemn, if possible, in standing before this small company, who, in the face of obstacles, of reproach and losses, had stepped aside from the multitude who were making void the law of God, and had turned their feet into the way of His commandments (HS, p. 162).

Sunday morning she again met with the believers, and in the evening she spoke in the town hall to an audience of about 1,200. Every seat was taken and some people stood. The Union Temperance Prize Choir of some 50 voices sang seven numbers—three at the opening, two at the close, and two after the benediction. The topic of Mrs. White's address was "The Love of God." She spent a busy week speaking and sightseeing in London and nearby cities, then on Friday took the train for Southampton and the house of J. H. Durland. That night she spoke to a small company of believers, and on Sabbath had two meetings.

Sunday night she spoke to 1,000 people in a rented hall. The public press asked her to write up the address for publication, and she spent the next two days in London preparing the copy. On Wednesday they took the train to the channel boat and were on their way to Basel, Switzerland.

ON TO BASEL, SWITZERLAND

Crossing the English Channel by ship is often an uncomfortable experience, and so it was on Wednesday, September 2. However, even though many were seasick, Ellen White reported that she was not sick at all. But "we were glad, after one hour and a half's ride, to step off the boat at Calais" (MS 16a, 1885). There they were met by Mr. Brown, a literature evangelist in the city.

To secure a sleeping compartment on the train to Basel would have cost $11 apiece, so they chose to spend an uncomfortable night and save the dollars. She reported on the experience:

> A bed was made for me between the seats on the top of the satchels and telescope boxes. I rested some, but slept little. The rest took their chances on the seats. We were not sorry to have the night pass (ibid.).

Morning came as they entered Basel. They were met at the train station by B. L. Whitney, president of the Swiss Mission, accompanied by R. F. Andrews and Albert Vuilleumier. Taking a hack, they drove to the publishing house on the corner of Weiherweg and Rudolphstrasse. There they were greeted by A. C. Bourdeau and were introduced to quite a number who had awaited their arrival (ibid.).

As they entered the building Whitney said to her, "Look at our meeting hall before going upstairs." Observing all the features of the large room, she said, "It is a good meeting hall. I feel that I have seen this place before." She stepped into the office across the hall for a brief look and then was taken to the pressroom, just below the ground floor. The press was running, and she said, "I have seen this press before. This room looks very familiar to me."

Two young men were at work, and they were introduced to Ellen. She shook hands with them and inquired, "Where is the other one?"

"What other one?" Whitney asked.

"There is an older man here," she replied, "and I have a message for him."

Whitney explained that the foreman of the pressroom was in the city on business (3LS, pp. 282, 283). Ten years before, in Battle Creek, on January 3, 1875, Ellen White was given a vision in which this publishing house and the foreman of the pressroom were shown to her. Needless to say, this experience brought courage to the heart of Whitney and his associates involved in the work in Basel.

ORGANIZATION OF THE WORK IN EUROPE

It was in Switzerland that J. N. Andrews had begun his work in 1874 and started to publish as he was learning the French language. Here in Basel he died and was buried in 1883.

In the late 1870s literature from America reached the countries of northern Europe. In various places the minds of individuals, in one way or another, were called to the Sabbath truth, and workers were sent to augment Andrews' work. The interests of the church stretched out of France, Germany, Italy, and Romania, and companies of believers emerged. With minimal steps in organization, what came to be known as the Central European Mission developed. Work that had begun in Norway, Denmark, and Sweden culminated rather quickly in what were designated as the Norway and Denmark conferences. In England the work was known as the British Mission.

At a meeting attended by S. N. Haskell in Switzerland in 1882, the several emerging units were bound together in a parent organization known as the European Missionary Council. Each of the local organizations was managed by a committee; the chairman of each was an ex-officio member of the European Missionary Council, which met annually.

In 1884 George I. Butler attended the second annual meeting of the European Missionary Council, held in Basel. At that time the loosely organized Central European Mission, the largest and strongest of the four local organizations in Europe, became the Swiss Conference. Organizational plans were perfected, and the decision was made to build a publishing house in Basel.

The publishing house, recently completed, was constructed of stone and consisted of three levels. In the subbasement were the furnace and two gas motors that provided power for the presses. The next level, the ground floor, provided room for the presses, bindery, stereotype foundry, storage space for the paper, and some storage space for the families living above. On the main floor to the right was the meeting hall, with seating capacity for 300; the other half was given to the business offices and the folding and mailing rooms.

Typesetting was done on the second floor; here also were rooms for the editors, translators, and proofreaders. On the left side there was some family housing. The third floor was devoted entirely to living apartments.

After meeting many of the workers, Ellen White was escorted into the hydraulic elevator and taken to the third floor, where the Whitneys had an apartment, for breakfast and a rest. Before long she was shown what was to be her apartment, close to the one the W. C. White family would occupy. These, apparently, were on the south side of the building and had the advantage of exposure to the winter sun.

She did not know it then, but this would be the place she would call "home" for the next two years—a place to rest between trips to Scandinavia, Italy, and Germany; a place to write and recoup.

Ellen White and her son were present for the first general meetings to be held in the publishing house chapel—first the Swiss Conference, scheduled to meet in session from September 10 to 14, and then the European Missionary Council, to open September 14.

The Swiss Conference consisted of 224 members in 10 churches, and an additional 39 Sabbathkeepers in groups. The members were served by one ordained minister and seven licensed ministers. There were 251 Sabbath school members, enrolled in 11 Sabbath schools.

Of the session that opened on Thursday evening, September 10, Mrs. White wrote:

> The conference was quite generally attended by our Swiss brethren, and by representatives from Germany, France, Italy, and Romania. There were nearly two hundred brethren and sisters assembled; and a more intelligent, noble-looking company is seldom seen. Although gathered from different nations, we were brought near to God and to one another by our eyes being fixed upon the one object, Jesus Christ. We were one in faith, and one in our efforts to do the will of God. The influence of the gospel is to unite God's people in one great brotherhood (RH, Nov. 3, 1885).

Of course, not all in the assembly could converse in one language. The congregation was divided into three parts, according to the language they understood. These were seated in different parts of the hall—French, German, and English.

Friday afternoon it was Ellen White's turn to speak, and she was surprised at the large number assembled. It was a new experience to have her with them, and the people did not want to miss a word. Her message was picked up by two translators, one speaking French, the other German. But with the audience divided into groups, time was conserved as the translators spoke to their respective groups simultaneously. She soon found this method of addressing the conference less taxing than her usual manner of continuous speaking, for she had more time for thinking of the construction of what she would say (*ibid.*).

She spoke again on Sunday afternoon for a half hour on missionary work, and again on Monday early afternoon, this time on the necessity of cultivating love and Christian courtesy and of being forbearing with one another (MS 16a, 1885).

Following her message more than 12 were baptized, using the new baptistry in the meeting hall for the first time. Then they united in celebrating the ordinances of the Lord's house.

A MINI-GENERAL CONFERENCE

The third session of the European Council of Seventh-day Adventist Missions opened Tuesday morning, September 15, 1885, in Basel, Switzerland. Twenty delegates from the Central European Mission, seven from the British Mission, six from the Scandinavian countries, and three representatives from North America were present. The delegates were joined by a substantial number of laymen who came in, largely from Switzerland but also a few from other countries. The meeting, which W. C. White described as a "miniature General Conference," was to convene for a week, but as the work got under way it was extended to two full weeks. It was a time of spiritual refreshing, a time of learning, and a time of constructive planning for the work of God in new and varied fields. Ellen White divided her time between writing and diligent public labor, as was usually the case in a meeting of this kind.

The daily program of the council contained most of the same features that characterized the General Conference. B. L. Whitney served as chairman and appointed committees. Mrs. White was the devotional speaker at 5:30 Wednesday morning. This was her first meeting with the workers who had come in especially for the council. She directed her remarks to the necessity of cultivating love and tenderness for one another.

A PROFITABLE COUNCIL

At the 9:00 business meeting W. C. White spoke of making the most profitable use of the time they would spend together. He suggested that a Bible institute, devoted to giving Bible readings and the investigation of difficult Bible subjects, be held during the council. Bible studies prepared in America could be revised and translated into French, German, and Danish-Norwegian and serve as the basis of their work. He suggested also that an English class could be held.

So the stage was set for a very profitable council, with daily reports from the various fields of labor, business sessions, and daily periods devoted to the study of the Bible and the English language.

Topics given special attention during the two weeks included: The evangelistic use of literature; the thrust of public evangelism; use of tents; problems unique to Europe: serving in the army? serving in the army on Sabbath? compulsory school attendance of Adventist children on Sabbath.

Daniel Bourdeau presented a potentially explosive proposition. Ellen White's diary gives the picture:

> Daniel then presented his plans that France and Italy be not encouraged to unite with Switzerland but become a separate conference and use their means among themselves to build up their own conference. This I earnestly opposed, for the influence would be bad. It would not lead to union and harmony in the work, but to separate interests, and they would not labor for that oneness that the Lord demands (*ibid.*).

Bourdeau argued that each one of the national groups was jealous and independent and therefore would resent being a part of the Swiss Conference. Mrs. White suggested that this was a strong reason that each group should learn to blend with other nationalities. As she reported the experience to the president of the General Conference, she said:

> I told Brother Daniel that this would not be in accordance with God's will. . . . The truth is one. It will take people from France and Italy, and, mingling them with other elements, soften and refine them through the truth (letter 23, 1885).

She pointed out that the cause was still in its infancy in the European countries and that to follow this suggestion would result in weakness. In the face of the dissent, Bourdeau grew excited and declared that he had been abused as he had labored in the cause, and cited examples. Ellen White walked out of the room. When she next wrote in her diary she declared: "I will not give sanction to any such spirit" (MS 16a, 1885).

Daniel Bordeau had accepted the third angel's message at the age of 22. Soon after his conversion he had been given strong evidence of Ellen White's call and work, for, on June 28, 1857, he had witnessed her in vision. He later declared, "Since witnessing this wonderful phenomenon, I have not once been inclined to doubt" (in MR, p. 24). But when the testimony of Ellen White touched his life, he almost floundered. He reported his experience of victory in the *Review and Herald* of November 10, 1885. His report opened with words that reflected his attitude:

> This council is among the precious gatherings of the past. Of all the general meetings of our people I have attended in twenty-nine years, I think of none that could be more properly pronounced a success, in every sense of that term, than this one. Christian love and union prevailed

throughout. There was a wonderful blending of nationalities, all seeming to feel that the cause was one, that our aim was one, and that we must unitedly push on the work to certain victory.

He then turned to the matter that came close to him in his personal struggle to relate to the Spirit of Prophecy counsels:

> The labors of Sister White and her son, Elder W. C. White, were highly appreciated at this general gathering. . . .
>
> How interesting and wonderful it was to hear Sister White correctly delineate the peculiarities of different fields she had seen only as the Lord had shown them to her, and show how they should be met; to hear her describe case after case of persons she had never seen with her natural vision, and either point out their errors or show important relations they sustained to the cause, and how they should connect with it to better serve its interests!
>
> As I had a fair chance to test the matter, having been on the ground, and knowing that no one had informed Sister White of these things, while serving as an interpreter, I could not help exclaiming, "It is enough. I want no further evidence of its genuineness."

A VISIT TO SCANDINAVIA

The summer months, rather than early winter, would have been more favorable to visit the countries of northern Europe, where the work of the church was developing quite nicely. But there was some uncertainty as to how soon Ellen White would return to America. So it was felt that the safest course was for her to visit the leading churches in Scandinavia at the earliest opportunity.

On October 6, just one week after the council closed, the party of four left Basel—Mrs. White, W. C. White, Sara McEnterfer, and Cecile Dahl. Cecile was from Christiania (Oslo), Norway, and would serve as guide and interpreter. It was an overnight trip to Frankfurt, Germany, then on to Hamburg. At Kiel, on the Baltic Sea, they took the ferry to Denmark. Ellen White found this trip through the northern countries an interesting experience.

VISIT TO DENMARK

They were met Thursday morning at Copenhagen, by J. G. Matteson. He took the travelers to his home and led them up six flights of stairs to the apartment occupied by his family. While it was somewhat of a struggle to get to the apartment, once there Mrs. White found it afforded a fascinating view.

Seventh-day Adventists in Copenhagen worshiped in a little hall on the fourth story of a building not far from the Matteson apartment. Friday evening Ellen White spoke to about 35 who assembled there. A third of these constituted the local church group; the others came in from adjacent churches. Her topic was "The Parable of the Fig Tree." She found the hall to be damp and cold, but Sabbath morning she was back. Although suffering from some teeth that had been improperly treated, a problem accentuated by the cold and dampness of the hall, she spoke to the well-filled room on the topic "The True Vine."

Halls where religious meetings might be held were difficult to secure in Denmark, but one was found, a basement room capable of seating 200 but equipped for only half that number. Meetings were held each evening throughout the week.

Ellen White spoke five times while in Copenhagen, and then the traveling worker group left by ship for Sweden.

A VISIT TO SWEDEN

"We left Copenhagen this morning," wrote Ellen in her diary for Thursday, October 15, on the steamer for Malmö, Sweden. A night's trip by train took them to Stockholm, where they were met by a Brother Norlin, who took the worker group to his home. Mrs. White wrote of him as one who, in humble circumstances, was earnestly seeking to spread the knowledge of the truth, laboring as a colporteur:

> Shouldering his pack, stocked with our books and papers, he goes on foot from place to place, often traveling many miles a day. His profits have been very small. . . . On one of the large bound books [imported from America] he received but five cents a copy, on some other books only three cents. On those works published at our office in Christiania he received one-third discount. . . .
>
> Brother Norlin's wife is an industrious worker, doing housecleaning, washing, or any other kind of hard work by which she can help in gaining a livelihood. They live in a very economical manner, occupying one good-sized room on a fourth floor, with the use of a small kitchen with another family (HS, p. 189).

After pointing out that this is a sample of how the work had to be done in Denmark, Sweden, and Norway, she declared:

> Those who are thus traveling on foot and carrying the books and papers in their leathern sacks are apparently engaged in a humble work; but they should not feel that it is in any sense degrading. It was in a humble manner that Christ labored when He was on the earth; He went on foot

from place to place teaching as He walked. Those who are spreading a knowledge of the truth are scattering precious light that some souls will accept. In the kingdom of God the fruit of their labors will be seen (*ibid.*).

While in Stockholm she and Sara were entertained in the home of a Sister Johanneson, who had lived in America and could speak English quite well. It was a comfortable home, heated by tall earthen stoves that reached nearly to the ceiling. Ellen much enjoyed and appreciated the comfort provided.

The worker group was in Stockholm from Friday to Wednesday morning, October 21, with meetings Friday evening, Sabbath morning, and then Sunday and Monday evenings. Of the Sabbath morning meeting held in a small public hall, Ellen noted in her diary, "We call this a *good day*. The Lord strengthened me to speak to His people with clearness and power."

The visit to Sweden included a few days at Grythyttehed, 150 miles (240 kilometers) northwest of Stockholm, and then Örebro, meeting with companies of believers at each place. In imagination she relived the days of the Reformation, and then the preaching of the Advent message in Sweden in 1842 and 1843, when the mouths of those who would herald the message were closed by authorities. In these circumstances the power of God came upon several children, and they heralded the message and called upon the people to get ready.

CHRISTIANIA, NORWAY

The last of the northern countries to be visited before it got too late in the season was Norway. It was Friday morning, October 30, when they reached Christiania (Oslo), and were taken to the home of A. B. Oyen, the minister sent from Battle Creek to Norway to translate the Ellen G. White books. It was a relief to Mrs. White to be residing in the home of English-speaking friends. Lest she be misunderstood, she hastened to record in her diary that "although we were welcomed and treated with every attention by our Danish and Swedish brethren and sisters, we felt all the time crippled because we could not converse together, and it was thus made impossible to do them all the good we much desired to do" (MS 27, 1885).

The church had a membership of 120, but 200 attended the Sabbath morning service, and 100 were present for the ordinances Sabbath afternoon (HS, p. 207).

Two full weeks, extending over three Sabbaths, were spent in Norway. Except for meeting a speaking appointment in Drammen, the entire time was devoted to the interests in Christiania, the principal city. Here a new publishing house was under construction, a sizable building that, as in Switzerland, would provide not only space for the publishing interests but a good meeting hall and living quarters for some of the workers.

After Ellen White had been in Christiania a week she had gained a feeling of the overall situation. She realized the need for these brothers and sisters to receive counsel on the high standards that God expects of His people, particularly in regard to the keeping of the Sabbath.

She dwelt on the point of the Sabbath. "It is God's test," she declared.

> It is no man-made test. This is to be the separating line to distinguish the loyal and the true—him that serveth God from him that serveth Him not (MS 27, 1885).

She was concerned that professed believers were sending their children to the public school on Sabbath. "They were not compelled to do this, but [they did it] because the schools objected to taking in their children unless they should attend the six days in the week" (ibid.). If they were unable to negotiate with the school authorities, then there was but one way—"to keep the Sabbath of the fourth commandment strictly," which might call for Seventh-day Adventists to establish schools among themselves.

She had opportunity to discuss some of these things in Christiania with a building contractor by the name of Hansen, a prominent and influential member but with rather lax views of Sabbath observance. Ellen described the visit as pleasant and profitable. They discussed health reform, and she related her experience in the rise and development of the work of the church.

When she came to the last weekend she knew it was a crucial time, for her pointed testimonies through the week had called for soul searching and reform.

During the week she had written a 16-page testimony to the Christiania church. A. B. Oyen had already translated much of it. Sabbath afternoon he read to the church the portion translated.

Ellen White's interest and concern is easily detected in her report to her son:

> There was not time for many testimonies to be borne afterward. Brother Hansen made no response, but he sent word that he would be pleased to take me over the city on Sunday forenoon, and I responded that I would be pleased to go.
>
> He showed me every attention and I managed to bring in again the vexed question of the Sabbath. He said he meant to get around to change his position just as soon as he could, and we had a very pleasant social time. He sat in the carriage where Sara generally sits. Annie sat beside him to interpret. He said if I would promise to come next spring he would make extra efforts to learn to talk and to understand English. I told him I thought without doubt I would come (letter 35, 1885).

Her last meeting in Christiania was held that Sunday afternoon at 3:00 in the

Good Templars' hall, where she had met with the church Sabbaths and evenings.

As she closed the service she bade the people farewell, and thought to slip away while the congregation was singing, to the carriage she saw waiting for her:

> But I was not to escape so easily. There was a rush for me and one and another took my hand, kissed it, and with tears running down their faces, told me how much good my message had done them. They held my hand so firmly and lovingly I could not withdraw it readily, while others were waiting to shake hands with me. The carriage was surrounded. We just had to wait, and then I was so sorry I had not waited in the house and shaken hands with every one of them. . . .
>
> This last meeting left a good feeling with nearly all, and I am inclined to think that all has been done that could be done on this visit (*ibid.*).

At 6:30 the next morning—long before daylight—she left by train. A large number of the believers, including Brother and Sister Hansen, were there to see her off.

RETURN TRIP TO SWITZERLAND

They took the southbound train, en route to Gothenburg, Sweden. When it became light, at about 9:00, she enjoyed what she termed "the romantic scenery." The trip on the ferry was tempestuous—six hours to Frederickshaven, Denmark (HS, p. 221); then by train south to Germany and across Germany to Basel.

Back home in Basel she summed up some facts about the tour:

> We reached Basel [Thursday] November 19, our homeward journey having occupied four days. We were absent six weeks on this Scandinavian tour, and traveled more than twenty-five hundred miles. . . . Wherever we went, our people warmly expressed their gratitude for the help which had been sent them and the interest manifested in their behalf by the brethren in America (*ibid.*, p. 225).

THE VISIT TO ITALY

Ellen White was weary and worn and would have welcomed a few weeks' rest, but she found herself immediately involved in plans for another trip, this time to Italy.

There were some problems in Italy. B. L. Whitney, president of the Central European Mission, suggested that she accompany him to Torre Pellice to bolster the spirits of the few discouraged believers there. "Weary and worn from the arduous labors of our northern trip," she wrote, "I would gladly have rested a few weeks in our home in Basel" (*ibid.*, p. 226). But arrangements were made to start out again the next Thursday, less than a week after reaching home.

Thursday morning, November 26, her fifty-eighth birthday, accompanied by Mary White and Whitney, Ellen White boarded the train for Torre Pellice. A. C. Bourdeau had just located there with his family. Ellen stated that the purpose of the visit was to "encourage the little company there who are striving under great difficulties to obey God" (*ibid.*, p. 231). The believers were meeting opposition on the question of the seventh-day Sabbath by one who had a few months before accepted it but was now a bitter opponent. Ellen White presented the picture of the beginning of her work in Torre Pellice:

> The next day, Sabbath, I spoke to the brethren and sisters in the hired hall in which they held their regular Sabbath meetings. Owing to a delay in getting out the appointment, few besides our own people were present. But I felt the same interest in speaking to the few that I would have felt in addressing hundreds. Choosing as my text Isaiah 56:1-7, I tried to impress upon them the importance of obeying God and walking in the light, regardless of the opinions or course of the world (*ibid.*).

She pointed out that the question might arise in some minds as to why commandment keepers are separated from the world into little companies, and she answered, "It is not because we choose to differ from those around us, but because we see the necessity of obeying all the requirements of God" (*ibid.*).

A secondary objective in her visit to Italy was to see the Waldensian valleys. During the week she did some sightseeing, going by carriage to nearby points of special interest. When the carriage could go no farther, several times she climbed the hills to points of historic interest relating to the experience of the Waldenses as they attempted to hide from their persecutors, and where many lost their lives.

They were now in the very heart of the Waldensian hideouts. Ellen White's heart thrilled as she recounted in her mind the history of God's noble, persecuted witnesses. Some of the surroundings had a familiar look to her, for in vision she had been shown the travails and persecutions of the Waldenses.

While she stayed in the Bourdeau home in Torre Pellice, council meetings were held to give study to the best way to conduct the work in Italy. "We keep asking the Lord," she wrote, "to open the way for the truth to find access to hearts in these valleys." Bourdeau spoke on the third Sabbath, giving Ellen a bit of rest, but Sunday afternoon she addressed an attentive audience. She spoke again Sunday night, her last meeting there.

At 4:30 in the morning of Tuesday, December 15, she and her companions were at the depot to catch the train back to Turin.

By the weekend she and Mary were home. She spoke to the believers Sabbath morning in the meeting hall at the publishing house. A large mail was waiting for her, and she picked up her work with no overshadowing of urgent travel plans. She had now made the rounds of visits to the principal countries of Europe where the message was reaching out. If she was to remain in Europe, she hoped to make progress with her literary work.

The length of her stay in Europe had not been determined. Widowed for five years, she missed James and his counsel in making decisions! Her son, W. C. White, was very helpful, but he was away at this time attending the General Conference in Battle Creek, Michigan.

As to her situation in general, Ellen White wrote to Willie on December 22:

> I can tell you, I find abundance of work that keeps coming ready to my hand and I see no place to rest, even in Europe. I think I will purchase a horse and carriage and ride out daily. I do not take pleasure in the rides taken with a coachman and hackman (letter 38, 1885).

Within a month she had made the purchase, which she described in a letter to J. D. Rise in California:

> I am now quite a cripple from the broken ankle. It was injured five years ago in Battle Creek. I cannot walk at times without a cane. I have had to purchase me a horse and carriage; cost something more than $300 for the whole outfit. All deemed it necessary for me as they surely saw I could not get exercise by walking (letter 18, 1886).

Continuing her December 22 letter to Willie, she wrote:

> Well, I am certainly doing more work than at any other period of my life, and I am thankful that the Lord has given me strength to work. . . .
>
> I see our work has but just begun here; I see so much to be done and I am doing too much. I wish I could do the work of ten. I would gladly do it. But I can only do the work of one—poor, frail at that. May God work Himself (letter 38, 1885).

"In regard to writing in the future," she commented, "I cannot say. I must write." One important literary task that loomed before her was the enlargement of the first of the great controversy books, *The Spirit of Prophecy*, volume 1—the one dealing with most of the Old Testament history, a volume that was to become *Patriarchs and Prophets*. She wrote:

> I think I can do it as well here in Europe as in America. Make just such arrangements as you please. If Marian is worn and has her plans

arranged to stay, I can send writing there, but if you think it advisable for her to come, all right *(ibid.)*.

The family now occupied five rooms on the third floor of the publishing house. After returning from Scandinavia Ellen had discovered that the unheated publishing house was "cold as a barn" and needed more furniture to make it comfortable. She had admired the stoves she had seen in Sweden, so she went down and selected "one of those earthen stoves" like the "white ones in Sweden, but this one we have purchased is about five feet [two meters] high, brown earthenware. It is a beauty for $20. . . . So you see we shall be nicely fixed here for the winter" (letter 37, 1885).

In this same letter she wrote:

> Brethren Whitney and Kellogg are true and earnest to do all they can for us. Brother Kellogg boards with us. They seem to think I must have everything I need to make me comfortable.
>
> But very little has been expended for furniture. Things picked up and borrowed have fitted us out with three good bedsteads and mattresses. Both rooms have carpets, not entirely covered, but answer all purposes *(ibid.)*.

During the winter and spring months of 1886 Ellen devoted her energies to writing, with occasional weekend trips to nearby churches in Switzerland. In addition to her almost-constant letter writing, her first literary work was to carry out the resolution, passed during the closing days of the European Missionary Council, that called for the publication in English of a "report of the European missions, with the report of Sister White's morning talks and a sketch of her visit to the missions" (see HS, p. 118). This would be for the information and encouragement of members in America.

MARIAN DAVIS JOINS THE FORCE

When W. C. White, in early February, returned from the General Conference session held in Battle Creek, Michigan, he brought with him quite a company of workers. It included Elder and Mrs. L. R. Conradi and Marian Davis. Commented Ellen when she got the word that they would soon be in Basel, "This settles the question that we shall remain in Europe during the best portion of the year 1886. We shall prepare books here and have them published here" (letter 94, 1886).

As spring came to Switzerland, plans were being laid for the work in Europe. Ellen White wrote in a newsy letter:

> We are now contemplating another journey to Italy. We should visit other churches; they are calling for us loudly. They call for us to again

visit Denmark, Sweden, and Norway. These places demand much hard work and I dread it, but I may feel that I must go. Jesus lived not to please Himself. I do not know as we will get away from here this winter. May the Lord direct (letter 11, 1886).

Ten days later, Thursday morning, April 15, Ellen, accompanied by Sara, Willie, and Mary, boarded the train for Italy. On Friday they were in Torre Pellice again at the home of A. C. Bourdeau (MS 62, 1886).

Six weeks intervened between their return to Basel and the time they had to be off for the second round of visits to the Scandinavian countries. These weeks were used by Ellen in literary work and in weekend visits to nearby churches.

ELLEN WHITE'S SECOND MISSIONARY JOURNEY

This was no pleasure trip for Ellen. She was not traveling as a tourist. She had work to do. In spite of forbidding circumstances, she determined to go. A few months before this she had stated, "I can, when I have to, do most anything" (letter 95, 1886). She looked to the Lord, and He gave her help.

SWEDEN

At the session of the Swedish Conference, which opened on June 23, 1886, about 65 church members were present from the 10 churches. Twenty-three were delegates sent from nine of the churches, representing a combined membership of 250. Leading ministers present were J. G. Matteson, O. A. Olsen, and W. C. White.

Mrs. White's meetings Sabbath and Sunday were well attended. She brought to the people practical instruction on true sanctification as contrasted with a spurious, no-cross experience in which perfection is claimed but is far from being attained. By the close of the general meeting she had spoken 11 times in 10 days.

"I think that the work here is going well," she wrote to Mary, back in Basel, "and I have felt much better healthwise than for months in the past. . . . The brethren are much encouraged. It is a good meeting and everything moves harmoniously. . . . I tell you, things look much different than when we were here last fall. There is a good hall, good seats to accommodate the people, and if Jesus will work with our efforts, we will be encouraged indeed and He will be" (letter 38b, 1886).

NORWAY—CHRISTIANIA

Before leaving America, Ellen White had been shown the low standard of piety in the Christiania church, and since she had been there only eight months before, she was constrained to bear pointed testimonies. The response was positive.

When she and Sara arrived in Christiania a little after 10:00 on Friday morning, July 2, they were met at the depot and driven to the old publishing house building, where two rooms were comfortably fitted up for them with a kitchen. She was pleased that Brother Hansen, the prominent Adventist building contractor, called on her soon after her arrival.

She was invited to take the Sabbath morning church service held in the commodious chapel of the newly constructed publishing house. The room was 41 feet (13 meters) by 55 feet (17 meters), with a 22-foot (7-meter) ceiling. Most of the 175 Seventh-day Adventists in Norway were members of this church, the balance being divided between two much smaller congregations (*SDA Yearbook* [1887], p. 94).

At some point in the several days Ellen White was there she had opportunity to look over the publishing house, now comfortably located in the new building. When she was shown through the several departments, she expressed great joy over the thought that, with these excellent facilities, periodicals and books suitable for the field could be printed quickly and sent on their mission. When she reached the pressroom, she took special interest and declared that she had seen that room and the presses years before—yes, nearly 12 years before, in the vision of January 3, 1875, in Battle Creek, Michigan (3LS, p. 299).

This was a crisis time for the church in Norway. Ellen continued her work to the close of the session on Tuesday evening, but spoke again to the church on Thursday evening before leaving the next day for Denmark:

> I presented before the church the necessity of a thorough change in their characters before God could acknowledge them as His children. I urged upon them the necessity of order in the church. They must have the mind which dwelt in Jesus in order to conduct themselves aright in the church of God. I urged upon them the importance of a correct observing of the Sabbath. . . . If it continues to go forward, then there will be a hearty repentance. . . . With this meeting my labors closed in Christiania (MS 66, 1886).

She commented, "The work was but just begun in the church."

DENMARK

Because of headwinds the ship bearing Ellen White and her party did not reach Copenhagen until too late for a Sabbath meeting. But on Sunday afternoon the hall was well filled, and many stood as they listened with good attention to her message.

At the Monday morning meeting 24 were present. It was a time of considerable unemployment in the city, and church members with work did not dare risk being away from their jobs. She divided the week in Denmark between the rather poorly attended meetings, her writing, and some sightseeing. On Monday, July 26, with Sara McEnterfer and W. C. White, she hastened back to Basel.

ENGLAND

After spending about a month at home she was off again to attend the Fourth European Missionary Council, to be held at Great Grimsby in England.

Although the business sessions of the council would not begin until Monday, September 27, tent meetings were being held in Great Grimsby, and Ellen threw herself into the work, with two meetings on Sabbath, September 18, two meetings on Sunday, and early-morning talks to the workers Sunday and Tuesday.

The Sunday night meeting was well attended, with the tent full and an overflow audience of half again as many outside. The congregation was attentive, and she spoke with freedom (letter 23a, 1886).

Many who came in during the week to attend the council were there for the Sabbath, September 25. Ellen White addressed them at 5:30 a.m. in a poorly ventilated, small room at the mission headquarters. The foul air almost paralyzed her.

The ventilation at the places chosen for the meetings was so poor that she finally became sick. She suffered with inflammation of head, stomach, and lungs.

Sara gave her hydrotherapy treatments, and she began to rally. But, although she attended some of the meetings of the council, she did not speak again, either through the week of the council or the week following, while she remained at Great Grimsby. However, she did labor in personal interviews, writing, and giving counsel.

The business of the Fourth Missionary Council was quite routine, with reports from the different fields of labor, resolutions aimed at improving the evangelistic thrust, and the election of officers.

FRANCE

In London for a day or two en route to France, and with improving health, Ellen White wrote several letters for B. L. Whitney to carry with him as he traveled to the General Conference session to begin in Battle Creek November 18. Then she and Sara, her son, and the Ingses were off for Nîmes, France, where tent meetings were being held.

D. T. Bourdeau had rented a home in Nîmes. He pitched an evangelistic tent there and for a few weeks had worked with a reasonable degree of success. He encountered some opposition, and some rowdies had attempted to break up the meetings, but by the time Ellen White joined in the work, matters were quite stable. On Sabbath, October 16, Ings spoke at the early-morning meeting; his message on the restoration of the Sabbath was well received. Mrs. White spoke in the worship service Sabbath morning and again in the evening. Sixteen people were keeping the Sabbath in Nîmes (MS 70, 1886). The meetings that were held through the two weeks Ellen and the Ingses were there were evangelistic—for the church and the general public—with Ellen taking the evening meetings in the tent. She did some sightseeing in this large city, which had a history that predated the life and ministry of Christ on earth.

As this was an evangelistic series, she preached Christ-centered, soul-winning sermons. And from day to day she was able to do a little sightseeing, some shopping, and as ever, write, write, write—100 pages while in Nîmes.

AT VALENCE, FRANCE

The travelers stopped at Valence, France, to meet with the few Sabbathkeepers who came together for two services. While at Valence they visited the cathedral and there saw a bust of Pope Pius VI. "This is the pope," Ellen wrote, "specified in prophecy, which received the deadly wound" (ibid.). She was intensely interested in the visit to the nearby tower where he had been confined and where he died.

THIRD VISIT TO ITALY

Ellen White expected to spend two weeks in Italy, but when they got to Torre Pellice they discovered that a man named Corcorda was attempting to neutralize the work A. C. Bourdeau had just done with the evangelistic tent; Corcorda got his ammunition from Miles Grant, an Advent Christian. With opposition coming early in Ellen's first visit to Italy and repeated now, it seemed impossible to accomplish much.

She spoke in Torre Pellice on Sabbath and in Villar Pellice on Sunday. After remaining a few days, however, she saw that little could be accomplished. She and the Ingses started home toward Basel, spending two weeks on their journey, visiting churches in Lausanne and Bienne in Switzerland on their way.

She reached Basel Tuesday, November 23. She had been gone for 10 weeks. As she gave a report to G. I. Butler the next day, she wrote:

> I have for weeks been exposed to fogs and rains and bad air in halls. I have talked in halls where it was sometimes very hot and the air was impure and then have gone out into a sharp, cutting air from the lakes, and taken cold again and again. . . . In two days, the twenty-sixth of this

month, I shall be 59 years old. I thank my heavenly Father for the strength that He has given me to do more work than I ever expected to do. I thank the Lord with heart and soul and voice. I am thinking we may not feel obliged to remain here in Europe much longer (letter 115, 1886).

THE GENERAL CONFERENCE SESSION OF 1888

PRE-1888

Ellen White had not been able to attend the General Conference session of 1886, because she was still in Europe, just concluding her third visit to Torre Pellice in Italy. But she was aware of the interest in the book of Galatians that was being taken by some of the leading brethren.

"That conference [1886]," she wrote to G. I. Butler, "was presented to me in the night season" (letter 21, 1888).

Records are meager, but the matter of the law in Galatians was discussed by a group of leading workers at the time of the General Conference session in Battle Creek in 1886 (3SM, p. 167). In her letter to Butler she said:

> My guide then had many things to say which left an indelible impression upon my mind. His words were solemn and earnest. . . .
>
> He stretched out his arms toward Dr. Waggoner and to you, Elder Butler, and said in substance as follows: "Neither have all the light upon the law; neither position is perfect" (letter 21, 1888).

In another account of this experience she told of how, while in Europe, she was shown what took place in Battle Creek at the 1886 General Conference session:

> Two years ago Jesus was grieved and bruised in the person of His saints. The rebuke of God is upon everything of the character of harshness, of disrespect, and the want of sympathetic love in brother toward brother (MS 21, 1888).

In Galatians 3:19 the apostle Paul wrote of the "added law," and in verse 24 of the "schoolmaster to bring us unto Christ." Among Seventh-day Adventists for two years there had been controversy over which law he meant.

This was not a new subject of interest to Seventh-day Adventists. J. H. Waggoner, in his book *The Law of God: An Examination of the Testimony of Both Testaments*, published at the Review office in 1854, took the position that the "added law" of verse 19 and the "schoolmaster" of verse 24 was the moral and not the ceremonial law. He took the controversial stance that "not a single dec-laration" in Galatians "referred to the ceremonial or Levitical law" (p. 24).

Opponents of the Seventh-day Sabbath commonly use lines in the book of Galatians to support their view that the law was done away with at the cross—phrases such as "curse of the law," "schoolmaster to bring us to Christ," "the yoke of bondage," etc. In trying to meet this argument early Sabbathkeepers ex-plained that Paul was referring to the ceremonial law which was fulfilled at the time that Christ was nailed to the cross.

According to Uriah Smith, "Sister White . . . had a vision in which this law question was shown her, and she immediately wrote J. H. Waggoner that his po-sition on the law was wrong," and the book was taken off the market (Uriah Smith to W. A. McCutcheon, Aug. 6, 1901). This settled the matter for a number of years. Then the question was raised as to whether the counsel given to Waggoner referred to the doctrinal positions in the book or to the matter of publishing conflicting views.*

In the mid-1880s E. J. Waggoner (son of J. H.), associate editor of the *Signs of the Times* in Oakland and teacher of Bible at Healdsburg College, was moved by an Ellen G. White address read at a camp meeting. He seemed to see Christ hanging on the cross as a sacrifice for his sins. He determined to delve into a study of this saving truth, a truth he felt he must make known to others (R. W. Schwarz, *Light Bearers to the Remnant*, p. 185).

The angel guide, who in vision took Ellen to the tabernacle in Battle Creek at the time of the 1886 General Conference session, declared:

> "There is much light yet to shine forth from the law of God and the gospel of righteousness. This message, understood in its true character, and proclaimed in the Spirit, will lighten the earth with its glory. The great decisive question is to be brought before all nations, tongues, and peoples. The closing work of the third angel's message will be attended with a power that will send the rays of the Sun of Righteousness into all the highways and byways of life" (MS 15, 1888 [see also A. V. Olson, *Thirteen Crisis Years*, p. 305]).

For Seventh-day Adventists generally the 1888 General Conference ses-sion in Minneapolis and the ministerial institute that preceded it bring to mind a matter of great importance—the message of righteousness by faith and the considerable resistance that met its presentation. Before we review the history of Ellen White's work at that crucial meeting, certain points of background and developments should be considered:

1. Although, as we look back, the subject of righteousness by faith is seen as one of great importance, it was but one of many pressing matters that called

for the attention of the delegates who met in Minneapolis for the twenty-seventh annual session of the General Conference and the ministerial institute that preceded it.

2. Other matters were: new missions, new churches, plans for a missionary ship (*Pitcairn*) to serve the work of the church in the South Pacific.

3. Consequently, the information concerning just what took place at Minneapolis in the way of theological discussions has come largely from the E. G. White documents and the memory statements of a few who were present.

4. As to establishing positions, no official action was taken in regard to the theological positions discussed.

WHAT HAPPENED IN MINNEAPOLIS

"It was by faith," wrote Ellen White, "I ventured to cross the Rocky Mountains for the purpose of attending the General Conference held in Minneapolis" (MS 24, 1888).

Overwhelmed with discouragement, she had been overtaken by sickness at her home in Healdsburg. "I felt no desire to recover," she later wrote. "I had no power even to pray, and no desire to live. Rest, only rest, was my desire, quiet and rest. As I lay for two weeks in nervous prostration, I had hope that no one would beseech the throne of grace in my behalf. When the crisis came, it was the impression that I would die. This was my thought. But it was not the will of my heavenly Father. My work was not yet done" (MS 2, 1888).

She remembered the solemn vows she had made at the bedside of her dying husband—vows "to disappoint the enemy, to bear a constant, earnest appeal to my brethren" (MS 21, 1888). This she now determined to do.

As she placed herself in the path of duty, the Lord gave her strength and grace to bear her testimony before the people. Day by day she found herself growing stronger.

On October 2 she, with a number of friends and fellow workers, and accompanied by Sara McEnterfer and Willie, was on the train bound for the East. To her disappointment, she found that in her reduced strength it was necessary to rest in her berth for most of the journey to Minneapolis. She could neither knit nor visit, but she did look over some papers.

Arriving at Minneapolis Wednesday morning, October 10, Ellen, Willie, and Sara were treated royally.

The General Conference session was to be held in the newly constructed Minneapolis church, opening Wednesday evening, October 17. A ministerial institute was to precede the session by a full week. It was not till the date for the General Conference session was announced in the *Review and Herald* of August 7 that the plans for an institute had begun to develop. Butler wrote:

"Leading brethren had suggested the holding of an institute to precede the General Conference the present year, and have presented many forcible reasons in its favor" (RH, Aug. 28, 1888). A week later the *Review* announced the institute plans as definite. Butler added:

> We cannot pretend to say what will be the exact order of exercises, or what subjects will be especially considered. . . . A week's time spent in instruction on important features of church and conference work, and in calmly considering and carefully studying perplexing questions relating to the Scriptures, as well as in seeking God earnestly for heavenly wisdom, will most likely be of vast benefit (*ibid.*, Sept. 4, 1888).

It seems that W. C. White, one of the "leading brethren" who suggested the institute, had something more specific in mind.

There was the question of the law in Galatians, which had been introduced at the session in 1886, and also the identity of the 10 horns, or kingdoms, of the beast of Daniel 7. Views on these points held by *Signs of the Times* editors E. J. Waggoner and A. T. Jones were in conflict with the traditional views held quite generally, and particularly by Butler and Smith.

In a letter to Mary, who was very ill at the health retreat at St. Helena, Ellen White said:

> Elders Smith and Butler are very loath to have anything said upon the law in Galatians, but I cannot see how it can be avoided. We must take the Bible as our standard and we must diligently search its pages for light and evidence of truth (letter 81, 1888).

In his report of the opening of the institute, Smith said:

> The subjects proposed to be considered in the hours for Biblical and historical study are, so far, a historical view of the ten kingdoms, the divinity of Christ, the healing of the deadly wound, justification by faith, how far we should go in trying to use the wisdom of the serpent, and predestination. Other subjects will doubtless be introduced (RH, Oct. 16, 1888).

Concerning the first hours of the institute, he wrote:

> At seven-thirty last evening Elder Haskell made stirring remarks upon the work of the message in foreign lands. At 9:00 a.m. today [the eleventh] a Bible reading was held by A. T. Jones, on the advancement of the work of the third angel's message. The point brought out was that personal consecration must lie at the foundation of all our success in this work (*ibid.*).

In his editorial report written on the second day Smith informed *Review* readers that about 100 ministers were present when the institute opened at 2:30 p.m. Wednesday, October 10. As Butler was detained in Battle Creek because of illness, S. N. Haskell was selected to chair the meetings. F. E. Belden was chosen secretary.

The daily program was a full one, beginning with a morning devotional meeting at 7:45 and continuing through the day and evening.

The meetings at 10:00 a.m. and 2:30 p.m. were occupied by A. T. Jones in an examination of the subject of the 10 kingdoms. At 4:00 p.m. E. J. Waggoner (both an ordained minster and physician), by arrangement, took up, in the form of a Bible reading, the duties of church officers.

Smith reported:

> Sister White is present, in the enjoyment of a good degree of health and strength. Much disappointment and regret is expressed by the brethren that Elder Butler is unable to be present on account of sickness. He is remembered fervently in their prayers. The prospect is good for a profitable meeting *(ibid.)*.

As Ellen White spoke at the Thursday morning devotional she was surprised at the large number of new faces in her audience. Many new workers had joined the forces in the three or four years since she had attended a General Conference session held east of the Rocky Mountains.

In writing of the institute to Mary, at the health retreat, she reported:

> Today, Friday [October 12], at nine o'clock, I read some important matter to the conference and then bore a very plain testimony to our brethren. This had quite an effect upon them.
>
> Elder Butler has sent me a long letter, a most curious production of accusations and charges against me, but these things do not move me. I believe it was my duty to come. I worry nothing about the future, but try to do my duty for today (letter 81, 1888).

Butler had dictated a 39-page letter in which, among other things, he attributed his five-month-long illness largely to the manner in which Mrs. White had counseled in dealing with the question of the law in Galatians. She had not condemned Waggoner for his positions, although they were in direct conflict with those held by Butler and Smith.

That the president of the General Conference, who had given Ellen White loyal support through the years, was writing "accusations and charges" against her was disheartening. It reflected the widening tide of negative attitudes toward the messages God was sending through His messenger to His people.

Butler was deeply suspicious of the work of Jones and Waggoner, and from reports that had come to him he felt certain Ellen White was in their camp. Thus the omens were beginning to appear of what was before them in the more than three weeks of the institute and the conference.

The Friday evening service, October 12, cast a cloud over the worker group. Mrs. White wrote of it:

> At the commencement of the Sabbath Elder [Eugene] Farnsworth preached a most gloomy discourse telling of the great wickedness and corruption in our midst and dwelling upon the apostasies among us. There was no light, no good cheer, no spiritual encouragement in this discourse. There was a general gloom diffused among the delegates to the conference *(ibid.)*.

She had the meeting Sabbath afternoon, and she used the opportunity to try to turn things around. She wrote:

> Yesterday was a very important period in our meeting. Elder Smith preached in forenoon upon the signs of the times. It was, I think, a good discourse—timely. In the afternoon I spoke upon 1 John 3.
>
> "Behold, what manner of love," et cetera. The blessing of the Lord rested upon me and put words in my mouth and I had much freedom in trying to impress upon our brethren the importance of dwelling upon the love of God much more and letting gloomy pictures alone.
>
> The effect on the people was most happy. Believers and unbelievers bore testimony that the Lord had blessed them in the word spoken and that from this time they would not look on the dark side and dwell upon the great power of Satan, but talk of the goodness and the love and compassion of Jesus, and praise God more. . . .
>
> The Lord gave me testimony calculated to encourage. My own soul was blessed, and light seemed to spring up amid the darkness *(ibid.)*.

On Monday, October 15, near the close of the institute, E. J. Waggoner introduced the subject of the law in Galatians. The discussion ran for almost a week at the Bible study periods in the General Conference session. Beginning with the second day, Waggoner placed the emphasis on justification by faith. He was scholarly, gentle, and earnest, his arguments persuasive. On Monday, October 22, just one week after beginning his studies, he wrote a report of the progress of the institute and the General Conference session for the readers of the *Signs of the Times*. After writing of the subjects presented in the Bible study hour during the first few days, he reported that taken up next were "the law and the gospel in their various relations, coming under the general head of justification by faith."

These subjects have aroused a deep interest in the minds of all present; and thus far during the conference, one hour a day has been devoted to a continuance of their study (ST, Nov. 2, 1888).

His audience generally was in sympathy with the much-loved and respected Uriah Smith. Many stood with Butler, who was absent. Because Ellen White was tolerant and wished to see a fair discussion of the vital question of Christ and His righteousness, it was assumed she was influenced by Waggoner. This she denied, testifying:

> I have had no conversation in regard to it with my son W. C. White, with Dr. Waggoner, or with Elder A. T. Jones (MS 15, 1888 [see also Olson, pp. 305, 306]).

All could see that she listened attentively to Waggoner's expositions. In her retrospective statement, written soon after the conference, she declared:

> When I stated before my brethren that I had heard for the first time the views of Elder E. J. Waggoner, some did not believe me. I stated that I had heard precious truths uttered that I could respond to with all my heart, for had not these great and glorious truths, the righteousness of Christ and the entire sacrifice made in behalf of man, been imprinted indelibly on my mind by the Spirit of God? Has not this subject been presented in the testimonies again and again? When the Lord had given to my brethren the burden to proclaim this message, I felt inexpressively grateful to God, for I knew it was the message for this time (MS 24, 1888 [see also 3SM, p. 172]).

It is interesting to note that several times Ellen White declared that she was not ready to accept some points made by Dr. Waggoner. Of this she wrote on November 1, while the conference was nearing its close:

> Some interpretations of Scripture given by Dr. Waggoner I do not regard as correct. But I believe him to be perfectly honest in his views, and I would respect his feelings and treat him as a Christian gentleman. . . .
>
> It would be dangerous to denounce Dr. Waggoner's position as wholly erroneous. This would please the enemy. I see the beauty of truth in the presentation of the righteousness of Christ in relation to the law as the doctor has placed it before us (MS 15, 1888 [see also Olson, p. 302]).

Quite naturally reports of the happenings at Minneapolis were sent from day to day to Butler, bedridden in Battle Creek. What he heard did not give him peace of mind. He telegraphed a message to the session, "Stand by the old landmarks." This stiffened the resistance to the Waggoner presentation. Shortly after the session Ellen White was to address herself to the point:

> In Minneapolis God gave precious gems of truth to His people in new settings. This light from heaven by some was rejected with all the stubbornness the Jews manifested in rejecting Christ, and there was much talk about standing by the old landmarks.
>
> But there was evidence they knew not what the old landmarks were. There was evidence that there was reasoning from the Word that commended itself to the conscience; but the minds of men were fixed, sealed against the entrance of light, because they had decided it was a dangerous error removing the "old landmarks" when it was not moving a peg of the old landmarks, but they had perverted ideas of what constituted the old landmarks (MS 13, 1889 [see also CWE, p. 30]).

Then she listed what she considered the "landmarks." She was listing, of course, the distinguishing characteristics of the Advent movement. She did not include such pillars of faith as authority of the Holy Scriptures, baptism, and justification by faith, but those that had been agreed upon by the early believers in the Second Advent after the passing of the time in 1844. She listed the cleansing of the sanctuary, the three angels' messages, the importance of the Sabbath, and the nonimmortality of the soul.

She said:

> All this cry about changing the old landmarks is all imaginary.
>
> Now at the present time God designs a new and fresh impetus shall be given to His work. Satan sees this, and he is determined it shall be hindered. He knows that if he can deceive the people who claim to believe present truth, [and make them believe that] the work the Lord designs to do for His people is a removing of the old landmarks, something which they should, with most determined zeal, resist, then he exults over the deception he has led them to believe (*ibid.* [see also CWE, pp. 30, 31]).

Forty years earlier Ellen White had been present when doctrinal matters were studied by those who were pioneering the work of the church. As she wrote of this in 1892 she recalled:

> We would come together burdened in soul, praying that we might be one in faith and doctrine; for we knew that Christ is not divided. One point at a time was made the subject of investigation. Solemnity characterized these councils of investigation. The Scriptures were opened with

a sense of awe. Often we fasted that we might be better fitted to understand the truth.

After earnest prayer, if any point was not understood, it was discussed, and each one expressed his opinion freely; then we would again bow in prayer, and earnest supplications went up to heaven that God would help us to see eye to eye, that we might be one, as Christ and the Father are one. . . .

We sought most earnestly that the Scriptures should not be wrested to suit any man's opinions. *We tried to make our differences as slight as possible by not dwelling on points that were of major importance*, upon which there were varying opinions. But the burden of every soul was to bring about a condition among the brethren which would answer the prayer of Christ that His disciples might be one as He and the Father are one (RH, July 16, 1892; italics supplied [see also TM, pp. 24, 25]).

But this was not the case at Minneapolis. The leaders there did not try to make their differences "as slight as possible." For two years the issue of the law in Galatians had smoldered, and when it was taken up, bitterness and accusations were unleashed.

The focal point was verse 24, chapter 3, which reads: "Wherefore the law was our schoolmaster to bring us unto Christ, that we might be justified by faith." There was no argument among Seventh-day Adventists concerning the believer's being justified by faith, although this vital truth was sadly neglected at the time. In 1888 the sharp difference of opinion, as when J. H. Waggoner wrote on the subject in 1854, was whether the law brought to view as the schoolmaster was the moral or the ceremonial law. Thus two issues were bound up in a study of "the law and the gospel" in such a way that if one topic suffered in bitter debate, both were affected. The great adversary took advantage of this.

To complicate matters, the discussion of the law in Galatians followed close on the heels of the bitter and extended debate over the Huns and the Alemanni (cf. Dan. 7:20), with key workers taking sides and reacting strongly.

As the meeting advanced and the positions of the participants became clear, Mrs. White developed a deep concern, amounting to anguish, for the sharp, hard feelings. She had little to say about righteousness by faith per se, but she emphasized the importance of tolerance and of unity among brethren, and the manifestation of a Christian attitude. She commented:

There are some differences of views on some subjects, but is this a reason for sharp, hard feelings? Shall envy and evil surmisings and imaginings, evil suspicion, hatred, and jealousies become enthroned in the heart? All these things are evil and only evil. Our help is in God alone.

Let us spend much time in prayer and in searching the Scriptures with a right spirit, anxious to learn and willing to be corrected or undeceived on any point where we may be in error. If Jesus is in our midst and our hearts are melted into tenderness by His love we shall have one of the best conferences we have ever attended (MS 24, 1888 [see also 3SM, p. 166]).

Ellen White felt she had done all that she could do in presenting the light the Lord had given her, and she thought to quietly withdraw from the conference (*ibid.*). But she discovered that this was not God's plan. She was not to be released from her responsibility to be there as His messenger.

Not released, she remained.

Before the close of the session, she had spoken nearly 20 times in many heart-searching appeals. Never before had she spoken so boldly to this group of responsible workers.

In a letter to Mary she commented:

We know not the future, but we feel that Jesus stands at the helm and we shall not be shipwrecked. My courage and faith has been good and has not failed me, notwithstanding we have had the hardest and most incomprehensible tug of war we have ever had among our people. The matter cannot be explained by pen unless I should write many, many pages; so I had better not undertake the job (letter 82, 1888; italics supplied).

This she did shortly after the session closed, in the 26-page statement "Looking Back at Minneapolis" (MS 24, 1888), a major portion of which appears in *Selected Messages*, book 3, pages 163-177.

By several expressions in this letter to Mary it seems clear that when the meeting at Minneapolis broke up, what the future held was not then seen but would be determined by what was in the hearts of individual ministers. This would not be known until there was a firming up and personal decisions were made.

LOOKING BACK AT MINNEAPOLIS

1. As to establishing positions, no official action was taken in regard to the theological questions discussed. The uniform witness concerning the attitude toward the matter of righteousness by faith was that there were mixed reactions. These were described succinctly by Jones in 1893: "I know that some there accepted it; others rejected it entirely. . . . Others tried to stand halfway between, and get it that way" (GCB 1893, p. 185). Ellen White and others corroborate this. It is not possible to establish, from the records available, the relative number in each of the three groups.

2. The concept that the General Conference, and thus the denomination,

rejected the message of righteousness by faith in 1888 is without foundation and was not projected until 40 years after the Minneapolis meeting, and 13 years after Mrs. White's death. Contemporary records of the time do not suggest denominational rejection. No E. G. White statement anywhere supports the concept of rejection.

3. The concept of denominational rejection, when projected, is set forth in the atmosphere of Ellen G. White statements made concerning the negative position of *certain individuals*—the "some" of Jones's report, above. The historical record of the reception in the field following the session supports the concept that favorable attitudes were quite general.

4. It has been suggested that the Minneapolis session marked a noticeable change in Ellen White's teaching on the law and the gospel. While Minneapolis brought a new emphasis in bringing to the front "neglected truth," the fact that there was no change in teaching is evidenced in the 19 articles from her pen comprising the 122-page book *Faith and Works*, with six written before 1888 and 13 written subsequent to the Minneapolis session.

5. Righteousness by faith is a vital truth, but it would seem that disproportionate emphasis has come to be given to the experience of the Minneapolis General Conference session. J. N. Loughborough, who authored the first two works on denominational history, *Rise and Progress of the Seventh-day Adventists* (1892), and a revision and enlargement in 1905, *The Great Second Advent Movement*, makes no mention of the session or the issues. True, he was not there, but if the matter was prominent at the time he wrote, he could not have overlooked it. *Life Sketches of Ellen G. White*, published in 1915, makes no reference to the General Conference session of 1888.

Perhaps the true attitude of the church and its leaders toward Jones and Waggoner after the 1888 conference session is best reflected by the invitations extended to these two men to conduct Bible studies in the General Conference sessions held during the next 10 years. It must be remembered that the General Conference Committee was responsible for planning General Conference sessions and choosing the speakers. The church organization had many able preachers. Here is the historical picture:

In 1889 Jones took the 8:00 daily Bible study, and spoke on righteousness by faith. Waggoner also addressed the conference.

In 1891 seventeen Bible studies were recorded in the *General Conference Bulletin*. All but one of these were given by Waggoner.

In 1893 Jones gave 24 consecutive Bible studies, which were published in the *General Conference Bulletin*.

In 1895 twenty-six consecutive studies by Jones were recorded.

In 1897 nineteen Bible studies were given by Waggoner, and 11 by Jones.

One man spoke on consecutive mornings, the other on consecutive afternoons. A large part of the *Bulletin* is made up of the reports of their 30 studies. In 1899 Waggoner gave three studies, and Jones seven.

It is clear that the rank and file of workers and laity alike respected and appreciated the men through whom light came at Minneapolis, and benefited from their earnest ministry of the Word. It is clear also that unprecedented opportunity was given for the presentation of whatever messages burdened their hearts.

In 1897 Jones was elected editor of the *Review and Herald*, a position he held for four years. During this time Smith took a secondary place on the editorial staff.

GOD'S GREATEST GIFT—CHRIST AND HIS RIGHTEOUSNESS

How could anyone in a group that had for 40 years, more or less, prayed together for hours at a time, studied the Scriptures earnestly to know the will of God, looked forward anxiously for the soon-coming Saviour, dedicated their lives to the cause of God, sacrificed their means to hasten the work, believed themselves to be the "remnant church," published thousands of pages proclaiming their faith—how could any of them not accept an inspiring message of "righteousness by faith"?

But some could, and some did.

Some even suggested that because Ellen White was tolerant and wished to see a fair discussion of the subject of Christ and His righteousness, she had been influenced by Elder Waggoner.

This she denied. She declared:

> Had not these great and glorious truths, the righteousness of Christ and the entire sacrifice made in behalf of man, been imprinted indelibly on my mind by the Spirit of God? Has not this subject been presented in the testimonies again and again? When the Lord had given to my brethren the burden to proclaim the message, I felt inexpressibly grateful to God, for I knew it was the message for this time (MS 24, 1888).

"Righteousness by faith"—had not this been part and parcel of the Protestant faith? Had it not been the fundamental cause of the split with the Roman Catholic Church? promoted by Luther, Calvin, and Wesley? a sort of "goes-without-saying" basic truth held by most Protestant congregations? It was not "present truth" in the same sense as the third angel's message. Hence, perhaps it was not in the forefront of subjects being proclaimed to catch attention by those attempting to warn of the end of the world.

When the early Adventists, in defense of the seventh-day Sabbath, enforced their position by emphasizing the perpetuity of the law and the authority of the Ten Commandments, they were accused of teaching salvation by works or obedience to the law. To get around this argument they tried to show that the law that was "nailed to the cross" was the ceremonial law, leaving the moral law still in effect. But Paul was teaching that salvation was gained not by lawkeeping, either moral or ceremonial, but by faith. The beauty of this concept as presented by Jones and Waggoner and sustained by Ellen White at Minneapolis thrilled most of the hearers, and they went forth to spread it to the churches.

With mixed emotions Ellen White traveled from Minneapolis to Battle Creek following the General Conference session. Her heart rejoiced with the precious revived truth of Christ our righteousness. Somewhat fearfully, however, she pondered what to expect in the attitude of the leaders residing in Battle Creek to whom the people looked. She did not have to wait long for the answer.

When she was invited to speak in the tabernacle on her first Sabbath, she urged the local elders to invite A. T. Jones to speak also. They answered that they would have to check with Uriah Smith.

"Then do this at once," she replied, "for time is precious and there is a message to come to this people and the Lord requires you to open the way" (MS 30, 1889).

It was now clear that those whose hearts were fired with the light revived at Minneapolis would have to work around the prejudice of some of the leaders who had long resided in Battle Creek, and take the message to the churches. Even the church paper, the *Review and Herald,* would be of little help under the circumstances.

And take it to the churches Ellen White and A. T. Jones did. Both began in the pulpit of the Battle Creek Tabernacle. In the normal order of things meetings of one kind or another were held in the local conferences through the coming months. Further, by special arrangement of the General Conference Committee, three institutes were held during the spring and summer.

As meetings were held through the spring and summer across the land, Mrs. White and Jones labored as a team. Truly, the presenting of righteousness by faith yielded good fruit.

THE REMARKABLE REVIVAL IN BATTLE CREEK

Late in the year, in Battle Creek, the real breakthrough came. J. O. Corliss, Jones, and Ellen White led out in the meetings of the Week of Prayer. It was scheduled from December 15 to 22—but it lasted a month. As the week opened, Mrs. White, because of infirmities of the moment, dared not leave the sanitarium. So she began her work there, with physicians, nurses, and the rest of the sanitarium staff. Jones and Corliss held meetings at the tabernacle, the publishing house, and the college. Reported Ellen White in the *Review:*

The revival services held during the Week of Prayer and since that time have accomplished a good work in the Battle Creek church. Elders A. T. Jones, J. O. Corliss, and others took an active part in conducting the meetings. The principal topic dwelt upon was justification by faith, and this truth came as meat in due season to the people of God. The living oracles of God were presented in new and precious light (RH, Feb. 12, 1889).

Meetings were held daily at the college, at the publishing house, at the sanitarium, and in the evenings in the tabernacle. Ellen White also found time to call on some families in personal visits.

In concluding her report of the victorious experience, in the *Review and Herald* of February 12 she exclaimed: "May the good work begun in the Battle Creek church be carried onward and upward till every soul shall be consecrated, purified, refined, and fitted for the society of heavenly angels!" But this wish was not to see fulfillment, for some who had been at Minneapolis and had resisted the light given there still held back. The decision in response to light is a personal one and some took the wrong course.

Back and forth across the land Ellen White went carrying the message of hope and faith. New York, Washington, D.C., Brooklyn, Des Moines, Chicago, South Lancaster, Healdsburg, Oakland.

Typical of her dauntless courage and determination is the story of her trip to the camp meeting at Williamsport, Pennsylvania, a few days after "the day the dam broke," causing the famous Johnstown Flood.

THE WILLIAMSPORT CAMP MEETING

Thursday night, May 30, Ellen White, accompanied by Sara McEnterfer, boarded the train in Battle Creek bound for Williamsport, Pennsylvania, where the camp meeting was to open Tuesday, June 4. Because of heavy rains, the train moved slowly. They had expected to reach Williamsport the next afternoon at 5:00, but soon they could see that this objective could not be met. Bridges had been swept away and roads washed out by the Johnstown Flood. When they reached Elmira, New York, they were advised to give up their journey.

But neither Ellen nor Sara was easily dissuaded. They were determined to go as far as possible, hoping that the reports concerning the conditions of travel were exaggerated. At Canton, some 40 miles (64 kilometers) from Williamsport, their car was switched onto a side track because of a washout; they spent the Sabbath there in a hotel. Determined to get through, Ellen and Sara put their heads together and left no stone unturned in their attempts to find a way. Traveling by carriage part of the way and walking part of the way, they compassed the 40 miles (64 kilometers) in four days, in a hair-raising venture described in her report in the *Review and Herald* of July 30, 1889. One interesting feature was the manner in which she was sustained physically. She reported:

> We were obliged to walk miles on this journey, and it seemed marvelous that I could endure to travel as I did. Both of my ankles were broken years ago, and ever since they have been weak. Before leaving Battle Creek for Kansas, I sprained one of my ankles and was confined to crutches for some time; but in this emergency I felt no weakness or inconvenience, and traveled safely over the rough, sliding rocks.

At one point they waited for three hours as, at their direction, a raft was constructed upon which to ferry the carriage in which they traveled across a swiftly flowing stream. A small boat pulled it across, the horses swam the stream, and the two women travelers were rowed across. Then they continued their journey by horse and carriage. The destruction reminded Ellen White of what is to come in the last days and encouraged her to be even more diligent in preparation for that day. Her report in the *Review* closes with these words:

> We arrived at Williamsport at three o'clock Wednesday afternoon. The experience and anxiety through which I passed on this journey greatly exhausted me in mind and body; but we were grateful that we had suffered no serious trouble, and that the Lord had preserved us from the perils of the land, and prospered us on our way.

When they reached the town they were told that the campground had been flooded out and that the tents had been taken down. Actually, they found the tents had been moved to higher ground and the meeting was in progress.

While it was a difficult meeting to get to, it was an easy meeting to work in. Wrote Ellen White:

> The Lord had a work for me to do at Williamsport. I had much freedom in speaking to the brethren and sisters there assembled. They did not seem to possess a spirit of unbelief and of resistance to the message the Lord had sent them. I felt that it was a great privilege to speak to those whose hearts were not barricaded with prejudice and evil surmising. My soul went out in grateful praise that, weary and exhausted as I was, I did not have to carry upon my heart the extra burden of seeing brethren and sisters whom I loved unimpressed and in resistance of the light that God had graciously permitted to shine upon them.
>
> I did not have to set my face as a flint, and press and urge upon them that which I knew to be truth. The message was eagerly welcomed; and although I had to speak words of reproof and warning, as well as words

of encouragement, all were heartily received by my hearers (*ibid.*, Aug. 13, 1889).

Ellen White spoke 13 times at the Williamsport camp meeting, including the early-morning meetings.

She worked her way west in the late summer to Colorado and then to California. After the camp meeting in Oakland she hastened back to Battle Creek for the General Conference session, which opened Friday morning, October 18.

THE 1889 GENERAL CONFERENCE SESSION

Carefully she watched developments at the 1889 General Conference session. When the meeting was well along she reported:

> The spirit that was in the meeting at Minneapolis is not here. All moves off in harmony. There is a large attendance of delegates. Our five o'clock morning meeting is well attended, and the meetings good. All the testimonies to which I have listened have been of an elevating character. They say that the past year has been the best of their life; the light shining forth from the Word of God has been clear and distinct—justification by faith, Christ our righteousness (MS 10, 1889 [see also 1SM, pp. 361, 362]).

The General Conference session late in October climaxed activities for the year. In a unique three-page statement near the close of 1889 she summarized in sweeping terms a review of her activities between the two General Conference sessions, 1888 and 1889:

> After the General Conference [of 1888] I journeyed to Battle Creek and commenced labor in Battle Creek. Visited Potterville [Michigan], by invitation, to attend the State ministers' meeting [November 22-27]. Returned to Battle Creek, and the same week felt urged by the Spirit of God to go to Des Moines, Iowa. Attended the Iowa ministers' meeting [November 29 to December 5]; spoke six times.
>
> Returned to Battle Creek and labored in speaking to the institutions in this place, the Sanitarium, especially during the Week of Prayer [December 15-22] in the early morning. I also spoke on other occasions to patients and helpers. Spoke to the workers in the office of publication. Spoke in the Tabernacle.
>
> Attended the South Lancaster meeting [beginning January 10]. Spoke there eleven times. Stopped on our way to Washington, D.C., and spoke in the evening to a goodly number assembled in the Brooklyn

Mission. Spoke six times in Washington. Spoke on our returning route one evening in Williamsport. Spent Sabbath and first day in [Syracuse] New York. Spoke three times and was several hours in important council.

Returned to Battle Creek [February 4] and labored earnestly. Attended two weeks' meeting in Chicago [March 28-April 8] [RH, May 7, 1889]. Spoke there many times. Returned to Battle Creek, attended special meeting for ministers in Battle Creek, and spoke several times. Continued to labor in Battle Creek until the Kansas camp meeting; was three weeks in that workers' meeting [May 7 to 21] and camp meeting [May 21-28]. Labored to my utmost strength to help the people assembled. Attended meeting at Williamsport [June 5-11]. Spoke ten times, including morning meetings.

Attended camp meeting in [Rome] New York [June 11-18] and labored as God gave me strength. Returned worn and exhausted to Battle Creek and was obliged to refrain from speaking for a time. Attended camp meeting at Wexford, Michigan [June 25-July 2], and the Lord strengthened me to speak to the people. After the meeting I was again prostrated through overlabor.

Attended the camp meeting in Kalamazoo [Michigan, August 25 to September 2], and the Lord strengthened me to speak and labor for the people. Returning home to Battle Creek, I was again prostrated, but the Lord helped me. I attended the meeting in Saginaw [Michigan, August 27 to September 3], and to praise of God He raised me above my feebleness, and I was made strong when before the people.

After the meeting I was again greatly prostrated but started on my journey to attend camp meeting in Colorado [September 10-17]. The Lord greatly blessed me in these meetings as I bore my testimony. I then continued my journey to California.

I spoke twice to the people in Healdsburg. Attended Oakland meeting and was very sick, but the Lord raised me up and strengthened me with His Spirit and power, and I spoke to the people eight times and several times before committees and ministers and in morning meetings. Then I came across the Rocky Mountains to attend the [1889] General Conference (MS 25, 1889).

E. G. WHITE *REVIEW* ARTICLES TELL THE STORY

Fifteen of the 31 E. G. White articles appearing in the *Review and Herald* for the first nine months of 1889 are stenographic reports of her addresses given throughout this period of special labor. These, together with her five reports of the convocations, carried the benefits of her arduous work to the church generally.

Some today ask why this movement in the church, emphasizing the subject of righteousness by faith, did not usher in the "loud cry." In answer, it might be suggested that the polarization of attitudes militated against such an advance. Further, that which proved to be so great a blessing to many individuals could easily be allowed to slip away if the recipient failed to renew daily the precious experience. With many the righteousness by faith message brought a turning point in their experience, lifting them to an enduring, victorious life. The numerous articles Ellen White published in the journals of the church and the E. G. White books published from 1888 onward, especially *Steps to Christ* (1892), *The Desire of Ages* (1898), and *Christ's Object Lessons* (1900), kept the theme of "Christ our righteousness" before Seventh-day Adventists and the world.

---

* On February 18, 1887, Ellen had written from Basel, Switzerland, earnestly admonishing Jones and Waggoner that the writers for the journals of the church should avoid coming before the public with divided or contradictory views.

ADVANCES IN
BOOK PUBLICATION

In 1889 it had been more than 40 years since Ellen White had seen in vision the streams of light bearing the third angel's message to all the world. The production of the first copy of *Present Truth* had been one person's job—the writing, editing, carrying in a carpet bag to the post office.

Since that time great advances in publishing had been made. There were now in 1889 a number of well-equipped publishing houses, well staffed, well organized, with goals to go into all the world.

From the publication of the first *Testimony* pamphlet in 1855, important instruction, admonition, encouragement, and reproof had reached the church through 31 *Testimony* pamphlets, each from 16 pages to 240 pages. In 1878 the General Conference session voted that these materials be kept in print and made available to the church in a more permanent form.

S. N. Haskell declared *Testimony* No. 31 to be "the most solemn one that has been published" (RH, Oct. 24, 1882). Early in the Ohio camp meeting a copy arrived, and frequently the entire camp was called together to hear portions read; the hearers were deeply affected (ST, Sept. 7, 1882). G. I. Butler, president of the General Conference, wrote of it, "Never before has so important a testimony been given to us. . . . It is filled with the choicest matter and the most stirring truths. Never were our dangers set before us as a people more clearly" (RH, Aug. 22, 1882). Reported Sanborn, a minister, "How thankful I feel that the Lord has not left us in our darkness and backslidings, but in mercy calls us to hear His special counsel" (*ibid.*, Sept. 19, 1882).

Many of the earlier writings, published in small printings, had been out of print for years, or partially incorporated in other publications.

Just before the opening of 1883 a little volume bearing the title of *Early Writings of Ellen G. White* came from the press. It was a book eagerly sought by Adventist families, for it provided Ellen's three earliest books, long out of print:

1. *Christian Experience and Views of Mrs. E. G. White*, a 64-page pamphlet published in 1851 that presented many of her early visions. This included her first vision, at this time found in no other work.

2. *Supplement to Experience and Views*, a 48-page pamphlet published in

1854. It explained some points in the preceding work that were not clear to all readers, and added some testimony-type articles on church order, et cetera.

3. *Spiritual Gifts*, Volume I, the 219-page presentation of the great controversy story, published in 1858.

Of these writings Butler wrote:

> These were the very first of the published writings of Sister White. Since they went out of print, many thousands have become interested in her writings. Many of these have greatly desired to have in their possession *all* she has written for publication. . . . It meets a want long felt (*ibid.*, Dec. 26, 1882).

In 1885 (the year Ellen White went to Europe) if a new Adventist had wanted to purchase all the E. G. White books available, he or she would have been able to secure the following:

Early Writings, an 1882 republication of the first three E. G. White books issued in the 1850s.

The Spirit of Prophecy, volumes 1-4, which told the great controversy story. The first three were 400-page books, and the fourth, 500 pages.

Testimonies for the Church, volumes 1-4, a reprint of 30 testimony pamphlets issued between the years 1855 and 1881 in four volumes of about 700 pages each.

Two *Testimony* pamphlets, Numbers 31 and 32.

Sketches From the Life of Paul, a 334-page volume.

Older Adventists might have had *Spiritual Gifts*, Volumes I-IV, the forerunners of *The Spirit of Prophecy* series. The second volume is a biographical work issued in 1860. They might also have had *How to Live*, comprising six pamphlets on health, each with one feature article from Ellen White, and the balance, related material selected and compiled by her; and a 64-page pamphlet, *Appeal to Mothers*.

THE GREAT CONTROVERSY THEME— DEVELOPED AND ENLARGED

The vision at Lovett's Grove, Ohio, on a Sunday afternoon in mid-March 1858 was one of great importance. In this the theme of the great controversy between Christ and His angels on the one side and Satan and his angels on the other was seen as one continuous and closely linked chain of events spanning 6,000 years. This vision has put Seventh-day Adventists into a unique position with clear-cut views of the working of Providence in the history of our world— a viewpoint quite different from that held by secular historians, who see events of history only as the interplay between the actions of human beings, often seemingly the result of chance or natural developments. In other words, this vision and others of the great conflict of the ages yield a philosophy of history that answers many questions and in prophetic forecast gives the assurance of final victory of good over evil.

The vision lasted for two hours, the congregation in the crowded schoolhouse watching with intense interest all that took place (WCW, in RH, Feb. 20, 1936).

In one brief paragraph Ellen White introduced what is thought of today as the principal topic of the March 14 vision:

> In this vision at Lovett's Grove most of the matter of the great controversy which I had seen ten years before was repeated, and I was shown that I must write it out (2SG, p. 270).*

STRICKEN BY SATAN

Ellen White was shown, in connection with the instruction to write out the vision of the controversy, that "I should have to contend with the powers of darkness, for Satan would make strong efforts to hinder me, but angels of God would not leave me in the conflict, that in God must I put my trust" (ibid.).

What did this mean? She was to learn before ever she reached home.

Monday the Tillotsons drove them in their comfortable carriage to the railroad station at Freemont, where the next day they took the train for Jackson, Michigan. At this point Ellen picks up the account:

> While riding in the cars we arranged our plans for writing and publishing the book called The Great Controversy immediately on our return home. I was then as well as usual.
>
> On the arrival of the train at Jackson we went to Brother Palmer's. We had been in the house but a short time, when, as I was conversing with Sister Palmer, my tongue refused to utter what I wished to say, and seemed large and numb. A strange, cold sensation struck my heart, passed over my head, and down my right side. For a while I was insensible; but was aroused by the voice of earnest prayer.
>
> I tried to use my left arm and limb, but they were perfectly useless. For a short time I did not expect to live. It was the third shock I had received of paralysis, and although within fifty miles (eighty kilometers) of home, I did not expect to see my children again. I called to mind the triumphant season I had enjoyed at Lovett's Grove, and thought it was my last testimony, and felt reconciled to die (ibid., p. 271).

As earnest prayer was continued in her behalf, she soon felt a prickling sensation in her arm and leg, and she praised God that the power of Satan was broken.

Three months later a vision given to her in Battle Creek opened to her what was really behind the distressing experience suffered in the Palmer home.

> I was taken off in vision. In that vision I was shown that in the sudden attack at Jackson, Satan designed to take my life to hinder the work I was about to write; but angels of God were sent to my rescue, to raise me above the effects of Satan's attack. I saw, among other things, that I should be blessed with better health than before the attack at Jackson (*ibid.*, p. 272).

The night after the stroke was one of great suffering, but the next day she seemed sufficiently strengthened to continue the journey by train to Battle Creek. On arrival home she was carried up the steep stairs to the front bedroom in their Wood Street home. She reported:

> For several weeks I could not feel the pressure of the hand, nor the coldest water poured upon my head. In rising to walk, I often staggered, and sometimes fell to the floor. In this condition I commenced to write *The Great Controversy.*
>
> I could write at first but one page a day, then rest three; but as I progressed, my strength increased. The numbness in my head did not seem to becloud my mind, and before I closed that work, the effect of the shock had entirely left me (*ibid.*).

While engaged in writing the great controversy story Ellen White had an opportunity to relate what had been shown to her in vision before some 400 believers assembled in Battle Creek for the General Conference called for May 21-24, 1858. In the morning she began her story with the fall of Satan, the plan of salvation, and the great controversy between Christ and His angels and Satan and his. In the evening she continued her narrative until nearly 10:00.

A month later it was reported that the forthcoming book was "in the press," meaning that the publishers had received some of the copy and were setting type. By mid-August Mrs. White had completed her writing, and the book was printed—*The Great Controversy Between Christ and His Angels and Satan and His Angels.* It was introduced by a 12-page statement from the pen of Roswell F. Cottrell that had appeared in the *Review and Herald* of February 25, 1858, under the title "Spiritual Gifts." For this wider use Cottrell amplified it somewhat.

The E. G. White text opens with the words:

> The Lord has shown me that Satan was once an honored angel in heaven, next to Jesus Christ. His countenance was mild, expressive of

happiness like the other angels. His forehead was high and broad, and showed great intelligence. His form was perfect. He had a noble, majestic bearing (1SG, p. 17).

The *Review and Herald* of September 9, 1858, carried on its back page, under the title "Spiritual Gifts," the notice that the book was ready. It read:

This is a work of 224 pages written by Mrs. White, with an introductory article on the perpetuity of spiritual gifts by Brother R. F. Cottrell. Price 50 cents.

This was the very first printing in book form of the great controversy theme. It was later bound with Volume II of a four-part series titled *Spiritual Gifts*. It traces the theme of the constant struggle between Christ and Satan that Mrs. White would continue to develop throughout her life.

Volume I   1858   *The Great Controversy Between Christ and His Angels and Satan and His Angels*

Volume II   1860   *My Christian Experience, Views and Labors in Connection With the Rise and Progress of the Third Angel's Message*

Volume III 1864   *Important Facts of Faith in Connection With the History of Holy Men of Old*

Volume IV 1864   *Important Facts of Faith: Laws of Health, and Testimonies Nos. 1-10*

The next book carrying the great controversy theme was Volume IV in the series titled *Spirit of Prophecy*.

Volume 1   1870   *The Great Controversy Between Christ and His Angels and Satan and His Angels*

Volume 2   1877   *The Great Controversy Between Christ and Satan. Life, Teachings, and Miracles of Our Lord Jesus Christ*

Volume 3   1878   *The Great Controversy Between Christ and Satan. The Death, Resurrection, and Ascension of Our Lord Jesus Christ*

Volume 4   1884   *The Great Controversy Between Christ and Satan. From the Destruction of Jerusalem to the End of the Controversy*

It may be observed from the above that for a period of 30 years, between 1858 and 1888, much of Ellen White's time and thought was given to producing *The Great Controversy*. During the same period, of course, she produced a great volume of writing for publication in journals, testimonies to individuals, and books.

"THE SPIRIT OF PROPHECY"—VOLUME 4

The first three volumes in the series had been published before James White's death in 1881. It was some time after his death before Ellen recovered sufficiently to settle down to a consistent program of book publication.

Weighing heavily on her mind was Volume 4 of *The Spirit of Prophecy* series—*The Great Controversy Between Christ and His Angels and Satan and His Angels*—dealing with the post-Christian Era from the destruction of Jerusalem to the new earth.

James and Ellen had hoped that the closing book in the series would be in the field without too much delay, but during the last two years of his life she could do little with it.

In an endeavor to keep the volumes close to the 400-page mark, volume 3 was held to 392 pages. This cut the story off in the midst of Paul's ministry, leaving him in Thessalonica. It was her plan to begin volume 4 at this point, and she continued writing five more chapters on this basis. But God had other plans; she was instructed through vision to adopt the format now seen in *The Great Controversy*. The fourth volume was to begin with the account of the destruction of Jerusalem. She followed this instruction. The five unused chapters on New Testament history were included in the second printing of volume 3, even though it made a book of 442 pages.

INSTRUCTED TO TRACE THE HISTORY OF THE CONTROVERSY

It was revealed to Ellen White that she should present an outline of the controversy between Christ and Satan, as it developed in the first centuries of the Christian Era and the great Reformation of the sixteenth century, in such a way as to prepare the mind of the reader to understand clearly the controversy going on in the present day. Writing of this in 1888 as she had occasion (just four years after its issuance) to enlarge and revise volume 4, she explained:

> As the Spirit of God has opened to my mind the great truths of His Word, and the scenes of the past and the future, I have been bidden to make known to others that which has thus been revealed—to trace the history of the controversy in past ages, and especially so to present it as to shed a light on the fast approaching struggle of the future.
>
> In pursuance of this purpose, I have endeavored to select and group together events in the history of the church in such a manner as to trace the unfolding of the great testing truths that at different periods have been given to the world, that have excited the wrath of Satan, and the enmity of a world-loving church. . . .
>
> In these records we may see the foreshadowing of the conflict before us. Regarding them in the light of God's Word, and by the illumination

of His Spirit, we may see unveiled the devices of the wicked one. . . . The great events which have marked the progress of reform in past ages, are matters of history, well known and universally acknowledged by the Protestant world; they are facts which none can gainsay (GC, p. xi).

VOLUME 4 —THE GREAT CONTROVERSY—FINALLY READY

A back-page note in the *Signs of the Times* for October 2, 1884, reported that volume 4, "so long looked for, is now out." It was published simultaneously by both the Pacific Press and the Review and Herald in editions of 5,000 copies each. Before the end of the year the first printing on the West Coast was sold out. Another milestone in Ellen White's writing was now passed. The book was sold to both Seventh-day Adventists and the general public, and 50,000 copies were distributed within several years' time.

By 1888 a far-reaching concept was emerging, with the use of *The Great Controversy*, volume 4 of *The Spirit of Prophecy* series, being successfully introduced by colporteurs to the general public. It was a popular book; 10 printings of 5,000 each had come from the presses of the Review and Herald and the Pacific Press in a short time. In 1886 its popularity was enhanced by the introduction of 22 illustrations, and it was printed in a larger page size. This, the sixth printing of the book, met with gratifying sale to the general public. Such a response broadened the vistas as to what could be done with the E. G. White books dealing with the controversy story.

It was the 1888 edition that Ellen White worked on so assiduously during her European tour, dividing her time between writing, public appearances, and traveling. Since the publication of her first vision she had responded to the compulsion to write with a wholehearted dedication of time and energy. Whether on a train or on a ship or in a caravan; whether in California or Basel, her one thought was, I hope I can find time to write. Writing, writing, writing— at all times and in all places. Always prepared with materials. Whenever it was at all possible, she was accompanied by members of her staff (paid from her personal exchequer).

In Europe she was inspired by visiting many of the places associated with the work of the Reformers; e.g., the Waldensian valleys and Switzerland. On a visit to Zurich, where Zwingli had labored and preached, she remarked, "We gathered many items of interest which we will use" (MS 29, 1887).

The manuscript was still unfinished when she arrived back in the United States. She made a number of stops—New England, Battle Creek, and other places—before reaching her home in Healdsburg, where the manuscript was finally finished.

SOURCES

In writing *The Great Controversy* Ellen White made use of the writings of others. She explained:

> In some cases where a historian has so grouped together events as to afford, in brief, a comprehensive view of the subject, or has summarized details in a convenient manner, his words have been quoted; but in some instances no specific credit has been given, since the quotations are not given for the purpose of citing that writer as authority, but because his statement affords a ready and forcible presentation of the subject (GC, p. xii).

She also drew from denominational authors, such as Uriah Smith and J. N. Andrews, in presenting views on prophecy. She had been with the pioneers of the church as they earnestly studied the Bible, and conclusions had been arrived at jointly, hence at times one would be the writer to set them before the public, and at times another. Thus she acknowledged: "In narrating the experience and views of those carrying forward the work of reform in our own time, similar use has been made of their published works" *(ibid.)*.

No one can mistake that in initially writing the great controversy story Ellen White is describing what she had seen—in vision, but nevertheless a very real experience. And so it is through the entire *Spiritual Gifts* volume, with such expressions as "I was shown" or "I saw" or the equivalent, averaging one a page.

The account passes from Creation very briefly down through the experiences of Old Testament history, touching those points prominent in the conflict between the forces of good and of evil. It deals in more detail with the life and ministry of Jesus and the experience of the apostles. At this point Ellen White goes beyond the Bible records and describes the apostasy, at times in symbolic representations. Then she moves into a brief chapter on the Reformation, describing what she saw of the ministry of Martin Luther and Melanchthon. This represented the conflict through postbiblical centuries, and bridged the story to the Advent movement. Twenty chapters fill the last half of the book, and trace the history, past and future, to the new earth. In this little volume there emerged for the first time the concept that links features in world history and church history as a part of the picture of the conflict of the ages.

Just where she may have begun her writing for the book is unknown. She mentions doing such writing two years before James White's death. In 1883 the May 31 issue of the *Signs* carried as its lead article the beginning of a series of 20 articles featuring Martin Luther as the central figure in the Protestant Reformation. In preparing this material for publication she was fulfilling the commission "to trace the history of the controversy in past ages," selecting and grouping "events in the history of the church." Much of this history had passed before her in vision, but not all the details, and not always in its precise sequence. In a statement presented to the Autumn Council of the General Conference Committee on October 30, 1911—a statement that had been carefully read by Ellen White and carried her written endorsement—W. C. White spoke of how she received light on Reformation history and the manner in which the writings of others were an aid to her in this work.

> The things which she has written out, are descriptions of flashlight [flashbulb] pictures and other representations given her regarding the actions of men, and the influence of these actions upon the work of God for the salvation of men, with views of past, present, and future history in its relation to this work.
>
> In connection with the writing out of these views, she has made use of good and clear historical statements to help make plain to the reader the things which she is endeavoring to present. When I was a mere boy, I heard her read D'Aubigné's *History of the Reformation* to my father. She read to him a large part, if not the whole, of the five volumes. She has read other histories of the Reformation. This has helped her to locate and describe many of the events and the movements presented to her in vision (3SM, p. 437).

At another time, in answering questions concerning his mother's literary work, W. C. White wrote:

> During her two years' residence in Basel, she visited many places where events of special importance occurred in the Reformation days. This refreshed her memory as to what she had been shown and this led to important enlargement in those portions of the book dealing with Reformation days (WCW to L. E. Froom, Dec. 13, 1934 [see also 3SM, p. 465]).

As *The Great Controversy* was being prepared for wide distribution to the general public, some materials were deleted. W. C. White explained this:

> In her public ministry, Mother has shown an ability to select, from the storehouse of truth, matter that is well adapted to the needs of the congregation before her; and she has always thought that, in the selection of matter for publication in her books, the best judgment should be shown in selecting that which is best suited to the needs of those who will read the book.
>
> Therefore, when the new edition of *Great Controversy* was brought out in 1888, there were left out about twenty pages of matter—four or five pages in a place—which was very instructive to the Adventists of

America, but which was not appropriate for readers in other parts of the world (WCW statement to the General Conference Autumn Council, Oct. 30, 1911 [see also 3SM, pp. 438, 439]).

One such deleted item was the first part of the chapter titled "The Snares of Satan," pages 337 to 340. In this she presented a view given her of Satan holding a council meeting with his angels to determine the best manner in which to deceive and mislead God's people. This presentation may be found in *Testimonies to Ministers*, pages 472 to 475, and, of course, in the facsimile reprint of *The Spirit of Prophecy*, volume 4.

THE STORY OF *THE MINISTRY OF HEALING*

In the early 1870s James and Ellen White had come to the rescue of the *Health Reformer*, the monthly health journal issued by Seventh-day Adventists, which was suffering a serious decline. In it, over a period of several years, James White published editorials on Bible hygiene. At the special session of the General Conference in the spring of 1876 he proposed preparing the manuscript for a book on the subject (RH, Apr. 6, 1876). The General Conference gave hearty support to this, but other tasks and then his death intervened.

The idea, however, did not die but found fruition in a volume issued in 1890 titled *Christian Temperance and Bible Hygiene*. Nine chapters from James White's pen filled the last section of the book, "Bible Hygiene." The first part of the volume, "Christian Temperance," was a compilation of a broad spectrum of E. G. White materials on the subject "Health and the Home"—19 chapters in all.

Dr. J. H. Kellogg was drawn in to assist in the compilation of this volume. In the preface, which he wrote, he paid high tribute to the major contribution to the world made by Ellen White in leading out in health teachings. Dr. Kellogg stated that up to that time "nowhere, and by no one, was there presented a systematic and harmonious body of hygienic truths, free from patent errors, and consistent with the Bible and the principles of the Christian religion" (p. iii). He wrote of the enduring nature of the principles she set forth. His closing paragraphs give the history of the book:

> This book is not a new presentation of the principles referred to in the above paragraphs, but is simply a compilation, and in some sense an abstract, of the various writings of Mrs. White upon this subject, to which have been added several articles by Elder James White, elucidating the same principles, and the personal experience of Elder J. N. Andrews and Joseph Bates, two of the pioneers in the health movement among Seventh-day Adventists. The work of compilation has been done under the supervision of Mrs. White, by a committee appointed by her

for the purpose, and the manuscript has been carefully examined by her.

The purpose in the preparation of this volume has been to gather together, in a condensed form, writings which were scattered through various volumes, and some that have never before appeared in print, so that the teachings of Mrs. White upon this subject might reach as large a number as possible of those for whom they were specially intended; and it is confidently believed that the work will receive a cordial reception, and the earnest consideration which its importance demands (*ibid.*, p. iv).

Christian Temperance and Bible Hygiene, with Ellen White's consent, was published in Battle Creek by the Good Health Publishing Company. For a number of years it was the standard E. G. White presentation on health. The "Christian Temperance" portion of the book—the E. G. White section—was in whole or in part issued in several of the languages of Europe. In 1905 *The Ministry of Healing* took its place as the prime E. G. White book on health written for the church and the world—a book for which no revision has ever been requested.

---

*Is this a reference to a particular vision in 1848, as it seems to imply? Or does it refer to phases of many visions received in the late 1840s, in which she witnessed segments of the conflict between Christ and His angels and Satan and his angels? A number of these presented the ultimate triumph of the righteous and the final destruction of sin and sinners. The absence of a contemporary reference to a specific, all-inclusive great controversy vision in 1848 would seem to point to the latter. Many of the visions of the late 1840s gave glimpses and at times rather detailed accounts of controversy and the triumph of God's people over the forces of Satan.

THE CALL TO AUSTRALIA

HASKELL PIONEERS WORK IN AUSTRALIA

Stephen N. Haskell was present at the dedication of Battle Creek College on January 4, 1875, and heard Ellen White mention that one of the countries shown her in vision where she had seen printing presses publishing the message was Australia, and he made up his mind he would proclaim the message in Australia. But it was 10 years before the church reached the point in growth that it felt it could support him in carrying the message to that faraway land in the South Pacific.

At its 1884 session the General Conference took an action to send Haskell to Australia. Being a practical man, he chose four families to help him start the work: J. O. Corliss, evangelist and editor; M. C. Israel, pastor and evangelist; William Arnold, a colporteur; and Henry Scott, a printer. The five families traveled to Australia in 1885, arriving in June, the winter season in Australia. They threw themselves wholeheartedly into the work. Through two evangelistic efforts, supplemented by book distribution, there soon was a church of 90 members in Melbourne and a fledgling monthly magazine, *The Bible Echo and Signs of the Times.*

Six years later, in 1891, the combined membership in Australia and New Zealand had reached 700. Among these were a number of young people eager to spread the church's message in the South Pacific. As Haskell, who had returned to the States, revisited the field, he saw clearly the need for a training school, and voiced his convictions in a letter to O. A. Olsen, president of the General Conference.

THE GENERAL CONFERENCE TAKES ACTION

The twenty-ninth session of the General Conference, held in Battle Creek, Michigan, commenced Thursday morning, March 5, 1891. It was a meeting marked with a broadening vision, particularly in lines of education. On Friday morning Haskell, having recently completed a tour among missions in Africa, India, and other countries, spoke on the importance of training workers in their native countries rather than sending them overseas, where they often lost touch with their home situations. Sunday morning W. W. Prescott, General Conference educational secretary, gave his report, in which he mentioned a number of calls for schools. He stated that "a request also comes in for the opening of a school in Australia" (GCB 1891, p. 39). On Monday morning the Committee on Education brought in the following recommendation:

> *We recommend,*
> 1. That as soon as practicable, an English Bible school be opened in Australia, to continue from twelve to sixteen weeks.
> 2. That at least two teachers be sent from this country to have charge of the school.
> 3. That the expense of maintaining this school be met by the brethren in Australia in such a manner as may seem best to them.
> 4. That the establishment of this school be regarded as the first step toward a permanent school for children of all ages, in case the brethren in Australia so desire (*ibid.*, p. 48).

Haskell was convinced that if Ellen White were to visit the field she could bring strength and inspiration, and promote the school idea as a training center. Others were inclined to side with him in this. So the idea of a visit by Ellen White to Australia began to develop.

Ellen White hoped that there would be no invitation for her to leave America. "I long for rest, for quietude, and to get out the 'Life of Christ,'" she wrote (MS 29, 1891). In fact, in anticipation of a concerted program of writing, she had purchased a lot in Petoskey, in a resort area on Lake Michigan, and was having a home built where she and her staff could work without the interruptions they would have to contend with in Battle Creek.

It was just at this point that word of the invitation of the Foreign Mission Board reached her, asking her to go to Australia. The Foreign Mission Board recommended the move if it agreed with her judgment and any light she might have from heaven; also that W. C. White accompany her. O. A. Olsen, president of the General Conference, informed the church at large through an article in the *Review and Herald* of June 2, 1891:

> There has been a long and urgent call from Australia for Sister White to come there, but the way has not been open; and even now it seems like an unreasonable undertaking for her, at her age and in her worn condition, to attempt such a journey; but she is of good courage, and has responded favorably, and it is quite probable that she and Elder White will sail for Australia next November.

TO GO OR NOT TO GO

The action of the Foreign Mission Board calling for Ellen White to go to Australia carried a clause that left the final decision with her. As the summer wore on she sought the Lord for light, but received none.

On August 5, 1891, she wrote in her diary:

> This morning my mind is anxious and troubled in regard to my duty. Can it be the will of God that I go to Australia? This involves a great deal with me. I have not special light to leave America for this *far-off country*. Nevertheless, if I knew it was the voice of God, I would go. But I cannot understand this matter.
>
> Some who are bearing responsibilities in America seem to be very persistent that my special work should be to go to Europe and to Australia. I finally did go to Europe and worked there in that new field with all the power and influence God had given me. My home and my goods in America became scattered, and I sustained much loss in this line. I offered my home for sale, and Dr. Kellogg purchased it. The price I received I needed, and it was a small price. I did wish it could have been double, for I had, with W. C. White, to open new fields, and I invested this means in school homes, in meetinghouses, and in opening new fields (MS 44, 1891).

Time was running out. Soon a decision had to be made. On August 20 she wrote, "I know that it is no use to tell them that all their flattering anticipations on my behalf does not lessen my ideas that going to Australia means work, responsibility to bear a message to the people who are not what the Lord would have them to be" (MS 29, 1891).

Nonetheless, she decided to go. As she later wrote of it, she had adopted the practice of responding to the requests of the General Conference unless she had special light to the contrary (letter 18a, 1892). The church leaders had asked her to go; and since she had no direct light, she decided to go, even though she wished she might be released from going.

In mid-August the Foreign Mission Board and the General Conference Committee took action appointing G. B. Starr and his wife to accompany Ellen White and her party to Australia (RH, Oct. 13, 1891).

ARRIVAL AT SYDNEY

At 7:00 Tuesday morning, December 8, 1891, the steamer S. S. *Alameda* entered Sydney harbor. The sea had rolled heavily in the night, and the passengers had kept close to their berths. But with the morning the whole party was on deck to see this harbor, reputed to be one of the most beautiful in the world. Coming from San Francisco were Ellen White, W. C. White, Emily Campbell, May Walling, and Fannie Bolton. Joining them in Honolulu were Elder and Mrs. Starr.

As they pulled near the wharf they could see a group of friends waiting to welcome them. Ellen White recognized A. G. Daniells and his wife, Mary, although it had been some years since they were together in Texas. With the others she was unacquainted. Before the ship touched the wharf, they were shouting back and forth, and when the gangplank was down they were soon shaking hands.

They took breakfast at the Daniells home, and while they were eating, others came in. Soon there was a season of worship, with praise to God for the safe passage across the broad Pacific.

On Friday evening, and again on Sabbath morning, Ellen White spoke in a hall in Sydney. She was gratified with the response and said, "I am not sorry that I am here" (letter 21, 1891).

Taking the train for the overnight trip to Melbourne, they arrived Wednesday morning, December 16. Here were located the publishing house and conference headquarters. A large group was assembled in Federal Hall, the meeting room on the second floor of the Echo Publishing Company, to extend a hearty welcome. G. B. Starr, W. C. White, and Ellen White each addressed the group. Gratitude was expressed to God for bringing the visitors safely to Australia (MS 47, 1891).

RECOGNIZED THE PRINTING PRESSES

The newcomers were taken to the printing office below the hall. As they entered the pressroom Ellen White recognized the presses as those shown to her in the vision of January 3, 1875. She declared, "I have seen these presses before," and continued, "I have seen this place before. I have seen these persons, and I know the conditions existing among the workers in this department. There is a lack of unity here, a lack of harmony" (DF 105j, WCW, "A Comprehensive Vision"). She had a message for the foreman. But she would have more of that to say and write later.

FOURTH ANNUAL SESSION OF THE
AUSTRALIAN SEVENTH-DAY ADVENTIST CONFERENCE

On the next Thursday evening, December 24, the fourth annual session of the Australian Seventh-day Adventist Conference opened in Federal Hall. About 100 people were present, representing the churches in Australia. Since the next day was Christmas, Mrs. White delivered an appropriate message on "the birth and mission of Christ, illustrating the love of God and showing the propriety of making gifts of gratitude, as did those who brought their gifts to Jesus, rather than to waste means in useless gratification" (BE, Jan. 1, 1892).

Federal Hall was too small for the Sabbath morning service, so Ellen White spoke in a larger hall. She was led to comment, "When they understand I am to speak, they have large numbers present" (MS 45, 1891). For the Sunday night meeting, the nearby Fitzroy Town Hall was secured. There she spoke on the plan of salvation and the love of God for fallen humanity, to an audience that sat attentively for an hour and a half.

In her diary she wrote:

> I was not well December 26 and December 27 [Sabbath and Sunday]. I had strong symptoms of malaria. I could eat but little through the day and had quite a fever, but the Lord strengthened me when [I was] before the people *(ibid.)*.

She little realized the ominous nature of the situation, for this was the onset of a prolonged and painful illness that was to affect her ministry in Australia materially.

THE BUSINESS SESSION OF THE CONFERENCE

On Monday morning, December 28, as 40 delegates took up the business of the session, two new churches were admitted, committees were appointed, and resolutions were brought before the delegates for consideration. These were not numerous, but they were important. The first read:

> 1. *Resolved,* That immediate attention be given to the Bible-reading work [Bible studies in private homes], and that suitable persons be selected and thoroughly trained for this kind of labor (BE, Jan. 15, 1892).

The next item had to do with the literature ministry and called for a faithful follow-up work where books were sold. This was followed by a resolution of gratitude to the General Conference for sending the newly arrived workers to "visit, counsel, and assist" at this present juncture of their experience.

The delegates were quite conscious of the action taken by the General Conference in its March session regarding starting a school. That matter was presented at the Melbourne session, with G. C. Tenney and W. C. White making appropriate remarks. Ellen White read important matter in regard to the church's schools and the work that should be done in them.

A. G. DANIELLS ELECTED PRESIDENT

The nominating committee brought in the name of A. G. Daniells for president of the Australian Conference, and he was elected. The choice was not an easy one. Writing of the experience to O. A. Olsen six months later, Mrs. White explained that there was an extremely short supply of leadership material available.

In later years Daniells told in rather general terms of this experience:

I was elected to the presidency of the newly organized Australian Conference, and continued in that office during the nine years of Mrs. White's residence in that field. This official responsibility kept me in unbroken association with her. Our mission field was vast. Our problems were heavy, and some of them very perplexing. . . .

Our membership increased encouragingly, and it became necessary to establish a training school for Christian workers, also church schools for the children of our believers. Then followed the erection of a sanitarium for the treatment of the sick, and the establishment of a factory for the manufacture of health foods.

I was young, and utterly inexperienced in most of these undertakings. As president, I was held more or less responsible for progress in all these endeavors. I needed counsel. This I sought at every important step from Mrs. White, and I was not disappointed. I was also closely associated in committee and administrative work with her son, W. C. White. His counsel was very helpful to me; it was based on a longer experience than my own, and also upon his intimate knowledge of the many messages of counsel that had been given through his mother during past years in meeting conditions similar to those we were facing (AGD, *The Abiding Gift of Prophecy*, pp. 364, 365).

ELLEN WHITE BEGINS WORK IN MELBOURNE

The conference session closed on January 3, but the program continued for another week in devotional meetings and "An Institute for Instruction in Christian Work." Mrs. White devoted this week to house hunting. She and her office family needed to have a place to live and work. The overall plan was that she would make Melbourne her headquarters for six months and write on the life of Christ. From there she would visit the principal churches and spend two months in New Zealand in connection with their conference session.

On Sunday morning, January 3, Stephen Belden drove Ellen White in his carriage five miles (eight kilometers) north to a suburb known as Preston. She was pleased with the country atmosphere and with the area generally, but the cottage they went to see was not large enough for the group that had to work together. Tuesday morning they were back in Preston, this time with better success. She noted in her diary:

> We found a nice brick house with nine rooms which, with a little squeezing, would accommodate Elder Starr and his wife and our workers. There is a beautiful garden, but it has been neglected and is grown up to weeds (MS 28, 1892).

Wednesday they were in Preston again, this time to make arrangements to rent the unfurnished house for six months. The next two days were spent in buying furniture, dishes, and other household necessities. Sunday morning Ellen White was up early packing and getting ready to move into their new home. By noon they were in their new quarters and quite content with the prospects: a large lot, pure, invigorating air; a yard full of flowers "of fine rich quality"; and good soil.

Because the new "home" was five miles (eight kilometers) from the city and the publishing house, she purchased a horse and carriage, a double-seated phaeton in which she could ride with comfort. They bought a good healthy cow to provide milk, and built a stable to accommodate the horse and cow (letter 90, 1892). A girl, Annie, was employed to assist with the housework. May Walling did the cooking. Because their plans called for only a six-month stay, they bought secondhand furniture and improvised somewhat with packing boxes. Some of the old carpeting used in packing the goods shipped from America served as floor covering. Economy was the watchword.

The women helpers took the yard work under their care, and the garden responded well. Wrote Ellen White:

> The girls went to work in the garden, pulling weeds, making flower beds, sowing seeds for vegetables. It was very dry, so we bought a hose, and Marian [Davis] was chief in the flower garden. With water, the flowers sprang up. Dahlias, the richest beauties, are in full bloom, and fuchsias flourish. I never saw them blossom as they do here; the geraniums, Lady Washingtons, in immense bunches of the richest colors to delight the eye (MS 4, 1892).

Just before the conference closed, Mrs. White was stricken with a severe illness. For 11 months she suffered from malarial fever and inflammatory rheumatism. During this time of extreme suffering she continued her writing only under great difficulties.

> I am now writing on the life of Christ, and I have had great comfort and blessing in my writing. It may be I am a cripple in order to do this work so long neglected (letter 90, 1892).

As her physical condition worsened she could not stand to speak, but she would not give up; she spoke while sitting in a chair on the platform. Finally it worsened to the point that she could no longer meet speaking appointments.

One happy event during this period was the arrival in the mail from America of a copy of *Steps to Christ*, published by Fleming H. Revell and Company of Chicago. It was announced on the back page of the *Bible Echo* for April 1.

The reception of the book in the United States was phenomenal, as indicated by another back-page note that appeared two months later. An announcement from the publisher, Revell, was reproduced under the title "A Remarkable Book":

> It is not often that a publisher has the opportunity of announcing a third edition of a new work *within six weeks of the first issue*. This, however, is the encouraging fact in connection with Mrs. E. G. White's eminently helpful and practical work, *Steps to Christ*. If you will read this work, it will *ensure* your becoming deeply interested in extending its circulation.
>
> *Steps to Christ* is a work to guide the inquirer, to inspire the young Christian, and to comfort and encourage the mature believer. The book is unique in its helpfulness.

ELLEN WHITE ANOINTED

Although Ellen White, as well as her husband, had responded a number of times to requests to join others in the service of anointing the sick and praying for their healing, she deferred making such a request for herself. But after long months of suffering and no evidence of improvement, and although she and her attendants had done all they could with proper hydrotherapy treatments, she was still almost helpless. Now her mind turned to what it was her privilege to do, to ask the brethren to come and anoint her and pray for her healing. While pondering this, and the whole matter of prayer for the healing of the sick in general, she wrote a statement:

> Praying for the sick is a most solemn thing, and we should not enter upon this work in any careless, hasty way. Examination should be made as to whether those who would be blessed with health have indulged in evil speaking, alienation, and dissension. Have they sowed discord among the brethren and sisters in the church? If these things have been committed they should be confessed before God and before the church. When wrongs have been confessed, the subjects of prayer may be presented before God in earnestness and faith, as the Spirit of God may move upon you (MS 26a, 1892).

In this statement, seemingly intended for herself, as well as others, Mrs. White wrote much in the vein presented in the chapter "Prayer for the Sick" in *The Ministry of Healing*. In fact, this manuscript probably formed the basis for the chapter.

After the preparation of heart that accompanied her writing on prayer for the sick, she called upon the brethren to come to her home and anoint her and pray for her healing. Of this experience, which took place on Friday, May 20, she wrote in her diary:

> Yesterday afternoon Elder [A. G.] Daniells and his wife, Elder [G. C.] Tenney and his wife, and Brethren Stockton and Smith came to our home at my request to pray that the Lord would heal me. We had a most earnest season of prayer, and we were all much blessed. I was relieved, but not restored.
>
> I have now done all that I can to follow the Bible directions, and I shall wait for the Lord to work, believing that in His own good time He will heal me. My faith takes hold of the promise, "Ask, and ye shall receive" (John 16:24).
>
> I believe that the Lord heard our prayers. I hoped that my captivity might be turned immediately, and to my finite judgment it seemed that thus God would be glorified. I was much blessed during our season of prayer, and I shall hold fast to the assurance then given me: "I am your Redeemer; I will heal you" (MS 19, 1892 [2SM, p. 235]).

THE BIBLE SCHOOL ESTABLISHED

One of the reasons the General Conference asked Ellen White and her son to go to Australia was the need there for a school to train the youth in their homeland. The principal item of business at the Australian Conference session that was held immediately after their arrival in Melbourne was the establishment of such a school. Provision was made for a committee to find a location, to which members representing Australia and New Zealand were named.

The next step was the securing of support from the believers in New Zealand, a conference with a membership about two thirds that of Australia. This was accomplished at the session of the New Zealand Conference held in Napier, April 1 to 14, 1892. Now it was time to move forward with the development of plans and to devise means of financial support.

Unfortunately Australia was moving into an economic depression. Not all believers saw the need of a school; nevertheless, they took the first steps in deciding where the school should be located. Some argued for Sydney, others for Melbourne. Mrs. White favored the latter.

Work had to begin in rented buildings. As the choice of a location narrowed down to Melbourne, it seemed that the area known as North Fitzroy, about two miles (three kilometers) from the publishing house, would serve best. There they found a complex consisting of four buildings, two of which were available, and the rent was within reason. On either side of the buildings was open land (letter 13, 1892).

School opened on August 24, 1892, with an enrollment of 25 students. What was not made public generally was how, in the face of adverse financial circumstances and the indifference on the part of many, the school actually got under way. Ellen White was to refer to it some months later. In a letter to Harmon Lindsay, treasurer of the General Conference, she said:

> Last winter when we saw that we must have a school to meet the demands of the cause, we were put to our wits' ends to know where we should obtain the funds. . . . [Ellen White tells of expenses.] Some thought it could not be done; yet we knew that it must be started in 1892. Some thought all that could be done was to hold a short institute for the ministers.
>
> We knew that there were many youth who needed the advantages of the school. While we were in such deep perplexity as to how we should be able to make a beginning, the same plan was suggested to Willie's mind that was suggested to mine, and that . . . on the same night.
>
> In the morning when he came to tell me his plan, I asked him to wait until I told him mine, which was that we use the royalty of the foreign books sold in America.
>
> Although in pain, my mind was exercised over this matter, and I prayed earnestly to the Lord for light, and it came. You know that I could not well use the money that is set apart for other purposes.
>
> Of the royalty above referred to I invested $1,000 to be used when most needed. But $500 must be used as a fund to bring to the school students who cannot and will not come unless they have help. Willie said [that] with this statement to place before the board we shall have their influence to sustain us. Thus our school was begun (letter 79, 1893).

THE BIBLE SCHOOL OPENS

At opening exercises for the school, A. G. Daniells and G. C. Tenney spoke first, then Mrs. White, who had to be carried onto the platform. She seemed to lose sight of the small constituency, of the adverse financial conditions, and the mere handful of students. With a vision of an unfinished task in a world with many continents yet untouched by the third angel's message, she declared:

> The missionary work in Australia and New Zealand is yet in its infancy, but the same work must be accomplished in Australia, New Zealand, in Africa, India, China, and the islands of the sea, as has been accomplished in the home field (BE, Supplement, Sept. 1, 1892 [quoted in 3LS, p. 338]).

W. C. White followed with a review of the development of school work among Seventh-day Adventists and set forth some of the conditions of success and some of the elements of danger.

One month after the school opened Mrs. White reported joyfully:

> The school is certainly doing well. The students are the very best. They are quiet, and are trying to get all the good possible. They all like Elder Rousseau and his wife as teachers (letter 54, 1892).

Three months later she wrote to Elder Olsen:

> The faculty have made few rules, and have not had one case where discipline was required. Peace and harmony have reigned from first to last. The presence of Jesus has been in the school from its beginning, and the Lord has wrought upon the minds of teachers and pupils (letter 46, 1892).

As she wrote to another of this, she explained:

> They [the students] would never have been able to enjoy the advantages of the school unless someone did help them, and as no one assumed the responsibility, it dropped on me. I carried several through the first term of school, and am paying the expenses of six during the present term, and the number may swell to eight (letter 65, 1893).

GROWING STRONGER

Beginning with July 10, the entries in Ellen White's diary began to take a new turn. On that day she wrote the words "I praise the Lord with heart and soul and voice that I am growing stronger" (MS 34, 1892). By the end of the school year she wrote jubilantly to the president of the General Conference: "The school has been a success!"

She had just attended the closing exercises of the Australasian Bible School, a simple service held in the chapel room. For almost three months she had been away, working in Adelaide and Ballarat, and had returned to Melbourne for this significant event. She had not forgotten that one of the basic reasons she and her son had been urged to spend a couple years in Australia was to aid in starting an educational work there. Despite indifference, financial depression in the country, and prolonged, debilitating illness, her persistence had won out.

Most of the students left immediately to enter the literature ministry in several of the Australian colonies. Church leaders turned briefly to planning for the next term of school, setting the time for opening as June 6. Then the ministers, including the president, scattered to the principal churches to lead out in the newly instituted Week of Prayer.

THE SECRET SIGNS
N. D. FAULKHEAD AND THE CONVINCING TESTIMONY

On the day school closed, W. C. White called a meeting of the available members of the school board. N. D. Faulkhead, treasurer of the publishing house, attended. As the meeting closed about 4:00, White spoke to him, telling him that Ellen White wanted to see him. As he started down the hall to the room where she was staying, there came to his mind a dream he had had a few nights before, in which Mrs. White had a message for him.

Faulkhead was a tall, keen, apt, and energetic businessman, genial and liberal in his disposition, but proud. When he became a Seventh-day Adventist, he held membership in several secret organizations, and he did not withdraw from these. As he wrote of his experience some years later in a general letter to "My Dear Brethren in the Faith," he told of these affiliations:

> I was closely connected with the Masonic Lodge. . . . I held the highest positions in the following lodges that could be conferred upon me: first, I was Master of the Master Mason's Lodge (or Blue Lodge); second, I was First Principal of the Holy Royal (of Canada); third, I was Preceptor of the Knights Templars, besides many other minor lodges, the Good Templars, Rechabites, and Odd Fellows, in which I also held high positions (DF 522a, N. D. Faulkhead letter, Oct. 5, 1908).

When the Faulkhead family—Mrs. Faulkhead was a teacher in the public school system—accepted the third angel's message, his unusual ability was recognized, and he was employed as treasurer in the Echo Publishing Company. He served well at first, but as time advanced he became more and more engrossed in his lodge work, and his interests in God's work began to wane.

This was his situation when Ellen White arrived in Australia in December 1891. As matters involving the publishing house workers were opened to her in a comprehensive vision a few days after her arrival, she wrote of conditions there in general; she also penned testimonies to a number of the individuals involved, including Mr. Faulkhead and his wife. The document addressed to them dealt with his connection with the publishing house and his affiliation with the Masonic Lodge. It filled 50 pages. She intended to mail it to him, but was restrained from doing so. She said, "When I enclosed the communication all ready to mail, it seemed that a voice spoke to me saying, 'Not yet, not yet, they will not receive your testimony'" (letter 39, 1893).

She said nothing regarding the matter for almost 12 months, but maintained a deep interest in the Faulkheads and their spiritual welfare. Some of his associates in the publishing house were very much concerned as they observed his growing infatuation with the work of the lodge and his waning spirituality and decreasing concern for the interests of the cause of God. They pleaded with him, urging him to consider the danger of his course. "But," as Mr. Faulkhead wrote, "my heart was full of those things; in fact, I thought more of them than I did of anything else" (DF 522a, N. D. Faulkhead letter, Oct. 5, 1908).

He defiantly met the appeals with the bold statement that "he would not give up his connection with the Freemasons for all that Starr or White or any other minister might say. He knew what he was about, and he was not going to be taught by them" (letter 21b, 1892). It was clear to those in charge of the work that unless a marked change came in his attitude, he would soon have to find other employment.

Mrs. White wrote of this experience: "None could reach him in regard to Freemasonry. He was fastening himself more and more firmly in the meshes of the enemy, and the only thing we could see to be done was to leave him to himself" (letter 46, 1892). His condition was shown to her to be like that of "a man about to lose his balance and fall over a precipice" (MS 4, 1893).

For a period of months Ellen White held messages for him and thought to send them, but was restrained.

In early December 1892 J. H. Stockton, one of the first Seventh-day Adventists in Australia, was talking with Mr. Faulkhead. He asked him what he would do if Mrs. White had a testimony for him in regard to his connection with the lodge. To this Faulkhead boldly retorted: "It would have to be mighty strong." Neither man was aware that almost a year before, the whole matter had been opened to her (DF 522a, N. D. Faulkhead to EGW, Feb. 20, 1908).

Shortly after this, on Saturday night, December 10, Faulkhead dreamed that the Lord had shown his case to Ellen White, and that she had a message for him. This, with his defiant reply to Stockton in regard to what would be his attitude toward a message through her, led him to serious thought. At the time of this dream Mrs. White was at Ballarat, but on Monday, December 12, as noted earlier, she had returned to Melbourne. The next day she attended the closing exercises of the first term of the Australasian Bible School.

With this dream vividly in his mind, Faulkhead sought out Mrs. White, who greeted him cordially. He asked her whether she had something for him. She replied that the burden of his case was upon her mind, and that she had a message for him from the Lord, which she wished him and his wife to hear. She called for a meeting in the near future, when she would present that message. Faulkhead asked eagerly, "Why not give me the message now?" (letter 46, 1892).

She was weary from her journey and her work that morning, but she went over to a stand and picked up a bundle of manuscripts. She told Faulkhead that several times she had prepared to send the message, but that she "had felt forbidden by the Spirit of the Lord to do so" (*ibid.*), for the time had not fully come that he would accept it.

She then read and talked. A part of the 50 pages that were read that evening was of a general nature, relating to the work in the Echo Publishing Company and the experience of the workers there. But the major part dealt with Mr. Faulkhead's experience and his connection not only with the work in the office but also with the Masonic Lodge. She pointed out that his involvement with Freemasonry had absorbed his time and blunted his spiritual perception. She read to him of his efforts to maintain high principles for which the lodge claimed to stand, often couching her message in Masonic language. She also told him where in the lodge hall she had seen him sitting and what he was endeavoring to do with his associates.

She spoke of his increasing interest in the work of these organizations and of his waning interest in the cause of God; of her seeing in vision his dropping the small coins from his purse in the Sabbath offering plate and the larger coins into the coffers of the lodges. She heard him addressed as "Worshipful Master." She read of scenes of drinking and carousal that took place in the lodge meetings, especially after Mr. Faulkhead had left (DF 522a, G. B. Starr, "An Experience With Sister E. G. White in Australia").

"I thought this was getting pretty close home," he later wrote, "when she started to talk to me in reference to what I was doing in the lodges" (*ibid.*, N. D. Faulkhead letter, Oct. 5, 1908).

ELLEN WHITE GIVES THE SECRET SIGNS

Mrs. White spoke most earnestly of the dangers of his connection with Freemasonry, warning that "unless he severed every tie that bound him to these associations, he would lose his soul." She repeated to him words spoken by her guide. Then, giving a certain movement with her hand that was made by her guide, she said, "I cannot relate all that was given to me" (letter 46, 1892).

At this, Faulkhead started and turned pale. Recounting the incident, he wrote:

> Immediately she gave me this sign. I touched her on the shoulder and asked her if she knew what she had done. She looked surprised and said she did not do anything unusual. I told her that she had given me the sign of a Knight Templar. Well, she did not know anything about it (DF 522a, N. D. Faulkhead letter, Oct. 5, 1908).

They talked on. She spoke further of Freemasonry and the impossibility of a man's being both a Freemason and a wholehearted Christian. Again she made a certain movement, which "my attending angel made to me" (MS 54, 1899).

Again Mr. Faulkhead started, and the blood left his face. A second time she had made a secret sign known only to the highest order of Masons. It was a sign that no woman could know, for it was held in the strictest secrecy—the place of meeting was guarded both inside and outside against strangers. "This convinced me that her testimony was from God," he stated (*ibid.*).

Speaking further of his reaction to this, he wrote:

> I can assure you . . . this caused me to feel very queer. But, as Sister White said, the Spirit of the Lord had come upon me and taken hold of me. She went on talking and reading as if nothing had happened, but I noticed how her face brightened up when I interrupted her again and spoke to her about the sign. She seemed surprised that she had given me such a sign. She did not know that she had moved her hand. Immediately the statement that I had made to Brother Stockton, that it would have to be mighty strong before I could believe that she had a message for me from the Lord, flashed through my mind (DF 522a, N. D. Faulkhead letter, 1908).

When Mrs. White finished reading, tears were in the man's eyes. He said:

> I accept every word. All of it belongs to me. . . . I accept the light the Lord has sent me through you. I will act upon it. I am a member of five lodges, and three other lodges are under my control. I transact all of their business. Now I shall attend no more of their meetings, and shall close my business relations with them as fast as possible (letter 46, 1892).

He also stated, "I am so glad you did not send me that testimony, for then it would not have helped me" (MS 54, 1899).

> Your reading the reproof yourself has touched my heart. The Spirit of the Lord has spoken to me through you, and I accept every word you have addressed especially to me; the general matter also is applicable to me. It all means me. That which you have written in regard to my connection with the Freemasons I accept. . . . I have just taken the highest order in Freemasonry, but I shall sever my connection with them all (letter 21b, 1892).

When Mr. Faulkhead left Ellen White's room, the hour was late. He took the streetcar to the railway station, and while traveling up Collins Street he passed the lodge hall. It suddenly dawned upon him that he should have been there attending a Knights Templar encampment that very evening. As he neared the station, he saw the train for Preston pulling out, so he was obliged to walk the rest of the way home. He chose an unfrequented road so that he might have opportunity for meditation. He enjoyed the walk very much, for there had come to him a new experience. He so much wanted to meet Daniells, Starr, or W. C. White and tell them that he was a new man, and how free and happy he felt in his decision to sever his connection with all secret societies. It seemed to him that a ton of weight had rolled from his shoulders. And to think that the God who rules the universe and guides the planets had seen his danger and sent a message just for him!

FAULKHEAD RESIGNS FROM THE LODGES

The next morning found Mr. Faulkhead at his office. Word spread quickly to the group of workers of his experience the night before. Again and again he recounted with one after another how God had sent a message to arrest him from a course of action that would have led him to destruction. As his first work he called in his assistant and dictated his resignation to the various lodges. Then A. G. Daniells came in, and Mr. Faulkhead told him of his experience. While the two were talking, his letters of resignation were passed to Mr. Faulkhead for his signature. He signed and enclosed them and handed them to Daniells to mail. In telling of it, Faulkhead says, "How his eyes did sparkle with pleasure to think that the Lord had gained His point at last, and that his prayers had been answered" (DF 522a, N. D. Faulkhead letter, Oct. 5, 1908).

But no sooner had Faulkhead given the letters to Daniells than a feeling of mistrust came over him; he felt he should have mailed the letters himself. Then he thanked the Lord for what he had done, for he felt that he could not have trusted himself to mail the letters.

ANOTHER INTERVIEW WITH ELLEN WHITE

On Thursday, December 15, Mr. Faulkhead, accompanied by his wife, had another interview with Mrs. White. A number of pages of new matter were read to both of them, and it was all accepted. "I wish you to know," he told Mrs. White, "how I look upon this matter. I regard myself as greatly honored of the Lord. He has seen fit to mention me, and I am not discouraged, but encouraged. I shall follow out the light given me of the Lord" (letter 21b, 1892).

The battle was not entirely won with the sending in of the resignations. His lodge friends refused to release him, so he had to serve out his terms of office for another nine months. Most determined efforts were put forth to hold him to their society, but he had taken a firm position and stood by it. At times his church associates trembled for him. Ellen White wrote encouraging letters in support of his stand.

With the expiration of his term as officer of several of the lodges, the complete victory was won, and Mr. Faulkhead was able, on September 18, 1893, to write to Mrs. White and her son:

Dear Brother and Sister White:

It gives me much pleasure to tell you that my term of office as Master of the Masonic Lodge expired last month. And I feel to thank God for it. How thankful I am to Him for sending me a warning that I was traveling on the wrong road. I do praise Him for His goodness and His love shown toward me in calling me from among that people. I can see now very clearly that to continue with them would have been my downfall, as I must confess that my interest for the truth was growing cold. But thanks be to God, He did not let me go on with them without giving me warning through His servant. I cannot express my gratitude to Him for it. . . .

I can praise God with all my might, and then I cannot express my gratitude to Him for the love that He has shown me. N. D. Faulkhead (DF 522a).

This experience brought great confidence to the hearts of church members in Australia, and it was ever a source of encouragement and help to Mr. Faulkhead. With the renewal of his first love and interest in the cause of God, he continued to serve the publishing house for many years, giving his time and strength and life to the spreading of the message.

In the testimony that was read by Ellen White to Mr. Faulkhead were recorded counsel and instruction of general application regarding the relation of Christians to organizations of the world.

ON TO NEW ZEALAND

In January 1893 longstanding plans for Ellen White to visit New Zealand were coming to fruition. These plans called for visiting the churches and for a camp meeting to be held in Napier in March. A conference session would be held in connection with it. Ellen White, W. C. White, and G. B. Starr and his wife would attend. The tour was expected to take about four months.

Leaving Melbourne on Thursday, January 26, the party arrived in Sydney the next day. Mrs. White met with the church at Parramatta on Sabbath morning, and this introduced a full week of meetings.

Here in Parramatta, a suburb of Sydney, was the first church building owned and operated by Seventh-day Adventists in continental Australia. A year previously Robert Hare and David Steed had held evangelistic meetings there and raised up a church of 50 members. The congregation was determined to have a house of worship. Beginning with donations amounting to £420 ($2,000), a good lot and building materials were purchased. Within three weeks' time of the laying of the foundations, the building was erected with donated labor, and Sabbath meetings were being held in it. It was dedicated on Sabbath, December 10. The next day 480 people crowded into the new church at what was called its opening meeting (BE, Jan. 15, 1893).

As funds were being raised in September, Ellen White, who had received a gift from friends in California of $45 with which to buy a comfortable chair for use during her illness, appropriated the money to aid in building the Parramatta church. She explained to her friends who had given the money that she wished them to have something invested in the Australian missionary field (letter 34, 1892).

Sunday night she spoke in the Parramatta town hall. It was well filled also, and she reported:

> The people listened with great attention, and the people here, believing the truth, are much pleased. But I do not feel satisfied. I needed physical strength that I could do justice to the great and important themes that we are dealing with. What a work is before us! (letter 127, 1893).

In addition to speaking in the church on Tuesday and Thursday nights, she visited in the community as well, where she was well received. She was told that the wife of a local minister had declared: "Mrs. White's words are very straight;

she has gone deeper than any of us in religious experience. We must study the Word to see if these things be so" (DF 28a, "Experiences in Australia," p. 316).

For the Seventh-day Adventist pastor in Parramatta, Robert Hare, she had words of counsel and instruction that she arranged to read to him and his wife. The testimony was received with profit.

VOYAGE TO NEW ZEALAND

At 2:00 Sabbath afternoon, February 4, Ellen White, together with her son William, her secretary, Emily Campbell, and Elder and Mrs. G. B. Starr, boarded the *Rotomahanna* for Auckland, New Zealand. She described the ship as a "beautiful steamer, and one of the fastest on these waters" (RH, May 30, 1893). She had a convenient and pleasant stateroom on the upper deck, and endured the journey well. Arriving at Auckland Wednesday morning, February 8, she and her companions were taken to a comfortable furnished cottage arranged for by the church. The next 12 days were devoted to meetings in the Auckland church. On two evenings she spoke to attentive audiences in a well-filled theater. In all, she spoke eight times while there.

ELLEN WHITE MEETS THE HARE FAMILY

The Hare family was already well known among Adventists "down under" and would be for generations to come. Edward Hare and his wife were among the very first in New Zealand to accept the third angel's message as S. N. Haskell began work in Auckland in late 1885. As soon as he accepted the Sabbath he was eager that his father, Joseph Hare, who resided in Kaeo, should also hear the message. So Haskell made a visit to Kaeo, 160 miles (256 kilometers) north of Auckland.

As a result of that visit many members of that family accepted the third angel's message, including Father Hare. Among the 24 children, 16 of whom were married, several were persons of more than ordinary ability, and many of them had means and extensive influence.

The little chapel at Kaeo was built by the Hare family, who largely composed its membership.

Now, eight years after Haskell's first visit, Ellen White was in New Zealand and was urged to visit Kaeo. Kaeo was a 24-hour journey from Auckland by a coastal boat, which made several stops en route. There was just time to squeeze in a two-week visit to Kaeo before entering into preparations for the camp meeting scheduled to open in Napier on Thursday, March 23.

So on Monday the White party, the same that had come from Australia, boarded the *Clansman* at Auckland for its weekly trip north.

When they arrived at their destination, Whangaroa Harbor, at 7:00 in the evening, Joseph and Metcalfe Hare were there to meet them. The men had come three miles (five kilometers) from Kaeo in their skiff. Travelers and baggage were transferred to the little boat, and they started on the two-hour trip to Kaeo. The water was smooth, the air was mild, and the new moon gave just enough light to outline the mountains (RH, May 30, 1893). Ellen White described the trip in her diary:

> Willie sat at the end of the boat at the helm, his back to my back to give support and to guide the boat. Brethren Hare stood up in the boat, each with an oar, and were guided by word and motion of head when the boat should go veering to right and left in the narrow passage, shunning rocks and dangerous places.
>
> The view on this passage must be grand when it can be seen, but it was night and we were deprived of the privilege of viewing the scenery. The water was as smooth as a beautiful lake. . . . The landing place was close to Joseph Hare's back yard. We stepped, with help, on the embankment and passed through the gate, and a few steps brought us to the back piazza [porch]. We climbed the steps and entered the open door and were welcomed by Sister Hare (MS 77, 1893).

In the morning Father Hare came with his carriage and took them the three miles (five kilometers) to his home. As they traveled, Ellen White became ecstatic by what she saw: fern trees in abundance, mountains "closely linked one to another, rounded or sharp at the top, and precipicelike at the sides; then uniting with this was still another and another, peak after peak presenting itself like links uniting in a chain" (ibid.). Father Hare's home was well located, close to a high, wooded mountain. A passing stream supplied pure water. There was a flourishing orchard of apples, pears, peaches, plums, and quince trees, and beyond, beautiful, fragrant pines.

Sabbath morning Mrs. White spoke in the little meetinghouse the Hare family had built. As she stood before her audience, she recognized faces she had seen in vision, as had happened to her many times. She was well aware of the experiences and attitudes of some present (ibid.). Sunday afternoon she addressed about 200 of the community folks at the Wesleyan church. George Starr spoke in the same church Sunday evening. Thus began a busy stay at Kaeo.

Some members of the Hare family had not yet confessed Christ. Of the youth she wrote that "there are some in Kaeo whom God has been calling to fit themselves for labor in His vineyard, and we rejoice that several are preparing to go to the Bible school" in Australia (RH, May 30, 1893). Because of bad weather and irregular boat schedules, the visitors stayed an extra week in Kaeo. They filled the time with meetings and in earnest visiting from family to family. Near the time for them to leave, Minnie and Susan Hare, ages 20 and 14, respectively, youngest daughters of Father Hare, were baptized.

Thursday morning, March 16, the visiting group caught the steamer for Auckland. Ellen White and the Starrs were taken to Whangaroa Harbor on Wednesday afternoon so that Mrs. White could speak in the town hall that evening. W. C. White and Emily Campbell came with the baggage early Thursday morning, and they were soon on the *Clansman* en route to Auckland.

At Auckland they changed to the *Wairarapa*, bound for Napier. Here the first Seventh-day Adventist camp meeting in the Southern Hemisphere was scheduled to open on Thursday, March 23.

FIRST SDA CAMP MEETING IN THE SOUTHERN HEMISPHERE

The little city of Napier was a beautiful place, the resident portion of the town having been built on a series of high hills overlooking the sea. Ellen White, W. C. White, and Emily were taken to the comfortable home of the Doctors Caro, not far from where preparations were already under way for the camp meeting. They were to be entertained there for the full time. A two-wheeled horse-drawn rig was made available for Ellen White's use in getting to the meetings.

Arrangements had been made for her to speak Sunday evening in the Theater Royal, and she presented her favorite theme, "The Love of God," to an attentive audience. The next three days were devoted to getting ready for the meeting. Two large tents were pitched. Notice had been sent to the churches weeks before, but the response was poor, so plans for a dining tent and a reception tent were dropped. Only a few family tents were pitched. It was expected that the restaurant in town could serve whatever food was needed.

However, by midweek boats and trains brought delegations from the churches, fully doubling the number expected. The camp meeting planners faced a minor crisis.

From the time plans were under way, Ellen White had urged that this first camp meeting must be a sample of what future camp meetings should be. Over and over she declared: "'See, saith he, that thou make all things according to the pattern shewed to thee in the mount.' As a people," she said, "we have lost much by neglecting order and method." She commented, "Although it takes time and careful thought and labor, and often seems to make our work cost more, in the end we can see that it was a paying business to do everything in the most perfect manner" (RH, June 6, 1893). For the people to go uptown for their meals would, she pointed out, "break into our program, waste precious time, and bring in a haphazard state of things that should be avoided" (*ibid.*).

The camp was enlarged; more tents were procured, a reception tent was fitted up, and also a dining tent.

The food provided was plain and substantial, but plentiful. Instead of the dozen people first expected, about 30 took their meals in the dining tent.

The first meeting in the big tent was on Tuesday evening, in advance of the opening, and Stephen McCullagh spoke. On the first Sabbath afternoon Ellen White was the speaker. At the close of her address she extended invitations for a response, first from those who had never taken their stand for Christ and then from those "who professed to be the followers of Christ, who had not the evidence of His acceptance." The responses were encouraging. A hard rain had come up, and the big tent leaked in many places, but this did not bother the audience, for the interest in "eternal matters" was too deep to be affected by the surroundings. As the rain continued, George Starr gave precious instruction and exhorted the people. The meeting continued until sundown (ibid.).

Sunday evening six were baptized. Monday was devoted to business meetings.

The messages presented at the camp were very practical, with Ellen White joining the ministers in their work.

The camp meeting was scheduled to close on Wednesday, April 5, but boat transportation was delayed, and so meetings continued another day. A meeting for literature evangelists followed over the weekend. Mrs. White remained for still another week in Napier; she and associate workers visited families and churches nearby. But much of her time was devoted to writing.

Two or three weeks after the camp meeting was over she wrote of its success to Harmon Lindsay in Battle Creek:

> Our camp meeting in Napier was excellent from the commencement to the close. Several decided to observe the Sabbath for the first time, and some who had left the church came back (letter 79, 1893).

THE WINTER IN NEW ZEALAND

With the Napier camp meeting over, Ellen White and her party moved on to Wellington at the southern tip of North Island, New Zealand. Wellington was the headquarters of the New Zealand Conference—if a book depository and the president's residence together could be called a headquarters. M. C. Israel served as president. Three rooms of this building were made available to Mrs. White and Emily Campbell (RH, June 13, 1893).

It was planned that Mrs. White would reside there for a month or six weeks, but it turned out to be the four months of the winter.

It was Tuesday, April 18, when they moved in, and she closed her diary entry for that day with the words "Now comes the taxing part of our work—preparing not only the American mail, which closes Thursday, but mail for Melbourne, which leaves every week" (ibid.).

As there was no church in Wellington, the whole worker group would drive six miles (10 kilometers) to Petone for Sabbath services.

There were many difficulties for the advancement of the work in New Zealand. Canright's books and a consistent opposition of Protestant ministers had a strong influence. Elder Daniells had had good congregations; Elder Israel had worked there for four years, but nothing had been successful in creating an interest. A deep sleep seemed to be upon the people.

Determined to make a break, the workers decided to rent the skating rink, which would seat about 1,000, for evangelistic meetings. Even though the rent seemed high, they would go forward in the name of the Lord and do something. At 3:00 Sunday afternoon, April 30, Ellen White spoke there on temperance to a good audience. She reported deep interest on the part of the hearers. In the evening Starr addressed an audience of about the same size on the inspiration of the Scriptures. An interest was created, and meetings continued for some time in the skating rink on Sabbath, Sunday, and some evenings.

Ever since crossing the Pacific nearly two years earlier Ellen White had been watching for an opportunity to write on Christ's life. Now in the winter months in New Zealand—June, July, and August—when travel would be somewhat curtailed, she determined to push the work forward as her strength and program would allow. She was glad to have found at the Tract Society Depository a quiet and comfortable place to write.

A MOTHER'S ANXIETY

During this time letters from James Edson White brought little comfort to his mother. While she was in New Zealand, he was in Chicago in the printing business, and quite involved in debt, which was not unusual for him. In one letter he stated, "I am not at all religiously inclined." There had been times when, with a heart dedicated to God, he had served in the Lord's work—Sabbath school, hymnbook preparation, publishing, et cetera. Now his letter, with these words, nearly crushed her.

Ellen White's response, in a letter that filled 10 double-spaced typewritten pages, described a dream in which was presented to her the case of a young man about to be carried away by the undertow, but was saved by the effort of one who risked his life to save him.

The letter, written in anguish, was attended by the winning and softening influence of the Spirit of God. Edson yielded his hard heart and experienced a reconversion. His immediate response and his experience of the next two or three weeks are not recorded in the files, but on August 10, 1893, he wrote to his mother:

I have surrendered fully and completely, and never enjoyed life before as I am now [enjoying it]. I have for years been under a strain, with so much to accomplish, and it has stood right in my way. Now, I have left it all with my Saviour, and the burden does not bear me down any longer. I have no desire for amusements and pleasures that made up the sum of my enjoyments before, but have an enjoyment in the meetings with the people of God such as I never had before.

As to his future, he declared he wanted to connect with the work of the church in some way. Later in the month he wrote his mother: "I have been thinking of going down into Tennessee to work among the colored people. . . . I shall go into the work somewhere in the spring. . . . I still hope and trust in God, and am sure He will care for me. I have proved my own way and it is a poor way. I now want God's way, and I know it will be a good way."

Through the next decade Ellen White thrilled to Edson's vivid reports of God's blessings as he pioneered the work among the Blacks in the great Southland of the United States.

DENTAL PROBLEMS

Mrs. White's teeth were causing her a good deal of trouble. Some were abscessing, and she concluded it was time to get rid of them. She had only eight left, and she wrote to Dr. Caro, the dentist in whose home she had stayed in Napier, inquiring whether she could come down to Wellington and have them pulled out. They settled on the date, Wednesday, July 5. At the end of the day she told the story in her diary:

> Sister Caro came in the night; is in the house. I met her in the morning at the breakfast table. She said, "Are you sorry to see me?" I answered, "I am pleased to meet Sister Caro, certainly. Not so certain whether I am pleased to meet Mrs. Dr. Caro, dentist."
>
> At ten o'clock I was in the chair, and in a short time eight teeth were drawn. I was glad the job was over. I did not wince or groan. . . . I had asked the Lord to strengthen me and give me grace to endure the painful process, and I know the Lord heard my prayer.
>
> After the teeth were extracted, Sister Caro shook like an aspen leaf. Her hands were shaking, and she was suffering pain of body. She had felt sick, she said, on the cars during her ten hours' ride. She dreaded to give pain to Sister White. . . . But she knew she must perform the operation, and went through with it (MS 81, 1893).

Ellen White took nothing to deaden the pain, for she suffered adverse aftereffects of such medication.

Then the patient turned attendant. She led Dr. Caro to a comfortable chair and found something to refresh her. As Mrs. White looked ahead she could see that she would have to give up public work for a while, perhaps for two months, when Dr. Caro would fit her for a new set of teeth. She pushed ahead with her writing.

DETERMINED TO WIN NEW ZEALAND

Of Wellington, and of New Zealand in general, Ellen White cried almost in despair: "God has a people in this place, and how can we reach them?" (letter 9a, 1893).

Writing to the churches in America, she described the difficulties for success in evangelistic effort. There was no church in Wellington; Adventists met in Elder Israel's house. People were not attracted to meetings in halls. Workers had tried everything possible to get people out. They circulated notices, leaflets, tracts. Workers went from house to house, sowing the seed upon ground that had hitherto proved unfruitful.

But the prejudice seemed like a granite wall. So far, except in a few places, almost every conventional means of reaching the people had failed.

A NEW APPROACH IN GISBORNE

As the little worker group counseled together, they decided to try a new approach to arrest the attention of the public. In letters to her son W. C. White and to her niece Addie Walling, Ellen White described what took place:

> We thought we would strike out on a new line. We would have Sunday-afternoon services in an open-air meeting. We did not know how it would come out. . . . Brother Wilson and Brother Alfred Wade secured the paddock just back of the post office. There was one large willow tree. Under this a platform was made and the organ and stand placed on the platform. Lumber for seats was right in the yard, costing nothing for their use (letter 140, 1893).

> There were seats without backs in abundance, and a dozen taken from the church with backs. . . . The weather was favorable, and we had an excellent congregation. The mayor and some of the first people in Gisborne were in attendance.

> I spoke upon temperance, and this is a living question here at this time. Hundreds were out to hear, and there was perfect order. . . . Mothers and any number of children were present. You would have supposed that the children had had an opiate, for there was not a whimper from them. My voice reached all over the enclosure (paddock is the name they give it here).

> Some of the hearers were very enthusiastic over the matter. The mayor, the policeman, and several others said it was by far the best gospel temperance discourse that they had ever heard. We pronounced it a success and decided that we would have a similar meeting the next Sunday afternoon (letter 68, 1893).

They did hold just such a meeting the next Sunday afternoon. It, too, was a decided success. Ellen White commented: "One thing we have learned, and that is that we can gather the people in the open air, and there are no sleepy ones. Our meetings were conducted just as orderly as if in a meetinghouse" (ibid.). A church member declared, "It is altogether the best advertisement of our people they have ever had in Gisborne" (letter 140, 1893).

Prejudice was broken down, and from that time on the meetings in the church and the Theatre Royal were well attended. At last they had witnessed a breakthrough.

THE WELLINGTON CAMP MEETING

It was finally decided to hold the New Zealand camp meeting, scheduled for November 23, 1893, at Wellington at the south tip of North Island instead of at Auckland in the extreme north of the island. The president of the General Conference, Elder O. A. Olsen, would be arriving from Africa. And the missionary brigantine *Pitcairn* would be in port. Also of importance, it was thought this might be the right time to add impetus to the breakthrough in evangelism in this most difficult place.

On Monday, November 20, Ellen White, with Emily, arrived at Wellington at 10:00 at night. W. C. White was on hand to meet the train. They hastened to rented rooms.

New tents, both large and small, had been shipped from Australia and were now being pitched on high dry ground in a beautiful fenced paddock within walking distance of the city of Wellington. It was with bated breath that church members and others watched the process. Wellington was well known for its fierce winds. Not long before this a circus tent had been torn to shreds by the high wind. Church leaders knew well the risks. "Our earnest prayer," wrote Mrs. White, "is that this encampment may have the favor of God. The winds and fountains of waters are in His hands, under His control" (MS 88, 1893).

God did hold His sheltering hand over the encampment. An early report to the *Bible Echo* indicated this:

> Every provision is made, and every care taken, to carry out the arrangements with facility and decorum. The tents are arranged in streets. The large tent has seating accommodation for about six hundred (Jan. 1, 1894).

O. A. Olsen arrived during the opening days of the meeting, and he became the main and much appreciated speaker. *Pitcairn* was in port, and her officers and crew were a help to the meeting. Dr. M. G. Kellogg, the medical missionary of the ship, was drawn into service and spoke from day to day on health topics and Christian temperance, which were reported to be one of the most telling and interesting features of the meetings *(ibid.)*.

From the very beginning Ellen White was often on the platform and almost every day addressed the congregation. Sabbath afternoon she spoke, and again on the afternoon of Sunday, her sixty-sixth birthday. She felt great freedom as she took pleasure in "showing our colors on which were inscribed the commandments of God and the faith of Jesus." Reporting the response, she wrote:

> I told them that we were Seventh-day Adventists, and the reason of the name which distinguished us from other denominations. All listened with deepest interest (letter 75, 1893).

Sunday evening the tent was full when G. T. Wilson was the speaker. Ellen White's disclosure of the identity of the people holding the meetings did not deter a good attendance. In a letter to Edson she told of their concern for the success of the meeting:

> We had much fear lest we would have a very slim attendance, but we were happily disappointed. From the first to the last there was a good appearance of congregation of the best class of our own people who fed on the bread of life during the meeting. Evenings there were good-sized congregations of outsiders. . . .
>
> We have had good, large, respectful audiences, and a very large number of people now understand what we do believe. . . . People listened as if spellbound. . . . The citizens were impressed with this meeting as nothing else could have transpired to impress them. When the winds blew strong, there would be many looking with wonder to see every tent standing unharmed (letter 121, 1893).

Ellen White wrote: "The camp meeting is a success. . . . The Lord is in the encampment" (letter 75, 1893). "Indeed, the whole meeting was a spiritual feast" (BE, Jan. 8, 1894).

Twenty-four persons were baptized as a result of the services.

Dr. Kellogg and G. T. Wilson remained in Wellington for a time to follow up the camp meeting interest. In the meantime the tents were quickly dismantled and shipped to Australia for use in their first camp meeting, scheduled to open in a suburb of Melbourne on January 5.

Within a week of the close of the camp meeting Ellen White had closed up her work and was one of quite a large group, which included W. C. White and O. A. Olsen, on their way back to Australia.*

In leaving New Zealand she left behind a number of friends with whom she had formed close relationships and who would later be known in the denomination. Among them were the Caros in Napier and the Browns in Long Point.

EVANGELISTIC THRUST IN AUSTRALIA

With the Wellington camp meeting fresh in their minds, the workers looked forward optimistically to plans for the first camp meeting in Australia. They entertained hopes that there would be a response similar to that witnessed in New Zealand. The meeting was scheduled to open in Melbourne on Friday, January 5, 1894, and there was just time to get the tents pitched for this innovation in gospel preaching.

The committee on location found a 10-acre (four-hectare) tract of land, grass-covered and partly shaded by eucalyptus trees (blue gum), in the suburb of Middle Brighton, nine miles (14 kilometers) from the Melbourne post office. It was south of the city, near the bay, and was served by an excellent railway line that had trains running every 30 minutes from morning till late at night.

Family tents were being made in three sizes for the camp meeting. Prices and styles of tents that might be purchased in the city did not fit the plans of the camp meeting committee, so good material was secured, and by early November, 35 tents were ready for sale or rent.

The *Bible Echo* for December 8 carried an Ellen White appeal for an outstanding attendance, as she pointed out the objectives of the meeting. It was to be a time of spiritual refreshing for the church and also an effective means of reaching the city with the third angel's message. "Come to the Feast" was the title of the three-column invitation.

Notice was also given of some of the best help the denomination could supply in making the meetings a success. The president of the General Conference of Seventh-day Adventists would be present; Ellen White and W. C. White would be there; and Dr. M. G. Kellogg, ship physician for the *Pitcairn*, would be giving instruction along health lines. One notice especially delighted the believers of a few years:

> Our readers will be pleased to hear that Elder J. O. Corliss, who spent some time in Australia five or six years since, is now on his way back, accompanied by Elder W. A. Colcord. They expect to be with us at our camp meeting (BE, Dec. 1, 1893).

It was announced also that there would be a dining tent on the campgrounds, "furnished with tables, dishes, chairs, et cetera, and with proper waiters to serve the meals" (*ibid.*, Nov. 22, 1893).

A weeklong workers' meeting would immediately precede the camp meeting, so the pitching of tents began on Tuesday, December 26. Initial plans called for 50 family tents, but these were taken so quickly that orders were given for 25 more.

The camp meeting opened on Friday, January 5, as scheduled. Through buying and renting, the number of family tents had more than doubled during the week of the workers' meetings. Even though the nation was passing through stringent economic times, every possible effort had been made to "make all things in the camp meeting after the divine order" (RH, Sept. 25, 1894).

The community in Brighton, a beautiful town, was stirred. The Sabbath meetings were a feast for the believers, and by then the grounds were being filled with people from the community whose interest had been aroused by the tent city and the distribution of reading matter. Ellen White wrote:

> People of the finest and noblest of society are coming from all places. The tent is filled in the afternoons and evenings, so there is scarcely room for them to find a seat (letter 125, 1894).

> In the afternoons and evenings throughout the week our congregations number about one thousand (letter 100, 1894).

> Many voices are heard expressing the gratitude of joyful hearts as men and women contemplate the precious truth of the third angel's message, and come to realize the paternal love of God (letter 86, 1894).

The visitors made good use of the dining tent. One hundred ninety were served on Sunday, January 14. The cost to the patrons was only sixpence, or twelve and a half cents. No meat was served, and the diners really enjoyed their meals (MS 3, 1894).

"This camp meeting is advertising us as nothing else could," Ellen White wrote in her letter to Mrs. Caro. "The people say it is a wonder of wonders, this city of clean, white tents. Oh, I am so thankful" (letter 100, 1894).

On Sunday, January 14, Mrs. White wrote to A. T. Jones in Battle Creek:

> The first Sabbath of the conference meeting [January 6] three commenced the observance of the Sabbath, and yesterday five more took their position on the truth. Two businessmen [A. W. Anderson[†] and his brother Richard] with their wives and relatives, numbering eight, begged for tents in order that they might remain on the ground and attend early-morning and evening meetings. One of the men will return every day with his horse and carriage to Melbourne, a distance of eight or ten miles (13 or 16 kilometers) and look after the business, returning at night.

These two brothers keep a large music establishment and are convicted of the truth, and we believe will yet take their position. Far and near the sound has gone out concerning this city of tents, and the most wonderful interest is awakened.

Other campers crowded together a bit to make two tents available to the Andersons, who camped there for a few days.

One of the attendees at the meetings was Mrs. Press, who was president of the Women's Christian Temperance Union and for several years had been a vegetarian. She sought an interview with Ellen White and visited with her in her tent. Mrs. Press requested Mrs. White to address her group, and urged participation on the part of Seventh-day Adventists in the work of the WCTU. The WCTU president called for someone to give the WCTU members lessons in hygienic cooking. When told the Adventists had no one in Australia well enough qualified, her response was, "Tell us what you do know" (letter 88a, 1894).

Not long after this Capt. and Mrs. Press hosted a private cooking school conducted by Mrs. Starr and Mrs. Tuxford in their home. Helpful guidance in food preparation was given to the Press family in connection with this cooking school (letter 127, 1894).

Thoroughly pleased with the response the meetings were receiving, Ellen White wrote enthusiastically to A. T. Jones in America:

> This is the first camp meeting that Melbourne has seen, and it is a marvel of wonder to the people. There is a decided interest to hear the truth. This interest we have never seen equaled among those not of our faith. The camp meeting is doing more to bring our work before the people than years of labor could have done. . . . Yesterday the most noted physician in North Fitzroy was here to listen. Some ministers have been here, and a large number of businessmen (letter 37, 1894).

Writing to Edson White, she said, "Taking it on all sides, this is the best camp meeting we have ever attended" (letter 86, 1894).

A UNION CONFERENCE IS BORN

Following the camp meeting a business session of the Australian Conference was conducted. Eight meetings were held, beginning on Monday morning, January 8, and running through the week.

As was the case with all local conferences and missions throughout the world, those in Australia were separate units under the direction of the General Conference, with headquarters in Battle Creek, Michigan. Local conferences, when formed, were accepted into the General Conference. The arrangement oftentimes proved awkward.

One problem was the time element. Mail to and from the United States took a month each way. Then there was the distance between local conference or mission and the General Conference. Institutions were developing to serve the peoples of the whole South Pacific, and they needed careful supervision. All this led A. G. Daniells and W. C. White to give study to a type of organization that would bind together the local organizations in a given area into an administrative unit, which in turn would be responsible to the General Conference. In several trips they took together to New Zealand and back they had time to canvass the matter carefully and to outline a course that might be followed.

With the business of the Australian Conference out of the way by the end of the second week, the key workers turned their attention to the creation of a new type of organization, which would stand between local conferences, missions, institutions, and the General Conference. In this way matters of local concern could be studied and acted upon by those nearby.

On Monday morning, January 15, with W. C. White, who had been appointed by the General Conference as the "superintendent of the Australasian Field," in the chair, some 250 persons came together to consider the matter of forming a union conference. Olsen was asked to preside at the meetings—nine in all during the next 10 days. Committees on organization, nominations, and resolutions were appointed.

The committee on organization presented a constitution that would foster the beginning of the new union conference and called for steps to be taken to enable it to hold church and school property. The nominating committee recommended for officers: president, W. C. White; vice president, A. G. Daniells; secretary, L. J. Rousseau; treasurer, Echo Publishing Company.

It was a trailblazing meeting, setting up in essence what the church as a whole would adopt within a few years. Olsen was strongly in favor of what was accomplished and worked closely with their church leaders. The development of the union conference organization would relieve the world headquarters of many administrative details. The union conference plan was well thought through and devised with understanding and care. It opened the door for true advancement throughout the Australasian field and in time the world field.

FAR-REACHING INFLUENCE OF THE BRIGHTON CAMP MEETING

About 100 souls were baptized as the immediate fruitage of the Brighton camp meeting, among them the two Anderson brothers (letter 40b, 1894). Their wives followed a few months later. An evangelistic tent was pitched in North Brighton, and Elders Corliss and Hare continued with a series of meetings that were all well attended. Another tent was pitched in Williamstown, across Hobson's Bay from Brighton and 12 miles (19 kilometers) south of Melbourne. Here M. C. Israel and W.L.H. Baker carried on the evangelistic thrust. Churches were raised up in both communities. Ellen White spoke at both places, several times in Williamstown, either in the tent or a hired hall (MSS 5, 6, 1894).

All in all, the first camp meeting held in Australia was a success and served to establish a pattern of fruitful evangelistic camp meetings.

---

*Mrs. White's ministry in New Zealand was confined to the North Island. She never visited Christchurch or other cities on the South Island.

† Father of the late well-known evangelist and teacher, Roy Allan Anderson, and his brothers, Ormond and Clifford.

THE AVONDALE SCHOOL

The Bible School, which had opened in August 1892 and closed in December, was regarded as a first step in the establishment of a permanent school for young people of all ages in Australia. The importance of training workers in their own land rather than sending them overseas had long been recognized.

When Elders Olsen and White returned with Ellen White from New Zealand to Australia in late December 1893, the search for a school site began in earnest. Following up investigations Arthur Daniells had made, they visited several places during their few days in Sydney. This continued off and on through the late summer and fall. The school had been made a union conference project, which drew W. C. White, the president, very closely into the task. By the time Ellen White had moved to New South Wales, the conviction seemed to prevail that the school should be located in that colony, with its warmer climate, perhaps within 75 miles (120 kilometers) of Sydney.

One very important consideration in the search for a site was the need for good soil and a large acreage to produce crops and provide labor. The majority of the constituents who would support the school would be in a low-income bracket.

The suffering of Sabbathkeeping families, not a few of whom had lost their homes, led some church leaders to feel that the school property should be large enough to provide little farms for some of these families. Thus they thought in terms of 1,000 or 2,000 acres (405 or 810 hectares).

W. C. White, now carrying the burdens of the new Australasian Union Conference in addition to other duties, was engaged in a feverish search for a site for the new school. Ellen White followed each move with keen interest. In his room in the Per Ardua home he not only administered the work of the union conference but also collected samples of soil taken from the different properties that he and other members of the locating committee visited.

In April 1894 the search had narrowed down to the Brettville estate on Dora Creek, which could be purchased for $4,500.

THE BRETTVILLE ESTATE

The Brettville estate was a tract of undeveloped land of 1,500 acres (610 hectares) 75 miles (120 kilometers) north of Sydney, near the villages of Cooranbong and Morisset on Dora Creek. ("Though the stream is called Dora

Creek," wrote Ellen White, "yet it has the appearance of a river, for it is a wide, deep stream" [letter 82, 1894]). The estate was attractive at the low price of $3.00 an acre (1 hectare) (high-priced land they could not buy); the physical features were very appealing, and the rural situation favorable for the location of the type of school that had been planned.

But a negative report had been given to the church leaders by the government fruit expert who had been requested to examine the soil. He had declared it for the most part very poor, sour, sandy loam resting on yellow clay, or very poor swamp covered with different species of Melaleuca. According to him, the whole of the land was sour, requiring liming and draining (DF 170, A. H. Benson, "Report of the Campbell Tract Near Morisset, N. S. W.," May 21, 1894; see also 4 WCW, pp. 410-412).

Legend has it that when Mr. Benson handed the report to a member of the committee he remarked that "if a bandicoot [a marsupial about the size of a rabbit] were to cross the tract of land he would find it necessary to carry his lunch with him" (see DF 170, "The Avondale School," WCW to F. C. Gilbert, Dec. 22, 1921).

Sometime before this Ellen White had made an appeal through the pages of the *Review* for members in America who might be willing to pioneer the work in Australia and share their time and abilities in getting the work started in some of these undeveloped places. She declared:

> What a great amount of good might be done if some of our brethren and sisters from America would come to these colonies as fruit growers, farmers, or merchants, and in the fear and love of God would seek to win souls to the truth. If such families were consecrated to God, He would use them as His agents (RH, Feb. 14, 1893).

In response to this the L. N. Lawrence family—father, mother, and daughter—had come from Michigan at their own expense to aid wherever they could with the work in Australia.

On Wednesday, May 16, 1894, W. C. White, with the Lawrences and others, traveled to Dora Creek to make a preliminary inspection of the Brettville estate. Ellen White reported:

> Brother and Sister Lawrence went yesterday [May 16] with a tent, W. C. White has taken a supply of bedding and provisions, and thus the party will be provided with board and lodging to save hotel bills. And the fact that they can spend their nights on the ground will expedite business. All will return Monday or Tuesday (letter 46, 1894).

While at Dora Creek the Lawrences found they could rent a small house—

three rooms and a kitchen. This would make it very convenient when the church leaders would come to inspect the property; they would have a place to stay.

ELLEN WHITE EXPLORES THE SCHOOL SITE

A group of church leaders planned to go up from Granville on Wednesday, May 23, to inspect the property. Although Ellen White had not been feeling well, she could not resist the desire to accompany them. The group included Brethren Daniells, Smith, Reekie, Humphries, Caldwell, Collins, and White.

Some time before Mrs. White made this first visit to Cooranbong, she had been given a dream. She described it:

> In my dream I was taken to the land that was for sale in Cooranbong. Several of our brethren had been solicited to visit the land, and I dreamed that I was walking upon the ground. I came to a neat-cut furrow that had been plowed one quarter of a yard [.23 meters] deep and two yards [1.8 meters] in length. Two of the brethren who had been acquainted with the rich soil of Iowa were standing before the furrow and saying, "This is not good land; the soil is not favorable." But One who has often spoken in counsel was present also, and He said, "False witness has been borne of this land." Then He described the properties of the different layers of earth. He explained the science of the soil, and said that this land was adapted to the growth of fruit and vegetables, and that if well worked it would produce its treasures for the benefit of man. . . .
>
> The next day we were on the cars, on our way to meet others who were investigating the land (MS 62, 1898).

> We found a good dinner waiting for us, and all seemed to eat as if they relished the food. After dinner we went to the riverside and Brethren Starr, McKenzie, and Collins seated themselves in one boat, Brethren Daniells, McCullagh, and Reekie in a still larger boat, and Willie White, Emily Campbell, and myself in another.
>
> We rode several miles upon the water. . . . It is somewhat salt, but loses its saltness as it borders the place which we are investigating. It required two rowers to pull the boat upstream. I should judge this is no creek, but a deep, narrow river, and the water is beautiful. . . . On our way we passed several houses upon farms of about 40 acres [16 hectares] of land. . . .
>
> When we landed on the ground to be explored, we found a blue-gum tree about one hundred feet [30 meters] long lying on the ground. . . . Around us were immense trees that had been cut down, and parts were taken out which could be used. . . . I cannot for a moment entertain the

idea that land which can produce such large trees can be of a poor quality. I am sure that were pains taken with this land, as is customary to take with land in Michigan, it would be in every way productive (letter 82, 1894).

She was escorted to some parts of the land, walking and resting and thinking. She later told about finding the furrow:

> When we came to Avondale to examine the estate, I went with the brethren to the tract of land. After a time we came to the place I had dreamed of, and there was the furrow that I had seen. The brethren looked at it in surprise. "How had it come there?" they asked. Then I told them the dream that I had had.
>
> "Well," they replied, "you can see that the soil is not good." "That," I answered, "was the testimony borne by the men in my dream, and that was given as the reason why we should not occupy the land. But One stood upon the upturned furrow and said, 'False testimony has been borne concerning this soil. God can furnish a table in the wilderness'" (letter 350, 1907).

But night was drawing on, and the party returned down Dora Creek to the cottage by the light of the stars. As the larger group came together near the boat-landing, they brought encouraging reports of their findings. Ellen White wrote:

> They came from their investigation with a much more favorable impression than they had hitherto received. They had found some excellent land, the best they had seen, and they thought it was a favorable spot for the location of the school. They had found a creek of fresh water, cold and sweet, the best they had ever tasted. On the whole, the day of prospecting had made them much more favorable to the place than they had hitherto been (letter 82, 1894).

Mrs. White retired early, but the committee earnestly discussed their findings on into the night. There were diverse opinions, for there was considerable variation in different parts of the land, but the majority felt the enterprise could be made to succeed. Added to this was their observation of Mrs. White's confidence in the potentialities of the property. Late that autumn night the committee voted to purchase the Brettville estate for $4,500.

REPORT TO THE FOREIGN MISSION BOARD

In his report written June 10 to the Foreign Mission Board in Battle Creek, W. C. White described the tract in considerable detail, filling four single-spaced typewritten pages:

Much of the land in this section of the country is a clayey gravel with subsoil of shale or rock, or a coarse red sand with a subsoil of red clay. So much of it is of this character that the district is generally spoken against. There is much good land to be found in strips, and some most excellent soil in places. . . . We estimate two hundred acres [80 hectares] fit for vegetables, two hundred fit for fruit, and two hundred good for dairying. The cost of clearing will vary considerably (4 WCW, pp. 420-422).

Twenty-five years earlier land in the area had been cleared for agriculture, and orange and lemon orchards had been planted. But the settlers neglected their orchards and turned to the cutting of timber to supply the nearby mines. W. C. White reported:

We have prayed most earnestly that if this was the wrong place, something would occur to indicate it, or to hedge up the way; and that if it was the right place, the way might be opened up. So far, everything moves most favorably. . . . We have signed a contract to buy the place, and have paid £25. At the end of this month, June 30, we are to pay £275, and then we have two years in which to pay the balance, with the privilege of paying all at any time (ibid., pp. 422, 423).

MAKING A BEGINNING

The first step was to find the funds with which to make the payment of 275 pounds, due on June 30. W. C. White reported to A. G. Daniells:

On Thursday, June 28, I borrowed £150 from Brother Sherwin and £105 from the Australian Tract Society, and scraped up all there was in our house, and made payment of the £275 due on the first payment (ibid., p. 488).

Their solicitor (attorney) said the title was good. Two weeks later Mr. Lawrence, the church member who had come from Michigan, rented an old 12-room hotel in Cooranbong, known as the Healey Hotel, and the furniture at the Bible school in Melbourne was sent for. Arrangements were made for surveying the land (6 WCW, p. 68). The last two weeks of August found quite a company of workers at Cooranbong.

Ellen White's enthusiasm for the Cooranbong property knew no bounds. She began making plans and looked forward to visiting as often as possible.

As soon as it had been decided to purchase the Brettville estate for the school, a horse and cart were purchased in Sydney and dispatched to Cooranbong for the Lawrence family and visitors to use. Mr. Collins, a colporteur leader suffering some eye difficulty, and Jimmy Gregory collected provisions for three days and started out on the 76-mile (122-kilometer) journey. At Cooranbong the rig proved very helpful. It was put to use by Mrs. White, Emily, and May Lacey while visiting Cooranbong in August. (May Lacey was the young woman Willie had met at the Bible school in Melbourne and had brought into the home to replace May Walling, who had returned to America.)

As they drove, or walked around the empty acres, Ellen White liked to visualize what might be planted here and there. She wrote to her close working companion, Marian Davis:

> I have planned what can be raised in different places. I have said, "Here can be a crop of alfalfa; there can be strawberries; here can be sweet corn and common corn; and this ground will raise good potatoes, while that will raise good fruit of all kinds." So in imagination I have all the different places in a flourishing condition (letter 14, 1894).

She little dreamed how long in the future that might be!

WORK AT COORANBONG BROUGHT TO A STANDSTILL

In late August, as W. C. White, L. J. Rousseau, L. N. Lawrence, and others were at Cooranbong with the surveyor, tramping over the newly purchased land, two letters were handed to W. C. White—one from F. M. Wilcox, secretary of the Foreign Mission Board in Battle Creek, the other from W. W. Prescott, educational secretary of the General Conference. White read them to Rousseau and Lawrence as they rested in the forest.

The two letters carried the same message. The writers of each had just attended a meeting of the Foreign Mission Board at which W. C. White's letter of June 10, with his description of the land at Cooranbong, had been read. Each conveyed the same word—that the board felt, from the description of the land, it would be well to look for other property that was more promising, even if, because of a higher price, not more than 40 acres (16 hectares) could be secured. White called a halt to the work in progress, and the surveyor was sent back to Sydney (DF 170, "Report of the Proceedings of the Executive Committee of the Australasian Union Conference for the Year 1894"; 6 WCW, pp. 126, 129).

To Prescott, White wrote on September 3:

> As regards the land, we are acting upon the suggestion of the Mission Board, and have suspended all operations as far as we can. How this will affect our future progress and prospects, we cannot now conjecture. If it were an enterprise of our own, we might have many forebodings, but as we are servants of a King, and as He has power to make light from dark-

ness, and to turn what looks to be failure into success, we shall wait and trust (6 WCW, p. 126).

Dreaded misgivings swept over W. C. White. He later described the circumstances in the report he prepared to present to the constituency at the camp meeting to be held at Ashfield, near Sydney. After noting the careful inspection of many properties and that there had been 28 meetings of the committee on school location between January 23 and August 29, he reluctantly wrote:

> Letters were received from the secretary of the Foreign Mission Board and the educational secretary of the General Conference acknowledging receipt of the description of the place sent them by W. C. White and intimating their fears that the place was not suitable for our work. The same fears were felt to some extent by W. C. White, L. J. Rousseau, and [A. G.] Daniells; therefore, at a meeting held in Sydney, August 27, White, Daniells, McCullagh, Reekie, and Rousseau being present, the following resolution was adopted:
>
> *Whereas,* The Mission Board has expressed doubts and cautions regarding our school location, therefore,
>
> *Resolved,* That we delay further proceedings at Cooranbong until we have time to consider the question of location (DF 170, "Report of the Proceedings of the Executive Committee of the Australasian Union Conference for the Year 1894").

Somewhat stunned, W. C. White found himself frequently humming the words "Wait, meekly wait, and murmur not" (6 WCW, p. 137), and threw himself into the search for what might be a more promising site for the school. To Ellen White also, the decision of the Foreign Mission Board was a blow, and she waited at Cooranbong for word on what action would be taken by the committee on school location to be held in Sydney, Monday, August 27. On that same day she wrote:

> The more I see the school property, the more I am amazed at the cheap price at which it has been purchased. When the board want to go back on this purchase, I pledge myself to secure the land. I will settle it with poor families; I will have missionary families come out from America and do the best kind of missionary work in educating the people as to how to till the soil and make it productive (MS 35, 1894).

On Wednesday, August 29, Ellen White received a telegram calling for her to return to Sydney the next morning. Cutting short her restful stay at Cooranbong, she and her women helpers took the morning train, arriving at

Sydney about noon. They were met by W. C. White, Daniells, Reekie, and Rousseau, and taken to the mission. Here, after refreshments, the news of the decision of the committee on Monday was broken to Ellen White. That evening she wrote of it in her diary:

> Brethren Rousseau and Daniells had propositions to lay before us that the land selected for the locating of the school was not as good land as we should have on which to erect buildings; we should be disappointed in the cultivation of the land; it was not rich enough to produce good crops, et cetera, et cetera.
>
> This was a surprising intelligence to us, and we could not view the matter in the same light. We knew we had evidence that the Lord had directed in the purchase of the land. They proposed searching still for land. . . . The land purchased was the best, as far as advantages were concerned. To go back on this and begin another search meant loss of time, expense in outlay of means, great anxiety and uneasiness, and delay in locating the school, putting us back one year.
>
> We could not see light in this. We thought of the children of Israel who inquired, Can God set a table in the wilderness? He did do this, and with God's blessing resting upon the school, the land will be blessed to produce good crops. . . . I knew from light given me we had made no mistake (MS 77, 1894).

It was clear where her confidence lay, and this was a point that neither the committee in Australia nor the Foreign Mission Board in Battle Creek could put out of mind, yet their best judgment led them to look with misgivings on plans to build a college at Cooranbong.

While to Ellen White the Brettville estate at Cooranbong was the right place, she knew that the final decision must be made by the church leaders, and they must be sufficiently confident of their decision to see the plans through not only in favorable circumstances but also in the face of the most foreboding difficulties.

The course now outlined seemed to her "very much like the work of the great adversary to block the way of advance, and to give to brethren easily tempted and critical the impression that God was not leading in the school enterprise. I believe this to be a hindrance that the Lord has nothing to do with. Oh, how my heart aches! I do not know what to do but to just rest in the Lord and wait patiently for Him" (ibid.).

The decision to search further for land remained firm, and the task was begun. Ellen White reluctantly joined the committee in inspecting new sites.

AVONDALE COLLEGE: ON HOLD

When Ellen White and her companions returned to Granville, it was to a different house. Her first home in Australia had been in Melbourne, where she made her headquarters for six months. When the next term of the Australasian Bible School was scheduled to open on April 4, the time had come when she must close up her work in Melbourne to free for student use the rooms she and her helpers were occupying. Also, the climate of New South Wales, being farther north, gave promise of being more comfortable than that of Melbourne. So in March a house was rented for her in Granville, a Sydney suburb.

The home in Granville, as do many houses in Australia, carried a name: Per Ardua. It was of brick and had 10 rooms, some oddly shaped. It stood on a three-acre (one-hectare) plot with an orchard, a place for a vegetable garden, and a grassy paddock, with some shade from gum trees. There were also shade trees in the front. In a letter to Willie, Ellen White commented favorably on the fireplaces, the broad porches, and the flower garden; she was pleased with the home generally. The building was large enough, with crowding, for her and her son, plus Elder and Mrs. Starr and several of her helpers.

W. C. White, a widower whose growing girls were living at his home in Battle Creek, was driven, as it were, from pillar to post in his living accommodations. Forced to the strictest of economy by a shortage of means, he contented himself with a room in his mother's home. He traveled the ocean by steerage; took low-fare, slow trains when there was a choice; and as union president often typed his own letters and worked prodigiously.

Per Ardua was at the foot of a hill, had low, rather small windows, and as time passed by Mrs. White became less pleased with it.

NORFOLK VILLA IN GRANVILLE

On looking around in June, as winter came on, they found a large house, Norfolk Villa, on top of a nearby hill in a neighborhood known as Harris Park. W. C. White described it as high, light, and dry, and planned more conveniently than where they had been living. It had 10 rooms and rented for the same rate as the previous property, $5.00 a week. "It is . . . real homelike," he said, with a "big dining room," which was a big comfort, for the whole family could gather (4 WCW, pp. 459, 489).

Ellen White's tent was pitched as an extra bedroom for the many visitors who came and went (letter 30a, 1894). The day after they were settled in the new home, July 9, she wrote to Edson:

> We are now in our new home. The house is the best we have ever lived in. It is two-story. I have the room above the parlor. Both parlor

and chamber have large bay windows, and the scenery is very fine. Everything is nice and pleasant here, and it is more healthful (letter 133, 1894).

The new home offered some relief to W. C. White, for his room, which served also as his office, was light and airy. He kept an observant eye on his mother and her welfare, and when at home made it a point to walk with her a few minutes after breakfast or dinner.

RUNNING A FREE HOTEL

With the interest developing at Cooranbong, the White home was a sort of stopping-off place, rather like a free hotel, a situation to which they tried hard to adjust.

Ellen White wrote of the heavy burden of entertaining. As preparations were being made to send off Jimmy Gregory and Mr. Collins with the horse and cart to Cooranbong, she wrote to Willie:

> We are supplying them with provisions for a three-day journey. We are expected to entertain all the saints who come and go, to shelter and feed all the horses, to provide provisions for all who go out, and to lunch all who come in.
>
> This would be all very well if it were only an occasional thing, but when it is continual, it is a great wear upon the housekeeper and upon those who do the work. They are continually tired and cannot get rested, and besides this, our purse will not always hold out so that we can run a free hotel.

She asked:

> But what can we do? We do not wish to say No, and yet the work of entertaining all who come is no light matter. Few understand or appreciate how taxing it can be; but if this is our way to help, we will do it cheerfully, and say Amen.
>
> But it is essential that we donate large sums of money to the work and that we lead out in benevolent enterprises. . . . Is it our duty also to keep a free hotel, and to carry these other burdens? May the Lord give us His wisdom and His blessing, is our most earnest prayer (letter 85, 1894).

Within a few days Ellen White felt remorse and self-condemnation for complaining. Repenting, she bravely wrote:

> I begrudge nothing in the line of food or anything to make guests comfortable, and should there be a change made in the matter of enter-

taining, I should certainly feel the loss and regret it so much. So I lay that burden down as wholly unnecessary, and will entertain the children of God whenever it seems to be necessary (letter 135, 1894).

It took some doing to feed a family of a dozen or 15 adults, with two to four visitors nearly every day. Now as the fruit came on, they prepared to move into a heavy canning program. On Thursday, December 20, as she wrote to Edson and Emma, she gave a little insight into the involvements:

> Well, we are now in the midst of fruit canning. We have canned one hundred quarts [ninety-five liters] of peaches and have a case more to can. Emily and I rode out five miles [eight kilometers] in the country and ordered twelve cases of peaches, one dollar a case. A case holds about one bushel [four pecks]. The ones we canned are the strawberry peach, called the day peach here. . . .
>
> Emily has canned fifty-six quarts [fifty-three liters] today of apricots, and we have twelve cases yet to can. We did have such a dearth of anything in the line of fruit desirable that we are putting in a good supply [letter 124, 1894].

A month later Ellen White could report, "We have canned no less than three hundred quarts [284 liters], and no less than one hundred [ninety-five liters] more will be canned"—some from the peach trees in their little orchard. She commented, "If I continue to keep open a free hotel, I must make provision for the same" (letter 118, 1895). She reveled in the fruit in the Sydney area, especially the peaches and the grapes.

THE ASHFIELD CAMP MEETING

On September 10 the *Bible Echo* carried an announcement that the Australian camp meeting for 1894 would be held at Sydney, October 18-30; there would also be a 10-day workers' meeting preceding the camp. The land selected was a five-acre (two-hectare) grassy plot in Ashfield, five miles (eight kilometers) from the Sydney General Post Office.

Granville, with easy access to Sydney and a number of rail connections, had become somewhat of a center of evangelistic operations. But all eyes were on the coming camp meeting and the annual session of the Australian Conference that would accompany it in late October.

To advertise the evangelistic meetings, which was a new thing for that area, a special camp meeting issue of the *Bible Echo*, dated October 15, was published. During the workers' meeting 20 young people distributed it to the homes in the various suburbs of Sydney. As they called on people, they sold copies of the

Echo and gave a hearty invitation to attend the camp meeting. Some 8,000 copies of the *Echo* were sold, and another 8,000 copies of the special cover, carrying an advertisement of the coming meeting, were given away.

As church members came in on Friday, October 19, they found more than 50 white canvas family tents among and under the shade trees. Another dozen were added by the end of the first week.

A large sign over the entrance to the enclosed grounds read, "WHOSOEVER WILL, LET HIM COME" (MS 1, 1895). In response to the advertising, Sabbath afternoon the attendance began to swell, and Ellen White reported to Olsen:

> On Sunday we had an immense congregation. The large tent was full, there was a wall of people on the outside, and the carriages filled with people in the street. The tents are a great surprise and curiosity to the people, and indeed, these white cotton houses interspersed among the green trees are a beautiful sight (letter 56, 1894).

Fully 1,000 were present as the afternoon discourse began, and W. C. White reported, "Before its close there were upwards of two thousand on the ground."

> Although many had apparently come from feelings of curiosity, the greater part of this multitude gathered in and about the large tent and listened attentively to Mrs. White as she presented the love of God and its effect upon the heart and character (BE, Nov. 5, 1894).

Throughout the week business meetings of the conference were held in the mornings, with various departments of the work given time for reports, discussions, and plans. Officers were elected for the ensuing year. A. G. Daniells was reelected president of the Australian Conference. Among the actions taken were two relating to the school. Since there was uncertainty over its location, the resolutions lacked precision and force.

After a second week of good meetings, the Ashfield camp meeting came to a triumphant close on Sunday with 2,500 people present. Ellen White described the climaxing service: "The last public service, on Sunday evening, was one long to be remembered. . . . At times the congregation was held as if spellbound" (DF 28a, "Experience in Australia," p. 789g).

Interest was high when the camp meeting closed. Many requested that the services continue, so it was decided to move the tent to another location, about a mile distant but with rail connections more convenient to several of the suburbs of Sydney. Corliss and McCullagh were commissioned to continue with meetings nightly; these were well attended. Other workers were drawn in to visit the people in their homes and conduct Bible readings (BE Dec. 3, 1894).

The Ashfield camp meeting closed November 5, 1894, with no decisive action concerning the location of the school. This was most disheartening.

A WEDDING IN THE FAMILY

W. C. White, like his father before him, had been pressed into service for the developing church almost beyond his capacity and time. From his early youth he had been involved in responsibilities of the publishing work, the health work, the educational work. His personal life, and such things as courtship, marriage, births, deaths, and family life had been wedged in between meetings, appointments, conventions, and travel.

Now at 40, a widower, he was president of the Australasian Union Conference and chairman of the locating committee for the proposed school at Cooranbong. He had a room in his mother's house and devoted as much time and attention to her as could be worked into his busy schedule.

On a recent visit to the Bible school in Melbourne he had noticed 20-year-old May Lacey and admired her. May had been at the Bible School for three terms and had developed her talents, giving Bible readings and visiting. She also played the piano and organ.

W. C. White encouraged his mother to bring May Lacey into the home in May Walling's place. "I have employed her," wrote Ellen White to Edson while she was at Cooranbong, "and she fills the bill nicely." She commented:

> I soon learned why Willie was anxious for May Lacey. He loved her, and she seems more like Mary White, our buried treasure, than anyone he had met, but I had not the slightest thought when she came to my home. . . . You will have a new sister in a few months, if her father gives his consent. She is a treasure. I am glad indeed for Willie, for he has not had a very happy, pleasant life since the death of Mary (letter 117, 1895).

W. C. White had seen May on only brief occasions when he was "at home" between meetings and conventions. So it was an utter surprise to her when he proposed that she become the mother to his motherless daughters now living in America. When Willie had left the United States to come to Australia, he had expected that the stay would be limited to not more than two years, and much of that would be in travel, so he had left Mabel, 4, and Ella, 9, in his home at Battle Creek in the care of Miss Mary Mortensen.

May could not give her answer to Willie's proposal on such short notice but agreed to make it a subject of prayer and conditional on solving several problems that she felt stood in the way. When these were resolved, plans for the wedding were made.

TASMANIA

The time for the wedding was chosen to coincide with a convention to be held in Hobart, Tasmania. The convention, according to an announcement in the *Bible Echo*, would be the first meeting of its kind to be conducted in that colony. It would be held in Hobart April 26 to May 6, 1895, and would include instruction on the duties of church officers and members, evening discourses on religious liberty, lessons on various lines of missionary work, and practical instruction given by Mrs. White.

May Lacey, accompanied by Ellen White and some of her staff, traveled by train from Norfolk Villa near Sydney to Melbourne, and then by ship, arriving at Launceston, Tasmania, on Wednesday morning, April 17. The travelers were taken to the Rogers home for lunch, and in midafternoon took the train south 125 miles (200 kilometers) to Hobart. It was 9:00 in the evening when they arrived. They were met by May's father, David Lacey, and several members of the family, and were taken to the comfortable and hospitable Lacey home in Glenorchy, just north of the city.

In his younger years David Lacey had filled the post of British police commissioner at Cuttack, in India, near Calcutta. Here May was born. She attended school in London, and on the retirement of her father joined the family in Tasmania. When colporteurs came to Hobart with *Thoughts on Daniel and the Revelation,* the family gained their introduction to Seventh-day Adventists. The careful follow-up work of evangelists Israel and Starr gathered the entire family into the church—Father and Mother Lacey and the four children, Herbert Camden, Ethel May, Lenora, and Marguerite. The mother died in 1890, and the father had by now married a widow, Mrs. Hawkins, who had four lively daughters and two sons. It was a loving and close-knit family that welcomed the daughter May and Ellen White that Wednesday.

A few days later the workers from New Zealand arrived by ship, among them W. C. White. It had been three months since he had parted from his fiancée and his mother at Granville in New South Wales, and this was a happy reunion. As the convention would not open until the next weekend, meetings were planned for the little country Adventist church built at Bismark in 1889.

Although the wedding was planned to follow W. C. White's three-month trip to New Zealand, there could be little detailed planning, since he and May were separated so widely. In fact, when W. C. White arrived in Tasmania on April 20, he did not know whether the marriage would take place in Tasmania or on the mainland of Australia. In a letter to his daughter Ella he told what took place:

> When we found that her father and sisters wished it to be there, at their home, and that Sister Lacey and her daughters all united in wishing us to have the wedding in Glenorchy, we decided to comply with

their invitation and so arranged to be married on Thursday afternoon, May 9, 1895 (7 WCW, p. 273).

In writing to Ella about the happy event, the groom told how the service was performed by a Methodist minister, Mr. Palfryman, an old friend of the Lacey family. There was no Seventh-day Adventist minister in that area qualified according to the laws of Tasmania. All went off well. The rooms in the Lacey home were nicely decorated with ferns and flowers. There were 10 members of the family present, and 11 friends of the bride who were invited guests. As they were in a British country, they were married with the wedding ring. Willie was 40 years old, and May, 21.

After the wedding service everyone was ushered into the dining room, where an attractive wedding supper was waiting for them. By 6:00 most of the friends were gone, and the bride and groom changed from their wedding garments. The bride finished packing, and her husband attended a committee meeting. At 8:30, with Ellen White, the couple took the train north to Launceston en route home (ibid., p. 274). A profitable weekend was spent in Launceston, the traveling workers meeting with the 17 newly baptized Sabbathkeepers there. With the children, there were about 40 at the Sabbath service who listened to Ellen White speak with freedom from the first chapter of 2 Peter. She also spoke to the group on Sunday (letter 59, 1895).

Good weather attended the traveling group as they left Launceston, but in the open ocean they encountered rough seas, and they arrived at Melbourne two and a half hours late. Ellen White was entertained in the Israel home and the newlyweds at the Faulkhead home. Mail from Granville told of the arrival from America on May 5 of W. C. White's two daughters, Ella and Mabel. The fond grandmother wrote: "Both are pronounced pretty, but Mabel is, they say, very pretty. We have not seen them for three years and a half, so they must have changed greatly. I wish to see them very much" (letter 120, 1895). But the reunion with the girls had to wait until committee work in Melbourne was completed, and speaking appointments were quickly made for Ellen White in Melbourne and its suburbs.

On Wednesday, May 29, the committee work was finished, and the three Whites—Ellen, W. C., and May—were on the train bound for Sydney and home in Granville. What a happy reunion it was that Thursday when, after more than three years, Ella and Mabel embraced Father, Grandmother, and their new mother, May Lacey-White! Exclaimed Ellen White a few days later:

> You cannot think how pleasant it is to have my family once more reunited. I have not seen more capable, ready, willing, obedient children than Ella May and Mabel. . . . They seem to have excellent qualities of

character. W. C. White is more and better pleased with his May. She is a treasure (letter 124, 1895).

STARTING A COLLEGE FROM SCRATCH

Because of the light given to Ellen White, there had never been any doubt in her mind that Cooranbong was the right place for the new school.

But several members of the locating committee hesitated and questioned. Even A. G. Daniells, influenced by the reports rendered by the government experts, had not taken a positive stand.

Since no decisive action had been taken at the close of the Ashfield camp meeting, Ellen White thought it was time for something to be done. She called W. C. White, chairman of the locating committee, and Elder Daniells, president of the Australian Conference, and repeated her strong convictions, ending her talk with a challenge: "Is there not a God in Israel, that ye have turned to the god of Ekron?"

In response to her firm convictions in the matter, the committee decided to return to Cooranbong and take another look at the Brettville estate.

In the meantime members of the Foreign Mission Board in America found it difficult to put out of their minds the fact that Ellen White was firm in her stand that the Brettville estate was the place for the school. By formal action they removed their objection to plans to establish the college there.

Word to this effect brought courage to the committee on the school location in Australia. On November 20, 1894, the Australian Union Conference committee took the following action:

> *Whereas*, The Foreign Mission Board has withdrawn its objections to our locating the Australasian Bible School in the Brettville estate at Cooranbong, and . . .
>
> *Whereas*, We believe that the Brettville estate can be made a suitable place for our proposed school. . . .
>
> *Resolved*, That we proceed to the establishment of the Australasian Bible School on the said Brettville estate (minutes of the Australasian Union Conference, Nov. 20, 1894, in 5 WCW, p. 197).

Returning from Tasmania and the wedding of W. C. White and May Lacey, Ellen White spent the month of June (1895) at her home, Norfolk Villa, in various activities: assisting in the work with the new companies of believers being raised up, planning for the evangelistic thrust in Sydney, and writing energetically. She felt much worn and was eager for a change that could come by being in Cooranbong.

So Monday morning, July 1, with W. C. White and his family, she took the train for Cooranbong, and stayed for three weeks, at first in the home of Herbert Lacey, newly come from America. They found 26 boys and young men living in the rented hotel building, and some sleeping in tents. They were clearing the land and building roads and bridges, making a beginning for the school. On February 25 Professor Rousseau had sent a letter to the churches announcing plans and inviting young men to come to the school and engage in a program of work and study. Each student would work six hours a day, which would pay for board, lodging, and tuition in two classes.

When Ellen White and W. C. White and his family came onto the school grounds, Metcalfe Hare was there managing a team of a dozen or more young men, Rousseau was managing a similar group in their work on the land, and good progress was being made.

Very early in the project to build a college at Cooranbong the idea of making it an industrial school, using students in manual training classes, and following the part-time-work, part-time-study plan, had been recognized as profitable and beneficial to the students both financially and healthwise.

Two years previously, when W. C. White was at the New Zealand camp meeting, he had scouted for young men interested in the industrial department.

On March 5, 1895, the manual training department opened, but it was without much support at first. In his efforts to get things moving at the school, W. C. White had been talking of such a plan for several months, and he wrote:

> You would be surprised to learn of the criticism, the opposition, and the apathy against which the proposition had to be pressed. The board said it would not pay, the teachers feared that it would be for them much labor with small results, and in many cases, the friends of those for whom the department was planned criticized severely, saying that young men would not feel like study after six hours of hard work (8 WCW, p. 32).

THE MANUAL TRAINING DEPARTMENT SUCCEEDS

But after watching the program in operation for six weeks, Ellen White reported:

> About twenty-six hands—students—have worked a portion of the time felling trees in clearing the land, and they have their studies. They say they can learn as much in the six hours of study as in giving their whole time to their books. More than this, the manual labor department is a success for the students healthwise. For this we thank the Lord with heart and soul and voice. The students are rugged, and the feeble ones are becoming strong (letter 126, 1895).

A START WITH BUILDINGS FOR AVONDALE COLLEGE

Land had been cleared on a high rise in the ground with the hope that when funds were available, a beginning could be made in putting up school buildings. The master plan worked out by W. C. Sisley and adopted by the union conference committee called for three structures as a beginning—the central building for administration and classrooms, flanked on either side at a distance of 100 feet (30 meters) by dormitories for the young men and the young women. These were to be erected on what L. J. Rousseau described in his letter to the churches, dated February 25, 1895, as "one of the prettiest elevations that could be found in the whole vicinity" (DF 170, "The Avondale School, 1895-1907").

But before there could be buildings, there had to be lumber, milled from trees cut from the forest. This called for a sawmill. W. C. White, writing to his brother Edson on August 3, described plans for the building to house the mill. He reported:

> Brethren Rousseau and Metcalfe Hare have been in Sydney for two weeks buying building materials, horses, wagons, farming implements, fruit trees, et cetera, et cetera. . . . Last night we advertised for a boiler, engine, circular saw, planer, turning lathe, and for a brickmaking plant (8 WCW, p. 31).

He commented, "We shall have very busy times at Avondale for the next few months."

Progress in erecting the school buildings was steady. Professor Rousseau, who had been connected with the school enterprise from the start of the Bible school in Melbourne, had returned to the United States. The chairman of the school board, W. C. White, who also served as president of the Australasian Union Conference, had been sent to America to attend the General Conference session and to take care of Australian interests, among them the production of health foods. Being on the grounds, Ellen White was expected to lead out. She felt quite alone in having to make decisions concerning the school enterprise. There was one ordained minister of experience in the whole colony of New South Wales, whose time was much taken up with the general interests of an advancing work.

THE SAWMILL LOFT PUT TO USE

It was midwinter as Ellen White wrote on July 5, 1896:

> One week ago yesterday I spoke in the upper room of the mill, partially enclosed, to eighty assembled, mostly our own people. . . . It is

rather a rustic place in which to meet, but when the sun shines in this country no other heating apparatus is needed.

I spoke again yesterday. We had a good meeting. We shall be glad to get a meetinghouse and school building. We are praying for means. We cannot advance until means shall come in from some source (letter 152, 1896).

The sawmill loft was often mentioned as a place of meetings that were held from week to week. It also became an assembly room for many of the young people at Cooranbong in a temporary school conducted by Prof. Herbert Lacey and his wife, Lillian. The Laceys had come from America to assist in what was to be the Avondale school. Hoping to get on with school work, and finding quite a number of young men and women eager to attend classes, Lacey saw an opportunity to make a beginning. On his own responsibility but with the consent of the school board, he began a night school in the mill loft. Some of the furniture and equipment, sent up to Cooranbong when the Bible school in Melbourne closed, was taken out of storage and put to use. Securing textbooks in Sydney and with his wife to help, Lacey conducted classes and collected tuition, with the understanding that the school board would not be held in any way responsible for expenses connected with the project, for the board had no money. Some 25 young people attended.

SETTING A TARGET DATE FOR AVONDALE COLLEGE TO OPEN

As the new year 1897 dawned, most activities at Cooranbong were geared to the proposed opening of the Avondale school, announced for April 28. On New Year's Day Prof. Lacey, who had returned to Australia to assist with the new school, was, with the help of his wife, Lillian, deep into the canning of fruit for the institution—starting with apricots. A donation of $60, just received to aid "where . . . most needed," was applied toward the purchase of other fruit, peaches, plums, et cetera, as they ripened. "There must be ample provision of fruit," declared Ellen White.

On New Year's Eve Lacey had been dispatched to ride horseback through the community to call the Adventists together for a meeting planned by Ellen White. She was determined that as they neared the target date enthusiasm for the school enterprise should not wane. It was an excessively warm evening, with the air "close and stifling," so instead of meeting in the loft of the sawmill, chairs were brought out to seat the crowd on the "green sward." Ellen White spoke, seated in her carriage with Sara McEnterfer to her right, holding a lantern, and Prof. Lacey standing on her left, also with a lantern. She reported that "all listened with interest" as she read from a manuscript and then spoke for a time, telling of "the establishment of the work in different localities, where buildings had been erected for schools, sanitariums, and places of worship."

In view of all that needed to be done before school could open on April 28, to accomplish the task seemed well nigh impossible.

Consider: The buildings were not finished. The carpenters were complaining about their wages and threatening to quit. As previously mentioned, W. C. White, the chairman of the board, had been sent to America to take care of the Australian interests. Prof. Rousseau, who had been connected with the school from the start of the Bible school in Melbourne, had returned to the United States. In addition, Herbert Lacey, who had been chosen as principal of the school, contracted typhoid fever during a visit in Tasmania to promote the school. He and his wife, Lillian, were both absent from Cooranbong until April 9. Haskell, whose strong support was needed, had been visiting in Africa for several months.

Metcalfe Hare, the business manager of the school, leaned heavily on Ellen White, and when important decisions had to be made she was looked upon as the senior officer in charge—a role she did not choose or covet. But those about her recognized that she had insights and experience others did not have.

One day she went over to see the progress being made on the second building, which would provide a dining room, kitchen, and storeroom for the school (letter 33, 1897). Taking in the overall situation, she had some questions to ask!

"What place have you prepared for the boys to room in?" I asked.

"The chamber above the sawmill," they answered. "Many students can sleep there, and we will also secure tents."

"Is that the best plan you have?"

"It is the best we can do. When the building is enclosed, our money will be expended."

"Have you thought of how much money it would take to run this building up another story?"

Several were present. "We cannot do that," Brother Hare said, "but I wish we could."

"You must do it, Brother Hare," I said. "What would the cost be?"

"Not less than £100," he answered.

"Then I advise you to put up the second story, and so provide sleeping rooms for the boys, and a meeting room for the church.". . .

"What shall we do?" they asked.

"Why," I said, "am I too late with my suggestions? Have the preparations gone so far that it would be a sacrifice to change now?"

"As to the matter of that," was the answer, "had your suggestions been a day later, we would have been at some loss.". . .

I said, "I will be responsible for the change made. If any censure comes, let it fall on me. You will be at expense of getting tents, and to the labor of pitching them. The students should not be put in the room over the mill. The influence would be demoralizing" (letter 141, 1897).

"Now," she wrote, "we have this two-story building nicely enclosed." The expansion provided a "room for Sabbath meetings" and "sleeping rooms for the young men" (letter 33, 1897).

She confided in a letter to Willie:

Be sure that Brother Hare is consulted in everything, and he will not move out in anything without consulting me. We move harmoniously in all our plans. Brother Haskell says it will not do for anyone to speak questioningly of anything I propose, for Brother Hare raises his right arm and says, "What Sister White advises to be done shall be done, without any ifs or ands about it" (letter 141, 1897).

She also stated:

All who see this upper story of the second building say, "Whatever could you do without it?" Brother Hare says he would not have taken the responsibility of changing anything if Sister White had not been right on the ground to say what was most needed. But that added story does Brother Hare lots of good (ibid.).

ELLEN WHITE CALLS A WORK BEE

When they were within three weeks of the target date for the school to open, Haskell was suddenly called to Adelaide to assist in meeting a crisis in the church there. With Haskell's leaving, even if for only a couple weeks, Hare's courage sank to an all-time low. He felt sure there was no hope of meeting the April 28 deadline for the opening of school. Taking in the situation, Ellen White began to plan a strategy, for she held that the school must open on time. She was not able to attend church on the Sabbath, but she sent an announcement to be read appointing a meeting for all who would, to attend on Sunday morning at 6:00. She had something to say to them. She sent word to Metcalfe Hare to come to her home after the Sabbath to meet with Mrs. Haskell, Sara, and herself.

Mrs. White wrote to Willie, telling what took place:

On Saturday evening we had our interview. Our means were gone, and the school building could not be finished to open school at the appointed time. Sister Haskell asked just how many hands could be put on to the building, how many on outside work, how many on the cistern, and how many inside. She wrote these down on paper, and after everything had been stated, she and I said, "We will have every position filled." Brother Hare argued that it was impossible.

We opened the morning meeting with singing and prayer, and then we laid the situation before them all. I told them that I would let them have Brethren Connell, James, and Worsnop, and pay them hire.

Brother Connell said that he had a two weeks' pledge to work out. Brother James said he would give one week's work in any line or place where they might put him. Brother Anderson also had pledged two weeks, and so one and another volunteered until men, women, and children were accepted.

I told them that I would give Sara to work in union with Sister Haskell, and they agreed to lay the floor with the help of Brother James to place the boards and press them into position, while Sister Haskell and Sara should drive the nails.

Our meeting lasted from six until eight o'clock. After [the] meeting the brother from Queensland made some depreciatory remarks about "lady carpenters," but no one to whom these words were addressed responded.

Every soul was put to work. There were over thirty in number. The women and children worked in the first building, cleaning windows and floors. Sister Worsnop came with her baby and children, and while she worked on the inside of a window, her eldest girl of 10 years worked on the outside. Thus the work in the first building was nearly completed in the first day.

Sister Haskell and Sara completed nearly one half on the dining-room floor. Brother Hare says everyone was enthusiastic. The women who engaged in the various branches of the work did well. Brother Richardson was putting the brick in the floor of the cellar. Some of the girls passed the brick from outside, while others inside passed them to Brother Richardson.

In the afternoon I was sent for to consult with Brother Hare in regard to making changes in the divisions of the dining room. . . . Then Brother Hare conducted me over the immediate premises, and we decided on the trees that must come down. . . .

Yesterday all the furniture in the mill loft was washed and cleansed from vermin, and prepared for the new building. One more floor is to be laid this afternoon. . . . The carpenters are siding up the building. Both ends are done, and quite a piece of the lower part on both sides. . . .

Monday, April 6, the workers, men, women, and children are all at work. . . .

The sisters had put the first coat of paint on the window frames. Brother Hare said that the women's diligent work had done more to inspire diligence in the men at work than any talk or ordering. The women's silence and industry had exerted an influence that nothing else could do. These women have worked until their hands and fingers are blistered, but they let out the water by skillful pricking, and rub their hands with Vaseline. They are determined to get at the work again. . . .

Brother Hare is full of courage now. Brother Haskell will be back in a week or two at most from the time he left. . . . His wife and Sara are heart and soul in the work. They make an excellent span just at this time. They will be in readiness to lay the upper floor after today, I think. Everything that is needed has come from Sydney and is right at hand, so that there will be no delay.

School will be opened April 28, 1897 (letter 152, 1897).

About the time the work bee began, word was received from W. C. White that at the General Conference session action was taken to send Prof. C. B. Hughes, principal of the school in Texas, to assist at Cooranbong. He was a well-qualified and experienced educator and would bring good help to Avondale. The word brought courage to all (11 WCW, p. 276).

Entering fully into the spirit of things, Sara McEnterfer set out to raise money to buy a school bell. From the families in the community she collected about £6, and what Ellen declared to be "an excellent sounding bell" was put in operation (letter 141, 1897).

As the target date for the opening loomed closer in April, there were some tense moments in Cooranbong. By an ill-advised action of the school board it was decided that there would be no primary school. Ellen White learned of this only after some announcements had been made, and she felt impelled to step in and take a firm position. She wrote of this, too, in her May 5 letter to Willie:

> The board met, and . . . decided that for this term there would be no primary school. On the next Sabbath morning, I told them that the primary school would commence when the other school did (ibid.).

> When Brother Lacey made the statement that there would be no primary school this term, Brother Hare felt much disappointed, for he wanted both of his children in the school. The officers are on his track, telling him that his children must attend the public school. . . .

> But in the first Sabbath meeting we held in the upper room, I presented this matter and called for a response, and you should have heard Brother Gambril's remarks. He came forward to the front seat, so that I

could hear him. He spoke of the influence of the public schools on his children, of the education they were receiving (ibid.).

It was in this setting that Ellen White made the rather familiar statement (found in *Testimonies*, vol. 6, p. 199): "In localities where there is a church, schools should be established if there are no more than six children to attend" (ibid.).

Steps were taken to rent the convent again for use in educating Adventist children in Adventist principles. Some of the children would be coming up Dora Creek by rowboat; Gambril's 15-year-old daughter would bring two Gambril children and two others to the primary school, which by mid-May had an enrollment of fifteen (ibid.; letter 126, 1897).

Elder Daniells had made a discouraging prediction about the attendance. He had said that they could not learn of one person in New South Wales and knew of only one in New Zealand who was planning to attend the school as a boarding student. He knew of only three or four from his conference. The matter became a subject of prayer, and his secretary, a woman named Graham, came up with a suggestion that he says "worked like a charm."

The suggestion was to ask each member of all the churches to pledge six-pence a week for 20 weeks toward the students' aid fund. Twenty-seven persons making such payments would meet the tuition of one student for the term of 22 weeks. This was to be a revolving fund, the student in time paying it back to aid another. The assignment of the students to be benefited would be in the hands of the conference committee. The people were pleased, and infused with a new spirit. The North Fitzroy church pledged to be responsible for two students, and other churches responded well. Daniells reported:

> One week ago tonight we sent six young men and women off by Cook's excursion. This morning at six o'clock we sent six more. One went alone in the middle of the week. This makes thirteen who have gone from this conference, and we are expecting to send four more (11 WCW, p. 435).

Plans called for the literature evangelists to sponsor one student, and the scattered believers another. Daniells wrote rather jubilantly:

> If these plans work, and from the way things are going I have reason to believe they will, we shall have a pretty good attendance after all. We shall pull hard to have from thirty-five to forty boarding students by the time Professor Hughes arrives. These with the day students will give us an attendance of about sixty students (ibid., p. 436).

Ellen White had declared: "There must not be one day of postponement.

. . . If there is but one student present, we must begin the school at the appointed time" (letter 149, 1897).

Her undaunted faith was a steadying influence. School would open on April 28, 1897.

THE AVONDALE SCHOOL OPENS

For some unknown reason, no official report of the opening of the Avondale school appeared in the *Bible Echo*. However, Metcalfe Hare stated in a report:

> The school opened the twenty-eighth of April, Mrs. E. G. White, Elder S. N. Haskell, and the teachers being present, with all those who had been associated with the work. The buildings were dedicated to their sacred mission by Elder Haskell (DF 170, "The Avondale School, 1895-1907").

Ellen White furnished a few more details in a letter to W. C. White a few days later:

> April 28 our school opened. At the opening exercises the upper room of the second building, above the dining room, was quite full. Brother Haskell opened the meeting by reading a portion of Scripture. He then prayed, and made a few remarks. I then followed (letter 141, 1897).

"The Spirit of the Lord was present," she wrote to Edson (letter 149, 1897), and in her diary for the opening day she wrote:

> We had the opening exercises in the last building erected. We had more in attendance than we had expected. We felt very thankful to make so good a beginning. We were very much pleased to have Brother and Sister Haskell with us. Brother Herbert Lacey and his wife were with us (MS 172, 1897).

So with a staff of six (four of whom were teachers) and with 10 students (LS, p. 365) the Avondale school commenced, and on the very day appointed.

One week after school opened, Ellen White reported that 40 students had enrolled. The *Bible Echo* dated June 7 reported that "about fifty students are in attendance at the Avondale school," rather more than expected. The next issue declared that they were "happy to revise these figures this week and state that there are sixty-two."

Ellen White felt comfortable with the Haskells taking the leading role at the school. She wrote of them as experienced laborers who "were a great help to us in the work of preparation, in devising and planning to get things in order" (letter 149, 1897). Prof. and Mrs. C. B. Hughes were on their way from Keene,

Texas. After the school was quite well organized and had continued for two months, the faculty was described in a report by G. T. Wilson in the *Bible Echo*:

> Prof. C. B. Hughes and wife arrived two weeks ago from America. He has been chosen by the school board as principal of the school, and is to have the general management of things on the place. He teaches the history class, who are now studying "Empires of the Bible." His wife teaches grammar, rhetoric, elocution, penmanship, and one Bible class.
>
> Prof. H. C. Lacey is teacher of mathematics, physiology, geography, singing, and voice culture; and his wife teaches the primary department.
>
> Pastor S. N. Haskell is the principal instructor in Bible study; and Mrs. Nettie Hurd Haskell, his wife, has charge of one Bible class, and acts as the matron of the school.
>
> Mr. T. B. Skinner, a graduate of St. Helena Sanitarium Nurses' Training Department, has charge of the kitchen and dining room, and on one day in the week gives practical instruction in cooking. The students are taught how to make bread, can fruit, and the other arts of healthful cookery (June 21, 1897).

In concluding his report, Wilson observed that "the students are mostly young men and women, of good, intelligent class, besides whom there are a few persons of more mature years." About one half were below the age of 16.

The school at Avondale was off to a good start.

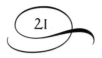

21

SUNNYSIDE— ELLEN WHITE'S FARM

From the very first, as plans began to develop for use of the 1,450 acres (587 hectares) of the Brettville estate, it was calculated that some of the land would be sold to Adventist families. By July 1895 there was talk of some 120 acres (49 hectares) being used in this way. On Sunday morning, July 7, Ellen White negotiated for the first of such land to be cut off from the estate, 40 acres (16 hectares) on the north side of the tract. For this she paid $1,350. "The reason I purchase now," she wrote, "is that I may furnish money which they [those connected with the school] need so much just now" (MS 61, 1895).

She planned to leave some of the land as woodland, use some for grazing, and some for orchard and garden. Of course, a choice spot would be selected for the homesite (letter 88a, 1895).

For some time she had felt that she should have her home in a location more conducive to her writing than the large rented house at Granville. There it seemed inevitable that she must run what seemed to be a "free hotel," with people coming and going almost every day. Now she determined to build a little cottage where such demands could not be made upon her. She also determined to develop a portion of her land in such a way as to provide an object lesson of what could be done in agricultural lines in that area. It was mid-July, and on inquiry she learned that whatever was to be done in planting an orchard must be accomplished in the next few weeks.

As the 40 acres (16 hectares) came into her possession, the first step in developing her little farm was clearing land for the orchard. Soon three good-sized tents were pitched on her property. She and her granddaughter Ella lived in one, and also, much of the time, one of her woman helpers. Another of the tents was used for cooking and dining, and the third was occupied by some of the men (8 WCW, p. 31) clearing land and planting trees. As construction of her little home progressed, Ellen White stood by to run errands for the workmen to save their time. She also did a little writing.

Starting almost from scratch, in early August the men made considerable progress on "the farm," and the foundation was in for the house (letter 156, 1896). Her August 28 description of the little camp at Sunnyside is revealing:

I am seated on the bed writing at half past 3:00 a.m. Have not slept since half past one o'clock. Ella May White and I are the sole occupants of a large, comfortable family tent. Close by is another good-sized tent, used as a dining room. We have a rude shanty for a kitchen, and a small five-by-five [1.5-meter-by-1.5-meter] storeroom. Next is another tent, which accommodates three of my workmen. Next is a room enclosed but not finished, for washhouse and workshop. This is now used as a bedroom by two men, Brother Shannon, my master builder, and Brother Caldwell. These five men we board. Several others are at work on the land who board themselves. Fannie Bolton occupies another tent, well fitted up with her organ and furniture. You see we have quite a village of tents (letter 42, 1895).

On a quick trip to Granville in late July Ellen White, with Hare, Rousseau, and W. C. White, spent a day driving around seeking information on securing fruit trees and orchard planting. She also had something else in mind.

I went into Sydney to see if I could find anything for the poor families, cheap. Money is so scarce we hardly know what to do and which way to turn to supply the demands in a variety of lines. The calamity of failure of banks has been and still will be keenly felt. We watch our chances where goods are offered for half price and purchase most excellent material to give to those who cannot buy that which they need (MS 61, 1895).

On Wednesday, the last day of July, they were shopping again:

All day W. C. White, Emily, and I spent in Sydney purchasing the things essential for our use in camp life. We thought it wisdom to select an outfit of granite ware [enameled cooking utensils] that will bear transporting and handling (ibid.).

Royalty income and some borrowing made it possible for Ellen White to do what others could not do in missionary lines.

Monday morning, August 19, 1895, Ellen White was exuberant as she took her pen to write to Edson. Paragraph after paragraph bubbled with good news:

Yesterday, August 18, 1895, the first [fruit] trees were planted on the Avondale tract. Today, August 19, the first trees are to be set out on Mrs. White's farm—an important occasion for us all. This means a great deal to me (letter 126, 1895).

The reason for her exuberance was that planting had begun.

PLANTING AND BUILDING AT COORANBONG

Two things were on Ellen White's mind as she hastened back to Cooranbong from Sydney—planting the orchard and constructing a place to live. Preparation of the land and planting had the priority. Right after she returned, W. C. White learned that J. G. Shannon, a good Adventist builder from Tasmania, was in Sydney looking for work. For the Whites it seemed most fortunate, for they were at a loss to know who to get to put up the home on the land just purchased. For eight shillings ($2) a day, this master builder was employed and dispatched to Cooranbong to begin work on a five-room cottage (8 WCW, p. 46). Ellen White wrote of the activities at her place:

> Today [Sunday] I am rushing the workmen on preparing ground for the orchard. We have today captured a part of the students' manual training company to clear the land for fruit trees which must be set this week and next, or give up the matter and lose one year.
>
> Emily and I are driving a span of horses hither and thither and are hunting for cows and gathering all the information possible in regard to planting, growing, et cetera (letter 125, 1895).

HOW TO PLANT A TREE—ACCORDING TO ELLEN WHITE

In search for information and guidance in putting in the orchards on her little farm and on the college estate, Ellen White was directed to a Mr. Mosely, a successful fruit grower.

On several occasions Mr. Mosely came over to plant trees and give instruction on orchard planting and care. The virgin land was well prepared. It took six spans of bullocks pulling an immense plow to break up the unworked soil. As she watched, Mrs. White marveled, and wrote that the bullocks were "under discipline, and will move at a word and a crack of the whip, which makes a sharp report, but does not touch them" (letter 42, 1895). At an early point in the tree planting, she had some input, about which she reminisced a little more than a decade later:

> While we were in Australia, we adopted the . . . plan . . . of digging deep trenches and filling them in with dressing that would create good soil. This we did in the cultivation of tomatoes, oranges, lemons, peaches, and grapes.
>
> The man of whom we purchased our peach trees told me that he would be pleased to have me observe the way they were planted. I then asked him to let me show him how it had been represented in the night season that they should be planted.

> I ordered my hired man to dig a deep cavity in the ground, then put in rich dirt, then stones, then rich dirt. After this he put in layers of earth and dressing until the hole was filled. . . . He [the nurseryman] said to me, "You need no lesson from me to teach you how to plant the trees" (letter 350, 1907).

Thus from the very start Ellen White was able to accomplish one of her objectives: to teach the people in the community what could be done by employing intelligent agricultural procedures. This was not just her own determined, ambitious plan. "The light given me from the Lord," she told Edson, "is that whatever land we occupy is to have the very best kind of care and to serve as an object lesson to the colonials of what the land will do if properly worked" (letter 126, 1895).

Rather jubilantly she wrote to Dr. Kellogg in late August of the influence of her work at Cooranbong, and of the appraisal of one expert on the quality of the land, a point her ears were attuned to:

> I came to this place and began work on my place so earnestly that it inspired all with fresh zeal, and they have been working with a will, rejoicing that they have the privilege. We have provoked one another to zeal and good works.
>
> The school workers were afraid I would plant the first trees, and now both they and I have the satisfaction of having the first genuine orchards in this vicinity. Some of our trees will yield fruit next year, and the peaches will bear quite a crop in two years. Mr. Mosely, from whom we bought our trees, lives about twenty miles [32 kilometers] from here. He has an extensive and beautiful orchard. He says that we have splendid fruitland.
>
> Well, the school has made an excellent beginning. The students are learning how to plant trees, strawberries, et cetera (letter 47a, 1895).

BUYING COWS

Ellen White also needed cows to provide a supply of milk and cream. In a letter written to friends in the United States she described the venture to supply the needs in this line:

> I drive my own two-horse team, visit the lumber mills and order lumber to save the time of the workmen, and go out in search of our cows. I have purchased two good cows—that is, good for this locality (letter 42, 1895).

The demonstration at Sunnyside was working well.

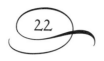

22

THE MEDICAL
MISSIONARY WORK

As Ellen White and other believers in the Advent message endeavored to spread the knowledge of the third angel's message in Australia they found that the subject of temperance was an opening wedge. The deep interest in temperance provided a receptive audience for new light in the broad field of healthful living: proper nutrition, exercise and rest, care of the sick, the relation of the mind to the body.

True temperance involves the total being: body, mind, and soul.

THE HEALTH HOME

The first step in the line of medical missionary work in Australia was the opening of the Health Home in Sydney in late 1896. The next step was the publishing of a health journal, the *Herald of Health*, launched in Melbourne in 1898.

Medical work was just getting a start in Australia. A. W. Semmens, a graduate nurse from Battle Creek, opened the Health Home in Sydney. A large residence was rented, and Ellen White noted, "As he had no money, I furnished him with £25 [$120] to make a beginning" (letter 70, 1897). To this was soon added £10 [$48]. The *Bible Echo*, on January 18, 1897, carried an advertisement for the newly developed Battle Creek health foods. The public was informed that "some of these valuable foods are already being shipped to this country, and that a proposition is on foot for their manufacture here at an early date." This was a significant project that was to take on large proportions in Australia.

On a Monday in early February 1897 a letter came to Ellen White from S. N. Haskell, who had just arrived in Sydney. He urged her to hasten to the city so they could counsel together. Although she was much involved in preparations for the opening of the Avondale school, she dropped everything and, with Sara, within three hours was "speeding to the train with" their "fastest team, conjecturing all the four miles and a half [seven kilometers] whether or not we would be able to catch the train to Sydney" (letter 82a, 1897). They did, and at 11:00 p.m. were at the Health Home at Summer Hill, where Haskell was staying. There they joined in planning.

To help keep the Health Home afloat financially, Haskell had rented and furnished one room. If the home proved a success, he would be paid back from earnings. Ellen White rented one room for $1 a week. She and Sara bought furniture in Sydney for this room so that she could have a place to stay when she was in the city. It could also be used by other workers as they passed through the city. Elder and Mrs. W.L.H. Baker took two rooms, for which they paid 10 shillings a week (letter 82a, 1897; letter 171, 1897). After explaining these steps to help get the enterprise going, Ellen White noted in a letter, "I hope this Health Home will prove a success, but it is an experiment" (letter 171, 1897). And to W. C. White she wrote on the same day:

> In regard to the Health Home, I cannot see anything very flattering in patients as yet. But it is no use to look on the discouraging side. We must walk by faith. We must talk faith and act faith and live faith (letter 188, 1897).

Dr. Kellogg had sent from Battle Creek a shipment of the newly developed health foods, apparently as a donation to the enterprise, so Ellen White reported to him:

> I have learned that Brother Semmens is doing well selling the health foods. . . . We feel thankful that you could give them this timely assistance. They appreciate it very much, for they have been in most straitened circumstances (letter 82a, 1897).

In mid-February the mail brought £50 ($240) from Peter Wessels. As Ellen White acknowledged the gift she declared:

> It came exactly at the right time. We were at the Health Home trying to get means to furnish some rooms in the humblest style. . . . When our means gave out, we had to wait; and when that money came, we rejoiced, and were glad. Now we can finish furnishing the rooms (letter 130, 1897).

The enterprise did succeed. By advertisements in each issue of the *Bible Echo* and in other media, the public was informed that at the Health Home they were prepared to "treat by the most approved rational methods paralysis, rheumatism, sciatica, neuralgia, and other disorders of the nervous system, also all manner of stomach and bowel disorders."

> These diseases will be treated by the most approved methods of hygiene, hydrotherapy, electrotherapy, massage, manual Swedish movement, diet, et cetera. Electric baths, electric vapour baths, sitz baths, salt glows, hot packs, wet sheet packs, massage, et cetera, can be had (BE, Jan. 11, 1897, and throughout the year).

After some months the *Bible Echo* on November 15 carried a back-page note to the effect that "the Sydney Health Home is having a good patronage at present—about all it can do."

THE SUCCESSFUL TREATMENT OF A VERY CRITICAL CASE

The little struggling health institution soon proved its worth as Professor Herbert Lacey, having become seriously ill during a visit in school promotion in Tasmania, was nursed back to health. On Friday, February 28, a telegram was received by his wife, Lillian, at Cooranbong to the effect that Lacey, desperately ill, would arrive by train in Sydney that day. Lillian hastened to Sydney and arrived just as her husband was arriving from Melbourne. They went immediately to the Health Home, where his case was thought to be typhoid fever. He had lost 20 pounds (seven kilograms) in one week, and his wife wrote that he was "very poor, nothing but skin and bones."

At the Health Home Elders Haskell and Baker were joined by Mr. Semmens in praying for his recovery (letter 189, 1897). Semmens began using hydrotherapy treatments. Lillian reported to her husband's father, who resided at Cooranbong, that "Brother Semmens was using ice on his bowels" (*ibid.*). His vitality was low, and when Ellen White learned of the ice remedy, she hastened off a telegram to Semmens, "Use no ice, but hot applications" (*ibid.*). Of course there was a reason for this, as she explained in a letter to W. C. White:

> In several cases light had been given me that the ice remedy was not as efficacious as the hot water. I was afraid. His vitality, I learned, was very low and to put ice on head and chest I knew was a mistake. It would tax his vitality. . . .
>
> There must be no risk run over Herbert's case. I was not going to be so delicate in regard to the physician as to permit Herbert Lacey's life to be put out. . . . There might be cases where the ice applications would work well. But books with prescriptions that are followed to the letter in regard to ice applications should have further explanations, that persons with low vitality should use hot in the place of cold. . . .
>
> Hot fomentations in fever will kill the inflammation in nine cases out of ten where ice applications will, according to the light given me, tax the vitality unsafely. Here is where the danger comes in of not using judgment and reason in regard to the subject under treatment (*ibid.*).

A week later in reporting to her son, she mentioned the steps being taken in connection with Lacey's illness:

> The case is critical, but I believe the Lord will raise him up. We are

praying for him. He is having everything done for him possible. . . . Brother Semmens gives his whole time to the sick man, and they are having Dr. Deek, who is watching the case of the hygienic methods of treatment with great interest. He says he is doing just as well as he could possibly do under this attack (letter 181, 1897).

In her diary she noted:

> We have made his case a special subject of prayer. We wrote a few lines to him each day to call his attention to that which the Lord was ready and willing to do for him. The angels of God have presided over him all through his sickness (letter 172, 1897).

Ellen White rejoiced when on Friday, April 9, she could send her carriage to the railway station to meet Herbert Lacey and his wife. She reported, "He is feeling real well and means to engage in the school at the beginning. I am so pleased."

But it was in the winter of 1898 that the various lines of medical missionary work really began to blossom in Australia. One matter of concern was that of priorities in the use of available funds. Responding in June to questions asked by A. G. Daniells, president of the union conference, Ellen White enunciated two principles:

> All should be able to see eye to eye before we determine how means shall be appropriated. It is necessary that we see how we stand financially in all our lines of work (letter 52, 1898).

In June she reported, "The Health Home is full. . . . We see a large number of people who are destitute of a knowledge of how to take care of themselves. We feel a great desire to advance the work" (letter 56, 1898). Then came a report indicating progress, published in the *Union Conference Record* of July 15.

> Those of our people who read the *Herald of Health* . . . will have noticed that the Sydney "Health Home" has changed its name. Henceforth this institution will be known as the "Medical and Surgical Sanitarium" of Summer Hill.
>
> Nor is this a change in name alone. The entire institution has been placed upon a higher scientific plane; in fact, a sanitarium plane.
>
> A physician has taken charge of the medical and surgical work. . . . A thoroughly competent chemist and microscopist is at the head of a new complete laboratory of investigation. Medical gymnastics and other special facilities are being added to assist in the recovery of the sick.

A SCHOOL FOR NURSES

The next step was the development of a school for nurses. The *Union Conference Record* of January 15, 1899, carried the following notice:

SANITARIUM TRAINING SCHOOL FOR NURSES

The sanitarium school for nurses is an institution for the training of young men and women to engage in various lines of medical and other philanthropic work under the direction of regularly organized missionary boards of the Australasian Medical Missionary and Benevolent Association. The school is evangelical, but highly scientific.

As to what might be expected in training and financial arrangements, the notice stated:

The Course: The course of instruction covers a period of three years, the terms commencing April 1 and October 1 each year. . . .

Remuneration: During the first year of the course, students receive uniforms and books, besides room, board, and tuition, and are required to work full time—ten hours each day. After the first year's examinations are passed, a small salary, as determined by the Sanitarium medical board, will be paid in addition to room and board, provided the work is done satisfactorily.

Soon Dr. S. C. Rand joined the forces, bringing the medically trained staff to four—two physicians and two graduate nurses. God blessed the work carried by the dedicated personnel laboring with limited facilities in cramped quarters. In response to Ellen White's almost heartbreaking pleas pointing out the dire need of building and equipping a sanitarium in Sydney, Dr. J. H. Kellogg, his brother, W. K. Kellogg, J. N. Loughborough, and others sent some funds with which to make a beginning in the erection of a well-planned medical institution.

It was reported that at the end of June there were 21 employees in the little Medical and Surgical Sanitarium of Summer Hill.

FIRM PLANS FOR ERECTING A SANITARIUM

In connection with the union conference session held at Cooranbong, a formal meeting was held of the Australasian Medical Missionary and Benevolent Association on Thursday morning, July 20, and recorded in the July 24 *Union Conference Record*. Fifteen resolutions were brought in for consideration. Three related to a proposed new building, the first of which read:

That we earnestly invite a hearty cooperation of our conferences and associations, and friends of our cause in general, in the erection and equipment of a medical and surgical sanitarium, to be located in the vicinity of Sydney; and that we suggest that this enterprise be undertaken according to plans for a building capable of accommodating one hundred patients.

This was followed by two lengthy resolutions relating to finance, the opening sentence reading:

That we undertake to raise the sum of £8,000 ($38,400) for the purpose named in the foregoing resolution.

The resolutions appealed to the constituency for strong support and the exercise of self-denial and "strict economy, that all may have means to offer for this cause." The common sentiment was that they should "look directly to God for help, committing our cause to Him and appealing through Him to the friends of the work."

At this point Ellen White was given an opportunity to speak. Her statement, which filled more than six columns in the July 21 *Union Conference Record*, opened with the words:

My husband and I took an interest in the sanitarium in Battle Creek from the time it was first started. It was very hard work to get right ideas fixed in the minds of the workers in regard to what the sanitarium should be. We had to go over the ground again and again, teaching them line upon line, precept upon precept, here a little and there a little.

After reviewing the initial steps taken in Sydney, she declared: "From the light I have received, I know that if ever there was a country where a sanitarium was needed, it is New South Wales, and I may say also, Victoria." She told of how the hospitals of the world could not suffice, and declared:

We should have a sanitarium under our own regulations, that the truth of God on health reform may be given to the world. Those connected with such an institution who are being educated as nurses should be trained to go forth from the institution as solid as a rock upon the principles of health reform and other points of truth.

She assured the delegates that it could be done. "The Lord has instructed me," she said, "that we can have a sanitarium here if everyone will do as I was reading this morning in the eighth and ninth chapters of Second Corinthians." She referred to the dire needs of the believers driven from Jerusalem and the manner in which means were raised for their relief.

"Their deep poverty abounded unto the riches of their liberality. For to their power, I bear record, yea, and beyond their power they were willing of themselves." Some who had no money gave part of their wearing apparel. Some divided the store of food they had, living poorly, that those who were suffering in Jerusalem might be fed. "Praying us with much intreaty that we would receive the gift."

She drew lessons from this experience and recounted God's providences in the beginning already made in Australia. "We need a sanitarium," she urged. "We desire that every soul here shall be interested in this work, because God is interested in it."

> This is the work the Lord desires to have done. Then let it be hindered no longer. God help us to take hold of it. No one man is to do the whole work. Let us all help to the best of our ability. . . . Nothing that we have is our own. All is the Lord's, and we are to do His work. God will put His Spirit upon those who will do something, and do it now.

At this point a vote was called for and the resolutions were adopted unanimously.

A SURPRISE MOVE

After the vote, E. W. Farnsworth stood and said that he did not know whether what he was about to propose was in order, but it seemed to him that they could not do better than to make a practical beginning of the matter right there. To start the fund, he would pledge £50 ($240). This pledge was quickly followed by others, and a list of the pledges (which was reproduced in the July 31 *Union Conference Record*) was made. The opening lines read:

	£	[$]
E. W. Farnsworth	50	[240]
Mrs. E. G. White	100	[480]
C. B. Hughes	40	[192]
S. N. Haskell and wife	55	[264]
G. B. Starr and wife	10	[48]
F. Martin	10	[48]

The list grew to 71 entries and £905, or the equivalent of more than $4,500.

A few months later Ellen White wrote of the fruitage of sanitarium work in Sydney:

> Several wealthy people who have come to our sanitarium in Sydney have embraced the truth, among them a man who has donated £500 ($2,400) to our sanitarium. He is an invalid. He and his wife have taken their stand fully (letter 11, 1900).

The sanitarium work in Australia was coming of age! The new sanitarium building in Sydney opened January 1, 1903, with Dr. D. H. Kress as medical director.

MEDICAL MISSIONARY WORK AT COORANBONG

In the vicinity of Cooranbong the medical missionary work was getting under way with a slow and humble beginning. First there was the selfless and dedicated work of Miss Sara McEnterfer, Ellen White's traveling companion, nurse, and private secretary. Sara, a graduate nurse from Battle Creek, involved herself in caring for the sick and injured in the community for some miles around. The nearest physician was 20 miles (32 kilometers) distant and charged £5 ($24) to make a visit.

Daily there were urgent calls for help. Many times it was children who had had accidents of various kinds. Sometimes the patient would be brought to either Ellen White's or W. C. White's home and nursed back to health.

A few excerpts from Mrs. White's diary through the early part of September 1897 yield a picture of this work of community ministry:

> *Wednesday, Sept. 1:* While I was reading the mail, a woman from Dora Creek came up with her baby for instruction on what to do for the child.
>
> *Thursday, Sept. 2:* We went to see the child that was brought to our house yesterday that was sick. Sara prescribed for her, and the mother followed the prescription. We learned today the child was relieved. . . .
>
> The father of the first child that had appealed for help asked me if we did not receive pay for our trouble. We told him no, we did not do the work for pay, only to relieve suffering humanity as Christ did when He was in our world. They seemed very thankful.

The Ellen G. White-sponsored medical missionary program right there in Cooranbong went quietly on. This was made possible because Sara McEnterfer was willing to serve as community nurse without charge, and to help families in which there was dire need of food, clothing, and bedding. But Mrs. White, in letters, and at times in her oral presentations, continued to call for a hospital at Cooranbong.

THE HEALTH FOOD WORK

It took quite a struggle to get the health food work in Australia on its feet. While the delegates and visitors in July 1899 were spending three weeks at Cooranbong attending the Australasian Union Conference session, they could observe the steps being taken to convert the sawmill structure into an efficient food factory.

The 1897 session of the Australasian Union Conference was held in connection with the Stanmore camp meeting. Ellen White attended but few of the meetings, but the groundwork was laid there for the manufacture of health foods in Australia. While in the United States, W. C. White, at the request of the union conference committee, had made quite a thorough investigation in Battle Creek of what might be done in health food manufacture in Australia.

On July 2, 1897, he had addressed a communication to the executive committee of the Australasian Union Conference reporting on his findings regarding the arrangements that could be made with the Kelloggs. In this letter he stated:

> Believing that the granose [wheat flakes] was a very valuable health food, that it would find a large sale in the colonies, and that it would aid us greatly in building up the market for a fine line of health foods, I had several conversations regarding its manufacture, during which I learned that the doctor [Kellogg] had expended more than £1,000 [$4,800] in experimenting with the manufacture of granose and developing the method of making it, and that his plan for permitting those in foreign countries to make the product was to lease them the mill and charge them a small royalty on all that they made. . . . I concluded to accept the terms and have ordered a granose mill which will be forwarded with some other machinery to Sydney to be held in bond there until we shall decide where it shall be put in operation (11a WCW, pp. 63, 64).

Two days later he reported in a letter to the Australasian Union Conference executive committee that he had secured the services of Mr. Halsey, who was skilled in the manufacture of the Battle Creek health foods, to come to Australia and lead out in making the new products. White also sent samples of the foods for the members of the board to taste, so they would be better prepared to make decisions on his return (*ibid.*, p. 80). So, following the union session in Sydney, and after spending just a few days at home, White was off to Melbourne, where he would give full reports to the appropriate committees, and actions could be taken in pioneering this new line of work in Australia.

As the church leaders worked in Melbourne, there emerged a "Report of the Committee on Health Foods" consisting of 13 points, among them:

> That we proceed at once to establish a health-food factory in Melbourne. . . .
>
> That immediate steps be taken to make and place upon the market

Granola, and Caramel Cereal, and that these be followed by Granose Biscuits, and a general line of healthful biscuits, and other foods, as quickly as possible (*ibid.*, p. 358).

The Adventist-sponsored manufacture and distribution of health foods in Australia was on its way.

THE MEDICAL AND SURGICAL SANITARIUM, AND THE USE OF MEAT

While at the sessions of the New South Wales Conference held in the Stanmore church, Ellen White attended an early-morning meeting on Monday, July 25, 1898, to discuss the dietary program of the new sanitarium. Drs. E. R. Caro and S. C. Rand, newly come to the institution, were present; also A. W. Semmens, W. C. White, and G. B. Starr. In her diary she reported what took place:

> The consideration was in regard to the meat question. Shall the sanitarium maintain the principle of nonmeat eating for the patients who have not been instructed in a vegetarian diet? The question was, "Would it not be well to let them have meat at first, educate them away from the appetite by lectures, and then bring them where they will be instructed by the lectures on the evil of meat eating?"
>
> I replied that to condemn meat eating and show its injurious effects and then bring the injurious article and give it to the patients, and prescribe it for some of the patients as some had thought best to do, was a denial of their principles and would not be in accordance with the teachings of our people on this question of health reform. We felt there must be no drawing back on this question (MS 184, 1898).

She pointed out that the increase of disease in the animal kingdom was a strong argument in favor of her position. The subject in various aspects came up in formal and informal discussions at the conference on both Monday and Tuesday, and Ellen White noted:

> We are to be sure that we commence the work in right lines. No tea, no coffee; avoid drugs. We are to take our position firmly in regard to the light given us that the consumption of the dead flesh of animals is counterworking the restoring of the sick to health. It is not a safe and wholesome diet. . . .
>
> However great the goodness of God and however abundant His promises to any people, continued transgression of the laws of God in our nature brings disease. Therefore we cannot present meat before the patients (*ibid.*).

The impact of the discussions and Ellen White's firm position were reflected in the resolutions passed at the session, two of which read:

> Resolved, That in the prosperity attending the work of the "Health Home," which has now grown into a "Medical and Surgical Sanitarium," we recognize the blessing of God upon right principles in dietetic reform, and the use of rational, or nature's remedies in the treatment of disease; . . .
> Resolved, That we pledge our support of these principles by our practice and our influence, and with our means (UCR, Aug. 15, 1898).

A few days after returning to Cooranbong, Ellen White wrote:

> We greatly hope that our physicians in the Health Home may be soundly converted to correct principles in health reform. I was glad that up to the present time flesh meat has not found its way upon the tables at the sanitarium, and we hope it never will disgrace the health-reform table (letter 180, 1898).

The next day, July 31, she reported that Willie "leaves Wednesday for Melbourne to have plans laid in regard to medical missionary work, to establish it upon a good basis" (letter 181, 1898). Medical personnel generally would be there, and, of course, plans would be laid for the developing health food business.

By this time health foods were being imported on a regular basis. P. B. Rudge was brought from New Zealand to manage sales, which were promising. The June 15, 1898, Record carried an interesting advertisement:

"TRY THEM"
> We invite all our readers to improve their diet by eating granola and nut butter, and by drinking caramel cereal. They are the great food correctives for indigestion and constipation. We also invite you to assist this good enterprise by selling the foods to others. Liberal discounts are offered to all agents. Address, Sanitarium Health Food Agency, 251 St. George's Road, North Fitzroy, Victoria.

Two months later the Record reported the arrival in Australia of G. W. Morse, who was to "devote his time to the interests of the Australasian medical missionary work, giving special attention to the health-food business." He was present at the Melbourne meeting of the newly formed Australasian Medical Missionary and Benevolent Association. An early and prime concern was where the food factory should be located. Melbourne was the well-established center of the work in Australia, and workers and believers there quite naturally felt that there was little need for such a study. Others felt there were other important considerations, and a committee on the location of the manufacturing plant was appointed, made up of A. G. Daniells, Dr. E. R. Caro, G. W. Morse, W. C. White, and E. R. Palmer.

LONG-DISTANCE COUNSELOR

During the nine years that Ellen White was in Australia she did not lose sight of what was going on in America. Although her mind was burdened and pushing forward the message in Australia and New Zealand, choosing sites for schools and tent meetings, she managed to keep up an almost overwhelming amount of correspondence across the sea.

Mail each way across the Pacific took a full month, and mail boats ran once a month. Preparing the mail to go on schedule was no small task for Ellen White and her secretaries. There were serious problems and agonizing situations. Her diary records the depth of concern she felt for leaders and individuals.

On April 9, 1894, she wrote of preparing the American mail while the house was full of visitors. "Elder Starr had to do most of the entertaining," she wrote, "for my letters must be prepared for the American mail" (MS 23, 1894). And on April 16, the day the mail closed, as she finished her letter to A. T. Jones, she, in weariness, declared: "I can write no more. This mail carries out more than one hundred pages" (letter 68, 1894). The May American mail carried 150 pages, some addressed to the president of the General Conference.

The communications ran from four to 12 pages of double-spaced typewritten material, and the few lines quoted in this volume, although selected as epitomizing the thrust of a respective message, represent but very brief samples of the many, many messages painstakingly penned.

MEETING OFFSHOOT TEACHINGS

The day before the New Zealand camp meeting opened in April 1893 Ellen White addressed a letter to a Mr. Stanton in America, who had begun to teach that the Seventh-day Adventist Church had, through apostasy, become Babylon. She wrote:

> Dear Brother Stanton,
>
> I address to you a few lines. I am not in harmony with the position that you have taken, for I have been shown by the Lord that just such positions will be taken by those who are in error. Paul has given us a warning to this effect: "Now the Spirit speaketh expressly, that in the latter times some shall depart from the faith, giving heed to seducing spirits, and doctrines of devils."
>
> My brother, I learn that you are taking the position that the Seventh-day Adventist Church is Babylon, and that all that would be

saved must come out of her. You are not the only man whom the enemy has deceived in this matter. For the last forty years, one man after another has arisen, claiming that the Lord has sent him with the same message. But let me tell you . . . that this message you are proclaiming is one of the satanic delusions designed to create confusion among the churches. My brother, you are certainly off the track (letter 57, 1893).

As she wrote most earnestly to him she touched on several points:

> Do not seek to misinterpret and twist and pervert the testimonies to substantiate any such message of error. Many have passed over this ground, and have done great harm. As others have started up full of zeal to proclaim this message, again and again I have been shown that it is not the truth. . . .
>
> God has a church upon the earth, who are His chosen people, who keep His commandments. He is leading, not stray offshoots, not one here and one there, but a people. The truth is a sanctifying power, but the church militant is not yet the church triumphant (*ibid.*).

GOOD NEWS FROM AMERICA

Mail, both going and coming, was an important part of the program of Ellen White and those who were with her in New Zealand.

Sunday, April 23, 1893, she arose early—at half past three—to prepare the mail bound for Melbourne, expecting it to leave on Monday.

That same Sunday, in came a large stack of letters. There was a long letter from O. A. Olsen, president of the General Conference, giving a full summary of the General Conference session and reporting on the confession of a number of prominent men who had taken a wrong position at the 1888 General Conference session.

Another letter was from Leroy Nicola, a prominent pastor in Iowa. It was the Nicola letter that brought her special rejoicing. It was "a most thorough confession of the part he acted in Minneapolis."

THE ANNA PHILLIPS EXPERIENCE

One of Ellen White's concerns at this time was the mishandling on the part of some leading brethren in America of Anna Phillips and her claims to special revelations from God.

Miss Anna Phillips—sometimes spoken of as Anna Rice, for she had been taken into the Rice family—felt she had been called by God to serve as a special messenger to the church, inspired by heavenly visions.

She wrote "testimonies," first to the Rices and then to other husbands and wives, touching on their personal experiences. These were earnest appeals for purity of life, with teachings that went beyond the Bible and the Spirit of Prophecy. Messages were directed to the leaders of the church aimed at giving guidance in administering the work.

Correspondence from America called the matter to Ellen White's attention. On November 1, 1893, she wrote to Elder and Mrs. Rice cautioning them not to become involved with Anna Phillips and her writings. Almost two months went by before she addressed herself again to the matter. On her journey back from New Zealand she had a few days in Sydney. There, on December 23, she wrote a general warning in the form of a 10-page letter addressed to "Dear Brethren and Sisters." It opened:

> I have a message to you from the Lord. Brother Rice is not engaged in the work which the Lord would have him to do. . . . He cannot see the outcome of this work which he has taken up. Anna Phillips is being injured; she is led on, encouraged in a work which will not bear the test of God.

In a nine-page letter written January 14, 1894, in Melbourne to A. T. Jones, Mrs. White discussed several matters. On page 5 she reported that word had reached her that Jones was giving encouragement to Anna Phillips, and even reading some of her messages in public in such a way that people found it hard to discern when he was reading from her writings and when he was reading from Ellen White's pen. She urged, "I want you to consider this carefully, for the Lord has given me light to the effect that the attention of the people is not to be called to Anna Phillips" (letter 37, 1894).

In the first paragraph of her 10-page letter to Jones, written March 15, 1894, she dealt quite fully with the situation. She pointed out that God had not called Anna Phillips to follow on after the testimonies. She wrote:

> Many things in these visions and dreams seem to be all straight, a repetition of that which has been in the field for many years; but soon they introduce a jot here, a tittle of error there, just a little seed which takes root and flourishes, and many are defiled therewith (letter 103, 1894 [see also 2SM, pp. 85-87]).

W. M. Adams, who was a student at Battle Creek College in 1894, has recounted his experience. He heard Elder Jones preaching in the Battle Creek Tabernacle. In the sermon Jones intermingled some of the messages of Anna Phillips with those he read from the testimonies, and asked the congregation whether they did not hear the same voice in each. The people were left in confusion.

The next morning Adams was at the post office in the Review and Herald building, writing a postcard home. Jones came in and asked for his mail. He was handed a long envelope with Ellen White's name in the return address. He dropped on the bench, tore the envelope open, and began to read. Adams reports that as Jones read, tears came to his eyes and fell on the sheets of paper.

Soon A. O. Tait came in, and Jones addressed him. "Oscar, come here. Sit down. You heard me preach that sermon yesterday?"

"Yes," replied Elder Tait.

"Well, read this," Jones said as he handed him the testimony he had just received from Ellen White. After Tait had read it, Jones asked, "Who told Sister White a month ago that I was going to preach that sermon about Anna Phillips as a prophetess?"

"Ah, you know, Alonzo," Tait answered in his calm yet firm way.

"Yes, I do know. God knew what I was going to do, and He impressed Sister White a month before I preached the sermon to send the testimony that I am wrong. Look at that date."

It was a thoughtful week for the brusque and ever-ready A. T. Jones. Adams reported that the next Sabbath he again preached in the tabernacle and that he read portions of the testimony he received Sunday morning. He said, "I am wrong, and I confess it. Now I am right" (RH, July 7, 1949).

Elder W. W. Prescott also became a supporter of Anna Phillips, but a few hours before he was to address the students at Walla Walla College, intending to introduce some of her messages, he was handed a copy of a letter from Mrs. White dealing with the matter. It was the first to come to his attention, and he dropped his plans. S. N. Haskell, president of the California Conference, happened to be at Walla Walla at the time. He exclaimed as he wrote to Ellen White of the incident, "I have heard about testimonies coming just in season, but I never experienced such providence before" (S. N. Haskell to EGW, Mar. 31, 1894).

J. H. KELLOGG AND THE MEDICAL MISSIONARY WORK

Another matter of vital importance that was pressing hard upon Ellen White in the year 1899 was the distressing course being pursued in the medical missionary work in America. Dr. John Harvey Kellogg was taking steps to divest this work of its denominational ties, in the Battle Creek Sanitarium, the medical school, and the work for the outcasts and socially deprived classes in Chicago. This last mentioned was a fast-burgeoning work that divided his interests and overburdened his body and mind.

Calling for earnest attention were the inroads of pantheistic philosophy insidiously creeping into the teachings of Seventh-day Adventists, threatening the basic theology of the church. A three-week-long General Conference session would open at South Lancaster, Massachusetts, on February 15, and Ellen White applied herself to the preparation of messages to sound solemn warnings and to guard the cause.

In progressive steps Dr. Kellogg worked toward placing the medical work of Seventh-day Adventists on a nondenominational basis. As Kellogg led out in the establishment of the American Medical Missionary College in 1895 (as explained in chapters 23 and 24 of *The Story of Our Health Message*), he rather stealthily imposed on this important phase of educational work an undenominational identity. The students who enrolled in this medical college were told by Kellogg:

> This is not a sectarian school. Sectarian doctrines are not to be taught in this medical school. It is a school for the purpose of teaching medical science, theoretically and practically, and gospel missionary work. It is not to be either a Seventh-day Adventist or a Methodist or a Baptist or any other sectarian school (*Medical Missionary*, October 1895 [quoted in SHM, pp. 294, 295]).

Through the year 1898 Ellen White penned 17 letters to Dr. Kellogg, aggregating some 113 pages; many were messages of caution. In 1899 she wrote another 26 letters to him, averaging nine pages each. The messages that dealt with various phases of medical missionary work were presented first. In the main these were but an amplification of what she had been writing in letters to him over a period of a year or two. Some of the letters contained words of commendation for certain phases of his work; some just newsy reports of developments in Australia, particularly in medical missionary lines; some sounded an alarm; some contained solemn warnings. All were written kindly, carefully, and with understanding. On February 13, 1898, she began her message to the doctor, whom she had known since he was a lad and whom she loved as her own son:

> It would give me great satisfaction to have a long visit with you. I have much to say to you, and you have much to say to me. Sometimes I have a strong impression that I shall again bear my testimony upon the old field of Battle Creek (letter 21, 1898).

To see the man, who had been used so mightily by God and by whose side she had stood through the years, veer away from the message and lose sight of the real objectives of medical missionary work tore Ellen White's soul. Nonetheless, she continued to labor and pray and to communicate through letters.

MEETING THE INROADS OF PANTHEISM

Only as God had revealed it to her could Ellen White have known that pantheistic teachings would be presented at the 1899 General Conference session. She was led to write and send in advance an article to be read entitled "The True Relation of God and Nature." At the Tuesday-morning meeting, February 21, as the health message was being discussed at the session, Dr. Kellogg declared that he would be glad to hear from Dr. E. J. Waggoner and W. W. Prescott "on this question of healthful living," for both had been giving interesting and helpful talks at the sanitarium. As Waggoner spoke, he did so in the framework of pantheistic philosophy, which carried apparent support of at least a part of the audience. Some days later the mail brought Ellen White's message, which was read to the session on Sabbath afternoon, March 4.

It opened with these words:

> Since the fall of man, nature cannot reveal a perfect knowledge of God, for sin has brought a blight upon it, and has intervened between nature and nature's God (GCB 1899, p. 157).

Excerpts from her address reveal the straightforward way she came to grips with the issues that had been so subtly raised at the church's world headquarters:

> Christ came to the world as a personal Saviour. He represented a personal God. He ascended on high as a personal Saviour, and He will come again as He ascended to heaven—a personal Saviour. We need carefully to consider this, for in their human wisdom, the wise men of the world, knowing not God, foolishly deify nature and the laws of nature. . . .
>
> The Father in heaven has a voice and a person which Christ expressed. Those who have a true knowledge of God will not become so infatuated with the laws of matter and the operations of nature as to overlook or to refuse to acknowledge the continual working of God in nature. Deity is the author of nature. The natural world has in itself no inherent power but that which God supplies. How strange, then, that so many make a deity of nature! God furnishes the matter and the properties with which to carry out His plans; Nature is but His agency (ibid.).

But at this time Kellogg was not prone to receive messages of caution and reproof. He took offense at the cautions Ellen White sounded and declared that she had turned against him. He threatened to resign from his work and all connection with Seventh-day Adventists. This almost stunned her. On August 15 she wrote in her diary:

> I lose my courage and my strength and cannot call to mind the very things I ought to write. I have a letter—two, yes, three—written for Dr. Kellogg, but I am so afraid of being misunderstood that I dare not send

them. I feel intensely, and want to help his mind in many things, but how can I do it? My words are misapplied and misunderstood, and sometimes appear to be so misunderstood by humans that they do more harm than good. This has been the case with Dr. Kellogg (MS 189, 1899).

CORRESPONDENCE WITH G. I. BUTLER

Some of her correspondence buoyed her soul. This was the case in the exchange with G. I. Butler. At the time of the General Conference session of 1888, held in Minneapolis, Minnesota, Butler, who had long served as president of the General Conference, was ill and could not be present. Relieved of his responsibilities at that meeting, he retired in Florida, planted an orange grove, and for more than a decade faithfully cared for his wife, who, soon after moving to Florida, suffered paralysis. Being for some years on the negative side of the issues that had surfaced at Minneapolis in 1888, he felt that Ellen White had written him off. When he received word that at her direction one of the first copies of *The Desire of Ages* to come from the press was to be sent to him, he was elated and took heart. He wrote to her expressing his gratitude for her thoughtfulness of him.

After five years in retirement he had come to see some things more correctly and had changed his attitude. He wrote a letter of confession in 1893, published in the *Review and Herald*. In this he stated:

> I freely admit that for a period I stood in doubt in regard to the agitation of these subjects ["the doctrines of justification by faith, the necessity of appropriating Christ's righteousness by faith in order to (attain) our salvation"] I have here so freely endorsed. I did not attend the General Conference in Minneapolis, where differences were agitated, being at the time sick in Battle Creek. . . . My sympathies were not with those leading out in bringing what I now regard as light before the people.

He was glad that he could testify:

> I am well satisfied that additional light of great importance has been shining upon these subjects, and fully believe that God has greatly blessed it to the good of those who have accepted it (June 13, 1893).

Thus while Ellen White was helping to pioneer the work in Australia, battling what seemed to be almost insurmountable difficulties, stalwart leaders at the home base of the church functioned as if she were in their presence, and benefited from her pen.

WRITING *THE DESIRE OF AGES*

In 1858 as Ellen White first wrote the account of what had been revealed to her in the great controversy visions of 1848 and 1858, she devoted 52 small pages to the life of Christ. Sixteen of these gave a very brief review of His ministry, and 36 were devoted to the few days of the last scenes of His life. These pages were expanded in volumes 2 and 3 of the Spirit of Prophecy series in 1877 and 1878; 387 larger pages were given to His general ministry and 254 pages to the Passion Week and His closing ministry. With *Patriarchs and Prophets* and *The Great Controversy* in the field, it was planned that the work, in its preparation called "The Life of Christ," would represent a further amplification, particularly of the account of the three years and more of the life and ministry of our Lord up to the Passion Week.

To this project, Ellen White and Marian Davis turned their attention in Australia. Bible study, visions, prayer, meditation, discussion with her literary assistant, even "hard thinking," all under the general superintendence of the Holy Spirit, were involved in the writing.

As the two women worked together with dedicated purpose, they had at hand for reference several standard works by other authors, such as William Hanna's *Life of Our Lord*, and Cunningham Geikie's *Life and Words of Christ*. Ellen White was acquainted with Daniel March's *Walks and Homes of Jesus* and his *Night Scenes in the Bible*. Geikie's *Hours With the Bible* and Edersheim's works on the Temple and its services and Jewish social life were known to her as well as some others. These books constituted an aid to her in her descriptions of places, customs, and historical events. It was a prevailing practice for one commentator to borrow the wording of another, considering truth common property. It could well be that some of the books to which Ellen White had easy access may have contained materials traceable to a number of authors. Ingram Cobbin in his preface to his *Condensed Commentary and Family Exposition of the Holy Bible*, page iv, declared: "All the commentators have drawn largely from the fathers, especially from St. Augustine," and then points out the borrowings of one from another, naming authors so involved.

Ellen White greatly appreciated the work of her helpers. Of Marian Davis she wrote:

I feel very thankful for the help of Sister Marian Davis in getting out my books. She gathers materials from my diaries, from my letters, and from the articles published in the papers. I greatly prize her faithful service. She has been with me for twenty-five years, and has constantly been gaining increasing ability for the work of classifying and grouping my writings (letter 9, 1903 [see also 3SM, p. 93]).

At another time, writing of Miss Davis' work, Ellen White explained:

She does her work in this way: She takes my articles which are published in the papers and pastes them in blank books. She also has a copy of all the letters I write. In preparing a chapter for a book, Marian remembers that I have written something on that special point, which may make the matter more forcible. She begins to search for this, and if when she finds it, she sees that it will make the chapter more clear, she adds it.

The books are not Marian's productions, but my own, gathered from all my writings. Marian has a large field from which to draw, and her ability to arrange the matter is of great value to me. It saves poring over a mass of matter, which I have no time to do. . . . Marian is a most valuable help to me in bringing out my books (letter 61a, 1900 [see also 3SM, pp. 91, 92]).

OTHERS WHO HELPED

A number of others helped Ellen White throughout the years. Among these were:

1. *Mary Clough.* In 1876 Ellen White was on the Pacific Coast, living in their new home in Oakland. James White, president of the General Conference, was detained in Battle Creek in administrative work. She had good literary help in her niece, Mary Clough, and she pushed ahead with her writing on the life of Christ.

The first drafts of her materials were in her own handwriting. Mary would edit the pages and put them into the form of a chapter, and then copy it. Of course, the finished work was also in handwritten form, for it was six or seven years later that typewriters came into use in Mrs. White's work. Every morning she would write diligently in her upstairs room. After the noonday meal she would go to Mary Clough's room, lie on a sofa, and listen as Mary read the materials prepared from her first written draft. "The precious subjects open to my mind well," she wrote in early April (letter 4, 1876).

2. *W. C. White.* Her son "Willie" helped with editing, reading manuscript, choice of illustrations; finding a publisher, business arrangements. He had no part in the writing, wording, or literary content of the work.

3. *Sara McEnterfer.* Sara McEnterfer, a graduate nurse from Battle Creek, assisted Ellen White in various ways and traveled with her in America and Europe. She was considered one of three "literary assistants" who helped Mrs. White in Australia, and was replaced by Fannie Bolton when she became ill and had to return to the States temporarily. She even took a turn at carpentry when the staff were pushing forward to the target date for the opening of Avondale College. She probably read copy occasionally, but did no share in the literary work.

4. *Fannie Bolton.* Fannie Bolton was one of three assistants who traveled with Ellen White on the S.S. *Alameda* when the party embarked from San Francisco for Australia. Fannie had been invited to join Mrs. White's staff in 1887. The daughter of a Methodist minister, she was brought into the Seventh-day Adventist Church in Chicago through the evangelistic efforts of G. B. Starr and his wife. At the time, she was a correspondent for the Chicago *Daily Inter Ocean.* She received her literary training at the ladies' seminary at Evanston, Illinois (DF 445, G. B. Starr to L. E. Froom, Mar. 19, 1933), and seemed well fitted for a promising future. Starr and others gave her a hearty recommendation. She was barely acquainted with Ellen White and W. C. White, but was employed when Mrs. White returned from Europe. She was to fit in where needed, but her work was to be largely in preparing Mrs. White's materials for the *Review and Herald, Signs of the Times,* and the *Youth's Instructor.* She traveled west with the White group and resided with them in the White home in Healdsburg, California. W. C. White reported that Fannie "proved to be brilliant and entertaining, and although somewhat erratic at times, was loved by the other members of the family."

Unfortunately, Fannie's years of service with Ellen White in Australia (1891-1896) brought mental anguish to Mrs. White because of Fannie's changeable moods, erratic course, and unfaithfulness. She was dismissed numerous times, but was graciously restored to her work. She finally resigned, recognizing her unworthiness and unsuitability to the work. She was replaced by Maggie Hare.

5. *Maggie Hare.* Maggie Hare was one of the large Hare family whose paternal home at Kaeo, New Zealand, Ellen White had visited (see chapter 39). A young secretary, Maggie assisted Sara in handling the immense amount of mail going out to the United States and coming in. She replaced Fannie Bolton in the task of selecting from Ellen White's manuscripts and letters material suitable for publishing in periodicals. When Mrs. White returned to the United States in 1900, Maggie was one of the four women assistants who accompanied her.

FINISHING THE WRITING ON *THE DESIRE OF AGES*

So the work in Australia on the life of Christ book did not consist in producing creatively, chapter after chapter, but rather in Ellen White's writing more fully what had been revealed to her on Christ's life in many visions.

Some years provided more favorable opportunities than others. While Mrs. White's work on the project was intermittent, Marian Davis kept right at the task. The latter often felt it was about finished and then would be frustrated and at the same time delighted when light was received by Ellen White in vision that, when written out, added rich sources of materials. The work on the manuscript stretched from 1892 through 1897 and into 1898. Even then, with the appearance of the finished book on December 10, 1898, there was still more to do on the life of Christ. That was presented in *Christ's Object Lessons*, published two years later.

THE PROPOSAL OF TWO VOLUMES

As the work progressed and the manuscripts grew, the staff working at Sunnyside proposed issuing two volumes of about 600 pages each. W. C. White felt that if this plan met the approval of the publishers, the materials for the first volume would be ready in March or April 1896 (9 WCW, pp. 198, 199). Assuming this would be done, Ellen White was reading the manuscript for the first volume (letter 90, 1896), and in writing to Edson on February 16, she indicated that "we now have it about ready for the printer" (letter 144, 1896).

ELLEN WHITE'S HUMILITY IN WRITING

In a letter to O. A. Olsen, president of the General Conference, she wrote of how as she undertook this work she was almost overwhelmed with the subject:

> This week I have been enabled to commence writing on the life of Christ. Oh, how inefficient, how incapable I am of expressing the things which burn in my soul in reference to the mission of Christ! I have hardly dared to enter upon the work. There is so much to it all. And what shall I say, and what shall I leave unsaid? I lie awake nights pleading with the Lord for the Holy Spirit to come upon me, to abide upon me. . . .

> I walk with trembling before God. I know not how to speak or trace with pen the large subject of the atoning sacrifice. I know not how to present subjects in the living power in which they stand before me. I tremble for fear lest I shall belittle the great plan of salvation by cheap words. I bow my soul in awe and reverence before God and say, "Who is sufficient for these things?" (letter 40, 1892).

Only occasionally at this time did she mention specific visions in which scenes pertaining to the life of Christ passed before her, but in connection with first writing on the subject in 1858, the terms "I saw," "I was shown," or other terms indicating divine revelation and inspiration, frequently occurred. In 1889 she told of how "the betrayal, trial, and crucifixion of Jesus" had passed before her point by point (letter 14, 1889). In 1900 she wrote:

Heavenly scenes were presented to me in the life of Christ, pleasant to contemplate, and again painful scenes which were not always pleasant for Him to bear which pained my heart (MS 93, 1900).

EXTRASCRIPTURAL INFORMATION

In her writing in the 1870s and again in the 1890s on the life and ministry of Christ, Ellen White often introduced significant extrabiblical points in historical narrative not mentioned by the Gospel writers—points in which she deals in sufficient detail to make it evident that her basic source in writing was the visions given to her. The following illustrations of this are drawn from three of her published accounts of the life of Christ.

At His trial before Herod, *Spiritual Gifts*, volume 1, page 51: "They spit in His face. . . . He meekly raised His hand, and wiped it off."

In feeding the 5,000, *The Spirit of Prophecy*, volume 2, pages 260, 261: "The disciples, seeing Him pale with weariness and hunger, besought Him to rest from His toil and take some refreshment. Their entreaties being of no avail, they consulted together as to the propriety of forcibly removing Him from the eager multitude, fearing that He would die of fatigue. Peter and John each took an arm of their blessed Master and kindly endeavored to draw Him away. But He refused to be removed from the place."

The Resurrection, *The Desire of Ages*, pages 779, 780: "'The angel of the Lord descended from heaven.' . . . This messenger is he who fills the position from which Satan fell. . . . The soldiers see him removing the stone as he would a pebble, and hear him cry, 'Son of God, come forth; Thy Father calls Thee.' They see Jesus come forth from the grave."

THE WORK OF THE HOLY SPIRIT

Looking back in 1906, Ellen White freely attributed to the work of the Holy Spirit the truths set forth in the books tracing the great controversy story. She mentioned only three of the Conflict books, for *Prophets and Kings* and *The Acts of the Apostles* were not yet published.

How many have read carefully *Patriarchs and Prophets*, *The Great Controversy*, and *The Desire of Ages*? I wish all to understand that my confidence in the light that God has given stands firm, because I know that the Holy Spirit's power magnified the truth, and made it honorable, saying: "This is the way, walk ye in it." In my books the truth is stated, barricaded by a "Thus saith the Lord."

The Holy Spirit traced these truths upon my heart and mind as indelibly as the law was traced by the finger of God, upon the tables of stone, which are now in the ark (letter 90, 1906 [CM, p. 126]).

WHO WILL PUBLISH IT?

This was a time, too, when the matter of the publisher had to be settled. Consideration had been given to offering the manuscript to Fleming H. Revell, who had handled *Steps to Christ* in a very acceptable manner. W. C. White wrote:

> [Mother] says that there are people who will be reached by the publications through outside publishers, who are not likely to get them from any of our agents; and she believes that much good has been accomplished through our placing *Steps to Christ* in the hands of Revell to publish (8 WCW, p. 36).

W. C. White felt that there were important and far-reaching advantages for Revell to do the publishing. He mentioned one, perhaps little known to the average person: "He is brother-in-law to Moody, [who is the] leading American evangelist and [who] as far as I can see has the lead in evangelical literature" (*ibid.*, p. 35).

Both the Review and Herald and the Pacific Press had issued a number of the E. G. White books, but things had become complicated since the enlarged and strengthened General Conference Association was handling denominational book publishing. That organization carried the responsibility of negotiating with the printers, and sent much of the work to the nearby Review and Herald. By contract, the Pacific Press stood in a reasonable degree of independence, and Ellen White could negotiate with them directly. The experience of the General Conference Association in publishing *Thoughts From the Mount of Blessing* in 1896 (a spinoff of the "Life of Christ" manuscript), particularly in the matter of illustrations, led W. C. White on May 10 to exclaim, "Never, *never*, NEVER!" (9 WCW, p. 436). Working through a second party in getting out books just did not work well.

On May 6, 1896, Ellen White wrote to Edson:

> I have decided to negotiate with Pacific Press to publish "Life of Christ." We are now waiting for them to obtain cuts to go in the book. The first book is completed; the second is in the process of completion (letter 150, 1896).

DECISION ON THE TITLE

Up to this point the project had been referred to as the "Life of Christ," and it was assumed that that would be the title. With the possible exceptions of *The Great Controversy* and the *Testimonies*, Ellen White did not select the titles for her books. As the time approached when a final decision on the title had to be made, suggestions came from various people in Australia and America. Writing to C. H. Jones, manager of the Pacific Press, on October 22, W. C. White said, "As regards the title, I do not wish to say much till I have the criticism of others" (11WCW, p. 20). Some, he felt, were "a hundred miles nearer being appropriate than the best of the others that have been recommended to us." He promised to send a cable after consulting "the wise men here, and have Mother's opinion, and that of Sister Davis." The suggestion of the publishers narrowed down to "The Desire of All Nations" and "The Desire of Ages," both based on Haggai 2:7, "The desire of all nations shall come."

THE LAST TOUCHES

On June 19 Ellen White was still producing material that needed to be included in the early chapters of the book. She wrote: "I am writing upon subjects which stir every fiber of my being. The preexistence of Christ—how invaluable is this truth to the believer!" (MS 65, 1896).

In July she was writing on the closing scenes of the life of Jesus. Her diary for July 28 shows how deeply she felt about her subject:

> In writing upon the life of Christ I am deeply wrought upon. I forget to breathe as I should. I cannot endure the intensity of feeling that comes over me as I think of what Christ has suffered in our world. He was a "man of sorrows, and acquainted with grief"; "he was wounded for our transgressions, he was bruised for our iniquities: the chastisement of our peace was upon him; and with his stripes we are healed," if we receive Him by faith as our personal Saviour! (MS 174, 1897).

The Desire of Ages first came from the press in two beautiful art volumes, with continuous numbering of pages. Shortly thereafter the books were combined into a single volume of 865 pages. Very near the close of the year, December 10, 1898, copies arrived at Cooranbong and were eagerly examined by Ellen White, W. C. White, and her staff of workers. The monumental task was completed. Now the book would bless millions in the years to come.

THE WORK IN
AUSTRALIA COMES OF AGE

Through the winter months of 1900—in the Southern Hemisphere that means May, June, and July—Ellen White was becoming more and more certain that she must soon go back to the United States. Conditions developing in connection with the work of the church in America, revealed to her in visions of the night, led to growing concern. The burden pressed heavily upon her heart. She could not forget that in January she had been shown a rather unusual outbreak of fanaticism at a camp meeting in America. She was deeply concerned over the increasing imbalance coming into the medical work, fostered by Dr. John Harvey Kellogg in Chicago. Of her plans to leave Australia, she wrote:

> Things have not been moving in right lines, and I must, in the fear of God, bear my testimony personally to those who are in danger of swaying the work disproportionately in the so-called medical missionary lines (letter 123, 1900).

Critical situations had developed in Battle Creek, adding to her anxiety. At first she talked of leaving Australia in November. She did not see how she could close up her work before that. But by all means she felt she should attend the General Conference session scheduled for the coming February.

When she proposed to her son William that she must return to the United States, it was hard for him to grasp. How could it be? The Avondale school was just getting well under way. Construction on the Avondale Health Retreat at the front corner of the school land, across the road from the church, was just recently completed, and that enterprise was developing nicely. Land had been purchased for a sanitarium in Wahroonga, a suburb of Sydney, and building plans were under way.

And then there was her book on which they were pressing hard. Willie, at his request, had been relieved of administrative responsibilities in Australia and from his membership on the General Conference Committee. Both he and his mother felt that he should give unbroken attention to assisting her in publishing her books. How could they pull up stakes and leave all this and reestablish themselves in the United States?

PROGRESS AT COORANBONG

Soon after meeting the target date for the opening of the college in April 1897, Ellen White initiated another project of equal importance. As winter gave way to spring and the end of the first school year at Avondale was in sight, she entertained one growing concern—the need of a church building. Could one be built by the close of the school year, now only seven weeks away? Such an accomplishment would crown this year that marked a new start in Christian education.

As the number of students had increased, and the staff had grown, and the families living in the community had increased, it had become increasingly evident that there was no suitable place for meeting. For a while they had met in the loft above the sawmill, but that became a place for storage. Just before school opened, a limited space on the second story over the kitchen and dining room became available, but this soon proved to be too limited.

"I am fully decided," exclaimed Ellen White, "that we must have a meetinghouse" (letter 70, 1897). On Wednesday morning, August 11, W.L.H. Baker and A. G. Daniells, the presidents of the two leading conferences, were on the campus to counsel with Ellen White and others concerning school matters and the coming camp meetings. Word had just been received at Cooranbong of the discovery of an accounting error in Melbourne. Eleven hundred pounds ($5,280) on deposit for the school—£600 ($2,880) from the Wessels family and £500 ($2,400) from the General Conference (letter 177, 1897)—had just been discovered. Construction of a dormitory for the men could now be undertaken, and £100 ($480) was allotted toward a church building. In reporting the interview, Ellen White wrote: "We feel the need of a church very much" (MS 175, 1897).

Careful consideration was given to the location and size of the proposed meetinghouse. Guidance in these particulars was given to Mrs. White in the "visions of the night":

> I received instruction to speak to the people, and tell them that we are not to leave the house of the Lord until the last consideration. . . . I was instructed that our place of worship should be of easy access, and that the most precious portion of the land should be selected as a place on which to build for God (letter 56, 1897).

There was need for haste, for they wanted to dedicate the building not later than the close of school.

THE NEW CHURCH AT AVONDALE IS DEDICATED

There were many visitors at Cooranbong for the church dedication and for the closing exercises of the school on Sunday evening, October 17. Sunday was a beautiful day, and in the afternoon all gathered in the church for the service of dedication. In a letter Ellen White described it:

> Every seat was occupied, and some were standing at the door. Between two and three hundred were present. Quite a number came from Melbourne and also from Sydney, and from the neighborhood, far and nigh.
>
> Elder Haskell gave the dedicatory discourse. Seated on the platform where the pulpit stands were Elders Daniells, Farnsworth, Haskell, Hughes, Wilson, Robinson, and your mother, whom they insisted should make the dedicatory prayer. Herbert Lacey conducted the singing, and everything passed off in the very best order. We felt indeed that the Lord Jesus was in our midst as we presented our chapel to God and supplicated that His blessing should constantly rest upon it (letter 162, 1897).

The *Bible Echo,* in reporting the dedication, described the building as situated on the school land near the Maitland Road and three quarters of a mile (one kilometer) from the school buildings, built of wood, well constructed, neatly painted, and presenting a very nice appearance.

> The land for the church was donated by the school. The building itself cost only about £550 ($2,640) and is capable of accommodating 450 persons. And one of the best features connected with the whole enterprise is that it was dedicated free from debt, every penny's expense having been provided for beforehand. So there was no collection called for on this occasion to clear the church from debt (BE, Nov. 8, 1897).

One feature of the developing enterprises at Cooranbong was the determination to avoid debt, even though the work was at times slowed, and all concerned had to sacrifice and deprive themselves of ordinary comforts and needs. Earlier in the year Ellen White had commented:

> There is no necessity for our meetinghouses to continue year after year in debt. If every member of the church will do his duty, practicing self-denial and self-sacrifice for the Lord Jesus, whose purchased possession he is, that His church may be free from debt, he will do honor to God (letter 52, 1897).

The last paragraph of the November 8 *Bible Echo* report of the dedication significantly declared:

> In conclusion, it should be stated that the erection of this building at this early stage of the school enterprise is mainly due to the faith and

energy of Pastor S. N. Haskell and Mrs. E. G. White, and the rich blessings of God on their efforts. But for them, the building would perhaps not have been built for some time yet. With but £100 ($480) in sight, they moved out by faith and began to build, and the results are as already stated.

But of special significance to Ellen White was the fact that in this new start in Christian education, not only was it a success, but was, as she observed, "the best school in every respect that we have ever seen, outside our people, or among Seventh-day Adventists" (letter 101, 1897).

Twenty of the students have been baptized, and some came to the school who had an experimental knowledge of what it means to be Christians; but not one student leaves the school but gives evidence of now knowing what it means to be children of God (letter 162, 1897).

COLLEGE HALL DEDICATED

Thursday, April 13, 1899, was a day to be remembered. College Hall was finished and ready for use. The first meeting of the day was held in the morning at 6:00. Ellen White explains why:

This early hour was chosen as appropriate to accommodate those who had worked with decided interest on the building. There was assembled the entire company of students and principal, preceptor and teachers. W. C. White and Brethren Palmer and Hughes spoke. I then spoke to the students and all present thirty minutes. At the close of the exercises there was the dedicatory prayer (MS 185, 1899).

The more formal dedication took place in the afternoon. Mrs. White reported in a letter to S. N. Haskell:

The room was decorated and festooned by flowers from our gardens, and beautiful tree ferns, some of which were placed before the entrance of the building. W. C. White spoke well. Brethren Palmer and Hughes followed. Herbert Lacey then addressed the people. . . . He spoke well (letter 70, 1899).

THE PUBLISHING HOUSE

When Seventh-day Adventists began activities in Australia in the winter of 1885, publishing work was begun almost at once. With borrowed type and equipment the type for the first numbers of the *Bible Echo* and *Signs of the Times* was set in the bedroom occupied by one of the workers. The form of set type was taken by a handcart to a nearby printer, where it was run on the press. As soon as they could purchase a press and small engine, quarters were rented. Four years later land was bought on Best Street in North Fitzroy and a building erected to house the emerging Echo Publishing Company and to provide a meeting hall on the second floor. Commercial work was taken in to supply work to justify the sophisticated equipment needed to produce denominational publications. After printing in a commendable manner a pamphlet for the governor of Victoria, the Echo Publishing Company was officially appointed "Publishers to His Excellency Lord Brassey, KCB." This gave the house standing and enhanced business. From one person employed in 1885 the work grew until in 1899 there were 83 employees. This gave it the third position among Adventist publishers, following the Review and Herald, which employed 275, and the Pacific Press, with 150 workers (UCR, July 19, 1899).

With an establishment standing first among the publishing houses operated outside of North America, the Echo Publishing Company was indeed "of age."

RETURN VOYAGE: TALES FOR THE GRANDCHILDREN

W. C. White took care of travel negotiations with the Union Steamship Company in Sydney and found that comfortable arrangements for the voyage back to the United States could be made on the S.S. *Moana*, which would sail from Sydney on Wednesday, August 29, 1990. Ellen White would have her four women assistants with her—Sara McEnterfer, Marian Davis, Sarah Peck, and Maggie Hare. The W. C. White family numbered seven—he and his wife, May; his two older daughters by his first marriage, 18-year-old Ella and 13-year-old Mabel; the twins, 4 years old; and Baby Grace, nearly 3 months old. Three other friends made up the traveling party—15 in all.

Before them was a 7,200-mile (11,520-kilometer), 23-day journey across the Pacific. Willie had been successful in securing the most comfortable room on the *Moana* for his mother, the bridal stateroom in the first-class section toward the stern of the ship. The tickets had cost $160 each for Ellen White and Sara McEnterfer. The rest of the party traveled second class. Willie reported that they had been successful in securing the four best rooms in that section, with tickets costing $70 each.

With anticipation and a little excitement they boarded the *Moana* in Sydney shortly after noon on Wednesday, August 29. Mrs. White was pleased with her room. "I have a wide bed," she wrote in her diary, "as I have at home. Sara has her berth opposite mine" (MS 96, 1900).

The journey would be broken by three stops—New Zealand, Samoa, and the Hawaiian Islands. All augured well. Ellen White was reported to be a good sailor, and she suffered only a touch of seasickness the first night out. Willie reported that they were soon on good terms with the stewards: "We feel as much at home as if we had lived with them for six months" (15 WCW, p. 861). The first 1,280-mile (2,048-kilometer) leg of the journey was almost due east to Auckland, New Zealand. Thursday and Friday were sunny days, and as the sun was setting behind them on Friday evening, they hunted up all the songbooks they could find and gathered for a little sing. They were pleased that about a dozen passengers joined them.

They found the food on the ship well prepared and appetizing, but to be certain of having a dietary to their liking they had brought some of their own food, particularly oranges and tangerines, zwieback, canned fruit, and canned grape juice. This greatly broadened their selection of menu choices. One favorite dish turned out to be fruit toast, made by pouring fresh hot water and then grape juice over zwieback. For their evening meal popular items were fresh fruit and crackers.

FIRST STOP: NEW ZEALAND

On Sunday morning, their fourth day out, the *Moana* was steaming down the east coast of New Zealand, past Great Barrier Island and into Auckland harbor. At 10:30 the ship dropped anchor opposite the quarantine station. Some of the sailors rowed over in a small boat, leaving the passengers in suspense about the possibility of going ashore. Willie was disappointed because he had hoped to see some of his friends from Auckland. "Here we lie," he wrote. "We cannot go ashore, and thus far no one has come to speak to us. It is a big lot of humbug, this quarantine business" (*ibid.*).

Finally George Teasdale, with Brethren Mountain and Nash and a few others, came out in a rowboat, but could not board. The White party found that by leaning over the rail they could converse with the folk in the rowboat. Willie Floding, a young man bound for Battle Creek to take the medical course, came on board at Auckland. The travelers were shocked to learn of the death of Mrs. F. L. Sharp, the wife of the treasurer and business manager of the developing Sydney Sanitarium, following major surgery. Willie and his mother sent messages of consolation back with the workers.

Ellen White spent as much time as possible in a steamer chair on deck, writing letters, mostly to friends left behind in Australia. She was fascinated and refreshed by the sea and the fresh salt air. From girlhood days she had loved the ocean. One day she wrote, "We now have a full view of the ever-changing, restless, beautiful sea" (letter 164, 1900). And at another time, "I am up on deck writing, and enjoying the fresh air. . . . This morning my soul is filled with praise and thanksgiving to God" (MS 96, 1900).

She spent many pleasant hours paging through the autograph album given her during the farewell service at Cooranbong. So did the Willie White family on the deck below, as day by day they read a few pages. These albums, gold embossed and bound in bright royal-blue velvet with gold-edged leaves, are now on display in the White Estate office at the General Conference headquarters. They still convey nostalgia and warmth. Visitors who read them feel drawn to those for whom they were so lovingly and carefully prepared. There was a section for every day of the voyage, and each section was introduced by an exquisite little watercolor painting, the *Moana* itself often appearing in the picture.

THE STOP IN SAMOA

The autograph album page designed for Sabbath, September 8, shows the *Moana* lying placidly in the harbor at Apia, largest of the Samoan islands. The artist's prediction came close to the fact. The ship arrived at 7:00 Friday morning. It would have been Sabbath morning if they had not just crossed the date line, thus adding an extra day.

As the anchor dropped, the White party spotted its welcoming committee—a large green boat powered by singing Samoans (15 WCW, p. 868). They were directed by Prof. D. D. Lake, who supervised the Samoan Mission. One by one members of the White party were helped down the rope ladder into the boat, and even 72-year-old Ellen White climbed down. One giant Samoan took Baby Grace in his arms and stood right on the point of the bow, much to the discomfiture of her mother, May, who had an innate fear of water. She could easily imagine those big bare feet slipping off the slick wood.

Even the smaller boat could not go all the way in to shore, so two of the men crossed arms to make a chair for Ellen White and carried her to the beach. May White was told to put her arms around the neck of the one who carried Grace, and Ellen White had a good laugh over the strange sight of this grown woman in her full skirts clinging to the bronzed back of a Samoan as he carried her and her baby ashore.

Two carriages were waiting to convey members of the party who were not up to walking the mile (two kilometers) to mission headquarters. The rest of the group enjoyed the little jaunt. Oh, how good the home-cooked breakfast tasted! While most of the party went sightseeing, Ellen White and Willie stayed behind with Professor Lake to discuss the possibilities of reopening the sanitarium that had been forced to close when Dr. F. E. Braucht left for New Zealand (*ibid.*).

The sightseers returned just as the interview was completed. After having prayer together, they collected the many baskets of fruit that had been gathered for them. There were bananas in abundance, mangoes, papayas, and oranges. Everybody then headed for the boat, except Mabel. One of the women had wanted to return early, so Mabel had volunteered to drive her to the dock with the horse and buggy. On the drive back to the mission she became lost. She could not ask her way, for the only words in Samoan she knew were "How do you do?" It was nearly time for the boat to leave. Just as the situation seemed almost hopeless, along came Willie Floding. He had worked on the island and knew his way around. Together they quickly found the ship.

Calm seas continued as they plowed their way north and east on the next leg of the journey—2,260 miles (3,616 kilometers) to Honolulu. Midway they would cross the equator and again be in the Northern Hemisphere. It was a pleasant week of travel. Ella, unable to restrain the desire to teach, had organized a little school for the twins, and soon other children joined. She even recruited Leonard Paap, one of the party, to teach the older children. The sunrise on Monday morning was outstanding. Ellen White wrote, "The sunrise was glorious. The whole sea was a river of yellow gold. We have on this journey a placid sea" (MS 96, 1900).

THE STOP IN HONOLULU

Friday morning, September 14, at 8:00, after a very hot night, the *Moana* reached Honolulu. Elder Baxter Howe, in charge of the work of the church there, welcomed the travelers and took them to Mrs. Kerr's, where the whole party enjoyed an early lunch. The Kerrs were an affluent family. Mr. Kerr, a businessman, was not a member of the church, but his wife, a generous-hearted and outgoing woman, had been a member for several years. Mrs. White had been entertained royally at their home on her trip to Australia nine years before.

The hours in Honolulu would be limited, so the party made a brief visit to the church, where both Ellen White and Willie addressed the people. Then they visited the Chinese school operated by W. E. Howell. By 6:00 that evening they were back on the boat, which soon was on its way eastward to San Francisco.

NEARING AMERICA: AN ENCOURAGING PROMISE

As they neared the California arrival time, late Thursday night, Mrs. White felt she could hardly endure the expected partying that traditionally marks the final day of a voyage. Willie came to her and said, "We are nearing the last night of the trip, when we shall have more noise than ever before; but I am praying for a storm" (MS 29, 1901). "So am I," his mother replied.

That Wednesday evening, still dreading the next day's carousal, Ellen White found a little anteroom and lay down. She fell asleep, but soon was awakened by a voice speaking to her. As she gained consciousness, she knew what it meant. "The room was filled with a sweet fragrance, as of beautiful flowers." Then she fell asleep once more and was awakened in the same way. Of it she wrote:

> Words were spoken to me, assuring me that the Lord would protect

me, that He had a work for me to do. Comfort, encouragement, and direction were given to me, and I was greatly blessed *(ibid.)*.

Part of the message that came to her at the time was an assurance that put her mind at rest on one particular point. This was the question of where she should make her home in America. In earlier years they had lived in Battle Creek, Michigan, as her husband led the church and managed the Review and Herald Publishing House. Then they had lived in Oakland, California, as James White started the *Signs of the Times*. After her husband's death, Ellen had lived in a home in Healdsburg, California, only a few blocks from the college. This home she still owned. Just before leaving for Australia she had lived in Battle Creek again. And now where should she settle? The question had concerned her from the time she planned to leave Australia.

The vision given to her that Wednesday evening during the last week of the journey set her mind at rest. She wrote of this, "The Lord revealed Himself to me . . . and comforted me, assuring me that He had a refuge prepared for me, where I would have quiet and rest" (letter 163, 1900).

What a comfort it was to know that God already had something in mind for her! How she wished she might know just what or where it was.

THROUGH THE GOLDEN GATE

Now they came to Thursday, the last full day of the trip. They would enter San Francisco Bay that night. The day was sunny and bright, but the sea was so rough the sailors could hardly keep their balance on deck. Most of the passengers remained in their berths. There was no trip-ending party. Ellen White lay in bed all day, fearful even to turn over. And then just before the *Moana* slipped through the Golden Gate, the sea suddenly quieted. It was 10:00. The ship could not dock until daylight, so the anchor was cast.

Through the long night hours the ship swung lazily at anchor in San Francisco Bay. The White party no doubt expected that with the coming of daylight the *Moana* would move into one of the Union Steamship Company piers, and that soon friends and fellow workers on the wharf would be welcoming them back to the United States. But such was not the case. Immigration officials, highly conscious of germs, required the Sydney passengers, even though they had been on the ship for nearly a month, to proceed by tugboat to a quarantine station on Angel Island, where their belongings and trunks could be fumigated. That whole weary Friday was spent going through these formalities.

Finally, by early evening, the contents of the trunks and suitcases having been properly fumigated and repacked, the party was taken by tugboat to San Francisco. They arrived at 8:00 and were met by G. A. Irwin, president of the

General Conference; C. H. Jones, manager of the Pacific Press; and J. O. Corliss, pastor of the San Francisco church. The traveling party soon dispersed. Elder Jones, a longtime friend and acquaintance, took Ellen White and some of her helpers to his home in Oakland. Others stayed with friends in San Francisco. W. C. and May White, with the twins and Baby Grace, were entertained by the Corlisses at their home in Fruitvale, an Oakland suburb. That night Elder Irwin sent a telegram to Battle Creek that carried the good news of the arrival of the party. It was published on the back page of the next issue of the *Review*. It read, "San Francisco, Cal., Sept. 21, 1900.—Sister White and party arrived this morning in good condition." The editor commented that this would be "good news to thousands." And it was.

ELMSHAVEN, A HAVEN FOR ELLEN WHITE

On arriving in California, Ellen White was eager to get to work. She hoped that she could quickly find a home, move in, and take care of the many tasks awaiting her attention. Not wanting to undertake the task of building a house, she hoped to find a place to rent.

On Monday morning, September 24, house hunting began. After three exhausting days driving from place to place in the Oakland area, Ellen White and Willie decided they would have to purchase. Rents were too high for their meager salaries. As W. C. White expressed it:

> For several days we have been trying to fit a number seven family into a number five house, with a number three purse to purchase furnishings (15 WCW, p. 871).

Ellen White had not forgotten that the Lord had shown His interest in her the last night while crossing the sea, so she declared she would just stop looking. "The Lord knows what our work is and where we should be located; and we shall wait the Lord's time" (letter 132, 1900).

At this point Willie suggested that she and some of her helpers go up to the health retreat at St. Helena, some 60 miles (96 kilometers) north of Oakland. This institution had just changed its name to St. Helena Sanitarium, or simply, "the san." There she could rest a bit and also attend some of the meetings to be held in connection with the nearby Napa camp meeting.

She had been there in the years following her husband's death and had purchased eight and one-half acres (three hectares) from William Pratt to preserve the land for the future use of the sanitarium. On the property she had erected a home, Eliel, which she thought could easily be turned into an expanded facility for the care of guests of the institution (DF 14).

At the sanitarium she met old friends—Mrs. J. L. Ings, Mary Thorpe, and others. When the topic of conversation turned to the frustration of house hunting in Oakland, Mrs. Ings volunteered: "Well, below the hill there is a place that is just the thing for you. It is Robert Pratt's place" (letter 158, 1900). Ellen White was definitely interested.

WAS THIS THE PROMISED REFUGE?

The next morning, Friday, September 28, she went down to see the "place under the hill" (letter 132, 1900). To her surprise, it was not the William Pratt place that she had envisioned (a home in which she and James White had stayed), but a large Victorian home built by his brother Robert. She had often admired it as she drove by.

Robert Pratt, a railroad executive, was a member of a family of three who had moved to California in search of gold. William had purchased the entire little valley and mountainside where the sanitarium was now nestled. Later Robert purchased a strip of some 74 acres (30 hectares), which stretched through rich farmland up onto the hillside.

William Pratt, with his wife and family, had responded to the preaching of J. N. Loughborough and I. D. Van Horn at St. Helena in 1873 and had become charter members of the St. Helena church. Three years later he gave land on the side of the mountain near Crystal Spring for a medical institution, the Rural Health Retreat. The spring, which yielded a bountiful supply of pure soft water, was shared with his brother Robert and was just above and to the east of the institution. William Pratt's gift of land also included his half share of the spring. At the time the sanitarium was opened, this seemed an adequate water supply.

Robert, not a Seventh-day Adventist, owned the land to the south and held the other half interest in the spring. He and his wife, facing advancing age, with their children grown and gone, accepted the invitation of their youngest daughter to make their home with her in the Bay Area (letter 146, 1900). So the Robert Pratt property was up for sale.

Farseeing Elder J. A. Burden, manager of the St. Helena Sanitarium, realized that the growing need for water would soon embarrass the institution, so he had already personally contracted to buy the Pratt property, making the initial payment of $1,000. Although the institution was in no financial position to buy the Pratt property, Burden was a man of deep faith and some daring and expected to dispose of the home and farm, retaining what was necessary for the institution and its growth.

The property represented an investment on the part of Robert Pratt of $12,000. It was sold to Elder Burden for $8,000, and in securing it he had arranged for long-term, easy payments.

Delighted with what she found, Ellen White with difficulty restrained her excitement. She wrote:

> This is a most beautiful location. The surroundings are lovely. Ornamental trees from various parts of the world, flowers, mostly roses of a large variety, an orchard containing a thousand prune trees which are

bearing, another orchard nearer the house, and still another orchard of live trees, are growing on the place (letter 158, 1900).

The home was situated on a knoll in the center of 35 acres (14 hectares) of level or nearly level land. The family orchard of about three acres (one hectare) lay to the north, with trees bearing peaches, apples, nectarines, figs, cherries, apricots, and pears. Back of this was about a half acre (one metric hectare) of olive trees. On the south side of the home was a vineyard of more than five acres (two hectares) of table and wine grapes, mostly the latter. The land to the west was divided between prune orchards—which the Whites soon discovered had 2,000 trees in prime bearing condition—a garden, and hayfield. The house itself was a well-constructed, seven-room, two-story frame building, completely furnished, including carpets, drapes, linens, and dishes. Ellen White continued her description:

> Well, to go back to my story, the Lord planned for me, and I found that I could buy this place here for less than I received for my house in Cooranbong and all its belongings. This included two horses, one rather old, four carriages and a platform wagon, much better than the one I gave away, and a house furnished throughout. It was like stepping out of my home in Cooranbong into a beautiful roomy one here. It has surprised me much that we should be thus favored (letter 132, 1900).

Back of the house to the east was "the farmer's cottage," which with a little adaptation could be turned into an office building. Beyond this was a barn and stable with four horse stalls and room for storing four carriages. The hayloft could store 20 or 30 tons of hay. The cow barn had space for 22 cows; to the one cow now occupying it, it must have seemed a bit lonely. A few chickens completed the farm population. Ellen White was delighted with the carriages and wagons that were included with the place: two farm wagons, one two-seated express wagon, one double-seated covered buggy, two phaetons, an old road cart, and one hand cart. In addition, there were plows, harrows, and other farm tools (15 WCW, p. 903).

That Friday, with its discovery, seemed all too short. There was a meeting at the sanitarium on Friday evening, and Ellen White spoke to the institutional family and to the guests. On Sunday morning she could not resist the temptation to slip away from council meetings and take another look at what she felt would surely be her future home. She pondered, as she wrote later:

> This place was none of my seeking. It has come to me without a thought or purpose of mine. The Lord is so kind and gracious to me. I can trust my interests with Him who is too wise to err and too good to do me harm (letter 132, 1900).

ELLEN WHITE PURCHASES THE PROPERTY

Ellen White and Elder Burden sat down to work out a settlement that was finally consummated on Tuesday, October 16, when she and her family moved in. Burden transferred to her the entire property—73.71 acres (30 hectares) of land—and half interest in the spring. Then, as agreed, the sanitarium bought back 8.7 acres (3.5 hectares) for a sewage-disposal area at the far west corner of the property, and 5.5 acres (2.2 hectares) for a food factory across Blackmon Canyon Creek to the east and south. For these two pieces of land and for the half interest in the spring, $3,000 was subtracted from the $8,000. Ellen White paid Burden $1,000 in cash and assumed a $4,000 mortgage with interest at 6¼ percent. "It is like stepping out of our home in Cooranbong," she wrote to her old friends the Farnsworths, "into one already prepared for us, without any time or care on our part" (letter 146, 1900).

On the day of the purchase they moved in, rather jubilantly, and she reported to Elder Irwin, "We are now located in our pleasant and much-appreciated home" (letter 127, 1900). She outlined the living arrangements. They were crowded, and would be until other buildings could be erected, particularly a home for William White and his family, who were temporarily staying at a nearby cottage. Beds were placed even in the living room.

One piece of furniture, in addition to what they found in the home, was squeezed in. It was Ellen White's comfortable writing chair, equipped with a writing board that she could swing to one side for freedom of movement. This was the only piece of furniture she had brought with her from Australia.

The general location of the home was ideal. It was two and one-half miles (four kilometers) northwest of St. Helena, and about 15 to 20 minutes' walk from the sanitarium, depending upon whether one was going or coming. In addition to its beautiful location, with hills to the south and mountains to the north and east, Ellen White particularly appreciated the fact that the home was not far from the sanitarium. Here she would often have an opportunity to address a changing audience of non-Adventists, which she enjoyed doing.

Mrs. White had traveled widely throughout her life. She had crossed the Rocky Mountains many times. She had lived in Colorado and in Switzerland. She had crossed the Alps into Italy, and traveled extensively in Europe, Australia, and New Zealand. But she exclaimed in 1905, perhaps with some bias, "Certainly no place I have ever seen equals the beauty of the scenery around here" (letter 111, 1905). At another time she wrote, "This world is not our abiding place, but I feel very grateful for the comforts of a good home. I consider the country here to be one of the most beautiful I have ever seen" (letter 117, 1905).

Almost 100 years have passed since Ellen White's happy evaluation of Robert Pratt's choice of an ideal place to build a home. The elms for which it was named have been replaced, but the haven they provided has been a blessing and an inspiration to thousands of visitors. (About 10,000 people annually visit Elmshaven on Glass Mountain Lane.) Robert Pratt built well, and the stately house represents the finest tradition of Victorian houses. Today, as a recognized historical site, it witnesses to the special work of Ellen G. White.

AND NOW, BACK TO WORK: THE PRIORITIES

Ellen White had always endeavored to obtain adequate living quarters for herself and staff. Much as she enjoyed the amenities of life, they were never the end but the means to the end—her special work. She moved into Elmshaven as quickly as she could, in mid-October, 1900.

In a number of visions in Australia, conditions, situations, and dangers that threatened the church were clearly revealed to her. Correspondence from America also disclosed some of the looming problems. Now she must face these unflinchingly and without delay.

There was the matter of the disproportionate development in the medical missionary lines, which was placing special emphasis on a work in Chicago directed toward outcasts, drunks, and prostitutes. The light given to Ellen White indicated that a certain amount of this type of work, carried out under proper safeguards, was essential and proper, but it would yield but little lasting harvest. There was grave danger of an imbalance that would divert attention from major objectives in the medical work of the church and, because of the heavy financial demands, curtail various lines of denominational work around the world. From a reliable source in Battle Creek she was informed that Dr. Kellogg had at last taken a position against her because she did not sustain him in the work he was carrying to such extremes.

Then there was the situation in which Dr. Kellogg was involved. His growing interest in and promotion of a great Christian medical work that would be undenominational in nature and not linked to a small religious body was a matter of growing concern.

Then too, Ellen White had been given views of an outbreak of fanaticism that, when developed, came to be known as the holy flesh movement. While in Australia she was shown in vision its perils and what would transpire.

There was the work among the Blacks in the South in which her son James Edson White was leading out.

These were some of the important matters that would be considered at the General Conference session, which was scheduled to meet in February. The reason she felt she must leave Australia in August was in order to be certain that she could attend this conference. Thoughtful church leaders sensed that this would be a particularly important meeting.

Where to hold the General Conference of 1901 was a matter of much discussion. At the Autumn Council in August the action taken was indecisive, with the feeling that Oakland was most likely the preferred location. Factors that seemed to point to Oakland as the logical place were the delicate nature of Ellen White's health, her dread of a long journey east in midwinter, and the state of the work in California. Nonetheless, while she dreaded returning to Battle Creek in winter, or anytime, because of the burdens that would fall upon her when she returned to that city after an absence of 10 years, deep down in her heart she knew that the time would come when she would have to spend some time in Battle Creek. In visions of the night she seemed to be bearing her testimony there in the tabernacle, and she knew that she must sometime return.

Finally, after careful consideration of the pros and cons of holding the conference at Oakland or Battle Creek, the available members of the General Conference Committee in Battle Creek voted on December 10, 1900, to hold the 1901 General Conference from April 2 to 23 in Battle Creek. Ellen White decided to attend, but her decision had not come without some cost to herself. She declared, "For a week before I fully consented to go to Battle Creek, I did not sleep past one o'clock. Some nights I was up at eleven o'clock and many nights at twelve. I have not moved from impulse, but from the conviction that at this time I must begin at Jerusalem" (letter 159, 1900).

During the last days of December she was very active working with the churches in the Bay Area and San Francisco and Oakland. She and Elder A. G. Daniells were the main speakers for the Week of Prayer. She was quite worn out when she returned to Elmshaven. She was happy, however, with the fruitage of the rather strenuous program. The following Friday she was exhausted, and during her evening bath she fainted. Sara and Maggie succeeded in getting her to bed, where she was confined for the next two weeks. Then, upon getting up too soon, she suffered a relapse and had another period of illness. Nonetheless, she maintained her plans to attend the General Conference session in Battle Creek, even though Sara declared that she was "not fit to go anywhere," and she dreaded the trip for her (MS 43a, 1901).

As the time neared for her to start her journey east, the question of where she should stay was uppermost in her mind. Dr. Kellogg invited her to stay at the sanitarium, but later invited her and her party to stay in his own home. He had a large, two-story frame house with sufficient room to accommodate the children he and his wife took in to rear. He promised to make a portion of the home available to Ellen White and her helpers, and urged that she accept the invitation.

But would it be wise to stay in the doctor's home when so much controversy swirled about him? At first she felt it would not be best. Would not people feel that she was under his influence? And then she thought, "No matter with whom I should stay, it would be said, 'Someone has been talking with Sister White, telling her about the state of the church. This is why she talks as she does'" (GCB 1901, p. 204).

The answer came in a very forceful way. Friday evening, February 15, as she met with her family in the sitting room for worship, she was deeply burdened with a decision about Dr. Kellogg's invitation. She began to pray about it. In reporting the experience, she wrote, "I was asking the Lord where I should go and what I should do. I was for backing out. . . . Well, while I was praying and was sending up my petition, there was, as has been a hundred times or more, a soft light circling around the room, and a fragrance like the fragrance of flowers, of a beautiful scent of flowers" (MS 43a, 1901). And a voice said, "'Respect the courtesy of My servant, John Kellogg, the physician by My appointment. He needs encouragement that you can give him. Let him put his trust in Me. My arm is strong to uphold and sustain. He may safely lean upon My strength. I have a work for him to do. He must not fail nor be discouraged'" (letter 33, 1901).

Did the others kneeling in worship that Friday evening see the light and notice the fragrance? This is a very natural question, which she answered as she recounted the incident on April 11 at the General Conference session: "Though none of the family saw what I saw, or heard what I heard, yet they felt the influence of the Spirit, and were weeping and praising God" (GCB 1901, p. 204).

So Dr. Kellogg's gracious invitation was accepted. Ellen White and her helpers would stay in his home.

THE LONG ROAD TO BATTLE CREEK

Now the decision must be made on the route to Battle Creek. To make the journey directly to Chicago and then Battle Creek would take them over the Sierra Nevadas and the Rockies. It would be a journey she had often taken and one she dreaded, for even when her health was seemingly good she was ill-equipped to stand the high altitude.

The alternative was to take a more extended journey via Los Angeles, New Orleans, and then to Chicago and Battle Creek. This route carried attractive features for both Ellen White and her son Willie. Since returning from Australia they had not traveled 100 miles (160 kilometers) from the Elmshaven home. The southern route would give them an opportunity to spend a few days in Los Angeles surveying the work that was beginning to develop nicely in southern California. Then there was Edson White and his work in Mississippi and Tennessee. They could go to Vicksburg, see the *Morning Star*, inspect the development of the work in Mississippi, then travel to Nashville. There Edson had his headquarters, engaged in publishing and managing the work of the Southern Missionary Society.

So, weighing the high mountains on the more direct and quick journey against the longer trip traveling at normal elevations; weighing the advantage of seeing James Edson White in his work, all of which had been developed since she had gone to Australia, Ellen White decided in favor of travel by the southern route. Tentative appointments were made for services she might hold with Adventist churches in Los Angeles, Vicksburg, and Chicago, even though it was a question from day to day as to whether she would even be well enough to make the journey.

The trip began Thursday afternoon, March 7, with her farm manager, Iram James, driving the party to the Southern Pacific Railroad station in St. Helena. The train would connect at Port Costa with the *Owl* on its nightly run from Oakland. In the party were Ellen White, Sara McEnterfer, Maggie Hare, and Willie White.

Willie White had made arrangements for them to stay at the sanitarium in Los Angeles (later known as the White Memorial Hospital), where they could have pleasant rooms and good food. On Sabbath morning Ellen White spoke at the Los Angeles church to an audience of more than 400 people, some of whom had come from as far away as 60 miles (96 kilometers). While standing before large congregations, not infrequently she had visions that opened up to her both general situations and the experiences of individuals in her audience.

In this case she saw, like a flash of lightning, the vast possibilities of the people before her. Her response to the challenge was almost too much for her sensitive nature, and the experience resulted in days of prostration in which serious misgivings were entertained as to whether she would be able to continue her journey.

By Tuesday she had rallied a bit, and they felt that they could go on. They boarded the *Sunset Limited* at 8:00, found the train not crowded and a first-class compartment ready for Mrs. White and her two women helpers. They also found two bushels of large, luscious oranges at the station waiting for them. The train pulled out on time for its 60-hour trip to New Orleans.

They arrived there Thursday evening in time to catch the train for Vicksburg, Mississippi, where Edson White had pioneered the work among the Blacks.

VICKSBURG AND *THE MORNING STAR*

How eagerly Ellen White had read all that Edson had written her about his ship while she was in Australia! Now she was actually to stay on it for a few nights. As she stepped aboard, she remembered how she had followed the boat with her prayers. She said, "Some most interesting scenes have been presented to me in connection with it. This boat has been a floating Bethel. At the gospel meetings held on it many have had the privilege of eating of the bread of life" (MS 29, 1902).

She was pleased with what she found, from the boiler room on the lower deck to the printing offices where two steam presses had printed the *Gospel Herald* for many months, to the two staterooms, the dining room, the galley, and finally the engine room.

Immediately behind the smokestacks, at the front of the upper deck, was a business office. Just behind this were the main cabin and Edson and Emma's stateroom. In the rear portion of the upper deck was a 16' x 40' (5 meter x 12 meter) chapel, where services were conducted. Even larger meetings could be held on the third, or hurricane deck, where 200 could be seated. The third deck also had a small pilothouse, with the steering apparatus and a bunk for the pilot.

Ellen White's eager glance missed nothing. She reported, "I was pleased with the arrangement of the boat and with the efforts made to make life on it as agreeable as possible. I found that everything about the rooms fitted up as a home for my son and his wife, and their helpers, was of the simplest order. I saw nothing expensive or unnecessary" (*ibid.*). Then she commented: "Perhaps some would have been unwilling to live in such narrow quarters" (*ibid.*).

The *Morning Star* had been built well to fulfill the many purposes for which it was intended. It provided a home for Edson and Emma; a place to print the gospel message; a place on board to hold meetings; a place to meet people. It was the means of spreading the good news to a broader field than any stationary chapel. And it pioneered the way for others who would meet the tough problem of race prejudice in the South. The small staff who heroically ran the boat were definitely pioneers in the fullest meaning of the word.

These early workers and believers faced two kinds of prejudice—racial and religious. The Black ministers opposed them because they were teaching Sabbath observance and tithe paying; the White people opposed them because they were educating the Blacks and introducing new and better agricultural methods, which threatened to break the stranglehold of poverty in the delta.

Edson had begun his Vicksburg work with Sunday schools and night classes in the Mount Zion Baptist Church on Fort Hill. When he was excluded from the church for his belief in the Sabbath, he built a little chapel at the corner of Walnut and First East streets. But this was only after 10 days of fervent prayer that had resulted in permission from adamant city councilmembers to grant a permit for building a church for the Blacks. Once the work had been established in Vicksburg, they had ventured into the heart of the delta, using the Yazoo River as their main highway. Halfway up the river to Yazoo City he had tried to establish a school for the hundreds of Black children in the area who had no facilities for education. He was soon informed by the county superintendent of education that his work must stop, and later learned that in the mob that accompanied the superintendent was one man who had volunteered to "hold a Winchester on ol' White while you-all fetch the rope."

A little later the *Morning Star* had been of great service to the plantation owners of the area, rescuing many of their animals during a flood. The next winter Edson brought in tons of food and clothing to relieve the suffering among the Black tenant farmers who were facing starvation from crop failures and severely cold weather. Then with some measure of confidence among both the Whites and the Blacks, they built a little chapel and schoolhouse at Calmar.

Later the work there was stopped also. On the boat Edson had edited and published a monthly journal, the *Gospel Herald*. One issue carried a mildly critical editorial of the sharecropper system, and this, along with the fact that so many of the Blacks were becoming Adventists and refusing to work on Saturdays, spurred the plantation owners to action. A mob of 25 men on horseback called at the school, sent the White teacher, one of Edson's men, out of town "on a rail," nailed the doors and windows shut, and burned books, maps, and charts in the schoolyard.

Then they found one of the leading Black believers in the area, N. W. Olvin, and thrashed him with a buggy whip. They stopped only when commanded to do so by a White man who brandished a revolver.

While the work was broken up at Calmar, it continued to thrive at Yazoo City and Vicksburg, and in the years shortly after Edson left for Nashville there were encouraging developments in a large number of other Mississippi towns.

One hair-raising episode occurred when the *Morning Star* escaped being dynamited in Yazoo City, having left town only hours earlier with the General Conference president and secretary on board. F. R. Rogers, who taught the Yazoo City school, was ordered by a mob to close his school, and was shot at in the streets.

Edson had informed his mother of these developments during her years in Australia, and her instruction was of caution and prudence as the only course available to the church if they wished to continue to witness and work in the South. This was as true for the work among the Whites as among the Blacks. Even though in his contacts Edson said nothing about political matters, even though he did not mention inequalities or the need for social justice, the mere fact that he was educating Blacks and trying to improve their economic condition nearly cost him his life and the lives of his wife, fellow workers, and believers.*

SERVICE IN VICKSBURG

Ellen White scrutinized the *Morning Star* because of the criticism she had heard of it. She knew her son was not always careful with money, and she was glad to report to the General Conference session a few weeks later:

> When I came to Vicksburg, I went on board my son's boat, the *Morning Star*. From the reports I had heard, I thought to find that boat fitted up very extravagantly. I found nothing of the kind. I want all to understand this (GCB 1901, p. 482).

Sunday morning, March 17, the new church, the second to be built in Vicksburg, was to be dedicated. It was a memorable weekend for Ellen White, her son William, and others in the traveling party. Just to be in the setting of the heart of Edson's activities and to witness the fruits of his dedicated labors and the labors of those who helped him was uplifting.

The crowning event of the visit was the Sunday dedication service. Ellen White was asked to preach the sermon. Word had gone up and down the river that the mother of James Edson White would be the speaker that Sunday morning. The report is that the church was packed. Pleased with the high caliber of people who made up the congregation, she wrote, "I know that Jesus and the angels were in the assembly, and that, as the church was dedicated to the Lord, He accepted it" (MS 29, 1902).

The present Vicksburg church stands on the site of this second building, and in the early 1970s three women who had been aboard the *Morning Star* were still worshiping there!

EN ROUTE TO BATTLE CREEK

The travel schedule called for the party to spend Sunday night on the train en route to Nashville via Memphis. Reaching Memphis in the morning, they found that a meeting had been arranged for 9:00 (16 WCW, p. 300).

Leaving Memphis at 1:00 they arrived at Nashville at 8:30. Edson, who had hurried on ahead, was at the station with his wife, Emma, when the train pulled in! He had brought what was called the "Gospel Wagon" to pick up the party (*ibid.*). They were to have two days in Nashville, with the time divided between inspecting the work that was being done there and a convention of the Southern Missionary Society.

Tuesday morning they climbed into the "Gospel Wagon," 14 in all, and Edson conducted a tour of the Adventist work in Nashville (*ibid.*). This included the printing establishment, which later grew into the Southern Publishing Association, treatment rooms for the Blacks, and the treatment rooms for Whites, operated by Louis Hanson and his wife.

At the meetings of the Southern Missionary Society Ellen White spoke strongly in favor of the establishment of an industrial school near Nashville.

She "gave a straight testimony upon this point, bringing out clearly the need of such schools, and in regard to other lines of work in the South. She also spoke about the necessity of our people arousing to the needs of this field, which has been so long neglected" (*Gospel Herald* Supplement, March 1901).

The party left Nashville on another night journey, arriving in Chicago at 10:00 Thursday morning, March 21. With the tenuous condition of Mrs. White's health when they left Nashville, no meetings were scheduled in Chicago. The general plan was that if she was able to do so, they would spend Thursday in Chicago and go on to Battle Creek on Thursday evening or Friday morning.

The Chicago visit was indeed an interesting one for Ellen White (MS 29, 1902). In visions the work in Chicago had been opened up to her. On the basis of these visions she had written encouraging words and had sounded warnings of the perils of a disproportionate work. Such endeavors would funnel too large a percentage of available funds into a work that was good in itself but that would yield only a limited fruitage.

The church's medical school, the American Medical Missionary College, had been started in 1895 with its clinical division in Chicago. She was deeply interested in this undertaking to train physicians within the church's educational and medical structure.

The train arrived late in Chicago, but they found a number of workers waiting to meet them. Ellen White was urged to remain over and speak on Sabbath, which she consented to do. When she was told that the medical workers in Chicago would like to hear from her, she also consented to speak at the medical school to students, helpers, and patients. She was pleased when it was suggested that she might have a hydrotherapy treatment at the sanitarium's branch at 33rd Place. Miss S. M. Gallion, a youthful Battle Creek Sanitarium nurse, gave her an hour of bath and massage.

Sabbath morning Ellen White spoke with freedom to a congregation of about 650 (16 WCW, p. 307). Looking back later, she wrote, "It was only by the Lord's help that I was enabled to do this work, for I was weary from traveling, and was not free from pain for a moment" (MS 29, 1902).

---

* For the account of James Edson White and the *Morning Star*, see Ron Graybill, *Mission to Black America*.

The General Conference Session of 1901: Time for a Change!

On Tuesday morning, April 2, 1901, an atmosphere of excitement and apprehension prevailed as workers and church members began to assemble in the Battle Creek Tabernacle. This would be the largest General Conference session yet held. Ellen White would be there, and it would be the first session she had attended in 10 years. The 267 delegates represented a church of 75,000 members, four fifths of whom resided in the United States.

For some years there had been a growing recognition that the church had outgrown its organization. The basic structure of church organization with its local conferences bound together in a General Conference had remained unchanged from 1863 to 1901.

There were two recognized organizational levels—the local conference and the General Conference. When the General Conference was organized in 1863, the church had one institution—a publishing house at Battle Creek. But the work of the denomination soon expanded. The health work began with the establishment of a sanitarium in 1866. Educational work was started with the opening of the denomination's church school in Battle Creek in 1872, and the college in 1874. Other publishing houses were added, and sanitariums and schools were opened.

As work in different lines developed, associations were formed to foster the interests. There were the International Medical Missionary and Benevolent Association, the International Sabbath School Association, the International Tract Society, the National Religious Liberty Association, and a foreign mission board.

These were all autonomous organizations represented by independent corporations, operated by Seventh-day Adventists but not integral parts of the General Conference organization. The various branches of the work were not thought of or directed as departments of the General Conference, but as independent entities.

As a diversified and growing denominational work with multiplied business interests rapidly developed, spiritual fervor waned, and in some areas there was a failure to heed the counsels God sent to alert of dangers and to guard the cause.

The General Conference Executive Committee, beginning with three members in 1863, was increased periodically as the church grew, and by 1899 had increased to 13. Even so, the group was widely scattered and did not often meet in a full session. Six of the 13 men were district leaders spread out across North America. Two men represented overseas work and resided overseas. This left four members of the General Conference Executive Committee resident in Battle Creek. These, with the secretary and the treasurer of the General Conference, who were not members of the committee, formed a sort of unofficial officer group that carried the day-to-day responsibilities of the operation of the church.

It is not difficult, then, to grasp the situation that developed with the world work outgrowing the organizational structure that was administering it. Those at headquarters naturally felt that they were prepared to give the wisest and best management to even the minute details of Seventh-day Adventist interest in the remotest parts of the world.

One area in particular in which serious problems developed was in financial support of the cause. Without carefully planned budgets to serve as guidelines in the expenditure of funds, great inequities developed, with the needs nearest at hand often gaining the favor of the treasurers.

Little wonder, then, that it was with apprehension that the delegates gathered for the General Conference session that Tuesday morning, April 2. All were profoundly thankful that Ellen White was to be there, and she carried a heavy burden for the meeting. It was this conference with its challenges and its opportunities that had in a large part led Mrs. White to close up her work in Australia and hasten back to the United States.

PREVIEW OF THE CONFERENCE

Two days before the General Conference session opened, church leaders held some unofficial precouncil meetings. Such a group gathered on Sunday evening, March 31. As they moved into their discussions, they decided to adjourn until a meeting could be held that would be more widely attended, and at which Ellen White could be present.

Quite a representative group met in the college library on Monday afternoon. It included the General Conference Committee, the Foreign Mission Board, conference presidents, and institutional leaders. The room was packed. Elder Daniells took along a secretary, Clarence C. Crisler; and Dr. Kellogg took his private secretary to report the meeting. The records of the meeting include the reports as transcribed by both men, with some understandable slight variations in wording.

Mrs. White had consented to be present and to lay before the brethren some matters that had been opened up to her mind.

Although Elder Irwin was president of the General Conference, Elder Daniells, who had recently come from Australia, was in the chair. In Australia he, with W. C. White, had developed a union conference, binding the local conferences in Australia together in an effective organization.

After making an introductory statement and telling of a meeting with Ellen White in the morning, at which time she had been invited to attend the afternoon meeting, Daniells expressed his pleasure that she was present, and invited her to speak. She replied: "I did not expect to lead out in this meeting. I thought I would let you lead out, and then if I had anything to say, I would say it" (MS 43a, 1901). To this Daniells replied, "Well, it seemed to me (and I think to all of us who counseled with you this morning) that we had said about as much as we wished to until we heard from you."

Ellen White came directly to the point:

> I would prefer not to speak today, though not because I have nothing to say. I have something to say.

Some of the points she brought out were:

> Never should the mind of one man or the minds of a few men be regarded as sufficient in wisdom and power to control the work and say what plans shall be followed. The burden of the work in this broad field should not rest upon two or three men. We are not reaching the high standard which, with the great and important truth we are handling, God expects us to reach. . . .
>
> There must be a committee, not composed of half a dozen men, but of representatives from all lines of our work, from our publishing houses, from our educational institutions, and from our sanitariums, which have life in them, which are constantly working, constantly broadening (MS 43, 1901).

She asked why more had not been done to open up new fields even in America.

From one point to another she moved. She branded as "contemptible in the sight of God, contemptible" (MS 43a, 1901) the selfish, grasping financial policies of some, particularly in the publishing houses, who demanded high wages. She called for men to "stand as true to principle as the needle to the pole" (MS 43, 1901).

She pointed out that God did not want the medical work separated from the gospel work, that the medical missionary work should be considered the pioneer work, "the breaking-up plow." She said that "God wants every soul to stand shoulder to shoulder with Dr. Kellogg." She referred to his work in Chicago as she had seen it a few days before. Then she went on to point out that Kellogg should work to reach the higher classes and the wealthy classes. Her closing words were in exaltation of the Word of God.

It was a solemn meeting. Mrs. White had not failed to deal with the matters that were heavy on her heart, matters that concerned the welfare of the General Conference session about to open and the welfare of the work of the church at large. Her talk pointed in the direction the General Conference should take in its work. The session, scheduled for a full three weeks, opened the next morning.

THE 1901 GENERAL CONFERENCE SESSION

At 9:00 Tuesday morning, with the president of the General Conference, G. A. Irwin, in the chair, the thirty-fourth session of the General Conference of Seventh-day Adventists was called to order. J. N. Loughborough read Psalm 106, and S. N. Haskell led in prayer. President Irwin then opened the way for business.

Following the preliminaries Ellen White, who was seated in the audience, arose and went to the front. The chairman gave her the floor. She first pointed out the privilege of the Advent people to stand high above the world, sanctified by the truth and having a close connection with Heaven. Then she turned to the immediate situation. The following statements were included in her address:

> Why, I ask you, are men who have not brought self into subjection allowed to stand in important positions of truth and handle sacred things? . . .
>
> The principles of heaven are to be carried out in every family, in the discipline of every church, in every establishment, in every institution, in every school, and in everything that shall be managed. You have no right to manage, unless you manage in God's order. Are you under the control of God? Do you see your responsibility to Him? . . .
>
> Here are men who are standing at the head of our various institutions, of the educational interests, and of the conferences in different localities and in different States. All these are to stand as representative men, to have a voice in molding and fashioning the plans that shall be carried out. There are to be more than one or two or three men to consider the whole vast field. The work is great, and there is no one human mind that can plan for the work which needs to be done (GCB 1901, pp. 24-26).

Thus Mrs. White gave what was in reality the keynote address. She spoke for an hour. The very serious nature of the situation that had developed she fearlessly and clearly delineated. Help from God was promised if they would take hold of Him. There must be a change. It was one of the most solemn messages ever delivered to the church in a General Conference assembly.

THE RESPONSE

A solemn silence pervaded the assembly as Ellen White made her way to a chair. Elder Irwin stepped forward and said in response:

> These are certainly very plain words that we have listened to, and it seems to me they come in very timely, right in the commencement of our conference. We notice the burden of the testimony was reorganization. This must first begin with us as individuals, and I trust that it may begin in each heart. I, for one, want to accept the testimony that has been borne, and I want that work of reorganization and regeneration to be not only begun, but completed, in my life. I am glad that these words were spoken right now (*ibid.*, p. 27).

What took place next came as no surprise to the president. A. G. Daniells, a man of 43 years of age and in his prime, who for the past 13 years had served in New Zealand and Australia, now asked for the floor. He walked down to the front of the tabernacle, mounted the stairs, and stepped up to the desk. He told of the meeting held in the college library the preceding day, at which Ellen White had given similar counsel. He declared:

> We all feel that our only safety lies in obedience, in following our great Leader. We feel that we should begin at the very beginning of this work at this meeting, and just as nearly as we know how, build on His foundation (*ibid.*).

Then he offered the following comprehensive motion:

> I move that the usual rules and precedents for arranging and transacting the business of the conference be suspended, and that a General Committee be hereby appointed, to consist of the following persons: The presidents and secretaries of the General Conference, of the General Conference Association, of the European and Australasian union conferences; of the Review and Herald, Pacific Press, and Echo publishing companies; of the Foreign Mission Board, Medical Missionary and Benevolent Association; of Battle Creek, Healdsburg, and Union colleges; and the following named persons—J. N. Loughborough, S. N. Haskell, A. T. Jones, W. W. Prescott, and such other persons as may be necessary to represent the important enterprises and interests connected with the work of the Seventh-day Adventists throughout the world, the

same to be named by the committee when organized, and this commit-tee to constitute a general or central committee, which shall do such work as necessarily must be done in forwarding the work of the confer-ence, and preparing the business to bring before the delegates" (ibid.).

Elder Daniells confidently predicted that if we "step out boldly to follow the light that He [God] gives us, whether we can see clear through to the end or not—if we walk in the light we have, go just as far as we can today, God will give us further light; He will bring us out of bondage into glorious liberty." In his closing remarks he expressed appreciation for the fact that "we have a defi-nite, certain voice to speak to us."

The delegates then entered upon an earnest discussion of the proposal be-fore them. When there seemed to be an overcautious attitude, Ellen White arose and urged that no one block what was being proposed. After a season of prayer, the matter was placed before the assembly, and after further discussion and the answering of questions, the chair put the matter to a vote. The record is that it "was carried unanimously" (ibid., p. 29).

Changes had been called for by the Lord. Changes had to be made. Steps must be taken that would distribute responsibilities to leaders near where the work was being done.

STEPS TOWARD REORGANIZATION

According to the General Conference Bulletin the first Sabbath of the General Conference session, April 6, was a great day. "Sister White spoke in the Tabernacle at 11:00 a.m. to an overflowing house. Not only was every available seating space occupied, but every foot of standing room was covered." The estimate was that approximately 5,000 people worshiped that Sabbath morning in Battle Creek, "making [it] the largest Sabbath meeting ever held" in that city (GCB 1901, p. 89).

If Ellen White's voice had not been heard in a General Conference session for 10 years, it was heard in this conference of 1901. This was the most largely attended session thus far held by Seventh-day Adventists. In addition to the delegates, there were 1,500 visitors from all parts of the United States, and the comment was made, "All of these seem of one heart and mind to make this the greatest and best occasion of their lives" (ibid., p. 65).

At 5:30 Tuesday morning, April 9, Mrs. White again gave the morning de-votional study. Her topic was the need of missionary effort. She thanked the Lord that He was working in their midst, and said that this could be so only when His people draw together. "There seems to be in this meeting an endeavor to press together. This is the word which for the last fifty years I have heard from the angelic host—press together, press together. Let us try to do this" (*ibid.*, p. 182).

Elder Daniells, with his implicit trust in the messages of the Spirit of Prophecy and his recent experience in leading in the organization of the work in Australia, was the man of the hour. Standing at the head of the Committee on Counsel, he was the man to step forward and fearlessly initiate steps toward reorganization. After reviewing the general needs and the directions in which the work should move, the first task was to set up subcommittees. First to be appointed was a committee on organization, with W. C. White as chairman. Then followed the naming of other committees, on education, on colporteur work, on publishing, on missionary work, et cetera. But it was the committee on organization especially that often brought its reports to the conference as a whole. And it was these reports that gained first attention.

SWEEPING CHANGES

The proposed changes were sweeping. They called for the various independent and separate international organizations—the Sabbath School Association, the Religious Liberty Association, the Foreign Mission Board, et cetera—to be blended into the General Conference. The Executive Committee was to be a much larger group with much wider representation. The medical missionary work, which had grown so strong, was to be integrated, with a definite representation on the General Conference Committee.

An early proposal was that union conferences, after the order of what had been done in Australia, be formed throughout North America and the European fields. At the business session held Thursday afternoon, April 4, a memorial was presented from the Southern field, or what might be termed the Southern district, embodying three conferences and six missions. On Tuesday, April 9, the organization of the Southern Union Conference was completed, a constitution adopted, certain officers elected, and members of the executive committee named. This represented the first full-fledged union conference to be organized in the United States. It was the bellwether, and before the conference closed two weeks later there were six union conferences in North America.

On this same day the basic action embodying reorganization was framed and presented to the General Conference in these words:

"5. That the General Conference Committee be composed of representative men connected with the various lines of work in the different parts of the world.

"6. That the General Conference Committee, as thus constituted, should take the place of all the present boards and committees, except in the case of the essential legal corporations.

"7. That the General Conference Committee consist of twenty-five members, six of whom shall be chosen by the Medical Missionary Association, and nineteen by the General Conference. That five of these members be chosen with special reference to their ability to foster and develop true evangelical spirit in all departments of the work, to build up the ministry of the word, and to act as teachers of the gospel message in all parts of the world; and that they be relieved from any special business cares, that they may be free to devote themselves to this work.

"8. That in choosing this General Conference Committee, the presidents of the union conference be elected as members" (ibid., p. 185).

BATTLE CREEK COLLEGE TO MOVE TO RURAL LOCATION

One matter of great concern to Ellen White at this conference was the location of the three institutions in Battle Creek: the publishing house, the sanitarium, and particularly the college. In the 25 years since the college had been dedicated, city growth had produced a congested environment far different from that which God had revealed as desirable.

At the time of selecting a location on which to build Avondale College she had said:

> Our schools should be located away from the cities, on a large tract of land, so that the students will have opportunity to do manual work. They should have opportunity to learn lessons from the objects which Christ used in the inculcation of truth. He pointed to the birds, to the flowers, to the sower and the reaper. In schools of this kind not only are the minds of the students benefited, but their physical powers are strengthened. All portions of the body are exercised. The education of mind and body is equalized (ibid., pp. 215, 216).

For some time the need for a change of location for the college had been the subject of discussion and correspondence between Ellen White and the president, Professor E. A. Sutherland, and the dean, Percy T. Magan.

At 5:30 on Friday morning Mrs. White dispatched one of her helpers to the Magan home with the message that she wished to see both men. They came at once.

Later that morning, in a meeting with the delegates, Magan gave his report on the relief book plan he was directing. Ellen White had dedicated her book, *Christ's Object Lessons*, to the financial relief of Seventh-day Adventist educational institutions. Thousands of dollars had been raised as church members sold the books to their neighbors and friends and used the proceeds for debt reduction. Mrs. White was seated on the platform with other workers who were leading out in this particular meeting. As Magan closed his report, he referred to the testimonies that called for a country location for Seventh-day Adventist schools and proposed that consideration be given to moving Battle Creek College to "a more favorable locality" (*ibid.*, p. 212).

Then Mrs. White rose to speak. After referring to the experience with *Christ's Object Lessons*, she challenged the audience with this declaration:

> The light that has been given me is that Battle Creek has not the best influence over the students in our school. . . . God wants the school to be taken out of Battle Creek. . . . Some may be stirred about the transfer of the school from Battle Creek. But they need not be. This move is in accordance with God's design for the school before the institution was established. But men could not see how this could be done. There were so many who said that the school must be in Battle Creek. Now we say that it must be somewhere else (*ibid.*, pp. 215, 216).

She urged:

> The best thing that can be done is to dispose of the school's building here as soon as possible. Begin at once to look for a place where the school can be conducted on right lines. God wants us to place our children where they will not see and hear that which they should not see or hear (*ibid.*, p. 216).

At this point the meeting adjourned to 11:00 a.m., which left just a short intermission. Much of the rest of the morning was devoted to a consideration of the relief of the denomination's schools from their debts through the sale of *Christ's Object Lessons* and to the moving of Battle Creek College.

Elder A. T. Jones, president of the Seventh-day Adventist Educational Society, asked for the floor. After referring to the appeal that the college be moved out of Battle Creek, he called for the stockholders of the Educational Society present, who favored carrying out the instruction that had been given, to rise to their feet. The report is that there was a hearty response and that when the negative vote was called for, no one responded.

Then the delegates of the General Conference session were asked to vote. They voted unanimously to move the school. Finally a third expression was called for from the congregation generally. Rising to their feet, they gave a unanimous affirmation to the decision to move the college from Battle Creek. History was made that day at the General Conference session, and when school took up that fall, it was at Berrien Springs, Michigan. This was the second marked instance of a wholehearted and immediate response at the General Conference session of 1901 to counsel by the messenger of the Lord that called for sweeping changes.

THE GENERAL CONFERENCE BECOMES A WORLD CONFERENCE

The General Conference was now a world conference, with an Executive Committee of 25 representing the various interests of the whole world field. The organization of union conferences provided for the leaders close to the problems to carry the burdens of the work. This was a point that had been emphasized again and again by Ellen White. It also led to the development of men in executive experience.

Provisions were made to bring the various auxiliary interests into the General Conference as departments. Though committees were named to represent these lines, to implement the changes would take a little time.

One weakness in the new constitution that did not show up clearly when it was adopted caused considerable concern in the months that followed. This related to the election of the officers of the General Conference.

According to the new constitution, the delegates attending a General Conference session were empowered to elect the General Conference Committee; this committee in turn was to organize itself, electing its own officers. It was recognized at the time that this could mean that someone might chair it for only one year.

Undoubtedly this provision came about as an overreaction to the desire to get away from any "kingly power" (letter 49, 1903), a point that was pushed hard by Elder A. T. Jones, a member of the committee on organization.

While this arrangement would clearly reduce the possibility of anyone's exercising kingly power, it also greatly undercut responsible leadership. It went too far, for it took out of the hands of the delegates attending the General Conference session the vital responsibility of electing the leaders of the church, and instead placed this responsibility in the hands of the General Conference Executive Committee of 25. This meant that there was no church leader with a mandate from the church as represented by its delegates.

That some of the delegates attending the session of 1901 were not clear on this point is evidenced in the insistence that the committee elect the chairman and announce its decision before that session closed. A. G. Daniells was chosen as chairman of the General Conference Committee. He was the leader of the church and nearly all the delegates were pleased, but they did not discern at this point how he would be crippled in his work, having no tenure and no mandate.

To take the position that Ellen White's urging that there be no kings meant, as interpreted by A. T. Jones, that the church should have no General Conference president was unjustified. At no time had her messages called for the abolition of the office of president of the General Conference; rather, her messages recognized such an office in the organization of the church. An earlier statement indicated that she understood that the work devolving upon the president of the General Conference was too large for one man to carry and that others should stand by his side to assist (TM, pp. 342, 343). She did condemn the exercise of "kingly power."

The weakness, which soon became apparent, was corrected at the next session of the General Conference—the session of 1903.*

LAST 10 DAYS: TAXING PROBLEMS

At midsession many burdens still rested heavily on Ellen White's heart. Perhaps one of the greatest was that of Dr. John Harvey Kellogg and the broad influence of the course of action that he might take. Along with this was the attitude of the ministry toward the medical work of the church, and further, the personal experience of the ministers toward the health reform principles to which God had called His people. Also, she was deeply concerned regarding the development of the work in the southern states, both among the Whites and the Blacks. Up to midsession little had been done along this line.

One disruptive element with which Ellen White had to contend at the 1901 General Conference session was the case of Helge Nelson, who claimed the prophetic gift and insisted that he be given a hearing by the conference. This being denied, he was granted an interview with Mrs. White and the General Conference leaders. His burden was that Mrs. White stood where Moses stood in the typical history of God's people, and he, Helge Nelson, was to stand where Joshua stood, for he claimed special guidance from God. Ellen White met the false claims squarely and in the interview declared, "I know that God never gave mortal man such a message as that which Brother Nelson has borne concerning his brethren. It is not like our God" (RH, July 30, 1901).

She was to meet Nelson again at the General Conference session of 1903 in a rather dramatic way.

MEETING THE HOLY FLESH FANATICISM

Another disruptive element that Ellen White met at the 1901 conference, and this time before all the ministers of the cause, was the "holy flesh" fanaticism, which centered in Indiana. This came on Wednesday evening, April 17.

Under the guise of a great revival and the outpouring of the latter rain, the "holy flesh" movement swept through the Indiana Conference. Late in 1899 the president, Elder R. S. Donnell, became a strong advocate of the movement and was joined by most of the ministers in Indiana. In arranging for the camp meeting of 1900 he planned great things. He was unwilling that the two visiting General Conference brethren, Elders S. N. Haskell and A. J. Breed, be given much opportunity to reach the people. He warned his workers that these men had not passed through Christ's Garden of Gethsemane experience, and the ministers should not allow themselves to be influenced by them.

As the conference president stood speaking one evening, he held his arms outstretched toward the congregation, and later reported that he had felt great power coursing down his arms and passing through his fingers out to the people.

Elder Haskell reported that there was indeed a power, a strange power, in this new message. The people were bewildered. None wished to miss the experience of the outpouring of the Spirit of God. Translation faith seemed desirable. The teaching was a mixture of truth, error, excitement, and noise.

This was not Ellen White's first introduction to this strange teaching. She responded to Haskell:

> Last January the Lord showed me that erroneous theories and methods would be brought into our camp meetings, and that the history of the past would be repeated. I felt greatly distressed. I was instructed to say that at these demonstrations demons in the form of men are present, working with all the ingenuity that Satan can employ to make the truth disgusting to sensible people; that the enemy was trying to arrange matters so that the camp meetings, which have been the means of bringing the truth of the third angel's message before multitudes, should lose their force and influence (letter 132, 1900 [2 SM, p. 37]).

The workers' meeting at 5:30 on Wednesday morning, April 17, was not only solemn but exciting. Mrs. White chose at that point in the session to meet the "holy flesh" fanaticism. She did so by reading a carefully prepared manuscript statement. Before the meeting closed, she told the audience that to meet this fanaticism was one of the reasons she had left Australia and returned to the United States. The situation with which she was dealing had been revealed to her in Australia in January 1900, "before I left Cooranbong." And she declared, "If this had not been presented to me, I should not have been here today. But I am here, in obedience to the word of the Lord, and I thank Him that He has given me strength beyond my expectations to speak to the people" (GCB 1901, p. 426). She said, in part:

> Instruction has been given me in regard to the late experience of brethren in Indiana and the teaching they have given to the churches. Through this experience and teaching the enemy has been working to lead souls astray.

> The teaching given in regard to what is termed "holy flesh" is an

error. All may now obtain holy hearts, but it is not correct to claim in this life to have holy flesh. The apostle Paul declares, "I know that in me (that is, in my flesh,) dwelleth no good thing" (Rom. 7:18). To those who have tried so hard to obtain by faith so-called holy flesh, I would say, You cannot obtain it. Not a soul of you has holy flesh now. No human being on earth has holy flesh. It is an impossibility. If those who speak so freely of perfection in the flesh could see things in the true light, they would recoil with horror from their presumptuous ideas. . . .

The manner in which the meetings in Indiana have been carried on, with noise and confusion, does not commend them to thoughtful, intelligent minds. There is nothing in these demonstrations which will convince the world that we have the truth. Mere noise and shouting are no evidence of sanctification (*ibid.*, pp. 419-421 [2SM 31-35]).

Ellen White stood before the congregation for an hour, first reading from the manuscript she had prepared for the occasion, then bearing impromptu testimony, which was also reported in the *Bulletin*.

The next day at the early morning workers' meeting, Elder Donnell rose and asked whether he might make a statement. It appears in the *General Conference Bulletin* under the title "Confession of Elder R. S. Donnell." He spoke in measured words:

I feel unworthy to stand before this large assembly of my brethren this morning. Very early in life I was taught to reverence and to love the Word of God; and when reading in it how God used to talk to His people, correcting their wrongs, and guiding them in all their ways, when a mere boy I used to say: "Why don't we have a prophet? Why doesn't God talk to us now as He used to do?"

When I found this people, I was more than glad to know that there was a prophet among them, and from the first I have been a firm believer in, and a warm advocate of, the *Testimonies* and the Spirit of Prophecy. It has been suggested to me at times in the past, that the test on this point of faith comes when the testimony comes directly to us.

As nearly all of you know, in the testimony of yesterday morning, the test came to me. But, brethren, I can thank God this morning that my faith in the Spirit of Prophecy remains unshaken. God has spoken. He says I was wrong, and I answer, God is right, and I am wrong. . . .

I am very, very sorry that I have done that which would mar the cause of God and lead anyone in the wrong way. I have asked God to forgive me, and I know that He has done it. As delegates and representatives of the cause of God in the earth, I now ask you to forgive me my sins, and I ask your prayers for strength and wisdom to walk aright in the future. It is my determination, by the help of God, to join glad hands with you in the kingdom of God (*ibid.*, p. 422).

With this confession the holy flesh fanaticism was broken.

---

*See A. V. Olson, *Thirteen Crisis Years*, pp. 326-330.

THE BATTLE CREEK
SANITARIUM FIRE

If the telegram that reached Elmshaven Tuesday morning, February 18, 1902, had said that the Review and Herald Publishing House had been destroyed by fire, Ellen White would not have been surprised. Five months earlier she had written to its managers a message that was read to the board:

"I have been almost afraid to open the *Review*, fearing to see that God has cleansed the publishing house by fire" (letter 138, 1901 [8T, p. 91]).

But the message that came that rainy morning was that the two main sanitarium buildings in Battle Creek had just burned to the ground. Mrs. White reached for her pen and somewhat in agony noted:

> I would at this time speak words of wisdom, but what can I say? We are afflicted with those whose life interests are bound up in this institution. Let us pray that this calamity shall work together for good to those who must feel it very deeply. We can indeed weep with those who weep (MS 76, 1903).

Why was it, she was led to ask, that this institution, which had been such a great means for good, should suffer such loss? As her pen traced the words, page after page, she wrote:

> I am instructed to say, Let no one attempt to give a reason for the burning of the institution that we have so highly appreciated. Let no one attempt to say why this calamity was permitted to come. Let everyone examine his own course of action. Let everyone ask himself whether he is meeting the standard that God has placed before him. . . . Let no one try to explain this mysterious providence. Let us thank God that there was not a great loss of life. In this we see God's merciful hand (*ibid.*).

Anxiously the staff at Elmshaven waited for word presenting in detail just what had happened. This in some larger features came in the West Coast newspapers and then in more detail in letters and in the next issue of the *Review and Herald*.

It was a winter night, with snow quite deep on the ground. The sanitarium had been ever gaining in popularity, and its main buildings were filled to capacity. Its guest list carried names of business and government leaders. Only a skeleton staff was on duty at 4:00 Tuesday morning, February 18, 1902, when fire broke out in the basement of the main sanitarium building, just beneath the treatment rooms. The two main alarms in the building were set off as well as the nearest fire-alarm box in the city. Equipment from Battle Creek and nearby cities hurried to fight the blaze. But spreading through the ventilating and elevator shafts, the flames soon enveloped the building, making it clear that it could not be saved.

The nurses and other staff members swung into their practiced fire-evacuation plan, first taking the 50 patients who were unable to get out of their beds, then assisting women and children to safety.

Ambulatory patients made good use of fire escapes. With the special blessing of God all patients were cleared from the building. This was made certain as physicians and nurses, wet towels about their heads, felt their way through the dense smoke to recheck the rooms and corridors. As the insurance inspector looked over the situation a few days after the fire, he declared: "Nothing but divine power could have assisted those nurses and doctors to do as they did in getting the people out" (DF 45a, S. H. Lane to AGD, Feb. 28, 1902).

But one man did lose his life. It was "old man Case," an eccentric patient in his late 80s, who, not trusting the banks, always carried his treasure with him in a satchel—"all the way from one to five thousand dollars" (*ibid.*). He, his wife, and daughter were led to a place of safety, and then, unnoticed, he must have gone back into the building to retrieve his satchel with its treasure. He never came out.

The fire from the main sanitarium building soon spread across the street to the hospital, a five-story structure. Situated as the building was on a hill, water pressure was insufficient to protect it. So it burned too.

By 7:00 that Tuesday morning it was all over. The principal sanitarium structures were gone. The patients, some 400 in all, had been moved to "the several large buildings which" were "rapidly adapted to the purpose, and the cottages which were not included in the disaster" (*Medical Magazine*, April 1902, p. 181). Immediately the staff swung into action to provide for the continued care of the patients. The treatment schedule, modified somewhat, continued that day.

Dr. Kellogg was on the train returning from the West Coast to Battle Creek at the time of the fire. He learned of it when he arrived in Chicago on Tuesday evening. As he continued his journey to Battle Creek he called for a table and utilized the two hours in drawing plans for a new sanitarium building.

The moving of Battle Creek College to Berrien Springs four months previous to the fire had left buildings vacant that were available to the sanitarium. The two dormitories, West Hall and South Hall, were soon filled with sanitarium patients. The old Battle Creek College classroom and administration building furnished space for the business offices. East Hall, the sanitarium-owned dormitory occupied by nurses, was able to accommodate 150 of the patients. The nurses moved elsewhere. Extensive bath and treatment rooms were quickly fitted up in the basements of two of these buildings. So within a few days' time the sanitarium program was moving forward quite normally.

W. C. White refused to believe the first report of the disaster. But the second report bore evidence of authenticity, and in a letter he explained his feelings: "I wish to join with all our people in mourning at this great loss to us as a people, and to the world" (18 WCW, p. 425).

The citizens of Battle Creek asked for the privilege of holding a mass meeting in the tabernacle on the evening of Wednesday, February 19. It was led by the clergy of the city. The tabernacle was packed; eulogies were spoken, and pledges given of moral and financial support.

As Ellen White pondered the first sketchy news of the fire, while the embers were still warm in Battle Creek, she wrote:

> Our heavenly Father does not willingly afflict or grieve the children of men. He has His purpose in the whirlwind and the storm, in the fire and in the flood. The Lord permits calamities to come to His people to save them from greater dangers (MS 76, 1903).

PLANS TO REBUILD

Plans were quickly drawn for a new sanitarium, "a temple of truth." Building concerns were consulted. Bids were called for. A special meeting of the General Conference Committee was called, and approval was given to the general plan for rebuilding the Battle Creek Sanitarium. One special point was the prospect of financial relief in Dr. Kellogg's proposal of writing a book to help raise money. The General Conference Committee considered it a "grand proposition." The doctor proposed providing 400,000 copies as a gift.

On March 25 A. G. Daniells reported this and other developments in a letter to W. C. White. Between $80,000 and $90,000 had been subscribed in the city of Battle Creek toward a new sanitarium; this, along with the insurance money, amounting to $154,000, would provide a "fair sum with which to erect a new building."

> We have accepted plans submitted by an Ohio architect. They are plain but dignified. We propose to erect an absolutely fireproof building,

and to pay the cash for everything. We suppose that when it is finished, furnished, and fully equipped for business, the cost will be between $250,000 and $300,000. But the board is determined that no debt shall be incurred by the erection of this building (DF 45a, AGD to WCW, Mar. 25, 1902).

Even the assurance of a modest building and of a debt-free building program did not put Ellen White's mind at ease. On the last night of April a vision was given to her concerning the rebuilding of the sanitarium, and she wrote in a letter addressed to Dr. Kellogg:

> I have been given a message for you. You have had many cautions and warnings, which I sincerely hope and pray you will consider. Last night I was instructed to tell you that the great display you are making in Battle Creek is not after God's order. You are planning to build in Battle Creek a larger sanitarium than should be erected there. There are other parts of the Lord's vineyard in which buildings are greatly needed (letter 125, 1902).

"It is not wise to erect mammoth institutions," she wrote in a letter to Dr. Percy Magan, now at Berrien Springs. "I have been shown that it is not by the largeness of an institution that the greatest work for souls is to be accomplished" (letter 71, 1902).

In the months that followed she wrote much more along these lines to those who were carrying responsibilities in Battle Creek, both in the sanitarium and in the General Conference.

LAYING THE CORNERSTONE

With the plans drawn and accepted and the bids let, the next step was to lay the cornerstone. Sunday afternoon, May 11, 1902, about 10,000 people gathered for the elaborate ceremonies, with guest speakers from the government and the clergy from the city. Sanitarium employees were seated back of the speakers' stand, and sanitarium guests and citizens, in front. W. W. Prescott led out in the main address of the afternoon. Appropriately, the cornerstone was laid by Dr. John Harvey Kellogg himself. In his address he reminded helpers, guests, and townspeople of the principles for which the institution stood. He referred to its history—a history he had often connected with God's providential guidance through the light given to Mrs. White.

He likened this new institution to the Temple city Jerusalem, to which the ancient Israelites looked from all over the world. In passing, we note that an element of pantheism appeared in this address, representing a philosophy he firmly held in his heart, but the perils of which had not yet been seen by his associates.

Kellogg was an energetic, forceful, persuasive man, and somehow the General Conference leadership through the middle 1890s found it difficult to resist his insistence on borrowing money for capital investments for institutions and then persuading the General Conference Association to assume the obligations. Debts piled on debts—debts assumed with no systematic plan for their amortization.

When Elder Daniells took up his responsibilities as leader of the church after the General Conference session of 1901, he was appalled to find that the total institutional indebtedness was close to $500,000. In the context of the times, this was a huge sum. The top pay of ministers, physicians, and publishing house employees at this time was $12 to $15 a week (DF 243d).

In the meantime, brick was being laid on brick in Battle Creek, and the sanitarium edifice was rising—an edifice that church leaders were soon to discover would cost between two and three times the amount estimated. What is more, not all the promises for financial help made when the institution was destroyed by fire were kept. Some of the pledges by the businesspeople and citizens of Battle Creek were never honored. The expected income from the sales of *The Living Temple*, Dr. Kellogg's gift book, did not materialize, for church leaders found it permeated with pantheistic philosophies. There is no indication that the pledge made by the sanitarium board or the General Conference Committee that no further debt would be incurred in the rebuilding of the sanitarium was kept or even remembered.

On July 6 a message from Ellen White addressed to the General Conference Committee and the Medical Missionary Board included this counsel:

> I am instructed to say that our people must not be drawn upon for means to erect an immense sanitarium in Battle Creek; the money that would be used in the erection of that one mammoth building should be used in making plants in many places. We must not draw all we can from our people for the establishment of a great sanitarium in one place, to the neglect of other places, which are unworked for the want of means (letter 128, 1902).

THE SANITARIUM UNDENOMINATIONAL?

Another deep concern on the part of Ellen White was regarding the position that Dr. Kellogg was taking and advocating, that the Battle Creek Sanitarium was undenominational. This was being heard more and more frequently. Its seeds went back for almost 10 years when Kellogg began to envision the medical work being done by Seventh-day Adventists as a great Christian benevolent work, not particularly denominational in its character. In 1893 the Seventh-day Adventist Medical Missionary and Benevolent Association had been formed to succeed the earlier Health and Temperance Association. But in 1896 the name had been changed, dropping out the words "Seventh-day Adventist" and adding the word "International" (SHM, p. 249).

Writing in 1898, Dr. Kellogg declared of this organization that it was developed to "carry forward *medical* and *philanthropic work independent of any sectarian or denominational control*, in home and foreign lands" (*Medical Missionary*, January 1898; quoted in SHM, p. 249; italics supplied).

The following year at a convention of the association it was declared that the delegates were "here as Christians, and not as Seventh-day Adventists." Nor were they present "for the purpose of presenting anything that is peculiarly Seventh-day Adventist in doctrine."

The growing number of undenominational declarations on the part of Dr. Kellogg and his close associates provided sound basis for alarm, and of this Ellen White spoke in midsummer, 1902:

> It has been stated that the Battle Creek Sanitarium is not denominational. But if ever an institution *was established* to be *denominational* in every sense of the word, *this sanitarium was.*
>
> Why are sanitariums established if it is not that they may be the right hand of the gospel in calling the attention of men and women to the truth that we are living amid the perils of the last days? And yet, in one sense, it is true that the Battle Creek Sanitarium is undenominational, in that it receives as patients people of all classes and all denominations (letter 128, 1902 [SHM, p. 253]).

And she pointed out:

> We are not to take pains to declare that the Battle Creek Sanitarium is not a Seventh-day Adventist institution; for this it certainly is. As a Seventh-day Adventist institution it was established to represent the various features of gospel missionary work, thus to prepare the way for the coming of the Lord *(ibid.)*.

DEDICATION OF THE NEW BUILDING

The institution was dedicated in a three-day service running from Sabbath morning, May 30, to Monday night, June 1, with meetings held in the tabernacle and on the grounds of the sanitarium. The Sabbath morning service was one of dedication on the part of the workers to this important phase of the Lord's work (RH, June 9, 1903).

In this dedication Ellen White could heartily agree. The Battle Creek Sanitarium was the Lord's institution. Even though some phases of counsel concerning its work had been brushed aside, it was still the Lord's institution. A few weeks before the dedication service, Mrs. White, speaking at the General Conference session of 1903, made this statement:

> Let me say that God does not design that the sanitarium that has been erected in Battle Creek shall be in vain. He wants His people to understand this. Now that the building has been put up, He wants this institution to be placed on vantage ground. . . . We are now to make another effort to place our institution on solid ground. Let no one say, because there is a debt on the sanitarium in Battle Creek, "We will have nothing more to do in helping to build up that institution." The people of God must build that institution up, in the name of the Lord. It is to be placed where its work can be carried on intelligently (GCB 1903, p. 58; see also p. 67).

She urged that one man was not to stand alone at the head of the institution. It was God's will that His servants should stand united in carrying forward the work in a balanced way.

Just how the sanitarium could be placed on vantage ground she declared she did not know nor could she tell the congregation. "But," she said, "I know that just as soon as the Holy Spirit shall come upon hearts, there will be unity in voice and understanding; and wisdom will be given us" (*ibid.*).

She arranged for a complete set of her books to be furnished to the sanitarium as her gift (letter 96, 1903). These were for the patients' library and were to be in the "best binding."

ELMSHAVEN:
NOT A REST HOME

Perhaps the beautiful home known as Elmshaven originally served as a single family residence, but in the years when Ellen White lived there (1900-1915) it became not only the residence for Mrs. White and an enlarging staff of helpers, but a center drawing people from home and abroad for counsel, interviews, and even conventions.

Changes involving the physical plant were necessary to accommodate a large number of visitors and improve working conditions not only for the staff but for Ellen White herself.

The house and surroundings of Elmshaven today are not the same as they were in 1900. When she purchased the home, the three upstairs rooms and a low attic room over the kitchen served as bedrooms. Soon arrangements were made to replace the attic room with a spacious writing room over the kitchen and back entryway.

This room extended across the complete east end of the home, over the kitchen and service porch. Even though it had been specified that old materials would be used as far as possible, the alterations, with the painting inside and outside, cost $1,000. But she felt she was justified in making this investment even though she thought she should defend it. She had to have working conditions that were conducive to efficiency and health. To an acquaintance she wrote:

> The building of this room took money. I held back for a year before consenting to have this room built; for I know how many places there were in which money was needed. But I saw that it was necessary, for the preservation of my life, that something be done. It would be wrong for me to shorten my life, for this would take me from the Lord's work (letter 165, 1902).

There was a bright bay-window arrangement on the southeast corner, with windows opening in all four directions, but principally east and south. Artistic shingles set off the tower on the outside. The room was fitted with a fireplace on the east side and with cabinets along the west wall, where her manuscripts, books, and papers could be kept. From the window on the north end of the room, between the cabinets and the door to the steep hidden stairway to the service porch, she could look up to the sanitarium on the hill above, and at the nearby office building when it was built shortly thereafter.

There were three features about this newly constructed writing room that especially pleased Ellen White: its roominess, its bay window with light and sunshine, and its fireplace. She was to spend a large part of her time here during the next 12 years, writing, writing. She would often come to the room at 2:00 or 3:00 in the morning, sometimes at midnight, sometimes earlier, to start her day of writing.

THE OFFICE BUILDING AND STAFF

There was an eight-room office building under construction about 30 yards (27 meters) north of the home. N. H. Druillard was in charge of construction.

Ellen White was eager to get on with the book work that awaited her attention. She now had a good staff: Sara McEnterfer was her personal secretary, nurse, and traveling companion; Marian Davis, Clarence Crisler, Sarah Peck, and Maggie Hare composed her secretarial force; Mrs. M. J. Nelson was cook; Iram James managed the farm; Mrs. N. H. Druillard was her accountant; and Mr. Druillard the builder. W. C. White gave general supervision and served his mother and the General Conference in varied capacities.

We turn our attention now to what was going on at Elmshaven from the standpoint of establishing Ellen White's work there. She occupied the northwest bedroom, at the top of the stairs. This overlooked the prune orchard, which had 2,000 trees and stretched just below the knoll and a quarter of a mile (.4 kilometer) to the west. She was to retain this bedroom until her death. Her office occupied the front bedroom across the hall, facing the south. The large writing room with a bay window that she later used as an office had not yet been built. She suffered somewhat because the room in which she worked had a stove instead of a fireplace. Very seldom did she light a fire in it, choosing rather to dress warmly enough to write.

The bedroom across the hall on the north side of the house was shared by her helpers, Sara McEnterfer, Sarah Peck, and Maggie Hare. Kitty Wilcox, niece of M. C. and F. M. Wilcox, who for a short time served as cook, stayed in the small attic room over the kitchen. The large downstairs formal parlor under Mrs. White's bedroom was converted to a bedroom and used by Mr. and Mrs. Druillard, for a time members of her staff. Others who intermittently helped with her literary work in those winter months were Eliza Burnham and Lillian Whalin, daughter of John Whalin, both borrowed from the Pacific Press.

THE EVERYDAY ENGROSSING ACTIVITIES

The work on *Testimony* 34 moved along at a torturous pace through the early weeks of 1901. Two things served to make the work difficult. The first was the time spent with the numerous letters and visitors that deluged the staff at Elmshaven as soon as Ellen White's new residence was established. Some people wrote wanting to work for her. One wrote that her doctor had recommended milk and she wondered whether it would be right to follow his advice. A young minister wrote asking whether he should try to convert the Protestant pastors of the town before visiting the members. Then there were questions of marriage and divorce and others about butter and eggs and cheese.

Sara McEnterfer, Mrs. Druillard, and W. C. White answered many of these letters in harmony with instructions given by Mrs. White. With many of these they enclosed a little duplicated appeal that read: "There are hundreds of people who desire to hear personally from Mother. Some write letters containing questions, others send us their life history, and others make donations to the cause. We have not time to write lengthy letters to these persons."

Often the answers said that Mrs. White had no special light on the case and urged the person to study what was already published. Sara told one woman who wanted Ellen White to inquire of the Lord, "I would say that the Lord is no respecter of persons and will hear your earnest cry to Him for help as quickly and willingly as He will should it be sent to Him through Sister White" (16 WCW, p. 184).

Two women appeared one day just as Ellen White was returning, worn and weary, from San Francisco. They said they had driven 60 miles (96 kilometers) in their little rig and they just had to see Sister White. She agreed to see them. The first thing they did was to present her with a demented child and ask what should be done. Then they produced a list of 10 questions for which they wanted Yes or No answers. Typical of these were: 1. Has the time come when we positively should eat no more meat, eggs, butter, milk? 2. Is it a sin to raise children? Is it a sin to raise bread? et cetera. Mrs. White referred them to her writings on each point, and told them that she was not commissioned to answer such questions, but the women would not desist (16 WCW, p. 55).

A daughter brought an invalid mother for whom she wanted special prayers. A divorcee wanted advice. Then an old friend fresh from the Klondike gold fields came to the home. It's not hard to see how Sara McEnterfer acquired the reputation of being Ellen White's "watchdog," for she bore much of the responsibility of protecting her from unreasonable demands upon her time and energy.

The great bulk of the mail received was of a justifiable and sensible nature, a good portion being from workers carrying heavy responsibilities. Many of those well acquainted with her and her work would address a letter to W. C. White and merely suggest that he discuss the matter with his mother at a time when she was free to give consideration to it. Some very personal letters she elected to answer herself.

Among the leaders who kept up active and continual correspondence were Elder Irwin, president of the General Conference; Dr. Kellogg; S. N. Haskell and his wife; and Edson. All wrote on a fairly regular basis, reporting their activities, outlining developments in their work, and asking for guidance and direction. Ellen White kept up an active correspondence with all of these. Her letters to them and to friends and relatives constitute the richest source of information about her day-to-day life. Whatever extra strength she could muster between her writing and bouts of illness she used in speaking to believers and unbelievers.

INFLUENCE OF THE MESSAGES IN CRITICAL SITUATIONS

The feeling was growing that some changes in politics and general plans should be made at the Pacific Press. With this there developed a feeling that implicated the manager, C. H. Jones, as the scapegoat, that he was the man mostly responsible for the commercial work and for the problems that it brought. A tide of criticism enveloped the employees.

As the time neared for the constituency meeting, at which a board would be chosen and officers selected to manage the institution, Jones wrote a nine-page letter to Ellen White in which he mentioned some of the problems that would be discussed, including: Should they dispose of the commercial work? (About half the time of the employees and half of the investment would be affected.) Should they sell the plant in Oakland, move to a more rural area, and build a plant of moderate size? et cetera.

On the closing page of his letter he bluntly stated that he did not plan to accept any responsibility in connection with the Pacific Press for the coming year. The situation, he felt, was such that he should take up other work, perhaps assisting his son, a physician in Santa Barbara. For 31 years he had been connected with denominational publishing work—eight with the Review and Herald and 23 with the Pacific Press. He declared:

> My life has been put into this institution. I have had no separate interest, but my whole time and attention has been given to building up the Pacific Press (C. H. Jones to EGW, Apr. 16, 1902).

He recognized that he had made mistakes, and he expressed his feeling of regret as he contemplated severing his connection with the institution, even though he thought that this was the best move. He invited any counsel that Mrs. White might have for him.

Soon after receiving this letter from Jones, she was shown "in the night season" how things were in the Pacific Press, and she was given "a most unexpected testimony," after which she wrote a kind letter of counsel to Brother and Sister Jones. Two days later she penned a message addressed to "My Brethren in

Positions of Responsibility in the Pacific Press." She came directly to the point, opening the letter with:

> The case of Brother C. H. Jones has been presented to me. Should he resign his position to take up some other line of work? If the Lord should say, "This is My will," it would be right for Brother Jones to do this. . . . When the Lord selects a man who in His sight is the proper man for this place, it will be right for Brother Jones to sever his connection with the Pacific Press. But at present the Lord does not accept his resignation (letter 67, 1902).

Mrs. White spoke at the sanitarium church on Sabbath, April 26, and then on Sunday made the journey to Oakland and to the C. H. Jones home, where she was to stay as a guest. The constituency meeting opened on Monday morning with a good representation present. On Monday afternoon Mrs. White was the principal speaker. As the letter to Jones was read to the constituency, followed by the reading of the 21-page testimony to the men in positions of responsibility in the Pacific Press, hearts were touched. In reporting the meeting the *Pacific Union Recorder* stated:

> The Spirit of the Lord came into the meeting, and many hearts were melted to tears. Following her remarks, there was a spirited social meeting, in which many confessions were made, and the entire audience manifested their desire to reconsecrate themselves to the service of the Lord by a rising vote (May 22, 1902).

What a contrast from the ordinary corporation constituency meeting! Among the actions taken were these:

> "That we instruct the incoming board of directors to make a continuous effort to reduce commercial work and develop the publication of religious, educational, and health literature. Also, that we recommend that the incoming board of directors dispose of the plant as a whole, or in part, as Providence may open the way.
>
> "We also recommend that, in case the plant is sold a smaller plant be established in some rural district convenient for our denominational work, for the training and education of missionaries" (*ibid.*).

A board of seven was chosen, and C. H. Jones was wholeheartedly and unanimously returned to his position as manager—a position he was to hold for another 31 years.

FINANCIAL HELP NEEDED FOR WORK IN THE SOUTH

The newly organized Southern Union Conference was facing an explosive situation. Neither Edson White nor W. O. Palmer, who had gone with him to the South to establish schools and churches and a publishing house, was known for his financial acumen. Ventures had been launched with borrowed money and were heavily mortgaged. Under these circumstances the Southern Union sent its president, George I. Butler, and the treasurer of the publishing house, W. O. Palmer, to California to interview Ellen White and gain counsel as to the course they should pursue.

The two men arrived at Elmshaven on Friday noon, May 16, and were given a hearty welcome. Mrs. White had worked very closely with Elder Butler down through the years. Will Palmer was a son of the Palmers who had helped in early days to establish the publishing work in Battle Creek.

When the brethren, early in the new week, spread before Ellen White and the Elmshaven staff their problems and the reasons for their coming, they were delighted to find that during the previous few months she had written much on the work in the South that answered their questions. As they looked over these materials, they found that the Lord had instructed her to appeal to the churches throughout America to assist in establishing the work in the Southern states on a firm basis. The needs, which were great, were to be made known to church members throughout the land, and an opportunity was to be given to them to help. The brethren found in this counsel that which brought courage to their hearts, and after several interviews in which the work was reviewed and counsel given, they felt that their mission had been accomplished.

Will Palmer returned to Nashville. Butler lingered a bit on the West Coast, speaking Sabbath morning in the sanitarium church. This was followed by a meeting Sunday night in which he made an appeal for the work in the South and obtained pledges for $500. This gave Butler the courage to go to other churches—Healdsburg, San Francisco, Oakland, and Fresno. Eighteen hundred dollars was raised to assist the Southern Publishing Association.

W. C. White, shortly after the visit, wrote of the surprise and amazement that came to the visitors and to the Elmshaven office staff in that "they found that before their arrival, their questions had been anticipated, and that Mother had already written many things which they can now use to excellent advantage for the advancement of the work in the Southern field" (19 WCW, p. 371).

LONG-RANGE PLANS FOR THE MEDICAL MISSIONARY WORK

When the delegates assembled for an important council at the St. Helena Sanitarium on Wednesday, June 18, 1902, Ellen White informed them that she would be pleased to talk with them for an hour each day. They quickly arranged for a session early every morning. Mrs. White read from manuscripts prepared especially for this convention. She explained the distinctive nature of the denomination's medical work as she urged that "conformity to the world is causing many of our people to lose their bearings. . . . Worldly policy has been coming into the management of many of our institutions" (MS 96, 1902).

At this four-day meeting long-range plans were laid that called for the establishment of the Pacific Union Medical Missionary and Benevolent Association. This meant that there would be on the Pacific Coast a strong medical organization under denominational control. The medical interests in the West would not be a part of the Battle Creek-controlled International Medical Missionary and Benevolent Association. The constituency of the new association sensed the impact of what they were doing. They stated that: "In view of the importance of the steps about to be taken, careful study should be given to the questions involved, as not only affecting the interests of the entire Pacific Coast, *but of the denominational work throughout the world*" (PUR, Aug. 14, 1902; italics supplied).

One feature of the long-range plans was that "medical missionary enterprises that may be started . . . shall be upon the basis that the financial and managing responsibility shall rest upon a local constituency or board" (*ibid.*). The way was being paved for very important decisions to be made by the General Conference Committee at a meeting to be held in November and the General Conference session the following spring.

ELLEN WHITE'S RECREATION

Though Ellen White spent much time in concentrated effort to meet her obligations as a messenger of the Lord, she also took time for activities she especially enjoyed: carriage rides to various scenic spots and picking fruit. She contrived to arrange her program so that short practical trips could be made that would rest her mind and body. Somehow, traveling by carriage did something for her that nothing else could.

On a Sunday in mid-July, feeling the need for a change, she spent the day in an excursion to find cherries. Accompanied by Sara McEnterfer and Iram James, she picked eight quarts (nine liters), largely for canning. She rejoiced in the progress in building her writing room over the kitchen and reported that she was "enjoying much better health" than she "ever enjoyed in the past" (MS 138, 1902). The fruit crop in northern California that summer was abundant, and she got some of her exercise picking peaches, plums, and apples.

BROADENING THE WORK IN CHRISTIAN EDUCATION

Christian education reached a high point of interest and activity among Seventh-day Adventists in the late 1890s and early 1900s. For 20 or 25 years the church had been operating colleges, but except for elementary schools in connection with these institutions of higher learning, little or nothing had been done for small children by way of "church schools" till just before the turn of the century.

Ellen White's counsels on education were published in 1893 by the International Tract Society in Battle Creek in the form of a 255-page book titled *Christian Education*. Its messages of instruction were eagerly read and began to influence the membership. Four years later *Special Testimonies on Education* in its 240 small pages added emphasis to the subject. With Ellen White calling the church to action and with instruction on the conduct of schools available, Seventh-day Adventists began to act.

In 1896 and 1897 at Battle Creek College, where G. W. Caviness served as president and Frederick Griggs headed a 12-grade preparatory school, dedicated instructors developed a normal school for the training of elementary teachers. (See A. W. Spalding, *Origin and History*, vol. 2, p. 361.) The next year, with E. A. Sutherland serving as college president, several church schools were opened in Michigan. The church school movement spread rapidly. All this intensified the interest of Seventh-day Adventists in Christian education and made the preparation of an Ellen G. White book on the subject particularly timely.

Work on the book *Education* was begun in Australia by Mrs. White and Sarah Peck. Considerable appropriate material was drawn from the two books just mentioned and from other sources such as her *Review*, *Signs*, and *Youth's Instructor* articles. Her addresses on education and letters of counsel to educators added more. Then she wrote new material to fill in where needed. Writing on April 11, 1900, while still in Australia, she reported:

> I have been reading some chapters of the book on education. Sister Peck has been gathering this matter from a mass of my writings, carefully selecting precious bits here and there, and placing them together in harmonious order. I have read three chapters this morning and I think the arrangement is excellent.
>
> I want all our teachers and students to have this book as soon as they possibly can. I can hardly await the process of publication. I want the principles contained in this book to go everywhere. We must take a higher stand on education (letter 58, 1900).

P. T. Magan made a bid to publish the book at Berrien Springs. He argued that it would be produced more economically there than at our regular denominational printing plants, and that it would thus have a larger circulation. The proposal was tempting, but on the basis of light she had received from God concerning independent publishing, she declined. The manuscript for *Education* was submitted to the Pacific Press and has been a publication of that house from

1903 to the present. Ellen White, especially led by God, refused to take steps that would bypass the divinely established organizational procedures that governed the publication and distribution of the literature of the church.

CRISIS IN NASHVILLE

James Edson White, after a reconversion in 1893, had unselfishly led out in the development of the work in the South, using the *Morning Star*, which he built, as a missionary boat. He prepared appropriate literature, such as *Gospel Primer*, to help finance the enterprise and to supply a teaching aid. With his new dedication and consecration, his labors were greatly blessed by God. He led out in the formation of the Southern Missionary Society, an organization the General Conference recognized, to carry the burden of developing work at a time when the church itself was largely underdeveloped in that area and for which finances were limited.

But Edson White had one great weakness—he was not a financier. Again and again he had been warned and counseled by his father and his mother in his younger years. As he pioneered the work in the South his mother warned him again about the perils of becoming involved in business ventures. He was a promoter, and to him every interest in which he was engaged gave promise of unfailing success. Often his close associates did not share his optimism. But he dared to do what others would not attempt. In so doing he brought about a work that was effective in the winning of souls for the kingdom.

A little printing press on the *Morning Star* made possible the issuance of literature to aid in the developing work. It was but logical that eventually a printing plant should be established at some permanent location in the South. Nashville gave promise of being a good location, so a building was secured and presses, paper cutters, and type were purchased. A dedicated staff launched into the work of a third publishing house in the United States. The overall scheme showed daring and optimism, but it had its weaknesses.

God had opened up to Ellen White the need of publishing in the South for the South, but under Edson White's unsteady financial hand, and with the use of worn-out equipment, losses mounted. And all this was taking place at a time when the attention of the denomination was being called to operating on a debt-free policy. In fact, this was a very strong point with A. G. Daniells, the new church leader in 1901. He saw disaster ahead if the cause were to plunge into debt and stay there year after year, as it had in the late 1890s.

As church leaders studied the worsening financial situation developing in Nashville, it seemed logical to take steps to reduce the newly established publishing house to that of a book depository and the printing of only some tracts and materials that would be especially useful in the Southern states. From a purely business standpoint this seemed sound, especially when the church had two well-established publishing houses in North America—one in Battle Creek and another in Oakland. Neither of these had sufficient denominational work to keep its presses active, and both continued to do commercial work. Why could not all of the literature that would be needed in the United States be issued from these two houses?

At a council meeting held at Elmshaven October 19, 1902, Elder Daniells said, "It has been repeatedly published that the brethren in Nashville were not going into debt, and everybody has understood that a new order of things had set in, and that they were going to have an institution put up without debt. And so they have sent their money in" (MS 123, 1902).

But the institution was badly in debt, and the people were beginning to discover it. It was suggested that the matter could be cared for if it were handled like other situations of a similar character, except that Ellen White's support of her son's work made it impossible for the brethren to step in and put things right.

The question was asked, "Shall we wait another period of time for things to evolve down there, or has the time come for General Conference leaders and the Southern Union Conference men to get together and in prayerful, thoughtful counsel readjust those matters . . . and bring the business where it will not continually be going into debt?" To this Ellen White replied:

> It has; and I say, Go ahead. God's cause must not be left to reproach, no matter who is made sore by arranging matters on a right basis. Edson should give himself to the ministry and to writing, and leave alone the things that he has been forbidden by the Lord to do. Finance is not his forte at all.
>
> I want the brethren to feel free to take hold of this matter. I do not want them to make any reference to me. I want them to act just as they would act if my son were not there (ibid.).

The report of the discussions was typed out the same day, and with a feeling of satisfaction Elder Daniells left California that night. In his pocket he carried a copy of the interview. On arriving in Battle Creek he called a meeting of the General Conference Committee and gave a report of the interview in California. He had the assurance that the Lord's messenger was with them in their plans to close up the Nashville printing establishment in a very short time.

But the publishing house was not closed. On Monday, within 24 hours of the interview that was held at Elmshaven, Ellen White wrote a letter addressed to "Dear Brethren."

> Last night I seemed to be in the operating room of a large hospital,

to which people were being brought, and instruments were being prepared to cut off their limbs in a big hurry.

One came in who seemed to have authority, and said to the physician, "Is it necessary to bring these people into this room?" Looking pityingly at the sufferers, he said, "Never amputate a limb until everything possible has been done to restore it." Examining the limbs which the physicians had been preparing to cut off, he said, "They may be saved, the first work is to use every available means to restore these limbs" (letter 162, 1902).

And another scene passed before her. She seemed to be in a council meeting. E. R. Palmer, leader of our publishing work, was speaking, urging that "all our book making should be done by one publishing house, at one place, and thus save expense." She described how "One of authority" was present and pointed out the perils of a consolidated work; then she declared, "Let the Southern field have its own home-published books" (ibid.).

When Elder Daniells received the letter, he was stunned. Commenting on the experience when the letter came to Battle Creek, he declared:

> The message to continue the work of the Southern Publishing Association was truly disconcerting. It brought great disappointment to many. Its contradiction to the counsel given to us in our interview threw some into perplexity (AGD, *The Abiding Gift of Prophecy*, p. 328).

He recalled the experience of Nathan and David:

> "Then Nathan said unto David, 'Do all that is in thine heart; for God is with thee.' And it came to pass *the same night*, that the word of God came to Nathan, saying, 'Go and tell David my servant, Thus saith the Lord, thou shalt not build me an house' (see 1 Chron. 17:1-4)" (ibid.).

He recalled that David accepted the message that had come by revelation in place of the counsel given in the interview the preceding day. And as he reported the experience, he said: "Our committee took the same action" (ibid.).

The whole experience was one in which Ellen White herself was reproved by God, as she explained in a letter to Elder Daniells, written December 7:

> When you were here, you laid before me the condition of things in the publishing house at Nashville. You spoke of the terrible financial embarrassment resting on the work there, and gave me the impression that the brethren did not think that anything could be done to set things in order, because Sister White would exert her influence to prevent them from doing what they thought necessary to put matters on a proper basis.

Questions were asked me, and I answered them in the light of your repre-sentations. I said, "If what you say is correct, I will not stand in the way of your doing what you think ought to be done." You said that if you could ad-just matters as they would be adjusted if the difficulties existed in any other place, the work would be placed on a sound basis (letter 94, 1902; italics supplied).

And then she significantly reported:

The Lord reproved me for accepting any man's version of matters, even Elder Daniells', when He had already given me instruction.
I never remember feeling more pained than I did after speaking as I did in the interview with you. I had nothing to say in favor of Nashville. *The Lord reproved me for this*, and pointed me to those who by His ap-pointment were laboring in Nashville (*ibid.*; italics supplied).

In a direct testimony of reproof she wrote:

That there should be an attempt to counterwork the Lord's plans, and to hinder the good work being accomplished in Nashville; that Elder Daniells and others, notwithstanding the light that God has given, should join in this attempt, is an offense to God. He will not endorse their work, nor countenance their course of action (*ibid.*).

Elder Daniells accepted the message of reproof for the course of action he had proposed on what he felt was sound argument and careful reasoning. The printing establishment was not closed.

How he rejoiced when a turn came in the tide. Within a few years the in-stitution began to gain ground. As he later told the story, he observed:

God who knows the end from the beginning sent us messages to pre-vent us from narrowing the work in a time of discouragement. These messages sometimes seemed difficult to understand. They called for su-perhuman effort. In these later days, we can rejoice more than ever in the guiding hand of God manifested through His servant. I number this experience as one among many that have confirmed my confidence in the divine leadership of God's people through the prophetic gift (AGD, *The Abiding Gift of Prophecy*, p. 329).

THE REVIEW AND HERALD FIRE

It was Tuesday, December 30, 1902, a quiet winter evening in Battle Creek. No snow was on the ground. Most of the 300 employees of the Review and Herald publishing house had left their machines and editorial offices for the day. A few workers had come in for the night shift. A. G. Daniells, the newly elected leader of the General Conference, was still in his office on the second floor of the West Building, just across North Washington Street. A little after 6:00 I. H. Evans, president and general manager of the Review and Herald Publishing Company, and E. R. Palmer had met with him to look over some new tracts in preparation. At 7:20 Palmer left, and Daniells and Evans were chatting.

It had been a good year for the Review and Herald—one of the most prosperous. There were bright prospects for a busy 1903 also (RH Supplement, Apr. 28, 1903).

The tabernacle bell rang, summoning the faithful to prayer meeting. Then the electric lights went out. Daniells stepped over to the window and saw flames coming from the publishing house.

A few minutes before, all had been normal in the big building. The night watchman had just made his rounds through the engine room. Then the few employees at work detected the smell of smoke. Immediately the lights throughout the plant went out, leaving everything in total darkness. The dense oily smoke that filled the building with incredible speed forced everyone to leave hastily; even now some found the stairways cut off and took to the fire escapes. All the workers got out, but one just barely made it, crawling through smoke-filled rooms to safety. The fire alarm had been turned on at the first detection of the emergency.

When Elders Daniells and Evans reached the street, the whole pressroom was in flames. A minute or two later fire engines from the city fire department arrived and soon were pouring water onto the blaze. The whole building seemed engulfed. At no place could any firefighter enter it. Attempts to check the fire were futile. All could see that the flames were beyond control. Brother Robert of the art department saved a few pieces of furniture and some precious art materials, but nothing could be saved from the editorial offices or library.

It was now a little past 7:30; the firefighters directed their efforts toward saving the two-story West Building across the street, and the stores on the east side of the Review plant. Fortunately, the breeze was from the southwest, and the smoke and flames were blown across Main Street into McCamly Park. At 8:00 the roof of the plant fell in, and the machinery on the upper floors began to tumble. By 8:30 the brick-veneer walls were collapsing.

Although there were a number of employees at work throughout the building, none had seen the fire start. It was generally agreed, however, that the fire had begun in the basement in the original engine room, under the dynamo room. The first published report of the fire said:

> The very day on which it occurred the chief of the city fire department, in company with the office electrician, made a tour of inspection throughout the building, examining the wiring for the lights and other possible sources of danger, and pronounced everything in satisfactory condition (RH, Jan. 6, 1903).

This had been done in consideration of the renewal of the insurance policy on January 1. Fire Chief Weeks, who had directed the fighting of a number of big fires in Battle Creek, was later to declare that he had tried to extinguish every one of the Adventist fires and his score was zero. "There is something strange," he said, "about your SDA fires, with the water poured on acting more like gasoline" (B. P. Fairchild to Arthur L. White, Dec. 4, 1965).

The Review and Herald publishing plant had grown to be one of the largest and best-equipped publishing establishments in the state of Michigan. Now it was just a pile of rubble. Why?

As some of the board members stood and watched the flames, there must have come to their minds one sentence in a letter from Ellen White, written from California and addressed to the manager of the Review and Herald. It had been read to the board 13 months earlier: "I have been almost afraid to open the *Review*, fearing to see that God has cleansed the publishing house by fire" (8T, p. 91).

THE WORD REACHES ELLEN WHITE

That Tuesday night Ellen White at her Elmshaven home had slept but little. In vision she had agonized over conditions in Battle Creek. As she came down for breakfast on Wednesday morning, Sara McEnterfer told her that the Review and Herald publishing plant had burned the night before; C. H. Jones had telephoned the news. It came as no surprise to Ellen White. Only a few days before, with pen in hand, she lost consciousness of her surroundings and again saw a sword of fire over Battle Creek, "turning first in one direction and then in another," with disaster following disaster (letter 37, 1903).

The sanitarium had burned in February; now the Review was gone. Picking up her pen, she wrote to Edson:

Oh, I am feeling so sad, because . . . the Lord has permitted this, because His people would not hear His warnings and repent, and be converted, that He should heal them. Many have despised the words of warning. Oh, how sad it is. How large the loss is of books and furniture and facilities. . . . May the Lord have mercy upon us is my prayer (letter 214, 1902).

For 10 years Ellen White had been noting the developments in the management of the Review and Herald publishing house, and the agony of soul she had suffered reached an almost unbearable level during the weeks before the fire. Managers had lost their sense of justice and responsibility. Employees had lost much of their unselfish dedication and consecration. Boards had lost their power to control in right lines. It was a gradual process that was frowned upon by Heaven, and warning after warning had been sounded by God's messenger. But these were for the most part ignored or scorned.

Primarily this was because of two situations: (1) injustice to authors by the instigation of policies that would deny them their just rewards for their literary work, and (2) inequity in dealing with publishing house personnel. Managers argued that it was because of the skill and ability of those in management that the work prospered, so the men in positions of responsibility should receive double the pay of the skilled workmen in the plant.

Added to this were the pressures being brought by men in the publishing house to put the Review office in control of all publishing work in North America. The Pacific Press in Oakland, California, would be but a branch of the Review and Herald, with all decisions made in Battle Creek. Steps that virtually would bring about the consolidation of the publishing work were introduced as early as 1889 at the General Conference session, and developed in 1891. In fact, propositions along this line had been made before James White's death in 1881.

From Australia Ellen White wrote in 1896:

The Lord has presented matters before me that cause me to tremble for the institutions at Battle Creek. . . .

The scheme for consolidation is detrimental to the cause of present truth. Battle Creek has all the power she should have. Some in that place have advanced selfish plans, and if any branch of the work promised a measure of success, they have not exercised the spirit which lets well enough alone, but have made an effort to attach these interests to the great whole. They have striven to embrace altogether too much, and yet they are eager to get more (letter 81, 1896).

Most distressing of all was the general deterioration of the spiritual experience of the Review management and workers and the eroding of a sense of right, which allowed for the commercial work to bring demoralizing publications into the manufacturing plant. Taking the stance that they were printers and not censors, management authorized the printing of publications that came far short of Adventist moral standards. There were no restraints established that regulated the type of literature that would be published. Presses poured forth fiction, Wild West stories, books promulgating Roman Catholic doctrines, sex literature, and books on hypnosis. The managers looked upon the publishing house as a commercial enterprise whose first obligation was to make money.

LAST-MINUTE WARNINGS

On July 8, 1901, Ellen White wrote to the manager of the Review and Herald:

> Unjust, unholy actions have brought the frown of God upon the Review and Herald office. Evil work has brought the cause of God into disrepute, and has kept the backslider from obeying His holy law (letter 74, 1901).

Conditions worsened during 1901, in spite of the many messages of warning. Frank Belden charged that the foreman was "brutal," and that he sometimes required employees to clean his bicycle on office time. One man still living in 1970 recalled his days in the Review pressroom where he began work at the age of 14 in 1896. He was still working there when the fire struck, and he left the building just minutes before the flames swept through it. He recalled a book on witchcraft being printed there, and a pressman printing copies of *Bible Readings* while spitting tobacco juice onto the press. This young man was ridiculed by other workers when he decided to be baptized. The terror engendered by the harsh manner of his superiors led him to wish that the next day would never come. There were young women workers who read proof on books that were filled with skepticism about religion and who then brought this skepticism into their talk around the office.

"We have no permission from the Lord," wrote Ellen White, "to engage either in the printing or in the sale of such publications, for they are the means of destroying many souls. I know of what I am writing, for this matter has been opened before me. Let not those who believe the message for this time engage in such work, thinking to make money" (7T, p. 166). About this time she made a most interesting observation, one that shows an insight God gave to her:

> Even the men who are endeavoring to exalt their own sentiments as wonderful science are astonished that men in positions of responsibility

in our office of publication—a printing office set for the defense of the truth of God—have consented to print their books (MS 124, 1901).

In her distress and in a desperate attempt to halt the satanic work, Ellen White called for a virtual boycott on the part of the employees in the publishing house. After depicting the demoralizing effects of the literature being printed on the Review and Herald presses—including love stores and books setting forth crimes, atrocities, and licentious practices—she pointed out that the position taken by the managers (that they carried no responsibility for the type of books coming from their presses and that the employees had no responsibility in the choice of the nature of the materials that passed through the publishing house) was wrong. She declared:

> In these matters a responsibility rests not only upon the managers but upon the employees. . . . Let typesetters refuse to set a sentence of such matter. Let proofreaders refuse to read, pressmen to print, and binders to bind it (7T, pp. 167, 168).

Somehow those who managed the work had become hardened against the messages that God had sent. Now on Wednesday morning, December 31, 1902, all that was left of the great Review and Herald publishing plant, except for the West Building book depository, were warm embers, collapsed brick walls, and twisted machinery. Nothing of any value was left.

The sword of fire over Battle Creek had fallen, and all knew that God had spoken.

THE 1903 GENERAL CONFERENCE SESSION

THE PRESESSION

Oakland, California, had been chosen as the site for the 1903 General Conference session. The session was to open on Friday, March 27, and run through a third Sabbath. Meetings would be held in the Oakland church. Most of the delegates would stay in the homes of church members and would breakfast with their hosts. A large tent was pitched across the street from the church, where noon and evening meals would be served by the staff of the San Francisco vegetarian restaurant. A vacant home in Oakland had been rented for the use of Ellen White and her staff during the General Conference session.

On Monday, March 23, Mrs. White traveled to Oakland. Willie had gone on one day in advance. Sara McEnterfer, Maggie Hare, C. C. Crisler, and D. E. Robinson went along with Ellen White. She had hoped that they could drive down, or at least that she could have access to a carriage while she was there, for carriage rides rested her when she was under pressure. This was not feasible, so a comfortable wheelchair was rented that would aid her in going from the rented home to the church where the meetings were held.

On Tuesday morning Elder Daniells, knowing that Ellen White had arrived in Oakland, went to greet her and welcome her. He wondered, How will she greet me? He knew of a 70-page letter Dr. Kellogg had written to prejudice her against him. He knew that if anyone could influence her it was Dr. Kellogg.[1] As he stepped up onto the porch he found the front door standing open. He looked down the hall and saw Ellen White seated in a rocking chair in the kitchen. He made his way down the hall to the kitchen. When she saw him approaching she called, "Come in, Brother Daniells." Grasping his hand in a warm greeting and looking him in the eye, she said, "Do you know we are facing a great crisis at this meeting?"

"Yes, Sister White," he replied.

She gripped his hand tighter and with a snap in her eyes said, "Don't you waver a particle in this crisis."

To this Daniells replied, "Sister White, those are the most precious words I ever heard. I know who you are and what you mean" (DF 15a, AGD, "How the

Denomination Was Saved From Pantheism," copy A, pp. 16, 17).

Then the Lord's messenger disclosed the forces behind the issues they faced. "Let me tell you," she said, "Satan has his representatives right here at this place now, and the Lord has bidden me, Have no interview with Dr. Kellogg, no counsel whatever with that man" (ibid., p. 17).

This session would be different from any that had preceded it. With the new union conferences functioning well, many matters that normally would come to the General Conference were being handled by union conference committees.

It was planned that this session would be "more a council of leading workers than an occasion for instructing the multitude" (20 WCW, p. 381). This would allow the rank and file of denominational workers to continue their labor in the field. There would be fewer delegates than assembled for the 1901 session at Battle Creek—initial provision called for 134.

This was the first General Conference session under the new constitution that had been adopted two years before. Not only was the plan for union conferences working well, but the various corporations and associations were being developed into departments under the direction of the General Conference Committee.

One weakness in the 1901 constitution had been early discovered, that the work as outlined by the delegates was to be administered by the General Conference Committee of 25, under officers of its choosing—a chairman, a secretary, and a treasurer. Under this arrangement the church officers had no mandate from the people. They were responsible only to a committee of 25.

ELDER DANIELLS' CONCERNS

Elder Daniells was weary from administrative conflicts and challenges. He pondered whether he should lay down the responsibilities of leadership and engage in another line of work, possibly in evangelism in some other part of the world field. But he was the man in the saddle. With other workers he made the trip from Battle Creek to Oakland in time for a week of presession meetings.

On several occasions Daniells related the experience that came to him at this time. He set apart Sabbath, March 21, preceding the General Conference session, as a day of special personal fasting and prayer. He felt he must know his duty. He went to one of the offices in the Pacific Press publishing house where he could spend the day in study, meditation, and prayer, longing for some omen that would give him courage to move into the session. Through the day and into the evening he remained there. As he knelt in a final prayer, the burden that he might get into true relationship with God's great work on earth rolled upon his heart.

In recounting the story just a few hours before his death, he said, "I struggled unto death, crying aloud, and I nearly reproached the Lord for not giving me some sign, some evidence of my acceptance, and His support of me in the awful battle that was before us." During this struggle he prostrated himself on the floor, clutching, as it were, at the floorboards as he agonized with God. All night he wrestled with the Lord. Then as the morning sun burst into the room, "as distinctly as if audibly spoken, the words burned into my mind as a message from heaven, 'If you will stand by My servant until her sun sets in a bright sky, I will stand by you to the last hour of the conflict'" (AGD, *The Abiding Gift of Prophecy*, p. 367).

"I couldn't talk any more with God," he said. "I was overcome. And although I have made mistakes, God has stood by me, and I have never repudiated that woman, nor questioned her loyalty, to my knowledge, from that night to this. Oh, that was a happy experience to me and it bound me up with the greatest character that has lived in this dispensation" (DF 312c, "Report of a Parting Interview Between AGD and WCW, Mar. 20, 1935," p. 5).

> "Every doubt was removed," he reported on another occasion. I knew that I must not run away from the work to which I had been called by my brethren, and that I must stand with them at my post of duty. I was deeply impressed that I must be as true as the needle to the pole to the counsels of the Spirit of Prophecy, that I must stand loyally by the Lord's servant, upholding her hands, and leading this denomination to recognize and appreciate her heaven-sent gift. . . . I then made my solemn promise to the Lord that I would be true to His cause, that I would do all in my power to prevent anything from arising in this denomination to dim the glory of the priceless gift and of the Lord's servant who had exercised this gift for so many years (AGD, *The Abiding Gift of Prophecy*, p. 367).

The experience, Elder Daniells said, "marked the beginning of an important era of wholehearted acceptance of the Spirit of Prophecy" (*ibid.*, p. 366).

Near the time for the opening of the session Ellen White put into the hands of the delegates and others some of the testimonies that touched on many of the points at issue. The 96-page pamphlet presenting *Selections From the Testimonies for the Church for the Study of Those Attending the General Conference in Oakland, California, March 27, 1903* was printed by the Pacific Press. A wide range of topics was represented in this pamphlet. There was special emphasis on the fires in Battle Creek, debt liquidation, and her vision of the 1901 session concerning "what might have been"; there were various items dealing with the churches, consolidation of the publishing work, the work in the South, the Southern Publishing Association, and the use of the *Morning Star*. It closed with references to the work at home and abroad.

THE BUSINESS OF THE CONFERENCE

The business of the conference proper began Monday morning at 9:30. After a roll call of the delegates, the chairman, Elder Daniells, gave his address. In his opening remarks he spoke of the efficient functioning of the union conferences and observed, "Scores of men are now getting the experience of burden-bearing that was previously confined to comparatively few" (GCB 1903, p. 18).

He then introduced the very difficult financial situation in which he found the denomination, and the improved security of its institutions. Speaking of God's leadings through the Spirit of Prophecy, he stated that "another phase of reform to which this people were called was to arise and roll away the reproach of debt that rested so heavily upon them" (ibid.). The General Conference had been operating on a cash basis, reported Daniells, and had reduced the debts of the denomination by $250,000 (ibid., p. 19). World membership at the end of 1902 stood at 67,000 (ibid., p. 120).

The first motion placed before the General Conference was significant and far-reaching:

> That Elder A. G. Daniells, chairman of the General Conference Committee, be, and is hereby, instructed to appoint a committee of five to examine into the financial standing of all our various institutions, and to investigate their relationship to the Seventh-day Adventist denomination, and to devise and recommend some plan to this conference whereby all institutions, as far as possible under existing corporation laws, be placed under direct ownership, control, and management of our people (ibid., p. 21).

The motion was right to the point and highlighted important work to be taken up at the session. It was referred to the Plans Committee, to be brought to the session in proper fashion. But another issue that threatened the cause lurked in the shadows—pantheism, propagated by Dr. Kellogg and his associates.

The business meetings of the General Conference session had been relieved of many of the details that had come before previous sessions, so there was time for discussion of two main items: the ownership of institutions, and the new constitution under which leading officers would be elected by delegates. A few days after the opening of the conference the Committee on Plans and Constitution submitted a partial report, recommending:

"That the General Conference offices be removed from Battle Creek, Michigan, to some place favorable for its work in the Atlantic States" (GCB 1903, p. 67).

As Dr. Kellogg occupied the second Sunday afternoon of the conference with his review of his experience with the Battle Creek Sanitarium, some rather sharp things were said at times. After lengthy debate, the following action was taken about control of institutions:

> All institutions created directly by the people, through either General Conference, Union Conference, State Conference, or mission field organization, to be owned by the people, through these or other such organizations as the people may elect (*ibid.*, p. 223).

THE NEW CONSTITUTION

The second major debate of the 1903 General Conference session, which came toward the end of the meeting, was centered upon the new constitution, specifically the provision for the election of a president and other appropriate officers for the General Conference. Although it was but a slight revision of the 1901 constitution, it was handled as a new document.

Two reports were filed with the session from the Committee on Plans and Constitution. The majority report supported the new constitution, which provided that the leading officers of the General Conference would be chosen by the delegates, thus giving them a mandate from the church. On this committee were a number of conference presidents and W. C. White. The minority report, signed by three men largely connected with institutional interests, claimed that the proposed new constitution would reverse the reformatory steps taken at the General Conference of 1901. These men argued that the constitution of 1901, which provided that the General Conference Committee could choose its officers, should not be "annihilated" without giving it a fair trial.

Dr. Kellogg strongly favored the minority report. In a letter written to Ellen White on the day of the opening of the session, he referred to "the schemes of Daniells and Prescott to become rulers over Israel," which would be "in direct opposition to the whole plan of reorganization which the Lord gave us through you at the last General Conference."

The matter was not settled quickly. A vote with a three-fourths majority was needed. At the close of the evening meeting, April 9, 1903, the vote was taken, with 108 delegates present. Eighty-five voted in favor of the majority report.

Another significant action provided for the use of tithe money for the support of widows and orphans of workers (GCB 1903, p. 135).

ELLEN WHITE'S MESSAGES TO THE DELEGATES

On Saturday night, March 28, Ellen White was shown in vision what she should bring to the session. This led her to request the privilege of addressing the delegates on Monday afternoon. In place of the regular business meeting she presented a sermon on Josiah's reign.[2] She spoke of the investigation that was made by the king and of the punishment for apostasy. She declared:

> Today God is watching His people. We should seek to find out what He means when He sweeps away our sanitarium and our publishing house. Let us not move along as if there were nothing wrong. King Josiah rent his robe and rent his heart. He wept and mourned because he had not had the book of the law, and knew not of the punishments that it threatened.
>
> God wants us to come to our senses. He wants us to seek for the meaning of the calamities that have overtaken us, that we may not tread in the footsteps of Israel, and say, "The temple of the Lord, the temple of the Lord are we," when we are not this at all (ibid., p. 31).

Sabbath morning she had said:

> God wants to work for His people and for His institutions—for every sanitarium, every publishing house, and every school, but He wants no more mammoth buildings erected, for they are a snare. For years He has told His people this (ibid., p. 10).

Wednesday morning, April 1, she spoke at the devotional service. She dealt with faultfinding and criticizing, backbiting and cannibalism. Then she began to deal with the church institutions and some of the problems faced by those institutions.

She reminded her audience of the financial embarrassment that had come to the publishing house in Christiania (Oslo), Norway. Some wanted to let the house sink in its financial problems, but she said that "light was given me that the institution was to be placed where it could do its work" (ibid., p. 58). Then she came to the question of the Battle Creek Sanitarium, which was on the minds of many, for the institution was being rebuilt at a cost of two or three times what had been estimated. Large debts were accumulating. Some in the meeting were probably surprised when they heard the words:

> Let me say that God does not design that the sanitarium that has been erected in Battle Creek shall be in vain. He wants His people to understand this.
>
> He wants this institution to be placed on vantage ground. He does not want His people to be looked upon by the enemy as a people that is going out of sight (ibid.).

She called for another effort to place the institution on solid ground, and declared, "The people of God must build that institution up, in the name of the Lord."

One man is not to stand at its head alone. Dr. Kellogg has carried the burden until it has almost killed him. God wants His servants to stand united in carrying that work forward (*ibid.*).

Before she closed her presentation, she declared:

Because men have made mistakes, they are not to be uprooted. The blessing of God heals; it does not destroy. The Mighty Healer, the great Medical Missionary, will be in the midst of us, to heal and bless, if we will receive Him (*ibid.*, p. 59).

Note Ellen White's relationship to situations of this kind. She knew that some institutions had been overbuilt, in disregard of counsel that God had given. But even though mistakes had been made, she contended that these were God's institutions, that the church was to stand by them and make them succeed.

At the close of Ellen White's devotional message on the second Sunday morning of the session, as she was stepping down from the platform, a man rushed forward and attempted to assault her. The man was Helge Nelson, who claimed to have the prophetic gift, and two years earlier had sought repeatedly for an opportunity to speak publicly at the General Conference. Of his attempted attack on Mrs. White this Sunday morning, a newspaper reported:

The venerable exhorter staggered against the pulpit platform steps and tottered feebly as she was grasped by a number of men who were close by, as the hand of her attacker descended upon the unsuspecting woman. Quickly, amid the scene of much commotion, "Angel Nelson" [the title assumed by her attacker] was hustled out of the church by some stout-armed elders. While others attended the stricken woman, Alonzo T. Jones, president of the California Conference of Seventh-day Adventists, summoned the police and Nelson was hustled off to the city prison by Patrolman Flynn and charged with battery.

The report stated that "Mrs. White regained her composure shortly, and happily received the congratulations of her friends that the assault had not caused more serious trouble" (DF 586).

Although Nelson had not been given an opportunity to speak in 1901, he did meet with some of the leading church workers. He related to the brethren his experience and what he understood to be his call. In this committee meeting Ellen White recounted her earlier contacts with Mr. Nelson. She told of how he had come to her home in California and she had spent time listening to him. She stated: "God has not given Brother Nelson the work of acting as Joshua in connection with His people. From the light that I have had, this could not be. It is an impossibility" (RH, July 30, 1901). She closed her remarks by saying:

> We love our brother. We want him to be saved, but we cannot allow him to take the time of this conference. It is not his time. God has given us a work to do, and we intend to do it, under His supervision, that souls may be brought to a knowledge of present truth (ibid.).

THE MOVE TO WASHINGTON, D.C.

To move the General Conference offices from their rented quarters in the West Building of the Review and Herald would be quite simple. But to close up the business of the publishing house in Battle Creek and reestablish it elsewhere would involve legal and deeply emotional factors.

The Review and Herald constituency meeting that convened in Battle Creek from April 21 to 29, 1903, was far from tranquil. Church leaders and the majority of the constituency favored the move from Battle Creek, but a relatively few constituent members bitterly opposed it. The Spirit of Prophecy counsels were clearly the deciding factor. The final vote was overwhelmingly in favor of moving. But the vote did not resolve legal matters. The General Conference and the publishing house had been closely connected through the years, and now in the proposed move, both were involved and both must be considered at the same time. The question was whether the move was to be to one location or two.

On May 15 Elder Daniells addressed a letter to Ellen White in which he indicated his need for divine guidance. This appeal for divine help was typical of his letters during the next five months. To this appeal Mrs. White replied immediately:

> Dear Brother Daniells: We have received your letter in regard to the selection of a place for the Review and Herald publishing house.
>
> I have no special light, except what you have already received, in reference to New York and the other large cities that have not been worked. Decided efforts should be made in Washington, D. C. . . .
>
> May the Lord help us to move understandingly and prayerfully. I am sure that He is willing that we should know, and that right early, where we should locate our publishing house. I am satisfied that our only safe course is to be ready to move just when the cloud moves (letter 95, 1903).

The committee that was appointed in mid-June to seek a suitable location found two promising sites. One was a 97-acre (39-hectare) tract 60 miles (96 kilometers) north of New York at Fishkill, New York, on the Hudson River, where a retired businessman had built a 40-room hotel with many attractive features. It was for sale for $12,000.

A portion of the locating committee, including Elder Daniells, mindful of Ellen White's instruction to give careful consideration to the advantages of Washington, spent four days there and were immediately impressed that the environs of that city possessed many favorable qualities as headquarters for the church.

TAKOMA PARK

The impression grew as the men investigated properties in the close vicinity of the nation's capital. Daniells reported to W. C. White and his mother:

> One of the finest places we have found was a place called Takoma Park. It is on the main line of the Baltimore and Ohio Railroad running to Chicago and St. Louis. It is also reached by an electric line. It is five or six miles (eight or ten kilometers) from the city. It is . . . a large wooded tract of land, lying on each side of the District line, part in the District and part in Maryland. It has an elevation of three hundred feet above the Potomac. It is a magnificent place. We could purchase all the land we required at a very reasonable rate (AGD to WCW, June 21, 1903).

As committee members studied the matter, their recommendation was to give Washington first consideration, but they wanted to retain the option to purchase the Fishkill property.

There were many Battle Creek Adventists who were not eager to see the General Conference and the Review and Herald printing plant leave the city. Three hundred people had been employed in the plant. Many owned their own homes and some had rental properties; they feared personal financial disaster. Then too, the burgeoning cereal food industry, pioneered by the Kelloggs but now far beyond their control, had made Battle Creek a boom town.

But more disturbing to church leaders were the lawsuits threatened by certain disaffected members of the Review and Herald constituency. These could tie things up in legal battles for years.

"We are in a dreadful place," wrote Daniells to the Lord's messenger. "God must help us. We are helpless" (AGD to EGW, July 5, 1903).

In agonizing words he poured out his soul:

> Sister White, the hour has struck for something to be done. We are in peril. The stability of this cause is at stake. This involves the honor of God and the welfare of thousands of innocent, faithful believers in this message. Unless I am altogether deceived, we are face to face with a crisis. . . .
>
> I want to tell you that I realize as I never have in all my life the need, and

the value to the church, of the Spirit of Prophecy. The working of Satan at this present time is surely with all power, and signs, and lying wonders (*ibid.*).

On W. C. White's arrival in Battle Creek the men hastened to the East to look at the New York and Washington properties. In spite of a pledge made by the real estate agent to hold the Fishkill property, they found it had been sold by another agent (AGD to EGW, July 23, 1903).

In Washington they hurried out to Takoma Park and found "a fifty-acre [20-hectare] block of land" about a mile (two kilometers) from the post office. This had been developed by a Dr. Flower, who founded a medical institution in Boston and planned to open one in the Washington area. After investing $60,000 in the land and clearing it, he ran into financial trouble. It was now in the hands of a man who, although he held a $15,000 mortgage on it, was willing to sell for $6,000. Daniells wrote: "We paid $100 to bind the bargain." They praised God for His opening providence (*ibid.*). Fifty acres (20 hectares) of well-located land seven miles (11 kilometers) from the U.S. Capitol, situated by a beautiful stream, Sligo Creek, for $120 per acre! In their initial planning the brethren saw this as most suitable for sanitarium and school purposes.

Recognizing the advantage of Seventh-day Adventist literature bearing a Washington, D.C., imprint, the men projected that they could also buy a tract of several acres just a mile [two kilometers] to the south, inside the District of Columbia, for a modest investment. Daniells promised Ellen White: "We shall counsel with you freely on this point" (*ibid.*).

Anticipating an immediate move, they sought and found in downtown Washington a building with 16 rooms, just a few blocks from the U.S. Capitol, which could serve as a temporary headquarters. It seemed to be "just the place." Some printing equipment could be installed in the basement and first-floor rooms. They would take possession August 15 or a little earlier.

Daniells went on to report to Mrs. White:

> There was not a dissenting voice among the brethren who were engaged in this important move. The blessing of the Lord rested upon us as we made our decisions day by day. . . . We believe that the good hand of our God is leading us (*ibid.*).

A new printing corporation was formed while the men were in Washington. The address, 222 North Capitol Street, would be shared by the new publishing concern and the General Conference office; operations would begin in Washington in three weeks' time—August 15, 1903.

Knowing Ellen White as he did, Daniells wrote: "I am expecting that before spring you will feel it your duty to come to Washington to see our situation, and counsel with us regarding the work" (*ibid.*). He even proposed putting up on the new land a little cottage that she could occupy. These propositions Ellen White would not forget.

BATTLE CREEK BELIEVERS RESPOND TO THE PROPOSED MOVE

The members of the Battle Creek Tabernacle church had to be apprised of the decision to move to Washington. Sabbath morning, July 25, Elder Daniells laid the whole matter before the congregation. He read from three or four of Ellen White's communications that gave instruction as to where they should go. The meeting continued in the afternoon. Elder Prescott read from other E. G. White testimonies and Elder Daniells followed, relating to the church "the providences of God that have opened before us as we have endeavored to walk in the light as given through the Spirit of Prophecy" (AGD to EGW, July 27, 1903).

The opposition that the leading men expected from many of the Battle Creek Adventists when it became known that they were leaving the city did not materialize. The plain instructions and the review of God's leadings and providences made a profound impression, and tears flowed freely.

"There was a softening and subduing influence present in our midst," wrote Daniells to Ellen White. He reported that he had learned that "this experience has given many of our brethren and sisters renewed confidence that the Lord is leading in this work" (*ibid.*). Further, he wrote: "I do not think I have seen the Tabernacle congregation so deeply interested and so thoroughly stirred over anything since the last conference here two years ago" (*ibid.*).

THE PROMPT MOVE TO WASHINGTON

Packing began at once. Two freight cars were loaded with General Conference furniture and documents on Monday and Tuesday, August 3 and 4. They left Battle Creek on the fifth and were in Washington on August 10. Printing equipment from the West Building followed shortly.

The last issue of the *Review and Herald* printed in Battle Creek carried the date Tuesday, August 11. The next issue bore the dateline, Washington, D.C., Thursday, August 20. To many Adventists across the land, the fact that their *Review* came two days late provided the first knowledge that the headquarters of the church and the printing equipment had been moved.

Elder Daniells and others were convinced that God had led in the move. This is apparent from Elder Daniells' letter to Ellen White, the first to be sent from the new Washington headquarters:

Dear Sister White: I am enclosing a copy of a letter I have just written to Brother White about our experiences this week in Washington. I know that you will be anxious to hear from us, and so I send you this copy. I cannot tell you, Sister White, what a blessing we experience as we enter upon our duties in this place. Surely the Lord's hand is in this move. I never felt such confidence in God's leadership in this work as I have since we started out from Battle Creek to find a location in the East.

I believe that He was speaking to us and that if we would obey His voice implicitly and not swerve nor follow our own notions He would give us unmistakable evidence regarding the right place; but, oh, what little conception I had of how clear and how comforting that evidence would be. I cannot tell you what this experience has done for my heart; but I can say that it leads me to a new and full surrender of my life to God and His work.

I see as never before the folly of doubting and hesitating and swerving from the instruction God gives His people. We shall never know until the books unfold it how much has been lost to this cause by failing to render prompt and implicit obedience to all that God calls upon us to do. I must write you again regarding some important matters, but will not write more today. Your letters and instruction never were so precious to me as at this time. I am praying God to help me to not falter whatever may come. Please be free to counsel me as the Lord instructs (AGD to EGW, Aug. 14, 1903).

---

[1] In December Dr. Kellogg dictated a 70-page letter to Ellen White—a letter clearly aimed at alienating her from Arthur Daniells and gaining her support for himself. It was a letter in which the doctor used every possible argument he could summon to influence her. A close associate of Elder Daniells' learned of the letter and reported the matter to him. He decided he must write to Ellen White, presenting his side of the story. That evening he sat down and wrote one page and started on another. Then he came to himself. "What are you doing?" he asked himself. "Are you helping the Lord to give Sister White information which she should have? I guess He is able to do it Himself." He tore up the sheet, "threw it into the wastebasket, and never wrote her a line" (DF 15a AGD, "How the Denomination Was Saved From Pantheism," copy A, p. 15).

[2] She likened the situation in modern Israel to that in the time of Josiah (see *Prophets and Kings*, pp. 392ff.), when the chosen people of God had neglected the counsels of God insofar as to allow the book of the law, which contained the statutes recorded by Moses, not only to be disobeyed but to be lost in the Temple for 100 years. The biblical record (2 Kings 23) reveals the depth of iniquity into which they had fallen, having adopted the idolatrous rites of the Canaanites: burning incense unto Baal and to the sun, moon, and the planets, and all the host of heaven; their "houses of sodomites"; and sacrifices of their children to Molech.

JOHN HARVEY KELLOGG AND *THE LIVING TEMPLE*

DR. KELLOGG INTRODUCES PANTHEISTIC TEACHINGS

Ellen White had had a long and close relationship with John Kellogg ever since he completed his medical training in 1876 and began teaching in the early days of the health institute. He had been a pillar of strength and influence as the medical work expanded. She had written him thousands of pages of letters and counsel and guidance. She had watched with a mother's love and interest his success in developing the medical work. Frequently she defended him against opposition and criticism of those less talented than he. She said:

> Many souls have been converted; many wonderful cures have been wrought. The Lord stood by the side of Dr. Kellogg as he performed difficult operations. When the doctor was overwrought by taxing labor, God understood the situation, and He put His hand on Dr. Kellogg's hand as he operated, and through His power the operations were successful. I wish this to be understood. . . .
>
> God has given Dr. Kellogg the success that he has had. I have tried constantly to keep this before him, telling him that it was God who was working with him, and that the truth of God was to be magnified by His physician. . . .
>
> God does not endorse the efforts put forth by different ones to make the work of Dr. Kellogg as hard as possible, in order to build themselves up. God gave the light on health reform, and those who rejected it rejected God. One and another who knew better said that it all came from Dr. Kellogg, and they made war upon him (GCB 1903, pp. 86, 87).

There is no question that Dr. Kellogg was an unselfish, dedicated, much-loved man. He was a generous, great man. But it was largely, yet not altogether, through Dr. John Harvey Kellogg that the great adversary introduced into the ranks of Seventh-day Adventists the seeds of error in the form of so-called new light, just at a time when the medical work was at its height.

Pantheism is the term used to designate the strange new teachings that were being introduced. Pantheism pictures God not as a great personal Being but as a mysterious essence—an impersonal influence pervading all nature. God is seen in all nature—in trees, flowers, sunshine, air, and human beings. The power of God in nature is confused with the personality of God.

Dr. Kellogg had toyed with these concepts before James White's death in 1881, and, considering it "great light," had discussed it with Ellen White. "Those theories are wrong," she told him. "I have met them before." He seemed dazed as she showed him the outcome of espousing such a philosophy. She then admonished, "Never teach such theories in our institutions; do not present them to the people" (MS 70, 1905).

Kellogg first introduced pantheism publicly in 1897 in a series of talks at the ministerial institute that preceded the General Conference session held in the College View church at Lincoln, Nebraska. He drew heavily upon Ellen White in laying out his position that God works through nature and in nature. His next presentation carried the title "God in Man." Under this title he gave several talks in which he set forth clearly the pantheistic philosophy he held:

> Gravitation acts instantaneously throughout all space. By this mysterious force of gravitation the whole universe is held together in a bond of unity. . . . We have here the evidence of a universal presence, an intelligent presence, an all-wise presence, an all-powerful presence, a presence by the aid of which every atom of the universe is kept in touch with every other atom. This force that holds all things together, that is everywhere present, that thrills throughout the whole universe, that acts instantaneously through boundless space, can be nothing else than God Himself. What a wonderful thought that this same God is in us and in everything (GCB 1897, p. 83).

In words that seemed to put humanity above God, he boldly declared:

> What a wonderful thought, that this mighty God that keeps the whole universe in order, is in us! . . . What an amazing thing that this almighty, all-powerful, and all-wise God should make Himself a servant of man by giving man a free will—power to direct the energy within his body! (ibid.).

Pantheistic views became popular and were taught in Battle Creek College. They were taught in the sanitarium, and were defended by some physicians and some ministers.

Ministers and physicians who had a high regard for Dr. Kellogg began to imbibe his philosophy and to develop it in their own work, not sensing the point to which it would lead. One such was E. J. Waggoner, who was also a physician. He was at one time editor of the *Signs of the Times* and the man who, with A. T. Jones, was used mightily of God at the General Conference session in 1888 to focus attention on the message of righteousness by faith. Elder Waggoner, one of the denomination's highly respected speakers, was repeatedly called upon at the time of General Conference sessions to conduct series of Bible studies.

At the General Conference session of 1899, held at South Lancaster, Massachusetts, Waggoner was a delegate from England, where he was engaged in editorial work. In a discussion of health and temperance, he was asked to make a presentation of some things he had been giving to the Battle Creek Sanitarium family. He opened with the rather bold statement:

> I thank God, brethren, that the Lord has taught me something in the last few months, and enabled me to teach something of how to live forever (GCB 1899, p. 53).

W. A. Spicer, who was serving with Elder Daniells in the General Conference as the newly appointed secretary of the Foreign Mission Board, had spent years of service in India. He was astonished at this teaching that was being proclaimed around Battle Creek. He recognized it as pantheism, which is the basis of Hinduism. He asked himself, "Could it be that the philosophies of heathenism are being taught by leading men in the Seventh-day Adventist Church?"

During the General Conference session held in Oakland in 1903, Ellen White spent most of the time in an agony of soul as she watched the crisis developing over the threat of pantheism, and Dr. Kellogg determinedly pushing ahead to override all contrary views. She knew that Elder Daniells was suffering with the weight of the responsibility. She wrote frequent letters to Dr. Kellogg urging him to rethink his position. "You are not definitely clear on the personality of God, which is everything to us as a people" (letter 300, 1903).

Again on April 5, while at the session, she wrote to the doctor:

> The specious, scheming representations of God in nature carry their charming, soothing influence as a peace and safety pill to give to the people, in the spiritualistic* views that Satan has instituted in your theories (letter 301, 1903).

She wrote to him a second letter on the same day. In this letter she said:

> Your ideas are so mystical that they are destructive to the real substance, and the minds of some are becoming confused in regard to the foundation of our faith. If you allow your mind to become thus diverted, you will give a wrong mold to the work that has made us what we are— Seventh-day Adventists (letter 52, 1903).

After the session closed, Ellen White wrote to Elder Daniells, "If you can move so wisely as to save Dr. Kellogg, and not sacrifice one principle of truth, if you can pass through this crisis without the loss of one soul, it will be because the Lord has worked with minds" (letter 49, 1903).

She knew that A. T. Jones, a General Conference Committee member, and Dr. Kellogg had worked very closely together, sympathized with each other on the principles of organization, and seemingly had a good rapport. Jones would be in a position to approach Dr. Kellogg. To Elder Jones she wrote:

> Dear Brother: I am sending to you three manuscripts to be read to the brethren assembled at Battle Creek in council. These I desire that you shall read to the brethren when you discern that the time has come. You know my anxiety regarding the work—my desire that everything possible shall be done to establish unity and drive out dissension. We must do all in our power to save Dr. Kellogg and his associates from the result of the mistakes they have made, and to help them to see and understand the way of the Lord (letter 59, 1903).

Elder Jones received the letter and the documents on Thursday, April 23, and shared them with Elder Daniells, who on Friday wrote to W. C. White:

> Our hearts are all made exceedingly glad by the arrival of the documents your mother has sent. They bring relief to the situation. . . .
>
> The crisis is here. The settlement must now be made. We shall do everything in our power to win every brother over to the right side, but we cannot compromise nor surrender the banner at this time (AGD to WCW, Apr. 24, 1903).

THE LIVING TEMPLE

On February 18, 1902, the Battle Creek Sanitarium burned to the ground, and the denomination was confronted with the matter of rebuilding. Dr. Kellogg came to the General Conference Committee and asked what the General Conference could do to help. Thinking of the effort being made in the selling of *Christ's Object Lessons* to help clear the debts of the church's educational institutions, Elder Daniells suggested that Dr. Kellogg write a simple book on physiology and health care that could be sold by Seventh-day Adventists throughout the United States. Perhaps they could sell a half million copies, and all income from the sale of this book could be used to help rebuild the sanitarium.

This appealed to Dr. Kellogg. But Daniells hastened to say:

> "Now look here, Doctor, that book must not contain a single argument

of this new theory you are teaching, because there are a lot of people [all] over the States who do not accept it. I know from what they say, and if it has any of what they consider pantheism they will never touch it" (DF 15a, AGD, "How the Denomination Was Saved From Pantheism," copy A, p. 3).

And the doctor replied, "Oh yes, oh yes, I understand that." And Daniells reiterated the point: "You must leave all that out" (*ibid.*). Dr. Kellogg fully agreed. (As Kellogg tells the story, it was he who proposed the book for popular sale. Perhaps the idea originated in the minds of both leaders.) In the summer of 1902 Daniells took the matter to the union presidents, and they promised to support the wide sale of a book that would help raise funds for the sanitarium.

As Elder Daniells took up residence in Battle Creek as the leader of the church following the General Conference of 1901, he found the teachings of pantheism rampant. For years he had been more or less isolated in Australia. He was amazed to hear the talk of God in flowers, in trees, in humankind. The expression was constantly heard: The acorn falls to the ground and a tree springs up. It was argued that one must say there is a tree maker in the tree. It was declared that the Creator, whatever He might be like, was in the things that were made, and some boldly said that there is no great Being sitting on the throne in heaven, but God is in all nature.

Daniells could not accept this, because, as he declared: "I knew that the Bible says that there is a great Supreme Being who had created all things. So I never felt in harmony with this idea" (*ibid.*, p. 2).

Dr. Kellogg was a tireless worker. He dictated a manuscript as quickly as he could, and sent it to the Review and Herald office to be set in type. In the form of galley proofs the book, to be called *The Living Temple*, came to W. W. Prescott, General Conference field secretary, who was serving as acting leader in the absence of Elder Daniells. It also was sent to Dr. Kellogg, who was in Europe.

Elder Prescott called Elder Spicer's attention to some of the chapters. Spicer in turn mentioned to one of Dr. Kellogg's medical associates that he felt wrong ideas were set forth in certain portions of the book.

The medical friend looked the matter over and wrote to Elder Spicer that it was his conviction that the matter in question was quite right and in harmony with the Advent message, although some truths might be expressed differently from a scientific standpoint. He felt that the church ought to be ready to accept advancing light. To this Elder Spicer replied in a letter written June 5, 1902:

> A book to be used as it is purposed that this shall be, in order to pay debts on our sanitariums, must be altogether above question and controversy. It is not a question as to whether our people ought to take advanced

light or not, but simply a question as to rallying everybody to undertake what at best will be a very difficult problem (DF 15c, W. A. Spicer, "How the Spirit of Prophecy Met a Crisis," copy A, p. 18).

Soon after Kellogg's return to Battle Creek, Spicer was invited by the doctor to come to his home for a discussion of the book. The men spent an entire Sabbath afternoon together. From the beginning they were in rather bitter controversy, as the doctor explained that the teachings of the book presented his views in a very modest fashion, and it was his intent to teach that God was in the things of nature.

Later Spicer wrote of the exchange:

> "Where is God?" I was asked. I would naturally say, "He is in heaven; there the Bible pictures the throne of God, all the heavenly beings at His command as messengers between heaven and earth." But I was told that God was in the grass and plants and in the trees. . . .
>
> "Where is heaven?" I was asked. I had my idea of the center of the universe, with heaven and the throne of God in the midst, but disclaimed any attempt to fix the center of the universe astronomically. But I was urged to understand that heaven is where God is, and God is everywhere—in the grass, in the trees, in all creation. There was no place in this scheme of things for angels going between heaven and earth, for heaven was here and everywhere. The cleansing of the sanctuary that we taught about was not something in a faraway heaven. "The sin is here . . . [Dr. Kellogg said, pointing to his heart], and here is the sanctuary to be cleansed" (*ibid.*, pp. 19, 20).

As he left the doctor on that Sabbath afternoon, Spicer reported:

> I knew well enough that there was nothing of the Advent message that could fit into such a philosophy. As I had listened, one light after another of the gospel message seemed to be put out. Religious teaching that to me was fundamental was set aside (*ibid.*, p. 21).

THE GENERAL CONFERENCE COMMITTEE REJECTS THE MANUSCRIPT

A committee of four had been appointed to give study to Kellogg's manuscript, *The Living Temple*, and make a report at the Autumn Council. The majority report stated:

> "That, we find in the book *Living Temple* nothing which appears to us to be contrary to the Bible or fundamental principles of the Christian religion, and that we see no reason why it may not be recommended by

the Committee for circulation in the manner suggested." [Signed] A. T. Jones, J. H. Kellogg, David Paulson (*ibid.*, p. 27).

The minority report, written by W. W. Prescott, read:

> "I am compelled to say that I regard the matter, outside those portions of the book which deal with physiology and hygiene, as leading to harm rather than good; and I venture to express the hope that it will never be published" (*ibid.*).

The General Conference Committee accepted the minority report. In the discussion that followed, according to the minutes, the author requested the privilege of withdrawing the book from consideration. But, according to Elder Daniells, it was not long before Kellogg jumped to his feet and demanded an open hearing so that everybody from the sanitarium and Review and Herald could hear both sides of the matter. He argued that it should not be confined to a small meeting of the General Conference brethren. So it was decided to hold such a meeting in the Review and Herald chapel. Daniells expected that only a relatively few people from the Review and Herald would be able to get off work to attend, although the chapel would hold a big crowd. However, when they met at 8:30 in the morning, the room was packed to the anteroom and down the stairs. The meetings lasted until noon.

Elder Daniells reviewed the history of the church's medical work, the steps being taken to bring the finances into line, and the pantheistic teachings in the galleys of *The Living Temple*. In the afternoon Dr. Kellogg presented his side of the story. Elder Daniells felt that he faced a real crisis in this situation and spent much of the night in study and prayer. The next morning as the Autumn Council attempted to proceed with business, Dr. Kellogg was present with a big pile of books. He asked for a point of privilege that he might present the fact that "from the first, Elder James White, George I. Butler, and all . . . leaders have been absolutely opposed to this medical department of the denomination" (DF 15a, AGD, "How the Denomination Was Saved From Pantheism," copy A, p. 13).

The brethren listened for a while. Finally one of the men stood and asked:

> "Mr. Chairman. I rise to a point of order. I cannot sit here in this committee and listen to these harsh terms that Dr. Kellogg is using against our venerable founder and leader [James White]. I wish the chairman to call him down" (*ibid.*).

The chairman accepted the proposition and declared, "I will say to Dr. Kellogg, 'We do not wish any more of this. You will please terminate your subject'" (*ibid.*, pp. 13, 14). He did, but under protest.

Undaunted, Dr. Kellogg placed a personal order with the Review to print *The Living Temple*. About a month later the Review and Herald burned, and the plates for the book, which stood ready for the press, were destroyed by the fire.

It had been hoped that in connection with the destruction of the book plates in the Review and Herald fire, Dr. Kellogg would abandon the matter of publishing *The Living Temple*. Instead he sent the manuscript to a commercial printer in Battle Creek. Three thousand copies of the book were printed and began to make their way among Seventh-day Adventists.

When the book came from the press, discerning readers clearly saw that certain chapters were literally peppered with pantheistic teachings. Those in sympathy with the new philosophy held that this understanding of God would lead to holy living and to a deeper religious experience. As Seventh-day Adventist workers met, the conversation inevitably turned to the "new light" set forth in *The Living Temple*. Ellen White was still silent on the matter. The book was now in the field and being pressed upon the conferences with the urging that its sale would help to meet the costs of rebuilding the Battle Creek Sanitarium.

The leading officers of the General Conference, on July 31, 1903, wrote a letter to conference presidents, pointing out that the book had been considered at the 1902 Autumn Council, and that certain teachings in it were seriously questioned.

In the meantime the attention of many church leaders was much taken up with moving the Review and Herald and the General Conference headquarters.

Eventually, in the summer of 1903, a copy of *The Living Temple* arrived at Elmshaven. Ellen White did not look at it. This was not unusual, for often in a crisis she refrained from reading materials that had a bearing on the situation, lest it be said she was influenced by what she had read. On the basis of the light she received from the Lord, however, from time to time she mentioned the book.

Finally, as the crisis developed, Willie suggested to her that perhaps she should read some of the passages. So on September 23 he sat down by her side and went over some of the statements dealing with theological matters (22 WCW, p. 219). This put her in a better position to speak more specifically in regard to the book.

When she was questioned as to why she had not spoken publicly about it earlier, she stated that she had assumed that those who were leading the church would have wisdom to know how to deal with problems of this character.

Ellen White fully intended on several occasions at the 1903 General Conference to meet pantheistic teachings explicitly and face-to-face in an open meeting where Dr. Kellogg and his views would be completely exposed. But in each case she had been restrained from doing so. While at the session she was instructed in vision that she "must not say anything that would stir up confusion and strife in the conference" (DF 15c, W. A. Spicer, "How the Spirit of Prophecy Met a Crisis," copy A, p. 30).

That the General Conference session should come to a close without the issues being squarely met was a matter of deep perplexity to not a few, including her own son, W. C. White. But most church leaders understood that God does not deal with such matters precipitously. He did not do so in dealing with Lucifer when he fell in heaven. Things must develop to a certain point before the issues could be met in a way that all would understand what they were and take a safe stand. And so it was seen in 1903 in the case concerning the pantheistic teachings.

THE 1903 AUTUMN COUNCIL

The Autumn Council of the General Conference Committee opened in Washington, D.C., according to plan on October 7, with meetings in the newly acquired M Street church. The brethren entered into their work with dedication and earnestness. In the early days of the council, E. J. Waggoner, A. T. Jones, and David Paulson arrived in Washington. Dr. Kellogg came Sabbath morning, October 17. As the men from Battle Creek presented themselves, it was evident to Elder Daniells and his associates that they would again be confronted with *The Living Temple* and the teaching of pantheism.

Although these elements were not included on the agenda for the council, the regular work was laid aside and a day was given to the consideration of the pantheistic philosophy. The representatives from the field were confused. All day they wrestled with the matter. Some wavered and waffled. About 9:00 in the evening Elder Daniells considered it time to adjourn the meeting, but he did not dare call for a vote. People were too confused and uncertain, and he did not wish to take a step that would solidify any conclusions. So he dismissed the meeting, and the people started to their lodging places.

Dr. Paulson, who was strongly supportive of Dr. Kellogg, joined Daniells. As the two walked along they continued with a discussion of the day. Reaching the home where Daniells was staying, they stood under a lamppost and chatted for a time. Finally Dr. Paulson shook his finger at Daniells and declared:

> "You are making the mistake of your life. After all this turmoil, some of these days you will wake up to find yourself rolled in the dust, and another will be leading the forces" (AGD, *The Abiding Gift of Prophecy*, pp. 336, 337).

Elder Daniells straightened up in his weariness and discouragement, and replied firmly:

"I do not believe your prophecy. At any rate, I would rather be rolled in the dust doing what I believe in my soul to be right than to walk with princes, doing what my conscience tells me is wrong" (*ibid.*, p. 337).

After parting, Daniells entered the home, where he found a group of people awaiting him. They seemed lighthearted and exclaimed: "Deliverance has come! Here are two messages from Mrs. White" (*ibid.*).

THE RIGHT MESSAGE AT THE RIGHT TIME

"No one can imagine," recounted Daniells later, "the eagerness with which I read the documents that had come in the mail while we were in the midst of our discussions. There was a most positive testimony regarding the dangerous errors that were taught in *The Living Temple*" (*ibid.*). The message had come just at the crisis hour. As he read, his eyes fell on these words:

> I have something to say to our teachers in reference to the new book *The Living Temple*. Be careful how you sustain the sentiments of this book regarding the personality of God. As the Lord presents matters to me, these sentiments do not bear the endorsement of God. They are a snare that the enemy has prepared for these last days. . . .
>
> We need not the mysticism that is in this book. Those who entertain these sophistries will soon find themselves in a position where the enemy can talk with them, and lead them away from God. It is represented to me that the writer of this book is on a false track. He has lost sight of the distinguishing truths for this time. He knows not whither his steps are tending.
>
> The track of truth lies close beside the track of error, and both tracks may seem to be one to minds which are not worked by the Holy Spirit, and which, therefore, are not quick to discern the difference between truth and error. . . .
>
> In the visions of the night this matter was clearly presented to me before a large number. One of authority was speaking. . . . The speaker held up *Living Temple*, saying, "In this book there are statements that the writer himself does not comprehend. Many things are stated in a vague, undefined way. Statements are made in such a way that nothing is sure. And this is not the only production of the kind that will be urged upon the people. Fanciful views will be presented by many minds. What we need to know at this time is, What is the truth that will enable us to win the salvation of our souls?" (letter 211, 1903).

The entire manuscript of seven pages was devoted to the subject and was published in the *Review and Herald* of October 22, 1903.

A second document, which Daniells also read, was addressed to "Leaders in

Our Medical Work," and dealt with medical missionary work, the control of medical institutions, and pantheism.

The next morning church leaders assembled for their council. After the prayer Elder Daniells arose and told the leaders he had received two important messages from Sister White. Everyone was eager to hear them. They sat in thoughtful silence while he read. As statement after statement setting forth the falsity of the teachings of *The Living Temple* was presented to the assembly, many loud amens were heard and tears flowed freely. At that moment the tide was turned.

As the reading ended, one of the ministers arose and stated that he felt impressed to ask all who proposed to take a firm stand with Sister White in this great struggle, to arise to their feet. Nearly every person in the room arose (AGD to EGW, Oct. 20, 1903).

At this session of the council Dr. Kellogg responded favorably, saying that he accepted the testimony and that he would modify the wording in *The Living Temple* dealing with theological matters. But his statements were rather erratic and changeable. His attitude alternated, and it finally turned out that the doctor never really changed.

So overwhelmed was Elder Daniells with these events that he could not refrain from mentioning them again and again in his correspondence in the days that followed. On Monday morning, October 20, he wrote to Ellen White:

> Never were messages from God more needed than at this very time; and never were messages sent from Him to His people more to the point than those you have sent to us. They have been exactly what we have needed, and have come at just the right time from day to day in our Council. You can never know, unless the Lord Himself causes you to know it, what a great blessing your communication regarding *The Living Temple* has been to us. It came at just the right time exactly (*ibid.*).

WHY THE MESSAGES CAME WHEN THEY DID

On receiving these communications from Elder Daniells, Ellen White wrote to him explaining why she had sent the messages just when she did:

> Shortly before I sent the testimonies that you said arrived just in time, I had read an incident about a ship in a fog meeting an iceberg. For several nights I slept but little. I seemed to be bowed down as a cart beneath sheaves. One night a scene was clearly presented before me. A vessel was upon the waters, in a heavy fog. Suddenly the lookout cried, "Iceberg just ahead!" There, towering high above the ship, was a gigantic iceberg. An authoritative voice cried out, "Meet it!" There was not a

moment's hesitation. It was a time for instant action. The engineer put on full steam, and the man at the wheel steered the ship straight into the iceberg. With a crash she struck the ice. There was a fearful shock, and the iceberg broke into many pieces, falling with a noise like thunder upon the deck. The passengers were violently shaken by the force of the collision, but no lives were lost. The vessel was injured, but not beyond repair. She rebounded from the contact, trembling from stem to stern, like a living creature. Then she moved forward on her way.

Well I knew the meaning of this representation. I had my orders. I had heard the words, like a living voice from our Captain, "Meet it!" I knew what my duty was, and that there was not a moment to lose. The time for decided action had come. I must without delay obey the command, "Meet it!"

This is why you received the testimonies when you did. That night I was up at one o'clock, writing as fast as my hand could pass over the paper (letter 238, 1903).

During the crisis of 1903 and in the years that followed, Ellen White wrote warnings concerning pantheism to the church and to individuals who were drawn to it.

On September 18, in a letter to Elder Daniells, she referred to Kellogg's experience as a young man back in 1882:

The Lord presented this matter to me, revealing that the result of such teaching was a subtle beguiling of the mind, and that the doctor himself did not foresee this result of his extreme views in regard to God in nature. . . . I told him that the Lord was greatly dishonored by being thus represented, and that such ideas would lead the people into spiritualism* (letter 271a, 1903).

Writing on October 2 to Dr. E. J. Waggoner, she said:

I am authorized to say to you that some of the sentiments regarding the personality of God, as found in the book *Living Temple*, are opposed to the truths revealed in the Word of God. . . . Had God desired to be represented as dwelling personally in the things of nature—in the flower, the tree, the spear of grass—would not Christ have spoken of this to His disciples? (letter 230, 1903).

---

* Note: This term was used several times in this setting to indicate a spiritualizing away of such basic truths as the personality of God.

THE ROUND-TRIP
TO WASHINGTON

From the day that the decision was made to purchase property in Washington, D.C., for the publishing house and the General Conference, it was Elder Daniells' hope and expectation that Ellen White would make a visit to the East so she could give counsel concerning the establishment of the work there. There was even some discussion of the possibility that she would make Washington her permanent place of residence. But this she felt she could not do. At Elmshaven she was in favorable circumstances for bringing out her books, and she felt she should not be called upon to move from place to place.

From time to time definite instruction was given to her in vision concerning the work in Washington. In fact, before the property was secured in Takoma Park, she had been shown that wherever the Review and Herald and the headquarters of the work were established, there should be a sanitarium and a training school. The church leaders had not planned on this. With the decision to make Washington the center in the East, then, the first steps were to get these institutions under way. The leaders felt they must now have Ellen White's help.

The plans being formed would keep her in the East for about a year, making Washington her headquarters. As it turned out, the trip to Washington and back took more than seven months and included side trips to a number of vital areas such as Berrien Springs, Nashville, New England, Chicago, Battle Creek, Omaha, and points west.

April 18, 1904, was the day set to leave for the East. Though on former trips she had traveled in the Pullman compartment to afford her as easy a journey as possible, this trip, for the sake of economy, would be made in a tourist sleeping car. Their car would go directly from northern California to Washington, D.C.

That evening in nearby San Jose they boarded the tourist sleeper and started their six-day trip east. In the party were Ellen White's traveling companion and nurse, Sara McEnterfer, and one of her secretaries, Maggie Hare. W. C. White had gone on in advance to attend to some business matters in southern California and would meet them there. Clarence Crisler, her leading secretary, would also join the party in Los Angeles.

The routing across the Southern states was to ensure comfort and to avoid the high altitudes that sometimes bothered Ellen White in travel. She remained in her berth for the entire trip, resting, watching the scenery, and doing a little reading and writing.

Nearing New Orleans they passed through great swamps, where many varieties of palms were heavily festooned with moss. Just west of New Orleans S. B. Horton, president of the Louisiana Conference, and E. V. Orrell, secretary of the Southern Union, met the train, bringing a basket of fruit. This supplemented the provisions they had taken from home and from southern California for their meals—malted nuts for soup, zwieback, cream sticks, oranges, bananas, apples, applesauce, olives, nuts, jelly, turnovers, boiled eggs, and bread.

In New Orleans some of the party went sightseeing with the Adventists who hosted them. Ellen White remained in the sleeping car. Then, under a full moon, the train started north, running for many miles along the shore of Lake Pontchartrain.

The train stopped for a time in Atlanta, and the traveling party was surprised to see about 20 or 30 believers at the station awaiting them. They came on board for a few minutes. Fathers, mothers, and children gathered around to shake hands.

ARRIVAL IN WASHINGTON

When they arrived in Washington, Ellen White was delighted to have Elder Daniells come into the car, greet them, and conduct them out through the station into the city. The station was the same one in which President Garfield had been shot more than 20 years before, in 1881.

It was nearly noon, and the party looked forward to a little change in the monotonous six-day dietary program.

Elder Daniells escorted Ellen White and the party to a carriage, a two-seated surrey with a canopy top, drawn by a large noble-looking horse named Charlie, very gentle and safe. Ellen White referred to the promise that she would have the use of this horse and carriage while she was in Washington. She felt this was a great favor.

Elder Daniells drove the visitors past the nearby temporary General Conference headquarters at 222 North Capitol Street, and then over to the Memorial church at 12th and M streets to see the building for which Ellen White had helped raise funds. Then he drove the seven miles out to Takoma Park to the Carroll Manor House, which had been rented for Ellen White's use. When they arrived, it was still full of people cleaning, repairing, painting, and furnishing, but a good dinner of tomato soup, hot boiled potatoes, and greens was ready.

Mrs. White, of course, was eager to see the property that had been purchased.

She had heard it described and had written about the work that needed to be done there. As soon as dinner was finished, Elder Daniells, leaving Clarence Crisler and Willie White to tend to the baggage, hitched up Charlie again and took Ellen White, Sara McEnterfer, and Maggie Hare the half mile (one kilometer) to see the site proposed for the college and the sanitarium.

Seeing the land, Mrs. White declared that the location "could not be bettered." She added, "That which is most valuable of all is the clear, beautiful stream which flows right through the land" (letter 141, 1904).

There were two important benefits to Ellen White's being in Washington at this time. First, her willingness to come, stay, and send out her letters and manuscripts with a Washington dateline added authority and prestige to the new Washington headquarters. This brought stability to the cause, as Adventists everywhere would turn their eyes eastward from Battle Creek. Second, construction was about to begin on the college buildings—the boys' dormitory was to be the first. She was intensely interested, and counseled that "every part of the buildings is to bear witness that we realize that there is before us a great, unworked missionary field, and that the truth is to be established in many places" (letter 83, 1904). There was to be no show or needless display.

MINISTRY IN THE WASHINGTON CHURCHES

Ellen White was immediately drawn into services in the Washington Adventist churches. On her first Sabbath there, the last day of April, she spoke in J. S. Washburn's Capital Memorial church (MS 106, 1904). She spoke again a week later at the rededication of this church. She had planned to speak on the Sermon on the Mount, but writing of the experience, observed, "This was taken from me," and John 15:1-17, "I am the true vine," was impressed upon her mind (MS 142, 1904).

From the day they had begun to make definite preparation for the trip to Washington, Ellen White had her eyes on the plans for the biennial session of the Lake Union Conference. This was called to meet at Berrien Springs, Michigan, from May 17 to 26. Not only would she attend the conference but she would also see the newly established Emmanuel Missionary College for the first time. This left just three weeks for the first part of her stay in Washington, and there was much to do.

OFF TO BERRIEN SPRINGS

The Lake Union Conference session held great importance. Dr. Kellogg and some of his supporters would be present. They were still in the throes of the pantheistic teachings. *The Living Temple* was being sold. The direction of the medical work and the control of the church's medical institutions were subjects of controversy.

Sunday evening, May 15, Ellen White, with the party traveling to the Lake Union session, boarded the cars in Washington en route to Berrien Springs. In the group were W. C. White, A. G. Daniells, W. W. Prescott, and Mrs. White's helpers, Sara McEnterfer and Maggie Hare.

The train left an hour late, which meant they were late reaching Milford Junction, Indiana, where they were to change trains for Berrien Springs. That caused a five-hour wait. Mrs. White utilized the time for a missionary visit. At 11:00 the train came through, and within a half hour it deposited them at Elkhart, Indiana, where they stopped at a hotel for the night. About noon the following day they reached Berrien Springs. Ellen White and her traveling companions were taken to the home of Professor P. T. Magan, where they were made comfortable. Professor Magan was at Kalamazoo at the time, taking care of his wife, who was very ill. So the party had the use of the Magan home.

Soon after her arrival Ellen White was urged to speak each morning at 11:00 during the union conference session, and this she consented to do.

MRS. WHITE BEGINS HER WORK AT THE SESSION

Weary from the journey, Ellen White retired early, then woke up at 10:00 p.m. Her mind turned to the subjects that she should present at the meeting. In vision she was instructed to speak clearly about *The Living Temple* controversy. The next morning she did just that. She declared:

> I am so sorry that *Living Temple* came out as it did, and was circulated, and the worst of it—that which struck right to my heart—was the assertion made regarding the book: "It contains the very sentiments that Sister White has been teaching." When I heard this, I felt so heartbroken that it seemed as if I could not say anything (MS 46, 1904).

She told her audience that silence was eloquence when it came to discussing God, what He is, and where He is. "When you are tempted to speak of what God is, keep silence, because as surely as you begin to speak of this, you will disparage Him" (*ibid.*).

The union conference session moved forward in the usual way, with reports, committee work, and elections. But Ellen White's concentration was on the crisis for the salvation of souls. On Thursday night, the nineteenth, she was again given a vision. The next day she wrote a message to Elders Daniells and Prescott in which she said that she had been strongly impressed that "now is the time to save Dr. Kellogg" (letter 165, 1904). She said a determined effort must be made and urged that Dr. Kellogg be called to the meeting. In this letter she wrote:

> Not one of us is above temptation. There is a work that Dr. Kellogg

is educated to perform as no other man in our ranks can perform. . . . We are to draw with all our power, not making accusations, not prescribing what he must do, but letting him see that we are not willing that any should perish (*ibid.*).

She asked, "Is it not worth the trial?" She said that Satan was drawing the doctor. In her visions she had seen someone slipping down a precipice; a company was looking on indifferently, making no effort to save him. But one hand, the hand of Christ, was stretched out, and the man was rescued (MS 52, 1904).

Then she heard Christ speaking, telling the ones who were watching that they must look to Him and not to this man (Kellogg), that they should take heed to themselves. She heard Christ appealing to Dr. Kellogg to put on Christ. She heard Kellogg exclaim, "I am sinful, but He hath covered me with His own righteousness, and henceforth I will go in the strength of the Lord God" (letter 165, 1904). Confessions by others followed.

The letter was written on Friday, May 20, copied by Maggie Hare the same day, and on the same day copies were given to Elders Daniells and Prescott, as well as to David Paulson and Edson White. Dr. Kellogg was urged to come to Berrien Springs. He arrived on Sabbath, May 21.

During the conference session subjects were presented having a bearing on pantheism. Kellogg and his cohorts engaged actively in the discussions. What went on behind the scenes was opened up to Ellen White in vision, and of this she said:

> In the scenes presented to me, I saw men talking together between the meetings about the mistakes and faults of their brethren. [Interlineation by EGW: Many things were not real mistakes, only in their own minds.] (MS 74, 1904).

Mrs. White had looked for a break in the situation over pantheism and Dr. Kellogg, but the matter had not turned out as she had hoped. The experience was a dark and disappointing one.

After the Berrien Springs meeting there was a strong effort on the part of Dr. Kellogg to draw some of the leading workers to Battle Creek for continued discussions on the question of *The Living Temple*. W. C. White and A. G. Daniells resisted this effort, and Ellen White supported them in that resistance (24 WCW, pp. 24, 25; 25 WCW, pp. 280-282).

THE CUMBERLAND RIVER TRIP

On Wednesday, May 25, near the close of the Lake Union Conference session, Ellen White left Berrien Springs for a trip into the South. With her on the train were Edson White, Sara McEnterfer, Maggie Hare, and Dr. and Mrs. David Paulson.

During the six-hour layover in Chicago Dr. Paulson arranged to take her out to Hinsdale to the site where plans were being laid to open a new sanitarium. She found Hinsdale something like Takoma Park. She thought the surroundings were perhaps even more beautiful, and she felt it would make an excellent place for a medical institution.

Back in Chicago in the late afternoon, with Edson and her two women helpers, Mrs. White boarded the train for Nashville. The overnight trip was comfortable, and in the morning they were met by W. O. Palmer, one of Edson's close helpers. He drove them to the plant of the Southern Publishing Association and then to Edson's home nearby. She made this her headquarters for the next six weeks.

During the Berrien Springs meeting both Professors Sutherland and Magan had resigned from their positions of leadership at Emmanuel Missionary College. They expressed their determination to go into the South, find a tract of land, and begin a self-supporting school. From Nashville they set out in various directions in search of a suitable property within their financial capability. They found one in particular—the Fergusen-Nelson place—but the quality of the land fell short of their desires. Then plans were developed for quite a large party to make a trip up the Cumberland River on the *Morning Star*, to continue the search for a school site. They would wait until W. C. White had closed up his work in the North and joined them in Nashville before making the trip.

Ellen White and all her party would be on the boat. She had visited the *Morning Star* in 1901 as she passed through Vicksburg, but had not traveled on the boat. A full week would be spent on the trip up the Cumberland River, and besides, she would be with her son and his wife. She eagerly looked forward to this.

While the *Morning Star* was being readied, she rested in Edson's home. He earnestly hoped that his mother would have an enjoyable experience living on the boat, and craved her counsel as he sought a site for another school for Blacks near Nashville.

Recounting the experience, she spoke of the bountiful supply of good things from Edson's garden—green peas, strawberries, potatoes, sweet corn. She felt that the good 10-acre (four-hectare) tract of land that had been secured for the publishing house was a favorable one.

As the Sabbath neared, some thought perhaps it would be better if Ellen White did not try to speak that day in Nashville, but she said, "I have a message to bear" (letter 183, 1904). She tells of how the Lord strengthened her, and "I bore a straightforward testimony. Maggie reported what I said. Afterward I was told that even had I known the real condition of things in the church, which I did not, I could not have spoken more to the point" *(ibid.)*.

Tuesday, June 7, was the day set for boarding the *Morning Star* and beginning the trip up the Cumberland River. That morning she wrote to her granddaughter Mabel:

> We are just about to leave here for a trip of six or seven days up the Cumberland River in the *Morning Star*. Our party will consist of Brethren Magan and Sutherland, your Uncle Edson and your Aunt Emma, your father, your grandmother, Sara, Brother Crisler, who returned from Graysville yesterday, Maggie, Edson's stenographer, and several others. We expect to start about noon today (letter 191, 1904).

As matters developed, some repairs had to be made on the boat, hence they were delayed until the next morning. The main object for the trip was to find land for a self-supporting school, but everyone looked forward to a change and a little vacation.

In addition to those who were named by Ellen White as being in the traveling party, there were the pilot, Will Palmer; Mr. Judd, Edson's stenographer; a fireman; an engineer; a cook; and a general hand. Several of these were Blacks. Passengers and crew numbered 16 in all. As they traveled north they stopped occasionally, sometimes for repairs, sometimes to purchase produce and milk or buttermilk from the farms they passed. From time to time they stopped to look at the land.

On the trip most of the men slept on the lower deck on double-wire camp meeting cots. The women slept on the upper deck, and the pilot slept in the pilothouse. The dining room also was on the upper deck. Each morning Crisler, Willie, and several others put on their bathing suits, which Ellen White described as "very becoming," and had a swim. The current was too strong to swim upstream, so they would dive off the front of the boat, swim along its side, and climb up on the framework around the paddlewheel (25 WCW, pp. 315-318).

On Sabbath, instead of having a church service, Willie, Edson, Will Palmer, Sutherland, and Magan climbed a nearby mountain and spent the morning in prayer and fellowship. Mrs. White recorded in her diary that "this precious Sabbath was a day long to be remembered by the passengers on this boat. I believe that all are being benefited" (MS 143, 1904).

By the time they reached Carthage, 170 miles (272 kilometers) north of Nashville, it had become apparent that the main object of the journey—to find land at reasonable prices—was not going to be accomplished. The land that was expected to be available for $2 or $3 an acre (.4 hectare), or $8 or $10, was running about $60 an acre. Willie concluded that the low prices he had heard about were those offered 20 or 30 years earlier. But nobody seemed to mind too much. Ellen White became more and more emphatic that any schools they would establish should be near Nashville. So on Monday morning the *Morning Star* started back down the river. Much better time was made with the river current carrying them along.

MADISON

In a letter written that Monday to Elder Daniells, Ellen White outlined their plans:

> Tomorrow morning we shall reach Edgefield Junction, which is only twelve miles [19 kilometers] from Nashville. We shall stay there for the rest of the day, for we wish to visit a farm which is for sale at Madison, about seventeen miles (27 kilometers) from Nashville, and two and a half miles [four kilometers] from the railway. It is said that this farm contains nearly 100 acres [40 hectares] of good bottom land, more than 100 acres [40 hectares] of second-quality agricultural land suitable for grain and fruit, and about 200 acres [80 hectares] of pasture land. We think that it can be purchased for about $12,000. It is said that there are on it over $2,000 worth of stock and farm implements.
>
> I desire to look at this farm, and if it be the will of the Lord, I shall do so tomorrow afternoon. The farm has a roomy house, barns, and other buildings, and two and a half miles [four kilometers] of good stone fence. Considering its advantages, its price is less than anything else we have seen in this part of Tennessee (letter 195, 1904).

She elaborated a bit about its general relationship to Nashville:

> I have been instructed that the lands on which our school shall be established should be near enough Nashville for there to be a connection between the school and the workers in Nashville (*ibid.*).

Tuesday, on looking over the Fergusen-Nelson place near Madison, Ellen White was pleased and thought it would serve well for the new school. "I felt so thoroughly convinced that it was a favorable location for the work that I advised our brethren to make the purchase" (letter 215, 1904). Brethren Sutherland and Magan were considerably less optimistic. They had hoped for something better for less money.

The price with standing crops was $12,723. The professors, as they recounted the story in later years, told of how, when they witnessed Ellen White's certainty about this matter and remembering the experience in Australia with the Avondale school, they felt they must move in this direction. So that Tuesday they made their decision to purchase.

But it proved to be anything but a simple transaction. Mrs. Fergusen, who had to sign the papers along with her husband, at first refused to sell the farm to men from the North, declaring, "I'll never sell to a Yankee" (Ira Gish and Harry Christman, *Madison, God's Beautiful Farm*, p. 23). After several interviews and many prayers, and a demand from Mrs. Fergusen for an extra thousand dollars, she put her signature by her husband's, and the contract was made secure.

There was some hesitation about the extra thousand dollars, and some took it as an omen that they should withdraw. But Ellen White exclaimed, "Do you think I'd let the devil best me out of a place for a thousand dollars? Pay the extra thousand. It's cheap enough. This is the place the Lord said you should have" (*ibid.*, p. 27).

With the property bargained for, the men hurried North to find friends who would help meet the purchase price. Wiring to a friend, Ellen White reported on the 400-acre (162-hectare) place:

> The size of the farm, its location, the distance that it is from Nashville, and the moderate sum for which it could be purchased seemed to point it out as the very place needed for our school work here. The house is old, but it can be used until more suitable buildings can be erected (letter 215, 1904).

Rather exuberantly she noted:

> Included in this sale are a number of horses, cows, and other stock, carriages and farming implements, also a house, that would be of use to the school. There are many beautiful cedar trees on the place. Fifty acres [20 hectares] of the land is under cultivation, and the crops are in a flourishing condition. Portions of this land can be sold to those connected with the school for dwelling houses (letter 249a, 1904).

In another letter she explained the cherished plans and objectives of Sutherland and Magan:

> The plan upon which our brethren propose to work is to select some of the best and most substantial young men and women from Berrien Springs and other places in the North, who believe that God has called them to the work in the South, and give them a brief training as teachers. Thorough instruction will be given in Bible study, physiology, the history of our message; and special instruction will be given regarding the cultivation of the land.
>
> It is hoped that many of these students will eventually connect with schools in various places in the South. In connection with these schools

453

there will be land that will be cultivated by teachers and students, and the proceeds from this work will be used for the support of the schools (letter 215, 1904).

OAKWOOD

While negotiations for the Madison property were under way, Ellen White and her party left on Wednesday, June 15, for a weeklong tour of several institutions in Tennessee and Alabama. The first was Graysville, where there was a school and a sanitarium. On Sabbath she spoke in the church and noticed that there were in her audience three ministers from other Protestant churches. On Sunday she made a grand tour of the school buildings, the farm—where she discovered peaches and corn and strawberries—and the sanitarium, where she urged that the pine trees be preserved, for there is healing in the pines. In their travels by carriage they stopped by homes of Adventists and met the families. She wrote of it: "Whole families, father, mother, and children, came out to speak to me, and I shook hands with each one, not forgetting the children" (*ibid.*).

Their travels took them west by train to Huntsville, Alabama, to visit the Oakwood school, which had been established for Blacks 10 years before. They arrived Monday afternoon at 1:00. After looking over the farm, she spoke to the few students who were there for the summer. She told them she wanted 100 students in the school the next year, and urged them to appeal to their friends to come to Oakwood. She told these students how pleased she was that they were training for service. She said she wanted to encourage them because she knew they had a battle to fight and strong prejudice to work against. She pointed out that the church needed them to work in places where racial hostility prevented Whites from working. She assured them of God's help and told them if she never saw them again on this earth she hoped to see them in the kingdom of heaven (MS 60, 1904).

On June 22 she returned to Nashville, where she spent another couple weeks resting, writing, speaking, and encouraging the workers in the area. During this time she went out to take another look at the Madison property. When the work for the new school was organized, Ellen White accepted an invitation to serve on the board of directors—the only time she ever served in such a capacity. She watched the developments at Madison with deep interest.

BACK IN WASHINGTON

On Friday, July 8, Ellen White and those traveling with her arrived back in Washington, where she would stay for another month in the Carroll Manor House. She was pleased that the construction of the college was underway. The basement for the boys' dormitory was about completed, as well as the excavating for the dining hall. A. S. Baird was managing the construction work well.

Almost every day Mrs. White and Sara drove out with the horse and carriage. She enjoyed these little journeys.

While living in the Carroll Manor House, she received a vision in which she seemed to be in a large company. "One not known to those present stepped forward" and sounded a message of warning to Dr. Paulson and Dr. Sadler, urging them to break their bonds with Dr. Kellogg and to be careful not to spoil their experience with philosophy and vain deceit. "Cut loose, cut loose is my message," she wrote in a letter to the physicians (letter 279, 1904). The text of the letter was much the same as in a letter addressed to Elders Jones and Waggoner, who were now associated with Dr. Kellogg in Battle Creek. The messenger who was speaking to them indicated that these men were in a mist and a fog, unaware of the seductive sentiments in *The Living Temple*.

The four final weeks spent in Washington were devoted to giving counsel about the developing work, speaking in the several churches on weekends, and in writing.

STARTING HOME

Ellen White and her helpers left Washington on Thursday, August 11, for the trip home. The trip would take them through New England, Michigan, Nebraska, and points west.

Monday, September 5, she was on her way by train to Battle Creek. She arrived there on Tuesday and was given one of the best rooms in the sanitarium. This was her first visit to Battle Creek since the fire and the building of the new sanitarium. She spoke the next morning to the patients in the parlor, dealing with basic Christian principles and the power of Christ to transform those who come to Him in simplicity and faith (letter 293, 1904). After the talk Dr. Kellogg introduced her to several of the guests. She was surprised to see how powerfully the Word spoken in simplicity and earnestness had affected them. She reported that that night she received a special blessing from God.

The next morning she spoke in the gymnasium to a group of about 300, composed mainly of physicians, nurses, and other workers. Her topic was the love of Christ, how He showed His love in good works, and how these good works gave birth to love in the hearts of others (*ibid.*).

At the last minute it was decided that she should try to speak in the tabernacle that afternoon. As there was not much time to get word out, she expected a rather slim attendance. To her surprise the tabernacle was crowded with 2,500 people and seemed to be packed as it had been at the 1901 General Conference session. Again her sermon was a simple exposition of Christian faith. She warmed to the subject, speaking for more than an hour (*ibid.*; MS 90, 1904).

Just before the service began, A. T. Jones asked her whether she would be willing to stay over the weekend. He urged her, she consented, and during the meeting he announced her decision. But that night W. C. White, who had been in Canada, arrived in Battle Creek and pointed out that they were committed to Sabbath meetings at the Omaha, Nebraska, camp meeting. So she promised to return to Battle Creek after the Omaha appointment.

One of the chief purposes of the Battle Creek visit was, of course, to help Kellogg, if that were at all possible. She had received letters from him at Melrose, Massachusetts, indicating some softening of his attitude. In writing from Battle Creek to W. C. White in Canada, she said she knew that Kellogg was like a blind man with a cane, striking about to find the road, but everything so far appeared to be surface work. But she said she must do her best to speak in Battle Creek. After her talk to the workers on Wednesday morning, September 7, Kellogg did make a brief attempt at confession. He declared:

> I want you to know that I feel in my heart to accept all the reproofs and all the instruction that the Lord has sent me through Sister White. I do not want to have any ambiguity about my position and attitude.
>
> The Lord has sent Sister White here, and she has given us instruction this morning for our good, and I hope the Lord will help us all to take this to our hearts and profit by her instruction (24 WCW, p. 325).

But Dr. Kellogg had become a very vacillating man, and the repentant attitude was shallow and short-lived.

Friday, September 9, Ellen White and W. C. White reached Omaha. She was feeling a little stronger than she had for the past few days and was pleased to observe that at the Omaha station she could walk through the large waiting rooms and up and down stairs as easily as ever (letter 283, 1904). Unfortunately, she caught a cold on the trip and was afraid she might have difficulty speaking on the Sabbath. But she went ahead and spoke anyway.

It was here at this Omaha meeting that one of the laymen, Jasper Wayne, sought an interview with her. He presented his newly developed plan for soliciting funds from non-Adventists by calling at their homes and leaving with them a church paper. This was the inception of what came to be known as the Harvest Ingathering Plan (later simply Ingathering), which has brought in hundreds of millions of dollars to help advance the work.

Ellen White spoke three times in Omaha, then went on to College View, where she and Willie were given rooms in the Nebraska Sanitarium, situated on the crest of the hill near Union College.

Then it was back to Battle Creek to fulfill her promise to be with the people there on Sabbath. She was given a hearty welcome, and spent five days there. She spoke three times in the tabernacle to large congregations, once to the medical students, and once to sanitarium workers.

Ellen White left Battle Creek on Monday, October 3. Because of delays she was unable to reach St. Helena by Sabbath, so she stayed in Reno on Friday and Sabbath and spoke to the people there. After a pleasant weekend she and her party hastened homeward. As she passed through Oakland, she found the workers at Pacific Press busily packing up the last of their things to take them to Mountain View. "The empty buildings at Pacific Press look lonesome," confessed Willie; he had known them since 1877 (24 WCW, p. 370).

When they reached home, they found Marian Davis desperately ill at the St. Helena Sanitarium. Illness that could be traced to a cold contracted during the 1903 General Conference session led to tuberculosis. During Ellen White's trip in the East Marian grew progressively weaker, although she continued with her literary work. This situation was exceedingly painful to Ellen White. For 25 years the two had worked together.

Although Marian rallied a bit when Mrs. White returned, she died early in the afternoon of Tuesday, October 25. On October 26 she was buried in the St. Helena Cemetery, where J. N. Loughborough and a number of other early workers await the call of the Life-giver. Of her and her work, Ellen White wrote:

> For twenty-five years Sister Davis had been a most faithful helper in my work. She was greatly appreciated by me and by all who were acquainted with her and her work, and we miss her very much. Of her it can truthfully be said, "Blessed are the dead which die in the Lord . . . , that they may rest from their labours; and their works do follow them" (letter 29, 1905).

"I WAS SHOWN": BEAUTIFUL PROPERTIES!

When Ellen White returned to the United States from Australia in 1900, she carried in her heart the memory of visions given her in which she was shown places in California suitable for building sanitariums. Now as she traveled in California she recalled these visions.

In August 1901, as she was attending the Los Angeles camp meeting, she began to think in practical terms of securing properties. In a vision of the night she seemed to be in a council meeting in which consideration was being given to establishing a sanitarium in southern California. She described what she saw and heard in this vision and made mention of One who often instructed her at such times: "There was among us One who presented this matter very clearly and with the utmost simplicity. He told us that it would be a mistake to establish a sanitarium within the city limits" (7T, p. 85).

Her Instructor continued:

> A sanitarium should have the advantage of plenty of land, so the invalids can work in the open air. For nervous, gloomy, feeble patients, outdoor work is invaluable. Let them have flower beds to care for. In the use of rake and hoe and spade they will find relief for many of their maladies. Idleness is the cause of many diseases.
>
> Life in the open air is good for body and mind. It is God's medicine for the restoration of health. Pure air, good water, sunshine, the beautiful surroundings of nature—these are His means for restoring the sick to health in natural ways (*ibid.*).

Ellen White envisioned sanitariums in the country "surrounded by flowers and trees, orchards and vineyards. Here it is easy for physicians and nurses to draw from the things of nature lessons teaching of God. Let them point the patients to Him whose hand has made the lofty trees, the springing grass, and the beautiful flowers, encouraging them to see in every opening bud and blossoming flower an expression of His love for His children" (*ibid.*, pp. 85, 86).

During the camp meeting itself, where she spoke daily, she went out with some of the brethren to look at two prospective properties. She was instructed that not only in various sections of Los Angeles but in San Diego and in other tourist resorts in southern California, health restaurants and treatment rooms should be established. This visit sparked the revival of concern for the medical missionary work throughout the world, but especially in southern California.

THE PARADISE VALLEY PROPERTY

After the camp meeting in September 1902, Ellen White went down to San Diego and twice visited the Potts Sanitarium property, about six miles (10 kilometers) south of the city. The buildings had stood idle for years, and the property was available for only a fraction of the original cost.

> Here was a well-constructed, three-story building of about fifty rooms, with broad verandas, standing upon a pleasant rise of ground, and overlooking a beautiful valley. Many of the rooms are large and airy. . . . Besides the main building, there is a good stable, and also a six-room cottage, which can be fitted up for helpers.
>
> The property is conveniently located, being less than seven miles [12 kilometers] from San Diego, and about a mile [two kilometers] from the National City post office. There are twenty-two acres [nine hectares] of land. About one half of this had once been planted to fruit trees, but during the long drought that this country has suffered, all the trees died except the ornamental trees and shrubbery around the buildings, and about seventy olive trees on the terraces. . . . I never saw a building offered for sale that was better adapted for sanitarium work. If this place were fixed up, it would look just like places that have been shown me by the Lord (Sp. T, Series B, No. 14, pp. 8, 9).

The Southern California Conference felt unable to invest in the enterprise, so Ellen White borrowed $2,000 from the St. Helena Bank at 8 percent interest, and Josephine Gotzian, a close friend, provided the other $2,000 toward the total price of $4,000. The two women "clasped hands in an agreement to unite in helping to purchase the Potts Sanitarium" (letter 97, 1904). With funds that were put into the enterprise by Prof. E. S. Ballenger and his parents, they paid $300 in back taxes and used $800 to buy eight acres (four hectares) of needed land adjoining the property. There were other expenses that brought the total cost of the property to $5,300. Of course, the two women and the Ballenger family had no intention of keeping the property as theirs. Nor did they have any intention of making it a matter of financial speculation. They purchased it to hold it until the business could be organized and the conference could take control.

But with the property in their hands, the next step was to find someone to

459

manage and develop it. For 15 years it had been unoccupied, and there was much to be done. Ellen White speaks of the next step:

> Having secured the place, we needed a manager, and we found one ready for the work. Brother E. R. Palmer and his wife, who had spent the winter in Arizona, were in San Diego. . . . They were willing to take charge of the work of fitting up the sanitarium building for use (RH, Mar. 16, 1905 [Sp. T, Series B, No. 14, pp. 10, 11]).

Elder Palmer arranged to have the building wired for electricity and had it cleaned up and painted outside. Then he began to assemble furniture for the new sanitarium.

He discovered that wealthy businessmen who went to California for the winter would rent a place and buy good-quality furniture for their use. When they wished to return to their homes in the East, they would make the furniture available at very reasonable prices. Thus Palmer was able to secure furniture, some of it bird's-eye maple, for furnishing at least a portion of the new institution.

A well and windmill furnished a limited supply of water, but it was known from the outset that the system could never supply the needs of a sanitarium. Palmer described the water situation: "The twenty-acre [eight-hectare] tract of land on which the building stands was as dry as the hills of Gilboa, with only a remote prospect for water underground" (DF 2a, E. R. Palmer, "The Paradise Valley Sanitarium").

Palmer and his fellow workers knew from their contacts with Ellen White that it was in the providence of God that the institution had been bought. They were confident that God would find a way to meet their needs. Still, through the summer of 1904 they suffered severely from the drought—a drought that had lasted eight or nine years (W. L. Johns and R. H. Utt, eds., *The Vision Bold*, p. 147). They watched the trees wither and die, and Mrs. White wrote: "The poor, drying up, dying trees are beseeching us by their appearance for refreshing streams of water" (MS 147, 1904). Palmer referred to their source of confidence in these words: "The Lord had spoken concerning these points, and His servants responded by purchasing the estate" (DF 2a, E. R. Palmer, "The Paradise Valley Sanitarium").

THE NEW WELL

Ellen White recommended that Palmer obtain the services of a good Adventist well digger of her acquaintance, Salem Hamilton, who was then living in Nebraska. Accordingly, he was called west to dig the well.

Palmer related:

> With what anxiety we surveyed the ground and tried the wizard water stick and discussed the possibilities. . . .
>
> Finally we chose a place and began digging down through the dry earth where the dust flew more than twenty feet [six meters] below the surface (ibid.).

The site selected was in a hollow just below the institution. Deeper and deeper Mr. Hamilton and his helpers continued to dig.

Ellen White, who was eager to be close to the sanitarium activities, was able to pull herself away from Elmshaven and travel south, arriving at the Potts property on Monday, November 7. Hamilton had reached a depth of 80 feet (24 meters) on the well. From day to day she listened with interest to reports of progress, and frequently talked with Hamilton. One day she asked, "'What are you going to do, Brother Hamilton?'

"'I have a question to ask you,' he answered. 'If you will answer that, I will give you my answer. Did the Lord tell you to buy this property?'

"'Yes! Yes!' Ellen White replied. 'Three times I was shown that we should secure this particular property.'

"'All right,' Mr. Hamilton said, 'I have my answer. The Lord would not give us an elephant without providing water for it to drink'" (Johns and Utt, p. 146). He declared that he would go on digging.

By now he was well past the 80-foot (24-meter) level, and there still was no sign of moisture. But one day he thought he heard the sound of a stream of water in the gravel at the bottom of the well. When Palmer visited the site and looked down the well, Brother Hamilton called up, "'Mr. Palmer, would you be afraid to come down? I think there is water not far away.'" Palmer did go down, and he heard it distinctly, "'like the tinkle of a bell or the sound of a small waterfall in the depths of a forest'" (ibid., pp. 146, 147).

Hamilton had tunneled in one direction, but to no avail. He now tunneled in another direction, and with a vigorous blow his pick broke through the clay into a fine stream of water as large as a man's arm. The well quickly began to fill. There wasn't even time to get all the tools out. That night the water rose 15 feet (five meters) in the well (ibid.).

Excitedly E. R. Palmer and W. C. White hastened to Ellen White's room to announce the good news. Writing of it the next day to her grandchildren, she said:

> "Yesterday morning Brother Palmer came to my room in company with your father . . . and told us there was fifteen feet [five meters] of water in the well. This morning there is twenty feet of water and their tools at the bottom of the well. I cannot express to you how glad we all

are made. Plenty of water for all purposes! This cannot be estimated by gold or by silver. Water means life. . . . The Lord has answered all our expectations, and we shall have reason for thanksgiving. . . . I want to praise the Lord with heart and soul and will" (*ibid.*, p. 147).

She wrote in her diary:

The water is now a certainty. The trees shall have their refreshing portion. Brother Palmer was so pleased. He expressed his gratitude to God for this great blessing, that labor and money invested for machinery for the water plant had brought returns (MS 147, 1904).

On the Thursday before the breakthrough in the well, a group from the sanitarium, including W. C. White, E. S. Ballenger, H. E. Osborne, and Mrs. Josephine Gotzian, set out to solicit financial support for the project. They drove 20 miles (32 kilometers) to San Pasqual, and then to Escondido, visiting families and churches and telling of the needs and providences of God in connection with the proposed sanitarium. They were able to raise $1,600 in cash to help carry the enterprise forward. Half that amount they were able to take home with them. They had also solicited material help that the farmers could provide from their land. They were glad for the cash because, in anticipation of a prosperous well, Palmer had purchased an engine, pipes, and pumps, and he needed money to pay the overdue bill.

When the party returned from Escondido on Tuesday, they were met by the cheering report that the well diggers had found an abundant flow of pure water. A few days later a four-horse team drawing a large, heavy wagon drove up to the sanitarium, bringing gifts from the churches of San Pasqual and Escondido. This timely donation included potatoes, squash, and canned fruit. Of special importance, the gift included two fine "Jersey cows" (RH, Mar. 16, 1905).

As to the organization for handling the business of the newly established sanitarium, various propositions were made and discussed, and counsel was sought from the conference brethren. It was finally decided to establish a stock company, not for profit but for managing the business, and to encourage those who could do so to make an investment in the institution. The plan was followed with some adjustments during the next two or three years until the Southern California Conference was in a position to take over the management and responsibility of the Paradise Valley Sanitarium.

Thus Ellen White, through the insights that came to her through the visions, through her persistence, through her soliciting the cooperation of those who had confidence that the Lord was speaking through her, and through heavy personal financial investment, led out in the establishment of this first Adventist sanitarium in southern California.

THE GLENDALE SANITARIUM

At Glendale J. A. Burden was leading out in the establishment of a second sanitarium in southern California. He was the manager of the St. Helena Sanitarium when Ellen White returned from Australia in late 1900. Shortly, however, he responded to a call to Australia to help lead out in the establishment of institutions there.

The Burdens returned to the States in February 1904. He picked up the words from Ellen White's pen that "a sanitarium should be established near Los Angeles" and "it is the expressed will of God that this shall be done" (letter 211, 1904). To Burden this was a challenge. He knew that she had also written:

> Light has been given me that a sanitarium should be established near Los Angeles, in some rural district. For years the need of such an institution has been kept before our people in southern California. Had the brethren there heeded the warnings given by the Lord, to guard them from making mistakes, they would not now be tied up as they are. But they have not followed the instruction given. They have not gone forward in faith to establish a sanitarium near Los Angeles (letter 147, 1904).

In response to her urging, Burden looked around for likely properties in southern California that could be secured for a reasonable sum. In the late 1880s many establishments had been built for tourists and health resorts, but the businesses had failed.

The building that now seemed most likely to provide what was needed was the castlelike Glendale Hotel, built in 1886 and situated on a five-acre (two-hectare) tract of land bordered by dirt roads. At that time Glendale was a country settlement of 500 inhabitants, eight miles (13 kilometers) from Los Angeles.

A 75-room, unfurnished structure that had cost $60,000 was available. Because of the business failures in southern California, it had never been used as a hotel. It served for four years as an Episcopal school for girls; then in 1901 and 1902 it was used as a public high school.

On the property were shade trees and orchards. Around it were chicken ranches and a scattering of modest homes. In 1904 a real-estate developer, Leslie C. Brand, controlled the property. The asking price was $26,000, which Burden knew was far out of his reach.

As he sat in his buggy looking over the hotel grounds, Burden decided that if he could buy it for $15,000 he would regard this as a sign of divine approval. Taking several of his brethren with him, he approached Mr. Brand and explained, "'Our money will have to come from church members. Can you help us by reducing the price?'"

Brand thought a moment and then asked, "'How does $12,500 sound?'"

Burden responded that it sounded fine. He took a $20 bill and gave it to Brand as a deposit on the purchase (Johns and Utt, p. 163).

At the conference headquarters Burden was dealing with the same administrators who had hesitated so long about investing in the Paradise Valley Sanitarium. The conference lacked even the $1,000 needed for a down payment on the Glendale property. The president of the Pacific Union Conference had made it clear to the local conference administration that there must be a stop to increasing indebtedness, and there must be a turnaround in financial affairs of the Southern California Conference.

Burden took the matter to the constituency at the camp meeting in September 1904, and, to his disappointment, they rejected the purchase for lack of money.

At last Elder Burden was able to enlist the help of Clarence Santee, the conference president. The two men decided to advance the money for the down payment out of their own pockets. Just at this time Mrs. White sent a message urging in strong terms the purchase of the property, and Elder Santee read it to the conference delegates in session.

"Why is this work delayed?" she asked. She also persuaded two of the church members to advance $1,000 each toward the purchase of the institution. The delegates rallied and pledged $5,200 to buy the Glendale Hotel. A cash payment of $4,500 was made, and a three-year mortgage was agreed upon for the balance. A board of trustees was set up, with Elder Santee as chairman. The board took steps at once to develop the institution.

This was the situation when Ellen White stopped at the new Glendale institution. She went through all the rooms of the new sanitarium, many of which were freshly painted. She wished there were more land than the five acres (two hectares) connected with the building, but she observed, "It is certainly in the country, for there are no buildings very near it. It is surrounded by large fields of strawberries, and by orange orchards" (letter 311, 1904).

LOMA LINDA, *THE HILL BEAUTIFUL*

Place: Elmshaven, living room.

Time: April 1905.

Those present: Ellen G. White; W. C. White; John Burden; the president of the California Conference; and one of his committee members.

Ellen White: "There is a sanitarium waiting near Riverside or Redlands, nearer Redlands, I think. You can find it if you really want to." (See DF8, J. A. Burden, "The Location and Development of Loma Linda," p. 96.)

In response to repeated messages from Ellen White, a committee was appointed to look for such a site. They felt it must be the Loma Linda resort hotel they had visited earlier, but as it carried a price tag of $85,000, they had turned from it. Now the hotel had failed and closed up on April 1; the committee found it could be bought for $45,000.

Elder Burden had hoped that Mrs. White, on her way to attend the 1905 General Conference session in Washington, would be able to stop long enough in Los Angeles to hear what they had learned about the Loma Linda property. Her party included her son W. C. White, his wife, May; and Maggie Hare. On Thursday, May 4, when the eastbound train stopped at the Los Angeles station, a few of the brethren, including Elder Burden, boarded the car to tell Mrs. White about Loma Linda. She was immediately interested and excitedly urged, "Look up all the particulars and write me at once in Washington" (*ibid.*).

The conference-bound party reached Washington on Tuesday morning, May 9. The session opened Thursday morning. Friday afternoon, May 12, the promised letter describing Loma Linda was placed in Ellen White's hands. She read it aloud to her son W. C. White. It read, in part:

> I am sending you a little pamphlet that contains a few views and a brief description of the property, but words and pictures can but faintly describe its beauty. It is simply ideal and grand for a sanitarium.
>
> The buildings are in excellent condition, well furnished, heated with steam heat, and lighted with electricity. Everything is complete to begin business at once. The main building has forty-six rooms, and there are four cottages having four rooms each, with bath and toilet. Three of these cottages have four porches each, with broad windows, so that beds can be wheeled right out on the porch and patients can sleep in the open air. There is another beautiful building—a two-story cottage of nine rooms, with bath and toilet. Another building which has been used as a recreation pavilion, and has four nice rooms, would make a fine gymnasium and chapel.
>
> There are barns and sheds, and a house for the workmen. There are ten acres (four hectares) of good bearing orange orchard, fifteen acres (six hectares) of alfalfa, eight acres (three hectares) of apricots, plums, and almonds. The rest of the grounds are beautifully laid out in lawns, drives, and walks, there being more than a mile of cement walk. The principal buildings are on a beautiful knoll about 125 feet (38 meters) above the valley. The main building is surrounded with pepper-wood trees from thirty to forty feet (12 meters) high.
>
> There are five horses, four cows, 150 chickens, thirty-five turkeys, some hogs, farm implements, buggies, carriages, and wagons.

The place has an ample supply of water from the mountains. An artesian well, which has a good pumping plant, yields an abundance of water, if for any reason the mountain water should fail. The water is piped all over the seventy-six acres (30 hectares).

The place cost the present owners $150,000. They have tried to run it as a tourist hotel, but it was a failure, and they lost money, so it was closed the first of April. The stockholders are financially embarrassed, and have ordered the property sold for $40,000. The furnishings in the building cost $12,000, and have been used for only about two years and a half.

A number of us went to see the place today, and we were deeply impressed that this is the place which the Lord has shown you, near Redlands and Riverside, in which sanitarium work should be carried on. It is five miles (eight kilometers) from Redlands.

The question is, what shall we do? We must act at once, for the company is anxious to sell, and there are others who want it. . . .

We do not wish to move hastily, and we should like to hear from you and the brethren in Washington who have gone from this field, as to how you and they feel about the matter. I wish that if it is at all possible you would take the matter up in council with them, and have them wire us. I do not know how long we can hold the offer open, but will try to do so until we hear from you (J. A. Burden to EGW, May 7, 1905 [Sp. T, Series B, No. 3, pp. 33-35]).

When she finished reading she told Willie that she believed the place was the one that had been presented to her several years before (28 WCW, p. 442).

The terms offered Elder Burden were $5,000 down and like amounts in August (due July 26), September (due August 26), and December (due December 31), making $20,000. The remaining $20,000 would come due in three years (SHM, pp. 349, 350).

What could they do? Elder Burden in California wanted an immediate answer. Conference officers and Ellen White were across the continent in Washington, D.C. It seemed that there could not have been a more inopportune time to deal with such a weighty and far-reaching matter. All in Washington were deeply involved in the General Conference session that had just opened. The Southern California Conference with 1,332 members was now involved in an indebtedness of about $75,000, stemming from the recently acquired San Fernando College and Glendale Sanitarium, the longer-established vegetarian restaurant and treatment rooms in Los Angeles, and the health food business there.

Three weeks earlier, at the Southern California constituency meeting, a new president had been chosen—a good man, but far from a seasoned executive. He had been charged to hold the line as far as indebtedness was concerned. The General Conference, too, was facing almost overwhelming financial problems. There was the possibility of having to raise between $75,000 and $90,000 to meet the deficit of the old medical association. So there was little to encourage the hope of help from that source.

"I'LL CONSULT NO ONE," SAID ELLEN WHITE

Without further ado Ellen White requested Willie to send a telegram to Elder Burden, saying, "Secure the property at once." She followed it with a letter, dated Sunday, May 14:

> Your letter has just been read. I had no sooner finished reading it than I said, "I will consult no one; for I have no question at all about the matter." I advised Willie to send you a telegram without spending time to ask the advice of the brethren. Secure the property by all means, so that it can be held, and then obtain all the money you can and make sufficient payments to hold the place. This is the very property that we ought to have. Do not delay; for it is just what is needed. . . .
>
> Here is the word of the Lord. Open up every place possible. We are to labor in faith, taking hold of a power that is pledged to do large things for us. We are to reach out in faith in Los Angeles and in Redlands and Riverside (letter 139, 1905).

In defense of her unprecedented action, she declared: "I considered that the advantages of this location authorized me to speak positively regarding this matter" (letter 247, 1905).

Here was the situation facing John Burden:

He had been directed to "secure the property"! With what?

The officers of the Southern California Conference had wired from Washington that they could take no responsibility whatever in the matter.

One telegram signed by conference officers and Ellen White urged Burden to delay action till they returned to the West. But circumstances did not warrant this. Burden could delay action on the deal only till Friday, May 26. On that date, if the property was to be held he must make a payment of $1,000 to bind the contract until Thursday, June 15. By then conference officers and Ellen White and her son would be back.

THE SEARCH FOR MONEY

But there was no money in sight. On Thursday, May 25, Burden and a close friend, R. S. Owen, a Bible teacher at the San Fernando school, took the interurban electric car down the coast to call on a farmer who was thought to have some means. He lived about a mile and a half (two kilometers) from the car stop. When they got to his cabin, no one was at home. A neighbor thought he was most likely somewhere on the ranch, but search as they would they found no sign of the man. The two men returned to the car stop and waited.

It was dark now, and as the interurban car sped toward them, they failed to signal it for a stop, so it did not even slow up. There would be a two-hour wait for another car, so the men went back to the cabin, which now had a light in it. Finding the farmer, his wife, and daughter, they introduced themselves and soon explained their mission. Elder Burden reports that as the telegram from Mrs. White and the letter that followed were read to the farmer, he suddenly exclaimed, "Praise the Lord!" (SHM, p. 355). He had been praying that the Lord would send someone to buy his place. It had been sold a few days before, and now he was ready to make available $2,400 for the Loma Linda enterprise.

The next day Elder Burden phoned the representative of the Loma Linda Association that he was ready to do business. The $1,000 was paid, and work was begun on a contract. This was finished the following Monday. Four thousand dollars more had to be on hand by June 15 to make up the first payment of $5,000, or the deposit would be lost. And this was only the first of four $5,000 payments that Burden had agreed upon. He was eager for Ellen White and the conference officers to see the property.

ELLEN WHITE INSPECTS LOMA LINDA

Travel plans called for Ellen White and her party to reach Redlands at 10:00 a.m. on Monday, June 12. Local and union conference workers would come out from Los Angeles and meet them at Loma Linda. A great deal depended on this meeting. Would approving action be taken, or would Elder Burden lose the borrowed $1,000 given to bind the contract?

Elder Burden, his wife, and fellow workers were inspecting the grounds and the buildings as the express wagon from Redlands drove up carrying Ellen White, W. C. White and his wife, and others. Mrs. White's gaze was fixed on the main building.

"Willie, I have been here before," she said as she stepped down from the wagon.

"No, Mother," he replied, "you have never been here."

"Then this is the very place the Lord has shown me," she said, "for it is all familiar."

She turned to one of the ministers and declared, "We must have this place. We should reason from cause to effect. The Lord has not given us this property for any common purpose." As they looked over the grounds and buildings, she said again and again, "This is the very place the Lord has shown me." Following Elder Burden into the recreation building, she commented:

> This building will be of great value to us. A school will be established here. Redlands will become a center as also will Loma Linda. Battle Creek is going down. God will reestablish His medical work at this place (Johns and R. H. Utt, p. 179).

It was past noon, and the representatives of the Loma Linda Association invited the entire party into the dining room to partake of a sumptuous vegetarian dinner. Then the manager opened a door and ushered the group into the parlor. All were waiting eagerly to hear from Ellen White; she did not disappoint them. She spoke on the work of the true medical missionary. Burden reports: "I think I never heard her paint in such glowing terms the work of the true medical missionary."

The manager of the Loma Linda Association stayed by Burden's side. Tears flowed down his cheeks. As Ellen White finished, he turned to Burden and said: "I would give the world to be with you people in a work such as this. It was what we had in mind, but we did not know how to carry it out. I am glad you people are obtaining this property, as I know our plans will now be realized." Burden invited him to stay and help carry forward the work. "Impossible!" he replied. "Only Christians of the highest ideals could carry out such a work" (DF 8, J. A. Burden, "The Location and Development of Loma Linda," p. 110).

In spite of the evidences of God's leading, both in circumstances and in Ellen White's counsel, the group facing such a stupendous project were unready to come to any decision. The financial problems loomed too large.

So before taking any steps, they felt that the matter should be placed before the Los Angeles Carr Street church, the largest in the conference. The meeting was called for 10:00 the next morning, June 12.

By 10:00 a.m. Monday, the church on Carr Street was crowded. Ellen White reviewed what had been revealed to her of the medical missionary work that should be carried forward in southern California. She told the audience that Loma Linda recalled to her mind visions of properties that ought to be secured for sanitarium work. The church members voted in favor of securing the property for a sanitarium.

THE FIRST $5,000 PAYMENT

However, the officers of the Southern California Conference felt that more than one church should be heard from before the conference could be brought into it. June 20 was set for a delegated meeting of the conference as a time for the decision. In the meantime June 14 would come with its payment of $4,000 due. It took considerable faith and courage just then to meet the payment to complete the first installment on the $40,000. The farmer down the coast had provided $2,400. Elder Burden talked with another church member, Belle Baker. She could see no reason to hesitate and said she would put up $1,000. "You may lose it," Burden suggested. "I'll risk it," she replied (SHM, p. 356).

Then Burden conferred with his friend, R. S. Owen. "I don't have the money," Owen declared, "but I'll mortgage my house for it." He was able to get an unsecured loan for the needed amount, and the June payment was made on schedule.

Five days later, on June 20, the constituency of the Southern California Conference met. They were faced with the matter of whether Loma Linda should be purchased, and, if so, whether it would be operated "by private corporation or by the conference assuming the financial responsibility of the enterprise" (PUR, July 13, 1905). Ellen White was on hand for the meeting. She spoke for more than an hour on the work that should be done in southern California and urged that the Loma Linda property be secured, as it fully met the descriptions of the properties shown to her in vision. She declared, "This is the very property that we ought to have" (ibid.).

Still the leading officers of the Southern California Conference hesitated. How, with the heavy debt on the conference, could they become further involved in securing properties and starting sanitariums? Conference officers cautioned the delegates to move guardedly.

Then G. A. Irwin, the newly elected General Conference vice president, rose to speak. He was on a mission to California, and while passing through Los Angeles had been urged to visit Loma Linda. He had just that morning come from there, and now spoke in favor of securing that institution. He rehearsed a number of incidents in which, when Mrs. White's counsel was followed and workers and church members responded to the guiding messages, God signally blessed and success came to the work.

The audience listened attentively as Elder Irwin spoke with measured words: "Although the conference is heavily in debt, I believe it to be to the glory of God that the conference should assume this responsibility" (ibid.).

Elder Irwin's speech, exuding confidence in the Spirit of Prophecy counsels and urging action, turned the tide. The constituency voted unanimously in favor of securing the Loma Linda property and opening a third sanitarium in southern California. Cash and pledges totaling $1,100 were offered in support of the action.

FAITH REWARDED: MEETING THE PAYMENTS

July 26, the fateful day when the second payment on the Loma Linda property was due, dawned with still no money in sight. If the payment was not made by 2:00 p.m., the property and the initial $5,000 would be lost. Would deliverance come, or would the enemy succeed in bringing defeat? A meeting of the conference committee had been called for that morning in Los Angeles at their new office on the second floor of 257 South Hill Street (PUR, June 22, 1905). A heavy cloud of perplexity hung over the assembly. Some felt the circumstances justified the misgivings they had entertained from the start. Others, Elder Burden recounted, "remembered the clear words that had come through the *Testimonies,* and refused to concede there should be failure" (SHM, p. 358). As they reached out for deliverance, someone suggested that the morning mail had not yet come and perhaps relief would come from that source.

Elder Burden tells the heartwarming story:

> Soon after this the postman was heard coming up the stairs. He opened the door and delivered the mail. Among the letters was one bearing the postmark Atlantic City, New Jersey.
>
> The letter was opened, and it was found to contain a draft for $5,000, just the amount needed for the payment.
>
> Needless to say, the feelings of those who had been critical were quickly changed. Eyes filled with tears, and one who had been especially critical was the first to break the silence. With trembling voice, he said, "It seems that the Lord is in this matter." "Surely He is," was the reply, "and He will carry it through to victory." The influence that filled the room that day hushed the spirit of criticism. It was as solemn as the judgment day *(ibid.).*

Among those to whom Ellen White had written appealing for funds was a woman in Atlantic City, and Elder Burden points out:

> The Lord put it into her heart to respond and to mail the letter just at the time when our faith had been tested almost to the limit, that it might be revived and strengthened *(ibid.,* p. 359).

TWO MORE PAYMENTS

Elder Burden had no reason to expect that it would be any easier to meet the remaining payments on the $40,000 contract that he had signed; the next payment was due within a month. The president and officers of the Southern California Conference were still holding back on their interest, support, and money.

It was hoped that the soon-coming Southern California Conference camp meeting would provide an opportunity to lift the level of support. Ellen White would be present and would have a message.

The camp meeting was scheduled for August 11 to 21 in Los Angeles, where evangelist W. W. Simpson's tent meetings were about to close. The big tent would be moved to Boyle Heights—an area that would become well known to Seventh-day Adventists a decade later, for the White Memorial Hospital was to be established there. The tent would be pitched on Mott Street, between First and Second (PUR, July 27, 1905).

The annual conference constituency meeting would be held in connection with the camp meeting, which made it a particularly crucial session. Writing of the experience a month later, W. C. White declared:

> We all saw that very much was at stake, and that much depended on how the sanitarium work was presented to our people at this meeting. We knew that there was sufficient means among our people in southern California to carry forward all the institutional work in that conference, but if they chose to keep it in the banks, to invest it in real estate, or to tie it up in farms, if they feared to trust it in our institutional work, then we should have great difficulty in securing funds.

Ellen White spoke six times in the large tent, at times to a packed tent of 2,000. And while some speakers found it difficult to make themselves heard by so large a crowd, the Lord gave her "strength to speak so that all could hear" (letter 241a, 1905). "The Lord greatly sustained me in my work at the camp meeting," she wrote later (letter 251, 1905).

> At the close of the three-hour meeting when the Loma Linda project was presented, the people began to testify to their confidence in the work, and to tell of the money they had in the bank, which they would lend to the enterprise. Others promised to sell property and to invest the proceeds in sanitarium enterprises. By one o'clock the blackboard showed the responses:
>
> | | |
> |---|---|
> | Gifts subscribed on June 20 | $ 1,100 |
> | Gifts subscribed today | $ 1,100 |
> | Money offered at moderate interest | $14,000 |
> | Property consecrated to be sold and the proceeds invested in sanitarium work | $16,350 |
>
> (28 WCW, p. 449).

The tide was turned in overwhelming favor of the sanitarium enterprises. Loma Linda would have full support.

This led the astonished conference president to comment in his report in the *Pacific Union Recorder:*

> This liberality on the part of a willing membership, few of whom are

well off in this world's goods, ought to stimulate confidence in our own conference and perhaps inspire other conferences to raise funds to liqui-date all indebtedness (Sept. 14, 1905).

The August payment of $5,000 was made on time, and a few days later the December 31 payment also was made. In fact, instead of taking three years to pay the second $20,000 of purchase price, as agreed to in the contract, it was taken care of within six months.

Reported J. A. Burden, who was closely involved in the enterprise:

> The counsel of the Spirit of Prophecy had been confirmed. As we moved forward in faith, the Lord opened the way before us, and the money came from unexpected sources (SHM, p. 361).

A detailed account of God's continued providence in connection with Loma Linda cannot be included here. Fuller accounts are to be found in such works as *The Story of Our Health Message; The Vision Bold, Legacy; Origin and History of Seventh-day Adventists*, volume 3; and the *Seventh-day Adventist Encyclopedia*.

DEDICATION OF LOMA LINDA SANITARIUM

By the first of October Elder and Mrs. Burden were residing at Loma Linda, and within days patients were coming. But pressed hard to meet the needs of an opening institution, the staff found it necessary to postpone the dedication.

This dedication was something Ellen White could not miss. Invited to give the dedicatory address, she made the trip south to meet the appointment and to attend, a week later, the dedication of the Paradise Valley Sanitarium. She, with her son W. C. White, Sara McEnterfer, her niece May Walling, and Clarence Crisler, reached Loma Linda on Friday afternoon, April 13.

She was glad to arrive a few hours before the Sabbath began. She sometimes found it necessary to travel on the Sabbath and sometimes arrived at her desti-nation after the Sabbath had begun, but she said, "It is very painful to me to be arriving on the Sabbath" (MS 123, 1906).

By the time the sun was setting over the orange groves, casting light on the snowcapped peaks beyond, Ellen White was comfortably settled in the "nine-room cottage," one of several on the eastern end of the sanitarium grounds. She found the surroundings beautiful—the air filled with the fragrance of orange blossoms, the lawns green and flower gardens colorful, and the glow on Mount San Gorgonio a rich pink from the last light of the sun.

Sabbath morning in the sanitarium parlor she gave a sermon on Second Peter. Sunday morning she looked over the property as guests came in from all over southern California for the dedication that afternoon. About 500 gathered in the chairs set up on the lawn under the pepper trees. Among the guests were "several physicians and other leading men from the surrounding cities." The speakers' platform was an improvised structure about three feet (one meter) off the ground and covered overhead and in back by a striped canvas.

Ellen White made her way to the platform for her talk and took a seat beside Elder Haskell (MS 123, 1906). When her turn came to speak, she stood just to the left of the small table in the center of the platform. Part of the time she placed her right hand on the table, while she gestured with her left.

In her talk she reviewed the providences of God in the purchase of Loma Linda, emphasized the values of its then rural location in the treatment of the sick, and delineated the purposes of establishing sanitariums (RH, June 21, 1906).

A MOMENTOUS YEAR: BALLENGER, JONES, KELLOGG

The year 1905 was only one hour old when Ellen White rose on a Sunday morning and made her way to her writing room.

> It is a cool morning. Built my fire. Bowed before the Lord in prayer. I have so many things burdening my mind. I ask the Lord Jesus to direct me, to guide me. . . .
>
> I need the Great Guide to control my mind. . . . Oh, how much I feel that I need the guidance of the Holy Spirit! (MS 173, 1905).

It was to be a momentous year. At the very hour she was writing, a part of the Melrose Sanitarium in New England was being ravaged by fire. She would learn of this later, of course. Two new sanitariums in southern California, started in response to her urgent calls, were struggling to their feet, and she would soon call for a third. The denomination was in the throes of agony over the defection of Dr. John Harvey Kellogg and his associates. The growing work in the South faced many needs.

The General Conference session of 1905 was scheduled to open on May 11 in Washington, D.C. Ellen White was invited, but questioned whether she should attend. In her correspondence she intimated that she probably would not make the trip. The work on her books called for her attention, and she felt that she should stay by this. Yet, as the time for the session approached, she laid plans to go if it seemed her duty to do so.

Night after night in visions she seemed to be either speaking to large congregations or attending important committee meetings. She wrote of how she had had "presentations regarding the deceptions that Satan is bringing in at this time" (letter 99, 1905).

Was she referring to the recent disclosure in correspondence that A. F. Ballenger, a worker in England, was teaching views on the sanctuary truth that would nullify the well-founded understanding of Christ's ministry in the heavenly sanctuary? Was it the intensification that was to come of the Kellogg views, which she once declared "virtually destroyed the Lord God Himself" (letter 300, 1903)? Could it be the growing apostasy of A. T. Jones?

When A. G. Daniells, president of the General Conference, learned that there was some question in Ellen White's mind as to whether she would attend the conference, he wrote to her:

> I did not know there was any question at all about your coming. . . . The members of the General Conference Committee located in Washington, and the leading brethren living here, desire that you shall attend this meeting, and we send you a hearty invitation to come (AGD to EGW, Apr. 19, 1905).

> As I fully expect you will come, I will not write more regarding this matter. We shall make the best arrangements we know how for your entertainment (*ibid.*).

With this urging by the General Conference president, Mrs. White decided to attend. Arrangements were quickly made to take care of personnel and travel plans. The southern route was chosen for the trip. Twenty to twenty-five people would be traveling together, their party almost filling the tourist car that would carry them to Washington.

Accompanying Ellen White was her son W. C. White; his wife, May; and Maggie Hare. The party arrived at the Washington station on Tuesday morning, May 9, at 10:00. After staying overnight at the little temporary sanitarium being opened in Washington in a rented building, the party moved to the newly completed boys' dormitory in Takoma Park, where four rooms were given over to them. Two rooms were for Mrs. White (a bedroom and a working room), one room was for W. C. White and his wife, and another for Maggie Hare.

Ellen White was pleased to witness the development of the work at the school. When she had left Washington in mid-August 1904, construction was just getting under way. Now this building was completed, and work was progressing on others.

She reported that she had "stood the trip remarkably well, and was stronger when I left the cars at Washington than when I got on board at San Francisco." She declared:

> I can but feel that the Lord is in my coming to Washington at this time. I have a message to bear. God helping me, I will stand firm for the right, presenting truth unmixed with the falsities that have been stealthily creeping in (letter 135, 1905).

Elder Daniells planned that this General Conference session would be deeply spiritual. He saw the importance of upgrading the ministry, so plans were laid for a ministerial institute to run though the session, with an hour each day devoted to the presentation of appropriate topics. Departmental meetings also would be held.

But it was the spiritual interest of the cause that weighed most heavily on his heart. This was reflected in the opening meeting at 10:30 a.m. on Thursday, May 11.

THE 1905 SESSION OPENS

Elder Daniells took Ellen White onto the platform with the group of ministers who were to open the important session. A spirit of solemnity pervaded the assembly as they gathered in the large tent pitched near the new college building. Many had the feeling that this would be "one of the most important gatherings of God's people ever assembled on the earth."

Behind the scenes, and not mentioned in the *Review and Herald* in the formal report of the session, a number of important things were taking place. One of these was three early-morning meetings in which church leaders heard A. F. Ballenger present his views on the sanctuary. Ellen White was to address these views in a somewhat veiled way in her talks, and more specifically in a face-to-face confrontation.

THE BALLENGER TEACHINGS

A. F. Ballenger, a brother of E. S. Ballenger in southern California, for a time was a minister in Great Britain. Associated with him in the work in Britain were such men as E. W. Farnsworth and E. E. Andross. The latter, in a series of talks given in 1911, gave a little of the background of the Ballenger experience:

> [In early 1905] A. F. Ballenger was over in Great Britain while I was there, and he had not been very thoroughly instructed in some points of the faith. He had been preaching around over the country on certain practical points of the faith, and had had considerable success in that line, but he had not been thoroughly grounded in the doctrinal points of the faith. One night while laboring with me in London, it came his turn to preach on the subject of the sanctuary. He did so, but he was very much discouraged over his efforts on the subject of the sanctuary that night. And then he said, "If the Lord will help me, I will never preach again until I know what I am preaching. I am not going to get it from our books. If our brethren could obtain it from the original sources, why can't I? . . . I will go to the books or commentaries and all these various sources from which Elder Uriah Smith obtained light on the subject of the sanctuary, and I will get it from the same sources that he did. I will not know it because Elder Uriah Smith knew it, but I will know it because God is

teaching it to me directly" (DF 178, E. E. Andross, "Bible Study No. II," July 13, 1911, pp. 13, 14).

Elder Andross then explained that Ballenger did not realize the source from which Elder Smith obtained the sanctuary truth. There was earnest Bible study by the pioneers of the Advent movement, and with them was the messenger of the Lord. As the brethren continued their study, there was in their midst one through whom the Spirit of God was able to point out what was truth and what was error.

Elder Ballenger considered his discoveries as new light and early in the 1905 session laid before the leading brethren his "discoveries." Not surprisingly, the brethren were unable to accept his reasoning, and pointed out the errors of his application of Scripture.

In her Tuesday afternoon address to the session, Ellen White's mind turned to the teachings on the sanctuary truth that were being quietly met by church leaders. She told of how in the early days errors crept in, and how the Lord sent her into the field to meet fanaticism and misleading teachings. She declared:

> We shall have to meet these same false doctrines again. There will be those who will claim to have visions. When God gives you clear evidence that the vision is from Him, you may accept it, but do not accept it on any other evidence; for people are going to be led more and more astray in foreign countries and in America. The Lord wants His people to act like men and women of sense (RH, May 25, 1905).

In an obvious reference to A. F. Ballenger and some of his friends attending the session, she said, "I am praying that the power of the Saviour will be exerted in behalf of those who have entered into the temptations of the enemy" (*ibid.*).

ELLEN WHITE SPEAKS OUT ON THE BALLENGER VIEWS

About this time Mrs. White met Elder Ballenger in the hallway of the dormitory where she was staying. Of this experience she wrote:

> As I spoke to him, it came vividly to my mind that this was the man whom I had seen in an assembly bringing before those present certain subjects, and placing upon passages in the Word of God a construction that could not be maintained as truth. He was gathering together a mass of scriptures such as would confuse minds because of his assertions and his misapplication of these scriptures, for the application was misleading and had not the bearing upon the subject at all which he claimed justified his position. Anyone can do this, and will follow his example to testify to a false position; but it was his own (MS 59, 1905).

She told Elder Ballenger that he was the minister that the Lord had presented before her in vision in Salamanca, New York, in 1890, as standing with a party who was "urging that if the Sabbath truth were left out of the *[American] Sentinel,* the circulation of the paper would be largely increased."

In her account of the experience, as recorded in her journal, Ellen White explained why she had come to Washington:

> I declare in the name of the Lord that the most dangerous heresies are seeking to find entrance among us as a people, and Elder Ballenger is making spoil of his own soul. The Lord has strengthened me to come the long journey to Washington to this meeting to bear my testimony in vindication of the truth of God's Word and the manifestation of the Holy Spirit in confirmation of Bible truth *(ibid.).*

On Wednesday, May 24, in a message entitled "A Warning Against False Theories," Mrs. White addressed herself to the subject in a document that most likely was read to a rather limited group. A copy was placed in Elder Ballenger's hands. In plain language she declared:

> Our Instructor spoke words to Brother Ballenger: ". . . Those who receive your interpretation of Scripture regarding the sanctuary service are receiving error and following in false paths. The enemy will work the minds of those who are eager for something new, preparing them to receive false theories and false expositions of the Scriptures" (MS 62, 1905).

A part of Elder Farnsworth's evaluation of Elder Ballenger's views follows:

> He has been studying the subject of the sanctuary a good deal lately, and he comes to the conclusion that the atonement was made when Christ was crucified and that when He ascended He went immediately into the Most Holy Place and that His ministry has been carried on there ever since.
>
> He takes such texts as Hebrews 6:19 and compares them with twenty-five or thirty expressions of the same character in the Old Testament where he claims that in every instance the term "within the veil" signifies within the Most Holy Place. He says the outer veil or the door of the tabernacle is never called the veil of the tabernacle . . . [except] once, and then by implication (Heb. 9:3), and does not think that one instance should be so construed as to practically overthrow the rest.
>
> He sees clearly that his view cannot be made to harmonize with the Testimonies, at least he admits freely that he is totally unable to do so, and even in his own mind, as far as he is able to see at present, there is

an irreconcilable difference. This, of course, involves the authenticity of the Testimonies and practically upsets them—I mean, in his mind.

It also upsets our views concerning the sanctuary and its work, though he does not really think that way. It also involves to a greater or lesser extent our views of the two covenants, and how much more I was not able to ascertain (E. W. Farnsworth to AGD, in AGD to WCW, Mar. 16, 1905).

Unlike his immediate and hearty response to the testimony of correction in 1891, Elder Ballenger this time turned from the message and appeal of Ellen White and the counsel of his brethren and held tenaciously to his cherished views. This led to his being dropped from the ministry of the Seventh-day Adventist Church. It was a bitter experience for all concerned.

ELDER A. T. JONES

The work of the 1905 General Conference session continued at an even pace. Ten times Ellen White addressed the session. "The Lord has helped me," she wrote near the close of the meeting, "to make the discourses impressive. . . . I still have a work to do on the grounds, for certain individuals" (letter 149, 1905). One of these individuals was A. T. Jones, still a member of the General Conference Committee but now closely associated with Dr. J. H. Kellogg and in full sympathy with him.

Sometime during the session a vision was given Ellen White in which "Elder Jones's case was again presented to me" (letter 116, 1906). This led her to have an extended interview with him in which she discussed the peril of his being in Battle Creek in close association with Dr. Kellogg. But the interview was unproductive, for Jones felt he was in no danger. His presence at the 1905 General Conference session marked the close of his connection with the church in an official capacity—a connection that in its earlier years was marked by outstanding contributions.

At the age of 23 Alonzo T. Jones, an officer in the United States Army, became a Seventh-day Adventist. An earnest, studious, self-made man, he prepared himself for the ministry, to which he was called in 1885. He soon distinguished himself as an associate editor of the *Signs of the Times*. Not long afterward he was joined by a physician-turned-minister, Dr. Ellet J. Waggoner. At the General Conference session of 1888 the two led out in presentations on righteousness by faith. They carried the strong support of Ellen White as advocate of this precious truth. When she could, she traveled and worked with them for two years following the session, carrying the message to churches, ministerial institutes, institutions, and camp meetings.

Elders Jones and Waggoner were catapulted into the position of the leading Bible expositors in the ranks of Seventh-day Adventists, a role they held through much of the 1890s. Jones attended all General Conference sessions, and it was not uncommon for each of the two men to lead out in 10 to 20 or more consecutive Bible studies. Jones spent much time in Battle Creek and stood as a prominent leader, holding several important positions.

But these two men, so highly honored of God because of their wide influence for good, became the special point of attack of the great adversary. The Ellen White communications to both men through a 15-year period following 1888 reveal that each had weaknesses in his experience, each was confronted with dangers, and each had made mistakes. This, however, did not disqualify them to do God's service.

Ellen White had occasion in April 1893 to caution Elder Jones regarding his extreme views in his presentation of the relation of faith and works (see 1SM, pp. 377-380). Again the following year she reproved him for giving wholehearted support to Anna Rice Phillips, who claimed the gift of prophecy (see 2SM, pp. 85-95). From time to time she counseled him to exercise caution in his manner of speaking and writing so as to avoid giving offense.

In February 1897 Jones was elected as one of the 13 members of the General Conference Committee, and eight months later was installed as editor of the *Review and Herald*, a position he held for four years. With this arrangement it was stated that "instead of speaking to comparatively few of our people in annual gatherings, he will address *all* of them *every week*" (RH, Oct. 5, 1897). Through a portion of this time he was chairman of the board of the Review and Herald Publishing Association.

Jones took a prominent place at the 1901 session of the General Conference, and urged that in the reorganization of the General Conference there be "no kings." He was influential in developing a constitution that did not provide for the election of leading General Conference officers by the delegates, but left the responsibility to an executive committee of 25.

Reappointed to the new General Conference Committee in 1901, Jones was assigned to general work that took him to the summer camp meetings in the West. After persuading local conferences in the Northwest to follow the lead of the General Conference and elect no presidents, he himself accepted the presidency of the California Conference. This conference, except for Michigan, was the largest and strongest local conference in the world.

His harsh, domineering spirit soon cost him the confidence of those with whom he worked. Ellen White labored with him diligently, and he promised to reform. Then, with her encouragement, he was elected to a second term in 1902.

In the summer of 1903, at a time when affairs in the California Conference were most uncomfortable, he had an interview with Ellen White at Elmshaven in which he told her that at the request of Dr. J. H. Kellogg he was planning to go to Battle Creek to teach Bible in the American Medical Missionary College. He hoped to be able to help Dr. Kellogg. She counseled him not to go. He promised her that he would be guarded. She had been warned in vision that such a move on his part would lead to his downfall.

Ellen White watched the inevitable results and agonized for his spiritual welfare. His plan to stay in Battle Creek only one year was soon forgotten as he became more and more entrenched there.

In vision Ellen White had been shown what Jones's attitude would be, and now she witnessed it. In "place of receiving the warnings, he was full of self-confidence" (letter 116, 1906).

"I warned Elder Jones," wrote Mrs. White, "but he felt that he was not in the least danger. But the fine threads have been woven about him, and he is now a man deluded and deceived. Though claiming to believe the Testimonies, he does not believe them" (ibid.).

To watch a man who had been used mightily of God rejecting light and spurning every appeal weighed heavily on the heart of the Lord's messenger, and deeply troubled church leaders. In this experience at the 1905 General Conference session A. T. Jones took an important step in his apostasy. Matters reached such a point that in 1909 it seemed necessary to drop his name from the church rolls.

DR. J. H. KELLOGG

On the final Tuesday morning of the session Ellen White spoke concerning Dr. Kellogg and Battle Creek problems. In her address on these sensitive points, she stated:

> It has been presented to me that in view of Dr. Kellogg's course of action at the Berrien Springs meetings [May 17-26, 1904], we are not to treat him as a man led of the Lord, who should be invited to attend our general meetings as a teacher and leader (MS 70, 1905).

The feelings of distress and some of the burdens she carried because of the defections of Dr. J. H. Kellogg and Elders A. T. Jones and A. F. Ballenger she could not lay aside. She had seen that Kellogg's pantheistic views, because they took away the personality of God and Jesus Christ, undercut the sanctuary truth, the cornerstone of the message, so precious to the pioneers. Now with Ballenger's direct attack on this point, there was occasion for added concern.

Two days after the close of the session she wrote words that forecast distressing times:

> The Lord now calls upon me to make plain to others that which has been made plain to me. . . . I have no liberty to withhold any longer the matters that I have written. There is much that must be brought out (letter 319, 1905).

Concerning the magnitude of the threat to the very existence of the Seventh-day Adventist Church, as shown to her in vision, she wrote a few months later:

> Had the theories contained in *Living Temple* been received by our people, had not a message been sent by the Lord to counteract these theories, the third angel's message would no longer have been given to the world, but pleasing fables would have been proclaimed everywhere. Men would have been led to believe a lie instead of the truth of the Word of God. An army of those who take pleasure in unrighteousness would have sprung into action.
>
> The roll was spread before me. The presentation was as though that against which the Lord was warning His people had actually taken place. I shall not attempt to describe the presentation, but to me it was a living reality. I saw that if the erroneous sentiments contained in *Living Temple* were received, souls would be bound up in fallacies. Men would be so completely controlled by the mind of one man that they would act as if they were subjects of his will. Working through men, Satan was trying to turn into fables the truths that have made us what we are (letter 338, 1905).

In document after document in the months that followed the 1905 General Conference session, Ellen White wrote not only of the threat of the Kellogg teachings but dealt explicitly with the error of Ballenger's positions on the sanctuary truth, basing her warnings on repeated visions. She made it clear that if there was one fundamental truth that had come to the pioneers by Bible study and revelation, it was the sanctuary truth, and she indicated that Satan would bring one attack after another on this fundamental point.

The year 1905 marked the rapidly growing rift between the medical interests, headed by Dr. John Harvey Kellogg, and church leaders and the church organization itself.

The steps taken following the General Conference sessions of 1901 and 1903 to bind the medical work to the denomination were seen by Dr. Kellogg as a challenge to the institution he dominated. The organization of a medical department and the appointment of a medical department secretary confirmed this in his mind. In seeming desperation he launched an aggressive program to develop Battle Creek Sanitarium into an even stronger base of influence, and entered upon an aggressive campaign to unsettle confidence in Ellen White and church leaders.

It was now clear to the leaders of the medical missionary interests in Battle Creek that medical work fostered by the Seventh-day Adventist Church was to be under the control of the church, for it was a branch of the work of the church. It was not to be dominated by leaders of medical interests in Battle Creek who had set about to make the medical missionary work undenominational.

Emissaries of Dr. Kellogg were sent out to hold a line of allegiance to him and the policies for which he stood. These Battle Creek-directed emissaries were sent to parts of the world where medical missionary work was promulgated. In a quiet and stealthy way they struck at the foundations of confidence in the Ellen White counsels (AGD to WCW, Oct. 12, 1905).

The groundwork for this had been established in the critical attitude toward church leaders and Ellen White's support for moving the headquarters of the church and the Review and Herald publishing plant to Washington, D.C. The issues were intensified as plans now blossomed to make Battle Creek a great educational center—greater and more influential than anything that had preceded it.

KELLOGG PLANS A UNIVERSITY IN BATTLE CREEK

A great deal concerning the Battle Creek situation had been written by Ellen White to church leaders, but the question with her was: When should it be broadcast generally? She explained the delay: she had been restrained until the appropriate time—when Dr. Kellogg made his first move.

The announcement in the September issue of the *Medical Missionary*, published in Battle Creek, of plans to launch a university in Battle Creek, was the "first move." Two years before, steps being taken to reopen Battle Creek College were laid aside because of Ellen White's clear counsel. Now the counsel itself was laid aside, and articles and catalogs proclaimed the opening of a number of schools—virtually a university (AGD to WCW, Oct. 12, 1905).

There would be "many courses of study offered by various schools carried on in connection with the Battle Creek Sanitarium"—"professional, scientific, literary, biblical, technical." Forty courses would lead to diplomas and degrees. In addition to the above, numerous trades would be taught, such as steamfitting, plumbing, blacksmithing, carpentry, painting, tinsmithing, steam and electrical engineering, shoemaking, and dressmaking.

All these were offered to Seventh-day Adventist youth who had no money. They could meet expenses by working at the sanitarium (*Medical Missionary*, October 1905; AGD to EGW, Oct. 11, 1905).

To draw Seventh-day Adventist youth to Battle Creek, most attractive inducements were made in courses and work opportunities offered. But there were the warnings sounded for two years that Seventh-day Adventist youth should not go to Battle Creek in pursuit of an education. The work of undercutting the Testimonies began with meetings held by Dr. Kellogg and A. T. Jones with the sanitarium workers and was advanced by correspondence with Seventh-day Adventist youth throughout the field.

In Daniells' opinion the whole denomination should be informed as to what was going on at Battle Creek. He pleaded with Ellen White: "Has not the time come to give the people enough of what God has revealed to you to fully inform and arouse them? . . . Has not the time come for the ship to strike the iceberg?"

VERY DECIDED TESTIMONY SENT TO ELDER DANIELLS

As the year 1905 was drawing to a close, the matter of a university at Battle Creek was coming to a crisis. Ellen White could no longer withhold her warning. On November 16 W. C. White left the West Coast to attend the first General Conference Medical Missionary Convention, to be held at College View, Nebraska, November 21-26 (29 WCW, p. 664; RH, Nov. 16, 1905).

Stirred by plans announced for the College View meeting, the medical people in Battle Creek launched countering measures. Dr. Kellogg called a convention of his new International Medical Missionary Alliance in Chicago for December 18-21 (*Medical Missionary*, November 1905).

The West Michigan Conference invited Elder Daniells to assist in the Week of Prayer in Battle Creek in mid-December. After taking counsel with Elders Irwin, Prescott, White, and Evans, he felt he should accept the invitation. This would give him an opportunity to present the testimonies dealing with the situation. The Week of Prayer would begin Friday night, December 15. Daniells, W. C. White, and one or two others went over on Tuesday, the twelfth. This gave them an opportunity to get the feel of the situation. One of the testimonies Daniells carried with him had been penned by Ellen White on June 28, 1905. It was titled "A Solemn Warning."

When Elders Daniells and W. C. White were in Battle Creek, Ellen White and her assistants continued to collect and copy material. That weekend she wrote to Elders Daniells and Prescott:

> I have lost all hope of Dr. Kellogg. He is, I fully believe, past the day of his reprieve. I have not written him a line for about one year. I am instructed not to write to him. . . .
>
> I have been reading over the matter given me for him, and the light is that we must call our people to a decision. . . . We are to be as wise as serpents and as harmless as doves (letter 333, 1905).

Her burden of heart intensified as the week progressed. To W. C. White she wrote:

> I have many things I wish you and Elder Daniells and those united with him in his labor in Battle Creek to have just as soon as possible. I have very decided testimony that I am sending in to Battle Creek to Elder Daniells. I fear he will leave before he gets this so I will send a telegraph message to him to tarry till he receives this that I send (letter 336, 1905).

The message was sent on Thursday, December 21, and Elder Daniells tarried in Battle Creek as the Week of Prayer meetings continued. Dr. Kellogg and many of the medical personnel were in Chicago attending the meeting he had called of the International Medical Missionary Alliance to convene Monday through Thursday, December 18-21. Daniells let it be known that he had changed his plans and was staying to await the message promised in Ellen White's telegram.

ARRIVAL OF THE PROMISED TESTIMONIES

On Tuesday, December 26, Daniells went to his office early (probably his old office in the West Building) to see whether the communications from Ellen White had come. They had not. A few minutes later one of the physicians from the Battle Creek Sanitarium came to see him.

The physician was in great perplexity of mind. He had been brought up to look upon all messages given by Ellen White as emanating from the Lord. But now he was bewildered and confused. The night before, he, with many other leading sanitarium workers, had attended a meeting lasting from 5:00 to 11:00 in which Dr. Kellogg had outlined the recent controversy as he saw it. Kellogg told this group of responsible sanitarium workers that he believed in the Spirit of Prophecy and believed Ellen White "is a good woman and that she had been inspired by the Lord." But, he continued, "all of the communications which were sent out could not be relied upon as coming from the Lord" (AGD to G. A. Irwin, Dec. 27, 1905).

"Now," said the doctor, addressing Elder Daniells, "I want, if possible, that you shall make it plain to me what messages we are to understand are from the Lord, and which ones emanate from men who are influencing Sister White."

Elder Daniells told him that he could not give him any light on the point, that to him they were "all genuine," that "they were all either from the Lord or from the devil."

While the men talked, there was a knock on the door, and a messenger handed Elder Daniells a large envelope with "Elmshaven," Sanitarium, California, as the return address. The next day Daniells told the story:

"Now," said I, "Doctor, we will open this envelope, and you shall be the first to look upon these testimonies; take them, look them over, and tell me whether they are genuine or spurious—whether they were given to her by the Lord, or by some man."

He took them and looked at the titles, the dates, and the signatures, and handing them over, he said to me, "Well, I cannot tell you whether these are from the Lord or from man, whether they are reliable or unreliable. It looks to me," said he, "that it is a question of faith on my part as to whether Sister White is a servant of God or a wicked pretender."

"Well," said I, "you are just as able to tell me who inspired these communications as I am to tell you; you have seen them first; you know just as much about them as I do; I cannot give you the slightest information that you do not possess.

"Now," said I, "the only ground for me to occupy is absolute confidence that God is revealing to His servant that which the church needs to understand, and that every single communication which she sends out emanates from God and not from man" (ibid.).

The physician said that he saw the whole point and that "he must stand fully on this ground."

A MARKED CONFIDENCE-CONFIRMING EXPERIENCE

Daniells could hardly wait to read the testimonies Ellen White had sent to him. With a fellow minister he read the communications. They noted that while each of the two documents had been copied on Thursday, December 21, 1905, one was penned in August 1903 and the other June 1, 1904.

Arrangements were made immediately for a meeting in the tabernacle that evening at 7:30, at which the testimonies would be read to the whole church. At 7:30 the tabernacle was full—auditorium, vestries, and gallery. Dr. Kellogg was not there. His brother, W. K., and a number of the doctor's supporters were there. Elder Daniells took the lead, telling the congregation of how, in times of old, God communicated with His people. Sometimes the prophet delivered in person God's message; sometimes it was delivered through others. He pointed out that "from the earliest days of this cause the Spirit of Prophecy had been in our midst, and had been recognized by those who were loyal to this message, and that the messenger had always claimed liberty to deliver the message either in person or by sending it to others to be read" (ibid.).

He read the telegram instructing him to wait in Battle Creek for the testimonies. Now he had the two documents in his hands: Manuscript 120, 1905, "The Result of a Failure to Heed God's Warnings," and Manuscript 122, 1905,

"A Solemn Appeal." He pointed out that both were penned by Ellen White in her journal, one as much as two years before, but were not copied until she was impressed to do so, Thursday, December 21. Both documents carried solemn messages pointing out that leaders who were spiritually blind were leading the blind, and unless "converted and transformed," "leaders and their followers" "cannot be laborers together with God" (MS 120, 1905).

Both of the testimonies were read without comment. As Elder Daniells read on, page after page, a number in the large tabernacle audience could not help noting how accurately they described the words and attitudes witnessed just the night before as Dr. Kellogg addressed sanitarium leaders. It was 9:00 when Daniells finished reading the 16 pages of the two documents. "It seemed to me as I read," he wrote the next day, "that I never felt the burning power of words reaching my own soul as these" (AGD to G. A. Irwin, Dec. 27, 1905).

"We ought to resort to earnest prayer," he told the hushed audience, and suggested that those who wished to do so "retire to the north vestry." But too many wished to pray, and so the audience turned back to the main auditorium.

During the break three men who had been in Dr. Kellogg's six-hour meeting came to Daniells and told him that the meeting held the previous night had been clearly described in the messages Ellen White had sent. They also said that "if there had been a doubt in their minds regarding the source of the testimonies, it would have been swept away by their own statements [as set forth by Ellen G. White] in the testimonies" (ibid.).

From 9:15 to 10:00 all united in prayer that their eyes might be opened to see things as God sees them. They prayed that Dr. Kellogg and his associates and all the sanitarium helpers might be led to receive and obey the solemn messages that had come to them.

The next few days in old Battle Creek there was much discussion of how the Spirit of the Lord on the previous Thursday had led Ellen White in California to have the message she wrote two years before copied and sent to Battle Creek to arrive just after the notable meeting was held by Dr. Kellogg in the college building. Some said of the Monday night meeting that "if they had not been well grounded, they would have been turned away entirely from the testimonies. One said that he would be driven into infidelity if he believed the things the doctor related to them" (ibid.).

Elder Daniells felt impelled to express his feelings. "I know," he firmly averred, "that God is rewarding us for our pledge of unswerving loyalty to the Spirit of Prophecy as well as all the rest of this message." "Victory has been given to this cause" (ibid.).

And indeed it was a victory.

As for Dr. Kellogg, no change was observed in his attitude. Two days after the memorable Tuesday night meeting he called the sanitarium family together and for three hours reviewed the history of the institution, endeavoring to prove that it was never a Seventh-day Adventist establishment but rather the property of the stockholders.

The *Review and Herald* of December 28, 1905, carried a six-column editorial by W. W. Prescott titled "The Battle Creek University." In it the editor bared his own soul as he stated:

> We know from personal experience something about the bitterness of the experience which results from listening to constant insinuations about the fundamental truths of this message borne to the world by Seventh-day Adventists. We know what it means to struggle with the doubts and fears aroused by skillful misrepresentations of warnings and counsels given through the Spirit of Prophecy. . . . We have learned our lessons through an experience from which we would gladly protect others, and therefore feel justified in speaking plainly when we see the snare set so seductively.

Battle Creek did not become the educational center some had anticipated; nor did it attract large numbers of Seventh-day Adventist youth. Union conference colleges were strengthened to meet the needs of the cause, and soon the College of Medical Evangelists was established by the church at Loma Linda.

ELLEN WHITE'S SPECIAL GIFT

Ellen White had a very special gift. She described it clearly:

> Some have stumbled over the fact that I said I did not claim to be a prophet; and they have asked, Why is this?
>
> I have had no claims to make, only that *I am instructed that I am the Lord's messenger;* that He called me in my youth to be His messenger, to receive His word, and to give a clear and decided message in the name of the Lord Jesus.
>
> Early in my youth I was asked several times, Are you a prophet? I have ever responded, I am the Lord's messenger. I know that many have called me a prophet, but I have made no claim to this title. My Saviour declared me to be His messenger. "Your work," He instructed me, "is to bear My word." . . .
>
> Why have I not claimed to be a prophet? Because in these days many who boldly claim that they are prophets are a reproach to the cause of Christ; and because my work includes much more than the word "prophet" signifies. . . .
>
> God has made plain to me the various ways in which He would use me to carry forward a special work. Visions have been given me, with the promise, "If you deliver the messages faithfully and endure to the end, you shall eat of the fruit of the tree of life, and drink of the water of the river of life" (1SM, pp. 31-33).

After describing the breadth of the work she was commissioned to do, she declared:

> To claim to be a prophetess is something that I have never done. If others call me by that name, I have no controversy with them. But my work has covered so many lines that I cannot call myself other than a messenger sent to bear a message from the Lord to His people, and to take up work in any line that He points out (*ibid.*, p. 34).

Because on one occasion she mentioned to a large audience in the Battle Creek Tabernacle that she did not consider herself a prophet or a leader of people, on the following Monday the newspapers at Battle Creek heralded the news: The woman the Adventists had believed in all these years as a prophet had now come straight out and said she was not a prophet after all! This naturally raised questions with some Adventists. Mrs. White and church leaders found that an explanation must be made. She took opportunity on several occasions to explain carefully the thoughts she intended to convey by her statement. W. C. White throws considerable light on the matter in the following statement:

> When she spoke these words she had in mind the ideas of the people regarding a prophet as one whose chief office was to predict events, and she wanted them to understand that that was not her place in the world.

MORE THAN A PROPHET

Ellen White was more than a prophet. She was a counselor, a comforter, guide, author, writer, public speaker.

All her life she had encountered opposition, antagonism, and criticism in all shapes and forms from the trivial to the serious. She was quoted and misquoted, interpreted and misinterpreted. But the value of her words was evidenced in schools, sanitariums, and churches all over the world.

Rarely did she defend herself. But now in the sunset of life she was forced into replying to her critics. It was a painful experience to her to know that there were members of God's family who were well acquainted with her and her work but who, on the basis of hearsay and flimsy evidence, had lost confidence in her prophetic mission. That they could so easily forget the many faith-confirming evidences of her call and work, burdened her heart.

What were some of these faith-confirming evidences?

The hundreds of letters crossing thousands of miles of land or sea to arrive at a critical time.

The many people who received letters of counsel on personal matters known only to themselves and God.

The numbers of times she had met individuals for the first time whom she recognized, having seen them in vision.

The credible eyewitness descriptions of the phenomena that accompanied her in vision in the early days of her work.

The lives of leaders such as Daniells, Bates, Loughborough, Haskell, whose doubts had been dispelled.

> I am now instructed that I am not to be hindered in my work by those who engage in suppositions regarding its nature, whose minds are struggling with so many intricate problems connected with the supposed

work of a prophet. My commission embraces the work of a prophet, but it does not end there. It embraces much more than the minds of those who have been sowing the seeds of unbelief can comprehend (letter 244, 1906 [see also 1SM, pp. 31-35]).

Battle Creek, where Dr. Kellogg and his cohorts, including Ballenger and A. T. Jones, were sowing seeds of unbelief, had been the center of the denominational work.

THE SEEDS OF UNBELIEF

After a vision in which she saw physicians of her acquaintance in a meeting setting forth what they considered valid reasons for their waning confidence, Ellen White told W. C. White that everything must be "ready for action." She felt she could, and must, meet many things she heard rehearsed in that meeting (letter 14, 1906).

Repeatedly in the early months of 1906 she mentioned her intention of getting a clear statement of facts from those who were troubled about the testimonies. "If statements have been made that there are contradictions in the testimonies," she wrote to E. W. Farnsworth, temporary pastor of the Battle Creek church, "Should I not be acquainted with the charges and accusations? Should I not know the reason of their sowing tares of unbelief?" (letter 84, 1906).

When in March the A. T. Jones attack came, she helped to meet it. On April 9 she sent out the letter she had written on March 30, addressed "To Those Who Are Perplexed Regarding the Testimonies Relating to the Medical Missionary Work":

> Recently in the visions of the night I stood in a large company of people. There were present Dr. Kellogg, Elders Jones, Tenney, and Taylor, Dr. Paulson, Elder Sadler, Judge Arthur, and many of their associates.
> I was directed by the Lord to request them and any others who have perplexities and grievous things in their minds regarding the testimonies that I have borne, to specify what their objections and criticisms are. The Lord will help me to answer these objections, and to make plain that which seems to be intricate (letter 120, 1906).

She pointed out that if the thought was being entertained that "Sister White's work can no longer be trusted," she wanted to know why that decision had been reached. "It may be," she conjectured, "that some matters that seem to you to be very objectionable can be explained." Making her position clear, she stated, "I am now charged to request those who are in difficulty in regard to Sister White's work to let their questions appear now."

This letter was sent not only to those named but to about a dozen others. Then three days later she and part of her staff were off to southern California for the dedication of the sanitariums at Loma Linda and Paradise Valley. Returning to Elmshaven on May 7, she found that question-laden responses were beginning to come in.

QUESTIONS CALLING FOR CAREFUL ANSWERS

The questions about Ellen White's work that came in from Battle Creek called for earnest attention, not only by her but by her staff. Some of the questions were serious; others were of a quibbling nature dealing with "supposed inconsistencies in the testimonies" (letter 142, 1906).

Many of the questions had their foundation in faulty concepts of inspiration. The prophet was thought of as a mechanical agent, speaking or writing each word dictated by the Holy Spirit. This "verbal inspiration" concept at times led to the expectation of more from Ellen White than was justified—more than was demanded of the prophets and apostles of old.

Her defense of the testimonies and of herself actually dated back to January. "I have been very busy of late," she wrote on January 19. "The Lord has sustained me in preparing matter to meet the unbelief and infidelity expressed regarding the testimonies He has given me to bear to His people. He has given me words to write" (letter 34, 1906).

Ellen White ignored some of the questions; many she answered, writing kind, tolerant letters that dealt in a straightforward way with the problems presented. At times the Elmshaven staff prepared answers. Sometimes the answer was readily available; sometimes the question itself was more a statement than a question (30 WCW, p. 333).

A letter from one prominent physician contained the most complete list of questions yet brought forward by the Battle Creek medical workers. A few illustrated the kind of trivia that the questions sometimes dealt with. Among the points presented in one of these letters were:

1. Is everything from Ellen White's pen a "testimony," or are some just "letters"?

2. Is one to assume that the conditions described in the Testimonies actually exist, or are they just designed to forestall such conditions?

3. What about the statement "I am not a prophet"?

4. Does W. C. White influence the Testimonies?

5. Do you approve of sending personal testimonies, which the Lord has given to certain men, to other people also?

6. Are the Testimonies a test of fellowship?

7. What about the recall of the volume 7 galley proofs for revision?

8. Is it right for any Seventh-day Adventist to work in the Battle Creek Sanitarium?

WHO MANIPULATED HER WRITINGS?

The questions raised concerning the manipulation of her writings, and the influence of W. C. White on the testimonies, distressed Ellen White, particularly such charges as were traced to careless statements made by James Edson White.

The two sons of James and Ellen White were much unlike in personality and character. The younger, William C., was steady, calm, loyal to the Testimonies, dependable, and endued with leadership qualifications. The older son, James Edson, while talented, creative, and a good author, was unsteady, a poor manager of finances, and, because his brother and church leaders could not and did not endorse all his ventures, very critical. The testimonies of his mother addressed to him from early years carried at times little weight; yet when fully consecrated to God he did a remarkable work, particularly among the neglected Blacks in the South.

Because he was the son of James and Ellen White, James Edson was able to borrow money, mainly from Adventists, to support his various enterprises, many of which failed. Again and again his mother and his brother came to his personal financial aid as various enterprises he had been warned against collapsed.

As Ellen White found she could not endlessly support him in these ventures, his brother attempted to counsel him. He in turn took the position that W. C. was influencing his mother. Among his personal friends in and around Battle Creek were a number who were voicing Dr. Kellogg's insinuations that Ellen White was being influenced by her son William and others. It was easy for James Edson to join in. He said some unfortunate things that were quickly picked up and, coming from Mrs. White's own son, capitalized on.

Finally, painful as it was, Ellen White had to step in and set the record straight. She wrote a six-page letter to Edson, ending with this firm statement:

> Your position is a grievous thing to your mother and wears upon the life of your brother. . . . I shall have to speak. I cannot and will not suffer reproach to come upon the cause of God, and my work that God has given me to do, by your saying he manipulates my writings. It is falsehood—but what a charge is this! Not one soul manipulates my writings (letter 391, 1906).

In another letter to Edson, written May 21, 1906, she stated:

> The position you have taken, the words you have said, are not a secret. Everywhere they are handled by those who would uproot confidence

in the Testimonies, and they have influence because you are WCW's brother and the son of Ellen G. White. . . . W. C. White is true as steel to the cause of God, and no lie which is in circulation is of the truth (letter 143, 1906).

Earlier in the year she had written:

There are those who say, "Someone manipulates her writings." I acknowledge the charge. It is One who is mighty in counsel, One who presents before me the condition of things in Battle Creek (letter 52, 1906).

Through June and the early part of July, Ellen White devoted much of her time to answering questions from the field. She wrote scores of letters totaling hundreds of pages. Many of these carried warnings concerning the perils of cherishing doubts in the face of the strong evidences God had given of the integrity of the Spirit of Prophecy.

When it became clear that "the most frivolous questions" were being asked (letter 180, 1906), instruction began to come to her that she need not pick up and answer "all the sayings and doubts that are being put into many minds" (MS 61, 1906). She and her staff, after providing answers to the principal questions, considered their work in this area quite well finished.

THE SAN FRANCISCO EARTHQUAKE

Ellen White spent much of the year 1906 at her Elmshaven home busily engaged in writing. She was deeply concerned about problems in Battle Creek involving Dr. Kellogg, A. T. Jones, and others. With the coming of April it was time for the dedication of two sanitariums in southern California. On Thursday, April 12, she left for the south. With her were her niece, May Walling, who had arrived at Elmshaven a week or two earlier (letter 124, 1906); Sara McEnterfer; and Clarence Crisler (MS 123, 1906).

After the dedication service at Loma Linda Sunday afternoon, April 15, Ellen White and her associate workers stayed on at the sanitarium through Monday. She was to return to Los Angeles on Tuesday and would speak at the Southern California Conference session held in the Carr Street church in Los Angeles on Wednesday. She would be en route to San Diego and the dedication of Paradise Valley Sanitarium the next week.

Monday night, April 16, while she was still at Loma Linda, a solemnizing vision was given to her. "A most wonderful representation," she said, "passed before me." Describing it in an article that now appears in *Testimonies for the Church*, volume 9, she wrote:

During a vision of the night, I stood on an eminence, from which I could see houses shaken like a reed in the wind. Buildings, great and small, were falling to the ground. Pleasure resorts, theaters, hotels, and the homes of the wealthy were shaken and shattered. Many lives were blotted out of existence, and the air was filled with the shrieks of the injured and the terrified. . . . The awfulness of the scenes that passed before me I cannot find words to describe. It seemed that the forbearance of God was exhausted and that the judgment day had come. . . .

Terrible as was the representation that passed before me, *that which impressed itself most vividly upon my mind was the instruction given in connection with it.* The angel that stood by my side declared that God's supreme rulership and the sacredness of His law must be revealed to those who persistently refused to render obedience to the King of kings. Those who choose to remain disloyal must be visited in mercy with judgments, in order that, if possible, they may be aroused to a realization of the sinfulness of their course (pp. 92, 93; italics supplied).

She woke up and switched on the lamp by her bed. It was 1:00 Tuesday morning. She was relieved to discover that she was safe in her room at the Loma Linda Sanitarium.

During the hours of Tuesday morning she seemed dazed (letter 137, 1906). In the afternoon she and her helpers took the train for Los Angeles and went on to Glendale.

That night she was given another vision:

I was again instructed regarding the holiness and binding claims of the Ten Commandments, and the supremacy of God above all earthly rulers. It seemed as if I were before many people, and presenting scripture after scripture in support of the precepts spoken by the Lord from Sinai's height (RH, July 5, 1906).

NEWS OF THE SAN FRANCISCO EARTHQUAKE

On Wednesday she attended a portion of the annual session of the Southern California Conference. As she neared the Carr Street church to fill her speaking appointment, she heard the newsboys crying: "San Francisco destroyed by an earthquake!"

A paper was purchased, and she and those with her in the carriage quickly scanned the "first hastily printed news" (9T, p. 94).

As to the visions on Monday and Tuesday nights, she later commented, "It has taken me many days to write out a portion of that which was revealed those two nights at Loma Linda and Glendale. I have not finished yet" (RH, July 5,

1906). She expected to write several articles on the binding claims of God's law and the blessings promised to the obedient.

After speaking at the dedication of the Paradise Valley Sanitarium in San Diego on April 24, Ellen White started back toward northern California via Loma Linda. Feelings of dread swept over her as she contemplated the trip home. She knew she would view with her own eyes destruction similar to what she had seen in vision. "I did not want to see the ruins of San Francisco," she declared, "and dreaded to stop at Mountain View" (*ibid.*, July 19, 1906), where the beloved Pacific Press had suffered severe damage. As the train neared San Jose, just south of Mountain View, that Thursday morning, May 3, she could see everywhere the effects of the earthquake.

Changing cars at San Jose, they traveled the 10 miles (16 kilometers) to Mountain View. Here they were met at the railroad station by C. H. Jones, manager of the Pacific Press, and W. T. Knox, president of the California-Nevada Conference, headquartered in Mountain View. The drive to the press took them through town, where they saw the new post office leveled to the ground and the largest stores totally destroyed. But "when we saw the fallen walls of the Pacific Press," she reported, "we were sad at heart." Yet there was one reason for rejoicing—"No lives were lost" (MS 45, 1906).

THE TOUR OF RAVAGED SAN FRANCISCO

Monday the group set out for San Francisco. At Palo Alto they saw the wreckage of Stanford University. When they arrived at San Francisco they hired a horse-drawn cab to spend an hour and a half touring the ruined city. With Ellen White was her son, W. C., and two women, May Walling and Minnie Crisler, wife of Clarence Crisler, her chief secretary (31 WCW, p. 293).

As they rode together, they recounted a good many things. Exactly what was said we do not know, but various and sundry reports give us a composite picture of what took place:

The quake came at 5:31 Wednesday morning, April 18. The first casualty was the Point Arena Lighthouse, 90 miles (144 kilometers) to the north. The huge lenses and lantern exploded in a shower of glass. Earth waves two and three feet (one meter) high were seen plunging south at an incredible rate. Giant redwoods were mowed down. Beaches were raised and lowered. Trains were derailed. At one ranch the earth opened directly beneath an unsuspecting cow. With a bellow of terror the animal plunged into the gaping hole, its cry cut short as the crevice clamped shut, leaving only a twitching tail visible (G. Thomas and M. Witts, *The San Francisco Earthquake*, pp. 66, 67).

The city was largely asleep as the wave of earth upheavals struck San Francisco in a 28-second tremor just at dawn.* First there was a terrifying roar, and then stone and bricks began to fall like rain from taller buildings; chimneys toppled from almost every home. The streets heaved, and in places dropped as much as 30 feet (nine meters).

CONSUMING FIRE THAT FOLLOWED THE EARTHQUAKE

A flicker of flame was seen in early dawn and then a dozen such tongues of fire here and there. The flames were started by broken power lines and fractured gas lines. Civilians and firefighters were soon at work, but to their dismay there was only a little water with which to quench the flames. And then no water. Some of the city's main water lines had been broken.

Some people looted breweries and liquor stores, and in certain areas drinking orgies added to the confusion. Drunken parents, unmindful of the perils about them, forgot babies and children, and in many cases were separated from them. One group of uncared-for, terrified children, thinking Telegraph Hill to be a safe place, flocked there, only to be consumed as the racing flames veered and took the hill (ST, May 30, 1906).

MARTIAL LAW

The city was put under martial law, and military personnel were called in to assist. Soon every able-bodied man was engaged in the work of fighting the flames and removing the injured and dead from the rubble. Early curious visitors from down the peninsula were pressed into service.

Looting continued, especially in liquor and food stores. Police officers and soldiers were ordered to shoot on sight anyone involved in looting or in stripping jewelry from the dead. Throughout Wednesday terror and confusion reigned. Telephones were dead, telegraph wires were down, rail lines were inoperative. Thousands sought refuge in the less-stricken cities and towns across the bay to the east; crowded ferries did a heroic work in moving people. From these towns news of the magnitude of the catastrophe began to reach the outside world.

Throughout the night the sky was bright with firelight, and those in the parks without bedding were comfortably warm from the heat of the inferno. Food was scarce and, when available, in most cases was very expensive. As the changing winds spread the fire in all directions, food stores commandeered by police and military were thrown open and were soon cleaned out; this eased somewhat the food emergency.

DESTRUCTION IN THE CENTRAL CITY

At the center of the city the earthquake took a heavy toll. Municipal and office buildings, as well as stores and hotels, were destroyed. Few buildings stood. Hundreds of people lost their lives in the collapse of several hotels.

498

Uncontrolled fires created more overall damage than the earthquake. Block after block succumbed to the flames in the three days following the quake. Since no cooking fires were allowed in buildings not inspected for safety, most cooking in areas where homes stood was done with improvised stoves on the sidewalks or in the parks. Water was treasured as gold. The military pitched tents in the parks to help care for the homeless. Bread lines measured a mile (two kilometers) long. In many cases families were separated; carriages carried signs and people wore placards stating, "I am looking for so and so."

It was only two weeks later that Ellen White viewed the 15 square miles (39 square kilometers) of rubble and devastation and listened to tales of the bizarre happenings. How similar it was to the scenes of the night at Loma Linda!

ADVENTISTS AND ADVENTIST PROPERTIES

But what of Seventh-day Adventists and Adventist Church properties in San Francisco? While there were a few injuries, no lives were lost. The treatment rooms, sometimes referred to as the branch sanitarium, superintended by Dr. Lamb at 1436 Market Street, were housing some patients when the earthquake struck. The brick walls fell away from the building, but the patients, uninjured, were soon placed in the custody of relatives. The vegetarian cafeteria at 755 Market Street and the health food store at 1482 Market withstood the quake but in a few hours were swept away by flames. A number of Adventists lost their homes.

But the large church on Laguna Street, with its accompanying clinic, which James and Ellen White helped to build in the 1870s, was saved. Being a frame building, it suffered only minor earthquake damage, and in God's providence the ravaging fire was held in check two blocks from the church. Members were able to continue to use it and were glad to allow the Presbyterians to use it on Sundays.

THE EARTHQUAKE SPECIAL OF THE SIGNS

What a unique opportunity this unprecedented catastrophe gave for telling the world the significance of such tragedies. The buildings of the Pacific Press were badly damaged (the loss was estimated at between $15,000 and $20,000), but managers, factory foremen, and editors quickly huddled to plan an "Earthquake Special" of the Signs of the Times, to be rushed through their undamaged presses. The journalism was good, illustrations outstanding, and the printing up to Pacific Press standards. Within a few days the first run of more than 150,000 copies was ready. From the initial planning, conferences across North America were appraised of the venture and orders in the multiple thousands poured in.

As banks in northern California were temporarily closed, the cash flow from the sale of the "Earthquake Special" into the Pacific Press was welcomed. Between press runs the illustrations were supplemented and in some cases upgraded. Of this project Ellen White declared:

> We shall do all we possibly can to get the truth before the people now. The special number of the *Signs of the Times* is a medium through which much good will be accomplished.

THE TRIP HOME TO ELMSHAVEN

After touring the scene of tragedy, Ellen White and those traveling with her made their way home to St. Helena and Elmshaven. In that area damage was very light, consisting mainly of cracked and twisted brick chimneys.

Mrs. White reported in the *Review and Herald* concerning her visit to San Francisco shortly after the earthquake, reminding readers that by both pen and voice she had predicted disaster in San Francisco. She had warned people to seek homes away from the crime-filled cities known for their wickedness and defiance of God.

Did Ellen White predict the San Francisco earthquake? No, she warned that San Francisco and Oakland would suffer God's judgments. Was the vision at Loma Linda on the night of April 16 a portrayal of what would happen to San Francisco? No city was named. But the scene and particularly the instruction given by the angel in connection with it prepared Ellen White to write forcefully as to the real significance of such disasters. Certainly it did fit the great earthquake of 1906.

FINDING A SITE FOR PACIFIC UNION COLLEGE

By 1908 the college at Healdsburg found itself needing room to breathe and grow. The attendance was dropping, and financial losses were heavy. The school building was now closely surrounded by the town, and the "boardinghouse" three blocks up the street was being choked by nearby residential housing. When built, the boardinghouse, on a five-acre (two-hectare) tract of land, was in the country, and it had been planned that as funds were available more land surrounding it would be purchased. But money was scarce, so part of the original acreage was sold. Houses soon sprang up.

Ellen White, who with W. C. White had led out in founding the college in 1882, was deeply interested in its welfare. At the California Conference session held in February a comprehensive resolution was passed calling for the disposal of the school properties in Healdsburg and establishing "an industrial college" in the country that would provide work for students and "furnish at least the agricultural and dairy products necessary for the college home" (PUR, Feb. 27,

1908). The Educational Society, which carried legal control, took official action to this effect three weeks later on March 19.

It was hoped that a property could be located rather quickly so that the school could open in the fall on the new site. Conference officials and Ellen White and her staff were on the constant lookout for a suitable place, perhaps with a building on it that could be put to immediate use.

At the well-attended Oakland camp meeting in early June, a special session of the California Conference was called. Here on June 9, after considerable discussion and a divided vote, plans to close Healdsburg College were approved and a committee of seven appointed to search for a new site. W. C. White, as well as conference officers, was on this committee. From time to time various sites were examined.

In August a property near Sonoma came to the attention of conference officers. This property, two or three miles (three or five kilometers) north of the town of Sonoma, consisted of 2,900 acres (1,174 hectares) of land, hills, mountains, valleys, and flatlands. On it was a spacious three-story, 38-room mansion called "The Castle" (36 WCW, p. 725; S. N. Haskell to EGW, Aug. 13, 1908). Since the property was less than a mile (two kilometers) from a tiny Western Pacific Railway station called Buena Vista, that was the name used in designating it for inspections and negotiations.

THE BUENA VISTA PROPERTY

On Wednesday morning, September 2, the day after she had gone north following her five-week stay in southern California, Ellen White, with some members of the committee on school location, visited the Buena Vista property.

Remembering the Loma Linda experience, during which she recognized the buildings when she came onto the grounds, everyone quite naturally was eager to hear whether the Lord had given direct light that this was the site to be purchased.

On leaving the grounds, she felt impressed "that this was just such a location for our school as we had been looking for" (letter 322, 1908). As to the suitability of the property, she noted that the tract of land was large, "away from the cities, where we could have an abundance of water and wood, and a healthful climate" (ibid.). The well-furnished house with "every convenience" was also an important factor (letter 324, 1908). But she did not identify the building as one shown to her.

Back in Oakland that night Ellen White was given instruction. Of this she wrote:

> That night in my dreams I seemed to be making plans in regard to this property. One spoke to me and said, "How were you impressed with

this location?" I replied, "Favorably; but I do not see how we can purchase: we have not the means. We might lessen the price by selling the stone winery."

"You cannot do that," our adviser said. "If you should do so, parties who do not regard the seventh day would be at work on the land on the Sabbath. Your only plan will be to purchase the entire property, and keep every part of it under your control. Not one foot of the land should be allowed to come under the control of those who would work it on the Sabbath day" (letter 322, 1908).

The committee members could easily see that Ellen White favored the property, but she did not have a "Thus saith the Lord" *that this particular property* should be secured. Further, she perceived that responsible committees made up of qualified men of experience must make the decision based on principles involved.

On Sunday morning, September 13, after a wakeful night, she wrote to Elder Haskell, who was now attending a camp meeting in Fresno, that she was afraid she might be taking too great responsibility in the matter. She declared:

> I do not feel that I want the decision of this question to rest with me. I had only a hasty view of the place at Buena Vista, and *while it corresponds to a place that had been shown* me, I do not want you to feel that you must secure it on that account (letter 256, 1908; italics supplied).

With a judgment enriched by the many visions God gave to her, she was influential in the making of important decisions, but never were the visions to take the place of study, initiative, faith, or hard work on the part of all concerned. The visions were not given to take the place of careful investigation and decision-making. Nor were her opinions, in the absence of special light, to be taken as authoritative.

So it was with the Buena Vista property. The principles that should guide in the selection of a site for a college were made clear, and any one of several places might have fitted these guidelines. In the absence of special light, Ellen White had to judge the same as her brethren as to the suitability of the property being investigated.

Here the matter rested for several months.

At the camp meeting in Fresno in late September, a special session of the constituency was held to consider, among other things, the matter of the college. The advantages and disadvantages of various sites were reviewed, and it was decided to accept whatever site might be chosen as long as the committee followed its best judgment and would be counseled by the Spirit of Prophecy.

Almost immediately definite steps were taken to purchase the Buena Vista property. The agreement was that 2,900 acres (1,174 hectares) would be purchased for $35,000 and the Healdsburg College properties. Only one thing remained—the owners must produce a proper abstract and clear title (36 WCW, p. 725).

But delay followed delay. When the transcript for the property finally was available, it was found that there were 22 defects in the title, some serious. The owner, in spite of his earlier promises, refused to do anything about it. Ellen White, when her counsel was sought, declared: "Tell them to put us in possession of the place, or to hand us back our money" (MS 65, 1909).

While she was in the midst of the General Conference session in Washington in May 1909, the deposit on the Buena Vista property was returned. Mrs. White said: "In the dreams of the night the assurance was given that we must not become discouraged; if we could not obtain the Buena Vista place, there would be a more advantageous place for our school" (letter 187, 1909).

THE ANGWIN PROPERTY A BETTER PLACE

Elder Haskell, president of the California Conference, recalled:

> When word came to us at Washington, D.C., that the trade could not be completed because of errors in the title and other reasons, the servant of the Lord said, "If this cannot be obtained, it is because the Lord has a better place for us" (PUR, Sept. 2, 1909).

With the time for the opening of school nearing, and now with considerable funds in hand for the purchase of a school property, the locating committee began a new search. In July H. W. Cottrell, president of the Pacific Union Conference and a member of the committee on school location, found what he considered the ideal place. S. N. Haskell wrote of it to Ellen White, who was on her protracted return journey from Washington, D.C., to California. It was Angwin's resort hotel atop Howell Mountain, about four miles (seven kilometers) beyond St. Helena Sanitarium. The property seemed most promising. So sure were the brethren that this place met fully the qualifications for a college site held before them by Ellen White that negotiations to purchase for $60,000 were commenced at once. It was with restless difficulty that they awaited Mrs. White's return home in early September to gain her full support in the steps taken.

After an absence of five months and four days Ellen White reached her Elmshaven home on Thursday afternoon, September 9, ill and exhausted. All were eager for her to visit the Angwin school site without delay. She was too. So, although ill-prepared to do so, on Friday morning she insisted on driving the five miles (eight kilometers) past the sanitarium and up the narrow, rocky road to the top of Howell Mountain to see the property everyone was excited about.

ELLEN WHITE DESCRIBES THE NEW SCHOOL PROPERTY

In letters to Edson and her granddaughter Mabel, Ellen White described what she found at Angwin. Selections from both letters tell the story:

We left home early on the morning of September 10, driving in my easiest carriage. It was a five-mile [eight-kilometer] climb to the top of the hill; then when about one mile [two kilometers] from the property the country became more level.

Elder [C. W.] Irwin met us at the place and showed us something of the grounds and buildings. As we drove along I marked the advantages over the Buena Vista property. True, there was not here the fine costly building that we found on the Sonoma property, but there were a number of buildings in good repair, and such as could be easily adapted to the needs of the school. The largest of the dwellings was a house of thirty-two rooms [the resort hotel], and in addition to this there were four cottages. All the rooms were well planned, and substantially but not extravagantly furnished. Everything about houses and grounds looked clean and wholesome (letter 110, 1909).

Many advantages came to us in the house furnishings. The beds were all supplied with two good mattresses, one hair mattress and one of cotton wool, feather pillows and woolen blankets, some of which are very good indeed. All the floors are covered, some of the rooms with carpets, but most with a straw matting. The bed linen was all in good order.

There are sixteen hundred acres [648 hectares] of land in the property, 105 [43 hectares] of which is good arable land. There are twenty acres [eight hectares] of orchards, bearing apples, pears, plums, prunes, peaches, figs, grapes, and English and black walnuts. There are thirty acres [12 hectares] of alfalfa. We were much pleased with the fruit that we saw. At the time of our first visit there were many workers on the ground taking care of the prunes, some gathering the fruits and others preparing it for drying. Forty-five tons [40,860 kilograms] of prunes have been gathered from the orchard this year (letter 114, 1909).

The large corn barn was filled to the roof with the best of lucerne [alfalfa] hay harvested from the land. In the carriage house we saw eight buggies and wagons. There were twenty milk cows, thirteen horses, and six colts included in this trade. . . .

We are thankful for the abundant supply of pure water flowing from numerous springs, and thrown into large tanks by three hydraulic rams; also for the good buildings, for the good farmland, and for the hundreds of acres of woodland, on which there are many thousands of feet of saw timber. We are thankful also for the machinery which is all in such good order, for the furniture, which though it is not fine, is good and substantial; for the fruit that is canned and dried, and which will be much appreciated by teachers and students this first year of school. . . .

We need have no fear of drinking impure water, for here it is supplied freely to us from the Lord's treasure house [300,000 gallons (1,135,500 liters) a day]. I do not know how to be grateful enough for these many advantages, but feel like putting my whole trust in the Lord, and as long as my life is spared to glorify my Redeemer (letter 110, 1909).

On the following Sunday, September 12, a phone call came from Oakland, where the camp meeting was being held. The discussion of the new college was slated to come up the next day. Could Ellen White come?

Indeed she could. She went down Monday morning and that afternoon spoke for 20 minutes on the advantages of the Angwin site. There was no legal action needed, since the purchasing committee—Elders Knox, Cottrell, and Haskell—had, at the Fresno camp meeting a year before, been given power to act. Ellen White's address went far to confirm the faith of the people in the new project and ensure that their pledges would be paid (PUR, Sept. 23, 1909; MS 59, 1909).

The Angwin resort property was not on the market when the search for a new school site was entered upon. The repeated delays held everything in abeyance until the ideal property became available. Then, with money in hand, the fully equipped and stocked Angwin property was purchased with confidence, and within a few weeks the school was ready for opening in late September. It was capable of caring for 150 students. Everything was on hand, just ready to put into use. All considered it providential. Of the experience Mrs. White wrote, "Now this lesson given us at this time of our great necessity was one of the most remarkable adventures in our experience" (letter 187, 1909). For nearly a year principles had been reviewed, sites inspected, and money raised. Guidance came through the Spirit of Prophecy, but responsible men were not relieved of diligent study, tireless seeking, and the making of decisions.

FACULTY AND STAFF

The faculty and staff for the new school were quickly assembled. Ellen White, at the General Conference session in Washington, had urged that C. W. Irwin, for eight years principal of the Avondale school in Australia, be released from his work there and kept on in the States to head the new college. Church leaders concurred in this and Professor Irwin stayed by, ready to head the new school when a site was found and school could begin.

The editor of the *Signs of the Times*, Oscar Tait, a man of broad experience, was prevailed upon to become Bible teacher. Others, seasoned and capable men and women, were drawn in. When school opened on Wednesday, September 29, fifty students were ready to begin classes. The dedication of the new college on that day, with services held in the dance hall, which could seat 200, was an impressive and joyous occasion. Ellen White was there and was one of the speakers. In her 20-minute address she said:

> We are very grateful to the Lord of hosts for this possession, for we have here just what we hoped to have in the Buena Vista estate. . . . God wanted us here, and He has placed us here. I was sure of this as I came upon these grounds. . . . The Lord designed this place for us, and . . . it has been the work of His providence that has brought it into our possession (MS 65, 1909).

And indeed, all recognized that the Lord had done just that.

---

*The description of the earthquake is fully supported by documents in DF 76, "The San Francisco Earthquake."

THE GENERAL CONFERENCE SESSION OF 1909

From an early date Ellen White seemed to be rather certain that she would attend the 1909 General Conference session to be held in Washington, D.C., May 13 to June 6. As early as September 1908 she wrote, "I expect to attend the next General Conference in Washington" (letter 274, 1908). In November she was discussing the best route to take. "But," she told Edson, "I dare not move in any action according to my own judgment."

As the time approached she wrote Edson on March 30:

> We have decided our family party—Sara McEnterfer, Minnie Hawkins, W.C.W., and your mother—will leave next Monday. . . . We must go to Los Angeles and direct from there to Paradise Valley, stay a couple of days and then visit Loma Linda, and then on to College View and then to Nashville. I think this is the route. Then to Washington (letter 183, 1909).

> My health is quite good. I am thankful that my lame hip is little trouble to me now. I have much to be thankful for that at my age—in my eighty-second year—I can be up (*ibid.*).

As planned, the party from Elmshaven left home Monday morning, April 5, and reached Mountain View in the early afternoon. After resting in Elder Cottrell's home for a few hours, they continued to San Jose to catch the 5:10 p.m. train for Los Angeles, and then it was on to San Diego and Paradise Valley Sanitarium.

Tuesday morning the party was again on its way, this time bound for College View, Nebraska, over the Salt Lake City and Omaha Railroad (37 WCW, p. 953). There Mrs. White spoke twice Friday morning, first to the students and faculty of Union College and then a few minutes later to the children in the elementary school room nearby (letter 88, 1909). The topic of the Sabbath morning sermon in the College View church, where she addressed 2,000 people, was "Individual Cooperation" (MS 31, 1909). Then again on Sunday she delivered her sixth sermon of the trip to those who gathered in the

College View church. This was followed by an address to the college faculty on educational principles (letter 84, 1909) and a tour of the school farm.

Tuesday morning, April 20, the group hastened on to Nashville, where she was entertained at Nashville Sanitarium for nearly a week, slipping out for a visit to the Hillcrest school and the Oakwood school.

Sunday afternoon she went out to the Madison school and addressed those attending a teachers' institute in progress there (letter 74, 1909; MS 15, 1909). She spent a few days at Madison, staying in their "new sanitarium" (letter 74, 1909).

The journey to Huntsville, Alabama, to visit the school was exhausting. The train made frequent stops in the stifling heat, and she suffered pain in her troublesome left eye (letter 74, 1909; 37 WCW, p. 959). But she talked to the students the next morning and visited the campus, the buildings, and the farm. That night she rode on the train to Asheville, North Carolina, and on Sabbath morning, May 1, took the service in the Haywood church.

On Sunday afternoon she addressed the congregation in the Black church pastored by M. C. Strachen, speaking on John 15. She tarried after the service to shake hands with the members. After dinner she left on the 2:05 p.m. train for Washington, D.C. By the time she reached Washington, she had spoken 14 times since leaving home.

In Washington she was entertained near the school grounds where the session was held, at the home of G. A. Irwin, General Conference vice president (37 WCW, p. 977). There she had two rooms—one for sleeping and the other in which to counsel with those who wished to see her. She quickly arranged for rooms in the nearby D. H. Kress home for Edson and Emma, and urged them to attend the conference at her expense, which they did.

THE 1909 GENERAL CONFERENCE SESSION

As in 1905, this General Conference session was held in a large tent pitched on the grounds of Washington Missionary College. The opening meeting convened at 10:45 a.m. Thursday, May 13. There were 328 delegates present, a number that swelled a little as the conference progressed.

The session itself was quite routine, with a great deal of time given over to reports of the progress of the cause around the world. A portion of each day was devoted to individual meetings of the various departments and to the business of the quadrennial session.

Sabbath morning, May 15, at 11:00 Ellen White addressed the session in the big tent. The *Bulletin* reported that it "was a day long to be remembered" as the "aged servant of God" stood in that large tent speaking to an audience of more than 1,000 people. She seemed to "lay upon those assembled representatives of the third angel's message the importance of rightly representing Christ to the world in our speech, in our character, in all our dealing with our fellow men, in order that we shall not be found fruitless in the great day of harvest" (p. 28).

She spoke 11 times in the big tent, taking the Sabbath morning services on three of the four Sabbaths of the session.

How did the voice of this little woman of 81 come through to the audience? Those who were there reported that they all heard her clearly and distinctly. One curious young minister, A. V. Olson, attending his first General Conference session, eager to find out for himself, sat near the front, where he heard her well. He went outside the tent, and even there her voice came through in clear tones. She did not shout. She had no public address system, but with a steady, low voice supported by her abdominal muscles, she spoke as she had been instructed by God (see Ev, p. 669). She made all hear, with no one straining to catch her words.

Reviewing instruction on the importance of healthful living, she listed strict temperance in eating as one reason for her ability to do so much work in speaking and writing (letter 50, 1908). Addressing one influential minister on March 28, 1909, she declared, "True conversion to the message of present truth embraces conversion to the principles of health reform" (letter 62, 1909). She also said:

> It is our duty to act wisely in regard to our habits of eating, to be temperate, and to learn to reason from cause to effect. If we will do our part, then the Lord will do His part in preserving our brain-nerve power (letter 50, 1908).

Ellen White used the opportunities given to her to speak in admonishing, encouraging, and instructing. Her prime theme was evangelistic outreach, with emphasis on both personal and city evangelism. Health reform and health interests were a close second. She had attended General Conference sessions from 1863 on, missing some while in Europe and Australia. She had been at the first general gathering of Sabbathkeeping Adventists in 1848, and at succeeding Sabbath Conferences had been with the brethren as they diligently studied the Word and formed the doctrinal structure of the church based on that Word.

The last meeting, Sunday afternoon at 3:00, June 6, was given to her. "Partakers of the Divine Nature" was her theme. It came too late to be included in the *Bulletin*, but it was referred to in the last issue under the title "A Touching Farewell."

Thus closed the last sermon Ellen White was to make at a General Conference session. She moved away from the desk and started to her seat, then turned and came back, picked up the Bible from which she had read, opened it, and held it out on extended hands that trembled with age. She admonished,

"Brethren and Sisters, I commend unto you this Book" (reported by W. A. Spicer, then secretary of the General Conference, in *The Spirit of Prophecy in the Advent Movement*, p. 30).

Thus in her last words to the leaders of the church officially assembled in conference Ellen White elevated the Word of God—that Word that had been so precious to her and that she freely used and ever kept before the church and the world.

THE DAILY

During the General Conference session in Washington in 1909, signals of potential doctrinal controversy surfaced in which the "daily" of Daniel 8 largely figured. "Yea, he magnified himself even to the prince of the host, and by him the daily sacrifice was taken away, and the place of his sacrifice was cast down" (Dan. 8:11).

" 'The daily'—this phrase is best limited to the usually accepted sense of the morning and the evening offering, though some prefer a more general sense as an expression of everything connected with the worship of the sanctuary" (F. C. Cook, *The Bible Commentary*, Vol. VI, p. 344).

The question of the meaning of the "daily" was not a new one in Adventist history. William Miller had taught that it referred to paganism, but even before the Disappointment that view was questioned. The classic 1843 chart produced by Fitch and used by all the Adventist preachers omitted reference to the meaning of the "daily."

In 1847 O.R.L. Crosier had expressed the view that the "daily" refers to the high-priestly ministry of Christ in the heavenly sanctuary. Uriah Smith in 1854 briefly expounded this position (RH, Mar. 28, 1854). But Smith, rising to prominence shortly afterward in his *Thoughts on the Book of Daniel* (1873 ed., p. 163), went back to the view of William Miller. Smith's became the accepted position until the turn of the century, and thus was known as the "old view." Prescott's position was similar to Crosier's but nevertheless acquired the less-than-accurate designation as the "new view."

As careful students took time to examine all the evidence, many were led to accept the new view—A. G. Daniells and W. C. White among them—and polarization began to develop. After the close of the Pacific Union Conference session at St. Helena in late January 1908, some of the workers lingered on to spend a little time at Elmshaven studying the question. They met in the Elmshaven office—Daniells, Prescott, Loughborough, the Haskells, W. C. White, C. C. Crisler, and D. E. Robinson (DF 200). The meeting, in place of bringing some solutions to the problem, served only to harden positions.

COUNSEL AGAINST AGITATING THE SUBJECT

Before Prescott left for the East on February 6, Ellen White spoke to him about the problem, telling him not to publish anything at that time that would unsettle the minds of the people regarding positions held in the past. She promised to write him on the subject (35 WCW, p. 217).

She did not write at once, but on June 24, 1908, she wrote to Prescott of perils that at times threatened his ministry. She spoke of a tendency on his part "to sway from clearly defined truth and give undue attention to some items which seem to require hours of argument to prove, when in reality they do not need to be handled at all." She wrote:

> You are not beyond danger of making mistakes. You sometimes allow your mind to center upon a certain train of thought, and you are in danger of making a mountain out of a molehill (letter 224, 1908).

A week later she wrote Prescott again, opening with the words:

> I am instructed to say to you, Let there be no questions agitated at this time in the *Review* that will tend to unsettle minds. . . . It will prove to be a great mistake if you agitate at this time the question regarding the "daily," which has been occupying much of your attention of late. I have been shown that the results of your making this question a prominent issue would be that the minds of a large number will be directed to an unnecessary controversy, and that questioning and confusion will be developed in our ranks. . . . My brother, let us be slow to raise questions that will be a source of temptation to our people (letter 226, 1908).

Then she referred to her own relation to the matter and the fact that God had given no special revelation on it:

> I have had no special light on the point presented for discussion, and I do not see the need of this discussion. . . . There have been different opinions regarding the "daily," and there will continue to be. *If the Lord has seen fit to let this matter rest for so many years without correcting the same, would it not be wisdom on your part to refrain from presenting your views concerning it?* (*ibid.*; italics supplied).

This letter was not sent off immediately and we do not know what Ellen White may have instructed him orally, but he published no articles on the subject in subsequent issues of the *Review*.

S. N. HASKELL AND THE 1843 CHART

On August 28, 1908, almost two months after writing to Prescott, Ellen White wrote to S. N. Haskell, a stalwart advocate of the old view. Because in

Early Writings she had made reference to "the 1843 chart" in connection with a mention of the "daily," Haskell had arranged for the publication of a facsimile copy of the chart and was circulating it. In her testimony to Haskell she stated:

> Now, my brother, I feel that at this crisis in our experience that chart which you have republished should not be circulated. You have made a mistake in this matter. Satan is determinedly at work to bring about issues that will create confusion.
>
> There are those who would be delighted to see our ministers at an issue on this question, and they would make much of it (letter 250, 1908).

While Ellen White was without special light from the Lord on the particular point in question, she did receive light on the controversy the discussion was causing, and she wrote, "I have been instructed that regarding what might be said on either side of this question, silence at this time is eloquence."

Significantly, in closing her letter, she declared:

> Elder Haskell, *I am unable to define clearly the points that are questioned.* Let us not agitate a subject that will give the impression that as a people we hold varied opinions, and thus open the way for those to work who wish to leave the impression on minds that we are not led by God. It will also be a source of temptation to those who are not thoroughly converted, and will lead to the making of rash moves (*ibid.*; italics supplied).

THE ISSUE OF INSPIRATION

In the case of the "daily," those who held the old view, with Haskell in the lead, maintained that to veer away from it would strike a mortal blow to confidence in the Spirit of Prophecy because of what they claimed was her endorsement of that view in the chapter "The Gathering Time," published in her first little book in 1851 and republished in *Early Writings*, pages 74-76. In this chapter, written in September 1850, in the context of time setting and containing such expressions as "Time has not been a test since 1844, and it will never again be a test" and "The message of the third angel . . . must not be hung on time," she wrote:

> I have seen that the 1843 chart was directed by the hand of the Lord, and that it should not be altered; that the figures were as He wanted them; that His hand was over and hid a mistake in some of the figures, so that none could see it until His hand was removed.
>
> Then I saw in relation to the "daily" (Dan. 8:12) that the word "sacrifice" was supplied by man's wisdom, and does not belong to the text, and

that the Lord gave the correct view of it to those who gave the judgment hour cry. When union existed, before 1844, nearly all were united on the correct view of the "daily"; but in the confusion since 1844 other views have been embraced, and darkness and confusion have followed. Time has not been a test since 1844, and it will never again be a test (EW, pp. 74, 75).

While some who were involved in the discussion attempted to follow the counsel against agitating the matter of the "daily" as one of importance, and no articles on the subject appeared in the *Review*, Haskell did not remain silent. Writing to Elder Daniells on March 22, 1908, he declared:

It is the *Early Writings* that I would defend, and as long as I believe they teach the view I take, and there are many others that believe the same, and if Sister White does not give any explanation in harmony with Prescott's idea to defend the testimonies for the sake of others I shall defend them. Must I be made to believe the testimonies teach a certain thing, contrary to my own judgment and the reading of the writings, when Sister White herself does not so explain it?

Thus, with not a few the discussion took on a major significance—namely, the integrity of the testimonies and loyalty to the Spirit of Prophecy. The question of revelation-inspiration was pressed to the front.

STUDY OF THE CONTEXT IMPORTANT

Concerning this whole matter W. C. White, after spending a day or two studying it carefully, on June 1, 1910, wrote to Edson, taking the position that the context of the statement must be considered.

It is evident that the vision of September 23, 1850, as published in *Early Writings*, new edition, pages 74-76, under the title "The Gathering Time," was given to correct the prevalent error of time setting, and to check the fanatical doctrines being taught regarding the return of the Jews to Jerusalem.

The statement concerning the "daily" of Daniel 8:9-14, as published in *Early Writings*, appeared first in *Present Truth*, Vol. I. No. 11, dated Paris, Maine, November 1850. During the same month and in the same place, there was published the first number of *Second Advent Review and Sabbath Herald*, which has continued as the church paper of Seventh-day Adventists ever since. In this first number appears an article by Elder Joseph Bates on "The Laodicean Church," in which he writes at considerable length on the confused state of various bodies of Advent believers, in contrast with the unity that the commandment-keeping

Adventists were endeavoring to maintain.

On the point of confusion of many bodies of Adventists at that period in their history, over the question of prophetic "time," he declares:

"For six successive years, viz: from the fall of 1844 to the spring and fall of 1850, the most of these leading members have been aiding and assisting each other in changing the chronology, i.e., the world's history, to prove that they were on the true position. What have they gained? Answer, nothing but disappointment and confusion."

At one point a little later in the discussions Elder Daniells, accompanied by W. C. White and C. C. Crisler, eager to get from Ellen White herself just what the meaning was of her *Early Writings* statement, went to her and laid the matter before her. Daniells took with him *Early Writings* and the 1843 chart. He sat down close to her and plied her with questions. His report of this interview was confirmed by W. C. White:

I first read to Sister White the statement given above in *Early Writings*. Then I placed before her our 1843 prophetic chart used by our ministers in expounding the prophecies of Daniel and Revelation. I called her attention to the picture of the sanctuary and also to the 2300-year period as they appeared on the chart.

I then asked if she could recall what was shown her regarding this subject.

As I recall her answer, she began by telling how some of the leaders who had been in the 1844 movement endeavored to find new dates for the termination of the 2300-year period. This endeavor was to fix new dates for the coming of the Lord. This was causing confusion among those who had been in the Advent Movement.

In this confusion the Lord revealed to her, she said, that the view that had been held and presented regarding the dates was correct, and that there must never be another time set, nor another time message.

I then asked her to tell what had been revealed to her about the rest of the "daily"—the Prince, the host, the taking away of the "daily," and the casting down of the sanctuary.

She replied that these features were not placed before her in vision as the time part was. She would not be led out to make an explanation of those points of the prophecy. . . .

The only conclusion I could draw from her free explanation of the time and her silence as to the taking away of the "daily" and the casting down of the sanctuary was that the vision given her was regarding the time, and that she received no explanation as to the other parts of the prophecy (DF 201b, AGD statement, Sept. 25, 1931).

Since charts figure in this matter, Ellen White's attitude in this interview is given strong support as the reckoning of the Cummings 1854 "prophetic chart" is studied.* In this the Jewish altar of "daily sacrifice" in 446 B.C. is used as the starting point for a new 2300-year time span set to end in 1854. This chart, published at Concord, New Hampshire, in 1853, was typical of charts that commenced the 2300 days with what was said to be the taking away of the "daily sacrifice."

A CALL TO HALT THE CONTROVERSY

Ellen White watched with growing anxiety and distress the time-consuming controversy between leading brethren on a point on which she repeatedly said she had received no light. On July 31, 1910, she could restrain herself no longer, and wrote:

> I have words to speak to my brethren east and west, north and south. I request that my writings shall not be used as the leading argument to settle questions over which there is now so much controversy. I entreat of Elders Haskell, Loughborough, Smith, and others of our leading brethren, that they make no reference to my writings to sustain their views of the "daily."
>
> It has been presented to me that this is not a subject of vital importance. I am instructed that our brethren are making a mistake in magnifying the importance of the difference in the views that are held. I cannot consent that any of my writings shall be taken as settling this matter. The true meaning of the "daily" is not to be made a test question.
>
> I now ask that my ministering brethren shall not make use of my writings in their arguments regarding this question; for I have had no instruction on the point under discussion and I see no need for the controversy. Regarding this matter under present conditions, silence is eloquence (MS 11, 1910 [see also 1SM, p. 164]).

A few days later, on August 3, she addressed a communication to the ministry of the church:

To My Brethren in the Ministry:

> Dear Fellow Workers: I have words to speak to Brethren Butler, Loughborough, Haskell, Smith, Gilbert, Daniells, Prescott, and all who have been active in urging their views in regard to the meaning of the "daily" of Daniel 8. This is not to be made a test question, and the agitation that has resulted from its being treated as such has been very un-

fortunate. Confusion has resulted, and the minds of some of our brethren have been diverted from the thoughtful consideration that should have been given to the work that the Lord has directed should be done at this time in our cities. This has been pleasing to the great enemy of our work (letter 62, 1910 [see also 1SM, p. 167]).

Then she referred to the last prayer of Christ calling for unity, brought to view in John 17, and commented, "There are many subjects upon which we can speak—sacred, testing truths, beautiful in their simplicity. On these you may dwell with intense earnestness. But," she urged, "let not the 'daily,' or any other subject that will arouse controversy among brethren, be brought in at this time, for this will delay and hinder the work that the Lord would have the minds of our brethren centered upon just now." And she pleaded, "Let us not agitate questions that will reveal a marked difference of opinion, but rather let us bring from the Word the sacred truths regarding the binding claims of the law of God" (ibid.).

As to the discourses of Seventh-day Adventist ministers, her counsel was:

> Our ministers should seek to make the most favorable presentation of truth. So far as possible, let all speak the same things. Let the discourses be simple, and treating upon vital subjects that can be easily understood. . . . We must blend together in the bonds of Christlike unity; then our labors will not be in vain. Draw in even cords, and let no contentions be brought in. Reveal the unifying power of truth, and this will make a powerful impression on human minds. In unity there is strength (ibid. [see also 1SM, pp. 167, 168]).

W. C. White repeatedly declared his position that statements in the Spirit of Prophecy must be taken in their proper context. On the question of the *Early Writings* statement in which the "daily" is mentioned, he considered it relevant that his mother had written much concerning the importance of the Advent movement and of the 2300-year prophecy, while the nature of the "daily" itself was "wholly ignored" in all her writings except in one 35-word sentence, found in the middle of the argument that "time has not been a test since 1844, and it will never again be a test." To him the context of the statement found in *Early Writings* seemed to involve the entire article in which the statement was originally written, the entire scope of the Ellen White writings on the subject, and the historical background of the original writing (DF 201b, WCW to J. E. White, June 1, 1910).

But larger issues than the identity of the "daily" concerned W. C. White:

> I have told some of our brethren that I thought there were two ques-

tions connected with this [daily] matter that were of more importance than the decision which shall be made as to which is most nearly correct, the old or the new view regarding the "daily." The first is, How shall we deal with one another when there is difference of opinion? Second, How shall we deal with Mother's writings in our effort to settle doctrinal questions? (WCW to AGD, Mar. 13, 1910).

---

* The original of this chart, probably never seen by Daniells, is now in the Advent Source Collection at Andrews University.

LOMA LINDA:
MORE THAN A SANITARIUM

On the basis of the visions given to her, Ellen White had insights into the future of the work at Loma Linda that far exceeded concepts held by those about her. At the General Conference session at Washington, on June 1, 1909, she addressed the delegates, reading from a manuscript entitled "The Loma Linda College of Evangelists." In this she declared:

> Loma Linda is to be not only a sanitarium, but an educational center. A school is to be established here for the training of gospel medical missionary evangelists. Much is involved in this work, and it is very essential that a right beginning be made. . . .
>
> In regard to the school I would say, Make it especially strong in the education of nurses and physicians. In medical missionary schools, many workers are to be qualified with the ability of physicians to labor as medical missionary evangelists. This training, the Lord has specified, is in harmony with the principles underlying true higher education (GCB 1909, p. 308 [see also 9T, pp. 173, 174]).

She spoke at length concerning the standards that should guide in the training of Seventh-day Adventists for medical missionary service, urging that "they are to be educated from the standpoint of conscience" and to follow right methods.

Step by step the counsels given by Ellen White seemed to be leading to a medical school fully recognized for the training given to physicians. Measures were taken with the view in mind that at Loma Linda one or two years of medical studies would be given, which might be accepted by a recognized medical college as part of a regular medical course. It seemed that the next step would be the securing of a charter that would give such work acceptance. Elder Burden, on September 20, 1909, counseled with Ellen White at her home about this. He found that she was distressed with any plan that called for "having medical students take some work at Loma Linda" and then "get the finishing touches of their education from some worldly institution." She exclaimed, "God forbid that such a plan should be followed," and commented, "I must state that the light I have received is that we are to stand as a distinct, commandment-keeping people" (MS 72, 1909).

As the steps were taken to secure a charter for medical education at Loma Linda, Ellen White on November 5, 1909, gave strong counsel:

> Some questions have been asked me regarding our relation to the laws governing medical practitioners. We need to move understandingly, for the enemy would be pleased to hedge up our work so that our physicians would have only a limited influence. Some men do not act in the fear of God, and they may seek to bring us into trouble by placing on our necks yokes that we could not consent to bear. We cannot submit to regulations if the sacrifice of principles is involved, for this would imperil the soul's salvation.
>
> But whenever we can comply with the law of the land without putting ourselves in a false position, we should do so. Wise laws have been framed in order to safeguard the people against the imposition of unqualified physicians. These laws we should respect, for we are ourselves protected from presumptuous pretenders. Should we manifest opposition to these requirements, it would tend to restrict the influence of our medical missionaries (letter 140, 1909 [MM, p. 84]).

A CHARTER SECURED

On December 9, 1909, with the full approval of the General Conference Committee, a charter was secured under the laws of the state of California authorizing the College of Medical Evangelists to grant degrees in the liberal sciences, dentistry, and medicine (see SHM, p. 383).

The biennial session of the Pacific Union Conference, held in the Mountain View church January 25-30, 1910, was a momentous meeting for the Seventh-day Adventist Church and one of deep concern for Ellen White. On the agenda was the matter of a medical school at Loma Linda. The future of medical education conducted by Seventh-day Adventists was in the balance.

In addition to the some 50 delegates in Mountain View for the opening meeting were both Ellen White and W. C. White; and from the General Conference, G. A. Irwin, vice president, and I. H. Evans, former treasurer, under appointment to a new assignment in eastern Asia. The usual reports, beginning with that of the union president, were presented and the various committees were appointed.

The nominating committee, working rather quickly, was ready with a report on Tuesday afternoon, but the secretary indicated that it failed to carry the signature of S. N. Haskell, a nominating committee member. Haskell was known to be a man of large experience and was the president of the largest local conference in the union—the California Conference—and someone proposed that the report, which included the name of the incumbent president of the union, be returned to the committee for further study. This was agreed upon. At this point the real issues, which had not been faced squarely earlier, came prominently to the front. In the nominating committee someone asked whether the incumbent "intended to stand as a stone wall to block the way of the Loma Linda College of Medical Evangelists" (WCW to AGD, Jan. 28, 1910).

It was agreed that before proceeding further, consideration be given to the development of the work at Loma Linda in the light of the counsel received through the Spirit of Prophecy. All knew that the issue was whether the developing school should be a full-fledged medical school. All knew that if it was, the costs would be large and the involvement deep.

FUTURE OF LOMA LINDA WITH PLANS COMMITTEE

Should the denomination attempt to organize and support a medical college? "The object to be gained was greatly to be desired, but the expense would be so large, and the difficulties so many, that they [the delegates] did not feel free to recommend the undertaking of such an enterprise, before satisfying themselves, first, that they correctly understood the instruction given in the communications received from Sister White" (PUR, Feb. 3, 1910).

Many of her statements relating to the point were reviewed, and there were differences of interpretation. Some held that the school she called for should be to train ministers in physiology and a knowledge of how to give treatments as a means of enhancing their ministry. Others held that the church was called upon to operate a school in which physicians would be trained. So at this point, on Tuesday, January 25, it was decided to make a specific inquiry of Ellen White. I. H. Evans, E. E. Andross, and H. W. Cottrell were authorized to place this before her in writing, with the hope that she would give a clear-cut answer in writing. Their letter opened:

> Dear Sister White: We have read the testimonies, as far as we have seen them, that you have given concerning Loma Linda, and the establishment of a medical school in connection with the work at that place. As far as we know, our people are anxious to carry out the light that the Lord has given; but there is a difference of opinion between us in regard to what you mean when you use the term, "a medical school" (ibid.).

Then the differences of interpretation were clearly outlined, probing especially the point as to whether the training along medical lines should "qualify the students who take the course to pass state board examinations and become registered, qualified physicians for public work."

This letter was submitted to Ellen White on Wednesday at noon. Early

Thursday morning, January 27, she penned her reply, and sometime Thursday it was placed in the hands of the committee. It was short and to the point and left no room for doubt as to what she meant or the course the church should follow:

> The light given me is, We must provide that which is essential to qualify our youth who desire to be physicians, so that they may intelligently fit themselves to be able to stand the examinations required to prove their efficiency as physicians. They should be taught to treat understandingly the cases of those who are diseased, so that the door will be closed for any sensible physician to imagine that we are not giving in our school the instruction necessary for properly qualifying young men and young women to do the work of a physician. Continually the students who are graduated are to advance in knowledge, for practice makes perfect.
>
> The medical school at Loma Linda is to be of the highest order, because those who are in that school have the privilege of maintaining a living connection with the wisest of all physicians, from whom there is communicated knowledge of a superior order. And for the special preparation of those of our youth who have clear convictions of their duty to obtain a medical education that will enable them to pass the examinations required by law of all who practice as regularly qualified physicians, we are to supply whatever may be required,* so that these youth need not be compelled to go to medical schools conducted by men not of our faith.

This response, far-reaching in its implications, made it clear both to the committee on plans and the nominating committee that the work of developing the educational interests at Loma Linda must be in the hands of those in full sympathy with steps that should be taken.

PROBLEMS FOR THE NOMINATING COMMITTEE

But not all were in sympathy with such an advanced step. Chief among them was H. W. Cottrell, the president of the Pacific Union Conference. Ellen White was aware of this, as also were some on the nominating committee. Someone asked, "Are we to reelect the incumbent who will stand as a stone wall to block the way of the Loma Linda College of Medical Evangelists?"

On Thursday afternoon two members of the nominating committee interviewed Ellen White regarding the names that should be brought forward as the future officers of the Pacific Union Conference. She advised "a change in the presidency" (WCW to AGD, Jan. 28, 1910). When this was reported to the delegates at the afternoon businesses session, it "created quite a sensation" (*ibid.*).

That afternoon Mrs. White wrote a six-page letter to the president that included these words:

I am instructed by the Lord to advise our brethren to choose some other man to stand in your place as president of the Pacific Union Conference. This would make it less difficult than otherwise for you to put away some traits of character that are not Christlike (letter 18, 1910).

She assured him that Jesus stood ready to help him overcome "objectionable traits" and fit him "for continued usefulness in His cause." She then spoke of the church's institutions as agencies of divine appointment, and stated that at times we should come into possession of favorable properties even though all the money for their purchase was not in hand. At such times, she said, "we are to learn to walk by faith when necessary."

The president received this testimony Thursday evening. Ellen White was to take the devotional hour on Friday morning. She chose to read to the congregation this letter that she had written the day before to the president, whose term would close with the session. This she followed with remarks that filled eight manuscript pages. She told of how since coming to the union session she had "been writing out the things that" she was "required to write," for, she explained, "the end desired could not be accomplished unless matters were brought before" the conference "plainly and decidedly." She told of the distress of soul this had caused her, but she said, "When messages come to me for the people of God, I must not conceal them, but must write them out, and speak of them" (MS 25, 1910).

In the light of these most earnest words a deep solemnity came over the delegates. Turning to the work before them in the few closing hours of the conference, they appointed a new nominating committee, for the original committee had lapsed.

Later, on Sunday morning, the nominating committee brought in its report, presenting the name of G. A. Irwin for president of the Pacific Union Conference. Irwin was a seasoned administrator; for four years he had been president of the General Conference (1897-1901), with subsequent experience as president of the Australasian Union Conference and then as General Conference vice president. He was known to have unbounded confidence in the counsels of the messenger of the Lord. J. J. Ireland, a son-in-law of J. N. Loughborough, would stand by his side as secretary-treasurer.

THE NIGHT OF THE DECISION

It was an eager but subdued group of workers and members that gathered that Saturday night in the Mountain View church. The outgoing president, who presided throughout the assembly, opened the meeting and then called Elder Irwin to the chair. Irwin reviewed the experience of the church in arranging in the 1890s for the education of physicians at the American Medical Missionary College in Chicago. He pointed out the church's responsibility in providing medical education for its youth under favorable spiritual conditions. Elder Burden followed with a review of the developments at Loma Linda. The letter to Ellen White and her response were read.

Burden was followed by I. H. Evans. The latter, on his way from Washington to Mountain View, had spent a few hours in Chicago conferring with the officers of the American Medical Association. This is the body that is recognized in the United States as establishing standards to be followed in medical education and practice. When Evans had presented the proposal that he had in mind, the medical men in Chicago laughed at the proposition, declaring that it was useless for Seventh-day Adventists, with their limited finances, personnel, and facilities, to consider starting a medical school. "Why," they said, "the best you could do would be to start a 'C' grade school, and we are closing all 'C' grade schools."

But Evans was a man of faith. He opened his remarks in the Mountain View Saturday night meeting by saying:

> I am deeply interested in what has been read to us tonight from the Spirit of Prophecy. The question before the meeting is one of great importance, and needs most careful consideration from every standpoint. . . .
>
> Now, if we always were wise-hearted, and saw everything as the Lord would have us view it, there would be no need of further light through the Spirit of Prophecy; but we are mortal, and our vision is limited, and we often see things in a perverted light. Because of our lack of clear perception, the Lord in mercy speaks to His people through the Spirit of Prophecy. He has had to do this in the past, and we may well hope that He may long continue speaking to us concerning our duty and the needs of His cause.

Most earnest attention was paid as this representative from the General Conference pressed the matter:

> Someone may say, "The time is most inopportune." But the question is, When the Lord reveals to us His desire that we shall establish a medical school and do it soon, is the time inopportune for doing such a work?
>
> I can conjure up many reasons why at this time we are ill-prepared to establish and operate a medical school. It is not hard for any man to say that we have not the money at hand. Any man need not be very wise to say, "We do not know where we shall get medical men trained and qualified to take up this work."

But the question is, Will we establish this medical school, when the Lord has indicated so plainly our duty?

I believe, brethren, if we step forward in the fear of God, and make an effort to establish this school, the Lord will help us and make the way clear.

W. C. White, in the last speech made, declared:

Brethren and friends, I believe that the Lord God of Israel is leader of this people, and I believe that it is He who is leading us to undertake this tremendous enterprise. . . .

And while the world will continue to say to us, as it has said in the past, "Ye are not able to go up and possess this field of usefulness," I believe that our people will unite in saying, "We are well able to go up and possess it, and do this great work" (PUR, Feb. 3, 1910).

THE VOTE TO ADVANCE

At this point the delegates were called upon to vote on the recommendations presented by the plans committee. This called for the establishment of a full-fledged medical school at Loma Linda. The vote was unanimous.

Then the delegates proposed that the matter be submitted to the whole congregation for their action. Again the vote favoring the establishment of a medical school was unanimous. The die was cast. The church would have a medical school at Loma Linda.

---

*In these words is found the justification for accrediting Seventh-day Adventist educational institutions, a point developed in *Counsels to Parents and Teachers* in the statement: "Our larger union conference training schools . . . should be placed in the most favorable position for qualifying our youth to meet the entrance requirements specified by state laws regarding medical students" (p. 479).

THE 1911 EDITION OF
THE GREAT CONTROVERSY
NOT A REVISION

As C. H. Jones, manager of Pacific Press, was preparing in early January 1910 for the annual constituency meeting to be held later in the month, he took stock of the accomplishments in 1909, the work in hand, and some things to which attention needed to be given in 1910. On January 5 he wrote to his close friend and long associate in the work of the church, W. C. White, listing things he felt needed consideration. Among these, under the heading "*Great Controversy*, English," he wrote:

> It will be necessary to print another edition of this book on or before July, 1910. You are aware that the plates are worn out. New plates ought to be made before printing another edition.

Ellen White owned the printing plates for her books; whatever would be done with *The Great Controversy* would be done under her direction and at her expense. In these matters W. C. White served as her business agent.

The work that eventually was done in what has come to be known as the 1911 "revision"—a term too strong for what actually took place—was not contemplated in the initial plans. In other words, no need was seen for changes in the book at the time that plans were initiated for resetting the type, nor were any alterations in the E. G. White text contemplated, beyond technical corrections as might be suggested by Miss Mary Steward, a proofreader of long experience and now a member of Ellen White's staff. Work on the book was undertaken in a routine fashion and according to plan. Miss Steward reviewed the book, checking spelling, capitalization, punctuation, et cetera. She finished her work late in February. By mid-March Pacific Press had copy for resetting the first five chapters and a portion of the sixth.

In the meantime, as a corollary to resetting *The Great Controversy*, thoughts began to develop both in the minds of Ellen White and the members of her staff regarding certain features of the new reset book. These related not only to the physical features of the book—typeface, illustrations, et cetera—but also to the text itself. Mrs. White wrote of this to F. M. Wilcox, chairman of the Review and Herald board:

> When I learned that *The Great Controversy* must be reset, I determined that we would have everything closely examined, to see if the truths it contained were stated in the very best manner, to convince those not of our faith that the Lord had guided and sustained me in the writing of its pages (letter 56, 1911).

These and other considerations led W. C. White to reach out for helpful suggestions. He reported:

> We took counsel with the men of the Publishing Department, with state canvassing agents, and with members of the publishing committees, not only in Washington, but in California, and I asked them to kindly call our attention to any passages that needed to be considered in connection with the resetting of the book (WCW to "Our General Missionary Agents," July 24, 1911 [see also 3SM, pp. 439, 440]).

As suggestions began to come in, he called a halt to typesetting and the making of printing plates. At this point 120 pages had been sent to the type foundry for platemaking, and type had been set for 100 more pages.

CONSIDERATIONS INITIATED BY PLANS FOR A NEW EDITION

The Great Controversy was Ellen White's most important book. She regarded it as a volume designed to win readers to an understanding and acceptance of the light of present truth. This lifted the matter of a new edition somewhat above the mechanical production of a volume for literature evangelists to introduce to the people of the world, to the excellence of the text itself, depicting the great controversy story in an accurate and winning way.

So, relatively early in 1910, there loomed before Ellen White, her staff, and the publishers the task of perfecting the text to reflect a precision of expression and the employment of words acceptable to both Catholic and Protestant readers. The steps to accomplish this were grasped somewhat progressively. While Ellen White, with a full sense of this implication, carried the responsibility for many changes in the text, she delegated the details of the work to several members of her experienced and trusted office staff. But she held herself as the ultimate judge, and she would from time to time consider specific points and finally review the text of the manuscript.

It should be stated here that neither Mrs. White nor her staff considered what was done as an actual "revision," and all studiously avoided the use of the term, for it was entirely too broad in its connotation.

It was agreed upon early that the new edition of the book should be held as nearly as possible, page for page, to the widely circulated 1888 printing. At the outset, work on the illustrations for the new book had been undertaken. This was a point of importance in a volume to be sold by colporteurs.

The typesetting that had begun was now being held in abeyance. W. C. White at first thought that the delay would be only a week or two, allowing, as he said in his letter to Jones on May 17, 1910, for "careful study of suggestions . . . recently received from brethren connected with the Review and Herald." White continued:

> You may be sure we will do all we can to minimize the changes, not only in the pages molded and in the pages set, but in the whole book. We feel, however, that now is the time to give faithful consideration to the suggestions that have been made to us.

FINDING SOURCES FOR THE QUOTATIONS

The most demanding of the tasks connected with readying the book for re-setting was the tracking down of all quotations employed in the book—417 in all, drawn from 75 authors, 10 periodicals, and three encyclopedias. It was while Ellen White was in Europe and had access to the library left by J. N. Andrews at the denomination's publishing house in Basel, Switzerland, that the manuscript for the 1888 edition was largely prepared. At Elmshaven Clarence Crisler was now in charge of seeking out the sources and verifying the quotations.

PROGRESS REPORT TO ELDER DANIELLS

In a letter to A. G. Daniells written on June 20, 1910, W. C. White reported:

> During the last two weeks, we have been busily engaged in studying those matters which demanded consideration in connection with the bringing out of the new edition of *Great Controversy*. When I presented to Mother questions as to what we should do regarding the quotations from historians and the references to these historians, she was prompt and clear in her opinion that we ought to give proper credit wherever we can. This has called for a good deal of searching of histories.
>
> Brethren Crisler and [D. E.] Robinson have taken much pains to look up the very best English authorities for the bulls and decrees and letters quoted and referred to, and they have been successful beyond my fondest hopes.

Then White wrote of the involvements in the preparation of the new edition of the book:

Further than this there will be very few changes made. In a few places where ambiguous or misleading terms have been used, Mother has authorized a changed reading, but she protests against any change in the argument or subject matter of the book, and indeed, we find, as we study into the matter, a clear and satisfactory defense for those passages to which our critics might take exception.

There are a few historical matters which we are still searching for. The most perplexing one is that regarding the three and a half days when the dead bodies of the two witnesses lay unburied, as referred to in Revelation 11:9-11 (DF 836).

E. G. WHITE SETTLES THE QUESTION OF THE D'AUBIGNÉ QUOTATIONS

Ten days after this report was made by W. C. White to A. G. Daniells, a question arose, sparked by the checking of all quoted materials in the book. It was found that the most frequently quoted historian was D'Aubigné, whose *History of the Reformation,* written in French, had been published in five translations in England and the United States. Three of the translations were represented in *The Great Controversy,* but it was discovered that only one had the wholehearted approval of the author. The question now was, "Should all the matter quoted from this author be from just the one that had the author's approval?" To do so would call for a good many changes in *The Great Controversy* text, and in some cases, provide a less desirable wording. Work on the pages involved was held up until this matter could be settled by Ellen White herself.

In the meantime, possibly with some intimation of the question that had to be settled, Mrs. White made a clear-cut statement to Mary Steward that Mary carefully wrote out, dated, and signed on July 31. Here it is:

> Whenever any of my workers find quotations in my writings, I want those quotations to be *exactly like the book they are taken from.* Sometimes they have thought they might change a few words to make it a little better; but it must not be done; it is not fair. When we quote a thing, we must put it *just as it is* (DF 83b).

To make any alterations in the text of the book written under the inspiration of the Spirit of God, especially a book as widely circulated and studiously read as *The Great Controversy,* was recognized by Ellen White and the staff at Elmshaven as something that would raise questions in the minds of Seventh-day Adventists. Many were jealous for Ellen White and the Spirit of Prophecy, and, not having thought the matter through, held, for all practical purposes, to a theory of verbal inspiration in the work of God's prophets. An action disavowing this stance was taken by the General Conference in session in 1883. But by 1911 this was either unknown or forgotten by Adventists generally. Here is the wording:

> We believe the light given by God to His servants is by the enlightenment of the mind, thus imparting the thoughts, and not (except in rare cases) the very words in which the ideas should be expressed (RH, Nov. 27, 1883 [in MR, p. 65, and 3SM, p. 96]).

And W. C. White, in the 1911 statement, approved fully by his mother, addressed himself specifically to the matter of verbal inspiration. He pointed out:

> Mother has never laid claim to verbal inspiration, and I do not find that my father, or Elders Bates, Andrews, Smith, or Waggoner, put forth this claim. If there were verbal inspiration in writing her manuscripts, why should there be on her part the work of addition or adaptation? It is a fact that Mother often takes one of her manuscripts, and goes over it thoughtfully, making additions that develop the thought still further (WCW letter, July 24, 1911 [see also 3SM, p. 437]).

CLARENCE CRISLER'S TESTIMONY

In January 1911 Clarence Crisler wrote to Guy Dail in Europe offering his testimony regarding what he saw of God's guiding hand in the writing of *The Great Controversy*:

> The more closely we examine the use of historical extracts in *Controversy*, and the historical extracts themselves, the more profoundly are we impressed with the fact that Sister White had special guidance in tracing the story from the time of the destruction of Jerusalem, down through the centuries until the end. No mortal could have done the work that she has done in shaping up some of those chapters, including, we believe, the chapter on the French Revolution, which is a very remarkable chapter, in more ways than one.
>
> And the more we go into these matters, the more profound is our conviction that the Lord has helped not only Sister White in the presentation of truth, but that He has overruled in the work of other writers, to the praise of His name and the advancement of present truth.
>
> Our brethren in years past have used many quotations, and, as a general rule, the Lord surely must have helped them to avoid making use of many extracts that would have led them astray. Of course there is still a

great deal of room for improvement, even in a book like Elder U. Smith's *Daniel and Revelation*. But not so much needs to be done, as might have had to be done, if the Lord had not given special help to these various writers (DF 84d, CCC to Guy Dail, Jan. 3, 1911).

A REVIEW OF WHAT WAS DONE TO THE BOOK

With the new printing of *The Great Controversy* now on the market it was important to take particular note of exactly what was done in preparing the copy for resetting the type for the 1911 edition. W. C. White was in charge of the work at Elmshaven; he was the principal spokesman during the period of work on the book, and quite naturally was the one to make explanations that might be called for.

On July 24, 1911, a few days after receiving a copy of the new book, he wrote a letter addressed to "Publishing House Managers," which he repeated the next day in a letter to "Our General Missionary Agents" (publishing department leaders). This he later included in a statement read to the General Conference Committee in its Autumn Council held in Washington, D.C. These W. C. White letters of explanation, quoted from in this chapter, carried Ellen White's written approval. Because of limitations in space, only excerpts can be included in this chapter. The reader is urged to pursue them in full in Appendix A of *Selected Messages*, book 3.

After mentioning that the new book runs page for page, he introduced the principal features:

> The most noticeable change in the new edition is the improvement in the illustrations. Each of the forty-two chapters, together with the preface, introduction, contents, and list of illustrations, has a beautiful pictorial heading; and ten new full-page illustrations have been introduced, to take the place of those which were least attractive.
>
> The thirteen appendix notes of the old edition, occupying thirteen pages, have been replaced by thirty-one notes occupying twelve pages. These are nearly all reference notes, intended to help the studious reader in finding historical proofs of the statements made in the book. . . .
>
> In the body of the book, the most noticeable improvement is the introduction of historical references. In the old edition, over 700 biblical references were given, but in only a few instances were there any historical references to the authorities quoted or referred to. In the new edition the reader will find more than 400 references to eighty-eight authors and authorities (WCW letter, July 24, 1911 [see also 3SM, p. 434]).

E. G. WHITE READS AND APPROVES CHANGES

From time to time as the work of *The Great Controversy* progressed, important matters were taken to Ellen White for decision, and the staff at Elmshaven worked under general instructions from her. Finally, when the type was set and proof sheets were available from the publishers, a set was marked showing clearly both the old reading and the new, and these were submitted to her for careful reading and approval. An envelope in the White Estate Document File No. 85e carries the notation: "*Controversy* Proofs Prepared for Mrs. E. G. White's Inspection and Approval." "All approved."

At last the work was done, a work much more demanding than was anticipated when those involved began in January 1910. By early July 1911 the book was in the binderies of Pacific Press and the Review and Herald. On Monday, July 17, copies of the newly published *The Great Controversy*—the 1911 edition—were received at Elmshaven. It was a joyous day.

TIME RUNNING OUT; IMPORTANT COUNSELS

Writing and book preparation occupied most of Ellen White's time during the last years of her life. She worked with a sense of time running out. But as in earlier years, her ministry was somewhat mixed. From time to time writing was laid aside for important interviews, occasional appointments in nearby churches, trips to Loma Linda, and camp meetings.

BOOK PREPARATION

THE ACTS OF THE APOSTLES. When the staff at Elmshaven late in 1910 learned that the Sabbath school lessons for 1911 were to be on the early Christian church, it was contemplated that materials on New Testament history, released week by week in *Review and Herald* articles, would serve as lesson helps.

Then the plan was that Clarence Crisler, as soon as the work on *The Great Controversy* was completed, would assemble materials on the life of Paul. He would take the 1883 E. G. White book *Sketches From the Life of Paul* as the foundation of this work. This book had been long out of print; Mrs. White had been looking forward to the time when she could expand its presentation. Now Crisler would draw from this as well as from other E. G. White sources of the past 25 or more years.

Because Maggie Hare (now Mrs. Bree), hard at work on the experiences of the early Christian church, became ill, the work was delayed; the deadline for copy for the January 5 issue of the *Review*, the time when the new series was to begin, was missed (WCW to F. M. Wilcox, Jan. 17, 1911). But four weeks later the *Review and Herald* carried two articles in time to parallel current Sabbath School lessons.

Ellen White was much involved in the task, going over the materials as they were assembled, doing some editing and writing to fill in gaps. All of this was done with an eye on the full manuscript for the forthcoming book to be known as *The Acts of the Apostles*. On October 6, 1911, she wrote:

> I feel more thankful than I can express for the interest my workers have taken in the preparation of this book, that its truths might be presented in the clear and simple language which the Lord has charged me never to depart from in any of my writings (letter 80, 1911).

The Acts of the Apostles was off the press and ready for sale in late November.

It was with satisfaction that Ellen White's staff noted her ability to engage actively in the preparation of book manuscripts at this late period in her life.

PROPHETS AND KINGS. When the year 1912 dawned, Ellen White was in her eighty-fifth year. Acquaintances, church leaders, and her family marveled at her continued ability to produce. In early January she wrote:

> There will be one more book—that dealing with the Old Testament history from the time of David to the time of Christ [*Prophets and Kings*]. The material for this book has been written, and is on file, but is not yet put into shape. When this book is complete, I shall feel that my work is finished. Yet I can hold my pen as firmly today as I have done in years past (letter 4, 1912).

Back in 1907 Clarence Crisler had assembled Ellen White's writings on Ezra for a series of *Review* articles. The Sabbath school lessons for the first quarter of 1907 were on the book of Ezra, and it was hoped these articles would provide collateral reading.

The task was larger than expected, and while the preliminary material on Nehemiah was printed in the *Review* in March and April, it was not until January and February 1908 that the five articles on Ezra were published. But the 18 articles on this phase of Old Testament history were steps in the preparation of *Prophets and Kings*.

The main thrust in preparing *Prophets and Kings*, however, was in the late summer months and fall of 1912. Ellen White wrote:

> Just now, what strength I have is given mostly to bringing out in book form what I have written in past years on the Old Testament history from the time of Solomon to the time of Christ. Last year *The Acts of the Apostles* was put into print, and is being widely circulated; and now we are making good progress with this Old Testament history. We are advancing as fast as possible.

I have faithful and conscientious helpers, who are gathering together what I have written for the *Review*, *Signs*, and *Watchman*, and in manuscripts and letters, and arranging it in chapters for the book. Sometimes I examine several chapters in a day, and at other times I can read but little because my eyes become weary and I am dizzy. The chapters that I have been reading recently are very precious (letter 20, 1912).

There had been a hastening of the work on Old Testament history, with the determination to bring it to completion while Ellen White could be involved. Now the task was well along, and Clarence Crisler went back to some of the chapters that in richness came short of most of the manuscript. With Ellen White's counsel and help, he was rounding them out. This is why the manuscript, which earlier had been spoken of as almost completed, was still in preparation. Wrote Crisler on New Year's Day 1915:

As we find new material from the file and add to the chapters that have already been prepared and passed upon, and reread these amplified portions to her, she seems to enjoy going over them anew. This perfecting of the manuscript is slow work, but very interesting; and we are hopeful of the outcome (CCC to WCW, Jan. 1, 1915).

This manuscript, published under the title of *The Captivity and Restoration of Israel*, had not been completed at the time of Ellen White's death, but was completed by Clarence Crisler from materials in the manuscript file. Later it was published as *Prophets and Kings*.

Other books that were being compiled from file material in much the same way but which were completed later were: *Gospel Workers*, *Education*, *The Ministry of Healing*, and *Life Sketches of Ellen G. White*.

ELLEN WHITE'S LAST TRIPS TO LOMA LINDA

On Thursday, March 30, 1911, Ellen White broke away from the work at Elmshaven. Taking with her Helen Graham, one of the secretaries, and Sara McEnterfer, her traveling companion and nurse, she set out for Loma Linda, where important meetings of the board were to be held early in April.

There were 76 acres (31 hectares) of land in the 1905 purchase of the Loma Linda property, 23 (9 hectares) in the hill site and the remaining 53 (21 hectares) in a strip of fertile valley land extending three fifths of a mile (one kilometer) toward the railway. The hill land was half occupied by buildings, lawns, drives, et cetera; the other half was orchard. Of the valley land, a portion provided a site for barns, stables, vegetable garden, and three acres of apricot trees. The balance was in alfalfa, and there was land suitable for grain.

Pressed as they were for money to meet the $40,000 purchase price, some looked hopefully to the sale of the valley land as building sites. When Ellen White heard of this, she urged that no land be sold.

None was sold. J. A. Burden and others associated with him felt there was a need of acquiring even more land for the institution. Within a few months a 30-acre (12-hectare) site just east was offered for something less than $100 an acre, and it was secured.

Shortly after this, Ellen White asked to see this land and was taken to the top of the sanitarium building where she could view it. G. A. Irwin, board chairman, reported that she scanned it carefully for a time, and then remarked, "Well, we are thankful we have it" (Sp. T, Series B, No. 17a, p. 2).

Then she turned and looked to the north, to the land in the front of the sanitarium that stretched to the railroad and Colton Avenue beyond. She waved her hand and declared: "The angel said, 'Get all of it.'" Somewhat startled, those with her reminded her of the financial difficulties experienced in securing what land they had, and she responded: "Well, we shall be thankful for what we have," and turned and went to her room. The brethren pondered just what was included in the words of the angel, "Get all of it."

The land north of the institution was in several tracts. One, of 150 acres (61 hectares), was held at $18,000; another, of 55 acres (22 hectares), was held for $20,000; another 27 acres (11 hectares) could be had for $2,250; and still another 20 acres (eight hectares) just north of the railway was available for $750. But who had the foresight, and where would the money come from? Nothing was done, and three years went by. But in those three years some of the tracts were sold, and what was left doubled in price.

When the decision to develop a medical school at Loma Linda was reached in 1910, the pattern of thinking began to change. In May, at the time of the organization meeting held at Loma Linda, at which Ellen White was present, steps were taken to secure land just in front of the institution. It was purchased for about $600 an acre.

ON HAND FOR THE 1911 CONSTITUENCY MEETING

Now it was April 1911, and Ellen White was at Loma Linda again. Her intense interest in the developments there led her for a year or two to go south to be present when the major board meetings were held in the spring and fall. Her counsel was much treasured by those who moved ahead, eager to see that the work was done in harmony with the mind of God as revealed through His messenger.

The 1911 constituency meeting was held during the first week of April. The record reveals that among other things, study was given to the importance of securing more land adjacent to the institution. A number looked over the

Kelly tract of about 85 acres (34 hectares), available at $300 an acre, but no action was taken to purchase it.

Immediately following the meetings of the constituency and the board, Ellen White went on south to spend a few days at Paradise Valley Sanitarium. But 10 days later she was back at Loma Linda, saying that her work there was not finished. The matter of securing more land rested heavily on her heart, and she talked of it and took several trips by carriage to look things over again. Repeatedly she stated that she had been instructed that the denomination should secure the land adjoining the sanitarium, and she urged that the brethren pray over the matter so that they might have light to know what to do. She mentioned the troubles that would come if others were allowed to secure the land and sell it to unbelievers.

Her rather relentless pressing of the matter led Elder Burden to call a council meeting of available workers on Thursday, April 20, to consider what should be done in the light of the availability of the Kelly tract. Ellen White was the principal speaker. After a few opening remarks she came right to the point:

> Today with Sister McEnterfer, and again with my son, I rode around the Loma Linda grounds, and took more particular notice of them than ever before; and I feel very thankful that we have such a place. . . . In our meetings during this council, we have been speaking of the higher education. What is the higher education? It is to understand Christ's works and teachings, and to follow on to know the Lord. It is to know that His going forth is prepared as the morning.

> Today, as I looked over the place more thoroughly than ever before . . . I felt gratitude in my heart toward God, that through His providence we had been brought into possession of Loma Linda. I felt thankful also to see the improvements that have been made since we have had the place. And I thought how important it is that we make every move in accordance with the will of God.

> As the Lord prospers us, we should manifest our gratitude by a willingness to advance. We should see the advantage of adding to that which we already have. I feel a burden regarding the danger of letting anybody come into the neighborhood to spoil the place.

> There is a piece of land across the railroad, lying next to a piece already purchased, which should be secured. . . . I am sure, from the representations that have been made to me, that this piece of land ought to come into our possession.

> If you are wise, the next time I come here you will have that land. I will try to help you all I can. Let us work intelligently.

She pledged $1,000 toward the purchase of the tract. Then she assured her audience that she was well pleased with what had been accomplished at Loma Linda. "When one sees the prosperity that has attended the work," she said, "and the spirit of consecration that prevails, the conviction deepens that you are working in harmony with God." In closing her remarks, she added:

> I am highly gratified as I look upon the land we already have. This will be one of the greatest blessings to us in the future—one that we do not fully appreciate now, but which we shall appreciate by and by. I hope that you will get the other land that I have spoken of and join it to that which you already have. It will pay you to do this (MS 9, 1911).

She made this interesting prediction:

> "The Loma Linda institution, if conducted according to the will of God, will become the most important in its work of all our institutions throughout the world" (WCW to AGD, June 16, 1912).

In the development of the medical school the point had been reached where provision had to be made for the clinical years of physician training. At first it was hoped that these needs could largely be met with the construction of a modest hospital at Loma Linda. Now it was clear that with the relatively sparse population in the area, the hospital at Loma Linda would be inadequate; they had to look to a populated area.

As the Loma Linda board wrestled with the problem, they were well aware of Ellen White's repeated advice that a sanitarium should not be located in Los Angeles. She was drawn in for counsel, and met with the board on the afternoon of April 4. W. C. White had discussed the matter of the clinical needs with his mother as they drove together that morning about the Loma Linda grounds. It now seemed overwhelmingly evident that the clinical work needed to be done largely in a center of population, and the question had narrowed down to a choice of going into Los Angeles for all of the clinical work or of doing part of the work at Loma Linda and part in Los Angeles.

Ellen White spoke up cheerfully and promptly and said that that was the better way—to do part of the work in Loma Linda, and part in Los Angeles. Both in the conversation with her son and now with the board, she supported this proposition (MS 14, 1912).

After spending another week or two at Loma Linda, she returned to Elmshaven where it was back to the work of reading manuscripts, writing, and occasionally filling speaking appointments.

After the monthlong stay in southern California, Ellen White found living and working conditions at Elmshaven more comfortable than they had been in former winters. A new steam central heating plant had been installed, with a large wood-burning furnace in the basement of a nearby tank house. While fireplaces would continue to enhance the attractiveness of the home, they would not be used exclusively to heat the large rooms with their high ceilings. And in the office steam radiators also took the place of the messy little wood stoves.

THE VISIT OF BOOKMEN

On Thursday, January 23, 1913, the staff at Elmshaven, except for W. C. White, who was in the East, played host to a group of about 40 men and women who arrived at the home about 4:00 p.m. For several days the literature evangelists working in the five union conferences in the territory of Pacific Press had been in Mountain View, together with conference leaders and others, for a convention. Now colporteurs, some of their wives, church leaders, and some others were spending the day visiting Pacific Union College, St. Helena Sanitarium, and Elmshaven.

Advance notice had been given and preparations were made to receive them. Appropriate exhibits showing books, documents, manuscripts, and letters that would be of interest to visitors were set up in the library room next to the manuscript vault.

As they crowded into Ellen White's living room and dining room, she came down to receive them and to read her message of greeting. It said, in part:

> I welcome you all to "Elmshaven," the refuge that I found prepared for me on my return from Australia. In this quiet and comfortable home we have been able to prepare articles and books for publication. I hope you will enjoy your visit, and that you may come again. In your prosperity and welfare I am deeply interested. . . .
>
> All who consecrate themselves to God to work as canvassers are assisting to give the last message of warning to the world. They are the Lord's messengers, giving to multitudes in darkness and error the glad tidings of salvation (letter 3, 1913).

After recounting some experiences in which Seventh-day Adventists were led to gain a broader grasp of the task before them, she urged her guests to pray for a deeper experience, and urged also that they go forth with hearts filled with the precious truths that God had given His people for this time.

After addressing them for about 30 minutes, she presented each with one of her books of their choice—*The Desire of Ages, The Acts of the Apostles,* or some other. The gift was made doubly memorable by a card in each book bearing a printed message of good cheer and her signature.

THE GENERAL CONFERENCE SESSION OF 1913

The thirty-eighth session of the General Conference was scheduled to be held in Washington, D.C. from May 15 to June 8, 1913. As with the 1909 session held four years before, meetings would be in a large tent pitched on the grounds of Washington Missionary College in Takoma Park, Maryland. The expectation was that Ellen G. White, now 85 years of age, would not attempt to attend. In early May she made her final decision, writing to Edson on the seventh, "I shall not attend. I desire to save my strength for the work here that is essential to be done" (letter 9, 1913). W. C. White wrote that she was quite content with the decision (WCW to AGD, May 1, 1913). She did, however, prepare two messages to be read to the session and sent them with her son.

On the first Sabbath afternoon of the session W. C. White was called upon to read Ellen White's message of greeting to the delegates. It contained a challenge to face the work with hopefulness and courage and venture to undertake by faith the work called for—a work they could not fully understand; as they went forward in the fear of God, they would receive rich blessing. She was referring to evangelizing the cities.

Ellen White had a continuing burden for the cities. In September 1909 *Testimonies for the Church*, volume 9, carried a section titled "The Work in the Cities," with a strong appeal to ministers and laymen. "Behold the cities," she urged, "and their need of the gospel!" (p. 97). She told of how the need of earnest laborers among the multitudes of the cities had been kept before her for more than 20 years (*ibid.*).

The *General Conference Bulletin* reported the response to Ellen White's message:

> The reading of this letter brought forth many hearty "amens" from the brethren on the rostrum and throughout the congregation. Tears flowed freely as Sister White's expressions of confidence in her brethren and in God's leadership of His people were read (GCB 1913, p. 32).

"COURAGE IN THE LORD"

The president of the General Conference, A. G. Daniells, presented Ellen White's second message to the delegates 10 days later at the business session on Tuesday morning, May 27. It opened:

> Recently in the night season, my mind was impressed by the Holy Spirit with the thought that if the Lord is coming as soon as we believe

He is, we ought to be even more active than we have been in years past (*ibid.*, p. 164).

Later in the message she declared:

> I long to be personally engaged in earnest work in the field, and I should most assuredly be engaged in more public labor did I not believe that at my age it is not wise to presume on one's physical strength (*ibid.*).

There was one part of her message to the session that touched a chord in the hearts of many of the delegates present, such as J. N. Loughborough, who with Ellen White had attended the very first session of the General Conference held in Battle Creek in May, 1863, exactly 50 years before, and G. I. Butler, an associate for many years. Here are her comforting and encouraging words:

> I greatly desire that the old soldiers of the cross, those grown gray in the Master's service, shall continue to bear their testimony right to the point, in order that those younger in the faith may understand that the messages which the Lord gave us in the past are very important at this stage of the earth's history (*ibid.*).

There was no word of pessimism in Ellen White's farewell message to the leaders of the church in assembly.

WINDING DOWN WITH COURAGE AND CHEER

The opening of the year 1914, the last full calendar year of Ellen White's life, was marked with an added convenience for Elmshaven—electricity. Just the year before, a beginning had been made in the use of steam in heating, and during the year her twin grandsons, Herbert and Henry, had secured their first automobile. Now the long-awaited convenience, electricity, had reached Pratt Valley.

W. C. White was away from home much of this year, and while it slowed the work at the office and left considerable loneliness, it had its benefits in the frequent reports to him from his wife, May, and C. C. Crisler. To keep White posted, Crisler wrote to him every day or two.

On March 18 the prune orchards were budding again. Ellen White was in good health and good spirits, and when the weather was favorable was still taking her daily carriage rides on the familiar roads and in the cherished lanes about Elmshaven. The next day Crisler reported to W. C. White of his conversations with Ellen White and of her outlook. Here is his statement:

> Last night Sister White assured me that her faith in God and her confidence in the Advent movement have been greatly strengthened of late by the excellent reports of success attending the labors of our ministers and workers. She declares that she has never doubted the providential leadership of God in connection with our denominational history, but that her confidence does grow stronger as the evidences of divine leadership multiply (CCC to WCW, Mar. 19, 1914).

As it was that day, so it pervaded the last months of her life.

FREQUENT VISITORS

On April 1 several visitors called—B. G. Wilkinson, M. N. Campbell, and O. Montgomery. Ellen White spent some time with them. The men were very glad for the opportunity to talk with her (*ibid.*).

When Elder Campbell asked if she had any light as to whether she would live till Jesus returned, she replied that she had no light on the matter. When he expressed his concern as to the welfare of the cause in her absence, she quietly replied, "The Lord is perfectly able to take care of His cause." On several occasions, by stating that she did not expect to live long, she opened the way for similar questions to be put to her by visiting brethren. Responding, she would step over to the book cabinet in her writing room, open the doors where her books and manuscripts could be seen, and declare, "Here are my writings; when I am gone they will testify for me" (WCW letter, July 9, 1922 [MR, p. 93]).

In mid-April Edson, who now resided in Marshall, Michigan, traveled west for a monthlong visit. It was a happy occasion for both mother and son, who had been separated so much for 25 or more years. They had good visits together, and went over many things of mutual interest.

Visits from prominent workers of long acquaintance were much appreciated by Ellen White. Among the visitors during this last year were: C. E. Andross, president of the Pacific Union Conference; C. H. Jones, manager of the Pacific Press; Mrs. Lida Scott, daughter of Isaac Funk of the Funk and Wagnalls Publishing Company (Mrs. Scott later made a liberal gift toward the establishment of the College of Medical Evangelists); and Elder and Mrs. G. B. Starr, former coworkers from Australia.

Her principal contributions to literary work in this her eighty-seventh year were on her books as she read and approved chapters and at times added a bit here or there. Chapters were brought to her; her son reported that "she read some, and asked us to read them to her. Sometimes I would read two or three pages, and then she would read one or two pages. . . . Sometimes I or Crisler do all the reading, and Mother comments on what we have read" (WCW to J. E. White, Dec. 15, 1914).

REVIEW AND SIGNS ARTICLES

Part of the overall literary program at Elmshaven in which Ellen White participated was the furnishing of articles most every week for the *Review and Herald* and *Signs of the Times*. Forty E. G. White articles were published in the *Review* in 1914. First was a series on Old Testament history, being portions of the book manuscript in preparation (*Prophets and Kings*), then 12 articles entitled "Early Counsels on Medical Work," followed by 18 on more general topics.

HER EIGHTY-SEVENTH BIRTHDAY ~ July 1915

On Thanksgiving Day, November 26, Ellen White reached her eighty-seventh birthday. She was not very strong, and Crisler could go over only three pages of manuscript with her. She received one birthday present, which some days before had come from Mrs. F. H. DeVinney, who was working with her husband in Japan. It was a warm, knitted vest, known as a "hug-me-tight," to be worn on cold days. When Ellen White tried it on, she showed that she had not lost her sense of humor. She told Dores Robinson to thank Sister DeVinney for the gift, but to tell her "that there is a great deal more to Sister White than some people thought" (D. E. Robinson to WCW, Nov. 3, 1914).

As the messenger of the Lord neared the close of her life, two tasks of a biographical nature emerged. Study was being given as to what would be said in the public press to inform the general public about her life and work.

Plans for a permanent biographical work that could be published immediately after Ellen White's death were also being developed. Soon her active labors would cease, fresh articles would no longer appear in the journals, and it was felt that a modest volume on her life was needed. So beginning in late 1914 consideration was given to the preparation of a manuscript that would at her death appear as *Life Sketches of Ellen G. White*. C. C. Crisler and D. E. Robinson, using what help W. C. White could give, undertook the work.

Tuesday, January 5, 1915, Crisler wrote to James Edson White:

> You will be pleased to learn that Sister White is keeping up fairly well, all things considered. . . . She can get about the house unaided and unattended, going freely from room to room and up and down stairs; but her steps are much slower and uncertain than in former years, and even than when you were last with us. She finds it possible to sit in easy chairs for hours at a stretch.
>
> Often during the past few months she has spent a good portion of the time downstairs, sitting in the sitting room by the fireplace; and Miss Walling has endeavored to sit much with her, to keep her company. . . . There is really more home life for your mother than during the years when her activities led her to isolate herself in her office room most of the time.

In correspondence Crisler mentioned often Ellen White's optimism, confidence, and simplicity of faith:

> It is in her hours of greatest physical weakness that your mother seems to rise to the highest spiritual heights; and yet in all this she simply does what any of us poor mortals can do—lays hold on the divine promises, and makes them her very own, and praises God for the comfort they yield. Thus her heart is filled to overflowing with joy, and she has perfect peace.
>
> The simplicity of her faith has made a profound impression upon my own mind, and constitutes one of the strongest evidences that during the years of her service for her Master she has lived with a conscience void of offense toward God and man. When one keeps full faith with himself

in his service for God, his efforts will bear the test of time, and will yield a rich fruitage (CCC to WCW, Dec. 23, 1914).

On Friday, February 12, 1915, W. C. White wrote to "Dear Friend" (February 15):

> Friday afternoon, February 12, as I was leaving the office for a quick trip to St. Helena, Mother came outdoors, and we spent ten minutes walking about in the bright sunshine and talking about the progress of the message in all the world.

On Sabbath, February 13, Ellen White broke her hip, and W. C. White telegraphed to relatives and friends:

> Sabbath noon, Mother, entering her study, tripped and fell, causing an intracapsular fracture of the left femur.

THE ACCIDENT AND ITS AFTERMATH

In his report of the accident, written Monday, February 15, sent to relatives and friends and published in the *Review and Herald*, W. C. White described what happened:

> Sabbath morning, Mother appeared to be as well as usual. About noon, as she was entering her study from the hallway, she tripped and fell. Her nurse, May Walling, who was in the hall about twenty feet away, hastened to her assistance, and endeavored to help her onto her feet. When Mother cried out with pain, May lifted her into a rocking chair, pulled the chair through the hall to Mother's bedroom and got her to bed. Then May telephoned to Dr. Klingerman at the sanitarium, and at once applied fomentations to the hip, where the pain seemed to be the greatest.
>
> When the doctor came, he said that it was either a bad sprain or a fracture, and advised an X-ray examination at the sanitarium. This examination showed an "intracapsular fracture of the left femur at the junction of the head and the neck." Mother bore very patiently all the painful experiences of being carried from her room to the sanitarium and back again.
>
> Sara McEnterfer, who was her traveling companion and secretary most of the time for thirty years, is with her; and so is May Walling, who was brought up in her home, and who has been her faithful nurse for about two years. Mrs. Hungerford, a trained nurse from the sanitarium, is also with her (RH, Mar. 11, 1915).

Sunday morning Dr. Klingerman arranged to have a hospital bed sent down to the White home. This was set up in her spacious and cheery writing room, close to the bathroom with its conveniences. As W. C. White told the story to readers of the *Review*, he continued:

> Mother occupies her study, where for the last ten busy years she did most of her writing. Sometimes when half awake she asks how long the journey will take, and when she will get home; and then, when fully awake, she says, "I am right here in my own room."
>
> In our seasons of prayer Mother unites with her usual fervor and clearness of thought, expressing complete confidence and entire resignation.
>
> Since her accident she has told me that she feels that her work is done, her battles ended, and that she is willing to lie down and sleep till the resurrection morning, unless there is yet some special work the Lord has for her to do (*ibid.*).

And thus it was for the next five months till mid-July. Her son's frequent reports through the *Review and Herald* and in his letters indicate that she had good days and days not so good, but that she was spared from any great suffering.

Soon after the accident, W. C. White reported that "when we ask her if she is suffering pain, she will start to say Yes; then she stops and says, 'It is not so painful as it might be, but I cannot say that it is comfortable'" (WCW to AGD, Mar. 1, 1915). A few weeks later, when asked what kind of day she had had, she replied, "A good day—in spots" (WCW to S. N. Haskell, Apr. 30, 1915).

By early June there was a rapid decline in her physical condition. One of the three nurses mentioned earlier was constantly with her. Relatives, friends, and neighbors were frequent visitors. A wheelchair was secured, and on pleasant days she was taken out on the little porch directly over the main entrance to the home, facing south. This she much enjoyed. On most days she would sit in a chair for several hours, and at nights she usually slept well. As time went on her appetite waned. On one occasion as Sara was coaxing her to eat, her response showed that she had not lost her sense of humor: "Well, Sara," she said, "I would not want to die before my time by overeating" (as told to A. L. White).

THE VISION OF MARCH 3

On the morning of March 3, about 10:00, Ellen White, on wakening, called her nurse, Mrs. Hungerford, to her side and began to tell of what took place in the night—her last vision. W. C. White was quickly called, and he wrote down the statement made rather slowly by his mother: "There are books that are of vital importance that are not looked at by our young people. They are neglected because they are not so interesting to them as some lighter reading" (RH, Apr. 15, 1915). She touched on a number of points and among them said:

> In the night season I was selecting and laying aside books that are of no advantage to the young. We should select for them books that will encourage them to sincerity of life, and lead them to the opening of the Word (*ibid.*).

She expressed confidence in her brethren in the cause, a theme often repeated as she faced the sunset of life.

> I do not think I shall have more *Testimonies* for our people. Our men of solid minds know what is good for the uplifting and upbuilding of the work. But with the love of God in their hearts, they need to go deeper and deeper into the study of the things of God (*ibid.*).

As she brought to the close this her last testimony for the church and especially its youth, she said:

> I have no assurance that my life will last long, but I feel that I am accepted of the Lord. . . . I have felt that it was imperative that the truth should be seen in my life, and that my testimony should go to the people. I want that you should do all you can to have my writings placed in the hands of the people in foreign lands. . . . I am impressed that it is my special duty to say these things (*ibid.*, [published in full in FE, pp. 547-549, and in MYP, pp. 287-289]).

WANING STRENGTH AND DEATH

But Ellen White's strength was waning fast now. Some days she was not aware of those in the room. She was not eating, and her body was wasting away, although she was given a little albumen water—the white of egg in water—from time to time as she would take it. On the morning of Thursday, July 8, she aroused sufficiently to say: "I do not suffer much, thank the Lord." And then to Sara she added: "It will not be long now" (WCW to "Friend," July 14, 1915; WCW to G. I. Butler, July 26, 1915).

Friday morning, July 9, she rallied enough to talk a little to Sara and to her son William. He prayed and told his mother that they would trust all in the hands of Jesus. She responded, saying in a faint whisper, "I know in whom I have believed" (3LS, p. 449).

Treatments were discontinued. On Thursday, July 15, W. C. White reported that everything was being done for her that kind hearts and willing hands could do. But now she lingered in silence, quietly breathing her life away.

The next day, Friday, July 16, about 2:00 the nurses saw that the end was very near and sent for W. C. White and his wife, May. They hastened to the home and her room. As her breathing slowed, others were notified and made their way one or two at a time to the second-floor room. C. C. Crisler and his wife, Minnie, soon joined the group. Then there were Ellen White's granddaughter, Mabel White Workman; her farm manager, Iram James, and his wife; her accountant, A. H. Mason, and Mrs. Mason; Mrs. Mary Chinnock Rhorp, a longtime acquaintance; her housekeeper, Tessie Woodbury. And of course there were the three nurses: Sara McEnterfer, who had been her faithful companion, nurse, and secretary of many years; May Walling; and Carrie Hungerford, who had waited on her night and day for 153 days since the accident.

In the morning Ellen White's respiration had been clocked at 50 per minute, but at 3:00 it was 38; at 3:20 it was 18, and a little later only 10. Then her breathing became slower and more irregular, until without a tremor the breathing stopped. It was 3:40. No one in the room stirred for several minutes, thinking she might take yet another breath. But she did not (WCW to David Lacy, July 20, 1915; WCW to G. I. Butler, July 26, 1915).

Describing the experience, W. C. White wrote:

> It was like the burning out of a candle, so quiet (WCW to David Lacy, July 20, 1915).

ELLEN WHITE AT REST; AWAITING THE LIFE-GIVER

Late Friday afternoon, July 16, 1915, the telegraph wires carried the word that Ellen G. White, the messenger of the Lord, was at rest. Through telephone and telegraph the message reached many of the churches in time to be announced Sabbath morning. For the public press, news stories had been prepared in advance, to be held until her death.

At Elmshaven carefully laid plans for funeral services were activated. One service was to be held on the lawn at her home, another in the San Francisco Bay area, and a third in Battle Creek, Michigan, where she would be laid to rest by the side of her husband. That Friday afternoon invitations to the Sunday funeral were quickly run off on the nearby "Elmshaven Press" operated by her twin grandsons, Henry and Herbert White, and these were mailed to 220 families in the valley (WCW to David Lacey, July 20, 1915). The invitation read:

FUNERAL NOTICE

Yourself and family are respectfully invited to attend the funeral of Mrs. Ellen G. White on the lawn at her residence, "Elmshaven," near the sanitarium, St. Helena, California, Sunday afternoon at five o'clock, July eighteenth, nineteen hundred fifteen (DF 756).

Word also was sent out that she would lie in state in her home on Sabbath and Sunday. Friends who called before Sunday noon were ushered to her writing room on the second floor, where they found her in a simple cloth-covered black coffin bearing a modest silver plate with the engraved words "At rest." If they called Sunday afternoon, as most did, they paid their respects to her in the living room, where so often she had received family and visitors.

Seating for about 300 people was provided on the lawn under the elm trees just in front of her house. Another hundred people sat on the lawn or in nearby parked automobiles. The sanitarium, the St. Helena church, and the college were largely represented. A few of the leading businessmen of St. Helena were present, and many friends came in from Napa, Santa Rosa, Sebastopol, and Healdsburg. A canopy was provided for the officiating ministers.

The service was simple and informal—ideal for the setting. Those participating were mostly ministers who had been long associated with Ellen White in the work of the church in America and overseas: J. N. Loughborough, George B. Starr, and E. W. Farnsworth. The pastor of the church of which she was a member, S. T. Hare, pronounced the benediction.

THE RICHMOND FUNERAL

"At Richmond, a northern suburb of Oakland, the California Conference was holding its annual camp meeting. Here were assembled many of Ellen White's old associates from the Oakland church, and many representatives of the churches that she had often visited in her earlier California labors. When they heard of Ellen White's death, they requested that her body be brought to the camp meeting, and that there be a service there. They said, 'If Sister White were alive and well, she would be right here at this meeting, telling us how to live a Christian life. Why not let her be brought here and someone tell us how she lived it?'" (WCW to David Lacey, July 20, 1915).

About a thousand people were present for the Monday-morning funeral service at the campground. E. E. Andross, president of the Pacific Union Conference, was in charge of the service and was assisted by A. O. Tait, *Signs* editor, and Elders Loughborough and Farnsworth. At 3:00 in the afternoon, following the service, W. C. White and Sara McEnterfer boarded the train, expecting to reach Battle Creek by Thursday evening.

THE BATTLE CREEK FUNERAL

It was Ellen White's request that she be buried by the side of her husband in Battle Creek's Oak Hill Cemetery, where also were buried her oldest son, Henry, and the little baby; and James White's father and mother. So the next Sabbath day, July 24, they planned to have a service at the Battle Creek Tabernacle, and from there the burial would take place (DF 757, E. W. Farnsworth funeral sermon, July 18, 1915).

As W. C. White and Sara McEnterfer neared Battle Creek on Thursday, July 22, two men boarded the train at Kalamazoo to travel the last 30 miles (50 kilometers) with them. One was James Edson White, Ellen White's older son; the other, George Israel, an officer of the Battle Creek church who was in charge of the funeral arrangements. The church had sent him to meet the travelers and to inform them of plans for the funeral.

Sabbath morning, sometime before 8:00, the people began to gather in front of the Battle Creek Tabernacle. The Battle Creek *Enquirer* of July 25 described what took place when the doors opened:

> During the two hours between eight and ten, there was a steady stream of humanity viewing the body. Men with gray heads and stooped shoulders, many who knew Mrs. White during the early days of the Advent movement, were at the Tabernacle to pay their last respects. They stood before the casket and tears flowed down their cheeks as they thought of her wonderful work for the denomination (DF 758).

> The casket was one of simple black, covered with a wreath of white carnations and forget-me-nots. But back of the casket were a wealth of elaborate flower pieces and wreaths (*ibid.*).

Among those who passed the casket that Sabbath morning was Dudley M. Canright, accompanied by his Adventist brother, Jasper. Dudley had served for years as a Seventh-day Adventist minister but had apostatized and was busily engaged in writing a book against Ellen White. He knew her well; they had worked together in earlier years. He had stayed for days in the White home, but when he was reproved for a course of action that was not right, he turned against her and through the last 28 years of her life had bitterly opposed her work. After passing the casket once, D. M. suggested to Jasper that they go down again, so they slipped into the line. As the two stood by the casket the second time, they paused. Dudley put his hand on the casket and with tears rolling down his cheeks declared, "There is a noble Christian woman gone" (W. A. Spicer, *The Spirit of Prophecy in the Advent Movement*, p. 127).

The Battle Creek Tabernacle proved much too small for the mourners that assembled. Some 3,500 crowded into the building. In the audience were many patients from the sanitarium, some in wheelchairs, and many of the older citizens of

Battle Creek who knew Ellen White personally (DF 758, *Evening News*, July 24, 1915). A thousand or more who could not get into the tabernacle remained quietly on the lawn outside. Many of these accompanied Ellen White to the cemetery.

THE FUNERAL SERVICE

As had been planned, A. G. Daniells presented the "sketch"; it was more of a history that recounted Ellen White's life and the contribution she had made to the church and the world. S. N. Haskell presented a well-prepared funeral sermon on the surety of the hope of one who dies in Christ Jesus. F. M. Wilcox, editor of the *Review and Herald*, read the Scripture lesson. His brother, M. C. Wilcox, longtime book editor at the Pacific Press, offered the prayer, thanking God for the light and blessing that had come through His servant.

Following the service, the throng made its way across the city to Oak Hill Cemetery. It was no doubt Battle Creek's largest funeral procession, with more than 100 vehicles. The July 25 *Enquirer* described it:

> Thousands followed the hearse to the cemetery. For this purpose every carriage in the city was used, and there were a number of automobiles. And then besides this, there were nine streetcars. No fares were collected on these cars, as they were provided by the church (DF 758).

The service at the cemetery was brief and impressive. A double quartet sang, I. H. Evans read appropriate scriptures, G. B. Thompson offered prayer, and then "the remains of our dear sister were tenderly and silently lowered into the grave to rest beside the body of her husband, Elder James White, who was buried in the same plot in 1881" (DF 756, *In Memoriam*, p. 24).

THE PUBLIC PRESS

Newspaper notices and articles of various lengths appeared throughout the United States, from the Bay Area, where San Francisco and Oakland papers gave good space, to New York, where a respectable item was published in the New York *Times*. The careful work done well in advance of her death bore fruit, for the leading newspapers had materials, prepared largely at Elmshaven, in hand when they received telegraph notice of her death.

Ellen White's hometown newspaper, the St. Helena *Star*, on its front page printed a large photograph and gave 33 column inches (84 centimeters) to tell the story of her life, work, and death. The San Francisco *Chronicle* and the Oakland *Tribune* each gave 15 column inches (38 centimeters), selecting materials from the sheets furnished from Elmshaven. The Mountain View *Register-Leader* was perhaps the most generous, with 147 column inches (373 centimeters) devoted to the story, together with a two-column picture of Ellen

White. The Detroit *News-Tribune* gave seven inches (18 centimeters).
The Battle Creek papers gave full coverage to the story.
The St. Helena *Star*, July 23, 1915, reported:

> LEADER OF ADVENTISTS DEAD. Mrs. Ellen G. White Passes
> Away After Over Seventy Years of Christian Labor.
> At 3:40 o'clock last Friday afternoon, at her home, "Elmshaven,"
> near St. Helena, Mrs. Ellen Gould White, leader and one of the founders
> of the Seventh-day Adventist Church, passed from this life to that re-
> ward promised the followers of Jesus Christ (DF 758).

Then followed a biographical account and a résumé of denominational accomplishments: in membership, nearly 100,000; 37 publishing houses; 34 sanitariums; 70 intermediate schools, academies, and colleges; and 510 elementary
schools scattered all over the world. Mrs. White's work as an author was mentioned, noting that some of her writings had been translated into 36 languages.
The report concluded:

> The prevailing sentiment of the speakers who addressed the congre-
> gations at St. Helena and at Richmond was that Mrs. White's most en-
> during monument, aside from her godly life and conversation, was her
> published works, which tend to the purest morality, lead to Christ and to
> the Bible, and bring comfort and consolation to many a weary heart. "She
> hath done what she could," and now "being dead, she yet speaketh."

"MY WRITINGS WILL CONSTANTLY SPEAK"

As W. C. White started westward after the Battle Creek funeral, his mind
turned to the care and publication of his mother's writings. They would be managed by the newly activated White Estate, under the direction of the five trustees
of Ellen White's appointment: A. G. Daniells, president of the General
Conference; F. M. Wilcox, editor of the *Review and Herald*; C. H. Jones, manager
of the Pacific Press; C. C. Crisler, for 14 years Ellen White's leading secretary; and
W. C. White, who had traveled and worked with his mother for 34 years.

Sunday morning, after his return from the east, Elder White took the eight-
minute walk from his home to the Elmshaven office and residence; there he knew
he would have to face new conditions. He stepped onto the porch of the
Elmshaven home. It was unoccupied, and the doors locked. He unlocked the door
and entered, as he had so often done. He described his findings and sentiments:

> Everything was in perfect order, but the life of the place had gone.
> Going upstairs to the big east room, where for fifteen years Mother had

studied and prayed and planned and written, I found it vacant. The old couch and the tables and chairs and chests of drawers were in their usual places, and the big armchair with its swing board in front was where it used to be, between the big bay window and the fireplace; but the dear mother, whose presence had made this room the most precious place in all the world to me, was not there. Then I recalled the many times I had returned from the Eastern states, and had hastened up to Mother's room, sure of a hearty welcome, and an eager listener to my reports of meetings attended and of the progress of the work in which she was so deeply interested. But now there was no one in the writing chair to listen to my report (WCW to "Dear Friend," Oct. 20, 1915).

It was the end of an era in the life of the church. A new era was about to begin.

As Elder White stepped over to the cabinets in the northwest corner and opened the doors to the shelves that held copies of the E. G. White books and copies of her manuscripts and letters, there must have come to his mind Ellen White's words as she at times opened these doors and displayed her books and her papers:

"Here are my writings; when I am gone they will testify for me" (WCW letter, July 9, 1922 [MR, p. 93]).

Appendix

A POWER PRESS FOR THE *REVIEW* OFFICE

For five years the *Review and Herald* had been printed on a press owned and operated by Sabbathkeeping Adventists. The printing of each sheet was virtually a "custom job"—the type was inked, a sheet of paper laid on it, and the lever pulled, making the impression. The same was true of all other publications put out between 1852 and 1857. Wrote James White in March:

> With our hand press, it takes three days of each week to print the *Review and Herald*. Should the circulation of the *Review and Herald* be doubled (which we may hope it soon will be), there would be no room for the *Instructor*; and a large amount of work . . . would be shut out.— RH, March 19, 1857.

A special conference to consider this urgent need was called for Friday, April 10, in Battle Creek. Joseph Bates was chosen to preside. First attention was given to the matter of a power press.

Two resolutions were passed. First, "that such a press be obtained for the Review office," and second, "that all business pertaining to the purchasing [of] the press, et cetera, be confined to the hands of the publishing committee."— RH, April 16, 1857.

It was thought that such a press could be secured for less than $2,500. James White made the purchase in Boston on their next trip to the east.